Encyclopedia of African-American Civil Rights

Blacks register to vote in Birmingham, Alabama, 1966. (Archives Collections, Birmingham Public Library, Birmingham, Alabama.)

ENCYCLOPEDIA OF AFRICAN-AMERICAN CIVIL RIGHTS

From Emancipation to the Present

Edited by
CHARLES D. LOWERY
and
JOHN F. MARSZALEK

Foreword by DAVID J. GARROW

GREENWOOD PRESS
New York • Westport, Connecticut • London

Library of Congress Cataloging-in-Publication Data

Encyclopedia of African-American civil rights : from emancipation to
   the present / edited by Charles D. Lowery and John F. Marszalek ;
   foreword by David J. Garrow.
      p.   cm.
   Includes bibliographical references and index.
   ISBN 0–313–25011–1 (alk. paper)
    1. Afro-Americans—Civil rights—Dictionaries. 2. Civil rights
   movements—United States—History—Dictionaries. I. Lowery,
   Charles D., 1937– . II. Marszalek, John F., 1939– .
   E185.61.E54   1992
   305.896′073—dc20   91–27814

British Library Cataloguing in Publication Data is available.

Library of Congress Catalog Card Number: 91–27814
ISBN: 0–313–25011–1

First published in 1992

Greenwood Press, 88 Post Road West, Westport, CT 06881
An imprint of Greenwood Publishing Group, Inc.

Printed in the United States of America

The paper used in this book complies with the
Permanent Paper Standard issued by the National
Information Standards Organization (Z39.48–1984).

10 9 8 7 6 5 4 3 2 1

In Memory of Those Who Died
So Others Might Be Free

CONTENTS

FOREWORD

David J. Garrow

This *Encyclopedia of African-American Civil Rights* is a valuable and informative reference volume, but it is also so rich a source of important sketches and instructive bibliographical references that it deserves—and encourages—a fairly thorough reading even by knowledgeable senior scholars.

The range and breadth of entries is oftentimes as impressive as it is informative. Most importantly, any thoughtful perusal of the volume—whether thorough or cursory—will quickly bring home to any reader what a large number of individuals, organizations, and events there are from these last ten decades of Afro-American history which deserve greater and more extensive historical research and study than has yet been the case.

As many scholars now recognize, current and future research in Afro-American history will increasingly treat a wider and wider range of participants and events. To date a disproportionate amount of historical attention has been focused on nationally prominent individuals and on organizations that received significant contemporaneous news coverage, but there is widespread appreciation that increased attention to "grass roots" individuals and organizations is our future direction, just as there also is growing appreciation of the importance of "local" history and events. Less and less will Afro-American history look at the black experience in America largely through a prism of national news and/or national politics.

No one can peruse this volume without thinking again and again about otherwise obscure and/or often unremembered individuals, protests, and court cases that merit a greater presence in secondary sources and textbook surveys than is presently the case. Probably every contributor hopes that this encyclopedia's publication will further stimulate and encourage such a broadening of secondary historical coverage, and such a hope is quite likely to be fulfilled. While many contributors to this encyclopedia are relatively senior scholars such as John Kirby, Steven Lawson, Jo Ann O. Robinson, Hans Trefousse, and Jerry Ward, many of the most thorough and impressive contributions come from promising junior scholars such as Cheryl Greenberg, Patricia Behlar, Peter Wallenstein, Francille Wilson, Lillie Johnson Edwards, and Glenn T. Eskew.

One very important and as yet largely unmined resource for an expanded and enriched Afro-American history since the late nineteenth century, which a number of significant entries highlight or touch upon, is black newspapers. Although many issues of a number of significant publications most tragically seem to have not been preserved, both national papers such as the *Pittsburgh Courier* and more regionally or locally oriented papers such as the *Birmingham World* can be exceptionally rich and instructive sources for future historical studies. Few scholars enjoy spending hundreds upon hundreds of hours reading microfilm, but there is no escaping the fact that far more use can and will be made of black newspapers as a significant historical source than has yet been the case.

The historical importance of black newspapers is just one notable research path that this rich and valuable volume suggests. Notwithstanding the thoroughness of many of this encyclopedia's more than eight hundred articles, hardly any scholar or student will be able to peruse the useful bibliographies that follow each entry without recognizing a significant number of subjects and individuals who undeniably deserve further or greatly increased research attention. If this volume's publication can stimulate even a modest number of such new research interests, it will have provided a significant scholarly service in addition to the very notable long-term reference value that it will offer to innumerable scholars and students. Such a goal is one which undeniably deserves to be fulfilled.

CONTRIBUTORS

DOROTHY A. AUTREY is Associate Professor of History at Alabama State University.

JAMES L. BAGGETT is a graduate student in history at the University of Mississippi.

MICHAEL B. BALLARD is Associate University Archivist at Mississippi State University.

LARRY T. BALSAMO is Associate Professor of History at Western Illinois University.

CHARLES T. PETE BANNER-HALEY is Assistant Professor of History at Colgate University.

ALWYN BARR is Professor of History at Texas Tech University.

JENNIFER J. BEAUMONT is a graduate student in history at the University of Maryland, Baltimore.

PATRICIA A. BEHLAR is Assistant Professor of Political Science at Pittsburgh State University.

ROBERT A. BELLINGER is Instructor in History at Suffolk University.

AMOS J. BEYAN is Assistant Professor of History at Youngstown State University.

MONROE BILLINGTON is Professor of History at New Mexico State University.

THOMAS E. BLANTZ is Associate Professor of History at the University of Notre Dame.

ROBERT BONAZZI is Editorial Director of *Latitudes*.

JAMES BORCHERT is Associate Professor of History at Cleveland State University.

JOSEPH BOSKIN is Professor of History at Boston University.

DORSEY OLES BOYLE is a graduate student in history at the University of Maryland, Baltimore.

RAY BRANCH is Instructor in History at Wood Junior College.

JEFF BROADWATER is Director of the John C. Stennis Oral History Project at Mississippi State University.

BRENDA M. BROCK is a graduate student in English at the State University of New York at Buffalo.

LISA BROCK is Assistant Professor of African History and Diaspora Studies at The School of the Art Institute of Chicago.

LESTER S. BROOKS is Assistant Professor of History at Illinois State University.

JOE LOUIS CALDWELL is Assistant Professor of History at the University of New Orleans.

ROBERT A. CALVERT is Associate Professor of History at Texas A&M University.

DOMINIC J. CAPECI, JR., is Professor of History at Southwest Missouri State University.

JOANN D. CARPENTER is Professor of History at Florida Community College.

JESSIE M. CARTER is Lecturer in African-American Studies at the State University of New York at Buffalo.

WILLIAM CASH is Professor of History at Delta State University.

JOAN E. CASHIN is Assistant Professor of History at Rutgers University at Camden.

SUZANNE ELLERY GREENE CHAPELLE is Professor of History and Geography at Morgan State University.

LAWRENCE O. CHRISTENSEN is Professor of History and Political Science at the University of Missouri-Rolla.

JAMES R. CHUMNEY is Associate Professor of History at Memphis State University.

ERIC C. CLARK is Assistant Professor of History at Mississippi College.

THOMAS D. COCKRELL is Lecturer in History at Mississippi State University.

WILLI COLEMAN is Director of the Center for Women and Ethnic Issues at California State University, San Luis Obispo.

W. LANCE CONN is a law student at the University of Virginia.

STEPHEN CRESSWELL is Assistant Professor of History at West Virginia Wesleyan College.

JEFFREY J. CROW is Adjunct Assistant Professor of History at North Carolina State University.

CHARLES CROWE, now deceased, was Professor of History at the University of Georgia.

LORENZO CROWELL is Associate Professor of History at Mississippi State University.

DONALD CUNNIGEN is a Fellow at the Center for Afro-American Studies at Wesleyan University.

ROBERT CVORNYEK is Assistant Professor of History at Rhode Island College.

JACK E. DAVIS is a graduate student in history at Brandeis University.

THOMAS J. DAVIS is Professor of African-American Studies at the State University of New York, Buffalo.

ALLEN DENNIS is Professor of History at Delta State University.

VINCENT P. DESANTIS is Emeritus Professor of History at the University of Notre Dame.

KENNETH DeVILLE is a law student at the University of Texas.

NANCY DIAMOND is a graduate student in history at the University of Maryland, Baltimore.

BRUCE J. DIERENFIELD is Associate Professor of History at Canisius College.

BERNARD DONAHOE is Professor of History at Saint Mary's College, Indiana.

MICHAEL S. DOWNS was Staff Historian, U.S. Air Force Space Command at Peterson Air Force Base, Colorado.

W. MARVIN DULANEY is Assistant Professor of History at the University of Texas, Arlington.

AINGRED G. DUNSTON is Assistant Professor of History at Eastern Kentucky University.

BRENDA M. EAGLES is Research Librarian and Bibliographer at the Center for the Study of Southern Culture at the University of Mississippi.

CHARLES W. EAGLES is Professor of History at the University of Mississippi.

LILLIE JOHNSON EDWARDS is Associate Professor of History and Director of American Studies Program at DePaul University.

GLENN T. ESKEW is a graduate student in history at the University of Georgia.

ROBERT FIKES, JR., is Associate Librarian at San Diego State University.

NANCY E. FITCH is Assistant Professor of History at Lynchburg College.

MARVIN E. FLETCHER is Professor of History at Ohio University.

LINDA G. FORD is Assistant Professor of History at Keene State College.

TONY A. FREYER is University Research Professor of History and Law at the University of Alabama.

DAVID J. GARROW is a Fellow of The Twentieth Century Fund.

PHILLIP A. GIBBS is Assistant Professor of History at Middle Georgia College.

BRUCE A. GLASRUD is Professor of History at California State University, Hayward.

IRA GLUNTS is Head of Technical Services at the American International College Library.

KENNETH W. GOINGS is Associate Professor of History at Rhodes College.

DANIEL GOMES is a graduate student in history at the University of Maryland, Baltimore.

HUGH DAVIS GRAHAM is McTyeire Chair Professor of History at Vanderbilt University.

BARBARA L. GREEN is Assistant Professor of History at Wright State University.

GEORGE N. GREEN is Professor of History at the University of Texas at Arlington.

CHERYL GREENBERG is Assistant Professor of History at Trinity College.

BERNICE F. GUILLAUME is Associate Professor of History at St. Louis University.

MICHELE M. HALL is a graduate student in history at the University of Maryland, Baltimore.

DAVID A. HARMON is a graduate student in history at Emory University.

ALFERDTEEN HARRISON is Professor of History and Director of the Margaret Walker Alexander National Research Center for the Study of the Twentieth-Century African-American at Jackson State University.

WANDA ANN HENDRICKS is Assistant Professor of History at the University of North Carolina at Charlotte.

CLARENCE HOOKER is Assistant Professor of American Thought and Language at Michigan State University.

GARY J. HUNTER is Assistant Professor of History at Glassboro State College.

MARSHALL HYATT is Director of the Center for Afro-American Studies at Wesleyan University.

JACQUELYN JACKSON is Assistant Professor of English at Middle Tennessee State University.

ROBERT L. JENKINS is Associate Professor of History at Mississippi State University.

LAVAREE JONES is a former Community Organizer for the Child Development Group of Mississippi, Jackson.

MAXINE D. JONES is Associate Professor of History at Florida State University.

MAGHAN KEITA is Assistant Professor of History at Villanova University.

JUDITH N. KERR is Assistant Professor of History at Towson State University.

AMM SAIFUDDIN KHALED is Assistant Professor of History at the University of Chittagong, Bangladesh.

WALI RASHASH KHARIF is Assistant Professor of History at Tennessee Technological University.

ALLEN KIFER is Associate Professor of History at Skidmore College.

ELIZABETH KIGHT is a graduate student in history at the University of Maryland, Baltimore.

JOHN B. KIRBY is Professor of History at Denison University.

STEPHEN P. LABASH is a graduate student in history at the University of Maryland, Baltimore.

JANE F. LANCASTER is a graduate of the Department of History at Mississippi State University.

STEVEN F. LAWSON is Professor of History at the University of South Florida.

JANICE M. LEONE is Professor of History at Middle Tennessee State University.

CHARLES D. LOWERY is Professor of History at Mississippi State University.

ANDREW M. MANIS is Assistant Professor of Religion at Averett College.

JOHN F. MARSZALEK is Professor of History at Mississippi State University.

JAMES MARTEN is Assistant Professor of History at Marquette University.

ROBERT F. MARTIN is Professor of History at the University of Northern Iowa.

MICHAEL S. MAYER is Associate Professor of History at the University of Montana.

EARLEAN M. MCCARRICK is Associate Professor of Government and Politics at the University of Maryland.

PHILLIP MCGUIRE is Dean of Arts and Sciences at Fayetteville State University.

NEIL R. MCMILLEN is Professor of History at the University of Southern Mississippi.

TENNANT S. MCWILLIAMS is Dean of the School of Social and Behavioral Sciences at the University of Alabama-Birmingham.

MARK E. MEDINA is a student at the Yale University Law School.

STEPHEN MIDDLETON is Assistant Professor of History at North Carolina State University.

GARY B. MILLS is Professor of History at the University of Alabama.

DENNIS J. MITCHELL is Associate Professor of History at Jackson State University.

GREGORY MIXON is Assistant Professor of History at Virginia Military Institute.

CHRISTOPHER MOBLEY is Assistant Professor of Political Science at DePaul University.

DANNY BLAIR MOORE is a graduate student in history at Mississippi State University.

BETSY SAKARIASSEN NASH is a Research Historian with the Stennis Oral History Project at Mississippi State University.

HORACE D. NASH is a graduate student in history at Mississippi State University.

WILLIAM A. PAQUETTE is Associate Professor of History at Tidewater Community College.

RANDALL L. PATTON is Assistant Professor of History at Radford University.

GLENN O. PHILLIPS is Assistant Professor of History at Morgan State University.

BETTY L. PLUMMER is Assistant Professor of History at the University of Tennessee.

JAMES B. POTTS is Associate Professor of History at the University of Wisconsin-LaCrosse.

STEVE REA is a graduate student in history at the University of Mississippi.

LINDA REED is Assistant Professor of History at the University of Houston.

RICHARD W. RESH is Associate Professor of History at the University of Missouri at St. Louis.

CHARLES A. RISHER is Professor of History and Political Science at Montreat-Anderson College.

JO ANN O. ROBINSON is Professor of History and Geography at Morgan State University.

WILLIAM WARREN ROGERS, JR., is Professor of History at Gainesville College.

STEVE SADOWSKY is a graduate student in history at Middle Tennessee State University.

JEFFREY SAINSBURY is a graduate student in history at Mississippi State University.

LOREN SCHWENINGER is Professor of History at University of North Carolina at Greensboro.

JAMES E. SEFTON is Professor of History at California State University, Northridge.

CAROLE SHELTON is Assistant Professor of History at Middle Tennessee State University.

MALIK SIMBA is Associate Professor of Ethnic Studies at California State University, Fresno.

FREDERICK G. SLABACH is Associate Dean of the Mississippi College School of Law.

JAMES G. SMART is Professor of History at Keene State College.

GERALD L. SMITH is Assistant Professor of History at Memphis State University.

THADDEUS M. SMITH is Assistant Professor of History at Middle Tennessee State University.

IRVIN D. SOLOMON is Instructor in History at Edison Community College, Florida.

ALLAN H. SPEAR is Associate Professor of History at the University of Minnesota.

JAMES W. STENNETT is a graduate student in history at Mississippi State University.

ARVARH E. STRICKLAND is Professor of History at the University of Missouri.

QUINTARD TAYLOR is Professor of History at the University of Oregon.

WILLIAM J. THOMPSON is Adjunct Professor of History at Essex Community College, Baltimore.

HANS L. TREFOUSSE is Distinguished Professor of History at City University of New York.

GLORIA WAITE is Assistant Professor of History at Southeastern Massachusetts University.

GEORGE E. WALKER is Associate Professor of History at George Mason University.

PETER WALLENSTEIN is Associate Professor of History at Virginia Polytechnic Institute and State University.

JERRY WARD is Professor of English at Tougaloo College.

VIBERT L. WHITE is Assistant Professor of African-American Studies at the University of Cincinnati.

LAWRENCE H. WILLIAMS is Assistant Professor of African and Afro-American Studies and History at Luther College, Iowa.

LEE E. WILLIAMS II is Associate Professor of History at the University of Alabama in Huntsville.

LEROY T. WILLIAMS is Associate Professor of History at the University of Arkansas in Little Rock.

CAROL WILSON is a graduate student in history at West Virginia University.

FRANCILLE RUSAN WILSON is Assistant Professor of History and Philosophy at Eastern Michigan University.

BARBARA A. WORTHY is Chair of the Social Science Department at Southern University in New Orleans.

BERTRAM WYATT-BROWN is Milbauer Professor of History at the University of Florida.

PAUL D. YANDLE is a graduate student in history at Wake Forest University.

DEAN K. YATES is a graduate student in history at the University of Maryland, Baltimore.

ALFRED YOUNG is Associate Professor of History at Georgia Southern College.

ROBERT L. ZANGRANDO is Professor of History at the University of Akron.

INTRODUCTION

The African-American's struggle for freedom and equality is one of the truly heroic episodes in American history. From the earliest colonial days to the present, that enduring struggle, in all its myriad forms, has been as relentless as it has been inevitable. Regardless of when they lived, black Americans have shared with white Americans—and all people everywhere—the innate, timeless, indomitable desire to be free. It is a cruel irony that a people who could so boldly assert as self-evident truth that "all men are created equal" and are "endowed by their Creator" with such "inalienable rights" as "life, liberty, and the pursuit of happiness," could at the same time so resolutely deny to blacks the exercise of these rights. In failing to remain faithful to their own creed, white Americans underscored the hypocrisy and deception, the contradiction of purpose and spirit, that characterized their relationship to blacks.

From the earliest time tragedy has marked race relations in America. The institution of slavery dominated the country's early years until a bloody Civil War opened the possibility for a new racial relationship. The coming of "Jubilee" contained more promise than reality, however, and slavery was soon replaced by segregation, at first through custom and then more firmly by law. Slave codes became Black Codes and then Jim Crow state constitutions and laws. Freed people saw their emancipation turn into the new prison of segregation. The United States Supreme Court in the landmark *Plessy v. Ferguson* case of 1896 legitimated this "separate but equal" Jim Crowism. The law of the land allowed segregation and enforced "separate" conditions for African-American citizens in all aspects of their lives, but the "equal" side of the equation was conveniently ignored.

For most of the twentieth century, the average black American's citizenship was a cruel hoax. Even when the Supreme Court in the momentous 1954 *Brown v. Board of Education* decision eliminated the constitutional justification for segregation, the battle was not won. Several more decades of struggle were required to achieve even minimal integration.

At the same time, though, there existed another dimension of race relations. There were blacks and whites who found slavery and segregation to be intolerable, and they battled it as best they could. The African who committed suicide rather than board a slave ship; the plantation slave who broke tools or nurtured aspects of the African past; the black and white abolitionists who served as national conscience; the free blacks who met in conventions of protest; and the politicians who finally took a stand, led the nation through a war of emancipation, and passed the Thirteenth Amendment—all these and many more individuals fought to eliminate the peculiar institution.

Once slavery was abolished, those who believed that the battle was over withdrew from the fray. Others, both blacks and whites, saw that the nation had much to do if the former slaves were ever really to be free. Theirs was a long, lonely, and often dangerous battle to try to eliminate pervasive racism and provide full citizenship to America's black population.

The battle seemed unending, and it had many fronts. These included the right to vote and hold public office; the chance for a good job and promotion; the opportunity for an education from kindergarten to professional school; access to decent medical treatment; the opportunity to eat in restaurants or at lunch counters, go to theaters, sleep in motels, use public restrooms and waiting areas, worship in churches; the chance to join the military, appear in films or on the stage, participate on amateur and professional athletic teams, have articles and books published, argue cases in court or serve on juries or testify as a witness; live in a decent home in a pleasant neighborhood; experience freedom from fear; and enjoy respect, courtesy, and acceptance. From 1865 through the twentieth century, the term "civil rights" came to mean the freedom and opportunity to enjoy, unimpeded, this whole complex of American citizenship rights. The civil rights movement, especially its intensification in the 1950s and 1960s, was the long struggle to bring African Americans into the promise of the American Dream.

Throughout this period, historical writing reflected the bias that the dominant American white society felt against black people. Assumptions of white superiority and black inferiority were as deeply imbedded in the history books as they were in society as a whole. When blacks were mentioned in the texts, if they were, it was in the most depreciative language. Favorable books or articles, when they saw print, were patronizingly or forcefully suppressed.

During the years of the modern civil rights struggle, workers in the movement have labored first and foremost to liberate black people, but they also have tried to liberate America's history. A torrent of literature on all aspects of the black-white experience poured forth when the dam of literary discrimination was breached. This literature has both influenced the civil rights struggle and been influenced by it. In this important body of books on race relations, however, there is a conspicuous void. There is no reference book that presents under a single cover an overview of the century-long struggle for civil rights. Excellent books and articles exist on all aspects of this subject, but there is no one convenient, accurate reference source.

This *Encyclopedia of African-American Civil Rights* was prepared to fill this void. It contains over eight hundred short articles on a wide variety of individuals, organizations, events, and court cases focusing on the period since emancipation. Librarians at all types of libraries, from the largest reference to the smallest public, will find it a convenient source for information on this topic. The bibliographical references with each article will also provide ready entry into the vast literature in the field.

In organizing and completing this volume, the editors faced several difficult decisions. The topic is broad and the available pages necessarily limited. The editors decided to include, for the most part, only that which, in their judgment, made a significant positive contribution to the advancement of black civil rights. Every state and community had its share of brave, resourceful individuals, influential organizations, and locally significant events and court cases. Unfortunately, all could not be included here, not because they were unimportant, but because there simply is not space enough for all of them. In order to include as many subjects as possible and be consistent with the purpose of an encyclopedia, the editors have kept the articles brief.

Another difficult decision concerned whether to include those who opposed the civil rights movement. Individuals such as Eugene "Bull" Connor, Ross Barnett, Orval Faubus, and George C. Wallace, and groups such as the Ku Klux Klan, the White Citizens' Council, and the State Sovereignty Commissions, were legion, outnumbering in the South, certainly, those people and organizations championing racial equality. In a perverse way the opponents of black civil rights, because of the depth of their racism and the brutish violence of their opposition, promoted the cause of freedom. But it would require another book to deal with all of them, and rather than include some and neglect others, we did not include any.

Similarly, we did not include presidents of the United States or every congressman, Supreme Court justice, black novelist, playwright, news-paperperson, soldier, sports figure, or "first black" whose activities contributed to the movement. We are acutely aware of how much we have omitted, but we also think that we have included a representative cross-section of the most significant people, organizations, events, and court cases of the black civil rights movement.

We were fortunate to be able to work with an outstanding group of conscientious and talented authors. They include some of the foremost scholars in the field as well as individuals just beginning their professional careers. We naturally appreciate the support of the former, but we particularly want to express our gratitude to the latter. Their willingness to undertake a wide variety of assignments enabled us to carry the project forward. All editors have horror stories to tell about working on a book such as this, and we have ours, too. Fortunately, our happy experiences far outnumber the unpleasant ones.

We are deeply indebted to a number of other people who have been instrumental in bringing this project to fruition. Undergraduate student-helper Marzett Jordan undertook a wide variety of clerical and research tasks and accomplished them in his usual quietly efficient manner. Graduate Assistant James Stennett was similarly productive, and Research Assistant Danny Blair Moore provided valuable assistance during the last stages of the project. Jean Whitehead and Karen Groce typed goodly portions of the manuscript. Peggy Y. Bonner and Lonna Reinecke not only typed the manuscript and letters to the authors, but provided invaluable assistance in other ways as well. Their organizational skills and their ability to remember where everything was filed saved us from a host of editorial problems. To say that this book could not have been completed without them is no exaggeration. To Professors David J. Garrow and Willard B. Gatewood, Jr., who read the manuscript and offered many discerning suggestions and criticisms, we are especially indebted. Our friend and colleague Allen Dennis not only authored entries for the *Encyclopedia*, but he also compiled the index for the volume. He has long experience as a professional indexer, and the finished product attests to his skill. We thank him for his help. At Greenwood Press, Executive Editor Cynthia Harris has provided from the outset, guidance and encouragement, for which we are deeply grateful. Production editor Penny Sippel has skillfully managed the editorial responsibilities of bringing the volume into production. Finally, to our wives, Susie and Jeanne, we are most indebted, not just for the freedom they gave us to complete this project, but for their support, love, and companionship in all things.

AN AID TO USING THE ENCYCLOPEDIA

The entries on individuals, organizations, events, and court cases that constitute this encyclopedia are arranged in alphabetical order. The entries are cross-referenced through the use of the asterisk; that is, any person, group, occurrence, or court case mentioned in an entry that has its own entry is so marked. A detailed index at the end of the volume provides a convenient way to locate desired information. Each entry includes a brief bibliographical list to guide the reader to other printed sources that contain valuable data on the subject in question.

Judicial citations conform to standard practice. Supreme Court decisions are officially published in *United States Reports* and are cited by volume and page number. The *Plessy v. Ferguson* opinion, for example, cited as 163 U.S. 537, is found in volume 163 of *United States Reports* at page 537. Recent opinions of the federal appeals courts are in *Federal Reporter, 2d Series*. Thus, the appellate decision in *Collins v. Walker*, cited as 339 F.2d 100, is in volume 339 of *Federal Reporter, 2d Series* at page 100. Federal district court opinions appear in *Federal Supplement* (F. Supp.), also cited by volume and page number.

Encyclopedia of
African-American
Civil Rights

A

ABBOTT, ROBERT S. (28 November 1868, St. Simon's Island, Ga.–28 February 1940, Chicago, Ill.). Known as "A Founding Father of Black Journalism and the Dean of Negro Publishers," he attended Beach Institute in Savannah, Georgia, spent time at Claflin College in Orangeburg, South Carolina, studied printing and graduated from Hampton Institute,* and received an LL.B. degree from Chicago's Kent College of Law in 1899. Abbott practiced law briefly in Kansas and Indiana before founding the *Chicago Defender** (the newspaper that revolutionized the black press) in 1905. From its inception, Abbott used the *Defender's* columns to urge a militant campaign against segregation and the racial injustices heaped upon African Americans. By the time of his death in 1940 he had urged a generation of black Southerners "to leave the lynching South."

SELECTED BIBLIOGRAPHY

Robert L. Green, *Robert S. Abbot: Negro Businessman* (1969); Roi Ottley, *The Lonely Warrior: The Life and Times of Robert S. Abbott* (1955); Edgar H. Toppin, *Biographical History of Blacks in America Since 1528* (1971); Roland E. Wolseley, *The Black Press, USA* (1971).

Phillip McGuire

ABERNATHY, RALPH DAVID, SR. (11 March 1926, Linden, Ala.–17 April 1990, Atlanta, Ga.). Abernathy was an African-American civil rights and religious leader and a top aide to the Reverend Dr. Martin Luther King, Jr.* He attended Alabama State College, which later became Alabama State University (B.S., 1950), and Atlanta University* (M.A., Sociology, 1951). He also received numerous honorary degrees. In 1951 he was appointed Dean of Men and sociology instructor at Alabama

State College. In the same year, he joined the National Association for the Advancement of Colored People* and became pastor of the black First Baptist Church in Montgomery (1951–1961). In 1955 he helped organize the Montgomery bus boycott.* Abernathy was a founder of the Southern Christian Leadership Conference* (SCLC) in 1957, and he became secretary/treasurer in 1961. He was arrested no fewer than nineteen times with King during civil rights marches, and in 1965 he was designated King's heir apparent as SCLC president. Following King's death in 1968, Abernathy assumed leadership of SCLC. Increasing SCLC's level of involvement in the civil rights movement, he directed the Poor People's March on Washington* in May 1968; led a demonstration at the July 1968 Republican National Convention in Miami; helped organize the 1968 Atlanta sanitation workers' strike; was jailed in June 1969 during the successful Charleston, South Carolina, hospital workers' strike; and helped plan the march from Perry, Georgia, to Atlanta in 1970. In 1977 Abernathy resigned leadership of SCLC and ran, unsuccessfully, for the Georgia congressional seat vacated by Andrew Young.* Afterward he became less influential in the civil rights movement. In 1980, he surprised many by endorsing Republican Ronald Reagan for president. Later, he founded the Foundation for Economic Enterprises Development, a nonprofit organization to improve black economic opportunities. He became more active on the lecture circuit and served as pastor of West Hunter Street Baptist Church in Atlanta until he suffered the first of several strokes in 1983. In 1989 Abernathy published *And the Walls Came Tumbling Down*, an autobiographical account of the civil rights movement, which contained statements regarding King's alleged sexual infidelities. The book was severely criticized, resulting in loss of prestige for the author. Nevertheless, Abernathy was an important actor in the civil rights struggle.

SELECTED BIBLIOGRAPHY
Ralph David Abernathy, Sr., *And the Walls Came Tumbling Down* (1989); A. John Adams and Joan Martin Burke, *A CBS News Reference Book: Civil Rights, A Current Guide to the People, Organizations and Events* (1970); *Jet* 7 (14 May 1990); Harry A. Ploski et al., eds., *The Negro Almanac* (1983).

                                                              Wali Rashash Kharif

ABOLISH PEONAGE COMMITTEE OF AMERICA. Following the demise of slavery, white landowners searched for ways to limit the freedom of movement of black laborers. Black peonage,* the forced immobility of labor based on indebtedness, was one of the measures implemented. This system of covert coercion began to be challenged effectively only with the growth of southern Progressivism in the early years of the twentieth century. The apogee of the movement came with the *Bailey v. Alabama** decision in 1911 whereby the Supreme Court declared an Alabama contract labor law unconstitutional because it violated the Thirteenth Amendment.* Despite the legal victory, peonage remained a prevalent practice and a constant encroachment upon civil rights. In 1939 William Henry Huff, a Chicago lawyer, learned of an attempt by a Georgia planter named Cunningham to extradite four of his indebted laborers back to his Ogelthorpe County farm. Huff intervened on their behalf and, aided by the International Labor Defense, formed the Abolish Peonage Committee of America, the first public organization to combat this practice. The committee at once joined the defense in the suit Huff initiated. The Cunningham case was catapulted into national prominence. Huff and other members of the committee were called on to testify before the Justice Department on the problem of peonage. The four laborers were acquitted but, to the dismay of the committee, the Georgia planter was not indicted. The Abolish Peonage Committee remained active into the World War II years, but never again was it to achieve such prominence. Huff's resignation in 1942 helped signal the demise of the organization's influence.

SELECTED BIBLIOGRAPHY

Pete Daniels, *The Shadow of Slavery: Peonage in the South, 1901–1969* (1972); Daniel Novak, *The Wheel of Servitude: Black Forced Labor after Slavery* (1978).

Steve Rea

ADAMS, HENRY (17 December 1802, Franklin County, Ga.–3 November 1872, Louisville, Ky.). A prominent African-American minister and pioneer educator, Henry Adams served the First African (later Fifth Street) Baptist Church in Louisville. Consisting of nine hundred members before the Civil War, it was the largest Baptist Church, black or white, in the area. Adams also started the first school for blacks in the city on 7 December 1841. Consisting of slave and free children, it continued to operate until public schools became available in 1870. Subsequently, Adams helped to organize the black public school system in Louisville. His contribution is important because it demonstrates the early connections among the black church, black education, and black social uplift.

SELECTED BIBLIOGRAPHY

Ira V. Birdwhistell, *Gathered at the River: A Narrative History of Long Run Baptist Association* (1978); William J. Simmons, *Men of Mark: Eminent, Progressive, and Rising* (1887); Henry C. Weeden, *Weeden's History of the Colored People of Louisville* (1897); Lawrence H. Williams, *Black Higher Education in Kentucky, 1879–1930: The History of Simmons University* (1987); George D. Wilson, "A Century of Negro Education in Louisville, Kentucky" (unpublished manuscript prepared by workers of the Works Progress Administration, 1941).

Lawrence H. Williams

ADDERLY v. FLORIDA, 385 U.S. 39 (1966). In September 1963, 107 Florida Agricultural and Mechanical University students were arrested for protesting outside the Tallahassee, Florida, Leon County Jail. The students were convicted of "trespass with a malicious and mischievous intent." Harriet Adderley and thirty-one others appealed their convictions before the Supreme Court, having failed in the Florida District Court and in the District Court of Appeals. Attorneys Richard Felder and Tobias Simon argued on 18 October 1966 that the students had been deprived of their "rights of free speech, assembly, petition, due process of law and equal protection of the laws under the 14th Amendment" (see also Fourteenth Amendment). Speaking for the majority, Justice Hugo Black ruled that "the state, no less than a private owner of property, has power to preserve the property under its control for the use to which it is lawfully dedicated." In the dissenting opinion, Justice William O. Douglas claimed that the Court had done "violence to the First Amendment" by permitting "this 'petition for redress of grievances' to be turned into a trespass action."

SELECTED BIBLIOGRAPHY

Henry J. Abraham, *Freedom and the Court; Civil Rights and Liberties in the United States* (1988); Richard Bardolph, ed., *The Civil Rights Record: Black Americans and the Law, 1849–1970* (1970); Glenda A. Rabby, "Out of the Past: The Civil Rights Movement in Tallahassee, Florida" (Ph.D. diss., Florida State University, 1984).

Maxine D. Jones

AFFIRMATIVE ACTION. Affirmative action applies to programs designed to eliminate discrimination against minorities and women, particularly in education and employment. The legal foundation on which it rests includes the Equal Protection Clause of the Fourteenth Amendment,* Title VII of the Civil Rights Act of 1964,* and President Lyndon B. Johnson's Executive Order 11246.*

Support for affirmative action crested in the late 1960s and declined thereafter, amidst a crescendo of complaints about "reverse discrimination." The *University of California Regents v. Bakke** (1978) and *United States Steel Workers v. Weber** (1979) Supreme Court cases demonstrated the "sharp and diverse points of view" provoked by this concept.

In his dissenting opinion on *Bakke*, Justice Thurgood Marshall* set forth an African-American point of view: "The experience of Negroes in America has been different in kind, not just in degree from that of other ethnic groups.... For far too long the doors to...positions of influence, affluence, and prestige...have been shut to Negroes. If we are ever to become a fully integrated society...we must be willing to open those doors."

SELECTED BIBLIOGRAPHY

Michael W. Combs and John Gruhl, eds., *Affirmative Action Theories, Analysis and Prospects* (1986); Gerald R. Gill, *Meanness Mania, the Changing Mood* (1980); Kathanne W. Greene, *Affirmative Action and Principles of Justice* (1989); Daniel C.

Maguire, *A New American Justice* (1980); Harrell R. Rodgers, Jr., and Charles Bullock III, *Law and Social Change: Civil Rights Laws and Their Consequences* (1972).

Jo Ann O. Robinson

AFRICAN BLOOD BROTHERHOOD. Founded in 1917 as a nationalist, revolutionary, Pan-African Movement* by Cyril Briggs (1888–1966), the short-lived African Blood Brotherhood for African Liberation and Redemption (ABB) sought to ally racial consciousness to the goals of class consciousness. This paramilitary organization, catapulted into national attention by the Tulsa Riot (1921) which destroyed that Oklahoma African-American community, proposed worldwide federation of all African groups and armed defense of all African-American communities. Its reported zenith "enlistment" was five thousand, mostly ex-servicemen, in fifty-six "posts." The ABB, prefigured by the Hamitic League of the World, became the first African-American auxiliary of the American Communist Party* in 1925.

SELECTED BIBLIOGRAPHY

Robert L. Allen, *Reluctant Reformers* (1974); Theodore Draper, *American Communism and Soviet Russia* (1960); Robert A. Hill, ed., *The Crusader* (1987).

Aingred G. Dunston

AFRO-AMERICAN. Founded by John Murphy, Sr., in 1892, the *Baltimore Afro-American* (and its editions in other cities) was a leader in the fight for civil rights. The newspaper campaigned against the inequities of Baltimore's and other segregated school systems, against Jim Crow* laws, and against attempts to disenfranchise black voters in the early twentieth century. It led the revival of the Baltimore chapter of the National Association for the Advancement of Colored People* in 1935 under the strong leadership of Lillie May Carroll Jackson. The *Afro-American* supported Democrat Franklin Roosevelt in 1936, liberal Republican mayoral candidate Theodore McKeldin in 1943, and black candidates, mostly Democrats, who won election to local and state offices beginning in the 1950s. It gave wide coverage to local and national racial abuses and civil rights protests of the 1950s, 1960s, and later decades.

SELECTED BIBLIOGRAPHY

Robert J. Brugger, *Maryland: A Middle Temperament, 1634–1980* (1988); George H. Callcott, *Maryland and America, 1940–1980* (1985).

Suzanne Ellery Greene Chapelle

AFRO-AMERICAN COUNCIL. In 1898 Timothy Thomas Fortune* and African Methodist Episcopal Bishop Alexander Walters* revived the defunct Afro-American League* under this new name. Initially the council adopted its predecessor's aggressive policies. Gradually, however, the moderate Booker T. Washington* and his supporters came to dominate it. The council attempted to censure Washington in 1899 for his apologetic tone in an appeal to southern white officials regarding lynching of accused black rapists. Washington's supporters blocked the censure, and by the turn of the century the council reflected his conciliatory position. Continuing white attacks on African Americans, plus the growing influence of the combative W.E.B. Du Bois's* Niagara Movement,* undermined the influence of the council which died out in 1908. Its brief history demonstrated the divisive philosophies of African-American leadership during the era of Jim Crow.*

SELECTED BIBLIOGRAPHY

Louis R. Harlan, *Booker T. Washington: The Making of a Black Leader, 1856–1901* (1972); Louis R. Harlan, *Booker T. Washington: The Wizard of Tuskegee, 1901–1915* (1983); August Meier, *Negro Thought in America, 1880–1915: Racial Ideologies in the Age of Booker T. Washington* (1963).

Michael B. Ballard

AFRO-AMERICAN LEAGUE. In 1887 Timothy Thomas Fortune,* the editor of the *New York Age,** conceived the idea of a protective league for African Americans. From this concept, the Afro-American League emerged in 1890. Under Fortune's leadership, the league espoused agitation and revolution as legitimate means of securing black rights. The league further emphasized black solidarity and proposed an economic program that included an Afro-American bank, the promotion of industrial education, cooperative enterprises, job training, nonpartisan politics, an immigration bureau to help scatter blacks more equitably around the states, self-solutions to black problems, and preservation of black cultural values. At one time or another the league counted as members most prominent black leaders. Internal friction and rivalry with the American Citizens' Equal Rights Association, however, soon caused the league to lapse into inactivity. By 1893 the national body and most of its local branches had ceased to function. The league did help keep alive black hopes for full and equal citizenship, and in 1898 it was revived under a new name, the Afro-American Council.*

SELECTED BIBLIOGRAPHY

Herbert Aptheker, ed., *A Documentary History of the Negro People in the United States,* vol. 1 (1951); Louis R. Harlan, *Booker T. Washington: The Making of a Black Leader, 1856–1901* (1972); August Meier, *Negro Thought in America, 1880–1915: Racial Ideologies in the Age of Booker T. Washington* (1963).

Michael B. Ballard

ALABAMA CHRISTIAN MOVEMENT FOR HUMAN RIGHTS. On 5 June 1956, more than one thousand people overflowed the Sardis Baptist Church in Birmingham, Alabama, to join the Reverends Fred L. Shuttlesworth,* Edward Gardner, R. L. Alford, and N. H. Smith in organizing the Alabama Christian Movement for Human Rights (ACMHR). Formed in response to the state attorney general's ban on the National Association for the Advancement of Colored People,* the ACMHR quickly became the leading civil rights organization in Birmingham. Using direct action,* the ACMHR challenged bus segregation in December 1956 and again in October 1958, attempted the integration of schools and the railroad station in 1957, and supported the student sit-ins in 1960 and the Freedom Riders* in 1961. This dedicated group of militant Christian activists elected Shuttlesworth president, and his association with the Southern Christian Leadership Conference* led to the Birmingham Confrontation* of spring 1963. When Shuttlesworth stepped down as president in 1969, Gardner, the longtime first vice president, assumed leadership—a position he still held in 1990. The ACMHR endorsed Richard Arrington for the Birmingham City Council in 1971 and worked to get him elected as the first African-American mayor of the city in 1979.

SELECTED BIBLIOGRAPHY

Jimmie Lewis Franklin, *Back to Birmingham* (1989); David J. Garrow, ed., *Birmingham, Alabama, 1956–1963* (1989); Howell Raines, *My Soul Is Rested* (1977).

Glenn T. Eskew

ALABAMA COUNCIL ON HUMAN RELATIONS. Founded in 1954 to promote racial harmony and goodwill, the council was the successor to the Alabama Commission on Interracial Cooperation. It was a state branch of the Southern Regional Council* organized by an integrated group who believed that the racial tensions of the times could be eased through dialogue and education. During the 1950s and 1960s, operating through its state headquarters and through its branches in major Alabama cities, the council sought to improve race relations. One of its most important roles was that of mediator in racial conflicts such as the Montgomery bus boycott* of 1955–1956 and the Birmingham Confrontation* of 1963. In 1965 the council shifted its focus from race relations to social programs to benefit the poor. Although hampered by a small membership and limited funding, the council was a positive force in Alabama for building a spirit of understanding and cooperation between the races.

SELECTED BIBLIOGRAPHY

Taylor Branch, *Parting the Waters—America in the King Years, 1954–63* (1988); Virginia Foster Durr, *Outside the Magic Circle, the Autobiography of Virginia Foster Durr* (1985); David J. Garrow, *Bearing the Cross, Martin Luther King and the Southern Christian Leadership Conference* (1986); Benjamin Muse, *The American Negro Revolution: From Nonviolence to Black Power, 1963–1967* (1968); Jan Gregory Thompson, "The History of the Alabama Council of Human Relations from Roots to Redirection, 1920–1968" (Ph.D. diss., Auburn University, 1983).

Dorothy A. Autrey

ALBANY, GEORGIA, MOVEMENT. *See* Albany, Georgia, Sit-In.

ALBANY, GEORGIA, SIT-IN. On Thanksgiving weekend 1961, African-American activists decided to test a recent Interstate Commerce Commission ruling on desegregation by using the whites-only facilities

Black protesters in Albany, Georgia, and elsewhere encountered the intimidating presence of the Klan. (Carl and Ann Braden Collection. State Historical Society of Wisconsin.)

at the Trailways bus station in Albany, Georgia. Their actions catapulted this southwest Georgia community of 56,000, 40 percent of whom were black, into national prominence. Albany became, in the early 1960s, both a catalyst for similar student-initiated actions, particularly those by the Student Nonviolent Coordinating Committee* (SNCC), and a symbol of organizational factionalism, especially regarding the role of Dr. Martin Luther King, Jr.,* in the ensuing "Albany Movement." On 22 November 1961, SNCC workers Charles Sherrod and Cordell Reagon, along with a group of black students from Albany State College and the local NAACP* Youth Council, sat down in the whites-only section of the Trailways terminal and refused to leave. Following their expulsion a coalition of local black organizations and student leaders began a co-ordinated attack on Albany's strict color line. Internecine squabbling among the participants prompted King to make an appearance in Albany, but he left without achieving the real or symbolic victories that earlier had won him national acclaim. The mass protest continued in Albany for another six years. Although King would call Albany his most glaring defeat, the actions there galvanized SNCC workers into a stronger commitment to direct-action* campaigns (e.g., the Freedom

Summer of 1964* struggles) and ushered in a new era in civil rights in which black spirituals, such as "Ain't Gonna Let Nobody Turn Me Around," were sung defiantly in the face of white oppression.

SELECTED BIBLIOGRAPHY

Taylor Branch, *Parting the Waters: America in the King Years, 1954–63* (1988); Henry Hampton and Steve Fayer, *Voices of Freedom: An Oral History of the Civil Rights Movement from the 1950s through the 1980s* (1990); Aldon D. Morris, *The Origins of the Civil Rights Movement: Black Communities Organizing for Change* (1984); Juan Williams, *Eyes on the Prize: America's Civil Rights Years, 1954–1965* (1988); Howard Zinn, *SNCC; The New Abolitionists* (1964).

                                                                Irvin D. Solomon

ALDRIDGE v. UNITED STATES, 283 U.S. 308 (1931). Although the trial judge in this case allowed the plaintiff's attorney to ask questions of prospective jurors regarding their knowledge of the facts in the case, their acquaintance with either the African-American defendant or the dead white policeman, and their reactions to circumstantial evidence and capital punishment, he refused to allow them to be questioned regarding their racial prejudices. Aldridge was convicted of murder, and the judge's decision was sustained by the District of Columbia Court of Appeals which ruled that such questions, proper elsewhere, were not appropriate in the nation's capital. The United States Supreme Court in its reversal recognized the propriety of such inquiries. Chief Justice Charles Evans Hughes ruled that the right to examine jurors on their voir dire regarding a disqualifying state of mind had been upheld in cases involving other races, "religious and other prejudices of a serious character." He maintained that the question of racial prejudice was not geared to the matter of civil rights but to the presence of bias in a particular juror. If prejudice of any kind would prevent a juror from "rendering a fair verdict, a gross injustice would be perpetrated in allowing him to sit."

SELECTED BIBLIOGRAPHY

Richard Bardolph, ed., *The Civil Rights Record, Black Americans and the Law 1849–1970* (1970); Derrick A. Bell, Jr., *Race, Racism and American Law* (1980); Alfred H. Kelly and Winfred A. Harbison, *American Constitution: Origins and Development* (1970).

                                                                Aingred G. Dunston

ALEXANDER, CLIFFORD L., JR. (21 September 1933, New York, N.Y.–). The first African-American chairman of the Equal Employment Opportunity Commission* (EEOC) (1967–1969), Alexander brought elite credentials to the commission at a turbulent time. A native of New York City with a Harvard B.A. (1955) and a Yale law degree (1958), Alexander served an Army tour during 1958–1959, then worked in New York City in the district attorney's office, Harlem youth work, and private law practice. In 1963 he joined the National Security Council staff under McGeorge Bundy, and in 1964 he became a presidential assistant to Lyndon B. Johnson. In 1967 the EEOC, created by the Civil Rights Act of 1964,* faced a troubled environment that included widespread urban violence, feminist demands for stronger enforcement of gender equality, administrative confusion within the agency, and a vacant chairmanship for the third time. Johnson appointed Alexander, who held a series of regional hearings to emphasize employment discrimination outside the South, especially in white-collar jobs. Alexander accelerated the agency's controversial shift from an equal-treatment model of nondiscrimination toward an equal-results model of affirmative action* that stressed proportional representation of minorities and women in the work force. In 1969 Senate minority leader Everett Dirksen attacked Alexander for harassing employers and for requiring racial quotas in employment. In May 1969 President Richard Nixon replaced Alexander as chairman with a black Republican, William A. Brown III. The EEOC continued its affirmative action program, but Alexander resigned from the commission in August 1969 to enter private law practice in Washington, D.C. In 1977 he was appointed Secretary of the Army by President Jimmy Carter and served until 1980.

SELECTED BIBLIOGRAPHY
Current Biography (1977); *The Ebony Success Library*, vol. 1 (1973); Hugh Davis Graham, *The Civil Rights Era* (1990).

Hugh Davis Graham

ALEXANDER, JOHN HANKS (6 January 1864, Helena, Ark.–26 March 1894, Springfield, Ohio). The son of slave parents, he attended Oberlin College in Ohio for one year until he scored higher on a test than the son of Ohio's Chief Justice and received an appointment to the United States Military Academy in 1883. Despite white ostracism, he did well in all his courses, particularly those in the languages, and in 1887 became the second black graduate in the history of West Point, ranking thirty-second out of a class of sixty-four. After graduation, he reported to the all-black 9th Cavalry Regiment (see Buffalo Soldiers) where he served for the next seven years and compiled an excellent record. Booker T. Washington* and other black leaders tried to get him assigned as an instructor of military science at Tuskegee Institute* or some other black college, but they were not successful until January 1894 when, through the efforts of the president of Ohio's Wilberforce College, he was assigned there. He had just begun his tour of duty when he died of a heart attack. Had he lived longer he might very well have become the ranking black officer in World War I; he outranked the later famous Charles Young* by two years. During the war, the War Department named a Virginia stevedore encampment Camp Alexander after him.

SELECTED BIBLIOGRAPHY
Williard B. Gatewood, Jr., "John Hanks Alexander of Arkansas: Second Black Graduate of West Point," *Arkansas Historical Quarterly* 41 (Summer 1982), 103–28; Rayford W. Logan and Michael R. Winston, eds., *Dictionary of American Negro Biography* (1982); Reverdy C. Ransom, *The Pilgrimage of Harriet Ransom's Son* (n.d.); William S. Scarborough, *A Tribute to Colonel Charles Young* (n.d.).

John F. Marszalek

ALEXANDER, MARGARET WALKER (7 July 1915, Birmingham, Ala.–). Daughter of a middle-class academic family, who taught at a series of southern colleges during her childhood, she graduated from Northwestern University during the Great Depression and went to work for the Works Progress Administration (WPA) in Chicago. She became friends with a group of writers on the South Side that included Richard Wright.* During that period, Walker wrote most of the poems later published in *For My People* (1942). When the WPA work ended, Walker went to Iowa for her master's degree in English and then taught at a series of black colleges. She married Firnist James Alexander in North Carolina and moved to Jackson, Mississippi, with three children in 1949.

Margaret Walker Alexander's relationship with Jackson State University proved stormy. She felt that the male administration discriminated against her because she was a woman; nevertheless, she worked hard and students considered her a demanding, master teacher who erased disciplinary lines seeking insight and understanding. In addition to continuing her writing, Alexander wrote grants, conducted workshops, and established the Institute for the Study of the Life, History, and Culture of Black People, one of the first academic organizations in the South devoted to black studies.

Walker has said that her teaching and writing are her contributions to the civil rights movement. She completed her Ph.D. at the University of Iowa and published her dissertation in 1966, which, as *Jubilee*, became a highly successful, popular novel, which describes the black debate in the 1870s in a manner relevant to the 1960s and 1970s. The main character, Vyry, a mulatto daughter of her master, remains faithful to her Christianity and refuses to hate despite the beatings and abuse heaped on her by whites. By contrast the main male character is pure black and espouses the black nationalist point of view. In her novel and in her life, Walker made many people uncomfortable because she lived Vyry's strong commitment to a Christian family while uncompromisingly condemning white racism and sympathizing with the black nationalist.

Alexander has written ten books and, since retiring from teaching, has devoted herself to writing full time. She published *Richard Wright: Daemonic Genius* in 1988 and is preparing a sequel to *Jubilee* which will tell the history of the black, southern middle class since Reconstruction.

Margaret Walker Alexander.
(Courtesy, Mississippi Department of Archives and History.)

SELECTED BIBLIOGRAPHY
Maryemma Graham, ed., *How I Wrote Jubilee and Other Essays on Life and Literature* (1990); Margaret Walker, *Jubilee* (1966); Margaret Walker Alexander Papers, Jackson State University Library, Jackson, Mississippi.

Dennis Mitchell

ALEXANDER v. HOLMES COUNTY BOARD OF EDUCATION, 396 U.S. 1218 (1969). On 29 October 1969, the U.S. Supreme Court unanimously declared that public school desegregation at "all deliberate speed," as allowed in the second *Brown v. Board of Education** case in 1955, was no longer constitutionally permissible. Instead, the court ordered that the dual school systems in Mississippi's thirty-three school districts had to be eliminated, and "unitary" school systems established "at once." District officials had argued that massive midterm integration would cause unjustified disruption in the schools. Serving as a precedent, *Alexander* was a major step away from the federal courts' post-*Brown* deliberate approach. It ensured widescale school integration across the South within the succeeding twelve months. *Alexander* also marked a milestone in changing federal policy from "desegregation," eliminating barriers to blacks and whites attending school together, to "integration," requiring blacks and whites to attend the same schools. The Justice Department and the Department of Health, Education and Welfare argued for the

Mississippi school districts' position. Prior to this case, the Justice Department and the NAACP* Legal Defense and Educational Fund,* the lawyers for the plaintiffs, were uniformly in agreement. Observers commonly saw President Richard Nixon's "Southern Strategy" to win southern votes as the cause for this change. Warren Burger, Nixon's newly appointed chief justice, concurred with his fellow justices.

SELECTED BIBLIOGRAPHY

" 'Desegregate Now'—But How to Do It?" *U.S. News and World Report* (10 November 1969), 45–46; Paul R. Dimond, *Beyond Busing: Inside the Challenge to Urban Segregation* (1985); Alfred H. Kelly, Winfred A. Harbison, and Herman Belz, *The American Constitution: Its Origins and Development*, 6th ed. (1983); "The Supreme Court: Integration Now," *Time* (7 November 1969), 19–20; J. Harvie Wilkinson III, *The Supreme Court and School Integration: 1954–1978* (1979).

Eric C. Clark

ALEXANDER, WILL W. (15 July 1884, Morrisville, Mo.–13 January 1956, Chapel Hill, N.C.). Born and raised in Missouri and ordained a Methodist minister, Alexander received a divinity degree from Vanderbilt University in Nashville where he first came in contact with southern poverty and racial segregation. In response to the racial violence of 1919, the resurgence of the Ku Klux Klan, and racial lynching, he founded the Atlanta-based Commission on Interracial Cooperation* (CIC) which he headed until the mid-1930s. Working within an isolated and racially hostile southern environment, Alexander did not directly challenge Jim Crowism (see Jim Crow) but sought social and economic opportunities for blacks while encouraging a more enlightened racial perspective among white religious, business, and civic groups. When Franklin D. Roosevelt took office in 1933, Alexander became a key adviser on racial matters to the New Deal and especially to individuals such as Eleanor Roosevelt.* He was also close to black leaders such as Walter Francis White* of the NAACP* and sociologist Charles S. Johnson.* In 1935 he left the CIC to become an assistant in the Resettlement Administration and shortly thereafter, head of the Farm Security Administration (FSA). Under Alexander, the FSA appointed blacks to national and state positions, and black farmers were included in various FSA programs such as farm loans. During World War II, Alexander and black economist Robert C. Weaver* worked to secure defense jobs for black workers, and in the late 1940s and early 1950s Alexander supported the interracial efforts of the Southern Regional Council* and the Southern Conference for Human Welfare.* Although he died prior to the southern civil rights struggles of the late 1950s and early 1960s, Alexander's long commitment to racial toleration and the rights of black people contributed to some of the later achievements won by blacks in the South.

SELECTED BIBLIOGRAPHY
Sidney Baldwin, *Poverty and Politics: The Rise and Decline of the Farm Security Administration* (1968); Wilma Dykeman and James Stokley, *Seeds of Southern Change: The Life of Will Alexander* (1966); John B. Kirby, *Black Americans in the Roosevelt Era* (1980); Harvard Sitkoff, *A New Deal for Blacks* (1978).

John B. Kirby

ALLEN, IVAN, JR. (15 March 1911, Atlanta, Ga.–   ). Allen entered Atlanta's business community in 1933 when he joined his father's office supply company upon graduation from the Georgia Institute of Technology. He became active in politics following World War II, serving two years as executive secretary to liberal Georgia Governor Ellis Arnall. After a failed attempt in the governor's race in 1954, Allen ran for mayor of Atlanta in 1961. Changing from his earlier defense of segregation to a liberal viewpoint that advocated economic growth and community development, he defeated segregationist Lester Maddox. His two terms as mayor saw public facilities and schools integrated and a basis laid for the economic transformation of Atlanta's commercial community. He was the only major southern white politician to support President John F. Kennedy's legislation to desegregate public accommodations.

SELECTED BIBLIOGRAPHY
Ivan Allen, Jr., *Mayor: Notes on the Sixties* (1971); "Atlanta: Voice of Confidence," *Newsweek*, (20 October 1969); Nelson Lichtenstein, ed., *Political Profiles: The Johnson Years* (1976).

Thomas D. Cockrell

ALLEN v. STATE BOARD OF ELECTIONS, 393 U.S. 544 (1968). As a result of the Voting Rights Act of 1965,* African Americans gained access to the polls, but they continued to encounter obstacles to the effective use of the ballot. To dilute the political power of the newly enfranchised blacks, white southern politicians changed electoral laws and practices by establishing multiseat electoral districts and at-large elections, all with the intent of reducing the effect of the black vote. It was not clear that the Voting Rights Act of 1965 prohibited such electoral manipulations. Southern conservatives predictably argued that the act simply prohibited restrictions limiting the right to register and vote but did not pertain to changes that might be made in the electoral process. In *Allen v. State Board of Elections*, a suit brought by the Legal Defense and Educational Fund* of the NAACP*, the Supreme Court swept aside a Mississippi statute that permitted a change from district to at-large elections of certain county officials. Because the statute had the effect of diluting black voting power and thereby nullifying or curtailing their ability to elect candidates of their choice, the Mississippi law violated the Voting Rights Act.

SELECTED BIBLIOGRAPHY
Derrick A. Bell, Jr., *Race, Racism and American Law* (1980); Thomas I. Emerson, David Haber, and Norman Dorsen, *Political and Civil Rights in the United States* (1967); Steven F. Lawson, *Black Ballots: Voting Rights in the South, 1944–1969* (1976); Donald G. Nieman, *Promises to Keep, African-Americans and the Constitutional Order, 1776 to the Present* (1991); Roland Young, ed., "Review of Recent Supreme Court Decisions," *American Bar Association Journal*, 55 (1969), 580–81.

Charles D. Lowery

ALSTON v. BOARD OF EDUCATION OF THE CITY OF NORFOLK,

112 F.2d 992 (4th Cir., 1940). Public education in the South in the era of "separate but equal" was anything but equal. In the late 1930s and the 1940s, the legal strategy of the NAACP* called for litigation that would produce greater racial equality, within a segregated public school environment, beginning with teachers' pay. Melvin O. Alston, a teacher at Booker T. Washington High School in Norfolk, Virginia, agreed in 1939 to bring suit against the city's school board. In federal district court, Alston lost, but, on appeal to the Fourth Circuit Court of Appeals, he won. That court ruled that racial discrimination in salary schedules for public school teachers violated the "due process" and "equal protection" clauses of the Fourteenth Amendment.* In turn, the city appealed, but the U.S. Supreme Court let the decision stand (311 U.S. 693 [1940]). The case was a good one, in the view of NAACP attorneys, in that it originated in the largest city of a border state, but, having won, they found that it took continued pressure for several years to approach equal salaries across Virginia. All such efforts—including suits for equal busing to black schools and then for equal physical facilities—constituted a prelude to the direct assault, after 1950, on segregation itself.

SELECTED BIBLIOGRAPHY
Richard Kluger, *Simple Justice: The History of Brown v. Board of Education and Black America's Struggle for Equality* (1976); Mark V. Tushnet, *The NAACP's Legal Strategy against Segregated Education, 1925–1950* (1987).

Peter Wallenstein

AMERICAN CIVIL LIBERTIES UNION. A national, nonprofit, nonpartisan legal organization dedicated to upholding the constitutional rights of Americans, the American Civil Liberties Union (ACLU) was founded in 1920 by Roger Baldwin—its president for thirty years—and others who opposed the government's treatment of World War I dissidents. Since its founding, the ACLU has worked mainly through the courts to safeguard the Bill of Rights for a large number of individuals and groups, including labor agitators, socialists and communists, religious nonconformists, political radicals, and antiwar protestors. In the matter of civil rights for minorities, it has helped to secure voting rights for blacks, has worked to desegregate public schools, and has defended blacks accused of a crime because of their race. The organization maintains a headquarters in New York City and has state and local offices throughout the nation.

SELECTED BIBLIOGRAPHY

Robert Justin Goldstein, *Political Repression in Modern America: From 1870 to the Present* (1978); Barbara Habenstreit, *Eternal Vigilance: The American Civil Liberties Union in Action* (1971); Peggy Lamson, *Roger Baldwin—Founder of the American Civil Liberties Union* (1977); Charles Lam Markmann, *The Noblest Cry—A History of the American Civil Liberties Union* (1965); Samuel E. Walker, *In Defense of American Liberties: A History of the ACLU* (1990).

Dorothy A. Autrey

AN AMERICAN DILEMMA. The Carnegie Foundation provided funds for this study of black-white relations and selected the Swedish economist Gunnar Myrdal to direct it. Myrdal came to the United States in 1938 and selected a group of black and white scholars to help him conduct the study. Many of them wrote monographs on specific aspects of race relations, and Myrdal used these in writing the final document. Myrdal concluded that black Americans were prevented from fully participating in American society. This posed a dilemma for Americans because this denial of equality violated the American democratic creed. Myrdal was optimistic that Americans would resolve the dilemma. When it was first published in 1944, the study received a welcome reception from white liberals, but it was strongly condemned by Southerners. Blacks were ambivalent. By the 1950s, however, Myrdal's study was the authoritative work on race relations. Lawyers cited it in arguing the civil rights cases of the 1950s and 1960s. By 1965, however, scholars were questioning Myrdal's optimistic prediction that racial equality would come within a decade. Moreover, the rise of the Black Power* movement caused black Americans to reconsider their favorable opinions of Myrdal's assimilationist views.

SELECTED BIBLIOGRAPHY

Gunnar Myrdal, *An American Dilemma: The Negro Problem and Modern Democracy* (1944); David W. Southern, *Gunnar Myrdal and Black-White Relations: The Use and Abuse of an American Dilemma, 1944–1969* (1987).

Arvarh E. Strickland

AMERICAN FRIENDS SERVICE COMMITTEE. Started in 1917 as a pacifist organization, the American Friends Service Committee (AFSC) soon extended its interest to benevolence and domestic reform. The committee followed the traditional belief of the Friends that there was no difference between idealism and practice, an emphasis that led it to join the struggle for civil rights. An important contribution by the AFSC was its espousal of merit employment, fair housing, and school desegregation after World War II. The migration of southern blacks to northern and western cities had disrupted normal patterns and had led to white resentment and discrimination. The AFSC exerted particular influence in Chicago with its merit employment drives in department stores and banks. It established the Housing Opportunities Program to work with white and black families in creating an open housing market in the area. In 1967 it issued a nationally important report on the difficulties blacks were experiencing in the suburban housing market. Though active in more renowned events like the activities of the Freedom Rides* and the Little Rock desegregation crisis,* the AFSC contributed significantly to public awareness of the less dramatic but no less real civil rights violations in housing and employment.

SELECTED BIBLIOGRAPHY

Gerald Jonas, *On Doing Good* (1971); Daisy Newman, *A Procession of Friends* (1972).

Steve Rea

AMERICAN MISSIONARY ASSOCIATION. The American Missionary Association (AMA) was founded on 3 September 1846 in Syracuse, New York, through an antislavery coalition of the Union Missionary Society, the Committee for West Indian Missions, and the Western Evangelical Missionary Society. In 1847 it established relief services for slaves escaping to Canada, but its principal goal was the nonviolent overthrow of slavery. The AMA's commitment to education began in 1859 when John G. Fee founded Berea College in Kentucky. Built on land donated by the ardent abolitionist, Cassius M. Clay, Berea was open to blacks and whites alike. Unfortunately, the college was closed shortly after opening because of growing fears among local whites after John Brown's raid at Harper's Ferry. As Union armies advanced across the South after 1862, the AMA followed behind, providing needed relief to the ever-growing contraband camps of former slaves. At Fortress Monroe in Virginia, the first AMA school for freedmen was established under the direction of Mary S. Peake. Out of this school grew a network of educational facilities for freedmen across the South. The AMA was soon associated with five hundred colleges and normal schools in the southern states. Of the 15,000 black teachers in the South in 1870, 7,000 were AMA graduates. Since 1900, the AMA has established services for the needy of all races. During the Great Depression, the AMA was a leader in the education of tenant farmers across the South, and the civil rights movement had several leaders who were graduates of AMA schools.

SELECTED BIBLIOGRAPHY

Augustus Field Beard. *A Crusade of Brotherhood* (1972); Clifton H. Johnson, ''The American Missionary Association, 1846–1861. A Study of Christian Abolitionism" (Ph.D. diss., University of North Carolina, 1958); Joe M. Richardson, *Christian Reconstruction* (1986).

James W. Stennett

AMERICAN NEGRO ACADEMY. Existing from 1897 to 1928, the American Negro Academy (ANA) was the first major black learned society in the United States. A small, select organization of authors, scholars, and artists, the ANA promoted the publication of scholarly work dealing with African-American culture and history. Several prominent scholars, including Alexander Crummell,* W. E. B. Du Bois,* Archibald Grimke,* John W. Cromwell, and Arthur Schomberg, served terms as president of the academy. The ANA went out of existence in 1928 because the scholarly elitist tradition embodied by ANA founders became difficult to defend during a decade when African-American leaders emphasized the courage, wisdom, beauty, and strength of the African-American masses.

SELECTED BIBLIOGRAPHY

Leon Litwack and August Meier, eds., *Black Leaders of the Nineteenth Century* (1988); Alfred A. Moss, Jr., *The American Negro Academy—Voice of the Talented Tenth* (1981).

Janice M. Leone

AMERICAN NEGRO LABOR CONGRESS. The American Communist Party* created this organization at a meeting held in Chicago in October 1925. Delegates representing black labor, fraternal, farmers', and benefit organizations attended. Lovett Fort-Whiteman, who had only recently returned from the Soviet Union, served as national organizer. He made it clear that the organization would have a distinct Marxist orientation. The American Negro Labor Congress (ANLC) was to be more than a labor movement, however. "The idea of the American Negro Labor Congress," according to the group's call to action, "is to bring together the most potent elements of the Negro race for deliberation and action upon those most irritating and oppressive social problems affecting the life of the race in general and the Negro working class in particular." Even so, the American Communist Party faced a dilemma in sponsoring an organization for black workers. The Communists declared that the problems faced by black Americans stemmed solely from class differences and that solutions to these problems required worker solidarity, not separation. Although the ANLC helped to call attention to the plight of black workers, it did not attract wide support, and it gradually faded from the scene.

SELECTED BIBLIOGRAPHY

Herbert Aptheker, ed., *A Documentary History of the Negro People in the United States 1910–1932* (1973); William H. Harris, *Keeping the Faith: A. Philip Randolph, Milton P. Webster, and the Brotherhood of Sleeping Car Porters, 1925–37* (1977); Sterling D. Spero and Abram L. Harris, *The Black Worker: The Negro and the Labor Movement* (1968).

Arvarh E. Strickland

AMERICAN STUDENT UNION. A Communist student group, which grew out of the Communist National Student League and the Socialist Student League for Industrial Democracy, the American Student Union (ASU) was one of several such Communist "front" organizations (the American League for Peace and Democracy and the American Youth Congress* were others) which sought control of U.S. public opinion during the socially turbulent 1930s. Like the American Youth Congress, ASU championed black interests and challenged Jim Crow.* Its principal journal, the *Student Advocate*, repeatedly called for an end to racial segregation in southern colleges and universities, intercollegiate athletics, and in ROTC units throughout the country. It called for the development of college studies in black history and culture, urged the hiring of African-American professors at white colleges and universities, and equated black civil rights with the universal struggle for freedom. Though short-lived, ASU served on many college campuses during the 1930s to focus attention on the great injustices African Americans suffered.

SELECTED BIBLIOGRAPHY
William E. Leuchtenburg, *Franklin D. Roosevelt and the New Deal* (1963); Arthur B. Link and William B. Catton, *American Epoch. A History of the United States Since the 1890s* (1963); Harvard Sitkoff, *A New Deal for Blacks: The Emergence of Civil Rights as a National Issue, The Depression Decade* (1978).

Charles D. Lowery

AMERICAN YOUTH CONGRESS. Founded in 1934 as one of several Communist "front" organizations, the American Youth Congress (AYC) pretended to speak for five million young people across the country who decried racism in every form. It joined hands with the Southern Negro Youth Congress* and the American Student Union* during the Depression decade to champion social, political, and economic equality for African Americans. At its periodic congresses, the AYC passed numerous resolutions, supporting such things as the enfranchisement of southern blacks, the abolition of Jim Crow* laws; and efforts of the Southern Negro Youth Congress to unionize black workers. It spoke out in defense of the "boys" in the Scottsboro Trials* and called for the implementation of black studies courses in public schools and universities. The AYC enjoyed the public endorsement of Aubrey Williams,* the director of the New Deal National Youth Administration, and the support of Eleanor Roosevelt.* Its Communist ties led to its demise after World War II.

SELECTED BIBLIOGRAPHY
Philip S. Foner, *Organized Labor and the Black Worker, 1619–1973* (1974); Note, *Journal of Negro Education* 5 (October 1936), 651–52; Harvard Sitkoff, *A New Deal for Blacks: The Emergence of Civil Rights as a National Issue, The Depression Decade* (1978).

                                                              Charles D. Lowery

AMERICANS FOR DEMOCRATIC ACTION. In 1947 Eleanor Roosevelt,* Reinhold Niebuhr, Chester Bowles, Walter Reuther,* Marquis Childs, David Dubinsky, and others led by James Loeb, Jr., founded the Americans for Democratic Action (ADA) as a political organization to support the advance of liberal causes. From the beginning, the ADA excluded Communists from membership although conservatives have often accused it of being, at best, a Communist front. The ADA rates the voting records of members of Congress to identify each one's degree of liberalness. The ADA is nonpartisan in its endorsements but usually supports Democrats. In 1948 the ADA selected civil rights as the issue to use to assert liberal influence in national politics. With Hubert Horatio Humphrey, Jr.,* leading on the floor, the ADA and other civil rights groups won a fight to include a strong civil rights plank in the Democratic party platform, which caused southern Democrats to walk out of the convention and run Strom Thurmond as the Dixiecrat candidate for president. ADA membership peaked at approximately 75,000 in the early 1970s.

SELECTED BIBLIOGRAPHY
Clifton Brock, *Americans for Democratic Action: Its Role in National Politics* (1962); Steven M. Gillon, *Politics and Vision: The ADA and American Liberalism, 1947–1985* (1987); Peter J. Kellog, "The Americans for Democratic Action and Civil Rights in 1948: Conscience in Politics or Politics in Conscience," *Midwest Quarterly*, 20 (Autumn, 1978), 49–63.

                                                              Lorenzo Crowell

AMSTERDAM NEWS. This weekly New York City African-American newspaper was established by James H. Anderson in December 1909. Armed with only "six sheets of blank paper, a lead pencil and a dressmaker's table," Anderson laid the foundation for one of the nation's oldest black newspapers. In 1936, physicians Philip Savory and Clelan B. Powell purchased the problem-plagued paper and chose not to crusade, but to feature instead "the accomplishments and progress of the Negro." It both praised and criticized public figures, editorially castigating its former columnist, Adam Clayton Powell, Jr.,* for example, and benefitted from his frequent inclusion of its activities into the *Congressional Record.* By the 1960s it was read by more blacks than any black newspaper in the nation. It was the only source for New York's large African-American population to get the black perspective of the news. In 1991 its circulation was down from its peak, but it continued to be a voice for black people in the nation's largest city.

SELECTED BIBLIOGRAPHY

Amsterdam News, 1909–1990; *The Crisis Magazine* 45 (April 1938), 105–6; Frederick Detweiler, *The Negro Press in the United States* (1968); J. Kirk Sale, *"The Amsterdam News," New York Times Magazine* (9 February 1969); Ronald E. Wolseley, *The Black Press, U.S.A.* (1990).

Maxine D. Jones

ANDERSON, CHARLES W., JR. (26 May 1907, Louisville, Ky.–14 June 1960, Louisville, Ky.). After graduating from Wilberforce University and Howard University* Law School, Anderson returned to his hometown, Louisville, Kentucky, and served as a distinguished politician, trial lawyer, and civil rights leader. In 1935 he became the first African American since Reconstruction to be elected to a southern state legislature. He successfully opposed a bill that advocated the use of glass partitions to segregate blacks and whites on buses. He also sought to expand educational opportunities for black Kentuckians. In 1936 he cosponsored the Anderson-Mayer State Aid Act which appropriated funds for the out-of-state education of blacks pursuing undergraduate work or advanced degrees in fields not taught at the state's black college. The following year Anderson convinced the legislature to pass a bill requiring Kentucky counties to support high school education for black students in rural areas. In 1944 Anderson presented a bill to amend the 1904 segregation Day law. It passed in the House but failed in the Senate. In 1959 President Dwight D. Eisenhower nominated Anderson as an alternate delegate to the United Nations.

SELECTED BIBLIOGRAPHY

Kentucky's Black Heritage (1971); *The Louisville Defender*, 27 August, 19 September, 1959, 16 June 1960; Gerald L. Smith, " 'Mr. Kentucky State': A Biography of Rufus Ballard Atwood" (Ph.D. diss., University of Kentucky, 1988).

Gerald L. Smith

ANDERSON, MARIAN. (17 February 1902, Philadelphia, Pa.–   ). As a child chorister at the Union Baptist Church of Philadelphia, this renowned opera singer's untutored voice so impressed the church members that they set up a trust fund to ensure that she could study with the great music and voice teacher, Giuseppe Boghetti. This education allowed her to launch a musical career in 1924; in one year's time she won first prize at New York's Lewisohn Stadium, defeating two hundred contestants in the competition sponsored by the New York Philharmonic Symphony. In the next four years she sang a debut recital in Berlin that was followed by even more successful concerts, usually consisting of a repertoire of Bach, Beethoven, and African-American spirituals. In 1939 the Daughters of the American Revolution (DAR) refused her permission to perform in Constitution Hall in Washington, D.C. The outraged First Lady Eleanor Roosevelt* immediately resigned her membership in the DAR. Anderson became a symbolic rallying point around whom others in agreement with Eleanor Roosevelt's position on racial equality could show their distaste for racial discrimination. Anderson accepted an offer to perform at the Lincoln Memorial on Easter Sunday. An integrated audience of 75,000 people, including members of the Supreme Court, Congress, and President Franklin Roosevelt's cabinet, came to hear her sing. In 1955, she became the first black person to appear on stage at the Metropolitan Opera House. That same year she served as an American delegate to the United Nations. In 1965 she gave a farewell recital at Carnegie Hall. She received honorary degrees from twenty-three American educational institutions and from one Korean institution, as well as decorations from numerous states and cities and from Sweden, the Philippines, Haiti, Liberia, France, and Japan.

SELECTED BIBLIOGRAPHY

Marian Anderson, *My Lord, What a Morning: An Autobiography* (1956); Marianna W. Davis, ed., *Contributions of Black Women to America, vol. 1: The Arts, Media, Business, Law, Sports* (1982); *Who's Who Among Black Americans* (1976).

                                                                                                    Linda Reed

ANNA T. JEANES FUND. *See* Jeanes (Anna T.) Fund.

ANTHONY v. MARSHALL COUNTY BOARD OF EDUCATION, 409 F.2d 1287 (5th Cir., 1969). In the wake of the U.S. Supreme Court's desegregation decision in *Green v. School Board of New Kent County, Virginia,** a group of black Mississippi school children, represented by their parents, brought a class action suit against the Holly Springs and Marshall County school districts. The U.S. District Court for the Northern District of Mississippi concluded that the only viable plan of desegregation for the two school districts was to continue under the existing "freedom of choice" plan, and the plaintiffs appealed. In view of the evidence that, during the 1967–1968 school year, only 21 of 1,868 black children in one district and only 22 of 3,606 in the other district attended white schools, along with the fact that no white students in either district had ever attended a black school, the U.S. Fifth Circuit Court of Appeals* ruled that the school districts remained dual systems. The court also said that "freedom of choice" plans had not been effective in eliminating dual systems and that the burden thus was on the two school boards to produce realistic and workable plans for realizing unified nondiscriminatory systems.

SELECTED BIBLIOGRAPHY

Richard Bardolph, ed., *The Civil Rights Record, Black Americans and the Law, 1849–1970* (1970). *Race Relations Law Survey* 1 (1969), 68, 167, 203; Francis B. Stevens and John L. Maxer, "Representing the Under-represented: A Decennial Report of Public Interest Litigation in Mississippi," *Mississippi Law Journal* 44 (1973), 298–314.

W. Lance Conn

ANTI-DEFAMATION LEAGUE OF B'NAI B'RITH. This organization was established in 1913 within the Independent Order of B'nai B'rith, a Jewish fraternal organization. Its founders saw its two goals as inextricably linked: to "stop . . . the defamation of the Jewish people" and to "secure justice and fair treatment to all citizens alike." From its inception, therefore, the Anti-Defamation League (ADL) concerned itself not only with anti-Semitism but also with racism and racial discrimination, and it was active in the modern civil rights movement. From its founding until the present, the ADL has monitored racist and anti-Semitic incidents and organizations (including the Ku Klux Klan and the Skinheads), and it takes action against them whenever possible. It also works proactively, promoting civil rights and defending civil liberties through the courts, the legislature, the press, and school and workplace educational programs.

SELECTED BIBLIOGRAPHY
Nathan Belth, "Not the Work of a Day: The Story of the Anti-Defamation League of B'nai B'rith," Anti-Defamation League pamphlet (1965); Oscar Cohen and Stanley Wexler, eds., *Not the Work of a Day: Anti-Defamation League of B'nai B'rith Oral Memoirs*, 6 vols. (1987–1989); Arnold Forster, *Square One* (1988); Murray Friedman, "One Episode in Southern Jewry's Response to Desegregation," *American Jewish Archives* 33 (November 1981); 170–83.

Cheryl Greenberg

ANTILYNCHING CRUSADERS. This group organized the first mass interracial attempt to stop lynching. When congressman L. C. Dyer proposed a federal antilynching bill in 1922, the Crusaders were organized by the NAACP* to mobilize women. These women, headed by Mary B. Talbert of the National Association of Colored Women,* had their own collective consciousness of sexual victimization and wanted to fight that, along with the myth of the black male rapist. Crusader volunteers tried to stop lynching with mass publicity. They mobilized black and white support and raised money for the Dyer bill's passage. Unable to reach their goal of $1,000,000, they did raise national consciousness and laid the groundwork for future antilynching activism.

SELECTED BIBLIOGRAPHY
Antilynching Crusaders Minutes, NAACP Papers, Library of Congress; Donald B. Grant, *The Anti-Lynching Movement, 1883–1932* (1975); Gerda Lerner, *Black Women in White America: A Documentary History* (1973); NAACP, *The AntiLynching Crusaders: A Million Women United to Suppress Lynching* (1922).

Linda G. Ford

A. PHILIP RANDOLPH INSTITUTE. *See*, Randolph Institute, A. Philip.

ARNOLD v. NORTH CAROLINA, 376 U.S. 733 (1964). Two black men, Jesse James Arnold and George Dixon, were found guilty of murder in state court in North Carolina. On appeal to the state supreme court, Arnold and Dixon argued that their convictions should be set aside under the equal protection clause of the Fourteenth Amendment* because local officials had routinely excluded blacks from grand jury service. According to evidence they presented in the state proceedings, county tax rolls listed 12,250 whites and 4,819 blacks. Although roughly a quarter of the local taxpayers were black, the clerk of the state trial court testified that during his twenty-four years in office, he could remember only one black ever serving on a grand jury. The North Carolina Supreme Court ruled that this was not sufficient evidence of the systematic exclusion of blacks. In a per curiam opinion, the U.S. Supreme Court reversed the state court. Comparing the case to its earlier decision in *Eubanks v. Louisiana*, 356 U.S. 584 (1958), the Court determined that the testimony of the defendants had established a prima facie case of the denial of equal protection.

SELECTED BIBLIOGRAPHY

Marvin E. Frankel and Gary P. Naftalis, *The Grand Jury* (1975); Richard D. Younger, *The People's Panel: The Grand Jury in the United States, 1634–1941* (1963).

Jeff Broadwater

ASHMORE, HARRY SCOTT (27 July 1916, Greenville, S.C.–   ). A graduate of Clemson College in 1937, Ashmore first worked for Greenville newspapers. He was a Nieman Fellow at Harvard (1941–1942) before he served in World War II. After working as an editor for the *Charlotte News*, he became in 1947 the executive editor of the Little Rock *Arkansas Gazette*. A southern liberal, he opposed the Dixiecrats in 1948 and campaigned with Adlai Stevenson in 1952 and 1956. In 1953–1954 he directed the Fund for the Advancement of Education's major study of the South's biracial educational system, which was published the day before the 1954 *Brown v. Board of Education** decision as *The Negro and the Schools*. During the 1957–1958 Little Rock desegregation crisis,* Ashmore editorially opposed Governor Orval Faubus and the segregationists. In 1958 he received the Pulitzer Prize for editorial writing, and the *Arkansas Gazette* won the Pulitzer Prize for meritorious public service. In 1959 Ashmore joined the Fund for the Republic's new Center for the Study of Democratic Institutions in California. He wrote *The Other Side of Jordan* (1960) about northern blacks and also served as editor of the *Encyclopedia Britannica*. As a critic of the war in Vietnam, he twice traveled to North Vietnam. In retirement, Ashmore wrote a personal history of American race relations, *Hearts and Minds: The Anatomy of Racism from Roosevelt to Reagan* (1982).

SELECTED BIBLIOGRAPHY

Harry Ashmore, *Hearts and Minds* (1982); *Who's Who in America*.

Brenda M. Eagles

ASSOCIATED NEGRO PRESS. Established by *Chicago Defender** reporter Claude Barnett in 1919 to provide black newspapers with national and international news, the Associated Negro Press (ANP) thrived during the next three decades, the hey-day of the black press. Only the *Pittsburgh Courier** and the *Chicago Defender* did not subscribe to it in 1919, but later they also signed on. The ANP successfully met its aim of providing news of interest to black readers. In 1945, after the failure to merge with the ANP, the National Negro Press Association formed the NNPA News Service. Most black newspapers continued to use the ANP and by the late 1950s over seventy African papers were also subscribers. American black newspapers went into decline during these years, however, which hurt the ANP. It went out of business in 1964.

SELECTED BIBLIOGRAPHY

Richard L. Beard and Cyril E. Zoerner II, "Associated Negro Press: Its Founding, Ascendancy, and Demise," *Journalism Quarterly* 46 (Spring 1969), 47–52; Lawrence D. Hogan, *A Black National News Service, The Associated Press and Claude Barnett, 1919–1945* (1984).

John F. Marszalek

ASSOCIATION FOR THE STUDY OF AFRO-AMERICAN LIFE AND HISTORY. Founded as the Association for the Study of Negro Life and History in Chicago on 9 September 1915, the association's purposes were the promotion of black history, the preservation of historical manuscripts, and the publication of books about black life and history. The cofounders were Carter Godwin Woodson,* George Cleveland Hall, W. B. Hartgrove, Alexander L. Jackson, and James E. Stamps. George C. Hall served as its first president. In its early years, the association received grants from the Carnegie Corporation, the Laura Spelman Memorial, and the Rockefeller Foundation.* Such foundation support was withdrawn in the 1920s, however, mainly due to some personal animosity for Woodson, whom opponents called a "propagandist." Woodson decided that the future of the association depended on securing support from blacks, and he actively launched a campaign for that purpose. For several years, the association suffered from lack of funds but by 1944 it was financially stable. In 1926 Woodson began a drive through the association to promote Black History Week, and the effort eventually resulted in the celebration of Black History Month. The association has also been responsible for the publication of *The Journal of Negro History** and the *Negro History Bulletin,** a mail campaign directed at home, club, and school study; and the publication of black history textbooks for colleges and secondary schools. Since 1915 the association has both sponsored and encouraged hundreds of young men and women to enter the field of historical research. Financial and personnel difficulties in the 1980s led to a reduction in the effectiveness of the organization and saw a reduction in active membership to only 3,500 in 1985.

SELECTED BIBLIOGRAPHY
Editorial, *Negro History Bulletin* 46 (July-September 1983), 74–77; *Jet* 67 (11 March 1985), 39; Rayford W. Logan and Michael R. Winston, eds., *Dictionary of American Negro Biography* (1982); Obituary of Carter G. Woodson, *The Journal of Negro History* 35 (July 1950), 344–48.

Thomas D. Cockrell

ASSOCIATION OF SOUTHERN WOMEN TO PREVENT LYNCH-ING. The Association of Southern Women to Prevent Lynching, organized in Atlanta in 1930 under the auspices of the Commission on Interracial Cooperation* (formed in 1919), existed for the express purpose of combatting the idea that lynching was needed "to protect Southern womanhood." Led by Jessie Daniel Ames of Palestine, Texas, the group collected thousands of signatures on antilynching petitions, worked to change public opinion and educate children away from racism, and "assisted" southern officials to uphold the law. Although the women suffered hostility and threats, they persisted and repeatedly succeeded in stopping lynchings and moving the public away from mob violence.

SELECTED BIBLIOGRAPHY
Jessie Daniel Ames, *The Changing Character of Lynching, 1931–41* (1973); Association of Southern Women to Prevent Lynching Papers, Atlanta University; Jacquelyn Dowd Hall, *The Revolt against Chivalry: Jessie Daniel Ames and the Women's Campaign against Lynching* (1979).

Linda G. Ford

ATLANTA [DAILY] WORLD. Founded in 1928 by W. A. Scott II as a weekly newspaper, the *Atlanta World* became a daily in 1932 and changed its name to the *Atlanta Daily World*. It also then became part of the Scott Newspaper Syndicate which by 1941 reached a peak of twenty-nine affiliates. It gained early notoriety by giving wide support to the accused black men in the Scottsboro Trials.* It was a consistent opponent of segregation, but when the sit-ins of the 1960s targeted some of the newspaper's biggest advertisers, it opposed the sit-inners. It survived this crisis, however, and remained staunchly Republican, but supported the moderates over the Goldwaterites. At its peak it was one of the nation's only black daily newspapers and had an influence far beyond its city limits.

SELECTED BIBLIOGRAPHY
Alton Hornby, Jr., "Georgia," in Henry Lewis Suggs, ed., *The Black Press in the South, 1865–1979* (1983); Vishnu K. Oak, *The Negro Newspaper* (1948).

John F. Marszalek

ATLANTA EXPOSITION SPEECH. On 18 September 1895, Booker T. Washington* delivered a speech at the Cotton States and International Exposition in Atlanta, Georgia. This Atlanta Exposition Speech has endured as his philosophical contribution to southern race relations. In his address, Washington, first principal of Alabama's Tuskegee Institute* and dedicated to the concept and practical application of industrial education, appealed to whites to work with and accept blacks as mutual partners in southern economic progress. He also called upon blacks to be patient and to accommodate themselves to the social system that had emerged in the post-Reconstruction South. The reaction to Washington's speech was overwhelmingly enthusiastic. From President Grover Cleveland to the white press, unstinting praise was bestowed upon Washington. Because the speech did not challenge southern race relations, Washington was elevated by white America as the spokesperson for the

Booker T. Washington addresses a Louisiana audience in 1915 with the same message he articulated in the Atlanta Exposition Speech. (Arthur P. Bedou Photographs, Xavier University Archives, New Orleans.)

black race. A majority of black Americans concurred. Some blacks, the well-educated, disagreed with Washington's philosophy and his approach to black economic and social progress. W.E.B. Du Bois* represented their thinking. The leader of this "Talented Tenth" group, he dubbed Washington's speech the "Atlanta Compromise." Du Bois accused Washington of compromising the human rights of black Americans by accepting their alleged inferiority by asking them to accommodate themselves to the racial injustices perpetuated against them. Washington's supporters have argued that this philosophy and formula for black success was correct in light of the sociopolitical, judicial, and economic climate of the times. His critics have maintained that Washington's speech and brand of racial politics retarded and prolonged black progress and, perhaps, further contributed to the segregationist and discriminatory mindset of the white South.

SELECTED BIBLIOGRAPHY

W.E.B. Du Bois, *The Souls of Black Folk* (1903); Leslie Fishel, Jr., and Benjamin Quarles, *The Black American: A Documentary History* 91970); John Hope Franklin and Alfred A. Moss, Jr., *From Slavery to Freedom: A History of Negro Americans* (1988); Louis R. Harlan, *The Booker T. Washington Papers*, 13 vols. (1972–1983); Louis R. Harlan, *Booker T. Washington: The Making of a Black Leader, 1856–1901* (1972). Booker T. Washington, *Up from Slavery: An Autobiography* (1900).

                                                                              Phillip McGuire

ATLANTA RACE RIOT (1906). Turn-of-the-century massacres of blacks by urban mobs with the connivance of local authorities in Wilmington, Delaware (1898) and Atlanta Georgia, and in the New Orleans race riot (1900)* and elsewhere can be described as American pograms. Although these bloody episodes were generally followed by new disfranchisement laws, blacks already lived in subjugation, and the new laws and pograms sprang largely from the expressive politics of white supremacy, a rage for more effective caste dominance. In Georgia violence was preceded by an eighteen-month ultraracist Hoke Smith–Clark Howell Democratic gubernatorial primary, a lurid Atlanta "crusade" against "vice" in black neighborhoods, and the increasingly hysterical yellow journalism of the city's highly competitive five dailies on a bogus "rape epidemic" in August and September. Between September 22 and 27 white mobs of several dozen to five thousand persons ranged the central city attacking blacks and black-owned or black-used property. The mobs left twenty-five persons dead, several hundred injured, and over a thousand in flight.

SELECTED BIBLIOGRAPHY

Charles Crowe, "Racial Massacre in Atlanta, Sept. 22, 1906," *Journal of Negro History* 54 (April 1969), 150–73; Charles Crowe, "Racial Violence and Social Reform: Origins of the Atlanta Riot of 1906," *Journal of Negro History* 53 (July 1968), 234–56.

                                                                              Charles Crowe

ATLANTA RACE RIOT (1967). Atlanta and its racially moderate mayor, Ivan Allen, Jr.,* were proud of the progress the city had made in race relations. Still there were wide economic, social, and political disparities between whites and blacks, and racial tension was evident in the existence of both civil rights and segregationist organizations. On Saturday, 17 June 1967, a black patron and a black security guard scuffled outside a tavern in the Dixie Hills Shopping Center, and a crowd gathered. The following night an even larger crowd appeared and began to discuss neighborhood grievances. Stokely Carmichael* arrived and was arrested after a heated discussion with police. The next day, police wounded a young black man during a disagreement in the same shopping center. A protest meeting that evening heard Carmichael urge those present "to take to the streets." Soon a crowd of one thousand people had formed. Rocks and bottles were thrown at police cars. Police reinforcements quickly put down the melee, and the next day work began on a long-delayed city playground for the community. Despite the opposition of the Student Nonviolent Coordinating Committee,* a youth patrol was established to help maintain calm that summer. A brief outburst of violence resulting in one death and a serious injury occurred on Tuesday, 20 June, but calm was maintained. State Senator Leroy Johnson and other black leaders circulated a petition, signed by one thousand people, calling on Carmichael to leave the neighborhood and allow it to work out its own problems.

SELECTED BIBLIOGRAPHY

Atlanta Constitution, June 1967; *Atlanta Inquirer*, June, July 1967; *New York Times*, June 1967; *Report of the National Advisory Commission on Civil Disorders* (1968).

John F. Marszalek

ATLANTA UNIVERSITY. Chartered in 1867 under the auspices of the American Missionary Association* (AMA), Atlanta University matriculated its first eighty-nine students in October 1869. Available to all people regardless of race, color, or creed, the school was nevertheless intended primarily to train African-American teachers to educate freedmen following the Civil War. Severing its ties with the AMA in 1892, Atlanta University developed as an undergraduate institution, offering both liberal arts and vocational training programs. In 1929 the university joined with Morehouse College* and Spelman College in Atlanta to form the Atlanta University Center, with Atlanta University offering only graduate and professional training. All three schools shared a common library funded by the General Education Board.*

SELECTED BIBLIOGRAPHY

Clarence A. Bacote, *The Story of Atlanta University* (1969); Florence Matilda Read, *The Story of Spelman College* (1961).

Janice M. Leone

ATLANTA UNIVERSITY CONFERENCE FOR THE STUDY OF NEGRO PROBLEMS. This conference, which convened annually during the period from 1896 to 1917, was the first systematic effort to examine black urban social and economic conditions. Its format of an annual

Atlanta University: First classes were held in railroad cars. (Negro Almanac Collection; Amistad Research Center; Tulane University, New Orleans.)

research study, spring meeting, and publication series was initiated in 1896 by trustees and alumni as an alternative to conferences held at Tuskegee Institute* and Hampton Institute.* Under the direction of William Edward Burghardt Du Bois* (1898–1914), a ten-year repeating cycle of comprehensive studies was implemented. Du Bois's research methods and results were widely accepted by contemporary social scientists and became the foundation for the serious study of black life. Du Bois's intent was "not only to make the Truth clear but to present it in such shape as will encourage and help social reform." The twenty conference monographs provided the first objective evidence of political and environmental causes of black poverty, crime, and disease as well as an analysis of such black social institutions as the family, the church, clubs, and businesses. The well-attended conferences also reported on regional efforts by black organizations to improve living conditions and to establish kindergartens and settlement houses. They were attended by black and white reformers and academics such as Lucy Laney, John Hope,* Jane Addams, and Franz Boas.

SELECTED BIBLIOGRAPHY

Clarence A. Bacote, *The Story of Atlanta University* (1969); W.E.B. Du Bois, *Autobiography* (1968); Ernest Kaiser, introduction, *Atlanta University Conference Publications* (1968).

Francille Rusan Wilson

ATTAWAY, WILLIAM (19 November 1911, Greenville, Miss.–17 June 1986, Los Angeles). William Attaway moved with his family to Chicago where he attended public schools and graduated from the University of Chicago. His career as a novelist began while he was involved in the Illinois Federal Writers Project during the Great Depression. Publishing two novels, *Let Me Breathe Thunder* (1939) and *Blood on the Forge** (1941), Attaway is primarily known for his second novel which concerns the Great Migration* and the effects of massive industrialization on poor laborers. He reveals that, for blacks, the northward movement was an exchange of "one master for another." In the 1960s, Attaway continued his involvement with the civil rights movement and later gained a considerable reputation as a radio, motion picture, and television scriptwriter, specializing in black scripts.

SELECTED BIBLIOGRAPHY

Robert Bone, *The Negro Novel* (1966); Robert Felgar, "William Attaway's Unaccommodated Protagonist," *Studies in Black Literature* 4 (Spring 1973), 1–3; Moody Simms, Jr., "In the Shadow of Richard Wright: William Attaway," *Notes on Mississippi Writers* 8 (Spring 1975), 13–18; Philip Vaughn, "From Pastoralism to Industrial Antipathy, in William Attaway's *Blood on the Forge*," *Phylon* 36 (December 1975), 422–25; Edward Waldron, "William Attaway's *Blood on the Forge*:

The Death of the Blues," *Negro American Literature Forum* 10 (Summer 1976), 58–60.

Jacquelyn Jackson

THE AUTOBIOGRAPHY OF AN EX-COLORED MAN. This novel, by James Weldon Johnson (printed anonymously in 1912 and reprinted with author acknowledgment in 1927), describes the wanderings, geographical and mental, of a light-skinned black person who at first believed he was white, but learned during elementary school that he was black. After graduation, the protagonist travels to the South, Europe, and the North in search of himself and his heritage. After witnessing a lynching in the South, he decides to "let the world take me for what it would." He divulges his "secret" to his wife and then he must decide how to raise his children. For him there was really no choice. Given the way black people were treated in America, he decided to continue "passing" and to raise his children as white. In a very poignant conclusion, the Ex-Colored Man does recognize that by remaining "an ordinary successful white man" he opted to discard his history and his race, and he concludes, "I cannot repress the thought that, after all I have chosen the lesser part, that I have sold my birthright for a mess of pottage."

SELECTED BIBLIOGRAPHY

Nathan Irving Huggins, *Harlem Renaissance* (1971); James Weldon Johnson, *The Autobiography of an Ex-Colored Man* (1927); Eugene Levy, *James Weldon Johnson: Black Leader, Black Voice* (1973).

Kenneth W. Goings

AVERY v. GEORGIA, 345 U.S. 559 (1953). This U.S. Supreme Court case helped clarify the issue of what constituted racial discrimination in a state's jury-selection process as proscribed under the "equal protection" clause of the Fourteenth Amendment.* James Avery, a black, was tried and convicted of rape in the Superior Court of Fulton County, Georgia, in 1952. He appealed on the grounds that racial discrimination in the selection of the trial jury had deprived him of the equal protection of the law. On 25 May 1953, the Supreme Court upheld his appeal, ruling that although the petitioner might be unable to identify particular acts of discrimination, the jury-selection process itself, in which prospective white jurors' names were handled on white tickets and prospective black jurors' names on yellow tickets, so lent itself to abuse of the sort alleged as to constitute *"prima facie* evidence of discrimination." The burden of proof in such instances falls upon the state, and, in the absence of countervailing evidence of blacks actually serving on juries, convictions obtained before juries so selected had to be reversed.

SELECTED BIBLIOGRAPHY

Richard Bardolph, ed., *The Civil Rights Record, Black Americans and the Law, 1849–1970* (1970); Marvin E. Frankel and Gary P. Naftalis, *The Grand Jury* (1975); Jack

Greenberg, *Race Relations and American Law* (1959); *New York Times*, 26 May 1953; *United States Supreme Court Reports*, vol. 73, 891–94 and vol. 97, 1244–50.

Robert A. Calvert

B

BAILEY v. ALABAMA, 219 U.S. 219 (1911). This case was one of a series of Supreme Court rulings between 1905 and 1914 that struck at black peonage,* a form of involuntary servitude for debt that developed in the South after Reconstruction and enslaved many impoverished blacks desperate for work. Alonzo Bailey, an illiterate Alabama black, received a small advance from an employer with whom he had entered into a twelve-month labor contract. When he walked off the job before the year had expired still owing the advance, he was promptly arrested and brought to trial. He was charged with having violated an Alabama statute which stipulated that a worker who accepted an advance from an employer and left before repaying it would be presumed to have taken the money with intent to defraud and would be liable to criminal action. Bailey's attorneys lost their case in state court and appealed to the Supreme Court in 1908. The plaintiff maintained that the Alabama statute contravened the Thirteenth Amendment* as well as certain congressional antipeonage statutes. In the first hearing, the Supreme Court remanded the case to the lower courts, but three years later, in 1911, it struck down the Alabama statute. Because the law prohibited Bailey from testifying that his intent was not to defraud his employer, he "stood stripped by the statute of the presumption of innocence, and exposed to conviction for fraud upon evidence only of breach of contract and failure to pay." The court went on to say that "the essence of peonage is compulsory service in payment of a debt." Although this decision did not completely end the new slavery, it did rule with finality that the state statutes that created a presumption of guilt from the mere signing of a contract and failing to carry out the agreement to work offended both the Thirteenth Amendment and federal antipeonage laws.

SELECTED BIBLIOGRAPHY
Pete Daniel, *The Shadow of Slavery: Peonage in the South, 1909–1969* (1972); Loren Miller, *The Petitioners: The Story of the Supreme Court of the United States and the Negro* (1966); Donald G. Nieman, *Promises to Keep: African-Americans and the Constitutional Order, 1776 to the Present* (1991); Benno C. Schmidt, Jr., "Principle and Prejudice: The Supreme Court and Race in the Progressive Era. Part 2: The Peonage Cases," *Columbia Law Review* 82 (1982), 646–717.

                                                                 Charles D. Lowery

BAKER, ELLA JO (1903, Norfolk, Va.–18 December 1986, New York, N.Y.). During most of her life, Ella Baker was active in civil rights and peace causes. When she came South in the 1960s to help in the Southern Christian Leadership Conference* of Martin Luther King, Jr.*, she had years of experience behind her. After the student sit-ins began, Baker organized a conference for students at her alma mater, Shaw University, in North Carolina. One hundred and fifty students came from nine states; the group became the Student Nonviolent Coordinating Committee* (SNCC). Baker fought for the students' autonomy from SCLC. Though her talk at the Shaw Conference, "More Than a Hamburger," was not very well received, many credited her with starting the organization and providing the initial vision. For this she had the enduring admiration of early SNCC members. Though she left the Southern Christian Leadership Conference, Ella Baker continued to provide counsel to SNCC. Ella Baker was clearly a living symbol of the "Beloved Community." She died in New York City well remembered and well loved.

SELECTED BIBLIOGRAPHY
Taylor Branch, *Parting the Waters: America During the King Years, 1954–63* (1989); Obituary, *New York Times*, 17 December 1986; Robert Weisbrot, *Freedom Bound: A History of America's Civil Rights Movement* (1990).

                                                      Charles T. Pete Banner-Haley

BAKER, GEORGE (FATHER DIVINE) (1877, Hutchinson Island, Ga.– 10 September 1965, Philadelphia, Pa.). The name George Baker is thought to be the given name of Father Divine. He was one of the most important social reformers and advocates of racial justice and equality in the twentieth century. During the Great Depression, he founded the Interracial Peace Mission, which was headquartered in Harlem and had branches throughout the United States and abroad. It was the largest movement of its kind during the Depression. Thousands of people received free meals at Peace Mission centers. Hundreds more were housed in properties owned by the mission or found work through the business cooperatives organized by the mission in urban and rural areas. Racial harmony and integration at Peace Mission centers were unprecedented. White members broke residential color barriers in several northern communities, by purchasing property for use by the Peace Mission. Father

Divine's followers also participated in the campaign for a federal anti-lynching law, which was a burning issue at the time. Prior to Father Divine, few black preachers were politically active or socially conscious. His Peace Mission was also the first interracial civil rights movement on a large scale in the twentieth century.

SELECTED BIBLIOGRAPHY

Arthur Huff Fauset, *Black Gods of the Metropolis: Negro Religious Cults in the Urban North* (1944); Robert Weisbrot, *Father Divine and the Struggle for Racial Equality* (1983).

Gloria Waite

BALDWIN, JAMES (2 August 1924, New York City–1 December 1987, Harlem, N.Y.). James Baldwin was an expatriate writer in Paris, France, when the civil rights movement began. His writings had a significant impact on students, intellectuals, and those in the movement. He emphasized in his books, especially in *The Fire Next Time*,* the urgent need for the civil rights movement to succeed. Born to a father who was an Alabama minister, James Baldwin grew up in Harlem. Early in his youth he became a boy preacher. As a young adult, he went to Greenwich Village where he worked at being a writer. His first novel, the semiautobiographical *Go Tell It on the Mountain*, recounted his early years and his wrestling with religion. It was this black spirituality that provided Baldwin with a keen sensitivity and perspective into the black urban condition. He felt stifled in this country because of its overwhelming racism, and he went to France where he lived for almost ten years. Though he returned to America and participated in the civil rights movement, he displayed impatience with the Kennedy administration for its slowness in dealing with southern segregation. This impatience showed itself during an intense meeting of several famous African-American writers and performers called by Kennedy. Baldwin continued to write about the movement and blacks, often becoming very pessimistic. In the end, however, he retained some hope that the racial situation in this country could be resolved.

SELECTED BIBLIOGRAPHY

James Baldwin, *The Fire Next Time* (1963); Taylor Branch, *Parting the Waters: America during the King Years, 1954–1963* (1989); William Weatherby, *James Baldwin: Portrait of a Writer* (1989).

Charles T. Pete Banner-Haley

BARNETT, IDA WELLS (16 July 1862, Holly Springs, Miss.–25 March 1931, Chicago, Ill.). From an early age, Ida Wells Barnett demonstrated the courage and persistence that were to become trademarks of her later life. In 1878 when a yellow fever epidemic left her and her siblings orphaned, she managed with her father's savings and assistance from the Prince Hall Masons, guardians for the Wells children, to keep the family together. Despite difficulties, she received an education at Rust College in Mississippi and became a teacher in Memphis, Tennessee.

When she was forced to give up her first-class seat on the Chesapeake and Ohio Railroad in 1884, she sued the company and became the first southern black to appeal to a state court since the U.S. Supreme Court's Civil Rights Cases* in 1883. The lower court ruled in Wells Barnett's favor, but the decision was reversed by the Tennessee Supreme Court in 1887. Recounting the story of the lawsuit, she launched a career in journalism in a black church weekly, *The Living Way*. She had established her prominence in Memphis literary circles by 1887 and was made secretary of the Afro-American Press Association; she was the first woman representative to attend the conclave. She became part owner of *Memphis Free Speech* in charge of editorial operations. When her criticism of the racist school system in Memphis caused her to lose her teaching job, she devoted more time and energy to speaking out forcefully for racial equality. She began a crusade against lynching, which caused a white mob to destroy *Free Speech*. Timothy Thomas Fortune* hired Wells to work at his *New York Age*,* where she continued her antilynching campaign.

Wells Barnett organized the Woman's Loyal Union in Brooklyn, New York, the first black women's antilynching club and established similar antilynching clubs in Boston, Massachusetts, Washington, D.C., and other cities. She toured Europe and was correspondent for the *Inter-Ocean*, later known as the *Chicago Herald Examiner*. She organized the first black women's suffrage group, and in 1909 she was among the prominent blacks and whites who formed the NAACP.* In the years thereafter, according to Langston Hughes,* "[H]er activities in the field of social work laid the groundwork for the National Urban League."*

SELECTED BIBLIOGRAPHY

Marianna W. Davis, ed., *Contributions of Black Women to America, vol. 1, The Arts, Media, Business, Law, Sports* (1982); Alfreda M. Duster, ed., *Crusade for Justice: The Autobiography of Ida B. Wells* (1970). Margaret L. Dwight and George A. Sewell, *Mississippi Black History Makers* (1984); John Hope Franklin and August Meier, eds., *Black Leaders of the Twentieth Century* (1982).

Linda Reed

BARROWS v. JACKSON, 346 U.S. 249 (1953). A racially restrictive covenant case, this decision barred damage awards when covenants were violated. The case grew out of efforts by whites to circumvent *Shelley v. Kraemer* (1948),* in order to maintain segregated neighborhoods or to gain damages from covenant violations. In *Shelley*, the U.S. Supreme Court forbade state action to enforce a deed restriction that would block African Americans and others from occupying property. In *Barrows*, Mrs. Leola Jackson, a white Los Angeles property owner, faced suit for damages from neighbors for selling property covered by a covenant to an

African American. Although both parties were white and no discrimination was directly involved, Loren Miller of the NAACP* defended Mrs. Jackson; plaintiffs gained support nationwide from white property-owners' associations. When California courts refused to award damages, Barrows appealed to the U.S. Supreme Court. In his majority opinion, Justice Sherman Minton concluded that damage awards would cause "a prospective seller of restricted land . . . either [to] refuse to sell to non-Caucasians or . . . require non-Caucasians to pay a higher price to meet the damage which the seller may incur," thus denying the third party's right to equal protection guaranteed by the Fourteenth Amendment.*

SELECTED BIBLIOGRAPHY

Charles Abrams, *Forbidden Neighbors: A Study of Prejudice in Housing* (1955); Kenneth T. Jackson, *Crabgrass Frontier: The Suburbanization of the United States* (1985); B. T. McGraw and George B. Nesbitt, "Aftermath of *Shelley v. Kraemer* on Residential Restrictions by Race," *Land Economics* 29 (August 1953), 280–87; C. Herman Pritchett, *Civil Liberties and the Vinson Court* (1954); Clement E. Vose, *Caucasians Only: The Supreme Court, the NAACP, and the Restrictive Covenant Cases* (1959).

James Borchert

BARRY, MARION S. (6 March 1936, Itta Bena, Miss.–). Longtime mayor of the District of Columbia from 1979 to 1991, Barry received his B.S. from Le Moyne College in Memphis, Tennessee, and a master's from Fisk University* in Nashville, Tennessee. Barry also pursued doctoral studies at the University of Kansas and the University of Tennessee. In 1960 he became actively involved in the civil rights movement when he participated in the Nashville sit-ins*, which included demonstrations at lunch counters. When college students met in April 1960 at Shaw University to form the Student Nonviolent Coordinating Committee* (SNCC), they chose Barry as the first national chairman. After a few months in this position, however, he began his doctoral studies in chemistry, and had to abandon his full-time commitment to the movement. However, while in Tennessee, he worked part-time, conducting nonviolent workshops, raising funds, and registering voters. In 1964 Barry dropped out of graduate school to work full-time for civil rights. He planned demonstrations and boycotts and was frequently jailed. SNCC headquarters sent him to New York City to open an office. From there he moved to Washington, D.C., and became the Washington director of SNCC. Eventually, Barry started his own "wildcat" movement, where he staged boycotts and struck out against police brutality and harassment. In 1990 he was sentenced to six months in prison for his conviction on a drug charge.

SELECTED BIBLIOGRAPHY

William C. Matney, ed., *Who's Who among Black Americans* (1988); George A. Sewell and Margaret L. Dwight, *Mississippi Black History Makers*, rev. ed. (1984);

Emily Stoper, *The Student Nonviolent Coordinating Committee* (1989); *Washington Post Magazine*, 16 December 1979, 26 April 1987.

Betty L. Plummer

BASSETT, EBENEZER DON CARLOS (16 October 1833, Litchfield, Conn.–13 November 1908, Philadelphia, Pa.). The first African-American diplomat to represent the United States government abroad, Ebenezer D. Bassett rose to prominence as a scholar and teacher. Immediately after his inauguration in 1869, President Ulysses Grant appointed Bassett as minister-resident to Haiti, a position he held with honor and distinction from 1869 to 1877. At the time of his appointment, he was principal of the Institute for Colored Youth, a Quaker school in Philadelphia. He had been educated at Wesley Academy in Wilbraham, Massachusetts, and at the Connecticut State Normal School.

Bassett served the United States in Haiti during a period of tense relations with Santo Domingo. He managed to ease the strong anti-American feeling there. When he completed his assignment in 1877, the Haitians expressed their confidence in his integrity by appointing him as their consul general to the United States for ten years. Upon his retirement, he returned to live as a private citizen in Haiti. He published his *Handbook of Haiti*—a valuable contribution to the geographical knowledge of the island—in French, English, and Spanish.

SELECTED BIBLIOGRAPHY

Nancy Gordon Heinl, "America's First Black Diplomat," *Foreign Service Journal* 50 (August 1973), 20–22; Rayford W. Logan, *The Diplomatic Relations of the United States with Haiti, 1776–1891* (1941).

George E. Walker

BATES v. LITTLE ROCK, 361 U.S. 516 (1960). In 1957 Little Rock, Arkansas, amended its license tax ordinance to require any organization operating within the municipality to supply the City Clerk, upon request: (1) its official name; (2) its headquarters or regular meeting place; (3) the names and salaries of officers, agents, servants, employees, or representatives; (4) its purpose; (5) its dues, assessments, and contributions paid (by whom and when), together with a statement reflecting the disposition of the funds and the total net income; (6) an affidavit stating whether the organization was subordinate to a parent organization and, if so, the latter's name. Daisy Bates, the records custodian of the local NAACP,* was convicted of violating the ordinance even though she supplied all the information required by ordinance except the names of the members and contributors, which she withheld due to the "anti-NAACP climate in this state." The Arkansas Supreme Court upheld the conviction, concluding that "compulsory disclosure of the membership list was not an unconstitutional invasion of the freedoms guaranteed." The U.S. Supreme Court reversed the conviction, ruling that compulsory disclosure of the membership lists would work unjustified interference with the members' freedom of association, a right protected by the due process clause of the Fourteenth Amendment.*

SELECTED BIBLIOGRAPHY

Daisy Bates, *The Long Shadow of Little Rock: A Memoir* (1962); Loren Miller, *The Petitioners, The Story of the Supreme Court of the United States and the Negro* (1966); George Rossman, ed., "Review of Recent Supreme Court Decisions," *American Bar Association Journal*, 46 (1960), 420–21; Roy Wilkins, *Standing Fast: The Autobiography of Roy Wilkins* (1982).

Michael S. Downs

BATTLE OF SEPTEMBER 14th (OR CANAL STREET) 1874. During Reconstruction, politically inspired violence was commonplace in Louisiana. The ultimate erosion of Republican strength in the state was tied directly to the existence of well-organized white paramilitary groups. The most violent and reactionary of this lot was the White League. Founded in Louisiana in April 1874, it had nearly blanketed the state by late summer. By September, the White League had overturned or neutralized the Republican governments of at least eight parishes. Emboldened by these triumphs and federal timidity, the New Orleans White League planned to force the resignation of the Republican Governor, William Pitt Kellogg, and thereby gain control of state government. They asked for his resignation in the early afternoon of 14 September 1874. When he refused to resign, fighting commenced. The might of the White League was opposed by the five-hundred-man Metropolitan Police, an integrated unit that was the most professional force New Orleans had prior to the twentieth century, and about three thousand black militiamen led by General James Longstreet. White Leaguers outflanked and vanquished the Metropolitan Police and the militia. Battlefield casualties were light on both sides; the Metropolitan Police force lost eleven men and sixty were wounded. Sixteen White Leaguers lost their lives and forty-five were wounded. The toppled state government was restored on 17 September by federal troops. To commemorate the event, conservative whites later erected a monument, which became an embarrassment to city officials and an affront to the black community.

SELECTED BIBLIOGRAPHY

Stuart Omer Landry, *The Battle of Liberty Place: The Overthrow of Carpet-Bag Rule in New Orleans. September 14, 1874* (1955); Oscar H. Lestage, Jr., "The White League in Louisiana and Its Participation in Reconstruction Riots," *The Louisiana Historical Quarterly* 18 (July 1935), 617–95; Lawrence Powell, "A Concrete Symbol," *Southern Exposure* 18 (Spring 1990), 40–43; Dennis Charles Rousey, "The New Orleans Police, 1805–1889: A Social History" (Ph.D. diss., Cornell University, 1978); Ted Tunnell, *Crucible of Reconstruction: War, Radicalism and Race in Louisiana, 1862–1877* (1984); Bennett H. Wall, ed., *Louisiana: A History* (1984).

Joe Louis Caldwell

BELL v. MARYLAND, 378 U.S. 226 (1964). The last sit-in case decided before the public accommodations provision of the Civil Rights Act of 1964* took effect, this was one of four such cases the Supreme Court adjudicated that year. The case involved twelve black students who were convicted of criminal trespass for their 1960 attempt to desegregate Hooper's Restaurant in Baltimore. The court reversed the convictions and returned the case to the Maryland court for further clarification because the city of Baltimore had passed a public accommodations law after the sit-ins occurred. Thus the Supreme Court avoided settling the constitutional issue of whether the Fourteenth Amendment* provided the right to service in public accommodations. Six justices, however, did issue statements on this question. In an opinion joined by William O. Douglas and Chief Justice Earl Warren, Arthur J. Goldberg discussed the history of the Fourteenth Amendment, explaining that its intent was to prohibit racial discrimination in public places. Hugo L. Black, joined by John Marshall Harlan* and Byron R. White, took the opposite position, stating that the amendment had not been designed to cover private businesses. If the Fourteenth Amendment was intended to prohibit segregation, he added, Congress would have had no reason to enact civil rights legislation.

SELECTED BIBLIOGRAPHY

Albert P. Blaustein and Robert L. Zangrando, eds., *Civil Rights and the Black American: A Documentary History* (1970); Leon Friedman and Fred L. Israel, eds., *The Justices of the Supreme Court, 1789–1976* (1980); *New York Times*, 23 June 1964; George Rossman, ed., "Review of Recent Supreme Court Decisions," *American Bar Association Journal*, 51 (1965), 78–79; Bernard Schwartz, *Super Chief: Earl Warren and His Supreme Court: A Judicial Biography* (1983).

Carol Wilson

BENSON, WILLIAM E. (1876, Elmore County, Ala.–14 October 1915, Tallapoosa County, Ala.). A graduate of Howard University,* William E. Benson attempted to establish a stable community of landowning African-American farmers. The nucleus of the enterprise was the Kowaliga Industrial Community* which he founded in 1897 or 1898. By 1915, Benson had organized the Dixie Industrial Company which owned ten thousand acres of land, a cottonseed-oil mill, a timber operation, a general store, a turpentine plant, and fifteen miles of railroad that linked the community to the larger society. The ideology of self-help was put into practice as African Americans built their own farms and the buildings that housed the community's businesses.

SELECTED BIBLIOGRAPHY

James D. Anderson, *Education of Blacks in the South, 1860–1935* (1988); August Meier, *Negro Thought in America, 1880–1915: Racial Ideologies in the Age of Booker*

T. *Washington* (1963); Elliot Rudwick, *W.E.B. Du Bois* (1969); U.S. Department of Interior, Bureau of Education, *Negro Education Bulletin* 39 (1917).

Aingred G. Dunston

BEREA COLLEGE v. KENTUCKY, 211 U.S. 26 (1908). In this decision, the U.S. Supreme Court upheld the Kentucky legislature's passage of the 1904 Day law, making it unlawful to teach white and black students in the same institution. After approximately fifty-eight years of integrated education, Berea was forced to segregate. Moreover, the Supreme Court had upheld the 1896 *Plessy v. Ferguson** decision making the "separate but equal"* philosophy the official law of the land. Yet there remained the question of whether a state legislature could compel a private institution to segregate. The Court responded by upholding the legality of the Day law. Earlier the Court had allowed each state to resolve the question on an individual basis.

SELECTED BIBLIOGRAPHY

Jacqueline G. Burnside, "Suspicion versus Faith: Negro Criticisms of Berea College in the Nineteenth Century," *Register of Kentucky Historical Society* 83 (Summer 1985), 237–66; Jack Greenberg, *Race Relations and American Law* (1959); Richard Allen Heckman and Betty Jean Hall, "Berea College and the Day Law," *Register of Kentucky Historical Society* 66 (1968), 35–52; George C. Wright, "The Founding of Lincoln Institute," *The Filson Club History Quarterly* 49 (1975), 57–70.

Lawrence H. Williams

BERRY, MARY FRANCES (17 February 1938, Nashville, Tenn.–   ). Distinguished historian and attorney, she earned her B.A. and M.A. from Howard University* and her Ph.D. and J.D. from the University of Michigan. As an undergraduate, she wanted to leave school and plunge into the civil rights movement, but a professor persuaded her to remain, arguing that some must earn degrees and become leaders. She followed this advice. In 1976 she was the first black woman appointed chancellor at a major white institution—the University of Colorado, in Boulder. In 1977 President Jimmy Carter appointed her as Assistant Secretary of Education, in the Department of Health, Education, and Welfare. In 1980 he named her as a commissioner on the Civil Rights Commission,* where she took positions for which President Ronald Reagan tried to have her removed.

SELECTED BIBLIOGRAPHY

Joan Barthel, "Mary Frances Berry," *MS* 15 (January 1987), 68–70, 95; Marianna W. Davis, ed., *Contributions of Black Women to America*, vol. 1, *The Arts, Media, Business, Law, Sports* (1982); William C. Matney, ed., *Who's Who among Black Americans* (1988).

Betty L. Plummer

BETHUNE, MARY McLEOD (10 July 1875, Mayesville, S.C.–18 May 1955, Daytona Beach, Fla.). Distinguished orator, executive, and educator, she was the founder and president of Bethune-Cookman College.

Mary McLeod Bethune, 1943. (Library of Congress.)

As early as 1914 a trustee at the then Daytona Normal and Industrial School for Negro Girls recommended her for a place on Vice President Thomas R. Marshall's Red Cross panel. During the administrations of Presidents Calvin Coolidge and Herbert Hoover, Bethune was the lone African American invited to participate in child welfare conferences. Eleanor Roosevelt* entertained Bethune at a 1934 luncheon for representative women leaders and often worked with her afterward, sometimes helping Bethune raise funds for her college and occasionally giving White House benefits for that purpose.

All of her adult life, Bethune remained active with national civil rights organizations, especially the NAACP* and the National Urban League.* The NAACP awarded her its Spingarn Medal* for distinguished services in 1935. She was vice president of the Commission on Interracial Cooperation* and the National Urban League,* president of the National Association of Colored Women,* and founder and president of the National Council of Negro Women*—all while simultaneously maintaining the presidency of Bethune-Cookman College. She was also one of the founders of the Southern Conference for Human Welfare* (SCHW) in Birmingham, Alabama, in 1938 and remained active in that organization until it ceased operations in 1948. By then SCHW had set up the Southern Conference Educational Fund, with which Bethune worked until her death in 1955. She was particularly noted as a counselor to Franklin D. Roosevelt on black affairs and the divisional director of the National Youth Administration. By 1940 she was cited as "among the fifty most distinguished American women." In 1974 the Mary McLeod Bethune Memorial, the first monument to a black person, or to a woman, erected on public land in the nation's capitol, was unveiled in Lincoln Park.

SELECTED BIBLIOGRAPHY
Mary McLeod Bethune, "My Secret Talks with FDR," *Ebony* 4 (April 1949), 43–48; Clarence Genu Newsome, "Mary McLeod Bethune in Religious Perspective: A Seminal Essay" (Ph.D. diss., Duke University, 1982); Linda Reed, "The Southern Conference for Human Welfare and the Southern Conference Education Fund, 1938–1963" (Ph.D. diss., Indiana University, 1986); *Who's Who in America: A Biographical Dictionary of Notable Living Men and Women of the United States* (1899–); *Who's Who in Colored America: A Biographical Dictionary of Notable Living Persons of African Descent in America* (1940).

                                                                    Linda Reed

BEVEL, JAMES (19 October 1936, Itta Bena, Miss.–). An African-American minister educated in Mississippi and at the American Baptist Theological Seminary in Nashville, Tennessee, Bevel was a member of the Student Nonviolent Coordinating Committee* (SNCC), the Southern Christian Leadership Conference* (SCLC), and other civil rights organizations. At Highlander Folk School* he came into contact with other civil rights activists who shared and reinforced his own commitment to the cause of freedom. In the early 1960s he helped to organize and lead protest movements in Nashville, Tennessee, Jackson, Mississippi, and Birmingham, Alabama. During the Birmingham Confrontation* of 1963 he organized and coordinated the children's marches. Having urged the Birmingham police in advance to eschew force in dealing with the young protesters, he led the children in a series of marches during the month

Sixteenth Street Baptist Church in Birmingham, shown here after it was bombed by white racists in 1963. James Bevel led children marchers during the Birmingham Confrontation. (Archives Collection, Birmingham Public Library, Birmingham, Alabama.)

of May from the Sixteenth Street Baptist Church. These marches infused new life into the Birmingham demonstrations and contributed significantly to the final victory. Parents who had previously remained on the sidelines joined their children in the city's streets and jails. Soon after the Birmingham demonstrations Bevel and his wife, Diane Nash, proposed the Selma to Montgomery March.* He was with Martin Luther King, Jr.* in Memphis, Tennessee, on 4 April 1968 when King was assassinated.

SELECTED BIBLIOGRAPHY

Taylor Branch, *Parting the Waters: America in the King Years, 1954–1963* (1989); James Forman, *The Making of Black Revolutionaries* (1972); David J. Garrow, *Bearing the Cross: Martin Luther King, Jr. and the Southern Christian Leadership Conference*

(1986); William Kunstler, *Deep in My Heart* (1966); Aldon D. Morris, *The Origins of the Civil Rights Movement: Black Communities Organizing for Change* (1984).

LeRoy T. Williams

BIRMINGHAM BUS BOYCOTT. When the U.S. Supreme Court outlawed segregated seating on buses in Montgomery, Alabama, in 1956, the Reverend Fred L. Shuttlesworth,* president of the Alabama Christian Movement for Human Rights* (ACMHR), notified the Birmingham City Commission that segregation was unconstitutional. Klansmen dynamited Shuttlesworth's house on Christmas night, but the next day he led an integration attempt on the city buses. When the subsequent appeal of the twenty-one blacks convicted of violating Birmingham's segregation ordinance reached federal court, the commission repealed the law on 14 October 1958 and passed a new one that authorized the Birmingham Transit Company to enforce segregated seating. The ACMHR challenged the new ordinance on 20 October 1958, and T. Eugene "Bull" Connor arrested fourteen blacks including Shuttlesworth. Charging them with vagrancy, Connor also arrested three members of the Montgomery Improvement Association*—the Reverends A. W. Wil-

Boycotts in Birmingham prompt use of police dogs, 1963. (Archives Collection, Birmingham Public Library. Courtesy *Birmingham News*.)

son, H. H. Hubbard and S. S. Seay—who had arrived in the city in support of the jailed protestors. This abuse of the law united the ACMHR with the Jefferson County Betterment Association, headed by the Reverend J. L. Ware, in a boycott of the city's buses which began on 31 October 1958. The total dependence of Birmingham's black community on the city transit system combined with the successful use of police intimidation and a press blackout caused the boycott to fail by the end of 1958. A federal court ruling on 14 December 1959 finally desegregated seating on Birmingham's buses.

SELECTED BIBLIOGRAPHY

Birmingham News, 18, 25 November, 13 December 1958; Glenn T. Eskew, "The Alabama Christian Movement for Human Rights and the Birmingham Struggle for Civil Rights, 1956–1963," in David J. Garrow, ed., *Birmingham, Alabama, 1956–1963* (1989); *Montgomery Advertiser*, 28, 29 October 1958.

Glenn T. Eskew

BIRMINGHAM CONFRONTATION. The Reverend Fred L. Shuttlesworth,* president of the Alabama Christian Movement for Human Rights,* invited the Southern Christian Leadership Conference* (SCLC) to Birmingham, Alabama, to lead demonstrations against segregation. Code-named Project C for "confrontation," the protests began on 3 April 1963 with sit-ins conducted by a few college students. On 7 April 1963, Public Safety Commissioner T. Eugene "Bull" Connor set police attack dogs on the marchers, gaining national attention for the fledgling campaign. Violating a state court injunction against further protest marches, the Reverends Martin Luther King, Jr.,* and Ralph David Abernathy,* among others, were arrested and jailed on Good Friday, 12 April 1963. While incarcerated, King wrote the "Letter from Birmingham Jail,"* which eloquently defended direct action.* President John F. Kennedy called Coretta Scott King* and expressed his concern for her jailed husband—foreshadowing the federal commitment for civil rights achieved by the Birmingham campaign. On 26 April 1963, King and the other ten defendants were convicted of criminal contempt and released on appeal, initiating the court case *Walker v. City of Birmingham.** James Bevel* of the SCLC suggested using school children to regain press attention, and the first student demonstrations began on 2 May 1963. As hundreds of youths marched on 3 May 1963, Connor turned the fire hoses on at pressures that tore the bark off trees in Kelly Ingram Park. Black spectators responded by throwing bricks and rocks at firemen. Kennedy sent Assistant Attorney General for Civil Rights Burke Marshall* to help negotiate a settlement that was announced on 10 May 1963. Despite the failure of Birmingham whites ever to implement the full accord, the action precipitated the Civil Rights Bill of 1963. On 11 May 1963, Klansmen bombed the A. G. Gaston Motel and the house of the Reverend

Birmingham Confrontation: Firemen hose marchers, 13 May 1963. (Archives Collection, Birmingham Public Library. Courtesy *Birmingham News*.)

A.D. King.* The first of the decade's riots began as black residents burned cars and buildings. Colonel Al Lingo directed the Alabama state troopers in the brutal suppression of the disorders. The climax of the civil rights movement occurred in Birmingham in 1963 inasmuch as the original goals of the movement were achieved with the passage of the Civil Rights Act of 1964.*

SELECTED BIBLIOGRAPHY

Glenn T. Eskew, "The Alabama Christian Movement for Human Rights and the Birmingham Struggle for Civil Rights, 1956–1963," in David J. Garrow, ed., *Birmingham, Alabama, 1956–1963* (1989); Adam Fairclough, *To Redeem the Soul of America: The Southern Christian Leadership Conference and Martin Luther King, Jr.* (1987); David J. Garrow, *Bearing the Cross: Martin Luther King and the Southern Christian Leadership Conference* (1986).

Glenn T. Eskew

BLACK BOY. Among African-American autobiographies, *Black Boy* (1945) by Richard Wright* is a classic example of the genre. Its achievement is to be located in Wright's yoking the pattern of slave narrative with perceptive social analysis, rendering his life story symbolic for a generation of black males who came of age in the South during the early twentieth century. In vivid, often painful detail, *Black Boy* documents the process of maturation in a racist society. As a record of hostility, alienation, violence, and the psychology of race, the autobiography illustrates why many blacks fled the South and why long-repressed black anger eventually burst forth in demonstrations to achieve civil rights and to dismantle the system of segregation. *Black Boy,* which covers the period from 1912 to 1927, emphasizes the limitations of a brutal environment and the impact of racism on the sensibility of a black youth. Race riots, lynchings, the degrading social norms blacks were expected to observe in the presence of whites, discrimination in schooling and employment, and exclusion from the use of public libraries were crucial elements in Wright's socialization and that of his peers. His autobiography is a powerful metaphor for one stage of the black struggle toward full citizenship in America.

SELECTED BIBLIOGRAPHY

Stephen Butterfield, *Black Autobiography in America* (1974); Charles T. Davis, "From Experience to Eloquence: Richard Wright's *Black Boy,*" in Michael S. Harper and Robert B. Stepto, eds., *Chant of Saints* (1979); Ralph Ellison, "Richard Wright's Blues," *Antioch Review* 5 (Summer 1945), 198–211; Richard Wright, *Black Boy* (1945).

                                                                                    Jerry Ward

BLACK CABINET. Given their already marginal status in American society prior to 1929, black Americans found themselves in particularly desperate circumstances in the 1930s depression. A key factor in the New Deal's ability to respond to black concerns was the appointment of prominent blacks to race relations advisory positions within federal departments and newly established federal agencies. A number of black advisers formed an informal network in 1936 which came to be known as the Black Cabinet, Black Brain Trust, or Federal Council on Negro Affairs. Prominent figures included Mary McLeod Bethune,* head of the Negro Division of the National Youth Administration; Robert C. Weaver,* adviser to Harold L. Ickes* in the Department of the Interior and later the United States Housing Authority; Lawrence Augustus Oxley,* Department of Labor; William Johnson Trent, Jr.,* Interior and Federal Works Agency; Eugene Kinckle Jones,* Department of Commerce; and Frank S. Horne, who served in various federal housing programs. This Black Brain Trust or Black Cabinet was never a formal organization nor did its members meet on any regular basis. Rather it consisted of a group of black advisers who came together on their own initiative, often at the urging of their most powerful members, Bethune and Weaver, to assess programs and develop strategies to ensure black participation in administration measures. The cabinet served also as an opportunity for many to share their personal problems in government, formulate common goals, and develop tactics to enhance the black perspective. In directly affecting policy, most black advisers had limited impact, and a number left the Roosevelt administration in frustration. But the cabinet was important because of its symbolic role in giving recognition to blacks within the federal government, educating white New Dealers to racial issues, and establishing a precedent within both the national government and the Democratic party for future black participation.

SELECTED BIBLIOGRAPHY

William A. H. Birnie, "Black Brain Trust," *American Magazine* 130 (January 1943), 26–37, 94–95; John B. Kirby, *Black Americans in the Roosevelt Era* (1980); Jane R. Motz, "The Black Cabinet: Negroes in the Administration of Franklin D. Roosevelt" (M.A. thesis, University of Delaware, 1964); B. Joyce Ross, "Mary McLeod Bethune and the National Youth Administration: A Case Study of Power Relationships in the Black Cabinet of Franklin D. Roosevelt," *Journal of Negro History* 60 (January 1975), 1–28.

John B. Kirby

BLACK CAPITALISM. This term refers to the accumulation of capital by individual African-American entrepreneurs, strategies designed to maintain African-American control over the African-American consumer market in the United States, and collective programs that are designed to improve the overall position of African Americans. Black capitalism has undergone two primary periods of development. Booker Taliaferro Washington,* through the National Negro Business League,* and Marcus Mosiah Garvey,* through the Universal Negro Improvement Association,* created the idea of concentrating on establishing entrepreneurial success via the African-American consumer market. "Buy Black" campaigns became popular in the 1920s and 1930s as a result of their efforts. In the contemporary period, beginning in the 1960s, the development of African-American participation in the corporate sector has constituted the primary emphasis of activities.

SELECTED BIBLIOGRAPHY

George Davis and Gregg Watson, *Black Life in Corporate America* (1982); Manning Marable, *How Capitalism Underdeveloped Black America* (1983).

Christopher Mobley

BLACK CODES. During 1865 and 1866, all the southern states except North Carolina passed a number of laws designed as substitutes for the old slave codes. The main purpose of these so-called Black Codes was to ensure an immobile, dependent black labor force for each state's agricultural interest. They were designed to immobilize penniless, unemployed, and powerless black laborers. If charged with being vagrants, such individuals had to post a bond or offer the required security. Failure to adhere to these stipulations resulted in arrest and being hired out for a period not to exceed one year. An antienticement provision made it a misdemeanor to lure an employee under contract away from his employer. While most Black Codes made no distinction based on race, they were worded in such a way as to exempt white workers. Moreover, a few counties and towns passed ordinances that were blatantly discriminatory against blacks. When Presidential Reconstruction came to a close, the Black Codes were made illegal. The maintenance of such southern practices as the convict lease system, black peonage,* and contract labor laws, well into the twentieth century, however, ensured continuing forms of forced labor in the South.

SELECTED BIBLIOGRAPHY

Eric Foner, *Nothing but Freedom: Emancipation and Its Legacy* (1983); Idus A. Newby, *The South: A History* (1978); W. C. Nunn, *Texas under the Carpet Baggers* (1962); Charles Vincent, *Black Legislators in Louisiana During Reconstruction* (1976); Michael Wayne, *The Reshaping of Plantation Society: The Natchez District* (1983); Vernon Lane Wharton, *The Negro in Mississippi: 1865–1890* (1947); Theodore Brantner Wilson, *The Black Codes of the South* (1965).

Joe Louis Caldwell

BLACK CONVENTIONS. Although state and national conventions of African Americans began in the 1830s, the primary focus of the conventions changed after the Civil War from antislavery, economic development,and some nationalism to voting, legal rights, and schools. These meetings debated the contradiction between being all black and their goal of greater participation in society. As political roles of African Americans declined at the end of Reconstruction, the sporadic conventions returned to an emphasis on economic improvement. In the 1880s, the conventions expanded their concerns to include education, lynching, and various forms of discrimination. They ceased in the 1890s with the formation of ongoing civil rights groups.

SELECTED BIBLIOGRAPHY

Philip S. Foner and George E. Walker, eds., *Proceedings of the Black National and State Conventions, 1865–1900* (1986); August Meier, *Negro Thought in America, 1880–1915: Racial Ideologies in the Age of Booker T. Washington* (1963).

Alwyn Barr

BLACK ECONOMIC DEVELOPMENT CONFERENCE. This organization began as a conference held by the Interreligious Foundation for Community Organization (IFCO) at Wayne State University, Detroit, Michigan, in April 1969. At the meeting, former Student Nonviolent Coordinating Committee* director James Forman* presented and led the adoption of the "Black Manifesto" which called for, among other things, reparations from American white churches and synagogues of $500 million. Although by 1970 only about $300,000 had been received, this action did result in the formation and funding of many black organizations within various major denominations. Disassociated from IFCO, the Black Economic Development Conference invested most of its funds in a revolutionary publishing house, Black Star Publications.

SELECTED BIBLIOGRAPHY
James Forman, *The Making of Black Revolutionaries* (1985); C. Eric Lincoln, *Race, Religion, and the Continuing American Dilemma* (1984); *New York Times*, 4, 5 May 1969.
                                                                        Ray Branch

"BLACK IS BEAUTIFUL." Coming into vogue around 1966, the slogan "Black Is Beautiful" signaled a mood of black racial pride and a rejection of white values of style and appearance. It was particularly popular with young black people, who expressed this attitude by foregoing the skin lighteners and hair straighteners used by their parents' generation and by adopting Afro hairstyles and such African forms of dress as dashikis. Along with the political concept of Black Power and the increasing interest in African-American and African history and culture, the slogan was one manifestation of black nationalism in the period after 1965.

SELECTED BIBLIOGRAPHY
Stokely Carmichael and Charles V. Hamilton, *Black Power: The Politics of Liberation in America* (1967); August Meier and Elliott M. Rudwick, *From Plantation to Ghetto: An Interpretive History of American Negroes* (1970).
                                                                        Carol Wilson

BLACK MUSLIMS. This term, coined by writer C. Eric Lincoln, refers to members of the Nation of Islam, a black nationalist and religious organization founded in Detroit, Michigan, in or around 1930 by W. D. Fard. Fard taught that blacks could obtain success through discipline, racial pride, knowledge of God, and physical separation from white society. In June 1934, Fard mysteriously disappeared and was succeeded by Elijah Muhammad (born Elijah Poole*). Muhammad proclaimed that Fard was Allah (God) and that he had selected him as his messenger. Muhammad moved the organization's headquarters to Chicago. The Black Muslims promoted integrity, honor, and cleanliness; they practiced abstinence from intoxicants and all controlled substances; they published their own newspaper; they purchased thousands of acres of southern farmland; they invested in business ventures; and they negotiated independently with foreign governments. The Nation of Islam also had its own educational system and a paramilitary force—Fruit of Islam. The most effective spokesman for the Black Muslims was Malcolm X* (El Hajj Malik al-Shabazz, born Malcolm Little). From the late 1950s to 1963 he served as Muhammad's national representative, and the Nation of Islam gained national attention and a strong following. In 1963, Malcolm X lost favor with Elijah Muhammad, and in 1964 he resigned from the Nation of Islam to form the Muslim Mosques, Inc., and the Organization of Afro-American Unity.* In 1965 Malcolm X was assassinated, allegedly by Black Muslims. When Elijah Muhammad died in 1975, the nation of Islam split. The American Muslim Mission, later called the Muslim American Community, is headed by Muhammad's son Imam (Reverend) Warith Deen Muhammad. Warith introduced his followers to internationally accepted practices of the Islamic religion. Those refusing to deviate from Elijah Muhammad's teachings comprise a smaller sect, retain the name Nation of Islam, and follow Louis Farrakhan (born Louis Eugene Walcott). Farrakhan became prominent when he replaced Malcolm X as Muhammad's national representative.

SELECTED BIBLIOGRAPHY

A. John Adams and Joan Martin Burke, *A CBS News Reference Book: Civil Rights, A Current Guide to the People, Organizations and Events* (1970); C. Eric Lincoln, *The Black Muslims in America* (1973); Louis E. Lomax, *The Negro Revolt* (1963); Barbara Ann Norman, "The Black Muslims: A Rhetorical Analysis" (Ph.D. diss., University of Oklahoma, 1985); Harry A. Ploski, et al., eds., *The Negro Almanac* (1983).

Wali Rashash Kharif

BLACK PANTHERS. The Black Panther party was organized in October 1966 in Oakland, California, by Bobby Seale* and Huey P. Newton.* Dedicated to the principle of self-defense in the face of racist aggression and police brutality, the Panthers captured instant media attention by combining militant rhetoric with overt brandishing of automatic weapons as they trailed Oakland police to monitor their dealings with the African-American community. The party was founded on the Ten Point Program, which took its inspiration from the Algerian freedom fighter, Frantz Fanon. Subscribing to the belief that African Americans constituted an oppressed black colony within a white mother country, the Panthers worked to liberate that colony. The party's platform demanded that African Americans be given freedom to decide their own destiny, control of their own communities, decent housing and education, exemption from military service, justice, and liberation from control by the white power structure. The party allied itself with the Weather Underground faction of Students for a Democratic Society, specifically because both groups sought to free themselves from American oppression. Panther workers organized many community-based programs, including a highly successful free breakfast program for school children.

SELECTED BIBLIOGRAPHY

Eldridge Cleaver, *Soul on Ice* (1968); Theodore Draper, *The Rediscovery of Black Nationalism* (1970); Philip S. Foner, ed., *The Black Panthers Speak* (1970); Gene Marine, *The Black Panthers* (1969); Gilbert Moore, *A Special Rage* (1971); Bobby Seale, *Seize the Time: The Story of the Black Panther Party and Huey P. Newton* (1968).

Marshall Hyatt

BLACK PEONAGE. Following the Civil War many southern blacks became victims of peonage, a form of involuntary servitude akin to slavery. The system developed because southern planters needed a cheap and stable labor force and because the recently freed slaves, lacking land and capital of their own, needed employment. Frequently employing deception, coercion, or intimidation, landowners entered into exploitive contractual labor arrangements with impoverished blacks. Because the labor contracts and other devices employed by whites to impose peonage were sanctioned by state laws, blacks were often victimized for years by the system. The sharecropping system so widely employed in the South after 1865 was itself a means sometimes used to convert Negro workers into peons. Indebtedness was the perpetual condition of sharecroppers, who went ever deeper into debt to the landowners whose land they farmed. Because the white landlord advanced the goods the sharecropper needed and kept the account ledgers himself, it was difficult if not impossible for the cropper to extricate himself from debt and get free from the oppressive system. The widespread practice of imposing fines for petty crimes and then allowing white employers to pay the fines for impecunious blacks in exchange for their labor was another easy avenue to peonage. Although the Peonage Abolition Act of 1867 was passed by Congress to end the practice, peonage persisted. Forced labor because of debt enjoyed legal sanction in the South until 1911, when in the decision *Bailey v. Alabama** the Supreme Court declared unconstitutional a state law that made peonage possible. Even then, peonage did not completely disappear. During the 1920s and 1930s the NAACP,* the Communist-backed Abolish Peonage Committee of America,* and other civil rights groups pressured the Justice Department to bring action against southern peonage bosses. In 1941 the Supreme Court in *Taylor v. Georgia** again struck down a state statute permitting coerced labor. After that time a sharp drop in peonage occurred, though peonage prosecutions were still being filed by the Justice Department as late as the 1950s.

SELECTED BIBLIOGRAPHY

Pete Daniel, *The Shadow of Slavery: Peonage in the South, 1901–1969* (1972); Daniel A. Novak, *The Wheel of Servitude, Black Forced Labor after Slavery* (1978); C. Vann Woodward, *Origins of the New South, 1877–1913* (1951).

Charles D. Lowery

BLACK POWER. On 17 June 1966, Stokely Carmichael,* the chairman of the Student Nonviolent Coordinating Committee* (SNCC), spoke at a rally in Greenwood, Mississippi, and called for Black Power. The speech split the civil rights movement and angered many of its supporters. Although the press interpreted Black Power as black violence against whites, Carmichael defined it as "a call for black people in this country to unite, to recognize their heritage, [and] to build a sense of community." He also defined Black Power as a call for African Americans to define their own goals, to lead their own organizations, and to reject the racist institutions and values of American society. While the press and conservative civil rights organizations such as the NAACP* and Southern Christian Leadership Conference* rejected and condemned Black Power as black racism, many of the young people in the civil rights movement adopted the slogan as a rallying cry for more aggressive action in the African-American liberation struggle.

SELECTED BIBLIOGRAPHY

Stokely Carmichael, "What We Want," *New York Review of Books* (22 September 1966), 5–8; Stokely Carmichael and Charles V. Hamilton, *Black Power: The Politics of Liberation in America* (1967); Henry Hampton and Steve Fayer, *Voices of Freedom: An Oral History of the Civil Rights Movement from the 1950s through the 1980s* (1990); Christopher Lasch, "The Trouble with Black Power," *New York Review of Books* (29 February 1968), 4–5, 8–14; Alvin Poussaint, "How the White Problem Spawned Black Power," *Ebony* (August 1967); Milton Viorst, *Fire in the Streets: America in the 1960s* (1979).

W. Marvin Dulaney

BLACK STAR STEAMSHIP LINE. Marcus Garvey* and his Universal Negro Improvement Association* operated a black-owned steamship line between 1919 and 1922. Stocks were sold inexpensively and widely within the black community. This corporation was established to foster black trade by linking black enterprises into a worldwide economic network and to provide transportation to Africa. The plan enjoyed widespread support among African Americans, suggesting as it did self-reliance and racial pride. Grave financial problems forced the closing of the Black Star Line, and it was replaced by the Black Cross Navigation and Training Company in 1924. This too failed. Garvey was convicted of mail fraud in connection with the Black Star Line, found guilty, and deported from the United States in 1927.

SELECTED BIBLIOGRAPHY

John Clarke, *Marcus Garvey and the Vision of Africa* (1974); Robert Hill, ed., *The Marcus Garvey and UNIA Papers*, vols. 1–6 (1983–1989); Tony Martin, *Race First* (1976); Judith Stein, *The World of Marcus Garvey* (1986).

Cheryl Greenberg

BLACK SUFFRAGETTES. By the end of the Civil War, African-American women in both the North and South had begun to demonstrate an interest in acquiring the right to vote. Viewing the ballot as a vehicle that could advance women as well as secure civil and social rights for blacks, they formed all-black organizations and also attempted to work within integrated groups. Throughout the country, black women's involvement in various forms of suffrage agitation and education continued until the passage of the Nineteenth Amendment.

SELECTED BIBLIOGRAPHY

Adele L. Alexander, "How I Discovered My Grandmother . . . and the Truth about Black Women and the Suffrage Movement," in Darlene C. Hine, ed., *Black*

Women in United States History, vol. 1 (1990); Angela Davis, *Women, Race & Class* (1983); Paula Giddings, *When and Where I Enter: The Impact of Black Women on Race and Sex in America* (1984); Dorothy Sterling, *We Are Your Sisters: Black Women in the Nineteenth Century* (1984).

Willi Coleman

BLAKE, EUGENE CARSON (7 November 1906, St. Louis, Mo.–31 July 1985, Stamford, Conn.). An influential white clergyman, scholar, and author, Blake attended Princeton (A.B., 1928), Princeton Theological Seminary (Th.B., 1932), and Occidental College (D.D., 1941). He received twenty honorary degrees. Blake headed the United Presbyterian Church and the National Council of Churches, and, after the 1963 Birmingham violence, challenged white clergymen: "Some time or other, we are all going to have to stand and be on the receiving end of a fire hose." Active in the civil rights movement, he was arrested in a Baltimore, Maryland, march, and he was a principal organizer of the 1963 March on Washington.* Blake supported nonviolence and opposed militancy in the civil rights movement.

SELECTED BIBLIOGRAPHY
Taylor Branch, *Parting the Waters: America in the King Years, 1954–63* (1988); Ebony, *Ebony Pictorial History of Black America*, vol. 3 (1971); John Hope Franklin and Alfred A. Moss, Jr., *From Slavery to Freedom: A History of Negro Americans* (1988); William Loren Katz, *Eyewitness: The Negro in American History* (1968); *Who's Who in America, 1980–1981* (1981).

Wali Rashash Kharif

BLOOD ON THE FORGE. Published in 1941 by African-American novelist William Attaway,* this novel, like *12 Million Black Voices*, by Richard Wright,* which appeared in the same year, deals with the harsh and disillusioning realities of northern working-class life faced by black Southerners who participated in the Great Migration* (1910–1920). Attaway's story is set in rural Kentucky and in a steel town outside Pittsburgh, Pennsylvania, where his protagonists, the sharecropping Moss brothers, flee to escape racial and economic oppression. *Blood on the Forge* was one of the first examples of African-American proletariat fiction.

SELECTED BIBLIOGRAPHY
Bonnie J. Barthold, *Black Time: Fiction of Africa, the Caribbean, and the United States* (1981); Arthur P. Davis, *From the Dark Tower: Afro-American Writers, 1900 to 1960* (1974); Phyllis R. Klotman, "An Examination of Whiteness in William Attaway's *Blood on the Forge*," *CLA Journal* 15 (June 1972), 459–64; Philip H. Vaughn, "From Pastoralism to Industrial Antipathy in William Attaway's *Blood on the Forge*," *Phylon* 36 (December 1975), 422–25; Edward R. Waldon, "The Death of the Blues in William Attaway's *Blood on the Forge*," *Negro American Literature Forum* 10

(Summer 1976), 58–60; Richard Yarborough, "Afterword" to William Attaway, *Blood on the Forge* (1941, reprint, 1987).

Judith N. Kerr

BLUES. Perhaps the best definition of the blues came from the Classic Blueswomen. These black women in the 1920s recorded the first blues discs for commercial distribution. Bessie Smith stated in 1924 that the blues were not funny songs. "Of course," she said, "the modern songs are greatly modified, but the original blues songs are deep, emotional melodies, bespeaking of a troubled heart." Two years later, the *Chicago Defender** featured a statement by Ethel Waters in which she claimed that one must feel the blues, not just sing them. Waters stated: "The blues are our own and they originated not from religious hymns as many people think, but from the feeling of sorrow and oppression born with the darky. Any religious Negro can sing a spiritual, but it takes a good one to sing blues." Although Ma Rainey, Bessie Smith, Alberta Hunter, Mamie Smith, and other blues singers often expressed personal pain, they also sang about the black poor. Songs such as these represented social protest and reflected the response in music to the oppressive racial injustices blacks experienced in America. Mamie Smith's success paved the way for other blues and black music artists to enter the world of professional entertainment. Thus began the "race record" industry that ended black exclusion from the commercial record industry. This was a civil rights milestone for black America. Although many African-American blues artists were exploited and experienced segregation and racial discrimination in recording, promoting, and performing the blues, eventually they were recognized as a significant aspect of American musical culture and, later, as a major force in the recording and performing industries.

SELECTED BIBLIOGRAPHY

William Barlow, *"Looking up at Down": The Emergence of Blues Culture* (1989); *Chicago Defender*, 25 December 1926; Daphne Duval Harrison, *Black Pearls: Blues Queens of the 1920s* (1988); LeRoi Jones, *Blues People* (1961); Phillip McGuire, "Black Music Critics and the Classic Blues Singers," *The Black Perspective in Music* 14 (Spring 1986); Paul Oliver, *The Story of the Blues* (1969).

Phillip McGuire

BOB JONES UNIVERSITY v. UNITED STATES, 461 U.S. 574 (1983). Until 1970 the Internal Revenue Service (IRS) granted tax-exempt status to private schools regardless of their racial admissions policies. In 1971 the District Court for the District of Columbia ruled in *Green v. Connally* that racially discriminatory private schools were not entitled to exemption under the Internal Revenue Code. Bob Jones University, a nonprofit corporation in Greenville, South Carolina, had excluded blacks until 1970 and, from 1971 to 1975, accepted only blacks married within their race.

After May 1975 the university enrolled unmarried blacks but prohibited interracial dating and marriage. On 16 January 1976, the IRS revoked the university's tax-exempt status, effective 1 December 1970, because of its racially discriminatory policy. The university filed suit to recover $21 it had paid in 1975 unemployment taxes, and the government counterclaimed for unpaid unemployment taxes for the years 1971–1975, totalling almost half a million dollars. The Federal District Court in South Carolina found in favor of the plaintiff, ruling that the IRS had exceeded its delegated powers in revoking the university's tax-exempt status. The Fourth Circuit Court of Appeals rejected the lower court's arguments and reversed the decision. The Supreme Court, on appeal, affirmed the decision of the Appellate Court.

SELECTED BIBLIOGRAPHY

Richard Nathan, "Reflections on Pragmatic Jurisprudence: A Case Study of Bob Jones University v. United States," *American Business Law Journal*, 22 (1984), 227–48; Donald G. Nieman, *Promises to Keep: African-Americans and the Constitutional Order, 1776 to the Present* (1991); J. Harvie Wilkinson III, *From Brown to Bakke: The Supreme Court and School Integration, 1954–1978* (1979).

Michael S. Downs

BOB-LO EXCURSION CO. v. MICHIGAN, 333 U.S. 28 (1948). When this case reached the U.S. Supreme Court, constitutional doctrine held that state laws based upon race affecting passengers in interstate commerce infringed upon the power of Congress to regulate interstate and foreign commerce. The effect of that doctrine in *Morgan v. Virginia** (1946) had been to protect black travelers on interstate buses from Virginia segregation law. Application of the doctrine to the *Bob-Lo* case, however, would have had the effect of permitting racial discrimination, which the Court was unwilling to allow. Bob-Lo Excursion Company operated an amusement park on an island in Canadian waters and used steamships to carry its customers there. It refused to serve blacks, and, when a group of thirteen young women, one of whom was black, boarded a Bob-Lo ship, the company required the black to leave. She brought charges against the company, which the state successfully prosecuted under its civil rights law. The company appealed. Rather than follow doctrine and hold the state civil rights act unconstitutional, the Court distinguished the *Bob-Lo* case, noting that the only access to the island was from Detroit, Michigan, and that most of the customers lived there, making the matter primarily local, rather than foreign, commerce. The state law did not infringe upon Congress's commerce power.

SELECTED BIBLIOGRAPHY

Note, "Discrimination and the Commerce Clause: Application of State Civil

Rights Acts in Interstate and Foreign Commerce," *Yale Law Journal* 58 (1949), 329–34; C. Herman Pritchett, *The American Constitution* (1977).

Patricia A. Behlar

BOLEY, OKLAHOMA. This was the most celebrated of the black towns established in Oklahoma as a result of black migration. When Congress created the Oklahoma Territory in 1889 and opened it for settlement, southern blacks moved in and claimed homesteads. The migrants brought with them dreams of a better life. They hoped to own land and to enjoy freedom and independence. Edwin P. McCabe, founder of the black town of Langston, thought it possible to carve an all-black state out of the Indian Territory. This dream soon faded, but it was still thought possible to gain control of Okfuskee County and have Boley named the county seat. Boley was founded in 1903 at the urging of W. H. Boley, president of the Fort Smith & Western Railroad, for whom it was named. By 1905, there were over two thousand people in the area, and economic, social, and cultural institutions were flourishing. On the eve of statehood, the white-dominated constitutional contention passed over Boley for the county seat. By gerrymandering Okfuskee County, white Oklahomans neutralized the black vote. Then, in 1910, black Oklahomans were disfranchised. This ended the dream of political power, and the cotton depression of 1913 ended Boley's economic prosperity. Soon, the town began losing population to northern industrial cities.

SELECTED BIBLIOGRAPHY
William E. Bittle and Gilbert L. Geis, "Racial Self-Fulfillment and the Rise of an All-Negro Community in Oklahoma," *Phylon* 18 (Third Quarter, 1957), 247–60; Jimmie Lewis Franklin, *Journey toward Hope: A History of Blacks in Oklahoma* (1982); Kent Ruth, *Oklahoma: A Guide to the Sooner State* (1958).

Arvarh E. Strickland

BOLLING v. SHARPE, 347 U.S. 497 (1954). On 17 May 1954, in *Brown v. Board of Education,** the Supreme Court ruled that school segregation violated the equal protection clause of the Fourteenth Amendment.* *Bolling v. Sharpe,* which dealt with the same issue in Washington, D.C., was decided because the Fourteenth Amendment specifically prohibited states from denying citizens the equal protection of the laws; it did not, however, apply to the federal government. The Court ruled in *Bolling* that discrimination could be "so unjustifiable as to be violative of due process" and that segregation in Washington's schools fell into that category and therefore violated the Fifth Amendment's guarantee of due process. If the legal reasoning seemed somewhat less than irrefutable, the Court concluded by stating the real rationale behind its decision:

"In view of our decision that the Constitution prohibits the states from maintaining racially segregated public schools, it would be unthinkable that the same Constitution would impose a lesser duty on the Federal Government."

SELECTED BIBLIOGRAPHY

Daniel M. Berman, *It Is So Ordered* (1966); David Chang, "The Bus Stops Here: Defining the Constitutional Right of Equal Educational Opportunity and an Appropriate Remedial Process," *Boston University Law Review*, 83 (1983), 1–58; Richard Kluger, *Simple Justice: The History of Brown v. Board of Education and Black America's Struggle for Equality* (1976).

Michael S. Mayer

BOND, (HORACE) JULIAN (14 January 1940, Nashville, Tenn.–   ). Bond was born into a family of educators which included his grandfather and his father, Horace Mann Bond, first black president of Lincoln University. Julian Bond dropped out of Morehouse College* to pursue a

Julian Bond. (Negro Almanac Collection, Amistad Research Center, Tulane University, New Orleans.)

career in journalism. His literary and analytical skills prepared him for his position as public affairs officer for the Student Nonviolent Coordinating Committee* (SNCC) which served as springboard for his election to the Georgia House of Representatives in 1965. Because of his outspoken opposition to the war in Vietnam, Bond was ejected from the legislature. In 1968, as one of the leaders of the civil rights and antiwar coalition within the Democratic party, Bond was nominated for the vice presidency at the Chicago Democratic Convention. In 1987 he lost a bitter congressional campaign to his former SNCC comrade in arms, John Lewis.* Bond still remains a highly regarded intellectual, political analyst, and historian of the late civil rights era.

SELECTED BIBLIOGRAPHY

Thomas E. Bell, *Julian Bond vs John Lewis* (1988); John Neary, *Julian Bond: Black Rebel* (1971); Roger M. Williams, *The Bonds: An American Family* (1971).

Maghan Keita

BONTEMPS, ARNA WENDELL (13 October 1902, Alexandria, La.–4 June 1973, Nashville, Tenn.). Bontemps was part of his home state's long tradition of producing outstanding nonwhite politicians, artists, educators, musicians, writers, and businessmen. He received his B.A. from Union Pacific College (1923) and his M.A. from the University of Chicago (1943), and his career included teaching and administration as well as writing. Among his various educational posts were positions at Oakwood School in Huntsville, Alabama (1930–1932); the University of Illinois (1966); Yale University (1969–1972); and Fisk University* (1943–1965 and 1972–1973). Scholarly recognition of his contributions is evidenced by his receipt of Guggenheim and Rosenwald Fellowships; his awards for writing include two Alexander Pushkin Prizes for poetry and *Crisis [*] Magazine*'s Poetry Prize. Bontemps was a novelist, historian, biographer, and playwright as well as a poet. Among his numerous works are *God Sends Sunday* (1931), *You Can't Pet a Possum* (1934), *Black Thunder* (1936), *Drums at Dusk* (1939), *Golden Slippers: An Anthology of Negro Poetry for Young People* (1941), *Story of the Negro* (1948), *George Washington Carver* (1950), *Frederick Douglass: Slave, Fighter, Freeman* (1959), *American Negro Poetry* (1963), *Famous Negro Athletes* (1964), and *The Harlem Renaissance Remembered* (1972). This productivity made him one of the most outstanding figures of the Harlem Renaissance;* however, his novel *Black Thunder*, depicting a slave insurrection amid the French Revolution, led to accusations that he was encouraging violent revolution. Arna Bontemps spent his last years as writer in residence at Fisk University, preparing his autobiography.

SELECTED BIBLIOGRAPHY

Bruce Kellner, *The Harlem Renaissance: A Historical Dictionary for the Era* (1984);

John O'Brien, ed., *Interviews with Black Writers* (1973); Wilhelmena S. Robinson, *Historical Negro Biographies* (1969).

Gary B. Mills

BOSTON GUARDIAN. This African-American protest newspaper was established in 1901 by the militant (William) Monroe Trotter* and George W. Forbes. The first issue pledged "to voice intelligently the needs and aspirations of the colored American." As managing editor, Trotter used the *Guardian* to demand full citizenship and equality for African Americans. The *Guardian's* editorials attacked Booker T. Washington* and his philosophy of accommodation. Trotter effectively used the *Guardian* as a forum not only to denounce Washington's policies, but also to fight increasing racism and to keep the protest tradition operative. The *Guardian* experienced a decline in the 1920s but continued in circulation even after Trotter's death in 1934.

SELECTED BIBLIOGRAPHY
The *Boston Guardian*, 1901–1957; Stephen R. Fox, *The Guardian of Boston: William Monroe Trotter* (1970); Louis R. Harlan, *Booker T. Washington: The Wizard of Tuskegee, 1901–1915* (1983); Charles W. Puttkammer and Ruth Worthy, "William Monroe Trotter, 1872–1934," *The Journal of Negro History* 43 (October 1958), 298–316.

Maxine D. Jones

BOSTON RIOT (1903). Appalled at the influence of Booker T. Washington's* doctrine of accommodation, (William) Monroe Trotter* and George W. Forbes of the *Boston Guardian* sought to challenge Washington's leadership directly. Drafting a series of probing questions on Washington's racial philosophy, Trotter and Forbes organized a group of about thirty people to interrupt Washington's speech to Boston's Negro Business League at the African Methodist Episcopal (A.M.E.) church on 30 July 1903. Trotter and his followers' attempts to ask questions disrupted the meeting, caused him to be arrested, fined fifty dollars, and sentenced to thirty days in prison. The incident, sensationalized and exaggerated in the local press as "the Boston riot," made the militant Trotter a martyr to other Negro radicals and he became a rallying point for anti-Washington forces. Later, Trotter and W.E.B. Du Bois* formed the Niagara Movement,* the first national organization of militant blacks, which favored direct political and social protest over Washington's accommodationist stance.

SELECTED BIBLIOGRAPHY
Robert H. Brisbane, *The Black Vanguard: Origins of the Negro Social Revolution, 1900–1960* (1970); W.E.B. Du Bois, "William Monroe Trotter," *Crisis* (May 1934), 134; Stephen R. Fox, *The Guardian of Boston: William Monroe Trotter* (1970); Charles W. Puttkammer and Ruth Worthy, "William Monroe Trotter 1872–1934," *Journal*

of Negro History 43 (October 1958), 298–316; Booker T. Washington, *My Larger Education: Being Chapters from My Experience* (1911).

Thaddeus M. Smith

BOSWELL AMENDMENT. The Boswell Amendment was representative of the system of legislative hurdles and literacy tests designed to exclude black voters from the polls in the post-Reconstruction period through the late 1960s. Authored by Alabama State Senator E.C. "Bud" Boswell in 1946, the amendment was offered especially "as a device for eliminating Negro applicants." The amendment was struck down along with other literacy restrictions by the federal courts in the 1949 litigation *Davis et al. v. Schnell et al.**

SELECTED BIBLIOGRAPHY

Loren Miller, *The Petitioners: The Story of the Supreme Court of the United States and the Negro* (1966): Mabel M. Smythe, ed., *The Black American Reference Book* (1976).

Maghan Keita

BOYNTON v. VIRGINIA, 364 U.S. 454 (1960). This case extended the prohibition against segregation in interstate travel to cover accommodations in terminals. The Supreme Court held that racial segregation practiced by a privately operated restaurant in an interstate bus terminal in Richmond, Virginia, violated the Interstate Commerce Act. Writing for the majority, Justice Hugo Black ruled that, if a bus company "has volunteered to make terminal and restaurant facilities . . . available to its interstate passengers as a regular part of their transportation," then the "terminal and restaurant stand in place of the bus company in the performance of its transportation obligations" and they "must perform these services without discrimination prohibited by the [Motor Carrier] Act." In spite of this decision and *Morgan v. Virginia** (1946), which had prohibited segregation on buses engaged in interstate travel, blacks who tried to sit in the front seat of buses or who tried to use terminal facilities other than those assigned to them were usually ejected or arrested. The Congress of Racial Equality* decided to test the *Boynton* decision with Freedom Riders.*

SELECTED BIBLIOGRAPHY

Catherine A. Barnes, *Journey from Jim Crow: The Desegregation of Southern Transit* (1983); James Farmer, *Lay Bare the Heart* (1985); Donald G. Nieman, *Promises to Keep, African-Americans and the Constitutional Order, 1776 to the Present* (1991).

Michael S. Mayer

BRADLEY, THOMAS (29 December 1917, Calvert, Tex.–). Bradley's family moved to Los Angeles when he was seven. A temporary police department job in 1940 turned into a career of twenty-one years during which time he rose to the rank of lieutenant, studied law, received the

LL.B. at Southwestern University in 1956, and was admitted to the California bar. He became the first black man elected to the Los Angeles City Council in 1963, and he was unopposed in 1967 and 1971 in a racially mixed district. A Democrat, he won 56 percent of the vote in a city with a 15-percent black electorate to defeat incumbent Sam Yorty to become the first black mayor of a predominantly white American city on 1 July 1973. Under his leadership, Los Angeles has received over $1 billion in federal grants, balanced the budget, and initiated ambitious transit and city planning programs.

SELECTED BIBLIOGRAPHY
Current Biography (1973); "How Blacks Are Faring as Government Leaders," *U.S. News and World Report*, 5 March 1984; "Los Angeles:A Black Mayor," *Newsweek*, 11 June 1973; *Roundtable* (1986); *Who's Who among Black Americans* (1988).

Thomas D. Cockrell

BRAITHWAITE, WILLIAM STANLEY BEAUMONT (6 December 1878, Boston, Mass.–8 June 1962, Boston, Mass.). The son of William Smith and Emma DeWolf Braithwaite, he was self-educated; as a youth, he became an apprentice typesetter at Ginn and Company. During his career, Braithwaite was literary editor and columnist for the *Boston Evening Transcript*; publisher of the *Poetic Journal of Boston* (1912–1914); editor, *Poetry Review* (1916–1917); founder and editor of B. J. Brimmer Publishing Co. (1921–1927); and a member of the editorial board of *Phylon*.* His works include collections of poetry (the first, *Lyrics of Life and Love* appeared in 1904), essays, novels, a Brontë biography—*The Bewitched Parsonage: The Story of the Brontës* (1950)—and an autobiography, *The House under Arcturus*, serialized in *Phylon* 1941–1942. He also contributed articles, essays, verse, and book reviews to periodicals. Braithwaite's poetry is classified as Romantic; but because it neither addressed social and political issues nor was identifiably African-American, some colleagues accused him of being ashamed of his race. Braithwaite chose to emphasize the aesthetic qualities of literature. Even so, as the editor of anthologies, he published the works of many black writers, who otherwise might not have attained public recognition. This was his contribution to the Harlem Renaissance.* In 1918, William Braithwaite was the first winner of the NAACP* Spingarn Medal* for literary achievement. He also received honorary degrees from Atlanta University* and Talladega College.

SELECTED BIBLIOGRAPHY
Benjamin Brawley, *The Negro in Art and Literature* (1918); Phillip Butcher, "William Stanley Braithwaite's Southern Exposure: Resume and Revelation," *Southern Literary Journal* 3 (Spring 1971), 49–61; Trudier Harris, ed., *Afro-American Writers*

Before the Harlem Renaissance (1986); Peter Quartermain, ed., *American Poets, 1880–1945*, 3rd ser. (1986); William H. Robinson, *Black New England Letters* (1977).

Judith N. Kerr

BREEDLOVE v. SUTTLES, 302 U.S. 277 (1937). The poll tax,* usually retroactive and cumulative, had the effect of disfranchising all indigent voters and on the surface was not aimed specifically at the African American. However, the Southern Conference for Human Welfare* condemned it as "patently a device for disfranchising Negroes." In 1937 a white, twenty-eight-year-old male challenged the Georgia poll tax as offensive to the rule of equality since it required a one dollar annual payment from all inhabitants between the ages of twenty-one and sixty as a prerequisite for voting in all elections. The U.S. Supreme Court ruled that the tax, properly administered, did not violate any protection or privilege guaranteed by the Fourteenth,* Fifteenth,* or Nineteenth Amendments and was, therefore, constitutional. Justice Butler stated that it was reasonable to exclude those under twenty-one years of age since the burden of payment would rest on their parents or guardians and those over sixty years since they were exempt from jury duty and military service. The final destruction of the poll tax occurred with the ratification of the Twenty-fourth Amendment (1964), the passage of the Civil Rights Act of 1964,* the Voting Rights Act of 1965,* and the Supreme Court decision reached in *Harper v. Virginia Board of Elections** (1966).

SELECTED BIBLIOGRAPHY

Richard Bardolph, ed., *The Civil Rights Record: Black Americans and the Law, 1849–1970* (1970); Paul Freund et al., *Constitutional Law: Cases and Other Problems* (1961); Jack Greenberg, *Race Relations and American Law* (1959); Alfred H. Kelly and Winfred A. Harbison, *American Constitution: Origins and Development* (1970).

Aingred G. Dunston

BRIGGS v. ELLIOT, 132 F. Supp. 776 (E.D. S.C., 1955). This case originally came before a federal appeals court in 1951 and then was added to a group of four other cases which went before the United States Supreme Court under the nomenclature of *Brown v. Board of Education.** The *Briggs* case concerned Harry Briggs, a black parent, who brought suit with other black parents against R. W. Elliot, the school board chairman of Clarendon County, South Carolina. The parents were represented by a team of NAACP* lawyers headed by Thurgood Marshall.* Marshall, arguing for the plaintiff, charged that the county schools provided for black children were unequal and inferior and that segregation was unconstitutional and detrimental to black children. Marshall's case relied heavily upon the testimony of psychologist Kenneth Clark whose "doll" studies demonstrated the effects of segregation. The attorney general of South Carolina did not even try to defend the unequal nature of the schools; he said that the state assembly was working to pass a bond issue that would rectify the NAACP's first argument. As for the second point, the attorney general stood on the *Plessy v. Ferguson** decision which upheld separate-but-equal* facilities. The Fourth Circuit Court of Appeals found for South Carolina. The case was then appealed by the NAACP to the U.S. Supreme Court.

SELECTED BIBLIOGRAPHY

Daniel Berman, *It Is So Ordered: The Supreme Court Rules on School Segregation* (1966); Richard Kluger, *Simple Justice: The History of Brown versus Board of Education and America's Struggle for Equality* (1976); George Rossman, ed., "Review of Recent Supreme Court Cases," *American Bar Association Journal*, 40 (1954), 618–19.

Kenneth W. Goings

BRIMMER, ANDREW FENTON (13 September 1926, Newellton, La.–). An African-American economist and public servant, Andrew Brimmer attended the University of Washington, where he earned bachelor's and master's degrees in economics. His master's thesis concerned economic aspects of fair employment. Noted for research on international monetary issues, he was appointed a governor of the Federal Reserve Board in 1966. Brimmer also researches and writes about the economic status of black Americans. He presented expert testimony on discrimination in interstate commerce for hearings on the Civil Rights Act of 1964* and initiated a study of the skewed income levels of blacks and whites after the 1968 Watts race riot.*

SELECTED BIBLIOGRAPHY

Andrew F. Brimmer, *Trends, Prospects, and Strategies for Black Economic Progress* (1985); *Current Biography* (1968).

Nancy E. Fitch

BROOKE, EDWARD WILLIAM (26 October 1919, Washington, D.C.–). Elected from Massachusetts in 1966, the liberal Republican Edward W. Brooke was the first African American to serve in the U.S. Senate after Reconstruction, and he has stood as a symbol of civil rights advances through moderate means. Educated at Howard University* (B.S., 1941) and Boston University (LL.B., 1948; LL.M., 1949), Brooke established a national reputation as an articulate and thoughtful spokesman for equality under the law while serving as Massachusetts attorney general (1963–1966). He pushed particularly for desegregated housing and, while a member of the Senate Banking, Housing and Urban Affairs Committee, he advocated open, private housing and low- and moderate-income public housing projects.

SELECTED BIBLIOGRAPHY

Edward W. Brooke, *The Challenge of Change* (1966); Edward W. Brooke, *United States Foreign Assistance for Haiti* (1974); *Washington Post*, 8, 10 November 1978.

Thomas J. Davis

BROOKS, GWENDOLYN (7 June 1917, Topeka, Kans.–). Nine years after graduation from Wilson Junior College (1936) in her native Chicago, Brooks published *Street in Bronzeville* (1945), which received an award from the American Academy of Arts and Letters. Her second volume *Annie Allen* (1949) won the 1950 Pulitzer Prize for Poetry. In 1960 Brooks published *The Bean Eaters* and was named Poet Laureate of Illinois in 1968. Marked by technical accomplishment and subtlety, Brooks's early poetry focuses on the lives of black Americans, particularly on the plight of urban existence, racial discrimination, and the special problems of women. After 1967 her poetry became more overtly political. The watershed volume *In the Mecca* (1968) contains poems on the assassinations of Medgar W. Evers* and Malcolm X,* the militant turn of the civil rights movement, and urban unrest as evidenced by Chicago street gangs. In *Riot* (1969), *Aloneness* (1971), the first volume of her autobiography *Report from Part One* (1972), *Beckonings* (1975), and *A Primer for Blacks* (1980), Brooks demonstrated her deepened commitment to the problems of racial injustice, empowerment, and independence. In recognition of her distinguished achievements as a poet and black American intellectual, Brooks was chosen poetry consultant to the Library of Congress for 1985–1986.

SELECTED BIBLIOGRAPHY
Mari Evans, ed., *Black Women Writers (1950–1980): A Critical Evaluation* (1983); D. H. Melhem, *Gwendolyn Brooks: Prophecy and Poetic Process* (1986); Maria K. Mootry and Gary Smith, eds., *A Life Distilled: Critical Essays on Gwendolyn Brooks* (1987); Claudia Tate, ed., *Black Women Writers at Work* (1983).

Jerry Ward

BROOKS v. BOARD OF EDUCATION OF THE CITY OF MOBERLY, MISSOURI, 3 R.R.L.R. 660 (E.D. Mo., 1958). The Board of Education in Moberly, Missouri, ordered the desegregation of its schools in 1955 in obedience to the 1954 *Brown v. Board of Education** decision, but it hired only white teachers. People of color were to teach only in segregated schools. Black teacher Naomi Brooks sued, alleging that she was a victim of racial discrimination. The board denied racial prejudice, and school officials insisted that they had looked for talent, not race. Although the court agreed that the school board had used subjective criteria, it ruled that the board's action had not constituted a policy of racial discrimination. The *Brooks* case illustrated that desegregation offered mixed blessings for African Americans. The promise of integration often meant loss of control over the few institutions blacks directed. In later cases NAACP* lawyers argued that a segregated staff meant a segregated school.

SELECTED BIBLIOGRAPHY
Jack Greenberg, *Race Relations and American Law* (1959); Leon Jones II, *From Brown to Boston, 1954–1974* (1979).

Stephen Middleton

BROTHERHOOD OF SLEEPING CAR PORTERS AND MAIDS. This union's founding and struggle for recognition was a dramatic episode in the history of black workers. From its beginning in 1867, the Pullman Company employed black workers as porters and maids. Through the years these workers became increasingly dissatisfied with their wages and working conditions. In 1925 a small group in New York City invited A. Philip Randolph* to lead their cause. Randolph formally organized the Brotherhood of Sleeping Car Porters and Maids (BSCP) on 25 August 1925. The Pullman Company refused to recognize the fledgling union and continued to deal with the porters through a company union. The BSCP leaders hoped to get federal help against the company under the provisions of the Watson-Parker Act of 1926, but this help did not come. Continued failure to receive company recognition caused the union to lose most of its members. New Deal labor legislation strengthened the BSCP's hand and finally led to recognition by the Pullman Company on 25 August 1937. In the meantime, Randolph had been carrying on a struggle for acceptance of the BSCP by the American Federation of Labor (AFL). In 1935 the AFL granted the BSCP an international charter, and Randolph carried on a fight against discrimination and on behalf of black workers from within the AFL and, after 1955, the AFL-CIO.

SELECTED BIBLIOGRAPHY

Jervis Anderson, *A. Philip Randolph: A Biographical Portrait* (1972); William H. Harris, *Keeping the Faith: A. Philip Randolph, Milton P. Webster, and the Brotherhood of Sleeping Car Porters, 1925–1937* (1977); Sterling D. Spero and Abram L. Harris, *The Black Worker: The Negro and the Labor Movement* (1968).

Arvarh E. Strickland

BROWDER v. GAYLE, 142 F. Supp. 707 (M.D. Ala., 1956). A landmark case in the demise of segregated public transportation, this case was filed by the Montgomery Improvement Association* (MIA) on behalf of five local black women. The MIA had intended to challenge Jim Crow* buses following the incident involving Rosa Parks* in December 1955 but feared endless delays in Alabama tribunals. By filing *Browder* in the federal district court in Montgomery, on which Judge Frank Minis Johnson* sat, they had a much better chance of success. NAACP* attorneys argued that segregated buses were unconstitutional and that Jim Crow laws should be struck down. The three federal judges who heard testimony, including Johnson and Fifth Circuit Judge Richard Taylor Rives,* ruled that statutes requiring segregated seating violated the due process and equal protection clauses of the Fourteenth Amendment.* *Plessy v. Ferguson*￼* had by implication been overruled in recent Supreme Court decisions, said Judge Rives, and there remained "no rational basis upon which the separate-but-equal* doctrine can be validly applied to public transportation." City and state officials appealed the decision, but the

Supreme Court unanimously upheld the lower court's ruling in *Gayle vs. Browder*, 352 U.S. 903 (1956). Thus was repudiated the momentous 1896 decision that had been the basis of the separate-but-equal doctrine and the mainstay of Jim Crow laws for more than half a century.

SELECTED BIBLIOGRAPHY

Richard Bardolph, ed., *The Civil Rights Record: Black Americans and the Law, 1849–1970* (1970); Catherine A. Barnes, *Journey from Jim Crow: The Desegregation of Southern Transit* (1983); Jack Bass, *Unlikely Heroes* (1981).

Charles D. Lowery

BROWN, EDGAR G. (2 March 1898, Sandoval, Ill.–10 April 1954, Washington Park, Ill.). Publisher and editor of the *St. Louis Standard News* and president of the National Lawn Tennis Association, Brown was also the founder and president of the United Government Employees which sought and won pay increases for the lowest ranks of government workers. A member of Franklin D. Roosevelt's Black Cabinet,* Brown served as director of public relations for the Negro press with the Civilian Conservation Corps. Later, as president of the National Negro Council, he was instrumental in instigating the U.S. Senate's investigation of Theodore Bilbo's win in the 1946 Mississippi primary election.

SELECTED BIBLIOGRAPHY

Ralph J. Bunche, *The Political Status of the Negro in the Age of FDR* (1973); *Negro Year Book, 1937–1938*; *New York Times*, 19 May, 7 September, 1946; *Who's Who in Colored America* (1940).

Ray Branch

BROWN, HUBERT GEROLD "RAPP" (JAMIL ABDULLAH AL-AMIN) (4 October 1943, Baton Rouge, La.–   ). Brown attended Southern University between 1960 and 1964, during which time he became involved in such youth-oriented civil rights organizations as the Nonviolent Action Group (NAG) and the Student Nonviolent Coordinating Committee* (SNCC). He rose quickly in these organizations, becoming director of the NAG in 1964, Alabama project director for SNCC in 1966, and national director of SNCC in May 1967 when he replaced Stokely Carmichael,* who had called Brown "a bad man." He also held office in the Black Panthers* in the late 1960s. His increasingly radical stance on black separatism and black power led him to turn away from—and to alienate—white liberal support for SNCC. The radical philosophy that became his trademark (symbolized by the phrase "Burn, Baby, Burn") is evident in his 1969 book *Die Nigger Die!* and in his speeches. He advocated black "self-defense" and economic and political control of ghettoes, and he agitated against the draft. Riots after some of his speeches; a disastrous fire in Cambridge, Maryland; and the importation of a weapon into Louisiana led to charges against him of inciting to riot, arson, and violating the Federal Firearms Act. His attorney, William Kunstler, attempted to brand Brown's troubles as harassment and to portray him as a political prisoner, but he gained little support from an unsympathetic public. In and out of trouble and jail from 1967 to 1970, Brown dropped out of sight until he eventually was shot and captured by New York City police during a robbery. He was sentenced to New York's Attica Prison in 1973 for a term of from five to fifteen years. He was paroled in 1976 after converting to Islam and changing his name to Jamil Abdullah al-Amin. Brown's perception of history sparked a philosophy that only violent revolution could bring about change. In that sense, he and his followers presented an extreme and unacceptable alternative to the inertia of the white power structure—the spectre of a violent race war. The incessant pressure of Brown and fellow radicals on the mainstream moderates did perhaps quicken changes. Had his radicalism gone unchecked, however, and had he secured adequate support from the masses, he could have been a serious impediment to progress in race relations.

SELECTED BIBLIOGRAPHY

Joan Martin Burke, *Civil Rights: A Current Guide to the People, Organizations, and Events* (1974); "Civil Rights: The Man from SNCC," *Newsweek* (22 May 1967); John D'Emilio, *The Civil Rights Struggle: Leaders in Profile* (1979); Herbert H. Haines, *Black Radicals and the Civil Rights Movement, 1954–1970* (1988); *New York Times*, 25 January 1975, 22 October 1976; Edward Vernoff and Rima Shore, *The International Dictionary of 20th Century Biography* (1987); "Where Have All the Soldiers Gone?" *Saturday Review* (28 April 1979).

Gary B. Mills

BROWN, JOHN ROBERT (10 December 1909, Funk, Nebr.–   ). Educated at the University of Nebraska (A.B., 1930) and the University of Michigan (J.D. 1933; LL.D., 1939), Brown was admitted to the Texas bar in 1932, and he joined a Houston and Galveston law firm that specialized in admirality law. In 1955 he was appointed to the United States Court of Appeals for the Fifth Judicial Circuit,* which he served as chief judge from 1968 to 1980. An active Presbyterian churchman, he believed strongly in the concept of brotherhood, which was evident in his decisions from the bench. On the Fifth Circuit Court he was an effective champion of minority rights. Together with fellow Fifth Circuit judges Elbert P. Tuttle,* Richard Taylor Rives,* and John Minor Wisdom,* he helped assure the success of the civil rights movement by making the federal courts, and especially the Fifth Circuit Court, whose heavy caseload made it the major battleground of the civil rights movement, a powerful vehicle for political and social change. As a regular member of three-judge panels, which usually included Rives and Wisdom, he helped implement the *Brown v. Board of Education** decision desegregating public education. He also helped to expand *Brown*'s mandate for equality beyond education to include landmark decisions that swept away racial discrimination in jury selection, employment, and voting.

SELECTED BIBLIOGRAPHY

Jack Bass, *Unlikely Heroes* (1981); Harvey C. Couch, *A History of the Fifth Circuit, 1891–1981* (1984); J. W. Peltason, *Fifty-Eight Lonely Men, Southern Federal Judges and School Desegregation* (1961).

Charles D. Lowery

BROWN, RICHARD JESS, SR. (2 September 1912, Muskogee, Okla – 31 December 1989, Jackson, Miss.). An African-American Mississippi lawyer educated at Illinois State University, Indiana University, and Texas Southern University Law School, Brown filed Mississippi's first civil rights lawsuit in the 1950s. In 1948, while a public school teacher, Brown joined Gladys Noel Baker in seeking equal salaries for black teachers in Jackson at a time when few blacks dared challenge white supremacy. In the 1960s, he filed lawsuits to desegregate school systems and transportation in Mississippi. Brown was coattorney for James Howard Meredith* when Meredith successfully enrolled at the University of Mississippi in 1962. He also defended Mack Charles Parker (accused of rape and subsequently lynched) and raised the issue of jury discrimination.

SELECTED BIBLIOGRAPHY

Alexander M. Bickel, "Impeach Judge Cox." *The New Republic*, 4 September 1965; *Jackson Clarion-Ledger*, 2, and 3 January 1990; *Martindale-Hubell Law Directory* (1984); *New York Times*, 3 January 1990; *Who's Who among Black Americans*, 5th ed., 1988.

Wali Rashash Kharif

BROWN v. BOARD OF EDUCATION, 347 U.S. 483 (1954). This decision removed the most important constitutional obstacle to equal rights for blacks. During Reconstruction, Congress inserted the equal protection clause into the Fourteenth Amendment* so that black as well as white Americans would be equal before the law. After Reconstruction, however, the willingness of the federal government and the states to enforce the clause in race cases abated. In 1896 the Supreme Court held in *Plessy v. Ferguson** that, as long as transportation facilities were theoretically equal, separation based on race was lawful under the equal protection clause. Shortly thereafter, amid the triumph of white supremacy throughout the South, the Court extended the separate-but-equal* doctrine to educational facilities. Over the next half century, the educational facilities provided blacks by southern and a few border states were always separate but never equal.

During the 1930s the Legal Defense and Educational Fund* of the NAACP* began to challenge the *Plessy* doctrine in federal court. Lawyers for the Legal Defense and Educational Fund argued that education was indispensable to the legal equality and economic opportunity of black Americans. After World War II, Thurgood Marshall* and other Defense Fund lawyers won victories in the Supreme Court which opened grad-

School Desegregation—white students protest the *Brown v. Board of Education* decision. (Archives Collection, Birmingham Public Library. Courtesy *Birmingham News*.)

uate and law schools to blacks. The Court's decision accepted Marshall's argument that, because of various intangible factors associated with the need to mix with peers in an academic setting, racial discrimination in education was inherently unequal.

Encouraged by these decisions, the Defense Fund attacked the *Plessy* doctrine in grade schools. Seeking to demonstrate the broad-based character of racial injustice, Marshall and the NAACP initiated suits simultaneously in South Carolina, Virginia, Delaware, Kansas, and Washington, D.C. The cases reached the Supreme Court in December 1952. The Court consolidated the four state suits under the style of the Kansas litigation, *Brown v. Board of Education*, while treating separately the federal questions raised in the Washington appeal.

Since the number of students involved was comparatively small, the Court had decided the graduate school cases unanimously. *Brown*, however, raised the larger issue of desegregating grade schools, touching virtually all southern families and the fundamental emotions underlying white supremacy. On this problem the Court was "severely divided." Not until Earl Warren became Chief Justice in 1953 was the Court able to agree on the constitutional status of grade schools under the equal protection clause and the *Plessy* doctrine. In 1954 the Court concurred unanimously in Warren's reversal of *Plessy*, holding that "in the field of public education the doctrine of 'Separate but equal' has no place." As a result, the black children in the four state suits, "by reason of the segregation complained of," had been deprived of the equal protection of the laws guaranteed by the Fourteenth Amendment. Separate facilities based on race were therefore "inherently unequal."

A year later, in the decision pertaining to the enforcement of *Brown*, the Court invited delay and massive resistance, declaring that state compliance with the desegregation could proceed "with all deliberate speed." Nevertheless, the 1954 *Brown* decision set in motion the most important social transformation of twentieth-century America.

SELECTED BIBLIOGRAPHY

Derrick A. Bell, Jr., *Race, Racism and American Law* (1980); Tony Freyer, *Hugo L. Black and the Dilemma of American Liberalism* (1990); Richard Kluger, *Simple Justice: The History of Brown versus Board of Education and Black America's Struggle for Equality* (1977); C. Vann Woodward, *The Strange Career of Jim Crow* (1955).

Tony A. Freyer

BROWN v. BOARD OF EDUCATION, 349 U.S. 294 (1955). A year after its landmark 1954 *Brown v. Board of Education** decision declaring that separate educational systems were inherently unequal, the U.S. Supreme Court handed down a second *Brown* decision, commonly called *Brown II*, which addresses the difficult question of implementation. In its 1954 decision the Court, hoping to defuse southern white resistance, had postponed answering the question of how the legal principle it had articulated was to be translated into practice. In *Brown II* the Court declared that implementation would be gradual and would be influenced by local conditions. School desegregation cases would be returned to the courts where they had been tried. There, federal district judges, who were familiar with local conditions, would be responsible for implementing *Brown I*. School officials were expected to "make a prompt and reasonable start" toward compliance, but the lower court judges might interpret the phrase "with all deliberate speed"* loosely when complex local problems and difficulties called for delays. In *Brown I* the Supreme Court had held unequivocally that segregated education deprived black children of "the equal protection of the laws guaranteed by the Fourteenth Amendment."* It also had affirmed that constitutional rights are always "personal and present"; in other words, petitioners challenging segregated schools could expect immediate relief. *Brown II* disappointed this expectation. Black victims of segregated education could be required to defer the exercise of their constitutional rights. *Brown II*, in the words of one prominent lawyer historian, was "a great mistake." It invited white Southerners to resist implementation and gave conservative federal judges, many of whom shared the social and political conservatism of their neighbors, power to postpone integration.

SELECTED BIBLIOGRAPHY

Derrick A. Bell, Jr., *Race, Racism and American Law* (1980); Harvey C. Couch, *A History of the Fifth Circuit, 1891–1981* (1984); Richard Kluger, *Simple Justice: The History of Brown versus Board of Education and Black America's Struggle for Equality* (1976); Loren Miller, *The Petitioners: The Story of the Supreme Court of the United States and the Negro* (1966); Donald G. Nieman, *Promises to Keep: African-Americans and the Constitutional Order, 1776 to the Present* (1991); David A. Strauss, "Discriminatory Intent and the Taming of Brown," *University of Chicago Law Review*, 56 (1989), 935–1015.

Charles D. Lowery

BROWN v. MISSISSIPPI, 297 U.S. 278 (1936). In 1934 Ed Brown and two other African Americans were convicted of murder in Mississippi based solely upon their confessions. Brown challenged the sufficiency of his confession, contending that it had been obtained through violent means. During Brown's trial, the deputy sheriff admitted that he had hung Brown from a tree and had whipped the other defendants to procure their confessions. Despite these admissions, Brown and the others were convicted. The United States Supreme Court reversed the convictions, stating that a confession obtained by force violated the due process clause of the Fourteenth Amendment.* The Court compared Brown's ordeal to medieval torture practices and found his trial and conviction to be an embarrassment to American justice. The *Brown* case is a milestone in the protection of individuals against police abuse, the use of involuntary confessions, and the complicity of prosecutors and judges. Following soon after the Scottsboro Trials, affirming the right of a defendant to adequate legal counsel and time to prepare a proper defense, *Brown* enlarged federal supervision of civil rights by declaring the use of coerced confessions to be a denial of due process.

SELECTED BIBLIOGRAPHY
Richard Bardolph, ed., *The Civil Rights Record: Black Americans and the Law, 1849–1970* (1970); Derrick A. Bell, Jr., *Race, Racism and American Law* (1980); Richard C. Cortner, *A "Scottsboro" Case in Mississippi: The Supreme Court and Brown v. Mississippi* (1986); Loren Miller, *The Petitioners, The Story of the Supreme Court of the United States and the Negro* (1966).

Steve Sadowsky

BROWNSVILLE, TEXAS, AFFRAY (1906). Despite local protests, in July 1906 three companies of the Twenty-Fifth Infantry, an African-American regiment, arrived at Fort Brown in the city of Brownsville. During the night of 13 August, some unknown men went on a rampage—shooting at buildings, wounding a policeman, and killing a bartender. Immediately the townspeople accused members of the garrison. Most Army officers accepted this conclusion. The soldiers' refusal to admit guilt was taken as evidence of a conspiracy of silence. In November 1906 President Theodore Roosevelt responded with an order discharging 167 of them. This miscarriage of justice greatly disturbed the African-American community, but Booker T. Washington* remained publicly silent. Despite a congressional investigation and an Army court of inquiry, only fourteen men were exonerated and offered a chance to rejoin the service. Though their guilt was never proven, the others lost everything including their pensions. In 1971 Representative Augustus F. Hawkins began an effort to have the conviction overturned and restitution made to the survivors. Eventually one soldier received some money and the discharges were changed to honorable. This travesty of justice indicated the powerlessness of African Americans in the Progressive era.

SELECTED BIBLIOGRAPHY
Marvin E. Fletcher, *The Black Soldier and Officer in the United States Army* (1974); Ann J. Lane, *The Brownsville Affair* (1971); John D. Weaver, *The Brownsville Raid* (1972).

Marvin E. Fletcher

BRUCE, BLANCHE K. (1 March 1841, Farmville, Va.–17 March 1898, Washington, D.C.). Born and reared a slave, he admittedly suffered few hardships under bondage. The tutor of his master's son provided him with the rudiments of an education. During the Civil War, Bruce emancipated himself. He briefly attended Ohio's Oberlin College before migrating in 1869 to Bolivar County, Mississippi, a delta region seemingly unlimited in its political opportunities for intelligent and ambitious freedmen. Fellow Republicans soon recognized his talents, and he rose to

Blanche K. Bruce. (Courtesy Mississippi Department of Archives and History.)

prominence rapidly. Numerous local and appointive posts preceded his election in 1875 to a full term in the U.S. Senate. Although he spoke infrequently in the Senate, Bruce was a fine orator and had a wide range of interests. A strong advocate of minority rights, he criticized the government's treatment of Indians and Congress's effort to restrict Chinese immigration into the country. Affected most by the plight of his own people, he appealed eloquently and emotionally for greater justice for southern blacks. He urged full compensation for black depositors of the failed Freedman's Bank* and sought to end segregated army units. He argued valiantly, but unsuccessfully, for federal assistance to Mississippi Republicans following the conservatives' violent overthrow of the Reconstruction government. Bruce seldom achieved the results he desired. Nevertheless, the Senate became an important forum for him to articulate his concerns for political justice, minority rights, and improved conditions for his race.

SELECTED BIBLIOGRAPHY

Henry C. Bruce, *The New Man, Twenty-Nine Years a Slave Twenty-Nine Years a Free Man* (1969); Maurine Christopher, *America's Black Congressmen* (1976); William Harris, *Day of the Carpetbagger: Republican Reconstruction in Mississippi* (1979); Howard Rabinowitz, "Three Reconstruction Leaders: Blanche K. Bruce, Robert Brown Elliott, and Holland Thompson," in Leon Litwack and August Meier, eds., *Black Leaders of the Nineteenth Century* (1988); Melvin Urofsky, "Blanche K. Bruce, United States Senator 1875–1881," *Journal of Mississippi History* 29 (February 1967), 118–41.

Robert L. Jenkins

BRYAN v. AUSTIN, 354 U.S. 935 (1957). In the mid-1950s, as the NAACP* began to make legal inroads to secure the civil rights of African Americans, several southern states reacted by denouncing the organization as destructive to the relations between the races. They made it illegal for state and school district employees to be members of the organization. In South Carolina, the legislature required school district employees to sign an oath swearing that they were not members of the NAACP. When seventeen African-American schoolteachers in Orangeburg County refused to complete the section of the oath concerning their membership in the NAACP and their views on school segregation, they were forced to resign. The schoolteachers filed suit in the Federal District Court in Charleston, seeking a ruling that the South Carolina law was unconstitutional and violated their rights to free speech and free assembly under the First Amendment. The federal district court refused to rule on the case, justifying its action on the ground that the South Carolina Supreme Court had not ruled on the constitutionality of the statute. The schoolteachers appealed this decision to the United States Supreme Court, but, in the meantime, the South Carolina legislature repealed the statute and the case had become moot. This case showed the power of African Americans to influence the repeal of oppressive state legislation by suing for their constitutional rights.

SELECTED BIBLIOGRAPHY

Thomas I. Emerson, David Haber, and Norman Dorsen, *Political and Civil Rights in the United States* (1967); Aldon D. Morris, *The Origins of the Civil Rights Movement: Black Communities Organizing for Change* (1984).

Steve Sadowsky

BUCHANAN v. WARLEY, 245 U.S. 60 (1917). This landmark civil rights case outlawed residential segregation ordinances—first passed in 1910 in Baltimore, Maryland. These laws had grown out of broader efforts by urban whites in southern and border states to legalize Jim Crow.* *Buchanan* tested a 1914 Louisville, Kentucky, racial residential zoning ordinance. Local NAACP* member William Warley, an African American, offered to buy a lot in a white neighborhood from a white real estate agent, Charles Buchanan, contingent on Warley's ability to occupy the property. As arranged, Buchanan accepted the offer; he then sued Warley for breach of contract when Warley refused to make payment because the ordinance prohibited his residence. When Kentucky courts upheld the local law, the NAACP, with national president Moorfield Storey* joining the case, appealed to the U.S. Supreme Court. A unanimous court found that the ordinances "destroyed the right of the individual to acquire, enjoy and dispose of his property," a right protected by the due process clause of the Fourteenth Amendment.* *Buchanan* stands as a major NAACP victory because it established a precedent against residential segregation, although racially restrictive covenants quickly replaced segregation ordinances as a legal device to segregate.

SELECTED BIBLIOGRAPHY

Charles Flint Kellogg, *NAACP: A History of the National Association for the Advancement of Colored People,* vol. 1 (1967); Roger L. Rice, "Residential Segregation by Law, 1910–1917," *Journal of Southern History* 34 (May 1968), 179–99; George C. Wright, *Life behind a Veil: Blacks in Louisville, Kentucky, 1865–1930* (1985).

James Borchert

BUFFALO SOLDIERS. Shortly after the Civil War, Congress established six regular army regiments consisting of black enlisted men and white officers. Two of these units were cavalry regiments (9th and 10th) and four were infantry regiments (38th, 39th, 40th, and 41st). In 1869, an army reorganization bill consolidated the four infantry regiments into two: the 24th and 25th Infantries. For over two decades, these black regiments of cavalry and infantry played prominent roles in settling the West, serving at diverse locations such as the Texas frontier, Indian Territory, New Mexico, Arizona, and the Dakota Territory.

"Buffalo Soldiers" were so named by Indians because the texture of their hair resembled the fur of the buffalo. A term of respect, the name was first applied to members of the cavalry; however, it soon became a term that also referred to the black infantrymen. These units served with distinction in campaigns against the Indians. During this period, fourteen black soldiers won the Medal of Honor. Despite inferior equipment and horses, their desertion rates soon came to be the lowest in the army. In addition to facing hostile Indians, the "buffalo soldiers" often faced discrimination and resentment in many civilian communities where they served, sometimes resulting in racial clashes. For the black male in the 1870s and 1880s, the Army, although not the epitome of democracy and equality, did provide as fair an opportunity as was available. For many black citizens of that time, these soldiers were symbols of pride and a hope for a better future.

All four black regiments took part in the fighting of the Spanish-American War period, serving in Cuba and later the Philippines. Many African Americans had hoped that the participation of black regulars and volunteers would improve the plight of their race in the United States. Instead, racism intensified in the post-frontier period, especially in the South where some of these units were being stationed. As a result, tension between soldiers and the local civilian communities heightened. When black soldiers objected to indignities inflicted on them by local whites, violent racial outbreaks occurred—in Tampa, Florida, in 1898, Brownsville, Texas* in 1906, and Houston, Texas, in 1917.* In some cases harsh punishment was meted out to some of the soldiers. After having served in the Mexican Punitive Expedition in 1916–1917 and along the U.S.–Mexico border during the Mexican Revolution, these units suffered from post–World War I military cuts. During and after service in World War II, they were either disbanded or merged into the integrated armed forces.

SELECTED BIBLIOGRAPHY

Monroe L. Billington, *New Mexico's Buffalo Soldiers, 1866–1900* (1991); Marvin E. Fletcher, *The Black Soldier and Officer in the United States Army, 1891–1917* (1974); Arlen L. Fowler, *The Black Infantry in the West, 1869–1891* (1971); Willard B. Gatewood, Jr., *Black Americans and the White Man's Burden, 1898–1903* (1975). William H. Leckie, *The Buffalo Soldiers: A Narrative of the Negro Cavalry in the West* (1976).

Horace D. Nash

BUNCHE, RALPH JOHNSON (7 August 1904, Detroit, Mich.–9 December 1971, New York, N.Y.). The son of Fred and Olive Johnson Bunch[e], this scholar and diplomat spent his childhood in the Midwest and the South before graduating summa cum laude in 1927 from the University of California at Los Angeles. An M.A. in political science (1928) and a Ph.D. (1934) in government and international relations, both from Harvard University, were achieved while Bunche taught at Howard University.* He received Rosenwald (Julius) Fund* and Social Science Research Council Fellowships in 1932 and 1936, respectively. Early in his career he displayed an analytical approach to studying the origins and results of racial discrimination. His energies found domestic focus by helping found the National Negro Congress* in 1936. In 1941 Bunche

Ralph Bunche and Adlai Stevenson. (Library of Congress.)

was a senior social science analyst in the Africa and Far East Section of
the Office of the Coordinator of Information. By the time he won appointment as adviser to the U.S. delegation at the San Francisco conference that drafted the United Nations (UN) Charter, he was regarded
as a brilliant mediator and an authority on peoples of color. Subsequent
international achievements include Acting Mediator of the UN Special
Committee on Palestine, 1948; successfully negotiating an armistice
agreement between Egypt and Israel in 1949 (and thereby establishing
a precedent for similar agreements elsewhere in the Middle East); receiving the Nobel Peace Prize in 1950; and appointment as Under Sec-
retary-General (without portfolio) of the United Nations, 1954. Bunche
received over sixty-nine honorary degrees, was a trustee of the Rockefeller Foundation* (1955–1971), and was awarded the Spingarn Medal*
of the NAACP* in 1949. He participated in the Selma to Montgomery
March* in 1965. Bunche produced over forty published monographs and
articles, including *A World View of Race* (1936); *Ideologies, Tactics, and
Achievements of Negro Betterment and Interracial Organizations* (1940); *The
Atlantic Charter and Africa* (1942); and *The Political Status of the Negro in
the Age of FDR* (1973).

SELECTED BIBLIOGRAPHY
Souad Halila, *The Intellectual Development and Diplomatic Career of Ralph J. Bunche* (Ph.D. diss., University of Southern California, 1988); Peggy Mann, *Ralph Bunche: UN Peacemaker* (1975); Saadia Touval, *The Peace Brokers: Mediation in the Arab-Israeli Conflict 1948–1979* (1982); Brian Urquhart, "Remembering Ralph Bunche," *Yale Review* 76 (Spring 1987), 448–52; Babatunde Williams, *Makers of Peace: Dr. Ralph Bunche and Chief Albert John Luthuli* (1965).

Bernice F. Guillaume

BURKE, YVONNE BRATHWAITE (5 October 1932, Los Angeles, Calif.–). An attorney, Yvonne Brathwaite Burke became the first black woman elected to the California Assembly and the first black congresswoman from California. The talented Burke worked for the McCone Commission's investigation of the Watts race riot,* chaired the California Assembly's Committee on Urban Development and Housing, was vice chair of the 1972 Democratic convention, chaired the Congressional Black Caucus,* campaigned unsuccessfully for state attorney general, and became a Los Angeles County supervisor. A civil rights advocate, she supported busing, voted to extend the Voting Rights Act of 1965,* vigorously backed the Equal Rights Amendment, and authorized the 1975 Burke Amendment, which provided equal opportunity for women and minorities on the Alaska pipeline.

SELECTED BIBLIOGRAPHY
Current Biography, 36 (1975), 59–62; Jeffrey M. Elliot, "An Interview with Yvonne Brathwaite Burke," *Negro History Bulletin* 40 (1977), 650–52; *Who's Who among Black Americans*, 6th ed. (1990); *Who's Who in America*, 45th ed. (1989); "Women Lawmakers on the Move," *Ebony* 27 (1972), 49–52.

Bruce A. Glasrud

BURTON v. WILMINGTON PARKING AUTHORITY, 365 U.S. 715 (1961). In the *Civil Rights Cases** of 1883, the Supreme Court held that there was a distinction between public and private action. However, the mixing of state and private activities in modern society made this distinction difficult to apply. In this case, the Eagle Coffee Shoppe, a private business located in a parking garage, refused service to blacks. Burton, the plaintiff, brought suit against the owner and operator of the garage, the Wilmington Parking Authority. According to Burton, the leasing arrangement between the garage and the coffee shop made the state a party to discrimination. The Supreme Court agreed, concluding that the coffee shop's policy was state action. Wilmington Parking Authority, an agency of the state of Delaware, leased space and services to the coffee shop. In return, the agency received rental fees which enabled it to sustain the garage. The interdependent nature of their relationship, said the Court, made the Eagle Coffee Shoppe and the garage a joint venture. Although the Court warned that no universal truth could be drawn from the case, its decision did broaden the scope of the equal protection clause of the Fourteenth Amendment.* In future cases, private racial segregation and discrimination would not be deemed private if the authority of the state loomed in the background.

SELECTED BIBLIOGRAPHY

Richard Bardolph, ed., *The Civil Rights Record: Black Americans and the Law, 1849–1970* (1970); Derrick A. Bell, Jr., *Race, Racism and American Law* (1980); Thomas I. Emerson, David Haber, and Norman Dorsen, eds., *Political and Civil Rights in the United States* (1967); Alfred H. Kelly and Winfred A. Harbison, *The American Constitution: Its Origins and Development*, 5th ed. (1976); Thomas P. Lewis, "Burton v. Wilmington Parking Authority—A Case without Precedent," *Columbia Law Review*, 61 (1961), 1458–67.

Phillip A. Gibbs

BUSH v. ORLEANS PARISH SCHOOL BOARD, 364 U.S. 500 (1960). This Supreme Court action was part of a prolonged constitutional controversy over the desegregation of New Orleans public schools, which had been ordered by J. Skelly Wright,* federal district judge for the Eastern District of Louisiana, as he sought to implement the requirements of *Brown v. Board of Education*.* The order to desegregate met resistance from state officials. In defiance of the desegregation order, in regular session and in special sessions called by Governor Jimmie Davis, the state legislature enacted numerous segregation laws, including an Interposition Act, in which the state of Louisiana claimed to interpose itself between the federal court and the people. The federal district court held the Louisiana legislature's enactments unconstitutional and enjoined the legislature, the governor, and several other officials from enforcing them. In December 1960, the Supreme Court, in the case cited above, refused to stay the injunctions pending appeal. In early 1961, in a one-sentence per curiam opinion, the Court affirmed the actions of the district court (*Orleans Parish School Board v. Bush*, 365 U.S. 569.). This prolonged controversy illustrated the extreme difficulty of the task placed by the Supreme Court upon the shoulders of southern federal judges in the 1955 *Brown v. Board of Education** (Brown II) decision.

SELECTED BIBLIOGRAPHY

Jack Bass, *Unlikely Heroes* (1981); Earlean M. McCarrick, "Desegregation and the Judiciary: The Role of the Federal District Court in Educational Desegregation in Louisiana," *Journal of Public Law* 16 (1967), 107–27; Arthur Selwyn Miller, *A "Capacity for Outrage": The Judicial Odyssey of J. Skelly Wright* (1984); J. W. Peltason, *Fifty-Eight Lonely Men: Southern Federal Judges and School Desegregation* (1961).

Patricia A. Behlar

BUTLER, BENJAMIN FRANKLIN (4 November 1818, Deerfield, N.H.–11 January 1893, Washington, D.C.). A prominent Massachusetts lawyer and politician, Butler enlisted in the Union Army in 1861 and was ap-

Benjamin F. Butler. (Library of Congress.)

pointed general by President Abraham Lincoln. While commanding Fortress Monroe, Virginia, he refused to return fugitive slaves to their masters, labeling them confiscated enemy property or "contrabands of war." On 6 August 1861 Congress incorporated this principle into law in the Confiscation Act,* authorizing the seizure of all property, including slaves, used in "aiding the rebellion." In April 1862, General Butler was named commander of the occupational forces in New Orleans where, on 22 August, he issued a general order authorizing the enlistment of free blacks. On 27 September, the First Regiment Louisiana Native Guards became the first unit of black soldiers mustered into the United States Army during the Civil War. Butler, concerned with educational aid to free blacks, supported many freedmen's relief associations. In

December 1864 he consolidated thirty-seven black regiments to form the Twenty-Fifth Corps and ordered regimental chaplains to teach the troops to read. By 1865 approximately twenty thousand black soldiers were literate. After resigning his commission, Butler served in the U.S. House of Representatives from 1866 to 1874 where he promoted the Civil Rights Act of 1875.*

SELECTED BIBLIOGRAPHY

James M. McPherson, *The Negro's Civil War: How American Negroes Felt and Acted During the War for the Union* (1965); Benjamin Quarles, *The Negro in the Civil War* (1953); William Preston Vaughn, *Schools for All: The Blacks and Public Education in the South, 1865–1877* (1974); Richard S. West, Jr., *Lincoln's Scapegoat General: A Life of Benjamin F. Butler, 1818–1893* (1965).

Betsy Sakariassen Nash

C

CABLE, GEORGE WASHINGTON (12 October 1844, New Orleans, La.–1 January 1925, St. Petersburg, Fla.). A late nineteenth- and early twentieth-century southern novelist and advocate of freedmen civil rights, he was born into a slaveholding family and served in the Confederate army. After the Civil War he became an occasional columnist for the *New Orleans Picayune*. His writing interests included short stories and novels focusing on themes of local color and southern black-white relationships. Subtle criticism of southern race relations in his novels angered his white reading audience, but his open and public attacks enraged them the most. His first public views were expressed in 1875 when he condemned New Orleans' efforts to reinstitute a segregated public school system. During the mid-1880s and 1890s his stand on the race question became uncompromising. Through speeches and essays he denounced segregation and black disfranchisement as unnecessary, unconstitutional, and oppressive. He dismissed as absurd the arguments of white supremacists that full black civil and political rights would lead to social equality. "We may reach the moon some day," he wrote, "not social equality." His periodic appeals to the "Silent South" to support racial justice found little audience. Essentially a lone white voice in the South, Cable's views jeopardized his career and forced him into exile in New England where he continued to oppose bigotry and racial injustice and to battle for what he believed.

SELECTED BIBLIOGRAPHY

George Cable, *The Silent South* (1885); Louis D. Rubin, Jr., *George W. Cable, The Life and Times of a Southern Heretic* (1969); Arlin Turner, *George W. Cable; A Biography* (1956).

Robert L. Jenkins

CAIN, RICHARD HARVEY (12 April 1825, Greenbrier County, Va.–18 January 1887, Washington, D.C.). Richard Harvey Cain stands as an outstanding example of an African American who combined the roles of gospel minister and political leader. At the age of six, Cain moved to Cincinnati, Ohio, where he attended public schools and then worked several years on steamboats of the Mississippi as porter and handyman. At nineteen, he joined the Methodist Episcopal Church and was licensed to preach, but, owing to racial discrimination, he cut short his affiliation and joined the African Methodist Episcopal (A.M.E.) Church. Ordained an elder in 1860, he pastored a church in Brooklyn but received an assignment to Charleston, South Carolina, after the victory there by Union troops. Almost immediately active in politics, Reverend Cain served successively as a delegate to the state constitutional convention, a member of the legislature, and one of the most prominent advisers to Republican governor Franklin J. Moses, Jr., a native white. In 1872 he was elected congressman at large by a tremendous majority. He served creditably in Congress, giving strong support to a civil rights bill and to public education. After leaving Congress in 1878, Cain continued his religious work, and in 1880 he was elected bishop of the A.M.E. Church for Louisiana and Texas. At Waco, Texas, he founded Paul Quinn College and became its first president while continuing in the duties of the episcopacy.

SELECTED BIBLIOGRAPHY

Maurine Christopher, *America's Black Congressmen* (1971); W.E.B. Du Bois, *Black Reconstruction in America* (1935); Peggy Lamson, *The Glorious Failure, Black Congressman Robert Brown Elliott and the Reconstruction of South Carolina* (1973).

George E. Walker

CALHOUN v. LATIMER, 377 U.S. 263 (1964). Vivian Calhoun initiated a lawsuit in Atlanta, Georgia, to bring city schools into compliance with *Brown v. Board of Education.** The court ruled in her favor, stating that the school board had violated the Fourteenth Amendment* by maintaining segregation. It ordered desegregation of city schools. Officials in Atlanta pursued a number of tactics to delay compliance, including the "grade-a-year-plan." Under this scheme, the school board proposed to transfer black children to a white school, beginning at the twelfth grade, at a rate of one grade per year. This plan would take more than a decade to reach the first grade. African-American parents, counseled by the NAACP,* challenged the plan, arguing that compliance with *Brown* meant reorganization of the school district on a nonracial basis. They complained that the Atlanta plan stalled desegregation. Ultimately, the Court approved a plan designed to achieve integration by 1968. Consequently, desegregation moved slowly in Atlanta in spite of the *Calhoun* case. NAACP lawyers also urged the Court to apply *Brown* to school personnel, arguing that a school with a one-race staff was a one-race school. This contention produced few changes in school personnel, however.

BIBLIOGRAPHY

Leon Jones II, *From Brown to Boston: Desegregation in Education* (1979); Stephen L. Wasby, *Desegregation from Brown to Alexander: An Exploration of Supreme Court Strategies* (1977).

Stephen Middleton

CAMBRIDGE, MARYLAND, DEMONSTRATIONS. The Cambridge, Maryland, demonstrations during spring 1963 marked a turning point in the civil rights movement from nonviolent demonstrations against legal segregation to violent protests that originated in the poverty and anger of the black community. African Americans, approximately one-third of the population of 11,000 in Cambridge, suffered from unemployment. Some town facilities remained segregated in January 1963 when college students from Baltimore, Pennsylvania, and New York began sit-ins. Cambridge resident Gloria Richardson, a recent graduate of Howard University,* emerged as a leader and quickly emphasized militance and black pride as students and local working-class residents joined in boycotts, sit-ins, pickets, and parades. Militance led to opposition by town police and angry whites. Fighting and arrests mounted. On 11 June windows of white-owned stores were smashed and shooting began. Martial law was declared. When Gloria Richardson refused to meet with state officials, U.S. Attorney General Robert Kennedy entered negotiations and promised open accommodations, a biracial commission to deal with unemployment, a new public housing program, and school integration at every grade level. Emotions remained high and troops stayed until May 1965. In July 1967 the National States Rights party, a racist organization, held a rally in Cambridge. Gloria Richardson replied in a radio special. Then on 24 July Hubert Gerold "Rapp" Brown* came to town, urged local blacks to take control, and said, "It's time for Cambridge to explode." A shooting occurred, then fires broke out in the black district. Two blocks burned to the ground. White firemen refused to enter the area without protection. Governor Spiro Agnew ordered the Maryland National Guard to Cambridge and the rioting ended.

SELECTED BIBLIOGRAPHY

Robert J. Brugger, *Maryland: A Middle Temperament, 1634–1980* (1988); George H. Callcott, *Maryland and America, 1940–1980* (1985); *Cambridge Daily Banner*, January–July 1963; *Washington Post*, January–July 1963, July 1967.

Suzanne Ellery Greene Chapelle

CANTY v. ALABAMA, 309 U.S. 629 (1940). Dave Canty, a twenty-three-year-old Montgomery, Alabama, black man was arrested and later convicted and sentenced to death on the charge of murdering a white woman, Eunice Ward, a county health nurse, on 21 March 1938. In his appeal to the U.S. Supreme Court, Canty's lawyers maintained that Alabama authorities had denied him due process of law. They argued that the lone witness had not positively identified him either before or during the trial, but the primary basis of their appeal was that Canty had been subjected to "persistent and prolonged" torture to extract a confession. Citing the precedent of *Brown v. Mississippi** (1936), attorneys for the petitioner reminded the Court that "the use of confessions obtained by coercion, brutality and violence constituted a denial of due process." The lawyers also pointed out that several witnesses supported Canty's alibi. In 1940, the Supreme Court reversed the murder conviction without comment. The Alabama court retried Canty, again convicted him, and sentenced him to life imprisonment.

SELECTED BIBLIOGRAPHY

Dorothy A. Autrey, "The National Association for the Advancement of Colored People, 1913–1953" (Ph.D. diss., University of Notre Dame, 1985); "Brief in Support of the Petition for Writ of Certiorari in Supreme Court of the United States, October Term, 1939," NAACP Files, Library of Congress, Washington D.C.; *Montgomery Advertiser*, 21, 23, 24, 25 March 1938, 6, 18 June 1942.

Dorothy A. Autrey

CAPON SPRINGS CONFERENCE (21–23 June 1899). In Capon Springs, West Virginia, about forty educators and businessmen adopted a platform calling for increased industrial education and the establishment of a universal system of secondary schools in the South. Presided over by H. B. Frissell of Hampton Institute* and including Presidents W. L. Wilson of Washington and Lee, Frank G. Woodworth of Tougaloo College,* and Dr. J.L.M. Curry of the Peabody Education Fund* and the Slater Fund,* the conference agreed to set up a committee to supervise the channeling of northern funds into worthwhile southern black schools. In its general philosophy of self-help, this conference was very similar to the Lake Mohonk Conference, the Hampton Conference,* and other such conferences that took place in the 1890s.

SELECTED BIBLIOGRAPHY

August Meier, *Negro Thought in America, 1880–1915: Racial Ideologies in the Age of Booker T. Washington* (1963); *New York Times*, 22–25 July 1899.

Ray Branch

CARDOZO, FRANCIS L. (1 February 1836, Charleston, S.C.–22 July 1903, Washington, D.C.). A free black man, Cardozo received enough education to make him one of the best-educated men in his state and probably one of the best-qualified persons to hold office during Reconstruction. After four years at the University of Glasgow, he continued his studies at seminaries in Scotland and England before returning to the United States in 1864. Serving briefly as a pastor in New Haven,

Connecticut, he accepted a post as head of an American Missionary Association* school in Charleston, South Carolina, in 1865. His later service to education included a position teaching Latin at Howard University,* It was in politics, rather than in education or religion, that Cardozo made his most noted contributions. Active in the Republican party and president of the Union League* in South Carolina, he was selected as delegate to the state's 1868 constitutional convention and was elected secretary of state—a term cut short by his tenure at Howard University. He won election as South Carolina's secretary of the treasury in 1872 and 1876. After Reconstruction, he continued in public service in the United States Treasury Department from 1878 to 1884. His remaining active years were spent as principal of a black secondary school in Washington, D.C., until 1896. His honesty, coupled with his intelligence and efficiency, made him one of South Carolina's most respected politicians. The *Abbeville Press* commended him as being an able officer of undoubted integrity.

SELECTED BIBLIOGRAPHY

Thomas Holt, *Black over White: Negro Political Leadership in South Carolina During Reconstruction* (1977); Wilhelmena S. Robinson, *Historical Negro Biographies* (1969); Francis B. Simkins and Robert H. Woody, *South Carolina During Reconstruction* (1932, 1966); Alrutheus Ambush Taylor, *The Negro in South Carolina During Reconstruction* (1924, 1969).

Gary B. Mills

CARMICHAEL, STOKELY (29 June 1941, Port-of-Spain, Trinidad–). A native of Trinidad, who emigrated to the United States in 1952, Carmichael became one of the most dynamic leaders of the civil rights movement. He attended Bronx High School of Science in New York City and then earned his bachelor's degree from Howard University* in 1964. While a student at Howard, he became active in the civil rights movement. In 1960 he participated in demonstrations, sit-ins, and picketing in the Washington, D.C., area. In 1961 he was a Freedom Rider,* was arrested in Jackson, Mississippi, and served forty-nine days in Parchman prison. After his release he became a member of the Student Nonviolent Coordinating Committee* (SNCC) and participated in demonstrations and voter registration projects in the South. He worked in the Freedom Summer of 1964* voter registration project in Mississippi and coordinated the project in Mississippi's Second Congressional District. His district was the best run of SNCC's five districts in Mississippi. As early as 1963, however, he began to disagree with other members of SNCC and other civil rights leaders over nonviolence and the value of peaceful demonstrations. Carmichael called for self-defense against the racist violence used against African Americans in the South and more emphasis on African Americans using the political process to control their own communities and their own destiny. He also believed that African Americans should control their own movement and repeatedly called for the expulsion of whites from SNCC. In March 1965 Carmichael went to Lowndes County, Alabama, to start a voter registration project that would showcase his ideas about empowering African Americans to control their own communities through the political process. In a county where only seventy African Americans had been registered to vote in 1964, Carmichael increased the number to over 2,600 and created an all-black political party, the Lowndes County Freedom Organization* (LCFO). In 1966, the LCFO challenged the Democratic party regulars in the county elections but failed to win any offices. Carmichael was also elected chairman of SNCC in 1966 and made the famous Black Power speech in Greenwood, Mississippi, which changed the focus of the civil rights movement from nonviolence and integration to self-defense and black nationalism.

SELECTED BIBLIOGRAPHY
Stokely Carmichael, *Stokely Speaks: Black Power Back to Pan-Africanism* (1973); Stokely Carmichael, "Toward Black Liberation," *The Massachusetts Review* 7 (Autumn 1966), 639–51; Stokely S. Carmichael and Charles V. Hamilton, *Black Power: The Politics of Liberation in America* (1967); Allen S. Matusow, *The Unraveling of America: A History of Liberalism in the 1960s* (1984); Cleveland Sellers with Robert Terrell, *The River of No Return: The Autobiography of a Black Militant and the Life and Death of SNCC* (1973); Milton Viorst, *Fire in the Streets: America in the 1960s* (1979); Robert Penn Warren, *Who Speaks for the Negro?* (1966).

W. Marvin Dulaney

CARNEGIE HALL MEETING (6–8 January 1904). This closed meeting of black intellectuals selected by Booker T. Washington* and W.E.B. Du Bois* attempted to articulate a common strategy toward racial uplift. Its most concrete outcome was the creation of the Committee of Twelve for the Negro Race, which was effectively controlled by Washington and secretly funded by Andrew Carnegie. Du Bois was offended by Washington's manipulation of the new organization and soon resigned, effectively limiting both its credibility and long-term significance. Ironically, Du Bois's prominent role at the Carnegie Hall meeting helped to propel him to the forefront of the anti-Bookerites. The meeting marked a last and lost opportunity for the two men to compromise before Du Bois founded the militant Niagara Movement* in 1905.

SELECTED BIBLIOGRAPHY
W.E.B. Du Bois, *Autobiography* (1968); The W.E.B. Du Bois Papers, University of Massachusetts, Amherst; Louis R. Harlan, *Booker T. Washington: The Wizard of Tuskegee, 1901–1915* (1983); Louis R. Harlan and Raymond Smock, eds., *The Booker T. Washington Papers* (1972).

Francille Rusan Wilson

CARTER, HODDING, II (3 February 1907, Hammond, La.–4 April 1972, Greenville, Miss.). Louisiana native Hodding Carter made his mark on the twentieth-century civil rights revolution through editorials in the

Greenville, Mississippi, *Greenville Delta Democrat-Times*,* which he purchased in 1938. In 1946 Carter won a Pulitzer Prize for a series of editorials that dealt primarily with racial issues. He criticized the racism of Mississippi senators James Eastland and Theodore Bilbo and called for equal public service facilities, such as playgrounds and hospitals, for the state's black citizens. By later standards a racial conservative, Carter called for gradualist solutions to southern racial problems. Opposing rapid change that might exacerbate race relations, Carter opposed such measures as the public accommodations provision of the Civil Rights Act of 1964.* Yet he never wavered in his contention that blacks should have equal rights. Carter denounced the segregationist white power structure in Mississippi; at one point, he described the citizens councils as uptown chapters of the Ku Klux Klan. An outraged Mississippi House of Representatives reacted by voting 89–19 to brand the *Delta Democrat-Times* editor a liar. Carter responded that, by a "vote of 1 to 0, . . . there are 89 liars in the State Legislature." Furthermore, "those 89 character mobbers can go to hell, collectively or singly, and wait there until I back down. They needn't plan on returning." Such was typical of the biting, humorous, controversial style of Hodding Carter, a courageous voice for reason and justice during a turbulent era.

SELECTED BIBLIOGRAPHY

Biloxi-Gulfport Sun-Herald, 11 February 1979; Biographical Sketches and Publication Series, Hodding and Betty Werlein Carter Papers, Manuscripts Division, Special Collections Department, Mississippi State University Library; Hodding Carter [II], "The Civil Rights Issue as Seen in the South," *New York Times Magazine* (21 March 1948), p. 15, 52–54; *Greenville Delta Democrat-Times*, 5 April 1972.

Michael B. Ballard

CARTER v. TEXAS, 177 U.S. 442 (1899). During the post-Reconstruction era, both legal and extralegal measures were utilized to diminish the recently acquired civil rights of African Americans. Throughout the South new laws separated the races in virtually every aspect of life. The United States Supreme Court reflected the mood of much of the nation as it affirmed separate but equal* as the law of the land. The Court also adhered to a strict interpretation of the provisions of both the Fourteenth* and Fifteenth* Amendments to the federal Constitution by ruling against "state action" to deprive blacks of certain rights while ignoring such violations engaged in by individual or private citizens. It would be decades before the Supreme Court broadened its interpretation and new laws would be enacted to include "individual action" against another's civil rights. In *Carter* the Court continued to hold against state action to deprive or deny individual rights and ruled that Seth Carter, a black resident of Galveston, Texas, had to be given a new trial on the charge of murder because the state had purposefully excluded blacks from jury service at the time of his conviction.

SELECTED BIBLIOGRAPHY
Richard Bardolph, ed., *The Civil Rights Record: Black Americans and the Law, 1849–1970* (1970); Joseph Tussman, ed., *The Supreme Court on Racial Discrimination* (1963).

                                                              LeRoy T. Williams

CASH, WILBUR JOSEPH (2 May 1900, Gaffney, S.C.–1 July 1941, Mexico City, Mexico). Descended from a long line of small-scale upland farmers and reared in a cotton-mill town in the southern foothills, Cash was imbued with romanticism and sentimentality toward the Old South as well as the racial doctrines of the New South. He enrolled at Wake Forest College in North Carolina in 1920, a small Baptist school that nurtured his already rebellious spirit. He was baptized into journalism as an associate editor of the campus paper, *Old Gold and Black*, and he thrived on satire and controversy. After graduation in 1922, Cash entered Wake Forest Law School, but quickly left. A summer stint on the *Charlotte Observer* preceded his move to the faculty of Georgetown College, in Georgetown, Kentucky, in the fall of 1923. Two years of disillusionment in Kentucky compelled him to leave teaching. After a brief period with the *Chicago Post*, he returned to the South in 1926 to the *Charlotte News*, and in 1929, he began to write articles for H. L. Mencken's *The American Mercury*. One such article, entitled "The Mind of the South," a theme he had been toying with since his college days, led to his book by the same title. After periods of unemployment and attempts to make it as a freelance writer, he returned to work with the *Charlotte News* in 1937. Cash's only book was finally completed in 1940 and published the following year. In Cash's own words:

My thesis is that the Southern mind represents a very definite culture, or attitude towards life, a heritage, primarily from the Old South, but greatly modified and extended by conscious and unconscious efforts over the last hundred years to protect itself from the encroachments of three hostile factors: the Yankee Mind, the Modern Mind, and the Negro. In other words, it is a combination of certain orthodoxies and a defense mechanism.

His criticism of the South, whether reserved in tone or not, made him unpopular. He was prounion but only because he supported the working man. He was antilynching and antiaristocracy; the latter he blamed for most southern problems. He also attacked the Vanderbilt Agrarians for unduly romanticizing the Old South. Cash's restless existence was cut short when he committed suicide in a Mexico City hotel room on 1 July 1941, just short of five months after the publication of his book.

SELECTED BIBLIOGRAPHY
Wilbur J. Cash, *The Mind of the South* (1941); Bruce Clayton, *W. J. Cash: A Life* (1991); Joseph L. Morrison, *W. J. Cash: Southern Prophet* (1967).

Gary B. Mills

CATHOLIC INTERRACIAL COUNCIL. The Catholic Interracial Council was started in New York City in 1934 by the Catholic Layman's Union, a group of black professional and businessmen organized by Father John La Farge. The organization soon grew to sixty branches throughout the United States and has survived into the 1990s. It seeks to perpetuate understanding and goodwill among people of different races and ethnic groups through the teachings of the Catholic Church. Local branches collect statistics on black employment, urge employers to hire black workers, and encourage Catholic colleges' admittance of black Catholics. From 1934 to 1971, the council also published a monthly newsletter, the *Interracial Review.**

SELECTED BIBLIOGRAPHY
Thomas J. Harte, *Catholic Organizations Promoting Negro-White Relations in the United States* (1947); *Interracial Review*, 1932–1971; John La Farge, *The Race Question and the Negro: A Study of Catholic Doctrine on Interracial Justice* (1943).

Carol Wilson

CAYTON, HORACE ROSCOE (12 April 1903, Seattle, Wash.–22 January 1970, Paris, France). A sociologist and writer, Cayton was an insightful commentator on black urban conditions. During the New Deal, Cayton was a special assistant to Secretary of the Interior Harold L. Ickes,* then directed a Works Progress Administration research unit studying black life in Chicago. Cayton's most important work was the award-winning *Black Metropolis* (1945), coauthored with St. Claire Drake.* Director of Parkway Community Center in Chicago (1940–1949) and longtime columnist for the *Pittsburgh Courier,** in his later years Cayton worked as a university lecturer and researcher. Cayton's autobiography, *Long Old Road* (1965), is a revealing account of the often turbulent life of the grandson of Reconstruction Senator Hiram R. Revels.*

SELECTED BIBLIOGRAPHY
Horace R. Cayton, "Ideological Forces in the Work of Negro Writers," in Herbert Hill, ed., *Anger and Beyond* (1966); Horace R. Cayton and George S. Mitchell, *Black Workers and the New Unions* (1939); Jack B. Moore, "Horace Roscoe Cayton," in *Dictionary of American Biography*, 8 (1988).

Francille Rusan Wilson

CHAMBERS v. FLORIDA, 309 U.S. 227 (1940). In *Chambers v. Florida* the U.S. Supreme Court ruled that the due process clause of the Fourteenth Amendment* prohibited the introduction of forced confessions as evidence in criminal trials. The case had originated in 1933 when four black men were convicted of murder in Broward County, Florida. The defendants were migratory farm workers who had been arrested for the crime, held without a warrant, and deprived of legal counsel. Interrogated relentlessly for a week, they had little opportunity to sleep or eat and were threatened and beaten. Finally, three of them confessed and also incriminated their companion, Isiah (Izell) Chambers. They were tried, convicted, and sentenced to death. Through appeals, the case dragged on in state courts for six years and resulted in guilty verdicts on three separate occasions. After the state's highest tribunal sustained the last conviction in 1939, the Supreme Court reversed it a year later. On 12 February 1940, Justice Hugo L. Black threw out the confessions because they had been obtained under duress. His opinion constituted a milestone in assisting those most vulnerable to harsh police interrogation: the poor, the uneducated, the unpopular, and the powerless. Without the admissibility of the tainted confessions, the case against the accused men collapsed, and they were set free.

SELECTED BIBLIOGRAPHY

Reed T. Phalen, "Comments," *Michigan Law Review*, 39 (1940), 274–83; Otis H. Stephens, *The Supreme Court and Confessions of Guilt* (1973); Rocco J. Tresolini, *Justice and the Supreme Court* (1963).

                                                                            Steven F. Lawson

CHANEY, JAMES EARL (30 May 1943, Meridian, Miss.–21 June 1964, Philadelphia, Miss.). An African-American plasterer and civil rights field worker who attended Harris Junior College, Chaney worked diligently with the Congress of Racial Equality* (CORE) and the Council of Federated Organizations* (COFO) recruiting workers and organizing freedom schools and voter registration activities. On 21 June 1964, on the eve of the launching of the Freedom Summer of 1964* in Mississippi, Chaney, along with Andrew Goodman* and Michael Schwerner,* was arrested in Philadelphia, Mississippi, released from jail, abducted by Klansmen, beaten with chains, and shot. Their bodies were found on 4 August 1964 and retrieved from an earthen dam. James Chaney was buried on 7 August 1964 in Memorial Park Cemetery atop Mount Barton in Meridian, Mississippi.

SELECTED BIBLIOGRAPHY

Seth Cagin and Philip Dray, *We Are Not Afraid: The Story of Goodman, Schwerner and Chaney and the Civil Rights Campaign for Mississippi* (1988); William Bradford Huie, *Three Lives for Mississippi* (1964); *New York Times*, 6 August 1964; Juan Williams, *Eyes on the Prize: America's Civil Rights Years, 1954–1965* (1987).

                                                                            Barbara L. Green

CHARLESTON RACE RIOT (1919). Economic, social, and historical causes of interracial maladjustment, compounded by years of physical and psychological abuses, combined to produce the Charleston, South

Carolina, riot. White sailors from the nearby naval yard and white civilians attacked black civilians after a black man was accused of shooting a white sailor. Fighting commenced near Market and West streets and spread through the city on Saturday night, 10 May, and continued into Sunday morning, 11 May, during which time more than one thousand sailors participated. Provost guards, marines, and city and county police were employed to quell the rioting. Four persons died and more than sixty sustained injuries. A naval board of inquiry indicted three white sailors for riot-related offenses; however, one was acquitted and the other two received one year's imprisonment at the Parris Island, South Carolina, naval prison with the possibility of parole after four months at which time they were dishonorably discharged.

SELECTED BIBLIOGRAPHY

Arthus I. Waskow, *From Race Riot to Sit-In, 1919 and the 1960s: A Study in the Connections between Conflict and Violence* (1966); L. E. Williams II, "The Charleston, South Carolina, Riot of 1919," in Frank A. Dennis, ed., *Southern Miscellany: Essays in Honor of Glover Moore* (1981).

Lee E. Williams II

CHARLOTTE, NORTH CAROLINA, SIT-IN. Approximately one hundred African-American students, primarily from Johnson C. Smith University, staged sit-ins at five different downtown Charlotte segregated lunch counters on 9 February 1960. The demonstration forced the closing of four of these counters and hurt business in the other store. Strongly supported by many African-American and white organizations, the students continued sporadic sit-down protests at lunch counters for several months. The movement was successful. On 9 July 1960 nearly one hundred African-American citizens of Charlotte exercised their civil rights by eating at desegregated lunch counters. This grassroots demonstration was a catalyst to the forceful integration of other public facilities in the area and to the demand for social, economic, and political equality.

SELECTED BIBLIOGRAPHY

The Charlotte News, 1960; *The Charlotte Observer*, 1960; Charlotte-Mecklenburg Community Relations Committee Papers, J. Murrey Atkins Library, University of North Carolina at Charlotte; Martin Oppenheimer, *The Sit-In Movement of 1960* (1989).

Wanda Ann Hendricks

CHASE, W. CALVIN (2 February 1854, Washington, D.C.–3 January 1921, Washington, D.C.). Born a free man, he was admitted to the Virginia and District of Columbia bar in 1889 and was a practicing attorney for the rest of his life. In 1882, he became editor of the *Washington Bee*, a black newspaper. In the *Bee*, Chase forthrightly attacked lynchings and race riots, utilizing cartoons after 1914 to make his argument. He pointedly criticized the federal government for the continued existence of American racism. He opposed the biased treatment of black soldiers in the Spanish American War and World War I and the widening segregation of black civilians in government offices. Chase helped found the Afro-American League* and the Afro-American Council,* but feuded with fellow journalist T. Thomas Fortune* and criticized W.E.B. Du Bois.* He was also critical of Booker T. Washington* until the *Bee* ran into financial difficulties and needed Washington's help. Chase was a life-long Republican, but he battled the increasing encroachment of lily-whitism into party thinking.

SELECTED BIBLIOGRAPHY
Hal S. Chase, "Honey for Friends, Stings for Enemies: William Calvin Chase and The Washington Bee, 1882–1921," Ph.D. diss., University of Pennsylvania, 1973; Rayford W. Logan and Michael R. Winston, eds., *Dictionary of American Negro Biography* (1982); I. Garland Penn, *The Afro-American Press and Its Editors* (1891, reprint 1969).

John F. Marszalek

CHATTANOOGA FREEDOM WALK. White Baltimore, Maryland, postman William L. Moore began an individual freedom walk from Chattanooga, Tennessee, to Jackson, Mississippi, on 21 April 1963 to deliver a message to Mississippi Governor Ross Barnett protesting southern segregation. Wearing a sign reading "Equal Rights for All—Mississippi or Bust," Moore was murdered two days later near Gadsden, Alabama. On 1 May 1963 an interracial group of Student Nonviolent Coordinating Committee* and Congress of Racial Equality* members left Chattanooga to complete Moore's pilgrimage. Physically assaulted, the freedom walkers were arrested after crossing into Alabama. Moore's death and subsequent Chattanooga Freedom Walks focused national attention on the social and economic grievances of African Americans.

SELECTED BIBLIOGRAPHY
The *Chattanooga Times*, 21 April–16 May 1963; Murray Kempton, "Pilgrimage to Jackson," *New Republic* 148 (11 May 1963), 14–16; *Nashville Tennessean*, 21 April–7 May 1963; *Newsweek* (6, 13 May 1963); Harvard Sitkoff, *The Struggle for Black Equality, 1954–1980* (1981).

Thaddeus M. Smith

CHESNUTT, CHARLES WADDELL (20 June 1858, Cleveland, Ohio–15 November 1932, Cleveland, Ohio). Chesnutt was the first African American to be recognized as an indisputable member of the American literati. His works, which pioneered realistic portrayals of African Americans, endowed black dialect characters with dignity. Chesnutt also poignantly described the effects of Jim Crow* and caste distinctions on black America's middle class. After an adolescence in Fayetteville, North Carolina, Chesnutt became a teacher and principal at its normal school.

Following his marriage to Susan W. Perry in 1878, Chesnutt moved to New York City and then back to Cleveland, Ohio. He passed the Ohio bar exam in 1887 with highest honors and became a legal stenographer. His professional debut into fiction was the short story "Uncle Peter's House," which appeared in the *Cleveland News and Herald* in 1885. Subsequent works include *The Conjure Woman*, *The Wife of His Youth*, and *Frederick Douglass* (all published in 1899), *The House behind the Cedars* (1900), *The Marrow of Tradition* (1901), and *The Colonel's Dream* (1905). The acceptance of Chesnutt's works by Houghton Mifflin, and his collegiality with William Dean Howells and George Washington Cable,* marked significant departures from the social and intellectual patterns of the "nadir" period. Chesnutt's civic activities included newspaper articles, memberships on the general committee of the NAACP* and the Cleveland Chamber of Commerce, and testimony before a senate committee against the Shipstead Anti-Injunction Bill. Additionally, he helped found the Playhouse Settlement of Cleveland (Karamu House). Chesnutt was awarded the LL.D. degree by Wilberforce University in 1913, and he received the Spingarn Medal* of the NAACP in 1928.

SELECTED BIBLIOGRAPHY
William L. Andrews, *The Literary Career of Charles W. Chesnutt* (1980); Helen M. Chesnutt, *Charles Waddell Chesnutt, Pioneer of the Color Line* (1952); J. Noel Heermance, *Charles W. Chesnutt; America's First Great Black Novelist* (1974); Frances P. Keller, *An American Crusade: The Life of Charles Waddell Chesnutt* (1977); Sylvia L. Render, *Charles W. Chesnutt* (1980).

Bernice F. Guillaume

CHICAGO BLACK BELT. Evolving between 1873 and the 1940s, the Chicago Black Belt was probably the most prominent black community after New York's Harlem. This narrow section of Chicago's South Side, seven miles long by one-and-one-half miles wide, grew in population from five thousand to over three hundred thousand residents. Political leaders such as Oscar Stanton DePriest,* elected to Congress in 1928, and William Dawson, leader of Chicago's black political community from the 1940s until the 1960s, were elected from this area, which contained 90 percent of Chicago's black population.

SELECTED BIBLIOGRAPHY
St. Clair Drake and Horace R. Cayton, *Black Metropolis* (1962); Dempsey J. Travis, *An Autobiography of Black Chicago* (1981); Dempsey J. Travis, *An Autobiography of Black Politics* (1987); James Q. Wilson, *Negro Politics* (1960).

Christopher Mobley

CHICAGO COMMISSION ON RACE RELATIONS. Established by Illinois Governor Frank Lowden to study the causes of the violent five-day Chicago race riot* of 27 July 1919 and composed of an equal number of blacks and whites, the commission examined the complex set of factors that led to thirty-eight deaths and over 537 injuries. The commission based its fifty-nine recommendations on the examination of discrimination in the areas of housing, employment, public accommodations, and the reluctance of police and courts to protect blacks from white violence. The commission recommended that laws prohibiting discrimination be strictly enforced.

SELECTED BIBLIOGRAPHY
Chicago Commission on Race Relations, *The Negro in Chicago: A Study of Race Relations and a Race Riot* (1922); Allen Spear, *Black Chicago: The Making of a Negro Ghetto, 1890–1920* (1967); William M. Tuttle, Jr., *Race Riot: Chicago in the Red Summer of 1919* (1970).

                                                                          Malik Simba

CHICAGO CONSERVATOR. Chicago's first black newspaper, the *Conservator* was founded in 1878 by attorney and civic leader Ferdinand L. Barnett. Reflecting the values of the city's black professional and business elite, the paper reported social and organizational activities within the black community and stressed the importance of education, self-improvement, and cultural refinement. After 1900, the *Conservator* became a pawn in the struggle between Booker T. Washington* and his more militant critics for the support of black Chicagoans. Editors and owners changed frequently, and editorial policy veered sharply from one position to another. The *Conservator* ceased publication in 1910; only a few scattered issues are extant.

SELECTED BIBLIOGRAPHY
Chicago Conservator (scattered issues) 1882, 1883, 1886, *Miscellaneous Negro Newspapers* (microfilm); Ralph N. Davis, "Negro Newspapers in Chicago" (M.A. thesis, University of Chicago, 1939).

                                                                          Allan H. Spear

CHICAGO DEFENDER. Begun by Robert S. Abbott* as a four-page weekly with a press run of three hundred copies in 1905, it grew into a thirty-two-page newspaper with a national circulation of 180,000 in the early 1920s. Proclaiming itself "The World's Greatest Weekly," the *Defender* combined sensationalist reporting with hard-hitting racial protest to become the country's leading black newspaper and the first to employ an integrated staff. The paper made Abbott into a millionaire and one of the country's leading black businessmen. Abbott's nephew, John H. Sengstacke,* took over the paper in 1940 and converted it to a daily in 1956. By then, the *Defender* was the flagship of the nation's largest black newspaper chain. In the 1910s, the *Defender*, which was widely read in the South, urged southern blacks to escape from racism. Letters from successful migrants and reports of plentiful jobs and southern cruelty encouraged the Great Migration* of 1916 to 1919. Over seventy years later, the *Defender*—with a morning circulation of 38,456—

still focuses on local and national events of interest to blacks and includes a sprinkling of important national and international news.

SELECTED BIBLIOGRAPHY

Frederick G. Detweiler, *The Negro Press in the United States* (1922); Roi Ottley, *The Lonely Warrior: The Life and Times of Robert S. Abbott* (1955); Allan H. Spear, *Black Chicago: The Making of a Negro Ghetto, 1890–1920* (1967).

James Marten

CHICAGO FREEDOM MOVEMENT. The movement was a coalition of the Coordinating Council of Community Organizations and the Southern Christian Leadership Conference* led by Dr. Martin Luther King, Jr.* These organizations sought to create a desegregated "Open City." Dr. King felt that Chicago's impoverished slums existed because someone profited from keeping Negroes poorly housed, educated, and employed. As the campaign progressed, dissension developed among the various organizations due to ideological differences heightened by Mayor Richard J. Daley's manipulative intransigence, by the deeply divisive race riot in March 1966, and by King's ill-fated march in Cicero during late August 1966. These strains doomed the movement.

SELECTED BIBLIOGRAPHY

Alan B. Anderson and George W. Pickering, *Confronting the Color Line: The Broken Promise of the Civil Rights Movement in Chicago* (1986); Mary J. Herrick, *The Chicago Schools: A Social and Political History* (1971); Mike Royko, *Boss: Richard J. Daley of Chicago* (1971).

Malik Simba

CHICAGO RACE RIOT (1919). The worst of the series of racial confrontations that swept America in the "red summer" of 1919, the Chicago race riot came in the wake of the World War I black migration from the South. Between 1916 and 1919, Chicago's black population doubled, and white Chicagoans reacted with hostility, often violence, to the newcomers. This racial tension came to a climax on 27 July 1919, when a black teenager, floating on a raft near a racially contested beach, was stoned by a white man and drowned. Fighting on the beach spread to nearby neighborhoods, and for the next five days, rioting raged throughout the city. White mobs assaulted black workers leaving the stockyards, dragged black passengers from streetcars, and fired shots into black homes from automobiles. Whites were, for the most part, the aggressors, but unlike in earlier riots, blacks fought back. The riot left 38 dead, 537 wounded, and hundreds homeless. Although Chicagoans of both races deplored the violence, the riot led to no real changes in the city's relations. Segregation in housing and jobs continued, and racial discrimination was evident in the disproportionate number of blacks who were brought to trial for participation in the riot. The one constructive reaction to the riot was the appointment of a biracial commission on race relations which published a comprehensive report on the causes of the riot (see Chicago Commission on Race Relations). Historians have emphasized three factors in explaining the riot: The large influx of black migrants into a rigidly segregated housing market led to bitter competition for residential space; white fear of black job competition exacerbated labor tension, particularly in the stockyards; and whites resented the growing political influence of black voters, which had been demonstrated in the 1919 mayoral election. The riot should also be viewed within the context of the worldwide racial, ethnic, and political tensions that followed World War I.

SELECTED BIBLIOGRAPHY

Chicago Commission on Race Relations, *The Negro in Chicago: A Study of Race Relations and a Race Riot* (1922); James R. Grossman, *Land of Hope: Chicago, Black Southerners and the Great Migration* (1989); Allan H. Spear, *Black Chicago: The Making of a Negro Ghetto* (1967); William M. Tuttle, Jr., *Race Riot: Chicago in the Red Summer of 1919* (1970).

Allan H. Spear

CHICAGO RACE RIOT (1965). On Friday, 13 August 1965, violence erupted in Chicago's West Garfield Park neighborhood when people gathered to hold a protest meeting near the site where a fire truck had accidentally swerved into and killed a black woman. Police were soon called to the scene to stop a bottle-throwing incident. The fire station had been a focal point of discontent in the area all summer as civil rights groups had sought repeatedly to have African-American firemen assigned to the station in this 85-percent black neighborhood. More than three hundred persons gathered at the protest meeting and clashed with police until shortly before dawn. By then, 104 persons had been arrested and 60, including 18 policemen, were hospitalized. The outbreak was characterized as "Chicago's worst racial rioting in thirteen years." The upheaval came in the midst of the Chicago civil rights movement and Dr. Martin Luther King, Jr.'s* launching of the Chicago Campaign (1965–1966), an unsuccessful attempt to secure significant changes in de facto segregation,* ghetto housing, and massive black unemployment. The Chicago and Watts race riots* that weekend brought the country's attention to the national issues of de facto segregation and other persistent dilemmas of democratic social change.

SELECTED BIBLIOGRAPHY

Alan B. Anderson and George W. Pickering, *Confronting the Color Line: The Broken Promise of the Civil Rights Movement in Chicago* (1986); David Garrow, *Chicago 1966: Open Housing, Marches, Summit Negotiations and Operation Breadbasket* (1989); *New York Times*, 15 August 1965.

Barbara L. Green

CHILDERS, JAMES SAXON (19 April 1899, Birmingham, Ala.–17 July 1965, Atlanta, Ga.). After education in the Birmingham public schools, Childers graduated from Oberlin College, served in World War I, and became a Rhodes scholar. For four decades he was a journalist, serving first as a columnist for the *Birmingham News* and later as an associate editor of the *Atlanta Journal*. Among Childers's numerous publications, none attracted more attention than his novel of racial liberalism, *A Novel about a Black Man and a White Man in the Deep South*, published in 1936. Here he reflects an extreme form of southern white liberalism of the day. The key characters, Gordon Nicholson, a young white, and Dave Parker, a young black, struggle to have friendship and normal, middle-class social exchange in Birmingham, Alabama, in the 1930s. Although Childers's personal experience suggests that such interracial friendship could, on occasion, exist in Birmingham, these characters ultimately are defeated by the racial tension of their environment. In telling this story, Childers provides, at times, a brilliant depiction of the terrains of the human heart sometimes overlooked in the broader story of American race relations. When Childers arrived in Atlanta, Georgia, in 1951, he found his racial liberalism at odds with the corporate community. He remained generally silent on racial matters. His staff writers wanted to cover the civil rights stories, however, and Childers was fired in 1956. In some ways Childers provides an example of the 1930s southern white liberal who did not turn the corner into the civil rights movement of the 1950s and 1960s. His later silence was not without torment.

SELECTED BIBLIOGRAPHY
Tennant S. McWilliams, "James Saxon Childers and Southern White Liberalism in the 1930s," in James Saxon Childers, *A Novel about a White Man and a Black Man in the Deep South* (reissue) (1988); Obituary, *Birmingham News*, 19 July 1965; Obituary, *New York Times*, 18 July 1965.

Tennant S. McWilliams

CHISHOLM, SHIRLEY ANITA ST. HILL (30 November 1924, New York, N.Y.–). Born to a Barbadian seamstress and a Guyanese factory worker in New York City's second most infamous ghetto, Brooklyn's Bedford-Stuyvesant, Shirley Chisholm received much of her early education in Barbados while living with her maternal grandmother. She attended Brooklyn College on a scholarship and graduated with a bachelor's degree magna cum laude. She soon earned her master's degree in education from Columbia University. She became a schoolteacher, a director of a child care center, and an educational consultant with New York's Day Care Division. Gradually, community activities brought her into Democratic party work in New York.

In 1964 Bedford-Stuyvesant sent Chisholm to the state assembly in Albany where she became only the state's second black female member. Her constituents liked her work so well that they reseated her three times. As an assemblywoman, Chisholm supported three significant measures: day-care centers, unemployment insurance for domestic workers, and the Search for Elevation, Education, Knowledge (SEEK) college students' program, a program that helps place talented, under-privileged students in college.

In 1968 Chisholm relinquished the assembly seat to seek a congressional seat in a revamped Twelfth Congressional District where she found James Farmer,* the former director of the Congress of Racial Equality,* her major opponent. The astute Chisholm made her decision to run upon learning that her district included a large number of registered female voters. Her victory was secured, however, because she was a native to the area whereas Farmer resided in Manhattan. As U.S. representative, she served on the Veterans Affairs Committee (her first appointment after she upset the traditional seniority rule in Congress), the House Education and Labor Committee, and the Select Education, General Education, and Agricultural Labor subcommittees. She was also a member of the Congressional Black Caucus.* Wishing to be a catalyst for change, Chisholm made a bid for the presidency of the United States in 1972, the first woman or black to do so. Unsuccessful in her candidacy, she now spends much of her time lecturing at various colleges and universities about the unfortunate rise of racism in these institutions.

SELECTED BIBLIOGRAPHY

Shirley Chisholm, The Good Fight (1973); Shirley Chisholm, Unbought and Unbossed (1970); Who's Who among Black Americans (1976).

Linda Reed

CINCINNATI RACE RIOT (1967). The death sentence of a black man for the murder of a white woman and the almost simultaneous suspended sentence for a white man convicted of the death of his girlfriend convinced the black community, once again, that justice in Cincinnati, Ohio, was racially biased. On 11 June 1967, a black man was arrested for soliciting money for a legal appeal of the death sentence. These events highlighted other social and economic wrongs inflicted on the city's blacks, grievances they felt powerless to enunciate. A protest meeting on the heels of an incident in which a policeman allegedly used the expression "young nigger punks" was followed by sporadic black youth violence on 12 June and a municipal judge's threat to mete out maximum punishment for any riot activity. The next night, the Avondale District of the city exploded. Fires were set, and responding firemen were attacked. Automobiles were stoned, and gunshots rang out. The mayor asked for the National Guard, and, although the violence continued for three more nights and Hubert Gerold "Rapp" Brown* arrived in the city to present demands, the rioting ended, leaving behind the conditions that had spawned the upheaval in the first place.

SELECTED BIBLIOGRAPHY

Cincinnati Enquirer, June 1967; Cincinnati Herald, June, July 1967; New York Times, June 1967; Report of the National Advisory Commission on Civil Disorders (1968).

John F. Marszalek

CITIZENS' LEAGUE FOR FAIR PLAY. Harlem citizens organized during the Great Depression to win clerical jobs for blacks in local white-owned businesses. The league, a coalition of sixty-two political, religious, fraternal, and social groups, picketed white-owned stores in 1934 and requested that Harlemites boycott discriminatory establishments. Several other groups worked alongside the coalition. Despite white resistance, the coalition's efforts brought some victories, but the "Don't Buy Where You Can't Work" movement* derailed over internal divisions and competition between the league and other groups. The league disbanded late in 1934 after a state court ruled that racially motivated picketing was illegal. In 1938 the Supreme Court ruled such picketing was in fact legal, and the league reformed as the Greater New York Coordinating Committee for Employment. Much larger, the committee soon won a crucial victory with the Harlem Merchants Association guaranteeing no discrimination in hiring.

SELECTED BIBLIOGRAPHY

Cheryl Greenberg, *"Or Does It Explode?" Black Harlem in the Great Depression* (1991); Gary Hunter, " 'Don't Buy from Where You Can't Work': Black Urban Boycott Movements During the Depression, 1929–41" (Ph.D. diss., University of Michigan, 1977); Mark Naison, *Communists in Harlem During the Depression* (1983); *New York Age*, 26 May, 9, 16, 23, 30 June, 7, 16, 21, 28 July, 4 August 1934; Adam Clayton Powell, Jr., *Marching Blacks: An Interpretive History of the Rise of the Black Common Man* (1945).

Cheryl Greenberg

CITIZENSHIP SCHOOLS. When Tennessee authorities closed down citizenship education of the Highlander Folk School* in 1960, the Southern Christian Leadership Conference* adopted the program. The Citizenship Education Program gave poorly educated, rural blacks a crash course in American government, focusing on overcoming obstacles to voting, such as teaching people how to fill out registration forms. Supervised first by black minister Andrew Young* and later by Dorothy Cotton, classes resumed in the summer of 1961 in Dorchester, Georgia. Septima P. Clark, a founder of the Highlander program, trained about thirty people a month; they returned home to teach classes.

SELECTED BIBLIOGRAPHY

Adam Fairclough, *To Redeem the Soul of America: The Southern Christian Leadership Conference and Martin Luther King, Jr.* (1987); David J. Garrow, *Bearing the Cross: Martin Luther King, Jr., and the Southern Christian Leadership Conference* (1986).

Carol Wilson

CITY OF MOBILE v. BOLDEN, 446 U.S. 55 (1980). After passage of the Voting Rights Act of 1965,* suffrage disputes shifted from restoring the right to vote to increasing the power of the ballot. *City of Mobile v. Bolden* involved the question of whether the at-large election of city commissioners unfairly reduced the voting strength of blacks in violation of the Fourteenth* and Fifteenth Amendments.* Blacks constituted about 35 percent of Mobile, Alabama's, population, but none had ever won election in the city commission. Wiley L. Bolden charged that citywide elections diluted black votes, particularly within a racially polarized electorate. The lower federal courts agreed and ordered the replacement of the commission form of government with a mayor and council elected from single-member districts. On 22 April 1980, the Supreme Court reversed the judgment. Speaking for a majority of six, Justice Potter Stewart held that official bias could not be inferred from its impact; rather, discrimination had to be intentionally motivated. Despite this stringent constitutional standard of proof, upon retrial in the district court, Bolden's attorneys exhibited the necessary evidence to win their suit. In 1982, Congress amended the Voting Rights Act to allow litigants to prove vote dilution based on the effect of discrimination, rather than its intent.

SELECTED BIBLIOGRAPHY

Chandler Davidson, ed., *Minority Vote Dilution* (1984); Steven F. Lawson, *In Pursuit of Power: Southern Blacks and Electoral Politics, 1965–1982* (1985); Abigail M. Thernstrom, *Whose Votes Count? Affirmative Action and Minority Voting Rights* (1987).

                                                                                    Steven F. Lawson

CITY OF RICHMOND v. DEANS, 37 F.2d 712 (1930). The city of Richmond, Virginia, adopted an ordinance in 1911 that restricted people of either race, white or black, from taking up residence on a block where a majority of the homes were occupied by people of the other race. In *Buchanan v. Warley** (1917), the U.S. Supreme Court ruled that such ordinances violated the Fourteenth Amendment,* but cities continued to enact them. In 1929, the Richmond city council replaced its old ordinance with one that placed a similar restriction on people who, under state law, could not marry members of the other group. J. B. Deans, a black resident of Richmond, forced a judicial ruling by buying a house in a white neighborhood and seeking an injunction from the federal district court against enforcement of the ordinance. When that court ruled in his favor, the city appealed, as attorneys for Deans and the city argued the relative merits of the Fourteenth Amendment and the state's police powers. The U.S. Supreme Court (273 U.S. 668 [1930]) let stand rulings of the district and appeals courts. Given the fact that the city's ordinance rested on state law that, in turn, rested on racial distinctions, the latest ordinance in no material way differed from the original, and it no better met the test of constitutionality. The concerns of the NAACP* moved on to restrictive covenants, the tool adopted by exclusionary groups to replace ordinances.

SELECTED BIBLIOGRAPHY

Richard Bardolph, ed., *The Civil Rights Record: Black Americans and the Law, 1849–*

1970 (1970); NAACP Papers, Library of Congress; *Richmond Times-Dispatch*, 20 May 1930; Christopher Silver, *Twentieth-Century Richmond: Planning, Politics, and Race* (1984).

Peter Wallenstein

CIVIL RIGHTS ACT OF 1866. Enacted on 9 April 1866 by an increasingly radical Congress over President Andrew Johnson's veto, the act declared that all persons (except Indians not taxed) born in the United States were now citizens, without regard to race, color, or previous condition. As citizens, they could make and enforce contracts, sue and be sued, give evidence in court, and inherit, purchase, lease, sell, hold, and convey real and personal property. Persons who denied these rights to former slaves were guilty of a misdemeanor and upon conviction faced a fine not exceeding one thousand dollars, or imprisonment not exceeding one year, or both. Authority for prosecuting the cases was given to United States district attorneys, marshals, and deputy marshals, who were instructed to submit indictments to United States district and circuit courts. The law did not mention the rights of blacks with regard to public education or public accommodations. Some of its language, however— that all persons born in the United States were citizens of the United States and that citizens of one state had the same rights and privileges as citizens of another—became part of the Fourteenth Amendment,* but, in the midst of racial violence, intimidation, the Ku Klux Klan, and political turmoil, the law failed to protect the civil rights of freedmen.

SELECTED BIBLIOGRAPHY

Richard Bardolph, ed., *The Civil Rights Record: Black Americans and the Law, 1849–1970* (1970); John and LaWanda Cox, *Politics, Principles and Prejudices, 1865–1866* (1963).

Loren Schweninger

CIVIL RIGHTS ACT OF 1875. Introduced by Massachusetts Senator Charles Sumner* in 1870, the bill did not become law until 1 March 1875, a year after Sumner's death. It promised that all persons, regardless of race, color, or previous condition, were entitled to full and equal employment of accommodations in "inns, public conveyances on land or water, theaters, and other places of public amusement." Nor could any citizen be denied the right to serve on grand or petit juries. Responsibility for enforcement fell to the federal district and circuit courts; those convicted faced a fine of between five hundred and one thousand dollars for each offense as well as a forfeiture of five hundred dollars to the aggrieved individual. Excluded from the law was a section concerning equal enjoyment of public education. Supporters of the bill argued that it was necessary to protect the rights of all citizens against class and race prejudice; opponents, including a number of prominent Republicans, deemed it an unconstitutional attempt to legislate "social equality" be-

"Outside of the Galleries of the House of Representatives During the Passage of the Civil Rights Bill," *Harper's Weekly*, 28 April 1866. (Library of Congress.)

tween the races. Although blacks asserted their rights under the law, federal officials were often indifferent to their claims of discrimination. In 1883, the Supreme Court struck down the law by declaring that Congress did not have the power to regulate the conduct and transactions of individuals.

SELECTED BIBLIOGRAPHY
David Donald, *Charles Sumner and the Rights of Man* (1970); John Hope Franklin, *Race and History* (1988).

Loren Schweninger

CIVIL RIGHTS ACT OF 1957. This act provided for the establishment of the Civil Rights Section, Justice Department,* empowered federal prosecutors to obtain court injunctions against interference with the right to vote, and established a federal Civil Rights Commission* with authority to investigate discriminatory conditions and to recommend corrective measures. Its chief importance, however, lay in providing a psychological lift for the black race; it was the first civil rights law Congress had passed since Reconstruction. Black Americans reasoned that, with additional pressure, further effective legislation might also be passed. They were correct.

SELECTED BIBLIOGRAPHY
John W. Anderson, *Eisenhower, Brownell, and the Congress: The Tangled Origins of the Civil Rights Bill of 1956–1957* (1964); Robert Fredrick Burk, *The Eisenhower Administration and Black Civil Rights* (1984); Congressional Quarterly Service, *Congress and the Nation, 1945–1964: A Review of Government and Politics in the Postwar Years,* vol. 1 (1965).

Monroe Billington

CIVIL RIGHTS ACT OF 1960. This act made unlawful flight to avoid prosecution for bombing offenses and interference with court orders regarding school desegregation. Federal judges were empowered to appoint referees to hear persons claiming that state election officials had denied them the right to register and vote. The law was difficult to enforce because, before a finding could be made and referee machinery started, the Justice Department had to bring forth specific cases to prove that qualified citizens had been denied the vote because of race or color.

SELECTED BIBLIOGRAPHY
Daniel M. Berman, *A Bill Becomes a Law: The Civil Rights Act of 1960* (1962); Robert Fredrick Burk, *The Eisenhower Administration and Black Civil Rights* (1984); Congressional Quarterly Service, *Congress and the Nation, 1945–1964: A Review of Government and Politics in the Postwar Years,* vol. 1 (1965).

Monroe Billington

CIVIL RIGHTS ACT OF 1964. During the civil rights struggle of the 1960s, Congress passed this landmark piece of comprehensive legislation. The most important provisions of this act banned discrimination by businesses offering food, lodging, gasoline, or entertainment to the public; forbade discrimination by employers or labor unions when hiring, promoting, dismissing, or making job referrals; authorized government agencies to withhold federal money from any program permitting discrimination; authorized the attorney general to file suit to force desegregation of schools, playgrounds, parks, libraries, and swimming pools; tightened provisions to prevent denial of black voting rights in federal elections by declaring that any person with a sixth grade education was presumed literate and that state literacy tests were not to be applied to him or her; established a federal agency to assist local communities in settling racial disputes; and granted additional powers to the Civil Rights Commission.* Congressional opponents, some of whom had participated in a three-and-a-half-month Senate filibuster, had directed most of their attention to the public accommodations section of this act, the most controversial section. Under threat of prosecution, most businesses generally accepted the fact that the issue of separate public accommodations for the races was settled permanently. Desegregated public facilities became the norm throughout the nation. No other act of Congress more directly affected the appearance of American society. The voting section of this act promised more than it could de-

Blacks attempt to integrate State House Restaurant, Raleigh, N.C., May 1963. The Civil Rights Act of 1964 prohibited segregation in public restaurants. (North Carolina Division of Archives and History.)

liver, and this weakness in the law stimulated black demonstrations, a large factor in the passage of the effective Voting Rights Act of 1965.*

SELECTED BIBLIOGRAPHY

Civil Rights Files, Lyndon B. Johnson Library, Austin, Texas; Congressional Quarterly Service, *Congress and the Nation, 1945–1964: A Review of Government and Politics in the Postwar Years,* vol. 1 (1965); Lyndon Baines Johnson, *The Vantage Point: Perspectives of the Presidency, 1963–1969* (1971); Charles and Barbara Whalen, *The Longest Debate: A Legislative History of the 1964 Civil Rights Act* (1985).

Monroe Billington

CIVIL RIGHTS ACT OF 1968. Stalled in Congress for two years, it was not until the heightened racial tension following the assassination of Martin Luther King, Jr.,* threatened to erupt into widespread rioting that the Civil Rights Act of 1968 gained the necessary support for passage. Its most important section prohibited discrimination in the rental or sale of housing. Fair housing was one of the most sensitive areas of civil rights legislation, which made it the last major area on which Congress took action. Not since 1866, indeed, had Congress passed any open housing legislation. (See Open Housing Act of 1968 for a full discussion of the open housing provision.)

Apart from open housing, the act contained several important provisions protecting civil rights and upholding civil obedience. It provided criminal penalties for anyone who interfered with or injured a person for exercising certain specified rights, such as voting, using public accommodations, serving on a jury, attending school or college, and the like. Civil rights workers who encouraged citizens to exercise the above and other fundamental rights were similarly protected. An antiriot provision provided criminal penalties for persons utilizing interstate commerce facilities, including the mails, telephone, radio, and television, with the intent to incite, organize, or take part in a riot. The act also provided federal penalties for persons who manufacture or teach the use of a firearm or explosive for use in a riot or public disturbance.

SELECTED BIBLIOGRAPHY

Hugh Davis Graham, *The Civil Rights Era* (1990); Donald G. Nieman, *Promises to Keep: African-Americans and the Constitutional Order, 1776 to the Present* (1991).

Charles D. Lowery

CIVIL RIGHTS BILL OF 1990. During his presidency, Ronald Reagan managed to roll back many of the hard-won civil rights gains of the 1970s. His political and judicial appointees were, for the most part, conservatives who shared his opposition to busing, affirmative action, quotas in hiring and promotion, and other similar measures which had been utilized with some success in the 1970s to redress the effects of racial discrimination. His appointees to the Supreme Court formed a new conservative majority which succeeded in the late 1980s in shifting the Court's direction on civil rights. In 1989, for example, it handed down no fewer than five separate rulings that weakened civil rights protections.

These controversial Supreme Court decisions spurred a coalition of civil rights and women's rights groups to pressure Congress in 1990 for legislation to reverse the most damaging rulings, primarily those relating to discrimination in the hiring and promotion of minorities and women. Senator Edward Kennedy and Representative Augustus Hawkins responded by sponsoring the desired legislation. The Kennedy-Hawkins bill strengthened Title VII of the Civil Rights Act of 1964* by providing stronger guarantees against discrimination in employment. Anyone suffering from job discrimination because of race, religion, national origin, or gender was empowered to bring suit against the employer, not just for job reinstatement and back pay, as provided for in the 1964 legislation, but for punitive damages as well. Despite strong opposition from business interests fearful of a flood of job discrimination litigation, the bill passed Congress in October. President George Bush vetoed the measure because, he said, it introduced "the destructive force of quotas into our national employment system." Since the early days of Ronald Reagan's administration, the White House's civil rights strategy had been to link almost every progressive measure affecting blacks to despised quotas. In vetoing the bill, Bush joined Reagan as one of only two presidents since the modern civil rights era began in the early 1950s to veto civil rights legislation. The Senate failed by two votes to override Bush's veto. In February 1991 House Democrats revived the bill.

SELECTED BIBLIOGRAPHY
Julian Bond, "Color Blinders," *The Nation* 251 (13 August 1990), 152–53; Diana R. Gordon, "A Civil Rights Bill for Workers," *The Nation* 251 (9 July 1990), 44–46; *New York Times*, 23, 25 October 1990; Donald G. Nieman, *Promises to Keep: African-Americans and the Constitutional Order, 1776 to the Present* (1991); "A Quota vs. Voters Dilemma," *Time*, 29 October 1990.

                                                                                Charles D. Lowery

CIVIL RIGHTS CASES, 109 U.S. 3 (1883). The Civil Rights Act of 1875* sought to combat private discrimination against blacks by punishing the denial of equal access or privileges on grounds of race in common carriers, hotels, and places of entertainment. For purposes of review, the Supreme Court consolidated five separate complaints, one on a railroad and the others at sites ranging from Maguire's Theater in San Francisco to the Grand Opera House in New York. Justice Joseph Bradley's majority opinion struck down the act's key provisions. The Fourteenth Amendment* gave Congress no power to prevent private wrongs, but only to supersede state laws that were discriminatory.

Bradley observed that at some point the black person had to take "the rank of a mere citizen" and cease being "the special favorite of the laws." The "state action" interpretation, based on the strict wording of the amendment, made it difficult to legislate against the traditional forms of social and economic discrimination. A vigorous dissent by Justice John Marshall Harlan* insisted that inns, amusement places, and conveyances were not private persons, but because of licensing and other regulatory laws they were public services operating with state permission and thus subject to public control. This philosophy has been central to federal civil rights legislation since 1964 and presents a continuing need to judicially interpret state action.

SELECTED BIBLIOGRAPHY

Charles Fairman, *Reconstruction and Reunion, 1864–1888* (1987); Milton Konvitz, *A Century of Civil Rights* (1961); Alan Westin, "John Marshall Harlan and the Constitutional Rights of Negroes: The Transformation of a Southerner," *Yale Law Journal* 66 (1975), 637–710.

James E. Sefton

CIVIL RIGHTS COMMISSION. The Civil Rights Commission is a temporary, independent, bipartisan agency established by Congress in 1957. The commission's purpose is to investigate any deprivation of voting rights complaints by citizens because of race, color, religion, or national origin, or due to fraudulent practices; to study and collect information on the denial of equal protection under law; to appraise federal laws and policies regarding equal protection enforcement; to serve as a national equal protection information clearinghouse; and to submit reports, findings, and recommendations to the president and Congress. The commission comprises eight commissioners appointed by Congress and the president.

SELECTED BIBLIOGRAPHY

Civil Rights Update (March 1984); Foster Rhea Dulles, *The Civil Rights Commission: 1957–1965* (1968).

Donald Cunnigen

CIVIL RIGHTS SECTION, JUSTICE DEPARTMENT. On 3 February 1939, Attorney General Frank Murphy established a Civil Liberties Unit within the Criminal Division of the Department of Justice. The unit increased its activity in the 1940s and 1950s and came to be known as the Civil Rights Section. The Civil Rights Act of 1957* elevated the Civil Rights Section to the status of a division of the Justice Department headed by an assistant attorney general. The creation of a separate Civil Rights Division also reflected the Eisenhower administration's desire to have access to civil as well as criminal remedies in civil rights cases.

SELECTED BIBLIOGRAPHY

Michael R. Belknap, *Federal Law and Southern Order: Racial Violence and Constitutional Conflict in the Post-Brown South* (1987); John T. Elliff, "The United States

Department of Justice and Individual Rights, 1937–1962" (Ph.D. diss., Harvard University, 1967; Steven F. Lawson, *Black Ballots: Voting Rights in the South, 1944–1969* (1976).

Michael S. Mayer

The Civil Rights Commission investigated complaints of demonstrators such as these in Raleigh, North Carolina, May 1963. (North Carolina Division of Archives and History.)

CLARK, KENNETH BANCROFT (24 July 1914, Panama Canal Zone–). An African-American educator and psychologist, Clark's research on the development of black children within segregated schools was used by the NAACP* as part of its strategy in winning *Brown v. Board of Education** (1954). A decade earlier, he had worked as a researcher on Gunnar Myrdal's landmark and controversial *An American Dilemma** (1944). Clark's "behavioralist" testimony before the Supreme Court introduced social science research into legal and constitutional issues, especially those relating to racial discrimination. Its use and validity generated debate then and continues to do so even decades later. In the 1950s, Clark also investigated the effects of segregated schools in the North, particularly in New York City, where he found de facto discrimination as effective as any southern law. One consequence he found was that segregated schools led to segregated neighborhoods. Clark earned bachelor's and master's degrees from Howard University* and his doctorate in experimental psychology from Columbia University. In 1967, he founded the Metropolitan Applied Research Center, a social research organization. Believing that the increasing numbers of black public officials would require research and technical assistance, he was instrumental in establishing the Joint Center for Political Studies, the nation's only black think tank, which is located in Washington, D.C.

SELECTED BIBLIOGRAPHY

Kenneth B. Clark, *The Black Man in American Politics* (1969); Harold Cruse, *Plural but Equal. A Critical Study of Blacks and Minorities and America's Plural Society* (1987); *Current Biography* (1964); David W. Southern, *Gunnar Myrdal and Black-White Relations: The Use and Abuse of "An American Dilemma," 1944–1969* (1987).

Nancy E. Fitch

CLARK, PETER HUMPHRIES (1829, Cincinnati, Ohio–21 June 1925, St. Louis, Mo.). A freeborn African American, Clark attended high school in Cincinnati and taught there for more than thirty years. As a youth, he helped slaves escape, served as national secretary of the Colored Convention in Rochester, New York, in 1853, and wrote the constitution for the National Equal Rights League.* During the Civil War, he organized a fighting unit that he memorialized in the book *The Black Brigade of Cincinnati*. A sometime Republican and a consistent race man, Clark became the first black socialist, and then a Democrat. He moved to St. Louis in 1887, where he taught at Sumner High School and engaged in politics. He retired in 1908, remaining in St. Louis until his death.

SELECTED BIBLIOGRAPHY

Lawrence Grossman, "In His Veins Coursed No Bootlicking Blood: The Career of Peter H. Clark," *Ohio History* 86 (January 1977), 79–94; Herbert Gutman, "Peter H. Clark: Pioneer Negro Socialist, 1877," *The Journal of Negro Education* 34 (Fall 1965), 413–15; Rayford W. Logan and Michael K. Winston, eds., *Dictionary of American Negro Biography* (1982).

Lawrence O. Christensen

CLEAVER, ELDRIDGE (31 August 1935, Wabbaseka, Ark.–). One of the most radical and articulate public spokesmen and revolutionary writers of the 1960s, Cleaver grew up in Watts, Los Angeles. Frequently in trouble with the law during his teens, he spent many of his early years in reformatories and prisons where he received most of his education. Cleaver turned to writing as a means of self-preservation, and in 1968 his first book *Soul on Ice*, highly influential and widely read, became a best-seller, "a classic contemporary black militant expression." Rising to national prominence as a writer for *Ramparts* and as the minister of information and major formulator of the Black Panther* party's ideology, Cleaver served as a symbol of growing black urban unrest and disillusionment and its bitter opposition to white America's oppression. Moreover, his pronouncement of "total liberty for black people or total destruction for America" signaled a new voice and a unique vision of the civil rights movement. Calling for a new assessment of the black condition and new strategies, Eldridge Cleaver helped raise the struggle for civil rights to a more militant level. Later in his life he disavowed many of his earlier radical views.

SELECTED BIBLIOGRAPHY

Jervis Anderson, "Race Rage and Eldridge Cleaver," *Commentary* 46 (December 1968), 63–69; Stokely Carmichael and Charles Hamilton, *Black Power: The Politics of Liberation in America* (1967); M. Karenga, *The Roots of the US/Panther Conflict* (1976); Manning Marable, *Race, Reform and Rebellion: The Second Reconstruction in Black America, 1945–1982* (1984); Joyce Nower, "Cleaver's Vision of America and the New White Radical: A Legacy of Malcolm X," *Negro American Literature Forum* 4 (March 1970), 12–21; Kenneth O'Reilly, *"Racial Matters": The FBI's Secret File on Black America, 1960–1972* (1989); Stanley Pacion, "Soul Still on Ice? The Talents and Troubles of Eldridge Cleaver," *Dissent* 16 (July–August 1969), 310–16; Harvey Swados, "Old Con, Black Panther, Brilliant Writer and Quintessential American," *New York Times Magazine* (7 September 1969), 38–39, 139–54.

Jacquelyn Jackson

CLEVELAND GAZETTE. Under the editorial direction of Harry C. Smith, this leading black weekly newspaper in Cleveland, Ohio, forcefully protested discrimination nationwide. During Neval Thomas's 1924–1928 Washington D.C.–based campaign against governmental mandated segregation in the federal civil service, the *Gazette* provided Thomas with a forum for disseminating information on his activities. Smith also utilized the paper as a vehicle to express his own civil rights convictions, including a controversial call for African Americans in Cleveland to buy guns for their self-defense during the Red Summer of 1919.

SELECTED BIBLIOGRAPHY

Larry Cuban, "A Strategy for Racial Peace: Negro Leadership in Cleveland, 1900–1919," *Phylon* 28 (Fall 1967), 299–311; Russell H. Davis, *Memorable Negroes in Cleveland's Past* (1969); Frederick J. Detweiler, *The Negro Press in the United States* (1968); Thelma T. Gorham, "The Negro Press, Past, Present, and Future," in *Dictionary of U.S. Negro Newspapers, Magazines and Periodicals* (1966); Marshall Hyatt, "Neval H. Thomas and the War on Federal Segregation," *Negro History Bulletin* 42 (October–December 1979), 96–102; Kenneth Kusmer, *A Ghetto Takes Shape: Black Cleveland 1870–1930* (1976).

Marshall Hyatt

CLINTON, TENNESSEE, SCHOOL INTEGRATION CRISIS. Building upon litigation precedents established by the NAACP,* African Americans in the East Tennessee community of Clinton filed suit in Knoxville's federal district court in 1951 seeking the integration of Clinton High School. District Judge Robert L. Taylor denied the plea, and Clinton's black students continued to be bused eighteen miles to Knoxville's segregated high school. After the 1954 *Brown v. Board of Education** ruling, Taylor directed Clinton school authorities to desegregate. Local citizens organized to delay integration, and racist agitator Frederick John Kasper of New Jersey successfully inflamed the area's antiblack sentiments until Governor Frank G. Clement sent troops to maintain order for the first nine days when integrated schools opened in August 1956.

SELECTED BIBLIOGRAPHY

Lester C. Lamon, *Blacks in Tennessee, 1791–1970* (1981); Neil R. McMillen, "Organized Resistance to School Desegregation in Tennessee," *Tennessee Historical Quarterly* 30 (Fall 1971), 314–28.

Thaddeus M. Smith

"CLOSE RANKS." This editorial, written by W.E.B. Du Bois,* appeared in the July 1918 issue of the *Crisis,** the organ of the NAACP,* after the United States had declared war against Germany. "We of the colored race," Du Bois wrote, "have no ordinary interest in the outcome. . . . Let us not hesitate. Let us, while the war lasts, forget our special grievances and close our ranks shoulder to shoulder with our own white fellow citizens and the other nations that are fighting for democracy." For Du Bois, as for many Progressives, the war represented an opportunity to battle militarism; unlike most whites, he also saw it as a struggle against racism. Over 2.2 million African Americans registered for the draft; 367,000 were called into service, and 50,000 went overseas. Taunted by *The Messenger** for supporting the war and stunned at army discrimination, Du Bois later repudiated his position: "We killed Faith and Hope." But in 1942, amidst the struggle against the Axis powers, he again endorsed the principles of "Close Ranks."

SELECTED BIBLIOGRAPHY

W. Manning Marable, *W.E.B. DuBois* (1986); Elliott M. Rudwick, *W.E.B. DuBois: Propagandist of the Negro Protest* (1960).

Richard W. Resh

CLYATT v. UNITED STATES, 197 U.S. 207 (1905). Samuel Clyatt was accused of holding two black Georgians, Will Gordon and Mose Ridley, in black peonage* as a repayment of debt. Clyatt was convicted by a jury and was sentenced to four years of confinement. He appealed his sentence contending that the Thirteenth Amendment* pertained to actions of a state and not to an individual. Justice David Brewer in the initial point of law stated for the majority that the Fourteenth* and Fifteenth Amendments* were state prohibitions, but that Congress held the authority to enforce the Thirteenth Amendment and had applied its law to an individual. In a second point of law, Brewer distinguished between peonage and voluntary actions in repayment of a debt, and he observed that Gordon and Ridley were forced to return to Georgia. In a more narrow ruling, Brewer stated that the specific charge against

Clyatt was "returning" the two men to peonage, and no evidence had been presented as to prior conditions of peonage. Thus, the lower court decision was reversed and remanded for a new trial. Justice John Marshall Harlan* dissented in the latter opinion. He argued that the men were returned to Georgia by force and against their will. He observed that Clyatt admitted the blacks owed him and did not object to a jury trial. Harlan held that the evidence "reflects barbarities of the worst kind against these negroes."

SELECTED BIBLIOGRAPHY
Richard Bardolph, ed., *The Civil Rights Record: Black Americans and the Law, 1849–1970* (1970); Pete Daniel, *The Shadow of Slavery: Peonage in the South, 1901–1969* (1972); Loren Miller, *The Petitioners: The Story of the Supreme Court of the United States and the Negro* (1966).

William Cash

COALITION OF BLACK TRADE UNIONISTS. Angered by the decision of the American Federation of Labor and Congress of Industrial Organizations (AFL-CIO) to remain neutral in the 1972 presidential election, nearly twelve hundred African Americans representing thirty-seven unions convened in Chicago, Illinois, on 23–24 September and established the Coalition of Black Trade Unionists (CBTU). Founded on the principle that a progressive trade union movement depends on black participation at all levels of the decision-making process, the coalition functions as a pressure group within the AFL-CIO to strengthen black influence throughout organized labor. Under the direction of such labor and civil rights activists as William Lucy and Charles Hayes, the CBTU sponsors a broad-based political and labor program to make trade unions more responsive to the needs and aspirations of African-American workers.

SELECTED BIBLIOGRAPHY
Coalition of Black Trade Unionists National Constitution and Bill of Rights, as Amended at the 17th Annual Convention, Washington, D.C., May 20, 1988; "Coalition of Black Trade Unionists: The Awakening Giant," *Bulletin* 3 (April 1974), 3; Philip S. Foner, Ronald L. Lewis, and Robert Cvornyek, eds., *The Black Worker: A Documentary History from Colonial Times to the Present,* vol. 8, *The Black Worker Since the AFL-CIO Merger, 1955–1980* (1984); Remarks by William Lucy, President, Coalition of Black Trade Unionists, 12th Annual CBTU Convention, 28 May 1983, Chicago, Illinois.

Robert Cvornyek

COFFEE v. RICE UNIVERSITY, 408 S.W. 2d 269 (1966). This case established the authority of Rice University, in Houston, Texas, to deviate from the terms of its endowment trust in order to charge tuition and admit qualified applicants regardless of race. This authority was conceded in state district court, Harris County, as the result of a suit brought by the university and its trustees in 1964, but was challenged in the Texas court of civil appeals by a group of former Rice students. On 27 October 1966, the court of appeals affirmed the judgment of the trial court, holding that the primary purpose of the trust created in 1891 by William Marsh Rice was to establish a first-class institution of higher learning and that this goal had fallen into conflict with subsidiary directives that the institution contribute to the "instruction of the white inhabitants of the City of Houston and the State of Texas" and that its benefits be "free and open to all." In such conflicts of intention the primary object of the trust controlled; were Rice's trustees to continue all-white and tuition-free admissions policies, the consequent loss of prestige and potential revenue would preclude the creation of a first-class university.

SELECTED BIBLIOGRAPHY
Richard Bardolph, ed. *The Civil Rights Record: Black Americans and the Law, 1849–1970* (1970); Thomas Emerson et al., *Political and Civil Rights in the United States* (1967); *Houston Post*, 22 February 1964.

Robert A. Calvert

COKE v. CITY OF ATLANTA, 184 F. Supp. 579 (N.D. Ga., 1960). On 23 December 1958 D. H. Coke, a Birmingham, Alabama, insurance executive, filed suit in district court attacking the segregated eating facilities •t the Atlanta Municipal Airport in Atlanta, Georgia. Dobbs House Inc., operator of the airport terminal restaurant, segregated its customers on the basis of race by seating African Americans behind a screen. Since Dobbs House was a lessee of the city of Atlanta, the central issue of this case was whether the restaurant's policy of segregation constituted private conduct or state action. Previous legal opinion held that only discriminatory conduct on the part of the state violated the Fourteenth Amendment.* The city of Atlanta and Dobbs House contended that the restaurant was a private organization. Since Dobbs House did not receive any instructions from the city regarding its operations, attorneys for the company maintained that its policy of segregation was "private conduct" and was not inhibited by the Fourteenth Amendment. On 5 January 1960 the court held that the conduct of Dobbs House was "state action" and that its policy of segregating customers on the basis of race violated the Fourteenth Amendment. This decision narrowed the definition of what constituted state and private action in regard to racial discrimination, and it defined the legal conduct of lessees of government property.

SELECTED BIBLIOGRAPHY
Henry J. Abraham, *Freedom and the Court, Civil Rights and Liberties in the United*

States (1988); *Atlanta Constitution*, 6 January 1960; Richard Bardolph, ed., *The Civil Rights Record: Black Americans and the Law, 1849–1970* (1970).

David A. Harmon

COLLINS, CARDISS ROBERTSON (24 September 1931, St. Louis, Mo.–). A graduate of Northwestern University in Evanston, Illinois, Collins became Illinois' first black congresswoman when she won the Seventh Congressional District seat vacated by the death of her husband, George Collins, in 1973. She won 87 percent of the vote in a district that was 55-percent black. Previously she had been a secretary, accountant, and revenue auditor with the Illinois Department of Revenue. She became the first African American to serve as majority whip at large, was chairperson of the Congressional Black Caucus,* and chaired the Manpower and Housing Committee.

SELECTED BIBLIOGRAPHY
Who's Who of American Women, 1989–1990.

Ray Branch

COLLINS, LEROY (10 March 1909, Tallahassee, Fla.–12 March 1991, Tallahassee, Fla.). Governor of Florida from 1955 to 1961, Thomas LeRoy Collins guided the Sunshine State along a course of racial moderation. Following the ruling in *Brown v. Board of Education,** he supported a pupil assignment program, based on criteria other than race, that allowed Florida to obey the law with a minimum of desegregation and racial confrontation. In this way, Collins averted school shutdowns and other forms of massive resistance that were popular throughout the South. By 1960, Collins had begun to bend with the moral force of the civil rights struggle. In response to the sit-in movement, he established a biracial committee to assist in desegregating lunch counters in stores where blacks shopped. A few years after leaving office, he was appointed by President Lyndon B. Johnson to head the Community Relations Service, a mediation agency created by the Civil Rights Act of 1964.* In this capacity in 1965, he went to Selma, Alabama, and worked out an arrangement with Dr. Martin Luther King, Jr.,* and local officials that prevented bloodshed during a voting demonstration. As Collins became more closely identified with the civil rights cause, he suffered politically at home. In 1968 he was defeated in his race for United States Senator by Edward Gurney, a Republican who used the race issue against him.

SELECTED BIBLIOGRAPHY
David R. Colburn and Richard K. Scher, *Florida's Gubernatorial Politics in the Twentieth Century* (1980); Tom R. Wagy, *Governor LeRoy Collins of Florida: Spokesman of the New South* (1985).

Steven F. Lawson

COLLINS v. WALKER, 339 F.2d 100 (5th Cir., 1964). Like the famous case of the Scottsboro Trials* in the 1930s, numerous legal decisions involving black defendants were challenged in the twentieth century because of the exclusion of blacks from juries. In an interesting twist on the theme of jury selection, the case of *Collins v. Walker* dealt with discrimination against the defendant, not because blacks had been excluded from his jury, but rather because they had been purposely included. Woodman J. Collins, a black man, had been convicted and sentenced to death for the aggravated rape of a white woman. This decision was upheld by the Louisiana Supreme Court in 1962. Collins appealed to the U.S. circuit court on three grounds. His attorneys claimed that Collins was mentally incompetent and unable to stand trial, and that his confession had been coerced. They also argued that Collins had been discriminated against because blacks had been intentionally placed on the jury for his case only. The grand jury that indicted Collins was composed of five blacks and seven whites. The judges agreed that the five black jurors had been deliberately added to the jury because the defendant was black; therefore, he had been discriminated against. The case was remanded to a new jury.

SELECTED BIBLIOGRAPHY

Derrick A. Bell, Jr., *Race, Racism and American Law* (1980); Thomas I. Emerson, David Haber, and Norman Dorsen, *Political and Civil Rights in the United States* (1967); Landman Teller, Jr., "Constitutional Law—Discrimination by Systematic Inclusion of Negroes on Grand Jury," *Mississippi Law Journal* 36 (1965), 243–45.

Carol Wilson

COLORADO ANTI-DISCRIMINATION COMMISSION v. CONTINENTAL AIRLINES, 372 U.S. 714 (1963). This Supreme Court case clarified the limits of the federal commerce power and preserved latitude for state initiative in defending civil rights by establishing that a state law forbidding racial discrimination in hiring did not place an unconstitutional encumbrance upon interstate commerce. The Colorado Anti-Discrimination Commission found Continental Airlines guilty of violating the 1957 Colorado Anti-Discrimination Act by denying pilot training to Marlon D. Green, a black, solely on grounds of race. When the Denver District Court reversed this ruling, the commission appealed to the U.S. Supreme Court. Restoring the commission's decision, the Court held that the facts of the case did not support the allegation of burden upon interstate commerce because of the virtual impossibility under federal law since the 1954 *Brown v. Board of Education** decision of encountering conflicting hiring regulations from state to state. Nor did Congress's previous adoption of less comprehensive antidiscrimination guidelines invalidate the tougher Colorado law under the federal supremacy clause, inasmuch as no goal of federal legislation in this field was frustrated by the state statute.

SELECTED BIBLIOGRAPHY
Richard Bardolph, ed., *The Civil Rights Record: Black Americans and the Law, 1849–1970* (1970); Loren Bell, *The Petitioners: The Story of the Supreme Court of the United States and the Negro* (1966); Thomas I. Emerson et al., *Political and Civil Rights in the United States* (1967); *New York Times*, 23 April 1963.

Robert A. Calvert

COLORED FARMERS' NATIONAL ALLIANCE AND COOPERA-TIVE UNION. Founded in Houston County, Texas, in December 1866, the Colored Farmers' Alliance was an appendage to the postbellum southern white Farmers' Alliance movement. Organized to educate black farmers in the agricultural sciences and to promote brotherhood, black rights, and communal support for black farm families, the alliance suffered from white paternalistic leadership and negative public reaction to its labor protests and other political activities. The alliance's general superintendent, R. M. Humphrey, and several of its state presidents, who were white, attempted to restrain the assertiveness of the black farmers. But the alliance established its own official newspaper, the *National Alliance*, set up a network of cooperatives, and pressured Humphrey to support alliance strikes and other forms of protest. White resistance to alliance activism grew rapidly. In 1891, a strike by cotton pickers in an Arkansas county led to several deaths, including the lynching of some of the instigators. By 1892 the white backlash had destroyed the alliance. Significant as an expression of agrarian protest and as an experiment in black self-determination, the alliance fell victim to the racist Jim Crow* milieu of the late-nineteenth-century South.

SELECTED BIBLIOGRAPHY
N. A. Dunning, ed., *The Farmers' Alliance History and Agricultural Digest* (1891); William F. Holmes, "The Arkansas Cotton Pickers Strike of 1891 and the Demise of the Colored Farmers' Alliance," *Arkansas Historical Quarterly* 32 (1973), 107–19; Floyd J. Miller, "Black Protest and White Leadership: A Note on the Colored Farmers' Alliance," *Phylon* 33 (1972), 169–74.

Michael B. Ballard

COLORED MERCHANTS' ASSOCIATION. Organized by Albon L. Holsey, of Booker T. Washington's* National Negro Business League,* the Colored Merchants' Association (CMA) established black-owned grocery stores which purchased merchandise cooperatively from selected dealers. The purpose was to stimulate black business, provide jobs for blacks, and pass on cost reductions to black consumers. The first CMA store opened in Montgomery, Alabama, in 1928; the concept soon spread to eighteen other cities. Despite initial enthusiasm and support from many black organizations, CMA stores failed within a few years because of the Great Depression. Few businesses joined, and consumers continued to buy national brands from white-owned chains, rather than chance the untested brands carried by the CMA.

SELECTED BIBLIOGRAPHY

E. Franklin Frazier, "Negro Business: A Social Myth," in Ronald W. Bailey, ed., *Black Business Enterprise: Historical and Contemporary Perspectives* (1971); Albon L. Holsey, "Business Points the Way," *Crisis* (July 1931); Albon L. Holsey, "The CMA Stores Face the Chains," *Opportunity* (July 1929).

Carol Wilson

COMMISSION ON INTERRACIAL COOPERATION. This organization was an interracial body of prominent blacks and whites who wished to address the social, political, and economic problems facing African Americans. Founded in December 1918 and incorporated eleven years later in Georgia, the commission consisted of state and local committees throughout the South. In 1920 a Department of Women's Work was created within the organization enabling black and white women to meet and discuss the problems they shared. The director of the organization was Will W. Alexander,* a white Methodist minister who devoted twenty-five years of service to the organization. Throughout its existence the commission used research and education to ameliorate race relations. It held conferences and published literature that espoused equal treatment. It endorsed various worthy causes including boy scout troops for African-American boys and training homes for delinquent girls. It called for the abolishment of the poll tax* and white primaries.* The organization was especially concerned about racial violence. In the early 1930s the commission engaged in a research project on lynching designed to give the public more information on the brutality of this crime. By the 1940s the organization was experiencing financial difficulties as support from northern philanthropists declined. The organization was dissolved on 16 February 1944 and succeeded by the Southern Regional Council.*

SELECTED BIBLIOGRAPHY

Edward F. Burrows, "The Commission on Interracial Cooperation," (Ph.D. diss., University of Wisconsin, 1954); Wilma Dykeman and James Stokely, *Seeds of Southern Change: The Life of Will Alexander* (1962); John Hope Franklin and Alfred A. Moss, Jr., *From Slavery to Freedom: A History of Negro Americans* (1988); Cynthia Neverdon-Morton, *Afro-American Women of the South and the Advancement of the Race, 1895–1925* (1989).

Gerald L. Smith

COMMONWEALTH OF PENNSYLVANIA v. BROWN, 270 F. Supp. 782 (E.D. Pa., 1967). Stephen Girard, a wealthy merchant and banker, established Philadelphia's Girard College in 1848. His will specified that this secondary school's enrollment was to be restricted to "poor, white, male orphans." Charged with administrating the school, the city of Philadelphia established a board of trustees which strictly enforced the will's terms. In 1957 the Supreme Court held that the board's refusal to admit blacks constituted governmental discrimination. In response, Philadelphia dissolved the board of trustees and appointed private persons to administer the school. Ten years later, seven black male orphans, together with the Commonwealth of Pennsylvania, its attorney general, and the city of Philadelphia, brought a class action suit against the private trustees in a federal district court to prevent the further denial of admission to blacks. Based on *Evans v. Newton*,* a 1966 Supreme Court case that involved a privately endowed park, the court ruled that the college had associated itself with the state in such a way as to suggest to the community that the institution's policy was approved by public authority. While Girard College was not accessible to the general public, said the court, it had always been an "institution whose benefits are available to any needy, fatherless boy—as long as he is 'white.' " In this way, the college was similar to a public boarding school or orphanage that practiced racial restriction. In addition, by requiring the trustees of the school to make periodic reports, Pennsylvania had become actively involved in overseeing the instruction and upbringing of Girard's students. The Court concluded that Girard's racial policy was "so afflicted with State action" that it violated the equal protection clause of the Fourteenth Amendment.*

SELECTED BIBLIOGRAPHY

Richard Bardolph, ed., *The Civil Rights Record: Black Americans and the Law, 1849–1970* (1970); Derrick A. Bell, Jr., *Race, Racism and American Law* (1980).

                                                                                                        Phillip A. Gibbs

COMMUNIST PARTY. The largest impact the American Communist Party (ACP) had on African Americans occurred during the Great Depression when the party sought to organize this most oppressed sector of America. The ACP offered equality in the party's organization, attacked social and economic discrimination, and promoted legal efforts at ending American racial injustice. In 1931 the International Labor Defense and NAACP* battled to handle the appeal of the Scottsboro Trials,* the focal point of the party's southern initiative. Also during the 1930s, the ACP, through the National Negro Congress,* attempted to join with other black organizations to form the United Front against Fascism and eventually to expand its political base. The party promoted expanded educational opportunities for black youth and black cultural enterprises which attracted such notables as Richard Wright* and Paul Robeson.* Politically, the ACP was an active force in Harlem political life during the period, and James Ford, recruited via the American Negro Labor Congress* in 1926, became the special organizer in Harlem in 1931 and ran as the party's vice presidential candidate in 1932, 1936, and 1940. The ACP's significance in the African-American community declined because of its failure to attract the aspiring black middle class firmly dedicated to the capitalist system.

SELECTED BIBLIOGRAPHY

Dan T. Carter, *Scottsboro: A Tragedy of the American South* (1969); Harvey Klehr, *Communist Cadre: The Social Background of the American Communist Party Elite* (1978); Harvey Klehr, *The Heyday of American Communism: The Depression Decade* (1984); Mark Naison, *Communism in Harlem During the Depression* (1983); Wilson Record, *The Negro and the Communist Party* (1951).

Thaddeus M. Smith

COMPROMISE OF 1877. When the vote was counted in the presidential election of 7 November 1876, neither the Republican Rutherford B. Hayes nor the Democrat Samuel J. Tilden had won the necessary majority of the electoral vote. Although Tilden had the majority of the popular vote (4,282,020 to 4,036,572), the electoral count was 184 to 165; the disputed votes of Florida, Louisiana, South Carolina, and Oregon had not been counted. Both candidates claimed the presidency. Tilden needed one vote and Hayes needed twenty to achieve the necessary majority. Rival canvassing boards and state governments pressed their claims and contrived a variety of deals, but the deadlock remained. Since there was no constitutional provision for resolving the dilemma, on 29 January 1877, the House and Senate created an Electoral Commission consisting of five members each from the House, Senate, and Supreme Court. The commission voted 8 to 7 in favor of Hayes. It is generally agreed that behind-the-scenes negotiating actually ensured congressional approval. The main parts of the so-called Compromise of 1877 consisted of a promise to end Reconstruction, to appoint a Southerner to the cabinet, and to support the building of southern railroads. The actual result of the compromise was the federal abandonment of black people to southern native whites.

SELECTED BIBLIOGRAPHY

Allan Peskin, "Was There a Compromise of 1877?" *Journal of American History* 60 (June 1973), 63–73; Keith I. Polakoff, *The Politics of Inertia* (1973); George C. Rable, "Southern Interests and the Election of 1876: A Reappraisal," *Civil War History* 26 (December 1980), 357–61; C. Vann Woodward, *Reunion and Reaction: The Compromise of 1877 and the End of Reconstruction* (1951); C. Vann Woodward, "Yes, There Was a Compromise of 1877," *Journal of American History* 60 (June 1973), 215–23.

Clarence Hooker

CONFISCATION ACTS (1861, 1862). The First Confiscation Act, approved on 6 August 1861, empowered the federal government to confiscate the property, including slaves, of disloyal Southerners who used such property in direct support of the Confederate war effort. The Second Confiscation Act, the product of intense and lengthy debate and complex parliamentary maneuvering, became law on 17 July 1862 only after Congress took the unusual step of attaching to the legislation an explanatory joint resolution that prevented a threatened veto by President Abraham Lincoln. The act gave disloyal Southerners sixty days to cease rebellious activity. At the close of that grace period, the government was authorized to confiscate the slaves and other property of rebellious Southerners. Such confiscated slaves were to be freed. In most cases confiscation took place after legal process in federal courts. However, slaves abandoned by disloyal masters or slaves who escaped to Union lines were immediately freed. Other provisions of this law authorized the president to enlist freed slaves into the Union military and appropriated $500,000 for colonization of ex-slaves out of the country. Both acts were cautiously enforced by the Lincoln administration and were overshadowed by the Emancipation Proclamation.*

SELECTED BIBLIOGRAPHY

Roy P. Basler, ed., *The Collected Works of Abraham Lincoln*, vol. 5 (1953); Leonard P. Curry, *Blueprint for Modern America: Nonmilitary Legislation of the First Civil War Congress* (1968); James G. Randall, *Constitutional Problems under Lincoln* (1951).

                                                                            Larry T. Balsamo

CONGRESS OF RACIAL EQUALITY. In 1942 George Houser and other pacifists affiliated with the Fellowship of Reconciliation* (FOR) formed a Committee of Racial Equality in Chicago, Illinois. Following a "Brotherhood Mobilization Plan" written by James Farmer,* they practiced nonviolent resistance* to public segregation. As Farmer and Bayard Rustin,* both FOR field secretaries, spread the concept to other cities, committees multiplied, and a national organization was formed with the name, Congress of Racial Equality (CORE).

After declining in the 1950s, CORE emerged as a major civil rights force in the 1960s. Among the first to respond to the 1960s sit-ins, which began at a Woolworths lunch counter in North Carolina, CORE leaders initiated picket lines and boycotts of northern Woolworths stores. In 1961 CORE Freedom Riders* tested a Supreme Court ban on segregated interstate transportation. Prevailing over vicious resistance in the Deep South, this strategy broke the back of Jim Crow.*

In 1962 CORE's emphasis shifted from direct action* to voter registration. Part of the Council of Federated Organizations,* CORE contributed leadership and resources to the Freedom Summer of 1964,* the Mississippi Freedom Democratic Party* (MFDP) and the MFDP's challenge of party regulars at the 1964 Democratic national convention. Meanwhile, northern CORE workers immersed themselves in "community organization" battles against poverty and racism in urban ghettos.

James Farmer, CORE's first national chairman and national director after 1961, retired in 1966. Floyd B. McKissick,* elected in his stead, was succeeded two years later by Roy Innis. Changes in leadership reflected changes in philosophy and tactics, and nonviolence and interracialism were eclipsed by the Black Power* movement.

While CORE veered toward separatism, historians began to assess its earlier strategies. Crediting the organization with contributing substantially to desegregation and landmark civil rights laws, they suggested that the record numbers of African Americans who attained public office in the 1970s were direct beneficiaries of the efforts of CORE.

SELECTED BIBLIOGRAPHY

Inge Powell Bell, *CORE and the Strategy of Nonviolence* (1968); James Farmer, *Lay Bare the Heart, an Autobiography of the Civil Rights Movement* (1985); George M. Houser, *CORE: A Brief History* (1949); August Meier and Elliot Rudwick, *CORE: A Study in the Civil Rights Movement* (1973); James Peck, *Cracking the Color Line: Nonviolent Direct Action Methods of Eliminating Racial Discrimination* (1962).

Jo Ann O. Robinson

CONGRESSIONAL BLACK CAUCUS. In 1969, when the number of black congressmen grew from six to nine, informal discussions of the group on matters primarily affecting the well-being of African Americans, chaired by Representative Charles Diggs* (D-Mich.), led to the official founding of the Congressional Black Caucus in January 1971. It quickly gained press attention when its members boycotted President Richard Nixon's State of the Union address, citing his failure to grant them an audience, a stance he soon reversed. With a less than sympathetic ear in the Oval Office and a conservative political trend in the nation, caucus members focused their energies on gaining seniority, acquiring political clout via important congressional committee assignments (Appropriations, Ways and Means, Budget), and mobilizing constituencies in support of caucus objectives ranging from minority set-aside legislation to voter registration. Its members sponsored and were instrumental in the passage of such measures as the Anti-Apartheid Act of 1986, the establishment of a national holiday in honor of Martin Luther King, Jr.,* in 1982; the Humphrey-Hawkins Full Employment and Balanced Growth Act and the Public Works Employment Act in 1977; and various civil rights legislation. In order to maximize its effectiveness, caucus members have voted as a bloc on legislation of common concern, maintained ties with black elected officials and organizations across the nation, formed coalitions with other special-interest groups, and disseminated information outlining its goals and activities through its periodic publications and seminars. Each year the caucus submits an "alternative budget" reflecting its national priorities and oversees a graduate legislative intern program. By 1990 there were twenty-four members in the caucus.

SELECTED BIBLIOGRAPHY
Mabel M. Smythe, ed., *The Black American Reference Book* (1976); Frank Dexter Brown, "The CBC: Past, Present, and Future," *Black Enterprise* (September 1990) 25–26; Lynn Norment, "Congressional Black Caucus: Our Team on Capitol Hill," *Ebony* (August 1984), 40, 42, 44, 46; Jeffrey M. Elliot, *The Presidential-Congressional Political Dictionary* (1984).

Robert Fikes, Jr.

COOPER v. AARON, 358 U.S. 1 (1958). After the 1954 *Brown v. Board of Education** decision, the city of Little Rock, Arkansas, drew up a plan for the gradual desegregation of its public schools (see Little Rock desegregation crisis). The parents of several black children, represented by the NAACP,* challenged the plan, contending that it provided for the continued operation of segregated schools. A federal district judge upheld the board's plan. Governor Orval Faubus declared the white schools off limits to blacks, but Judge Ronald Davies ordered the board to proceed with the plan forthwith. After the Arkansas National Guard turned away black students attempting to enter Central High School, the board filed a petition for a temporary suspension of the plan. Davies denied the petition and issued a preliminary injunction prohibiting the governor and officers of the National Guard from interfering with black students entering Central High. Faubus withdrew the National Guard, and on 23 September 1957 black students again entered the school. A large and threatening crowd prompted authorities to remove the black children from the school, and Mayor Woodrow Wilson Mann requested aid from President Dwight Eisenhower, who nationalized the guard and sent 1,000 troops from the 101st Airborne Division to escort the black students into Central High. On 23 June 1958, District Judge Harry J. Lemley granted a request by the school board to delay implementing the desegregation plan until 1961. The Eighth Circuit Court of Appeals reversed Lemley's decision. Sitting in special session, the Supreme Court affirmed the decision of the Eighth Circuit on 12 September 1958.

SELECTED BIBLIOGRAPHY
Tony Freyer, *The Little Rock Crisis: A Constitutional Interpretation* (1984); George Rossman, ed., "Review of Recent Supreme Court Decisions," *American Bar Association Journal* 44 (1958), 1078–79; Robert G. Webb, "Constitutional Law—Little Rock Litigation," *North Carolina Law Review* 37 (1959), 177–84.

Michael S. Mayer

CORRIGAN v. BUCKLEY, 271 U.S. 323 (1926). In the early part of the twentieth century, it was a common practice for white urban homeowners to enter into agreements that excluded certain groups from owning property in their neighborhood. The agreements, directed most often against African Americans and Jews, bound not only the signatories to the agreement but also any future purchasers of the property.

In 1921, Irene Corrigan, a homeowner in Washington, D.C., entered into an agreement with her neighbors to exclude African Americans from purchasing, leasing, or otherwise occupying any property in her neighborhood. A year later, Corrigan attempted to sell her property to an African-American woman in violation of the neighborhood agreement. Corrigan's neighbors filed suit to stop her. The United States Supreme Court decided that it had no jurisdiction in this case, stating that the provisions of the Fifth Amendment and the Fourteenth Amendment,* relating to equal protection under the laws, applied only to governmental actions, not to private contracts such as the one Corrigan had signed. In so ruling, the Supreme Court inferred that although restrictive covenants were instruments of racial discrimination, they were not unconstitutional because no governmental action was involved.

SELECTED BIBLIOGRAPHY

Richard Bardolph, ed., *The Civil Rights Record: Black Americans and the Law, 1849–1970* (1970); Loren Miller, *The Petitioners: The Story of the Supreme Court of the United States and the Negro* (1966); Gilbert Osofsky, *Harlem: The Making of a Ghetto* (1971); Clement E. Vose, *Caucasians Only: The Supreme Court, the NAACP, and the Restrictive Covenant Cases* (1959).

Steve Sadowsky

COSTIGAN-WAGNER ANTILYNCHING BILL. In 1934 the NAACP* led the fight to obtain from Congress an antilynching measure designed to give equal protection of the law to African Americans, to challenge the complacent acceptance of mob murder, and to make lynching a punishable crime in every state. Senate Democrats Edward Costigan (Colorado) and Robert Wagner (New York) sponsored the NAACP measure. The Costigan-Wagner bill was aimed at state and local law enforcement officials who permitted lynching. The bill also proposed a $10,000 fine on the county in which the lynching occurred. The NAACP maintained that the bill would pressure local authorities and that federal jurisdiction would protect judges, juries, attorneys, and witnesses against reprisals. Although President Franklin D. Roosevelt reportedly favored the measure, he refused to publicly endorse it and risk a congressional battle at the expense of other national reform measures. The NAACP was not successful in the Senate, but the bill did pass in the House of Representatives and progress was made toward gaining broad-based congressional support for a national antilynching law. Likewise, the NAACP secured its position as a major lobbying voice in Congress for African Americans for the next two decades.

SELECTED BIBLIOGRAPHY

Joseph Huthmacher, *Senator Robert F. Wagner and the Rise of Urban Liberalism* (1968); James R. McGovern, *Anatomy of a Lynching: The Killing of Claude Neal* (1982); George C. Rable, "The South and the Politics of Antilynching Legislation,

1920–1940," *Journal of Southern History* 51 (May 1985), 201–20; Robert L. Zangrando, *The NAACP Crusade against Lynching, 1909–1950* (1980).

Thaddeus M. Smith

COUNCIL OF FEDERATED ORGANIZATIONS. In 1962 Robert Moses* of the Student Nonviolent Coordinating Committee* (SNCC) and David Dennis* of the Congress of Racial Equality* led in the formation of this statewide coalition of civil rights organizations in Mississippi. Moses served as director, Dennis as assistant director, and Aaron Henry* of the NAACP* as president. During 1962 and 1963, the Council of Federated Organizations (COFO) conducted a voter registration campaign, which was supported by funds from the Voter Education Project.* White Mississippians responded to the campaign by harassing and terrorizing COFO workers and would-be black voters, with the result that few blacks were registered. Recognizing the need for new tactics, in August 1963 COFO mobilized about a thousand black voters to cast protest votes in the August Democratic primary. As a next step, COFO leaders wanted to show the desire and willingness of black Mississippians to vote. The "freedom vote" campaign provided a way to do this without having voters face intimidation at the regular polling places and by giving them the opportunity to vote for candidates of their own choosing. COFO members selected Aaron Henry of the NAACP and R. Edwin King, Jr.,* a white minister who was chaplain of Tougaloo College,* as candidates for governor and lieutenant governor. About a hundred northern white students came to Mississippi to help with the campaign. This experiment with white volunteers led to the Freedom Summer of 1964* in Mississippi. Moses and Dennis decided that the only way to get the country to respond to what was going on in Mississippi was to involve white college students. The National Council of Churches provided support. In spite of opposition to white participation from some SNCC staff members, COFO undertook the project. Northern students responded with enthusiasm to the invitation to come help in the all-out campaign in Mississippi. In addition to working in voter registration campaigns, the summer workers set up schools to teach reading and writing and voting procedures. The numerous reports of murders, beatings, arrests, church burnings, and home bombings attest to the response of white Mississippians. The killing of James Earl Chaney,* Andrew Goodman,* and Michael Henry Schwerner* in Neshoba County was the most tragic event that occurred that summer. The most spectacular result of the project was the organization of the Mississippi Freedom Democratic Party* and the challenge this group made to the seating of the regular Democratic delegates to the National Democratic convention in 1964. COFO disbanded soon after the summer project ended.

SELECTED BIBLIOGRAPHY
Clayborne Carson, *In Struggle: SNCC and the Black Awakening of the 1960s* (1981); August Meier and Elliot Rudwick, eds., *Black Protest in the Sixties* (1970); August Meier and Elliot Rudwick, *CORE: A Study in the Civil Rights Movement, 1942–1968* (1973); Benjamin Muse, *The American Negro Revolution: From Nonviolence to Black Power, 1963–1967* (1968); Howell Raines, *My Soul Is Rested: Movement Days in the Deep South Remembered* (1977).

Arvarh E. Strickland

COX v. LOUISIANA, 379 U.S. 559 (1965). This U.S. Supreme Court case helped define the limits of state regulation of First Amendment rights. B. Elton Cox was conducting an officially sanctioned student demonstration in Baton Rouge when he was arrested for violating a Louisiana law prohibiting protests near courthouses. His subsequent conviction in district court in East Baton Rouge Parish was upheld by the Louisiana Supreme Court. The U.S. Supreme Court reversed Cox's conviction. It noted that the Louisiana statute prohibiting demonstrations near courthouses was not itself unconstitutional; the state's interest in safeguarding its judicial system renders such picketing and protesting subject to regulation. Yet in this case, where the defendant had in effect received permission from officials of the city government to demonstrate in a specified area across the street from the courthouse, the application of the regulation violated Fourteenth Amendment* due process guarantees. Prosecution of the defendant once he had received official permission to conduct a peaceful protest was tantamount to entrapment. Citizens had to know the restrictions on peaceful protest; otherwise, the breadth of regulatory power would stifle First Amendment freedoms, which "need breathing space to survive."

SELECTED BIBLIOGRAPHY
Derrick A. Bell, Jr., *Race, Racism and American Law* (1980); Morroe Berger, *Equality by Statute: The Revolution in Civil Rights* (1968); Thomas I. Emerson et al., *Political and Civil Rights in the United States* (1967); *New York Times*, 19 January 1965; George Rossman, ed., "Review of Recent Supreme Court Decisions," *American Bar Association Journal* 51 (1965), 369–70.

Robert A. Calvert

CRISIS. The journal of the NAACP,* the *Crisis* was first published in November 1910. Its founder and first editor was W.E.B. Du Bois,* who served in that office until 1934 when he resigned over differences with NAACP leadership. The *Crisis* set out to be "A Record of the Darker Races." It has served as a vehicle for the dissemination of information by and about African Americans, "to set forth those facts and arguments which show the danger of race prejudice." Throughout its history, regular columns, including "Along the Color Line" and later "Along the NAACP Battlefront," have documented developments relating to race or racism as well as the activities of the NAACP. The artwork, poetry, stories, and photographs of both prominent and newly emerging black artists are highlighted in its pages. Every important issue of interest to the black community has been discussed in both its editorials and feature articles including nationalism, integration, voluntary segregation, protest strategies, the black press, education, and examples of racism. The journal also covers events or individuals of interest to the community and reviews new music and literature. It is published monthly.

SELECTED BIBLIOGRAPHY

Crisis, November 1910–present, particularly Kenneth Jones, "Seventy-Five Years on the Cutting Edge," Crisis 92 (December 1985), 16–28, 30, 34, 62; NAACP Papers, Manuscript Division, Library of Congress; Elliot M. Rudwick, W.E.B. DuBois, Propagandist of the Negro Protest (1968).

Cheryl Greenberg

CROW, JIM. See Jim Crow.

CRUMMELL, ALEXANDER (c. 1819, New York, N.Y.–10 September 1898, Point Pleasant, N.J.). A religious leader, intellectual, nationalist, pan-Africanist, and integrationist, Crummell received his secondary education in New York and New Hampshire. Having been denied admission to the General Theological Seminary of the Episcopal Church in 1839 because he was black, Crummell decided to attend Queen's College in England, where he earned his A.B. degree in 1853. Following his graduation, Crummell went to Liberia, West Africa, where he served as a missionary for twenty years. Crummell's return to the land of his ancestors was a manifestation of the Pan-African movement.* But Crummell was not only a Pan-Africanist, he was also an African-American nationalist. After his return to America in 1873, he told blacks that they would be treated with respect if they improved their spiritual and material well-being. Crummell founded the American Negro Academy* in 1897; its primary goal was to help blacks acquire mainstream American values that would win them respectability. In this sense, Crummell was also an integrationist like most of his contemporaries.

SELECTED BIBLIOGRAPHY

Alexander Crummell, Africa and America, Addresses and Discourses (1891); Floyd Miller, The Search for a Nationality: Black Emigration and Colonization, 1787–1863 (1975); Wilson J. Moses, Alexander Crummell: A Study of Civilization and Discontent (1989); Wilson J. Moses, The Golden Age of Black Nationalism 1850–1925 (1978).

Amos J. Beyan

THE CRUSADER. Launched in 1918, by Cyril Briggs (1888–1966), this New York–based monthly magazine called for a separate African-American nation within the United States, an "Africa for Africans," and the defeat of the imperialist League of Nations. The publication, supported by African-American socialists, journalists, businessmen, and entertainers, operated as the publicity organ of the Hamitic League of the World (1919–1920) and the African Blood Brotherhood* (1920–1921). It ceased to exist in 1922. If one of the most significant features of post–World War I revolution was the emergence of African-American radicalism, then one of the most important documents of the phenomenon was *The Crusader*.

SELECTED BIBLIOGRAPHY

Robert L. Allen, *Reluctant Reformers* (1974); Philip S. Foner and James Allen, eds., *American Communism and Black Americans* (1986); Robert A. Hill, ed., *The Crusader* (1987).

Aingred G. Dunston

CULLEN, COUNTEE (30 May 1903, Louisville, Ky.–9 January 1946, New York, N.Y.). Like many of his contemporaries, Cullen was preoccupied more with the problems of art than sociopolitical issues. Cullen believed that success in art would dispel notions about black inferiority and would thus ameliorate the American dilemma. Cullen possessed what W.E.B. Du Bois* called the "double consciousness" of being at once American and something apart. This ambivalence about identity led him to write in the foreword to his anthology *Caroling Dusk* (1927) that "Negro poets, dependent as they are on the English language, may have more to gain from the rich background of English and American poetry than from any nebulous atavistic yearnings toward an African inheritance." Cullen had gained recognition as a talented poet before he graduated Phi Beta Kappa from New York University in 1925. The following year he earned an M.A. degree from Harvard University. His first collection of poems, *Color* (1925), secured his place as a leading poet of the Harlem Renaissance.* He served as assistant editor of *Opportunity*,* the official journal of the National Urban League* (1926–1928), and he won a Guggenheim Fellowship in 1928. He published two books of poetry in 1927, *Copper Sun* and *The Ballad of the Brown Girl*. These were followed by *The Black Christ and Other Poems* (1929), the novel *One Way to Heaven* (1932), *The Medea and Some Poems* (1935), two children's books, *The Lost Zoo* (1940) and *My Lives and How I Lost Them* (1942), and the posthumously published selection of his best poems, *On These I Stand* (1947).

SELECTED BIBLIOGRAPHY

Houston A. Baker, Jr., *A Many-colored Coat of Dreams: The Poetry of Countee Cullen* (1947); Blanche E. Ferguson, *Countee Cullen and the Negro Renaissance* (1966); Margaret Perry, *A Bio-Bibliography of Countee Cullen* (1971); Alan R. Shucard, *Countee Cullen* (1984).

Jerry Ward

CUMMING v. RICHMOND COUNTY BOARD OF EDUCATION, 175 U.S. 528 (1899). *Cumming* was the first case to apply the separate-but-equal* doctrine to education, and it demonstrated that separation would be enforced more vigorously than equality. Richmond County, Georgia, maintained separate high schools for whites and blacks. Enrollments in the black primary schools exceeded their capacity. The school board addressed the problem by converting the black high school into an elementary school, thus leaving sixty black high school students without a school to attend. Several black parents went to court seeking a prohibition against operating the white high schools until secondary education was made available to blacks as well. The trial court granted their request but suspended the order until the Georgia Supreme Court could hear the case. The Georgia Supreme Court reversed the decision, and the black parents appealed to the United States Supreme Court. A unanimous Supreme Court, speaking through Justice John Marshall Harlan,* the lone dissenter in *Plessy v. Ferguson*,* accepted the county's argument that it could not afford to maintain a high school for black students and rejected the sought-after remedy. Not providing any high school, ruled the Court, was not appropriate because the black students would not benefit. Richmond County continued to provide high schools for whites but not for blacks.

SELECTED BIBLIOGRAPHY

Richard Bardolph, ed., *The Civil Rights Record: Black Americans and the Law, 1849–1970* (1970); "Recent Cases," *Yale Law Journal* 9 (1900), 235; Mark V. Tushnet, *The NAACP's Legal Strategy against Segregated Education, 1925–1950* (1987).

Michael S. Mayer

CUNEY, NORRIS WRIGHT (1846, Sunnyside Plantation, near Hempstead,Tex.–1896, Galveston, Tex.). One of the most powerful African-American politicians of the post–Reconstruction era, Cuney was one of eight children born to white planter Colonel Philip Cuney and his slave Adeline Stuart. In 1856, Colonel Cuney sent Norris and two brothers to Wylie Street School in Pittsburg, Pennsylvania. They might have attended Oberlin College, but the Civil War disrupted their financial support. After the war, Norris Cuney settled in Galveston, Texas, where he became interested in politics. In 1870 black carpetbagger George T. Ruby helped secure his appointment as first assistant to the Twelfth Legislature's sergeant at arms. Subsequently, Cuney became affiliated with the E. J. Davis wing of the Republican party. His career advanced steadily after that. He was inspector of customs, 1872–1877; collector of customs, 1889–1893; secretary of the Republican State Executive Committee, 1874; delegate to the Republican national convention, 1896; and alderman in Galveston, 1881–1883. Cuney's rise to power reflected the strength of the black vote, which he was said to control by 1884. Conversely, the lily-white political movement in Texas contributed to his decline.

SELECTED BIBLIOGRAPHY

Maud Cuney-Hare, *Norris Wright Cuney: A Tribune of the Black People* (1913);

Virginia Neal Hinze, "Norris Wright Cuney" (Master's thesis, Rice University, 1965); Lawrence Rice, *The Negro in Texas, 1874–1900* (1971).

Judith N. Kerr

CUNEY, WILLIAM WARING (6 May 1906, Washington, D.C.–30 June 1976, Washington, D.C.). This Harlem Renaissance* poet was the son of Norris Cuney II and Madge Baker Cuney. He attended Howard University* and Lincoln University, where he became a friend of Langston Hughes.* He studied music at the New England Conservatory of Music, in Boston, Massachusetts, and at the Conservatory, in Rome, Italy. In 1926, *Opportunity** awarded him first prize for "No Images," a poem capturing the militancy of the Harlem Renaissance. Reflecting the rhythm of urban life, it is his most anthologized work. Cuney authored several poetry collections—*Chain Gang* (1930), *Puzzles* (1960), and *Storefront Church* (1973)—a number of broadsides, and songs. "Southern Exposure" and "Hard Times Blues," for example, were created for balladeer and protest singer Josh White.

SELECTED BIBLIOGRAPHY

Black World 20 (November 1970), 20–36, 52–58; Arna Bontemps, *The Harlem Renaissance Remembered* (1972); Trudier Harris, ed., *Afro-American Writers from the Harlem Renaissance to 1940*, vol. 51 (1986); Linda Metzger et al., *Black Writers: A Selection of Sketches from Contemporary Authors* (1988).

Judith N. Kerr

D

DAHMER, VERNON FERDINAND (10 March 1908, Hattiesburg, Miss.–10 January 1966, Hattiesburg, Miss.). Vernon Dahmer, merchant, farmer, and sawmill owner, was a leading member of the black community in Hattiesburg, Mississippi. By the mid-1960s, commensurate with his local status, Dahmer was taking an active role locally in the civil rights drive. Passage of the Voting Rights Act of 1965* precipitated problems in previously quiet Forrest County. Dahmer urged blacks to vote; he even offered to pay their poll taxes.* Not long thereafter, early on the morning of 10 January 1966, Klansmen fire-bombed his home. Family members escaped the blaze that consumed his residence and nearby store while Dahmer fired after the assailants. The fifty-eight-year-old Dahmer, suffering from facial burns and smoke inhalation, was rushed to the local hospital where he soon died. Speaking from his hospital bed, Dahmer reasoned, "I figure a man needs to do his own thinking." The *Hattiesburg American* condemned the act as "a revolting, cowardly crime." President Lyndon B. Johnson telegraphed his condolences and ordered a federal investigation which resulted in the arrest of fourteen Klansmen who were charged with arson and the murder of Vernon Dahmer.

SELECTED BIBLIOGRAPHY
Sara Bullard, ed., *Free at Last* (1989); *Hattiesburg American*, 10–12 January 1966; *Jackson Clarion-Ledger*, 11 January 1966.

William Warren Rogers, Jr.

DANIEL AND KYLES v. PAUL, 395 U.S. 298 (1969). The Civil Rights Act of 1964* banned racial discrimination in a wide range of areas. Under its authority to regulate interstate commerce, Congress, in Title II of the act, specifically prohibited racial bias in public accommodations. Many white businesses, however, sought to evade the act's restrictions by claiming status as private clubs. The Lake Nixon Club, a privately owned recreation center with swimming, boating, dancing, and a snack bar near Little Rock, Arkansas, routinely admitted whites but excluded blacks. The Pauls, the owners of the club, claimed that their establishment was not a public accommodation covered under Title II of the act. The plaintiffs, Daniel and Kyles, maintained that the snack bar, which was located on the club's premises, brought the recreation center within the coverage of Title II. The Supreme Court agreed with Daniel and Kyles. The fact that the snack bar both served interstate travelers and sold food and drink that had moved in interstate commerce brought the entire Lake Nixon facility within the provisions of Title II. The Court's ruling, consequently, extended the power of the federal government to prevent private discrimination.

SELECTED BIBLIOGRAPHY

Derrick A. Bell, Jr., *Race, Racism and American Law* (1980); Alfred H. Kelly and Winfred A. Harbison, *The American Constitution: Its Origins and Development*, 5th ed. (1976).

Phillip A. Gibbs

DANIELS, JONATHAN MYRICK (20 March 1939, Keene, N.H.–20 August 1965, Hayneville, Ala.). After graduating from the Virginia Military Institute in 1961 and studying English for a year at Harvard University on a Woodrow Wilson Fellowship, Jon Daniels entered the Episcopal Theological School in Cambridge, Massachusetts. He joined a dozen others from the theological school who responded to Martin Luther King, Jr.'s* call for clergy to join a voter registration drive in Selma, Alabama. After the Selma to Montgomery March,* Daniels continued his Christian witness in Selma under the auspices of the Episcopal Society for Cultural and Racial Unity.* He lived in the black community, worked in voter registration, integrated the local Episcopal church, and publicized the social services available to blacks. In August Daniels began working with the Student Nonviolent Coordinating Committee* in adjacent Lowndes County. He was one of two whites arrested with two dozen blacks on 14 August for demonstrating in Fort Deposit. After six days in jail in Hayneville, they were all suddenly released. When Daniels, the Reverend Richard Morrisroe (a white Catholic from Chicago), and two young black women approached a store to buy soft drinks, Tom L. Coleman ordered them away. When Daniels questioned the middle-aged local white man, Coleman shot and killed Daniels instantly, then wounded Morrisroe. Six weeks later an all-white Lowndes jury found Coleman not guilty for reason of self-defense. In 1979 Daniels was honored as one of the twelve representative martyrs listed in Canterbury Cathedral's Chapel of Saints and Martyrs of Our Own Time.

SELECTED BIBLIOGRAPHY
Marshall Frady, "A Death in Lowndes County," in *Southerners: A Journalist's Odyssey* (1980); Jack Mendelsohn, *The Martyrs: Sixteen Who Gave Their Lives for Racial Justice* (1966); William J. Schneider, ed., *The John Daniels Story, with His Letters and Papers* (1967).

Charles W. Eagles

DANIELS, JONATHAN WORTH (26 April 1902, Raleigh, N.C.–6 November 1981, Raleigh, N.C.). Writer and newspaperman, he edited the family paper, the Raleigh *News and Observer*, from 1933 to the mid-1960s, except for 1941 to 1948 when his father, Josephus Daniels, resumed control. Partly because of his racial views, Daniels became known as a southern liberal. In the 1930s he advocated equal treatment for blacks, but he did not challenge segregation. By the late 1930s he called for equal treatment without regard to race. During World War II, he served as President Franklin D. Roosevelt's assistant in charge of monitoring domestic race relations. In the late 1940s Daniels supported many of President Harry Truman's racial policies, opposed the Dixiecrats, and served on the United Nations Subcommission for the Prevention of Discrimination and the Protection of Minorities. After the *Brown v. Board of Education** decision, Daniels advocated compliance through voluntary segregation of "free choice schools," but he also condemned proposals to close the public schools, denounced interposition and massive resistance, and criticized white supremacist groups. Though he opposed poll taxes,* unequal protection of the law, and discriminatory health care and housing, he preferred moderate, informal compromises instead of disruptive confrontations and demonstrations. He endorsed the Civil Rights Act of 1964* and the Voting Rights Act of 1965,* but he maintained that economic advancement remained the key to black progress.

SELECTED BIBLIOGRAPHY
Jonathan Daniels Papers, Southern Historical Collection, University of North Carolina, Chapel Hill; Charles W. Eagles, *Jonathan Daniels and Race Relations: The Evolution of a Southern Liberal* (1982).

Charles W. Eagles

DAVIS, ANGELA (26 January 1944, Birmingham, Ala.–). Born in a city particularly known for steel and racial violence, in a segregated middle-class neighborhood called "Dynamite Hill," Davis graduated magna cum laude from Brandeis University in 1965 and received her master's and doctoral degrees from the University of California at San Diego several years later. In California she worked with the Student Nonviolent Coordinating Committee,* the Black Panthers,* and the Communist party,* which she joined in 1968.

While completing her dissertation, Davis served as an instructor at the University of California at Los Angeles. The California board of regents declined to renew her contract, and she was dropped from the staff when Federal Bureau of Investigation leaks identified her as a member of the Communist party. UCLA objected to her speeches in support of the Soledad brothers. In 1970 Davis became involved in an alleged kidnapping attempt of three San Quentin prisoners from the Marin County Civic Center. Accused of planning the incident and supplying the gun that killed four people during the incident, Davis was charged with murder, kidnapping, and conspiracy and eventually was incarcerated. In 1972, however, after sixteen months in jail, she was acquitted of the charges, after only thirteen hours of deliberations by the jurors. Davis has since spent much of her time traveling to the Soviet Union and several other Communist countries. In the United States, she lectures on long-range goals that affect blacks and all working people.

SELECTED BIBLIOGRAPHY

Angela Davis, *Angela Davis: An Autobiography* (1974); Angela Davis, *If They Come in the Morning: Voices of Resistance* (1971); Angela Davis, *Lectures on Liberation* (1972); Regina Nadelson, *Who Is Angela Davis? The Biography of a Revolutionary* (1972); J. A. Parker, *Angela Davis: The Making of a Revolutionary* (1973).

Linda Reed

DAVIS, BENJAMIN O., SR. (28 May 1880, Washington, D.C.–26 November 1970, Chicago, Ill.). In 1898 Davis joined the army and in 1940 he became the first African American promoted to the rank of brigadier general. As a member of the Inspector General's Office during World War II, he grappled with the problems in the United States and Europe caused by segregation and discrimination. Despite Davis's abhorrence of racial separation, his low-key approach led some blacks to charge that he was ineffective and too conciliatory. One of his accomplishments was the partial integration of combat units in Germany and France. Until his retirement in 1948, he continued to act as a military adviser on race relations.

SELECTED BIBLIOGRAPHY

Marvin E. Fletcher, *America's First Black General* (1989); Ulysses Lee, *The Employment of Negro Troops* (1966).

Marvin E. Fletcher

DAVIS et al. v. SCHNELL et al., 81 F. Supp. 872 (S.D. Ala., 1949). *Davis v. Schnell* struck down the Boswell Amendment* to the Alabama state constitution. The 1944 Supreme Court ruling outlawing the white primary* alarmed many of Alabama's conservative white Democrats. To prevent increased black voter registration, state representative E. C. Bos-

General Benjamin Davis, Sr., reviews plans with General Patton (WWII). (Negro Almanac Collection, Amistad Research Center, Tulane University, New Orleans.)

well in 1946 sponsored a state constitutional amendment to require that voter applicants be able to "understand and explain" any article of the U.S. Constitution. Hunter Davis and other black Mobile residents who had been refused voter registration filed a federal suit against the Mobile County Board of Registrars, including Milton Schnell. The decision in *Davis v. Schnell*, written by District Judge Clarence Mullins, found that the Boswell Amendment gave local boards "arbitrary power to accept or reject any prospective elector." The Mobile registrars had routinely rejected black applicants who could not fulfill the requirements of the Boswell Amendment, but the same requirement was not made of most white applicants. E. J. Gonzales, one of the Mobile registrars, had confirmed this in testimony before the court. The court held that this practice violated the Fifteenth Amendment* to the U.S. Constitution, and it also cited Democratic party propaganda and newspaper editorials published before the general election as proof that the amendment's sponsors, and the voters of Alabama, understood that the purpose of the Boswell Amendment was to limit black suffrage.

SELECTED BIBLIOGRAPHY

William D. Barnard, *Dixiecrats and Democrats: Alabama Politics, 1942–1950* (1974);

Steven F. Lawson, *Black Ballots: Voting Rights in the South, 1944–1969* (1976); "Recent Cases," *Vanderbilt Law Review* 2 (1949), 696–98.

James L. Baggett

DAVIS, JOHN P. (1905–12 September 1973, New York City, N.Y.). Trained at Harvard Law School where he knew Robert C. Weaver,* William H. Hastie,* and Ralph J. Bunche,* Davis was a major spokesperson for black civil rights and black and white working-class alliances during the 1930s and early 1940s. With Weaver, Davis established the Negro Industrial League in 1933 to argue the cause of black workers and farmers before congressional hearings then debating proposed New Deal reform and recovery measures. With financial backing from the NAACP* and the Rosenwald Fund,* Davis and Weaver established an umbrella organization of black rights groups called the Joint Committee on National Recovery,* which sought support for black needs within and outside the Roosevelt administration. After Weaver joined the New Deal, Davis became the joint committee's chief organizer, researcher, and spokesperson.

After the joint committee lost the support of the NAACP and Rosenwald, Davis turned to a grass-roots black movement allied with progressive white and labor groups. Following the Howard University conference of 1935, organized with Ralph Bunche, which critically assessed the New Deal's impact on the black American, a National Negro Congress* (NNC) was formed with A. Philip Randolph* as president and Davis as executive secretary. By constructing a coalition of national and local black groups, left-wing political parties, and organized labor, the NNC hoped to build an independent movement and force greater social and economic reforms from the New Deal. Davis was never successful in his efforts because the NNC was later dominated by the Communist party* and certain Congress of Industrial Organization unions and lost the support of both Bunche and Randolph. In the early 1940s, Davis left the NNC and became a political writer for the *Pittsburgh Courier.** A tireless organizer, Davis's efforts to build an independent political base for black protest in the 1930s provided an important precedent for the later civil rights struggles.

SELECTED BIBLIOGRAPHY

Robert H. Brisbane, *The Black Vanguard: Origins of the Negro Social Revolution, 1900–1970* (1970); John B. Kirby, *Black Americans in the Roosevelt Era* (1980); John Baxter Streater, "The National Negro Congress" (Ph.D. diss., University of Cincinnati, 1981); Raymond Wolters, *Negroes and the Great Depression* (1970).

John B. Kirby

DAVIS, (WILLIAM) ALLISON (14 October 1902, Washington, D.C.– 21 November 1983, Chicago, Ill.). A social anthropologist, Davis's most influential work, *Deep South* (1941) was the first comprehensive analysis of caste, class, and race relations in a southern town. A graduate of Williams College, in Williamstown, Massachusetts, and Harvard University, Davis received a Ph.D. from the University of Chicago in 1942 where he was a member of the Department of Education from 1939 until his death. One of the first blacks to become a tenured professor at the university, Davis was named John Dewey Distinguished Service Professor in 1970. Davis was an early critic of the effect of I.Q. tests on educational opportunities for low-income children, and he also studied the psychological effects of segregation on blacks. He was a member of the president's Civil Rights Commission,* 1966–1967.

SELECTED BIBLIOGRAPHY
Allison Davis, *Leadership, Love, and Aggression* (1983); Allison Davis, *Social-Class Influences upon Learning* (1948); Allison Davis and John Dollard, *The Children of Bondage: The Personality Development of Negro Youth in the Urban South* (1940); St. Clair Drake, "In the Mirror of Black Scholarship: W. Allison Davis and *Deep South*," *Harvard Educational Review* 2 (1974), 42–54.

Francille Rusan Wilson

DEACONS FOR DEFENSE. Based in Louisiana, the Deacons for Defense advocated self-defense in the face of white supremacist aggression and violence. Over the vehement objections of Martin Luther King, Jr.,* the Deacons were an armed presence during the 1966 James Meredith march.* At the invitation of the Student Nonviolent Coordinating Committee* and the Congress of Racial Equality,* armed Deacons patrolled the sides of the highway along which demonstrators were to pass, making certain that no snipers were in hiding. Fashioned as a vigilante organization, the Deacons sought to protect themselves and other African Americans because they believed that southern law enforcement neither could nor would do that on their behalf.

SELECTED BIBLIOGRAPHY
Clayborne Carson, *In Struggle: SNCC and the Black Awakening of the 1960s* (1981); Vincent Harding, "Black Radicalism: The Road from Montgomery," in Alfred F. Young, ed., *Dissent: Explorations in the History of American Radicalism* (1968); Stephen B. Oates, *Let the Trumpet Sound: The Life of Martin Luther King, Jr.* (1982); Harvard Sitkoff, *The Struggle for Black Equality, 1954–1980* (1981); Milton Viorst, *Fire in the Streets: America in the 1960s* (1979); Robert L. Zangrando, "From Civil Rights to Black Liberation: The Unsettled 1960s," *Current History* 57 (November 1969), 281–86, 299.

Marshall Hyatt

DE FACTO SEGREGATION. This term refers to segregation that existed without the sanction of law. Constitutional provisions and laws in the South required segregation, and this legal segregation was called de jure segregation. In the North, segregation existed even though there were no laws requiring it and often in spite of civil rights laws prohibiting discrimination and inequality of treatment. De facto segregation resulted from custom, policies of real estate firms, actions of school officials and school boards, governmental policies, and the actions of private persons and groups. Civil rights organizations often found it more difficult to fight segregation in the North than in the South. The Congress of Racial Equality* began as a movement to end segregation in the North. Long legal battles led to court decisions outlawing racially restrictive covenants in housing, and civil rights groups urged changes in those federal housing policies that promoted segregated housing developments. The most bitter struggle was the continuing one to end de facto segregation in schools. This campaign received stimulation from the 1961 ruling of a federal district court in a case involving segregation in the schools of New Rochelle, New York. The judge held that segregation resulting from the action of school boards was as unconstitutional as that resulting from laws creating a dual school system.

SELECTED BIBLIOGRAPHY
Richard Bardolph, ed., *The Civil Rights Record: Black Americans and the Law, 1849–1970* (1970); John Hope Franklin and Alfred A. Moss, Jr., eds., *From Slavery to Freedom: A History of Negro Americans* (1988); Gunnar Myrdal, *An American Dilemma: The Negro Problem and Modern Democracy* (1944).

Arvarh E. Strickland

DELANY, MARTIN ROBINSON (6 May 1812, Charles Town, Va.–January 1885, Wilberforce, Ohio). Born in what is now West Virginia, Martin R. Delany became an advocate for black self-reliance and uplift through education, skilled labor, property ownership, and entrepreneurship. He championed the cause of black freedom and equality as an abolitionist, a journalist, a Union Army major and recruiter of black troops during the Civil War, and an important member of the Republican party in South Carolina Reconstruction politics. Best known for his claim that African Americans constituted "a nation within a nation," he advocated the establishment of an African-American nation in Africa as the cornerstone for the freedom and elevation of black people. Although the masses of black people never adopted his elitist ideas for racial uplift and his campaign for African emigration, future generations used Delany's philosophies as the foundation for the contemporary black nationalist ideology.

SELECTED BIBLIOGRAPHY
Martin R. Delany, *The Condition, Elevation, Emigration and Destiny of the Colored People of the United States* (1852); Cyril F. Griffith, *The African Dream: Martin R. Delany and the Emergence of Pan-African Thought* (1975); Floyd J. Miller, *The Search for a Black Nationality: Black Emigration and Colonization, 1787–1863* (1975); Wilson J. Moses, *The Golden Age of Black Nationalism 1850–1925* (1978); Nell Irvin Painter, "Martin R. Delany: Elitism and Black Nationalism," in Leon Litwack and August Meier, eds., *Black Leaders of the Nineteenth Century* (1988); Frank A. Rollin, *Life*

and Public Services of Martin R. Delany (1883); Victor Ullman, *Martin R. Delany: The Beginnings of Black Nationalism* (1971).

Lillie Johnson Edwards

"DELIBERATE SPEED." When the U.S. Supreme Court ruled segregation unconstitutional in *Brown v. Board of Education** on 17 May 1954, it did not order immediate relief. On 31 May 1955, the Court handed down its ruling on implementation, known as *Brown II*. In that decision, the Supreme Court remanded the cases to the lower courts with instructions that school districts "make a prompt and reasonable start toward full compliance with our May 17, 1954 ruling" and that the lower courts "enter such orders and decrees consistent with this opinion as are necessary and proper to admit to public schools on a racially non-discriminatory basis with all deliberate speed the parties to these cases." The phrase "all deliberate speed" was added at Felix Frankfurter's suggestion; its origin remains obscure. Southerners took the phrase as an invitation to obstruction, and it became the basis for a generation of litigation.

SELECTED BIBLIOGRAPHY
Daniel M. Berman, *It Is So Ordered* (1966); Alexander Bickel, "Integration, the Second Year in Perspective," *New Republic* (8 October 1956); Jack Greenberg, *Race Relations and American Law* (1959); Dennis J. Hutchinson, "Unanimity and Desegregation: Decisionmaking and the Supreme Court, 1948–1958," 68 *Georgetown Law Journal* 1 (1979); Richard Kluger, *Simple Justice: The History of Brown versus Board of Education and America's Struggle for Equality* (1976).

Michael S. Mayer

DELTA MINISTRY. An outgrowth of the National Council of Churches' involvement in the Freedom Summer of 1964* in Mississippi, the Delta Ministry was organized in September 1964 with the dual goals of reconciling the black and white communities and ameliorating economic, health, and social conditions among Mississippi blacks. The Delta Ministry established community centers for day care, recreation, and education; provided health education in hygiene, nutrition, first aid, and other areas through local health committees; created programs for literacy, vocational training, and liberal arts studies; instituted workshops to teach basic constitutional rights and to train black political candidates; and organized community Head Start* programs and government surplus food distributions despite state government opposition. The ministry supported striking plantation workers, organized picketers against companies guilty of job discrimination, and filed allegations of noncompliance with antidiscrimination clauses against plants with government contracts. A center of controversy during its twenty-year existence, the Delta Ministry is an example of the mobilization of the liberal church in support of civil rights; it was the first civil rights or church project in the United States to receive funds from foreign countries as a foreign mission.

SELECTED BIBLIOGRAPHY

Eric D. Blanchard, "The Delta Ministry," *The Christian Century* (17 March 1965), 337–38; Bruce Hilton, *The Delta Ministry* (1969); Henry J. Pratt, *The Liberalization of American Protestantism: A Case Study in Complex Organizations* (1972); Mary Aickin Rothschild, *A Case of Black and White: Northern Volunteers and the Southern Freedom Summers, 1964–65* (1982); Wilmina Rowland, "How It Is in Mississippi," *The Christian Century* (17 March 1965), 340–42.

Carole Shelton

DENNIS, DAVID (17 October 1940, Omega, La.–). A sharecropper's son, Dennis joined the New Orleans Congress of Racial Equality* (CORE) in 1960 while attending Dillard University. He immediately began to organize new CORE chapters and projects in Louisiana. As CORE representative in Mississippi, he was instrumental in the founding of the Council of Federated Organizations* (COFO), along with Aaron Henry,* of the Mississippi NAACP,* James Forman,* of the Student Nonviolent Coordinating Committee* (SNCC) national office; and Robert Moses,* of the Mississippi SNCC. Setting up a CORE chapter in Canton, Mississippi, Dennis worked to organize demonstrations there and to help launch the Mississippi Freedom Democratic party's* challenge to the regular state Democrats in 1964. In September 1964, he became CORE's Southern Regional Office program director.

SELECTED BIBLIOGRAPHY

Taylor Branch, *Parting the Waters: America in the King Years, 1954–1963* (1988); James Forman, *The Making of Black Revolutionaries* (1985); August Meier and Elliott Rudwick, *CORE: A Study in the Civil Rights Movement, 1942–1968* (1973).

Ray Branch

DEPARTMENT OF RACIAL AND CULTURAL RELATIONS, NATIONAL COUNCIL OF CHURCHES. Organized in 1949 as the council's successor to its Commission on Race Relations, the Department of Racial and Cultural Relations under director J. Oscar Lee was primarily involved in mobilization for civil rights legislation. In January 1963, working with Catholic and Jewish organizations, it helped to sponsor the National Conference on Religion and Race which issued the "Appeal to the Conscience of the American People" on the eradication of racism. When its educational philosophy proved to be too slow to deal with political events, it gave way in strategy to the Commission on Religion and Race, which eventually superseded it and went on to develop such projects as the Delta Ministry.*

SELECTED BIBLIOGRAPHY
Henry J. Pratt, *The Liberalization of American Protestantism* (1972); Mark Silk, *Spiritual Politics: Religion and America Since World War II* (1988).

Ray Branch

DePRIEST, OSCAR STANTON (9 March 1871, Florence, Ala.–12 May 1951, Chicago, Ill.). The first African American elected to Congress during the twentieth century and the first ever elected from outside the South, Oscar DePriest championed equal protection of law, especially in employment. Like many he represented, DePriest made his way from southern rural poverty to northern urban opportunity during the Great Migration.* His parents moved from his native Florence, Alabama, To Salina, Kansas, when he was seven years old. He attended public schools and completed a business curriculum at the Salina Normal School. At seventeen he moved to Dayton, Ohio, and then to Chicago, Illinois, where he worked his way up to become a successful real estate agent and a controversial, longtime Republican party ward boss. He served as Cook County commissioner (1904–1908), and in 1915 he became Chicago's first black member of the city council, where he served until 1917 and again from 1943 to 1947. In 1929 he entered the U.S. House of Representatives, where he pressed for blacks to have their share of federal jobs, appointed blacks to the United States Military Academy at

Oscar DePriest. (Library of Congress.)

West Point and the United States Naval Academy at Annapolis, and pushed for a federal antilynching bill. He was unseated by black Democrat Arthur W. Mitchell* in 1934.

SELECTED BIBLIOGRAPHY

Biographical Directory of the American Congress, 1774–1971 (1971); Maurine Christopher, *America's Black Congressmen* (1971); Thomas J. Davis, "Oscar Stanton De-Priest," *Encyclopedia USA* (1991); Harold F. Gosnell, *Negro Politicians: The Rise of Negro Politics in Chicago* (1935); Rayford W. Logan and Michael R. Winston, eds., *Dictionary of American Negro Biography* (1982); Obituary, *New York Times*, 13 May 1951.

Thomas J. Davis

DERRINGTON v. PLUMMER, 240 F.2d 922 (5th Cir., 1957). After the *Civil Rights Cases** of 1883, and before the Civil Rights Act of 1964,* the equal protection clause of the Fourteenth Amendment* provided limited protection against the discriminatory acts of private individuals. In *Derrington* the United States Court of Appeals for the Fifth Judicial Circuit* provided reasoning that allowed the invocation of constitutional protections in cases where the state and the private discriminator were engaged in close, mutually beneficial relationships.

Harris County, Texas, had built a courthouse with a basement specifically designed for use as a cafeteria. The county leased the cafeteria to Derrington who agreed to keep the facilities open whenever the courthouse was open, paid the county a percentage of his gross sales, and promised to give county employees a discount on their food. Derrington routinely refused to serve blacks in the cafeteria "solely because they were negroes." A group of blacks sued in federal court claiming that they had been denied equal protection of the law. The county and Derrington argued that the Fourteenth Amendment only prohibited discrimination that arose from state action and that the cafeteria restrictions constituted permissible, individual action.

The court of appeals ruled that Derrington could not constitutionally discriminate against blacks; the majority opinion reasoned that the cafeteria had been built with county funds and therefore was serving county purposes. When state purposes are served through the "instrumentality of a lessee," the court explained, the lessee "stands in the place of the County." As a result, "[h]is conduct is as much state action as would be the conduct of the County itself." The *Derrington* rationale provided constitutional protection in those situations in which an individual and the state maintained a close symbiotic relationship and in which the private individual was acting in the interest of the state.

SELECTED BIBLIOGRAPHY

Charles Black, "Forward: 'State Action,' Equal Protection, and California's Proposition 14," *Harvard Law Review* 80 (1967), 69–109; William W. Van Alstyne, "Mr.

Justice Black, Constitutional Review and the Talisman of State Action," *Duke Law Journal* (1965), 219–47.

Kenneth DeVille

DETROIT RACE RIOT (1943). The worst riot to take place during World War II began in Detroit, Michigan, on 20 June and raged for forty-eight hours; its toll in lives and property set national records. The Detroit outbreak manifested black-white strains wrought by historical, perennial, and, most significantly, wartime circumstances. A heritage of interracial violence plagued the city, as did employment discrimination and slum conditions which confined most blacks to the eastside ghetto, known as Paradise Valley. Two hundred thousand in-migrants of both races, particularly from the South, compounded the usual antagonisms. The competition and rising expectations clashed several times, primarily in the spring of 1943 when 35,000 black newcomers joined black natives in their "Double V" protest for democratic victories at home and abroad.

The riot began on Belle Isle, spread quickly to the ghetto, and then reached the city's major thoroughfare: Woodward Avenue. At Belle Isle Park, black youth harassed white picnickers who, with the aid of numerous sailors, fought back. Paradise Valley residents attacked white bypassers, white policemen, and white-owned stores, which they ultimately looted. Soon whites along Woodward Avenue beat black citizens and laid siege to the black community (which police repulsed). The Belle Isle and Woodward Avenue clashes were typical of interracial combat or communal riots of earlier eras. Whites fought with police support to uphold the very system challenged by blacks; indeed, Detroit police killed seventeen blacks but no whites. The Paradise Valley destruction resulted from the anger and frustration of blacks, who struck at the symbols of their degradation and whites who lived beyond the riot zone. Both races employed violence as protest.

Signaling the decline of communal outbursts and the emergence of commodity uprisings, the Detroit riot pointed to shifting patterns of racial disorder and future conflicts whenever whites blocked opportunities and blacks sensed the failure of nonviolent strategies. It also resulted in the creation of the Mayor's Interracial Committee, the first permanent municipal body designed to ease tensions and promote civil rights. Unfortunately, these efforts fell short in Detroit—and elsewhere—and large-scale rioting recurred in the 1960s.

SELECTED BIBLIOGRAPHY

Dominic J. Capeci, Jr., *Race Relations in Wartime Detroit: The Sojourner Truth Housing Controversy of 1942* (1984); Dominic J. Capeci, Jr., and Martha Wilkerson, "The Detroit Rioters of 1943: A Reinterpretation," *Michigan Historical Review* 16 (Spring 1990), 49–72; Alfred M. Lee and Norman D. Humphrey, *Race Riot* (1943, 1968); Robert Shogan and Thomas Craig, *The Detroit Race Riot: A Study in Violence* (1964, 1976); Harvard Sitkoff, "The Detroit Race Riot of 1943," *Michigan History*

53 (Fall 1969), 183–206; Walter White and Thurgood Marshall, *What Caused the Detroit Riot?* (1943).

Dominic J. Capeci, Jr.

DETROIT RACE RIOT (1967). On 23 July 1967, the Detroit, Michigan, police raided an afterhours club on Twelfth Street in the center of the African-American ghetto. The club was crowded with celebrants, and it took the police longer than usual to clear the premises of the revelers and to arrest them. Onlookers threw bottles and broke out the windows of the police vehicle. The riot that erupted that Sunday morning lasted until the following Thursday. Of the fifty-nine urban riots that occurred in 1967, the one in Detroit took the most lives, forty-three people, mostly blacks shot by the National Guard, and caused the most property damage. Most white Americans were shocked by the Detroit riot. Mayor Jerome P. Cavanagh, a Democrat, had instituted model programs in urban renewal and in poverty programs. Nevertheless tensions between the black community and the police had been increasing, exacerbated by a recall petition led by conservatives to remove Cavanagh from office for his alleged failure to fight crime. When the tensions exploded into a riot, Republican Governor George Romney sent in the National Guard, but the 700 guardsman, 200 state police, and 600 Detroit policemen could not restore order. President Lyndon B. Johnson reluctantly ordered into Detroit, on 25 July, 4,700 troops of the elite 82nd and 101st Airborne units. Some Republicans criticized Johnson, asserting that he had delayed sending in troops to embarrass Romney, a potential Republican nominee for the presidency. Republicans, including Barry Goldwater, Ronald Reagan, and Richard M. Nixon, cited the riot as an example not only of the lawlessness sweeping the nation because of the refusal of Democrats to be tough on crime but also of a planned insurrection caused by radicals rather than a spontaneous uprising. Johnson denied vehemently all charges. His position has been supported by most historians and by the Kerner Commission* (National Advisory Commission on Civil Disorders), which blamed "white racism" and emphasized needed social reform as the alternative to violence.

SELECTED BIBLIOGRAPHY

Godfrey Hodgson, *America in Our Time* (1976); *New York Times*, 24, 25, 30 July 1967; Harvard Sitkoff, *The Struggle for Black Equality, 1954–1980* (1981).

Robert A. Calvert

DIGGS, CHARLES C., JR. (2 December 1922, Detroit, Mich.–). The youngest member of the Michigan State Senate from 1951 to 1954, he became the first African American elected to represent Michigan in the U.S. Congress. Elected twelve times in Detroit's Thirteenth Congressional District, he became a powerful and respected congressman. He

Aerial photo of 1967 Detroit Riots. Estimates of property damage ranged upward of $100 million in the two days of arson and looting. (UPI/Bettmann.)

and twelve others founded the Congressional Black Caucus* in 1971; he became chairman of the House Committee on the District of Columbia in 1973; he was instrumental in winning home rule for the capital city; and he rose to the chairmanship of the House of Representatives' Subcommittee on African Affairs. After thirty years in public office, his career was interrupted in 1978 when a federal grand jury charged him with using taxpayers' money for personal, business, and office expenses. Censured by the House in July 1979, he resigned in 1980.

SELECTED BIBLIOGRAPHY

Lenore Cooley, *Ralph Nader Congress Project Citizens Look at Congress: Charles Diggs Jr.* (1972); *Detroit Free Press*, 16 May 1976; *Detroit News Magazine*, 22 July 1979.

Clarence Hooker

DIRECT ACTION. Ordinarily associated with the nonviolent ideology espoused by Martin Luther King, Jr.,* direct action actually predated his rise to civil rights leadership. Early protests against segregation in the federal civil service, the "Don't Buy Where You Can't Work" movement* in the depression decade, and the Congress of Racial Equality's* desegregation activities in the 1940s all utilized direct action. The sit-ins of 1960, modeled after similar protests by industrial workers in the 1930s, also employed nonviolent, public demonstration tactics and initiated many new and creative ways of combatting segregation and discrimination. It was King, however, who strove to adapt direct action protest

Black Civil Rights activists engage in direct action in Raleigh, N.C., February 1960. (North Carolina Division of Archives and History.)

to the changing realities of American racism and eventually merged that philosophy into creative tension.

SELECTED BIBLIOGRAPHY
Kenneth B. Clark, "The Civil Rights Movement: Momentum and Organization," in Talcott Parsons and Kenneth B. Clark, eds., *The Negro American* (1966); Adam Fairclough, *To Redeem the Soul of America: The Southern Christian Leadership Conference and Martin Luther King, Jr.* (1987); James Farmer, *Lay Bare the Heart: The Autobiography of the Civil Rights Movement* (1985); David J. Garrow, *Bearing the Cross: Martin Luther King, Jr., and the Southern Christian Leadership Conference* (1986); Martin Luther King, Jr., *Stride toward Freedom: The Montgomery Story* (1958); Martin Luther King, Jr., *Why We Can't Wait* (1963).

Marshall Hyatt

DISTRICT OF COLUMBIA v. JOHN R. THOMPSON COMPANY, 346 U.S. 100 (1953). This case upheld the validity of Washington, D.C.'s "lost" antidiscrimination laws which were passed during Reconstruction. Although they had not been enforced for years, these laws required that restaurants, bars, and similar establishments serve all "respectable, well-behaved" persons and sell to them "at their usual prices." In 1950, Washington's board of commissioners brought suit against a segregated cafeteria owned by the John R. Thompson Restaurant Company. Municipal Judge Frank Myers decided that the laws had been repealed "by implication" and quashed the case. The following year, the municipal court of appeals reversed Myers's ruling on the law regarding prices but upheld his position on the law requiring service. The United States Court of Appeals for the District of Columbia voted to overturn the municipal court of appeals and affirm Myers's decision. Throughout the course of the case, President Harry Truman's attorneys general had declined to become involved. With the case pending before the Supreme Court, the Eisenhower administration filed an amicus curiae brief arguing for the validity of the "lost laws." Attorney General Herbert Brownell argued the case himself. On 8 June 1953, the Supreme Court unanimously sustained the validity of both Reconstruction era ordinances.

SELECTED BIBLIOGRAPHY
Robert Fredrick Burk, *The Eisenhower Administration and Black Civil Rights* (1984); Constance McLaughlin Green, *The Secret City* (1967); Michael S. Mayer, "The Eisenhower Administration and the Desegregation of Washington, D.C.," *Journal of Policy History* 3 (January 1991), 24–41.

Michael S. Mayer

DOAR, JOHN M. (3 December 1921, Minneapolis, Minn.–). A Republican and a graduate of Princeton University and the law school at the University of California, Berkeley, in 1960 Doar became an attorney and in 1965 assistant attorney general in the Civil Rights Section, Justice Department.* He gained the respect of civil rights protesters as a trial lawyer and troubleshooter in the South. Following the murder of Medgar W. Evers* in Jackson, Mississippi, in 1963, Doar helped calm a tense confrontation between angry blacks and hostile whites at the funeral of the civil rights leader. Despite his close association with civil rights workers, Doar maintained that the federal government lacked the constitutional authority to protect them from racist intimidation. He preferred to rely on negotiation and cooperation with state and local officials to obtain compliance with federal law. However, in the face of violent, criminal wrongdoing, he brought federal prosecutions against the murderers of civil rights activists in Mississippi and Alabama. Combining conciliation with pressure, he helped enforce the Voting Rights Act of 1965,* which enfranchised a majority of southern blacks. From 1967 to 1973, he served as director of the Bedford-Stuyvesant Development and Service Corporation in Brooklyn.

SELECTED BIBLIOGRAPHY

Michael R. Belknap, *Federal Law and Southern Order: Racial Violence and Constitutional Conflict in the Post-Brown South* (1987); John Doar, "Civil Rights and Self-Government," in Dona Baron, ed., *The National Purpose Reconsidered* (1978); Steven F. Lawson, *In Pursuit of Power: Southern Blacks and Electoral Politics, 1965–1982* (1985); Victor Navasky, *Kennedy Justice* (1971).

Steven F. Lawson

"DON'T BUY WHERE YOU CAN'T WORK" MOVEMENT. Prominent in the black political revival of the 1930s were numerous organized boycotts and picketing of any white-owned businesses within black communities that had refused to hire black employees. By the early 1930s, what became known as "Don't Buy Where You Can't Work" campaigns existed in many cities. First begun in Chicago, Illinois, in late 1929, the Chicago "Don't Buy" movement had the support of the black newspaper, the *Chicago Whip*, the local NAACP,* and black church groups. Successful in breaking the color line in a number of local industries and securing white-collar jobs for some blacks, the Chicago campaign spread during the early 1930s to New York, Washington, D.C., Cleveland, and Los Angeles, as well as to smaller communities like Evansville, Indiana, and Alliance, Ohio. By the time the movement died out during the war, some thirty-five cities had experienced it. Despite their mixed impact, the "Don't Buy Where You Can't Work" movement sharpened black political consciousness and reflected the ability of blacks to build indigenous grass-roots organizations seeking economic and social equality. Many of the struggles of the 1940s and later drew from the efforts of these campaigns.

SELECTED BIBLIOGRAPHY

Ralph J. Bunche, "The Programs, Ideologies, Tactics, and Achievements of Negro Betterment and Interracial Organizations" (unpublished ms. for Carnegie-

The boycotts of the 1960s and 1970s were inspired by the same spirit of the earlier "Don't Buy Where You Can't Work" Movement. (Charles H. Ramberg Collection; Courtesy Mississippi Department of Archives and History.)

Myrdal Study, 1940); August Meier and Elliott Rudwick, *Along the Color Line* (1976); Edward Peeks, *The Long Struggle for Black Power* (1971).

John B. Kirby

DOUGLAS, AARON (26 May 1898, Topeka, Kans.–2 February 1979, Nashville, Tenn.). The murals of Aaron Douglas, one of the best-known painters of the Harlem Renaissance,* revealed an awakened interest in black life. Following his graduation from the University of Kansas, he came under the tutelage of Winold Reiss, who influenced many black painters of the period. Douglas painted murals for the New York Public Library and Fisk University,* where he later served on the faculty. He became well known for his illustrations in black periodicals and magazines in addition to his work for such black authors as James Weldon Johnson,* Langston Hughes,* and Alain Locke.*

SELECTED BIBLIOGRAPHY

Richard Bardolph, *The Negro Vanguard* (1958); John P. Davis, ed., *The American Negro Reference Book* (1966); Bruce Kellner, ed., *The Harlem Renaissance: A Historical Dictionary for the Era* (1984).

Michael S. Downs

DOUGLASS, FREDERICK (February 1818, Tuckahoe, Md.–20 February 1895, Anacostia, Washington, D.C.). Born a slave, probably of white paternity, Douglass learned to read and write as a hired ship's caulker in Baltimore, Maryland. He escaped to the North in 1838 and settled in New Bedford, Massachusetts, where he became an agent and orator for the Massachusetts Anti-Slavery Society. During the 1840s, he published his *Narrative of the Life of Frederick Douglass* (the first of three autobiographies), spoke at numerous abolitionist rallies, and travelled to England. In 1847, he moved to Rochester, New York, and brought out the *North Star*, wielding his pen, as he put it, against the evils of slavery. His remarkable abilities as an orator and writer pushed him to the forefront among reform leaders during the antebellum period. He favored women's rights, temperance, better working conditions, and the abolition of slavery. Following the passage of the Fugitive Slave Act of 1850 (giving slave catchers the authority to journey north and secure fugitives), Douglass wrote that the best remedy for the law was a "good revolver, a steady hand, and a determination to shoot down any man attempting to kidnap." In 1852 he gave his support to the Free Soil party, and, four years later, to the newly formed Republican party. Although espousing standard middle-class values—industry, thrift, honesty, and sobriety—Douglass, called "the father of the civil rights movement," opposed unceasingly all forms of racial discrimination. Following the Civil War, he urged President Andrew Johnson to extend the franchise to freedmen, advocated equal rights as the editor of the *New National Era*, a weekly newspaper, and spoke against convict lease, the crop-lien system, the prevalence of lynching, and anti-Negro rulings of the Supreme Court. After moving to Washington, D.C., in 1872, he continued his strong support for the Republican party and served in patronage positions both as marshal (1877–1881) and recorder of deeds (1881–1886) for the District of Columbia. Later, he served as minister-resident and consul-general to the Republic of Haiti, and chargé d'affaires for the Dominican Republic. During the 1870s and 1880s, he continued to speak out and write on the issues of the day, but he was criticized by some blacks when, in 1884, two years after the death of his wife, he married a white woman, Helen Pitts. While some of his postwar stances might be considered conservative—supporting a proposed annexation of Santo

Frederick Douglass. (Library of Congress.)

Domingo in 1871 and opposing the black "Exodus" from the South in 1870—Douglass never vacillated from his belief that black Americans should be accorded equal civil and political rights. Only then, he said, would America begin to solve its "color problem."

SELECTED BIBLIOGRAPHY

John W. Blassingame, ed., *The Frederick Douglass Papers* (1979); Eric Foner, *Frederick Douglass* (1964); Frederic Holland, *Frederick Douglass: The Orator* (1891); William S. McFeely, *Frederick Douglass* (1991); Waldo E. Martin, Jr., *The Mind of Frederick Douglass* (1984); Michael Meyer, ed., *Frederick Douglass: The Narrative and Selected Writings* (1984); Benjamin Quarles, *Frederick Douglass* (1948).

Loren Schweninger

DOWELL *v.* SCHOOL BOARD OF OKLAHOMA CITY PUBLIC SCHOOLS, 244 F. Supp. 971 (W.D. Okla., 1965). *Dowell v. School Board of Oklahoma City Public Schools,* a class action suit, was filed in federal district court in 1963 by A. L. Dowell on behalf of his son Robert L. Dowell and other black Oklahoma City school children. It challenged the school board's policy of allowing white students to transfer from schools that were predominantly black to schools that were predominantly white. The U.S. district court ruled in July 1963 that the student transfer policy was unconstitutional and ordered the school board to submit an integration plan within ninety days.

Before ruling on the school board's new integration plan in January 1964, the court appointed three educational experts to study the Oklahoma City schools. Based on this panel's report, the court ordered the school board to submit another integration plan by 30 October 1965. The court ruled that the system of "neighborhood" schools proposed by the board would perpetuate racial segregation, and it outlined measures that the new plan must include. Certain segregated schools within the city were to be combined, and teachers would be transferred to achieve faculty integration. The student transfer policy had to be standardized and revised so that black students could transfer from predominantly black to predominantly white schools. The court retained jurisdiction to issue "additional orders which may become necessary" to "complete desegregation."

SELECTED BIBLIOGRAPHY

Richard Bardolph, ed., *The Civil Rights Record: Black Americans and the Law, 1849–1970* (1970); Thomas I. Emerson, David Haber, and Norman Dorsen, *Political and Civil Rights in the United States* (1967); Leon Jones II, *From Brown to Boston: Desegregation in Education* (1979).

                                                                      James L. Baggett

DRAKE, ST. CLAIR (2 January 1911, Suffolk, Va.–14 June 1990, Palo Alto, Calif.). A distinguished scholar and author of several books and articles in professional journals on topics in African and Pan-African studies, urban anthropology, and race relations theory, Drake received numerous honors and honorary degrees, awards, and fellowships, including being named an Honorary Fellow of the Royal Anthropological society of Great Britain and Ireland. He taught at Dillard University, in New Orleans, Louisiana (1935–1936), Roosevelt University, in Chicago, Illinois (1946–1968), the University of Liberia (1954), the University of Ghana (1958–1961), and Stanford University, in Stanford, California (1969–1976). An activist for interracial harmony and economic justice, Drake advocated nonviolent approaches to social change, and he refused to serve in the segregated armed forces during World War II.

SELECTED BIBLIOGRAPHY

George Clement Bond, "A Social Portrait of John Gibbs St. Clair Drake: An American Anthropologist," *American Ethnologist* 15 (November 1988), 762–81; St. Clair Drake, *Black Folk Here and There: An Essay in History and Anthropology* (1987); St. Clair Drake, *The Redemption of Africa and Black Religion* (1970); St. Clair Drake, "Value Systems, Social Structure and Race Relations in the British Isles" (Ph.D. diss., University of Chicago, 1954); St. Clair Drake and Horace R. Clayton, *Black Metropolis: A Study of Negro Life in a Northern City* (1945); St. Clair Drake (with

George Shepperson), "The Fifth Pan-African Conference, 1945, and the All African Peoples Congress, 1958," *Contributions in Black Studies: A Journal of African
and Afro-American Studies* 8 (1986–1987), 35–66; Obituary, *New York Times*, 21 June
1990.

Gloria Waite

DREW, CHARLES RICHARD (3 June 1904, Washington, D.C.–1 April
1950, Haw River, N.C.). Charles R. Drew, a researcher in the use of
blood plasma, was educated at Amherst College (B.A., 1926), McGill
Medical College (M.D., 1933), and Columbia University Medical School
(M.D.Sc., 1940). He was the first black person in the United States to
earn the Doctor of Science degree. His professional positions included
assistant professor of surgery, Howard University* School of Medicine
(1940); medical director of "Blood for Britain Project" (1940); director of
the American Red Cross Blood Bank (1941); assistant director of blood
procurement for the National Research Council (1941); professor and
chairman, Department of Surgery, Howard University School of Medicine (1941–1950); and medical director, Freedman's Hospital (1944–
1950). Dr. Drew believed that excellence of performance would transcend
racial bias, and he focused his energies on training and educating black
medical students, interns, and residents in general surgery. He was
honored for his work with the Spingarn Medal* (1944), a fellowship in
the International College of Surgeons (1946), and two honorary Doctor
of Science degrees (1945 from Virginia State College and 1947 from Amherst College).

SELECTED BIBLIOGRAPHY
Claude H. Organ, Jr., and Margaret M. Kosiba, *A Century of Black Surgeons—
The U.S.A. Experience*, vol. 1 (1987); Harold Wade, Jr., *Black Men of Amherst* (1976);
Charles E. Wynes, *Charles Richard Drew—The Man and the Myth* (1988).

Robert A. Bellinger

DU BOIS, WILLIAM EDWARD BURGHARDT (23 February 1868,
Great Barrington, Mass.–27 August 1963, Accra, Ghana). W.E.B. Du
Bois dedicated his life to the struggle for race advancement by using
research and scholarship as tools of propaganda to elevate the African-
American's political status. His writings were a brilliant articulation of
black protest in the twentieth century. Educated in the public schools
of Great Barrington, Massachusetts, he received baccalaureate degrees
from Fisk University* and Harvard University and, in 1896, a doctorate
from Harvard. After teaching at Wilberforce University in Ohio from
1894 to 1896, Du Bois became an instructor at the University of Pennsylvania where he produced the first sociological study of an African-
American community. Du Bois spent thirteen years conducting similar
research at Atlanta University* and produced a series of sixteen monographs. In 1903 Du Bois compiled fourteen essays into a book entitled

W.E.B. Du Bois. (Special Collections Department, Robert W. Woodruff Library, Emory University.)

*The Souls of Black Folk.** In a prophetic voice, he defined "the color line" as the problem of the twentieth century, and he created the metaphors of the "veil" and "double consciousness" to describe the political and cultural dilemma of being black in America. Du Bois promoted a black nationalist platform of racial unity, leadership by the black elite which he called "The Talented Tenth," and full participation of African Americans in American society. In one particular essay, Du Bois courageously challenged Booker T. Washington's* accommodationist strategies and his platform of vocational education. He told blacks that, in order to achieve social justice, they must demand their rights insistently and continuously, using a college education to gain the wisdom and knowledge to serve the race. Having alienated Washington, Du Bois left Atlanta University in order to protect the institution from Washington's retaliation. In 1909, Du Bois became one of the founders of the National Association for the Advancement of Colored People* (NAACP). From 1910 to 1934 he served as editor of the *Crisis,** the official publication of the NAACP. *Crisis* gave him a national audience to campaign for the rights of African Americans and to protest against racial discrimination in the United States and throughout the colonial worlds of Africa, Asia, and South America. Du Bois's message was not only political, it was also cultural. In *Crisis* and in the children's publication *The Brownies' Book*, Du Bois educated the public about African culture, promoted African-American artists, and proclaimed that "Black Is Beautiful."* In 1934, Du Bois resigned from *Crisis* and the NAACP to chair the Department of Sociology at Atlanta University for the next eleven years. After a brief return to the NAACP as a consultant from 1945 to 1948, Du Bois left the organization for the last time. His perception of the world had changed. In his search for the most appropriate political philosophy for the liberation of African-American people and all other oppressed peoples, Du Bois came into conflict with many of the policies of the NAACP. An early prophet of the Pan-African Movement,* Du Bois helped to organize five Pan-African congresses from 1919 to 1945. Though he demanded full participation of blacks in American society, Du Bois also called for racial unity. In 1911 he had joined the Socialist party and in 1961 he joined the Communist party.* In a final act of Pan-Africanism and black nationalism, Du Bois emigrated to Ghana, where he died in 1963 at the age of ninety-five. Having championed social justice for seven decades, Du Bois, by the time of his death, had incorporated into his thinking the full range of black political and social thought and strategies.

SELECTED BIBLIOGRAPHY

Francis L. Broderick, *W.E.B. DuBois: Negro Leader in Time of Crisis* (1959); W.E.B. Du Bois, *The Autobiography of W.E.B. Du Bois*, (1968); W.E.B. Du Bois, *Black Reconstruction in America* (1935); W.E.B. Du Bois, *Darkwater* (1920); W.E.B. Du Bois, *Dusk of Dawn* (1940); W.E.B. Du Bois, *The Philadelphia Negro* (1899); W.E.B. Du Bois, *The Souls of Black Folk* (1903); W.E.B. Du Bois, *The Suppression of the Slave Trade to the United States of America* (1896); W. Manning Marable, *W.E.B. DuBois* (1986); Arnold Rampersad, *The Art and Imagination of W.E.B. Dubois* (1976). Elliott M. Rudwick, *W.E.B. DuBois: A Study in Minority Group Leadership* (1960); Elliott M. Rudwick, *W.E.B. DuBois, Propagandist of the Negro Protest* (1969).

Lillie Johnson Edwards

DUNBAR, PAUL LAURENCE (27 June 1872, Dayton, Ohio–9 February 1906, Dayton, Ohio). An African-American poet, novelist, and journalist, Dunbar was the son of ex-slaves. Born in Dayton, Ohio, in 1872, he was educated in the city's public schools. Dunbar's service as editor in chief of the *High School Times*, as president of the literary society, and as the class poet early indicated his literary interest. Publication of his first poem in the *Dayton Herald* when he was just sixteen formally signaled the beginning of a prolific literary career. In 1893 *Oak and Ivy*, Dunbar's first full-length volume of poetry, was published. An 1896 review of Dunbar's *Majors and Minors* written by William Dean Howells praised Dunbar's gift for writing dialect and brought him to the attention of American literati. Dunbar's *Lyrics of a Lowly Life* (1898) published in

New York and England brought him international fame. In 1898 his first novel, *The Uncalled*, appeared in *Lippincott's* and in book form. While highly praised for his poetry, Dunbar also published four novels and numerous articles in his later years. Booker T. Washington* called him "The Poet Laureate of the Negro People." His legacy to American literature is a rich body of prose and poetry which reflects the African-American experience in American culture.

SELECTED BIBLIOGRAPHY

Rayford W. Logan and Michael R. Winston, eds., *Dictionary of American Negro Biography* (1982); Doris Lucas Laryea, "Paul Laurence Dunbar," *Dictionary of Literary Biography*, vol. 50 (1986); Jay Martin, ed., *Centenary Conference on Paul Laurence Dunbar* (1972); Jay Martin and Gossie H. Hudson, eds., *The Paul Laurence Dunbar Reader: A Selection of the Best of Paul Laurence Dunbar's Poetry and Prose* (1975).

Brenda M. Brock

DURHAM, NORTH CAROLINA, SIT-INS (1957–1964). North Carolina's introduction to the sit-in technique came in Durham in August 1957 when the Reverend Douglas E. Moore of Asbury Temple, accompanied by a few students from North Carolina College, asked for service at the white section of the Royal Ice Cream Company store. The group sat down and was arrested for trespassing. No further attempts were made until 1960 when the NAACP* chapter at North Carolina College, led by Lacy Streeter, Callis Brown, and other students from Durham Business College, Bull City Barber College, DeShazor's Beauty College, and Hillside High School, moved against segregated lunch counters, movie theaters, recreational facilities, and the bus station. Inspired by visits from Martin Luther King, Jr.,* Ralph Abernathy,* and Roy Wilkins,* and with the support of the Ministerial Alliance and of students and professors from other local colleges, the sit-ins made progress toward integrating retail services in Durham. By 1962 a local chapter of the Congress of Racial Equality* (CORE), organized by longtime participant and advisor Floyd B. McKissick,* joined in the effort. Additional visits by Roy Wilkins, James Farmer,* and Jim Peck served to rally the cause. In one sit-in on 12 August 1962, four thousand people participated, seven hundred of whom were arrested. On the night of Mayor Wense Grabarek's election on 18 May 1963, protesters held a rally followed by a march through the city and sit-ins at six eating places. The NAACP and CORE announced that thirty days of mass demonstrations would begin on 20 May. Mayor Grabarek met with the protesters at Saint Joseph A.M.E. Church and set up the Durham Interim Committee (DIC). Two if its eleven members were black. Grabarek met repeatedly with McKissick, the students, and the restaurant owners, and the combined efforts were productive. Although sit-ins would continue in a few places until 1964, relative peace was achieved. The DIC was later replaced by the biracial Committee on Community Relations. Grievances and racial confronta-

Following the example of students in Durham, Greensboro, and Raleigh, students in Chapel Hill, N.C., sit-in at a local store, 1964. (North Carolina Division of Archives and History.)

tions continued to the end of the decade, but bolder and more strident attention-getting methods replaced the sit-ins.

SELECTED BIBLIOGRAPHY

Jean Bradley Anderson, *A History of Durham County, North Carolina* (1990); *Durham Morning Herald*, 5, 17, 23 February, 1 March, 7, 12 May 1960; 2, 17 January 1961; 15 March, 10, 19 April, 31 July, 13, 20 August, 1962; 19, 20, 22, 24 May, 5, 9 June 1963.

Charles A. Risher

DURR, CLIFFORD J. (2 March 1899, Montgomery, Ala.–12 May 1975, Montgomery, Ala.). Educated at the University of Alabama and Oxford University, where he was a Rhodes scholar, Durr earned a degree in jurisprudence from Oxford in 1922 and returned to his native Montgomery to practice law. In 1933 he went to Washington, D.C., to assume the position of assistant general counsel of the Reconstruction Finance Corporation. For almost two decades he continued in government service, holding a number of positions in New Deal agencies, including a stint as the federal communications commissioner. An able administrator of liberal political persuasion who was related by marriage to Supreme Court Justice Hugo Black, he was an outspoken champion of civil liberties. He declined reappointment to the Federal Communications Commission in 1948 because he would not support President Harry Truman's Cold War loyalty program, some of whose early victims he represented. His defense of these innocent people during the McCarthy era isolated him from mainstream politics, and he returned in 1951 to Montgomery to resume his private practice of the law.

He soon found himself again isolated from mainstream politics, ostracized by Montgomery's white society because of his defense of another group of hapless citizens victimized by unjust laws and oppressive political authority—the black community. In the early 1950s Montgomery's long-suffering black citizens were, unwittingly, about to launch the civil rights revolution. When Rosa Parks* challenged segregation on the city's buses and precipitated the 1955–1956 Montgomery bus boycott* that thrust Martin Luther King, Jr.,* on to the national stage, Clifford Durr and his wife Virginia Foster Durr* were among a mere handful of white Alabama liberals who stood unflinchingly with the blacks in their struggle for freedom. Durr was confidante and counsel to Montgomery's black leaders, especially E. D. Nixon,* and he quietly worked with a young black attorney, Fred Gray, to prepare a solid legal challenge to segregated public transportation. Success came in late 1956 with the *Browder v. Gayle** decision which ended segregated busing. His championship of civil rights cost Durr most of his white Montgomery clients, but he never reckoned personal cost when human dignity, individual rights, and equal justice under the law were at issue.

SELECTED BIBLIOGRAPHY

Taylor Branch, *Parting the Waters, America in the King Years, 1954–1963* (1988); Virginia Foster Durr, *Outside the Magic Circle: The Autobiography of Virginia Foster Durr*, ed. Hollinger F. Barnard with a foreword by Studs Terkel (1985); Obituary, *New York Times*, 13 May 1975; John A. Salmond, *Conscience of a Lawyer: Clifford J. Durr and American Civil Liberties, 1899–1975* (1990); Harvard Sitkoff, *The Struggle for Black Equality, 1954–1980* (1981); J. Mills Thornton III, "Challenge and Response in the Montgomery Bus Boycott of 1955–1956," *The Alabama Review* 33 (July 1980), 163–235.

Charles D. Lowery

DURR, VIRGINIA FOSTER (6 August 1903, Birmingham, Ala.–). Virginia Durr has been a civil rights activist for many years. She did relief work during the Great Depression, and, after her husband Clifford J. Durr* accepted a job with the Roosevelt administration, she lobbied in Washington, D.C., against the poll tax* and later took part in Henry Wallace's presidential campaign. In 1951 the family moved to Montgomery, Alabama, where she worked with integrated women's groups and the Southern Regional Council,* while Clifford Durr practiced law. The Durrs became friends with E. D. Nixon,* Ralph D. Abernathy,* and Rosa Parks;* Nixon and Clifford Durr secured Parks's release from jail after she was arrested in 1955. Virginia Durr supported the Montgomery bus boycott* by organizing car pools for black workers. The Durrs were scorned and ostracized by many other whites, yet they continued to support the civil rights movement after the boycott ended. Virginia Durr's memoir, *Outside the Magic Circle*, which recounts these experiences in rich detail, is filled with insights on family, sex roles, and southern culture.

SELECTED BIBLIOGRAPHY

Virginia Foster Durr, *Outside the Magic Circle: The Autobiography of Virginia Foster Durr*, ed. Hollinger F. Barnard with a foreword by Studs Terkel (1985); David J. Garrow, ed., *The Montgomery Bus Boycott and the Women Who Started It: The Memoir of Jo Ann Gibson Robinson* (1987); J. Mills Thornton III, "Challenge and Response in the Montgomery Bus Boycott of 1955–1956," *The Alabama Review* 33 (July 1980), 163–235.

                                                                        Joan E. Cashin

E

EAST ST. LOUIS RACE RIOT (1917). East St. Louis, Illinois, an industrial satellite of St. Louis, was, in 1917, a city of about 75,000 with a long history of labor strife, inept political leadership, poor living conditions, and widespread corruption. The World War I Great Migration* from the South brought migrants to the city in search of jobs and created a climate of fear and prejudice among white residents, especially industrial workers. On 1 July, two police detectives were killed, probably by blacks who mistook them for marauders who had been shooting into black homes. Convinced that black "armies" were mobilizing for a race war, white mobs formed the next morning and rampaged through the city, indiscriminately beating and killing black residents on the streets and in their homes. Police and militiamen did little to stop the carnage. The official death toll of thirty-nine blacks and nine whites made East St. Louis the deadliest urban race riot of the twentieth century. Only a few white rioters were prosecuted or convicted, and city officials did little to correct the conditions that had led to the riot. Nationally, there were numerous protests, and a congressional committee conducted an investigation. Historians attribute the riot to the economic insecurity of the city's white workers, which led to exaggerated fears of black competition for jobs, and to the political corruption and mismanagement that had bred disrespect for the law.

SELECTED BIBLIOGRAPHY

Elliott Rudwick, *Race Riot at East St. Louis: July 2, 1917* (1964); U.S. House of Representatives, "Report of the Special Committee Authorized by Congress to Investigate the East St. Louis Riots" (1918).

Allan H. Spear

EBONY. *Ebony* magazine was founded by the young black entrepreneur, John H. Johnson, just after World War II. Johnson wanted a magazine that would reflect the unknown contributions and achievements of African Americans. The magazine, though it had a decidedly middle-class bent and was in many ways modeled after *Life* magazine, was a major source of information about the civil rights movement. One feature was its annual August special issue devoted to a theme of particular interest to the black community at that moment. One such issue of the early 1960s focused on the civil rights movement. *Ebony* continues to explore various facets of that movement.

SELECTED BIBLIOGRAPHY
Taylor Branch, *Parting the Waters: America During the King Years, 1954–1963* (1989); *Ebony* (August 1963); John H. Johnson, *Succeeding against the Odds* (1989).

Charles T. Pete Banner-Haley

EDWARDS, HARRY (22 November 1942, St. Louis, Mo.–). An African-American sociologist and sports activist who has conducted seminal research on black participation in American sports, Harry Edwards is best known as the force behind an attempted boycott by black track and field athletes in the 1968 Olympic Games in Mexico because of South Africa's participation. It was during these games that two African-American medal winners gave the Black Power* salute while the national anthem was being played. Edwards saw the "revolt of black athletes [as] the newest phase of the black liberation movement in America." Edwards has served as the chairman of the Olympic Committee for Human Rights.

SELECTED BIBLIOGRAPHY
Joan Martin Burke, *A CBS News Reference Book: Civil Rights, A Current Guide to the People, Organizations, and Events* (1974); Harry Edwards, *The Revolt of the Black Athlete* (1969); *Who's Who among Black Americans 1990–1991* (1990).

Nancy E. Fitch

EDWARDS v. SOUTH CAROLINA, 372 U.S. 229 (1963). In the spring of 1961, James Edwards, Jr., along with almost two hundred other African-American high school and college students, marched to the South Carolina State House in Columbia to protest against segregation and racial discrimination. The protesters carried placards to publicize their grievances and marched in an orderly fashion on the public sidewalks surrounding the state house. When a crowd of onlookers gathered to watch, the police ordered the protesters to disperse. The students responded by singing patriotic and religious songs, clapping their hands, and stomping their feet. They were arrested and convicted of breaching the peace in violation of South Carolina law.

The United States Supreme Court overturned the protester's convictions, finding that the students were within their First Amendment rights of free speech, free assembly, and freedom to petition against grievances in their peaceful demonstration. The Supreme Court did not find any evidence that would support Edwards's conviction and declared that the states could not subvert the principles of liberty found in the First Amendment by criminally prosecuting individuals peacefully expressing their political views.

SELECTED BIBLIOGRAPHY

Richard Bardolph, ed., *The Civil Rights Record: Black Americans and the Law, 1849–1970* (1970); Derrick A. Bell, Jr., *Race, Racism and American Law* (1980); Loren Miller, *The Petitioners: The Story of the Supreme Court of the United States and the Negro* (1966); George Rossman, ed., "Review of Recent Supreme Court Decisions," *American Bar Association Journal* 49 (1963), 1494–95.

Steve Sadowsky

ELAINE, ARKANSAS, RACE RIOT (1919). Blacks protesting the traditional pattern of economic exploitation by white landlords organized tenant cotton farmers into the Organization of the Progressive Farmers' and Household Union of America. This occurrence led to rumors in Elaine that blacks were plotting an uprising to slaughter a large number of whites in the county. Allegations concerning the planning of the presumed uprising brought sheriff's deputies to investigate proceedings at a union meeting at Hoop Spur on the night of 1 October 1919. Gunfire erupted, and fighting spread to a fifty-mile radius. At least two persons died, and many were injured. An investigation ordered by the governor incorrectly found "a mature plan of insurrection" by the union and twenty-one white men marked for death. In a kangaroo-court–like atmosphere, some fifty blacks were found guilty of second degree murder, and ten received twenty-one-year terms in the state penitentiary. Eleven blacks received one-year terms for night-riding, and twelve blacks were sentenced to die; however, these sentences were overturned by the Supreme Court in 1924.

SELECTED BIBLIOGRAPHY

Robert H. Brisbane, *The Black Vanguard: Origins of the Negro Social Revolution, 1900–1960* (1970); J. W. Butts and Dorothy James, "The Underlying Causes of the Elaine Riot of 1919," *Arkansas Historical Quarterly* 20 (Spring 1961), 95–104; Richard C. Cortner, *A Mob Intent on Death: The NAACP and the Arkansas Riot Cases* (1988); Ralph H. Desmarais, "Military Intelligence Reports on Arkansas Riots: 1919–1920," *Arkansas Historical Quarterly* 33 (Summer 1974), 175–91; O. A. Rogers, Jr., "The Elaine Race Riots of 1919," *Arkansas Historical Quarterly* 19 (Summer 1960), 142–50; Lee E. Williams II and Lee E. Williams, Sr., *Anatomy of Four Race Riots* (1972).

Lee E. Williams II

ELIJAH MUHAMMAD. *See* Elijah Poole.

ELLISON, RALPH (1 March 1914, Oklahoma City, Okla.–). In his fiction, essays, and reviews, Ellison insists upon the necessity of coming to grips with the multiethnic composition of American society and seeking to be tolerant of differences in a highly diversified culture. "Our pluralistic democracy," Ellison said in a 1979 address at Brown University, "is a difficult system under which to live, our guarantees of freedom notwithstanding. Socially and politically we have yet to feel at ease with our principles, and on the level of culture no one group has managed to create the definitive American style." After completing high school in Oklahoma, where one of his teachers was the former black West Point cadet, Johnson C. Whittaker,* Ellison studied music for three years (1933–1936) at Tuskegee Institute,* a model for the college portrayed in his novel *Invisible Man*. He them moved to New York with the intention of becoming a musician. There he met Richard Wright* and Langston Hughes,* both of whom encouraged Ellison to develop his writing talents. After 1937, Ellison wrote reviews and short stories for such magazines as *New Masses, Tomorrow, Partisan Review*, and *Common Ground*. He worked on the Federal Writers Project from 1938 to 1942. Ellison received a Rosenwald Fellowship (see Rosenwald Fund) in 1945 and published *Invisible Man* in 1952. This book, now recognized as the most distinguished novel published between 1945 and 1965, won the National Book Award (1953), the Russwurm Award, and the National Newspaper Publishers' Award. In it, Ellison deals with the phenomenon of invisibility, the failure of the dominant American society to see or to understand the humanity of black Americans. Through the adventures of the nameless hero, Ellison sketches the racial rituals of American civilization in tragicomic detail: education about the Negro's "place" in the South, the duplicity involved in accommodationist postures, militant rebellion and black nationalism, and Marxist attempts to create a black proletarian advance guard in the class struggle. Indeed, *Invisible Man* might be considered a fictional companion to Gunnar Myrdal's classic study of race problems, *An American Dilemma** (1944). In his two collections of essays, *Shadow and Act* (1964) and *Going to the Territory* (1988), Ellison has written brilliantly about literature, music, and American culture. His ideas about race and civil rights are succinctly summarized in the closing of his essay "Perspective of Literature" (1976): "The great writers of the nineteenth century and the best of the twentieth have always reminded us that the business of being an American is an arduous task, as Henry James said, and it requires constant attention to our consciousness and to our conscientiousness. The law ensures the conditions, the stage upon which we act; the rest of it is up to the individual."

SELECTED BIBLIOGRAPHY

John Hersey, ed., *Ralph Ellison: A Collection of Critical Essays* (1974); Robert List, *Daedalus in Harlem: The Joyce-Ellison Connection* (1982); Robert O'Meally, *The Craft of Ralph Ellison* (1980); John Reilly, ed., *Twentieth Century Interpretations of Invisible Man* (1970).

                                                                                        Jerry Ward

Union soldier reads the Emancipation Proclamation. (Negro Almanac Collection, Amistad Research Center, Tulane University, New Orleans.)

EMANCIPATION PROCLAMATION. Issued by President Abraham Lincoln on 1 January 1863, the Emancipation Proclamation freed all slaves in areas still in rebellion. The proclamation, promulgated after considerable pressure by radicals and designed to make foreign recognition of the Confederacy difficult, was the president's way of dealing with a formidable problem. A minority executive personally committed to freedom but held back by constitutional limitations and the necessity of keeping the border states loyal, he also had to consider the Democrats' opposition to abolition. He solved the dilemma by giving the insurgents a chance to return to their proper allegiance before freeing the slaves only in rebellious territory. In June and July 1862, Lincoln, who, while signing two Confiscation Acts* and the bill freeing the blacks in the District of Columbia, had vetoed individual generals' attempts at emancipation, wrote his proclamation of freedom. He presented the document to the cabinet on 22 July, but, upon William H. Seward's advice, he delayed its publication pending some Union victory. The Battle of Antietam provided him with the success he needed, and on 22 September Lincoln issued the Preliminary Emancipation Proclamation announcing his intention of freeing all slaves in places that had not returned to their allegiance within the following three months. In spite of pressure to desist, he promulgated the final document on 1 January 1863. Clearly indicating that he was acting in his capacity as commander in chief of the army in times of actual armed rebellion and ending with a felicitous conclusion suggested by Salmon P. Chase, the president declared free all slaves in areas still in rebellion and invited blacks to enlist in the armed forces. Tennnessee and part of Louisiana and Virginia were specifically exempted, so that on the day of issue only a few slaves in the Department of the South were legally affected by the document. As time went on, however, and as more and more territory fell to the Union, the proclamation became effective in the rest of the Confederacy. Although it was not the sweeping measure advocated by the radicals, it nevertheless signaled the end of slavery in the United States.

SELECTED BIBLIOGRAPHY

John Hope Franklin, *The Emancipation Proclamation* (1963); Hans L. Trefousse, *Lincoln's Decision for Emancipation* (1975).

Hans L. Trefousse

ENFORCEMENT ACTS. In order to protect black rights under the Fourteenth* and Fifteenth Amendments,* and more specifically to break up the Ku Klux Klan, Congress passed a series of three Enforcement Acts. The acts of 31 May 1870 and 20 April 1871 were quite similar; they define a number of crimes and provide punishments for these crimes. Among the crimes defined are intimidating or hindering voters, failing to do one's duty as an election officer, and "going in disguise upon the public highway" with intent to deny a citizen his constitutional rights. Punishments ranged as high as ten years' imprisonment and a fine of $5000. The Enforcement Act of 28 February 1871 provided for federal supervision of elections in northern and southern cities with a population of more than 20,000.

Federal prosecutors won some notable victories under the Enforcement Acts. In South Carolina over 1,500 and in northern Mississippi about 1,070 indictments were found. On the other hand, 85 percent of the cases in South Carolina were dismissed before trial. In northern Mississippi, the conviction rate was a respectable 55 percent, yet the federal judge's mild sentencing provided little deterrence to further violations. Overall, these laws led to the breakup of the Ku Klux Klan, but black voting had nevertheless become rare in the South by 1900.

SELECTED BIBLIOGRAPHY

Stephen Cresswell, "Enforcing the Enforcement Acts: The Department of Justice in Northern Mississippi, 1870–1890," *Journal of Southern History* 53 (1987), 421–40; Everette Swinney, "Enforcing the Fifteenth Amendment, 1870–1877," *Journal of Southern History* 27 (1962), 202–18.

Stephen Cresswell

EPISCOPAL SOCIETY FOR CULTURAL AND RACIAL UNITY (ESCRU). An unofficial church organization, founded in 1959 at St. Augustine's College in Raleigh, North Carolina, the Episcopal Society for

Cultural and Racial Unity (ESCRU) both participated in the civil rights movement and tried to reform the church. From 1959 to 1967, the Reverend John B. Morris served as executive director of ESCRU, which had a membership of about five thousand. In its first year, ESCRU supported the sit-ins and opposed bars to interracial marriage. In September 1961 it staged an interracial prayer pilgrimage by bus from New Orleans, Louisiana, to the General Convention in Detroit, Michigan, which led to arrests in Mississippi and demonstrations at the University of the South. ESCRU opposed segregation throughout the country, from a church hospital in Brooklyn, New York, to Lovett School in Atlanta, Georgia, and it participated in the March on Washington* and the Selma to Montgomery march.* In 1966 ESCRU charged the Episcopal Church with racism in clergy assignments, education, and investments. Affected by the Black Power* movement and torn by disagreements between liberals and radicals over its objectives, ESCRU in 1967–1968 decided to commit its "primary attention to combatting white racism." Internal dissension, declining membership, and a lack of funds led to its demise in November 1970.

SELECTED BIBLIOGRAPHY
John L. Kater, Jr., "The Episcopal Society for Cultural and Racial Unity and Its Role in the Episcopal Church, 1959–1970" (Ph.D. diss., McGill University, 1973); Papers of the Episcopal Society for Cultural and Racial Unity, the Martin Luther King, Jr., Center for Nonviolent Social Change, Atlanta, Georgia; David E. Summer, "The Episcopal Church's Involvement in Civil Rights: 1943–1973" (S.T.M. thesis, University of the South, 1983).

Charles W. Eagles

EQUAL EMPLOYMENT OPPORTUNITY ACT OF 1972. Passage of the Equal Employment Opportunity Act of 1972 on 8 March 1972 represented both the culmination of a seven-year drive by civil rights groups to provide enforcement powers for the Equal Employment Opportunity Commission* (EEOC) and a legislative victory for the Nixon administration. The EEOC had been stripped of direct enforcement powers during Senate debate over passage of the Civil Rights Act of 1964,* and the compromise version of Title VII which created the new agency allowed only the attorney general to file pattern or practice suits against discriminating employers in cases in which EEOC mediation had failed. Between 1965 and 1968, President Lyndon B. Johnson failed to persuade Congress to grant cease-and-desist authority to the EEOC. In 1969, the Nixon administration countered with its own bill that would deny cease-and-desist authority but would allow the EEOC to file suit against discriminating employers. Committee hearings and debate on EEOC enforcement bills continued in stalemate throughout the period from 1969 to 1971, and in 1972 the Republican president and the Democratic Congress compromised on a bill that established a presidentially appointed

EEOC counsel authorized to bring suit in federal court and extended Title VII coverage to state and local governments and educational institutions. The EEOC subsequently filed class-action suits that won large awards for minorities and women in numerical requirements for hiring and promotion, back pay, and damages for past discrimination.

SELECTED BIBLIOGRAPHY

Hugh Davis Graham, *The Civil Rights Era* (1990); U.S. Equal Employment Opportunity Commission, *A History of the Equal Employment Opportunity Commission, 1965–1984* (1984).

Elizabeth Kight

EQUAL EMPLOYMENT OPPORTUNITY COMMISSION. The Equal Employment Opportunity Commission (EEOC) was established through Section 705 of the Civil Rights Act of 1964* and was charged with enforcing the provisions of Title VII of that act. The 1964 law provided for a bipartisan commission composed of five members appointed by the president for staggered five-year terms. The commission is staffed by over three thousand employees in its Washington, D.C., headquarters and regional offices. The EEOC enforces nondiscrimination by private employers, unions, and employment agencies (excluding federal contractors, who are regulated by the Office of Federal Contract Compliance Programs.* The powers available to the EEOC to accomplish Title VII compliance represent compromises reached after heated battles in Congress and constraints placed upon it by Supreme Court decisions. In its first seven years, the EEOC lacked the authority to compel employers to conform, but instead relied on investigation and conciliation to achieve voluntary compliance with Title VII. Unlike the antidiscrimination commissions that were created by legislation in most of the non-southern states following World War II, the EEOC was denied cease and desist powers. The Equal Employment Opportunity Act of 1972* added educational institutions and government agencies to the commission's coverage, and gave the EEOC the authority to bring class action suits. Jurisdiction was further expanded by the Age Discrimination in Employment Act and Amendments (1974, 1978) and the Fair Labor Standards Act Amendments of 1974. In 1978 Chairperson Eleanor Holmes Norton executed major reorganization to increase efficiency. Clarence Thomas, who chaired the EEOC during the Reagan administration, criticized the agency for pursuing affirmative action* quotas.

SELECTED BIBLIOGRAPHY

Norman C. Amaker, *Civil Rights and the Reagan Administration* (1988); Hugh Davis Graham, *The Civil Rights Era* (1990); Kathanne W. Greene, *Affirmative Action and Principles of Justice* (1989); U.S. Equal Employment Opportunity Commission, *A History of the Equal Employment Opportunity Commission, 1965–1984* (1984).

Michele M. Hall

EUROPE, JAMES REESE (22 February 1881, Mobile, Ala.–9 May 1919, Boston, Mass.). James Reese Europe was at the center of American music from 1910 to 1919. He formed one of the first black musicians' unions, the Clef Club, in April 1910. The Clef Club bands were among the first black bands to make recordings. From 1913 to 1915 Europe provided the music and many of the dances for Vernon and Irene Castle. As a member of the U.S. Army he was responsible for organizing and conducting the 369th Division "Hellfighters" band. Known as "the best damned brass band in the United States Army," it introduced the music of black Americans to the world. Europe was instrumental in the development of orchestral jazz and was a major force in countering the return of white minstrelsy to the American stage.

SELECTED BIBLIOGRAPHY

Reid Badger, "The Conquests of Europe: The Remarkable Career of James Reese Europe," in *Alabama Heritage* 1 (Summer 1986), 34–49; Robert Kimball and William Bolcom, *Reminiscing with Sissle and Blake* (1973); Eileen Southern, *Biographical Dictionary of Afro-American and African Musicians* (1982); Eileen Southern, *The Music of Black Americans: A History* (1971).

Robert A. Bellinger

EVANS v. NEWTON, 382 U.S. 296 (1966). Under the terms of the 1911 will of Senator Augustus Bacon, the city of Macon, Georgia, was appointed the trustee of a privately owned park that was to be reserved for whites only. When the city failed to keep the park racially segregated, members of the park's board of managers sued to remove the city as trustee and return the park to private trustees who would enforce racial segregation in accordance with Senator Bacon's will. Macon's African-American citizens sought to block the return of the park to private trustees who would exclude them.

The United States Supreme Court ruled that, although the park was privately owned, the city had operated and managed it in such a way that the equal protection clause of the Fourteenth Amendment* applied. Under the Fourteenth Amendment, the city could not exclude members of any race from the enjoyment of a public facility, whether it be a park, golf course, or pool. Once the city has taken on the operation of a recreational facility, it must make it available to all members of the public, without regard to race.

SELECTED BIBLIOGRAPHY

Derrick A. Bell, Jr., *Race, Racism and American Law* (1980); Thomas I. Emerson, David Haber, and Norman Dorsen, *Political and Civil Rights in the United States* (1967); "Recent Cases," *Vanderbilt Law Review* 19 (1966), 939–45.

Steve Sadowsky

EVERS, JAMES CHARLES (11 September 1922, Decatur, Miss.–). A civil rights leader, businessman, and politician educated at Alcorn A&M College, Evers's life was shaped early by the racism characteristic of

Mississippi's "closed society." Acute poverty, rigid segregation, disfranchisement, and mob violence permeated the environment, causing him to lament the misery of growing up black in the Magnolia State. Outspoken and direct in his reaction to prejudice and discrimination, Evers became state chairman of a voter registration campaign in the 1950s, frequently using radio time to encourage blacks to register and vote. His activities antagonized many whites in the area. An abortive assassination attempt by irate segregationists followed by job reprisal forced him to leave Mississippi in 1956 for Chicago where he prospered financially from both legal and illegal pursuits. He kept abreast of the Mississippi situation through his younger brother, Medgar Evers,* the state's most indefatigable civil rights leader. Medgar's assassination in 1963 shook Charles tremendously, and it brought him back to Mississippi on a permanent basis to continue Medgar's work. Charles succeeded Medgar as NAACP* field secretary for Mississippi and committed himself to nonviolent racial change. His advocacy of political and economic tactics as keys to eradicating white racism focused on voter registration drives and boycotts. Targeting several key defiant cities, he helped organize economic boycotts and selective buying campaigns in an effort to end discriminatory business practices, and to promote black employment in private and public sector jobs. He was jailed and harassed, but his leadership helped lead to significant cracks in the Mississippi monolith by the 1960s. In 1969 Evers personally tested the extent of the state's racial progress by running for mayor of the biracial town of Fayette. He won that election and three subsequent mayoral contests between 1973 and 1981. He became the first of his race to launch serious, though unsuccessful, statewide campaigns for governor and the U.S. Senate. His efforts have inspired other blacks to seek public office in a state where, until recently, participation in politics had been restricted to "white only."

SELECTED BIBLIOGRAPHY

Jason Berry, *Amazing Grace* (1973); Charles Evers, edited by Grace Halsell, *Evers* (1971); Charles Evers, "Playboy Interview: Charles Evers," *Playboy Magazine* (October 1971); Walter Rugaber, "The Brothers Evers," *New York Times*, 4 August 1968; George A. Sewell and Margaret Dwight, *Mississippi Black History Makers* (1977).

Robert L. Jenkins

EVERS, MEDGAR W. (2 July 1925, Decatur, Miss.–11 June 1963, Jackson, Miss.). For nearly a decade, Medgar Evers was a central figure in Mississippi's civil rights struggle. Like countless other Deep South blacks of his generation, Evers daily experienced the region's bigotry and racism. In 1946 he returned from World War II determined to work to change what was perhaps the South's most segregated and oppressive state. After graduation from Alcorn A&M College, he sold insurance in the Mississippi Delta where black conditions were among the South's most deplorable. There he employed economic boycotts to mobilize blacks against inequality. He joined the largely inactive NAACP* and helped organize and revitalize branch chapters all over the state, accepting in 1954 the NAACP's offer of full-time work as state field secretary. Much of his new job involved monitoring, collecting, and publicizing data concerning civil rights violations, but he also organized campaigns against racial injustice in Jackson, Mississippi's largest and most densely black populated city. In defiance of the conservative NAACP national leadership, he often pursued a policy of mass direct action,* which both unified the Jackson black community and antagonized the recalcitrant white power structure. He conducted numerous mass meetings and led and participated in sit-ins and lunch counter demonstrations. Like many of those who followed his leadership, Evers was frequently beaten and jailed. Although his life was constantly threatened, Evers never allowed fear to discourage him. In the early morning of 11 June 1963, however, the threats became a reality when he was ambushed in the driveway of his home. Although his death left the civil rights movement void of one of its most influential and dedicated leaders, it also greatly enhanced his historical position in African-American communities everywhere, and he became a major symbol of the struggle to overcome racial bigotry and oppression.

SELECTED BIBLIOGRAPHY

Ronald Bailey, *Remembering Medgar Evers . . . for a New Generation* (1988); Cleveland Donald, Jr., "Medgar Wylie Evers: The Civil Rights Leader as Utopianist," in Dean Faulkner Wells and Hunter Cole, eds., *Mississippi Heroes* (1980); Charles Evers, edited by Grace Halsell, *Evers* (1971); (Mrs.) Medgar Evers, with William Peters, *For Us the Living* (1967); George R. Metcalf, *Black Profiles* (1968); John Salter, *Jackson, An American Chronicle of Struggle and Schism* (1979); George A. Sewell and Margaret Dwight, *Mississippi Black History Makers* (1977).

Robert L. Jenkins

EVERS v. DWYER, 358 U.S. 202 (1958). Plaintiff O. Z. Evers, a black resident of Memphis, Tennessee, boarded a city bus on 26 April 1956 and seated himself in the front. He refused to move to the back of the bus as instructed by the driver, and he left the vehicle only when faced with arrest by city police officers. Evers brought a class action suit in federal district court against Memphis city officials, the transportation company, and the bus driver. He sought a declaratory judgment as to his claimed constitutional right to travel on buses within the city without being subjected, as required by Tennessee statute, to segregated seating arrangement on account of race. The district court dismissed the complaint on the grounds that no "actual controversy" within the meaning of the Declaratory Judgment Act had been shown because appellant had ridden the bus only on one occasion, had done so for the purpose of instituting litigation, and was not "representative of a class of colored citizens who do use the buses in Memphis as a means of transportation." The Supreme Court reversed the lower court's decision and remanded the case for further adjudication, ruling that evidence in the case had established the existence of an actual controversy.

SELECTED BIBLIOGRAPHY

Stewart A. Baker, "A Strict Scrutiny of the Right to Travel," *UCLA Law Review* 22 (1975), 1129–60; James Peck, *Freedom Ride* (1962); George Rossman, ed., "Review of Recent Supreme Court Decisions," *American Bar Association Journal* 45 (1959), 283–84.

Michael S. Downs

EXECUTIVE ORDER 8802. In 1942, as billions of dollars flowed into defense industries, African Americans were excluded from all but menial jobs. Protests yielded only weak responses. A. Philip Randolph,* president of the Brotherhood of Sleeping Car Porters and Maids,* proposed a 1 July march of from 50,000 to 100,000 African Americans on Washington, D.C., to force President Franklin Roosevelt to issue an executive order abolishing discrimination in all government departments, the armed services, and national defense jobs. To prevent the march Roosevelt, on 25 June, issued Executive Order 8802 prohibiting discrimination in government departments and defense industries and establishing a Fair Employment Practice Committee* to enforce the order. Although enforcement was sometimes lax and the armed services remained segregated, the order's impact was widespread. Randolph's threat to march anticipated the direct action* techniques of the civil rights leaders of the 1950s and 1960s.

SELECTED BIBLIOGRAPHY

Jervis B. Anderson, *A. Philip Randolph: A Biographical Portrait* (1973); John H. Bracey, Jr., August Meier, and Elliott Rudwick, ed., *The Afro-Americans: Selected Documents* (1972); Joseph P. Lash, *Eleanor and Franklin* (1971).

Suzanne Ellery Greene Chapelle

EXECUTIVE ORDER 9808. Signed by President Harry S. Truman on 5 December 1946, this order created the President's Committee on Civil Rights. The fifteen-member committee's task was to determine how existing powers of federal, state, and local governments could be "improved to safeguard the civil rights of the people," to submit a written report, and to make recommendations for the more adequate protection of civil rights. The report, published on 29 October 1947, included the following recommendations: (1) establishing a permanent Civil Rights Commission,* a joint Congressional Committee on Civil Rights, and a Civil Rights Section Justice Department*; (2) strengthening existing civil rights statutes; (3) providing federal protection against lynching; (4) protecting more adequately the right to vote; and (5) establishing a Fair

Employment Practices Commission (see Fair Employment Practice Committee). While the order resulted in little legislation, it did succeed in dramatizing the civil rights problem.

SELECTED BIBLIOGRAPHY

William C. Berman, *The Politics of Civil Rights in the Truman Administration* (1970); President's Committee on Civil Rights, *To Secure These Rights* (1947).

Clarence Hooker

EXECUTIVE ORDER 9981. Moved by political and military expediency and apparently by genuine concern for racial justice, President Harry S. Truman issued an executive order on 26 July 1948 directing the armed forces to provide "equality of treatment and opportunity for all personnel without regard to race, color, religion, or national origin." Truman's directive also established a presidential committee—chaired by Charles Fahy—to make appropriate recommendations to ensure equality of treatment and opportunity. Prodded by the Fahy Committee,* the U.S. Air Force and U.S. Navy moved toward integration in 1949; the U.S. Army, with far more blacks, grudgingly adopted a gradualist policy the following year. With full integration spurred by the Korean War and nearly complete by the end of 1954, the armed services had become the most completely integrated segment of American society. Desegregation of the military may have been Truman's most significant civil rights accomplishment.

SELECTED BIBLIOGRAPHY

Richard M. Dalfiume, *Desegregation of the U.S. Armed Forces: Fighting on Two Fronts, 1939–1953* (1969); Morris J. MacGregor, *Integration of the Armed Forces, 1940–1965* (1981); Bernard C. Nalty, *Strength for the Fight: A History of Black Americans in the Military* (1986); Lee Nichols, *Breakthrough on the Color Front* (1954).

James B. Potts

EXECUTIVE ORDER 10577. In response to recommendations by the Committee on Government Contracts, President Dwight D. Eisenhower issued this order on 3 September 1954. Its purpose was to clarify existing orders obligating contractors and subcontractors not to discriminate against an employee or applicant for employment because of race, creed, color, or national origin. The recommended clarification specified that nondiscrimination applied to "employment, upgrading, demotion or transfer; recruitment or recruitment advertising; layoff or termination, rates of pay or other forms of compensation; and selection of training, including apprenticeship." Contractors were required to post nondiscrimination clauses in conspicuous places. Excluded from the order were contracts to meet special requirements or emergencies and contracts executed outside the United States for which American workers had not been recruited.

SELECTED BIBLIOGRAPHY
The Code of Federal Regulations; Thomas R. Wolanin, *Presidential Advisory Commission* (1975).

                                                                    Clarence Hooker

EXECUTIVE ORDER 10590. President Dwight D. Eisenhower signed this order on 18 January 1955, establishing the President's Committee on Government Employment Policy and abolishing the Fair Employment Board of the Civil Service Commission. The five-member committee consisted of representatives from the Civil Service Commission, Department of Labor, the Office of Defense Mobilization, and two presidential appointees. The committee's mandate was to ensure that government agencies did not discriminate because of race, color, religion, or national origin in employment or application for employment in the federal government. The order provided for an employment policy officer in each department or agency; empowered the committee to undertake necessary research; and authorized it to advise, make recommendations, and act as a consultant to the president and government agencies.

SELECTED BIBLIOGRAPHY
Dwight D. Eisenhower, *Mandate for Change* (1963); Thomas R. Wolanin, *Presidential Advisory Commissions* (1975).

                                                                    Clarence Hooker

EXECUTIVE ORDER 10925. President John F. Kennedy signed this order which established the president's Equal Employment Opportunity Commission* on 6 March 1961. The committee, consisting primarily of cabinet officers and chaired by Vice President Lyndon B. Johnson, was charged with eliminating race, creed, color, and national origin as barriers to employment in the government as well as in firms employed on government contracts. Unlike similar efforts made in the Roosevelt, Truman, and Eisenhower administrations, this order demanded affirmative action* to make the policy effective. The committee was empowered to publish the names of noncomplying contractors and unions and to recommend that the Justice Department file suits to compel compliance and institute criminal suits for filing false information.

SELECTED BIBLIOGRAPHY
Howard J. Anderson, *Primer of Equal Employment Opportunity* (1978); Paul Burstein, *Discrimination, Jobs, and Politics: The Struggle for Equal Employment Opportunity in the United States Since the New Deal* (1985).

                                                                    Clarence Hooker

EXECUTIVE ORDER 11063. During the presidential campaign of 1960 Senator John F. Kennedy criticized the civil rights record of the Eisenhower administration and promised, if elected, to ban racial discrimination in federally assisted housing "with the stroke of a pen." Kennedy did not redeem that pledge until 20 November 1962, when he issued Executive Order 11063. The order prohibited racial discrimination in federally owned and operated housing, in public housing built with federal assistance, and in new housing funded through FHA and VA loans. This represented approximately 25 percent of all housing; it excluded housing built through commercial mortgages from banks and savings and loan associations. Kennedy omitted commercially funded housing on Justice Department advice that the president lacked the authority to enforce social programs through independent agencies of financial regulation. Kennedy delayed the "penstroke" order for two years because he feared it might jeopardize his plan to create a Department of Housing and Urban Affairs and to appoint Robert C. Weaver* to head it as the first black member of the cabinet. Kennedy was also urged by northern Democrats in Congress, who feared a white backlash at the polls, not to issue the order until after the 1962 elections. Kennedy's order had little observable effect on housing patterns, and it was superseded by the Open Housing Act* of 1968, signed by President Lyndon B. Johnson, which made nondiscrimination in housing a national policy.

SELECTED BIBLIOGRAPHY

Carl M. Brauer, *John F. Kennedy and the Second Reconstruction* (1977); Hugh Davis Graham, *The Civil Rights Era* (1990).

Hugh Davis Graham

EXECUTIVE ORDER 11114. Issued by President John F. Kennedy on 22 June 1963, Executive Order 11114 extended Kennedy's fair employment and affirmative action* order of March 1961 (Executive Order 10925)* to cover federally assisted contracts in the construction industry. The issue was politically difficult for the Kennedy administration because it brought two Democratic constituencies into conflict: minority workers and union members. Hiring decisions in construction were made not by the builders who signed the contracts, but rather by white-dominated craft unions whose collective bargaining agreements gave them hiring-hall authority. To blue-collar union members, the order threatened seniority and labor solidarity. But civil rights leaders pointed to a black unemployment rate that doubled the white rate, and demanded that minority workers help build the tax-subsidized hospitals, highways, schools, and urban renewal projects. The threat of federally enforced minority hiring, like the parallel issue of housing desegregation, split the Democrats' northern constituency in much the same way that the school desegregation issue split the party in the South. Kennedy withheld the construction order until the Birmingham Confrontation* in the spring of 1963. Then he sent Congress for the first time, on 19 June, a strong civil rights bill. Three days later, on a news-quiet Saturday, Kennedy released Executive Order 11114 without ceremony or comment. Subsequent difficulties in enforcing the order led to the controversy over the Philadelphia Plan* during the Nixon administration.

SELECTED BIBLIOGRAPHY
Hugh Davis Graham, *The Civil Rights Era* (1990).

Hugh Davis Graham

EXECUTIVE ORDER 11246. Signed by President Lyndon B. Johnson on 24 September 1965, Executive Order 11246 distributed authority among federal agencies for enforcing the Civil Rights Act of 1964.* To enforce Title VI, it established the equal opportunity obligations for federal contractors and subcontractors by requiring procuring agencies to insert an equal opportunity clause into each contract. Under this clause, contractors were barred from discriminating against employees and applicants on the basis of race, color, religion, or national origin (sex discrimination was added in 1967 by Executive Order 11375). Such employers were required to take affirmative action* (a term first mentioned in 1961 in Kennedy's Executive Order 10925,* but not defined until the Labor Department issued regulations regarding the program's implementation in May 1968) to employ and advance in employment, all applicants and employees without regard to such factors. Evidence of these nondiscriminatory policies alone did not ensure compliance, however. By 1970 federal officials were requiring contractors to provide minorities and women with a share of jobs that reflected their representation in the labor force or population. The goal of compliance became a form of numerical parity between those minority workers who were available and the percentage who held jobs. Johnson's directive granted responsibility for enforcement to the Secretary of Labor, who was to administer the program through the Office of Federal Contract Compliance Programs.*

SELECTED BIBLIOGRAPHY
Hugh Davis Graham, *The Civil Rights Era* (1990); Floyd D. Weatherspoon, *Equal Employment Opportunity and Affirmative Action: A Sourcebook* (1985).

Nancy Diamond

EXECUTIVE ORDER 11478. Executive Order 11478 was issued by President Richard M. Nixon on 8 August 1969, during the height of the Labor Department's struggle to regulate federal construction contracts as outlined in the revised Philadelphia Plan.* While the Labor Department was being accused by congressional conservatives and by the General Accounting Office of trying to enforce minority hiring quotas on private contractors, the president, in his memorandum announcing Executive

Order 11478 to the heads of all federal agencies, declared, "Equal employment opportunity must become an integral part of the day-to-day management of Federal agencies and interwoven with every action which has an effect on employees." Under Section 2 of the order, each agency was required to establish and maintain an affirmative action* program of equal employment opportunity. Executive Order 11478 proved to be redundant, since it superseded President Lyndon B. Johnson's similar Executive Order 11246* of 1965 and its amendment of 1967 for gender discrimination. Nixon's requirement of "affirmative programs" in all federal agencies supplanted the Johnson orders as the source of policy for equal employment opportunity in the federal government.

SELECTED BIBLIOGRAPHY
Codification of Presidential Proclamations and Executive Orders, April 13, 1945–January 20, 1989 (1989); Hugh Davis Graham, The Civil Rights Era (1990); Public Papers of the Presidents of the United States: Richard M. Nixon (1971).

Dorsey Oles Boyle

EX PARTE VIRGINIA, 100 U.S. 339 (1880). The Civil Rights Act of 1875* stated that no person could be disqualified from jury service because of race and that any officer who disqualified a potential juror because of his or her race was subject to a fine of up to $5000. In this dramatic case, a Virginia county judge named J. D. Coles was indicted for excluding blacks from juries and was imprisoned by the U.S. marshal. In petitioning for a writ of habeas corpus, Coles argued that he could not be tried by a United States court for actions he had taken as a state judge. He argued that, although his actions might be overruled by a federal court, he could not be punished for these actions. The Supreme Court refused to issue the writ of habeas corpus, declaring that the jury rights provisions of the Civil Rights Act of 1875 were firmly based upon the Thirteenth* and Fourteenth Amendments.* The court's decision also held that, in enforcing the Constitution, Congress cannot punish the abstract entity called a state but must punish individuals—including officials in charge of jury selection. As a civil rights victory, ex parte Virginia was effectively watered down by another decision handed down the same day: Virginia v. Rives.*

SELECTED BIBLIOGRAPHY
Stephen Cresswell, "The Case of Taylor Strauder," West Virginia History 44 (Spring 1983), 193–211; Benno C. Schmidt, "Juries, Jurisdiction, and Race Discrimination: The Lost Promise of Strauder v. West Virginia," Texas Law Review (1983), 1402–99; Charles Warren, The Supreme Court in United States History (1926).

Stephen Cresswell

EX PARTE YARBROUGH, 110 U.S. 651 (1884). Jasper Yarbrough and seven accomplices beat Berry Saunders to discourage his voting in a federal election in Georgia. Indicted under the enforcement legislation for the Fifteenth Amendment,* which prohibited intimidation of voters and conspiracy to do so, the defendants sought a writ of habeas corpus. They claimed that Congress could not control the actions of private individuals in the guise of regulating elections. The Supreme Court unanimously denied their appeal. Justice Samuel Miller observed that democratic government required free elections, and that free participation in federal elections was a federal right guaranteed by the Constitution without reference to state law. This case was the Court's strongest statement on electoral freedom in the aftermath of Reconstruction. It concluded a ten-year period of vacillation in which the Court took several contradictory positions about the nature of the right to vote, its source, and its relation to the privileges and immunities clause. The *Yarbrough* case raised the Court's contemporary statements on protection of federal elections higher than its positions on most other aspects of civil rights. The doctrine of the *Yarbrough* case remained significant in the voter registration movement of the 1960s and forms part of the philosophical foundation of the constitutional law of all civil rights.

SELECTED BIBLIOGRAPHY

Charles Fairman, *Reconstruction and Reunion, 1864–1888* (1987); William Gillette, "Samuel Miller," in Leon Friedman and Fred Israel, eds., *The Justices of the United States Supreme Court, 1789–1969: Their Lives and Major Opinions* (1969).

James E. Sefton

F

FAHY COMMITTEE. The Committee on Equality of Treatment and Opportunity in the Armed Forces, commonly called the Fahy Committee, after its chairman Charles H. Fahy, was authorized to examine the rules, procedures, and practices in the armed services to determine how these might be altered or improved in order to abolish racial discrimination. Beginning in January 1949, the committee not only investigated the racial practices of the Army, Navy, and Air Force but also worked directly with them to bring about desegregation. From the beginning, the Air Force and the Navy cooperated with the committee, making the necessary changes with little difficulty. After first resisting the committee's desegregation suggestions, the Army finally accepted the committee's basic recommendations. In less than a year and a half, the committee helped establish nondiscriminatory racial policies in the military services, even though the policies on paper were not always carried out in practice. The Fahy Committee was an important factor in the eventual total desegregation of the armed forces of the United States.

SELECTED BIBLIOGRAPHY

Monroe Billington, "Freedom to Serve: The President's Committee on Equality of Treatment and Opportunity in the Armed Forces, 1949–1950," *Journal of Negro History* 51 (October 1966), 262–74; Richard M. Dalfiume, *Desegregation of the U.S. Armed Forces: Fighting on Two Fronts, 1939–1953* (1969); Records of the President's Committee on Equality of Treatment and Opportunity in the Armed Forces, 1949–1950, Harry S Truman Library, Independence, Mo.

Monroe Billington

FAIR EMPLOYMENT PRACTICE COMMITTEE. In 1941 President Franklin D. Roosevelt declared that racial discrimination in defense industries was a violation of public policy, and he established a temporary

Committee on Fair Employment Practice to receive and investigate complaints of discrimination. The committee had no enforcement powers. Following World War II, blacks pressured Congress to establish a permanent Fair Employment Practice Commission to outlaw job discrimination in industries receiving government contracts. Southern members of Congress successfully filibustered against establishing a permanent FEPC, and not until the passage of the Civil Rights Act of 1964* were many of the objectives of its supporters incorporated into law.

SELECTED BIBLIOGRAPHY

FEPC File, Harry S Truman Library, Independence, Mo.; Louis Coleridge Kesselman, *The Social Politics of FEPC: A Study in Reform Pressure Movements* (1948); President's Committee on Fair Employment Practice File, Franklin D. Roosevelt Library, Hyde Park, N.Y.; Louis Ruchames, *Race, Jobs, & Politics: The Story of FEPC* (1953).

                                                                Monroe Billington

FARMER, JAMES (12 January 1920, Marshall, Tex.–   ). During the civil rights movement of the 1960s, Farmer became one of the nation's most recognizable and influential black leaders. Educated at Wiley College, in Marshall, Texas, and Howard University,* he began his civil rights activism in 1942 when he and several Christian pacifists founded the Congress of Racial Equality.* The interracial organization's purpose was to apply direct challenges to American racism by using Gandhian tactics of nonviolence. Farmer participated in the organization's pioneering demonstrations in 1947, a campaign of sit-ins which successfully ended two Chicago restaurants' discriminatory service practices against blacks. CORE quickly recognized Farmer's leadership abilities, and his influence in the group increased considerably. Articulate, aggressive, and charismatic, he became CORE National Director in 1961 and led it to its greatest successes during the decade. It was in the South that he achieved for himself and for CORE national exposure and recognition. In 1961 he initiated the dangerous activities of the Freedom Riders* throughout the Deep South. Opposition to the rides highlighted southern intransigence to the U.S. Supreme Court decision prohibiting segregated interstate terminal facilities. Farmer was arrested with the courageous young riders when they tested Mississippi's resistance in the Jackson Trailways Bus Station. When convicted, he and hundreds of other riders chose to serve prison terms in the state penitentiary to focus further national attention on their cause. CORE increased its direct action* activities as Farmer expanded the organization's branches throughout the nation. While much of the activity involved purely local campaigns of the autonomous chapters, Farmer's leadership was notable in numerous CORE–led projects of voter registration and antisegregation protests, not just in the South but throughout the country. In 1964, for example, he led a CORE demonstration at the New York World's Fair to protest black conditions in that city. In 1966 Farmer resigned as CORE's leader to direct a national adult literacy project. By then both he and CORE were prominent members of the "Big Four" of the civil rights leaders and groups. In 1969 he accepted a minor post in the Department of Health, Education, and Welfare under the conservative President Richard M. Nixon. Militant black activists, unimpressed with Nixon's civil rights agenda, criticized him for his decision, but Farmer viewed the appointment as another opportunity to further black causes. He served the administration less than two years, but he succeeded in establishing several programs increasing black employment in the agency. Until 1981 he devoted most of his energy to lecturing; directing the Council on Minority Planning and Strategy, a Washington, D.C.–based black think tank; and administering a public employees labor group. Farmer will be remembered for helping to popularize the nonviolent direct action methods that became synonymous with the civil rights movement and which led to many of the gains of the era.

SELECTED BIBLIOGRAPHY

Inge P. Bell, *CORE and the Strategy of Non-Violence* (1968); James Farmer, *Freedom When?* (1965); James Farmer, *Lay Bare the Heart; An Autobiography of the Civil Rights Movement* (1985); August Meier and Elliott Rudwick, *CORE: A Study in the Civil Rights Movement, 1942–1968* (1973); Charles Moritz, ed., "James Farmer," in *Current Biography Yearbook* (1964).

Robert L. Jenkins

FATHER DIVINE. *See* Baker, George.

FAUSET, JESSIE REDMOND (26 April 1882, Camden County, N.J.–30 April 1961, Philadelphia, Pa.). One of the major African-American women writers to come out of the Harlem Renaissance,* Jessie Redmond Fauset was born in Camden County, New Jersey, and she was the only black to be educated in Philadelphia's High School for Girls. After graduating Phi Beta Kappa from Cornell University, she taught French and Latin to middle-class black youth in Washington, D.C., at the M Street High School (later renamed Dunbar). Jessie completed her education at the Sorbonne in Paris and received an M.A. from the University of Pennsylvania in 1919. She was deeply involved in the Harlem Renaissance as literary editor for the *Crisis*,* where she developed a strong working relationship with W.E.B. Du Bois.* She encouraged the work of many of the leading writers and artists of that period. Her own writing addressed the issues confronting the black middle class. Her political work revolved around helping Du Bois put together the Pan-African Conferences of 1919–1921. She was later involved in national politics; her brother Arthur Huff Fauset, an anthropologist, was vice president of the National Negro Congress.* Jessie married Herbert Harris, a businessman, in 1929. They lived in New Jersey until his death in 1958 when Jessie moved to Philadelphia, where she died in 1961. Her most enduring contributions are her novels: *There is Confusion* (1924), *Plum Bun* (1929), and *Chinaberry Tree* (1931), which depicted the world of middle-class African Americans.

SELECTED BIBLIOGRAPHY
Bruce Kellner, ed., *The Harlem Renaissance: A Historical Dictionary for the Era* (1984); David Levering Lewis, *When Harlem Was in Vogue* (1981).

Charles T. Pete Banner-Haley

FELLOWSHIP OF RECONCILIATION. Members of this Christian pacifist organization, which originated during World War I, believed that peace meant not simply an absence of war but a spirit of unity and harmony among people of all nationalities, races, and classes. Throughout the 1920s, Fellowship of Reconciliation (FOR) members, such as James Weldon Johnson,* Hollingsworth Wood, and Will W. Alexander,* engaged in pioneering interracial work. From the late 1920s to the late 1930s the fellowship focused considerable attention upon the South. FOR secretaries Howard Anderson Kester* and Claude Nelson traveled across the region speaking about economic and social problems before black and white students and organizing interracial fellowship conferences at which the race problem was an important topic for discussion. Meanwhile, across the nation, fellowship members labored quietly to defuse tense racial situations, promote integration, and register black voters. During the early 1940s, under the leadership of Abraham John Muste,* FOR attempted to develop effective nonviolent tactics with which to combat American racism and promote Christian fraternity. Among fellowship members involved in this endeavor were James Farmer,* Bayard Rustin,* and George Houser. Their efforts led to the establishment of the Congress of Racial Equality* which soon disassociated itself from the fellowship. For a time, however, the leadership of the two groups overlapped, and FOR members assisted in CORE fundraising and organizational work into the early 1950s.

During the 1950s and 1960s fellowship members either participated in or supported emerging groups such as the Southern Christian Leadership Conference* and the Student Nonviolent Coordinating Committee.* As the civil rights movement became more militant in the mid-1960s, the fellowship continued to endorse peaceful means to achieve just ends but refused to abandon its financial or legal support of those for whom frustration led to violence.

SELECTED BIBLIOGRAPHY
Betty Lynn Barton, "The Fellowship of Reconciliation: Pacifism, Labor, and Social Welfare, 1915–1960" (Ph.D. diss., Florida State University, 1974); Fellow-

ship of Reconciliation Papers, Friends Historical Library of Swarthmore College, Swarthmore, Pa.; John N. Sayre, *The Story of the Fellowship of Reconciliation, 1915–1935* (1935).

Robert F. Martin

FELLOWSHIP OF SOUTHERN CHURCHMEN. This interracial, interdenominational fellowship was founded in 1934 by neoorthodox Christian social activists who believed that southern Protestantism had failed to bring a prophetic voice to bear upon the economic and social ills plaguing their region. From the mid 1930s to the early 1960s this little band of a few hundred radical Christians worked quietly but courageously to resolve the problems of the South's industrial workers, impoverished farmers, and disinherited blacks. In the years before the civil rights movement, fellowship members of both races traveled and ate together in violation of law and custom. Whites opened their homes to black travelers denied public accommodations. Whenever racial tensions flared they worked behind the scenes to defuse explosive situations before these erupted into violence. At their periodic conferences and through the pages of their journal, *Prophetic Religion*, fellowship members denounced lynching and all other forms of racial violence, called for the integration of the labor movement, advocated political equality for all races, demanded justice for blacks in the courts, and supported the integration of schools, churches, and other social institutions. During the 1950s the fellowship was eclipsed by other, more dramatically active, groups, but for more than a quarter-century it was the most radical expression of Christian social consciousness in the South.

SELECTED BIBLIOGRAPHY

Anthony P. Dunbar, *Against the Grain: Southern Radicals and Prophets, 1929–1959* (1981); Fellowship of Southern Churchmen Papers, Southern Historical Collection, University of North Carolina at Chapel Hill; Robert F. Martin, "Critique of Southern Society and Vision of a New Order: The Fellowship of Southern Churchmen, 1934–1957," *Church History* 52 (March 1983), 66–80; Robert F. Martin, *Howard Kester and the Struggle for Social Justice in the South, 1904–1977* (1991).

Robert F. Martin

FERRIS, WILLIAM H. (20 July 1874, New Haven, Conn.–23 August 1941, New York, N.Y.). An African-American intellectual, nationalist, Pan-Africanist, and integrationist, Ferris earned his M.A. degrees at Yale and Harvard. He argued that blacks are not naturally inferior, as was alleged by the American popular culture, and that their poor conditions had been imposed on them by the American system. Like W.E.B. Du Bois,* Ferris repudiated Booker T. Washington's* vocational educational philosophy. Ferris became a member of the American Negro Academy and later a vice president of the Universal Negro Improvement Association,* an organization founded by Marcus Garvey* to send blacks to

Africa. Ferris also recognized with pride the achievements of African intellectuals such as Fadumah Orishautukeh and Ka Issaka Seme, who were students in the United States. Despite his Pan-Africanist sentiment, Ferris had strong admiration for Western civilization and was therefore a strong advocate of black assimilation into the dominant American culture.

SELECTED BIBLIOGRAPHY

William H. Ferris, *The African Abroad: Or, His Evaluation in Western Civilization, Tracing his Development under Caucasian Milieu,* 2 vols. (1913); Wilson J. Moses, *The Golden Age of Black Nationalism, 1850–1925* (1978).

Amos J. Beyan

FIFTEENTH AMENDMENT. The Fifteenth Amendment, ratified by Congress in 1870, enfranchised black males. The amendment states that "the right of citizens of the United States to vote shall not be denied or abridged by the United States or by any State on account of race, color, or previous condition of servitude" and that "Congress shall have power to enforce this article by appropriate legislation." This legislation produced a small cadre of African Americans in southern politics—black legislators, judges, superintendents of education, lieutenant governors

Georgetown Election: These first black votes in D.C. were made possible by the passage of the Fifteenth Amendment. (Negro Almanac Collection, Amistad Research Center, Tulane University, New Orleans.)

and other state officers, members of Congress, and two United States senators. Fearful of black political participation, the white southern leadership enforced measures to disenfranchise black voters. The poll tax,* the grandfather clause,* literacy tests, confusing election procedures, gerrymandering, and intimidation effectively eliminated black political participation in the South until the passage of the Voting Rights Act of 1965.*

SELECTED BIBLIOGRAPHY

William Gillett, Retreat from Reconstruction, 1869–1879 (1979); William Gillett, The Right to Vote: Politics and the Passage of the Fifteenth Amendment (1965); Thomas Holt, Black over White: Negro Political Leadership in South Carolina during Reconstruction (1977); Harold M. Hyman, A More Perfect Union: The Impact of the Civil War and Reconstruction on the Constitution (1973); Stanley I. Kutler, Judicial Power and Reconstruction Politics (1968); Michael Perman, The Road to Redemption: Southern Politics, 1869–1879 (1984); Harold N. Rabinowitz, Southern Black Leaders of the Reconstruction Era (1982).

Lillie Johnson Edwards

FIFTY-FIRST COMPOSITE DEFENSE BATTALION. Pressure from President Franklin D. Roosevelt and the need for manpower caused the U.S. Marine Corps in February 1942 to enlist one thousand blacks for general service, ending 167 years of black exclusion. Montford Point Camp, a new facility near Camp Lejeune, North Carolina, provided segregated infantry, armor, and artillery training for these first black marines who formed the 51st Composite Defense Battalion in 1943. Though trained for combat, the 51st remained at Montford Point until 1944, providing reception and specialized training for black marines who followed. In all, some 20,000 recruits served, mostly in all-black service units; many of them saw combat in Saipan, Iwo Jima, and other Pacific battles. Marines continued to bar blacks from their main combat divisions, the air arm, and commissions as officers.

SELECTED BIBLIOGRAPHY

Jack D. Foner, Blacks and the Military in American History (1974); Morris J. MacGregor, Integration of the Armed Forces, 1940–1965 (1981); Bernard C. Nalty, Strength for the Fight: A History of Black Americans in the Military (1986); Henry I. Shaw, Jr., and Ralph W. Donnelly, Blacks in the Marine Corps (1973).

James B. Potts

FIKES v. ALABAMA, 352 U.S. 191 (1957). In 1953 William Earl Fikes was sentenced to death in Alabama for burglary with intent to commit rape. Fikes's conviction rested on a confession that had been obtained by psychological intimidation in violation of the due process clause of the Fourteenth Amendment.* Fikes was an Alabama African American of limited mental ability. He had been taken to jail in a distant county where he was confined in isolation except for periods of interrogation, which lasted several hours at a time over the course of five days. He was denied contact with his father and a lawyer who had come to see him. After his extended confinement and interrogation, Fikes confessed to the crime for which he was later sentenced. The United States Supreme Court ruled that Fikes's confession had been coerced and could not be used against him. Although no physical brutality had been employed, the circumstances of his interrogation were reminiscent of the Inquisition and had the same effect as physical brutality in forcing his confession. The Supreme Court affirmed that only voluntary confessions were consistent with the Fourteenth Amendment's guarantee of due process and that coercion by physical or psychological means could not be reconciled with this fundamental principle of justice.

SELECTED BIBLIOGRAPHY
Robert Frederick Burk, *The Eisenhower Administration and Black Civil Rights* (1984); Loren Miller, *The Petitioners: The Story of the Supreme Court of the United States and the Negro* (1966); George Rossman, ed., "Review of Recent Supreme Court Decisions," *American Bar Association Journal*, 43 (1957), 254–55.

Steve Sadowsky

THE FIRE IN THE FLINT. Walter Francis White's* first novel was a significant historical landmark in American fiction. Written from within the southern black experience, which White knew so well because of his extensive knowledge and experience as a lynching investigator for the NAACP,* the 1924 novel exposed the terrible truth about the American South: its double standard of justice and heinous crime of lynching. Realistically portraying the violent, oppressive racial atmosphere, this serious work of fiction was designed to destroy the plantation tradition myth of the innately "happy," "stupid" Negro, to jolt America's social conscience, and to force the nation's attention to the dire need for antilynching legislation. More important, it paved the way for other Negro writers to voice opinions on previously taboo subjects.

SELECTED BIBLIOGRAPHY
Arna Bontemps, ed., *The Harlem Renaissance Remembered* (1972); Nathan Irving Huggins, *Harlem Renaissance* (1977); James Weldon Johnson, *Black Manhattan* (1930, reprint, 1969); Amrithit Singhn, *The Novels of the Harlem Renaissance: Twelve Black Writers* (1976); Edward E. Waldron, *Walter White and the Harlem Renaissance* (1978); Cary D. Wintz, *Black Culture and the Harlem Renaissance* (1988).

Jacquelyn Jackson

THE FIRE NEXT TIME. Published for the 100th anniversary of the Emancipation Proclamation,* *The Fire Next Time* (1962), by James Baldwin,* expressed a prophetic vision of what would happen if the Negro's grievances were not addressed. In the first of two essays, Baldwin urged his nephew (and all black Americans) to develop a black consciousness so that they could resist the temptation to become socially accepted by becoming "white." In the second essay, "Down at the Cross," Baldwin related his earlier religious experiences, his rejection of white Christianity, and his understanding (but not acceptance) of the Black Muslims'* teachings. He concludes this extremely powerful work with the prophetic words, "If we do not now dare everything, the fulfillment of that prophecy, recreated from the Bible in a song by a slave, is upon us: God gave Noah the rainbow sign, no more water, the fire next time."

SELECTED BIBLIOGRAPHY

James Baldwin, *The Fire Next Time* (1962); Therman B. O'Daniel, ed., *James Baldwin: A Critical Examination* (1977); Louis H. Pratt, *James Baldwin* (1978); W. V. Weatherby, *James Baldwin: Artist on Fire, A Portrait* (1989).

Kenneth W. Goings

FIREFIGHTERS v. STOTTS, 467 U.S. 561 (1984). The Department of Justice under President Ronald Reagan attempted to roll back gains blacks had made in the 1970s under affirmative action* programs. Taking its cue from administration officials who vociferously denounced all "race conscious remedies which require preferential treatment for blacks," the department encouraged whites to challenge affirmative action policies and sometimes filed amicus curiae briefs in affirmative action cases. *Firefighters* was such a case. In it the Justice Department, intervening on behalf of aggrieved white male firefighters, sought to overturn a federal district court ruling which set aside the seniority rights of white firefighters. The trial court had ruled that because blacks had been discriminatorily excluded from the fire department in question until very recently, layoffs based on seniority alone would be discriminatory. To apply the last-hired, first-fired rule would have the effect, in this instance, of eliminating only blacks from the force. Therefore, the court decreed that the fire department must develop a work reduction plan that would not reduce the proportion of blacks on the force, even if the plan meant that whites with seniority would have to be laid off in order to retain blacks with less seniority. On appeal, the Supreme Court reversed the lower court. It declared that, under federal civil rights statutes, courts could not set aside seniority systems in the workplace unless they had been adopted with discriminatory intent. The scope of the *Firefighters* ruling was quite limited, but Reagan officials interpreted it to mean that the courts lacked authority under Title VII of the Civil Rights Act of 1964* to establish employment goals and quotas.

SELECTED BIBLIOGRAPHY

Derrick A. Bell, Jr., *And We Are Not Saved: The Elusive Quest for Racial Justice* (1987); Dawn D. Bennett-Alexander, "The State of Affirmative Action in Employment: A Post-Stotts Retrospective," *American Business Law Journal*, 27 (1990),

565–97; Donald G. Nieman, *Promises to Keep: African-Americans and the Constitutional Order, 1776 to the Present* (1991).

                                                                    Charles D. Lowery

FISHER v. HURST, 333 U.S. 147 (1947). Oklahoma operated a law school for whites but did not provide one for blacks. A black woman, Ada Sipuel, applied for admission to the University of Oklahoma Law School on the ground that Oklahoma provided no opportunity for black students to receive a legal education. A trial court refused to order Sipuel's admission, and the Oklahoma Supreme Court upheld that decision. The United States Supreme Court reversed the decision, ruling that Oklahoma had an obligation to provide Sipuel with equal opportunity for a legal education. Oklahoma responded by creating a black law school; it set aside three rooms in the state capitol and hired three white attorneys to serve as faculty. However, even this flimsy excuse for a law school could not open by the same date as the University of Oklahoma's. Sipuel, who had married and changed her name to Fisher, refused to apply to the newly created black law school. Her attorney asked that the trial court order her admission to the University of Oklahoma Law School. The trial court ruled that Oklahoma could either admit Fisher or refuse to enroll any white students at the University of Oklahoma until the black law school began to operate. The Supreme Court ruled that the trial court's decision met the requirement of the Supreme Court's ruling in *Sipuel v. Board of Regents*.* Justices Wiley Rutledge and Frank Murphy dissented.

SELECTED BIBLIOGRAPHY
"Notes and Comments," Boston University Law Review 28 (1948), 240–42; *Sipuel v. Board of Regents* 199 Oklahoma 36 (1947); *Sipuel v. Board of Regents* 332 U.S. 631 (1947); Mark V. Tushnet, *The NAACP's Legal Strategy against Segregated Education, 1925–1950* (1987).

                                                                    Michael S. Mayer

FISK UNIVERSITY. Founded in 1866 in Nashville, Tennessee, by the American Missionary Association,* the school was incorporated as Fisk University on 22 August 1867. Fisk graduated its first college class in 1872 and became the first black college to receive a class A rating by the Southern Association of Colleges and Secondary Schools. In spite of poverty and white hostility, Fisk fulfilled the vision of its founders by becoming a leading black educational institution and cultural center. It has and continues to train many educational and civil rights leaders, including W.E.B. Du Bois,* Henry Hugh Proctor, John Hope Franklin,* and Constance Baker Motley.*

SELECTED BIBLIOGRAPHY
American Missionary Association Archives, Amistad Research Center, Tulane University, New Orleans, La.; Fiskiana Collection, Fisk University Library,

Graduating Class of 1893, Fisk University. (Negro Almanac Collection, Amistad Research Center, Tulane Univeristy, New Orleans.)

Nashville, Tenn.; Joe M. Richardson, *A History of Fisk University, 1865–1946* (1980).

Maxine D. Jones

FLETCHER, ARTHUR ALLEN (22 December 1924, Phoenix, Ariz.–). Following his graduation from Washburn University of Topeka, in Topeka, Kansas, in 1950, Fletcher played professional football with the Baltimore Colts and the Los Angeles Rams. He also worked in public relations for the highway commission in Kansas (1954–1957) and became involved in Republican politics in 1960 as a paid staff member of the Nixon-Lodge campaign. After a losing race for lieutenant governor in Washington State in 1968, he worked as special assistant to Governor Dan Evans (1969). He also served as alternate delegate to the United Nations General Assembly.

Fletcher's most important early position was assistant secretary for wage and labor standards for the U.S. Department of Labor, which made him at the time the highest-ranking black official in the Nixon administration. Working closely with Secretary George Schultz, in 1969 Fletcher supervised the redesign of the Philadelphia Plan.* During the summer of 1969 Fletcher held hearings in Philadelphia that produced official findings of discrimination by seven different construction trade unions.

Based on these findings, the Labor Department required contractors to establish target ranges for minority employment in order to qualify for bidding. When the Nixon administration defeated a congressional attack on the Philadelphia Plan in December 1969, and a federal appeals court upheld it in April 1970, Fletcher pushed its expansion to include all federal contractors. During 1971–1972 Fletcher was executive director of the National Urban League.* In 1989 President Bush appointed Fletcher chairman of the U.S. Civil Rights Commission.*

SELECTED BIBLIOGRAPHY
Hugh Davis Graham, *The Civil Rights Era* (1990); William Safire, *Before the Fall* (1975); Mary Mace Spradling, ed., *In Black and White* (1980).

Daniel Gomes

FLIPPER, HENRY OSSIAN (21 March 1856, Thomasville, Ga.–3 May 1940, Atlanta, Ga.). The first African American to graduate from the United States Military Academy in West Point, New York, Flipper had

Lieutenant Henry O. Flipper, first black graduate of the U.S. Military Academy. (Negro Almanac Collection, Amistad Research Center, Tulane University, New Orleans.)

a brief career in the U.S. Army but achieved much greater success as an engineer. In 1882, seven years after his graduation, Flipper was convicted (under questionable circumstances) of "conduct unbecoming an officer" and dismissed from the service. During the next thirty years, while continually appealing the verdict, he worked as an engineer, surveyor, and translator for the United States and Venezuela and a number of corporations. In 1921 Flipper again was in the black vanguard when he became an assistant to the Secretary of the Interior.

SELECTED BIBLIOGRAPHY

Paul H. Carlson, *"Pecos Bill"; A Military Biography of William R. Shafter* (1989); Bruce J. Dinges, "The Court-Martial of Lieutenant Henry O. Flipper," *The American West* 9 (January 1972), 12–17, 59–61; Henry O. Flipper, *The Colored Cadet at West Point* (1878).

Marvin E. Fletcher

FLORIDA ex rel. HAWKINS v. BOARD OF CONTROL OF FLORIDA, 347 U.S. 971 (1954), 350 U.S. 413 (1956). In 1949 Virgil D. Hawkins, a graduate of Pennsylvania's Lincoln University, was denied admittance to the University of Florida Law School in Gainesville. Hawkins turned to the courts for assistance. In August 1952 the Florida Supreme Court upheld the board of control's decision and dismissed the case on the grounds that Hawkins could get an adequate legal education at the recently created law school at the all-black Florida Agricultural and Mechanical University in Tallahassee. Hawkins appealed the decision to the U.S. Supreme Court, which on 24 May 1954 ordered the state court to reconsider the case in light of the recent *Brown v. Board of Education.** In March 1956 it directed the board of control to register Hawkins without further delay. Claiming that violence would result, the state Supreme Court employed stall tactics. The U.S. Supreme Court refused to hear a Hawkins appeal in 1957 but suggested that he "seek relief in an appropriate United States District Court." Federal district court Judge Dozier De Vane on 18 June 1958 ordered the University of Florida graduate schools opened to qualified blacks. The law school then admitted African-American George H. Starke in the fall semester of 1958.

SELECTED BIBLIOGRAPHY

Algia R. Cooper, "*Brown v. Board of Education* and Virgil Darnell Hawkins: Twenty-Eight Years and Six Petitions to Justice," *Journal of Negro History* 64 (Winter 1979), 1–20; George Rossman, ed., "Review of Recent Supreme Court Decisions," *American Bar Association Journal* 42 (1956), 450; Samuel Selkow, "Hawkins, the United States Supreme Court and Justice," *Journal of Negro Education* 31 (Winter 1962), 91–101; Joseph A. Tomberlin, "Florida and the School Desegregation Issue, 1954–59: A Summary Review," *Journal of Negro Education* 43 (Fall 1974), 457–466; Joseph A. Tomberlin, "The Negro and Florida's System of Education: The Aftermath of the Brown Case" (Ph.D. diss., Florida State University, 1967).

Maxine D. Jones

FORCE BILL (1890). The Federal Elections, or "Force," bill introduced by Republican Congressman Henry Cabot Lodge of Massachusetts in April 1890 was the last significant federal effort to protect black suffrage until the Civil Rights Act of 1957.* The bill authorized oversight of congressional elections by federal officers when five hundred voters petitioned for it. Although applicable nationally, its primary intent was to ensure enforcement of the Fifteenth Amendment* for black Republican voters in the South. The bill passed the House of Representatives by a narrow margin in July 1890, but it failed in the Senate because of Democratic resistance and defection by Republican leaders who needed

The White Leaguers, shown here denying blacks the vote, would have been outlawed by the Force Bill. (Negro Almanac Collection, Amistad Research Center, Tulane University, New Orleans.)

southern votes for the McKinley Tariff, desired by northern business. Subsequently, northern Republicans returned control of black rights in the South to white supremacists.

SELECTED BIBLIOGRAPHY

Carl N. Degler, *The Age of Economic Revolution, 1876–1900* (1977); John A. Garraty, *Henry Cabot Lodge: A Biography* (1953); Stanley P. Hirshson, *Farewell to the Bloody Shirt: Northern Republicans and the Southern Negro, 1877–1893* (1962); H. Wayne Morgan, *From Hayes to McKinley: National Party Politics, 1877–1896* (1969).

James B. Potts

FORD, JAMES W. (1893, Pratt City, Ala.–21 June 1957, New York, N.Y.). Son of an Alabama steel worker and a domestic working mother, Ford graduated from Fisk University* in 1920 where he earned high marks as an athlete and scholar. During the 1920s, Ford migrated to Chicago where he worked as a parcel post dispatcher, joined the Postal Workers Union, read widely in the trade union movement, and became a member of the Communist party.* He traveled to the Soviet Union in 1927 and 1928, rose through the ranks of the American Communist party, and in 1929 became head of the International Trade Union Committee of Negro Workers. In the early depression years, he left Chicago for New York City where he became chief organizer for the Harlem section of the Communist party and was deeply involved in leftist politics. A consistent supporter of Communist ideology and Marxist class theories, Ford was committed to building alliances between the black and white working classes. Running with William Z. Foster, he was the Communist party's vice presidential candidate in 1932, 1936, and 1940. In 1938 he was an unsuccessful candidate on the Communist ticket for a seat in the United States Senate. When party ideology shifted in the mid-1930s to the "united front," Ford gave his support to traditional black rights organizations, progressive unions, and the newly formed National Negro Congress.* Despite a rather unyielding commitment to party ideology, Ford and Harlem Communists helped to spotlight civil rights issues such as the Scottsboro Trials* and worked tirelessly against racial discrimination in public and private employment.

SELECTED BIBLIOGRAPHY

Harold Cruse, *Crisis of the Negro Intellectual* (1967); Claude McKay, *Harlem: Negro Metropolis* (1940); Mark Naison, *Communists in Harlem During the Depression* (1983); Wilson Record, *The Negro and the Communist Party* (1951).

John B. Kirby

FOREMAN, CLARK H. (19 February 1902, Atlanta, Ga.–15 June 1977, Atlanta, Ga.). Born in a well-known Georgia family whose grandfather owned the *Atlanta Constitution*, Foreman studied at Harvard University, Columbia University, and the London School of Economics. As an undergraduate at the University of Georgia, he witnessed the lynching of a black man. He committed himself to the cause of racial justice. In the 1920s, he worked for the Commission on Interracial Cooperation* and the Rosenwald Fund.* In 1933, he was chosen by Harold L. Ickes* to be Special Adviser on Negro Affairs for the Department of Interior and Public Works Administration. Although appointment of a white Southerner was initially criticized by many blacks, Foreman's strong support for the inclusion of blacks within New Deal programs and his selection of black economist Robert C. Weaver,* who later replaced him, as his assistant, won over many of his critics. Leaving Interior in 1935, he held a number of other positions within the Roosevelt administration. In 1942 he was dismissed from the Federal Works Administration because of his strong condemnation of the racial conflict that occurred at the Sojourner Truth Housing Project in Detroit, Michigan. From 1942 to 1948, he led the Southern Conference for Human Welfare,* one of the few organizations within the South during the 1940s and postwar years that continued to work for the improvement of race relations and black justice. At the time of his death, Foreman had long been associated with the Emergency Civil Liberties Committee and the cause of equal rights. He symbolized a small but influential group of white, southern, racial liberals who helped shape racial thought during the Roosevelt era and provided encouragement to the civil rights struggles of the 1950s and 1960s.

SELECTED BIBLIOGRAPHY
John B. Kirby, *Black Americans in the Roosevelt Era* (1980); Thomas A. Krueger, *And Promises to Keep* (1967); Morton Sosna, *In Search of the Silent South* (1977).
John B. Kirby

FORMAN, JAMES (4 October 1928, Chicago, Ill.–). A persistent African-American leader, James Forman grew up in a working-class neighborhood in Chicago's southside. After high school, he entered the U.S. Air Force, became a veteran of the Korean War, and graduated from Chicago's Roosevelt University in 1957. On assignment for the *Chicago Defender* in 1958, reporting on the aftermath of the Little Rock desegregation crisis* in Little Rock, Arkansas, he became active in the civil rights struggle. Later as a leader in Fayette County, Tennessee, he joined the Student Nonviolent Coordinating Committee* (SNCC). The following year he became SNCC's executive secretary, a post he held for five years (1961–1966). Forman's most widely publicized act was the demand for the United States to give reparations to the African-American community. Forman first voiced this view in 1969 during a surprise speech at New York City's Riverside Church. He called for $500 million in reparations for the injustices of slavery, racism, and capitalism. Detailed in his 1969 Black Manifesto, the demand effectively raised the consciousness of white America to the enduring socioeconomic disadvantages experienced by African Americans. During the 1970s he continued to speak and work for civil rights causes across the country. He served several terms as president of the Unemployment and Poverty Action Council (UPAC) during the mid-1970s. He pursued educational goals and received his M.A. degree from Cornell University (1980) and his Ph.D. from the Union Institute (1982). In April 1990 he received the 1990 National Conference of Black Mayor's Fannie Lou Hamer Freedom Award. A prolific writer, Forman has published several books about the civil rights movement, including *Sammy Young, Jr.: The First Black College Student to Die in the Black Liberation Movement* (1968); *The Political Thought of James Forman* (1970); *The Makings of Black Revolutionaries* (1972); and *Self Determination: An Examination of the Question and Its Application to the African-American People* (1985).

SELECTED BIBLIOGRAPHY

Afro-American Encyclopedia, vol. 4 (1974); Derrick A. Bell, Jr., *And We Are Not Saved* (1987); Michael Harrington and Arnold S. Kaufman, "Black Reparations—Two Views," *Dissent* 16 (July-August 1969), 317–20; Robert S. Lecky and H. Elliot Wright, eds., *Black Manifesto* (1969); Arnold Schuchter, *Reparations* (1970).

                                                                Glenn O. Phillips

FORTUNE, TIMOTHY THOMAS (3 October 1856, Jackson County, Fla.–2 June 1928, New York, N.Y.). Born into slavery, Fortune received a limited education but did briefly attend a school sponsored by the Freedmen's Bureau.* He learned the printer's trade in Jacksonville, Florida, where he became an expert compositor, and later moved to Washington, D.C., in the mid-1870s to work on the *People's Advocate*, a black newspaper.

In 1879, Fortune moved to New York City and took part ownership of the *Rumor*, which became the *Globe* in 1881 with Fortune as its editor. Following the failure of the *Globe* in 1884, Fortune became sole owner of the *New York Freeman*, which changed its name to the *New York Age** in 1887. Within a few years, the *Age* became the premier black newspaper published in the United States, and Fortune rose to become the dean of African-American journalists in America. The program and methods proposed in his contentious editorials in the *New York Age* and other publications anticipated the direction that would be taken by the civil rights movement in the twentieth century. Through the columns of his newspaper, Fortune waged a militant struggle against all forms of discrimination and racial repression. He was the prime mover in the formation of the Afro-American League* in 1890; this organization, though short-lived, later merged with the Afro-American Council,* organized in 1898 at Rochester, New York. During the early 1920s, Fortune became editor if the *Negro World*,* the organ of Marcus Garvey's* Universal Negro Improvement Association.*

SELECTED BIBLIOGRAPHY
New York Age, 27 February 1886; *New York Amsterdam News*, 13 June 1928; Emma
Lou Thornbrough, *T. Thomas Fortune, Militant Journalist* (1970).

George E. Walker

FOURTEENTH AMENDMENT. The Fourteenth Amendment to the
Constitution of the United States was ratified in 1868. Of the amendment's five sections two directly punished the former Confederate states
by repudiating the Confederate debt, guaranteeing the war debt of the
United States, and prohibiting prominent Confederates from political
participation. The final section delegated to Congress the power to enforce the provisions of the article.

The first two sections of the amendment tried to redress the violence
and discrimination of the Black Codes* instituted to resubjugate the freed
black population after the end of slavery. It conferred citizenship on
African Americans; guaranteed the privileges and immunities of citizenship; prohibited states from depriving "any person of life, liberty,
or property, without due process of law"; and guaranteed "equal protection of laws." In addition, it empowered African Americans to exercise their citizenship and punished Confederate politicians by reducing
state representation in Congress in proportion to the number of male
voters denied the right to vote.

By 1877 southern politicians overlooked the civil rights guaranteed by
the Fourteenth Amendment and, with the complicity of all branches of
the federal government, neutralized the black vote and all black political
participation. However, when enforced, the civil rights sections of the
amendment were used throughout the twentieth century to guarantee
the civil rights of African Americans.

SELECTED BIBLIOGRAPHY
Mary Frances Berry, *Military Necessity and Civil Rights Policy: Black Citizenship and
the Constitution, 1861–1868* (1977); Richard C. Cortner, *The Supreme Court and the
Second Bill of Rights: The Fourteenth Amendment and the Nationalization of Civil
Liberties* (1981); Robert John Kaczorowski, *The Nationalization of Civil Rights: Con-
stitutional Theory and Practice in a Racist Society, 1866–1883* (1972); Hermine Herta
Meyer, *The History and Meaning of the Fourteenth Amendment: Judicial Erosion of the
Constitution through the Misuse of the Fourteenth Amendment* (1977); United States
Supreme Court, *The Civil Rights Cases [109 U.S. 3] in the Supreme Court of the
United States, October 15, 1883* (1963).

Lillie Johnson Edwards

FRANKLIN, JOHN HOPE (2 January 1915, Rentiesville, Okla.–   ). After
he graduated magna cum laude from Fisk University* in Nashville, Tennessee, in 1935, Franklin enrolled at Harvard University where he received his M.A. in 1936. After he spent a year as an instructor at Fisk
(1936–1937), he returned to Harvard to work for his Ph.D., which he

earned in 1941. A teaching position at St. Augustine's College (1939–1943) in Raleigh, North Carolina, afforded him access to the sources he needed to complete his dissertation on free blacks in that state. When that work was published in 1943, he went to North Carolina College at Durham; and in 1947, he moved to Howard University* in Washington, D.C. Brooklyn College invited him to join its faculty in 1956, and in 1964 he became a professor of history at the University of Chicago, where he served as department chair and was named the first John Matthews Manly Distinguished Service Professor of History. After retirement in 1982, he accepted appointment as the James B. Duke Professor of History at Duke University. Prominent among his works are *The Free Negro in North Carolina, 1790–1860* (1943); *From Slavery to Freedom: A History of Negro Americans* (1947; sixth edition, 1988); *The Militant South* (1956); *Reconstruction after the Civil War* (1961); and *A Southern Odyssey; Travellers in the Antebellum North* (1975); *George Washington Williams: A Biography* (1985). He became the first black to read a paper before the Southern Historical Association in 1949, and subsequently he was elected president not only of that organization but also of the American Historical Association and the Organization of American Historians. His honors—which include other professional offices, fellowships, and honorary doctorates—are too numerous to list. He has also donated his professional expertise to public causes. Notable among his contributions was the research he did on the Fourteenth Amendment* for the plaintiff's case in *Brown v. Board of Education.**

SELECTED BIBLIOGRAPHY

William C. Matney, ed., *Who's Who among Black Americans* (1976); August Meier and Elliott Rudwick, *Black History and the Historical Profession, 1915–1980* (1986); Charles V. Willie, *Five Black Scholars: An Analysis of Family Life, Education, and Career* (1986).

Gary B. Mills

FRASIER v. BOARD OF TRUSTEES OF THE UNIVERSITY OF NORTH CAROLINA, 134 F. Supp. 589 (M.D. N.C., 1955). Some states continued to enforce segregation in higher education in 1955, despite the Supreme Court rulings in *Sipuel v. Board of Regents** and *Brown v. Board of Education.** The University of North Carolina (UNC) system pursued such a policy, although it had admitted blacks to graduate and professional programs. Leroy Benjamin Frasier and two other African-American students challenged this policy in the spring of 1955. The university declined their application because of their race. The students appealed to the board of trustees without success. In May, the board affirmed its policy: "It is hereby declared to be the policy of the Board of Trustees . . . that applications of Negroes to the undergraduate schools of the three branches of the Consolidated University be not accepted." It assumed that segregated colleges satisfied the terms of the Fourteenth Amendment.* The students then filed a class action suit in federal courts. Attorneys argued that the policy of the UNC system violated the equal protection of the law clause of the Fourteenth Amendment. The court agreed. That fall, the university enrolled three black students in its undergraduate program.

SELECTED BIBLIOGRAPHY

Richard Bardolph, ed., *The Civil Rights Record, Black Americans and the Law, 1849–1970* (1970); *U.S. Commission on Civil Rights: Equal Protection of the Laws in Public Higher Education* (1957).

Stephen Middleton

FRAZIER, EDWARD FRANKLIN (24 September 1894, Baltimore, Md.–17 May 1962, Washington, D.C.). After graduating from Howard University* with honors in 1916, Frazier taught at Tuskegee Institute* in Alabama; St. Paul's Normal and Industrial School at Lawrenceville, Virginia; and Baltimore High School. Entering graduate school at Clark University in Worcester, Massachusetts, in 1919, he completed his master's degree in sociology in 1920. A Russel Sage Foundation fellowship financed a year's study at the New York School of Social work; then, aided by an American Scandinavian Foundation Fellowship, he studied another year at the University of Copenhagen. Returning in 1922, he accepted a position at Atlanta University* as director of its school of social work, but his stay there was terminated in 1927 by white reactions to an article he wrote for *Forum Magazine*, "The Pathology of Race Prejudice." He entered the doctoral program in sociology at the University of Chicago, and his dissertation, "The Negro Family in Chicago," was completed in 1931 while he was teaching at Fisk University.* He returned to his alma mater in 1934, where he served in various capacities until his death. Among his published works are *The Negro Family in Chicago* (1932), *The Negro Family in the United States* (1939), *Black Bourgeoisie* (1957), and *Race and Culture Contacts in the Modern World* (1957). His intellectual achievements won him elective offices in numerous professional organizations—most significantly the presidency of the American Sociological Society in 1948. He was one of the first blacks to serve as the head of a national professional association in the United States. His major contributions were his studies of the black family and race relations. His analysis of the impact that slavery, sudden freedom, urban migrations, and dislocations had had on the family produced sociological explanations rather than racial or genetic condemnations; thus Frazier helped find a plausible cause for African-American problems that was prerequisite to any cure. He also attacked the theories of Melville Jean Herskovits* on the survival of Africanisms, for enabling whites to blame black antisocial behavior upon surviving African traits rather than upon societal oppression. Although he argued for equal rights and integration,

Frazier nevertheless felt that blacks should not sacrifice their positive cultural identity for the sake of equality. He was not an assimilationist as some have asserted.

SELECTED BIBLIOGRAPHY

Rayford W. Logan and Michael R. Winston, eds., *Dictionary of American Negro Biography* (1982); August Meier, *Negro Thought in America, 1880–1915: Racial Ideologies in the Age of Booker T. Washington* (1963); August Meier and Elliott Rudwick, *Black History and the Historical Profession, 1915–1980* (1986); Anthony M. Platt, *E. Franklin Frazier* (1991).

Gary B. Mills

FREE SOUTHERN THEATER. During the fall of 1963, three civil rights workers in Mississippi conceived the idea of using drama to communicate the aims of the civil rights movement to masses of black people in the rural South. John O'Neal and Doris Derby of the Student Nonviolent Coordinating Committee* and Gilbert Moses, a reporter for the *Mississippi Free Press*, established an integrated touring company whose productions were intended to educate southern blacks about the institutional barriers to progress and to encourage people to either join or support the civil rights movement in their local communities. During Freedom Summer of 1964,* the Free Southern Theater conducted a theater workshop for students from Tougaloo College* and Jackson State College. After opening with *In White America* in Jackson with an integrated cast drawn from the Mississippi Summer Project volunteers, Free Southern Theater made a twenty-one-town tour of Mississippi, Louisiana, and Tennessee. The successful tour touched audiences in much the way the organizers had envisioned. After the 28 November 1964 performance of *Waiting for Godot*, for example, Fannie Lou Hamer* is reported to have remarked that the play was "somewhat similar to any person in a suffering condition who just keeps on waiting and nothing happens." Drama of the absurd could intensify the meaning of what the ardent struggle for civil rights entailed. By 1970, Free Southern Theater was less a touring company than a community theater project in New Orleans, Louisiana, where it ceased to be a cultural arm of the civil rights movement.

SELECTED BIBLIOGRAPHY

Tom Dent, Gilbert Moses, and Richard Schechner, eds., *The Free Southern Theater by the Free Southern Theater* (1969); Genevieve Fabre, *Drumbeats, Masks, and Metaphor: Contemporary Afro-American Theater* (1983); Larry Neal, "Free Southern Theatre, the Conquest of the South," *The Drama Review* 14 (1970), 169–74; John O'Neal, "Motion in the Ocean: Some Political Dimensions of the Free Southern Theatre," *The Drama Review* 12 (Summer 1968), 70–77.

Jerry Ward

FREEDMAN'S BANK. The Freedman's Bank, chartered by Congress on 3 March 1865 as the Freedman's Savings and Trust Company, was "designed to furnish a place of security and profit for the hard earnings of the colored people, especially at the South." It began operations on 4 April 1865. The business of the bank was confined to blacks. Its thirty-four branches were located in every state of the South as well as in New York City and Philadelphia. Although it was an independent institution, the bank worked closely with the Freedmen's Bureau* in encouraging blacks to deposit their money in the bank's offices. During the nine years that the bank operated, total deposits amounted to fifty-six million dollars. The Freedman's Bank was forced to close its doors on 28 June 1874, and its depositors lost their savings. The failure of the bank was partially due to a general business depression in the country, but the major cause was mismanagement of its funds by its officers, many of whom were influential members of the Republican party.

SELECTED BIBLIOGRAPHY

George R. Bentley, *A History of the Freedmen's Bureau* (1974); W.E.B. Du Bois, *Black Reconstruction in America* (1935); Walter L. Fleming, *Documentary History of Reconstruction* (1906).

Robert A. Bellinger

FREEDMEN'S BUREAU. Many have viewed the Freedmen's Bureau as the original federal civil rights agency for blacks. Congress created the bureau in March 1865 under its official title, the Bureau of Refugees, Freedmen, and Abandoned Lands. It initially fed, clothed, sheltered, and gave medical care to more whites than blacks; it became identified only with freedmen after Congress directed it to promote their general welfare. President Andrew Johnson criticized the bureau in 1866 and attempted to kill it, charging that it "would not be consistent with the public welfare." Headed by Commissioner Oliver Otis Howard,* a veteran U.S. Army major general, the bureau supervised freedmen's labor and legal relations. To secure justice in hostile jurisdictions it sometimes conducted court proceedings. Its services reached far, even to establishing a missing persons agency to help reunite families separated by slavery. The bureau had established more than forty hospitals by 1867 and had distributed twenty-one million meals by 1869. By 1870 it had initiated 4,239 schools with 9,307 teachers and 247,333 students. Many of the oldest historically black colleges and universities owe a debt to the bureau. A feeble congressional and national commitment to full and equal citizenship for blacks permitted the bureau to die after 1868.

SELECTED BIBLIOGRAPHY

George R. Bentley, *A History of the Freedmen's Bureau* (1955); John A. Carpenter, *Sword and Olive Branch: Oliver Otis Howard* (1964); William S. McFeely, *Yankee Stepfather: General O. O. Howard and the Freedmen* (1968); Donald G. Nieman, *To Set the Law in Motion: The Freedmen's Bureau and the Legal Rights of Blacks, 1865–*

Black women teaching at Freedmen's Bureau School. (Negro Almanac Collection, Amistad Research Center, Tulane University, New Orleans.)

1868 (1979); Claude F. Oubre, *Forty Acres and a Mule: The Freedmen's Bureau and Black Landownership* (1978); Paul S. Pierce, *The Freedmen's Bureau* (1904).

Thomas J. Davis

FREEDOM RIDERS. James Farmer,* national director of the Congress of Racial Equality* (CORE), planned the first freedom ride of the 1960s as a nonviolent direct action* test of *Boynton v. Virginia** (1960), which had declared segregation in railway and bus terminal accommodations to be unconstitutional. Thirteen persons including Farmer left Washington, D.C., on 4 May 1961 for Georgia, Alabama, and Mississippi. In Anniston, Alabama, one bus was destroyed and riders on another were attacked. The interracial Freedom Riders continued the protest throughout the summer. By the time the Interstate Commerce Commission prohibited segregated accommodations in November 1961, over a thousand participants had attempted a freedom ride, and CORE's credentials as a militant pacifist organization had been established. Later Freedom Riders met with similar violence but with eventual success.

Freedom Riders met with violence in Anniston, Alabama. (Archives Collection, Birmingham Public Library. Courtesy *Birmingham News*.)

SELECTED BIBLIOGRAPHY
Catherine A. Barnes, *Journey from Jim Crow: The Desegregation of Southern Transit* (1983); Robert H. Brisbane, *Black Activism: Racial Revolution in the United States, 1954–1970* (1974); James Farmer, *Lay Bare the Heart: An Autobiography of the Civil Rights Movement* (1985); August Meier and Elliott Rudwick, *CORE: A Study in the Civil Rights Movement: 1942–1968* (1973); August Meier and Elliott Rudwick, "The First Freedom Ride," *Phylon* 30 (Fall 1969), 213–22; Kenneth O'Reilly, "The FBI and the Civil Rights Movement during the Kennedy Years—From the Freedom Rides to Albany," *The Journal of Southern History* 54 (May 1988), 201–32.

Thaddeus M. Smith

FREEDOM SUMMER OF 1964. Approximately one thousand northern, predominantly white, college students joined a cadre of predominantly African-American freedom fighters in Mississippi. They registered thousands of black voters and provided health and education services through community centers and freedom schools. The Student Nonviolent Coordinating Committee,* initiated this project, which was jointly supported through the Council of Federated Organizations* and directed by Robert Moses.*

Volunteers received prior training in nonviolence, self-defense, Mississippi mores, and how to behave under arrest. On 21 June three volunteers were reported missing from Neshoba County. The search for James Earl Chaney,* a local African American, and New York volunteers Michael Henry Schwerner* and Andrew Goodman* continued until 4 August when their bodies were unearthed from a dam. (Seven members of the Ku Klux Klan, convicted of the murders in 1967, were later paroled and set free). Terrorism pervaded the summer. Workers endured at least eighty beatings, one thousand arrests, and sixty-seven incidents of bombings and arson.

A major focus of the project was building the grass-roots Mississippi Freedom Democratic party* (MFDP). An MFDP delegation challenged the all-white regulars for their seats at the Democratic national convention in August 1964. Party chiefs responded with overt compromises and covert sabotage and suppression.

Short-term perceptions of Freedom Summer emphasized disillusionment with liberal politics and increasingly strained relations between African-American activists and white volunteers. Later perspectives credited the project with hastening passage of the Voting Rights Act of 1965* and opening the way for federally funded health clinics and Headstart* programs. The most famous of the MFDP delegates, Mrs. Fannie Lou Hamer,* observed that "before the 1964 summer project there were people that wanted change but they hadn't dared to come out. After 1964 people began moving. To me it's one of the greatest things that ever happened in Mississippi."

Freedom School class, Mississippi, Summer 1964. (Staughton Lynd Collection. State Historical Society of Wisconsin.)

SELECTED BIBLIOGRAPHY
Seth Cagin and Philip Dray, *We Are Not Afraid: The Story of Goodman, Schwerner and Chaney and the Civil Rights Campaign for Mississippi* (1988); Sara Evans, *Personal Politics* (1980); Mary King, *Freedom Song: A Personal Story of the 1960s Civil Rights Movement* (1987); Doug McAdam, *Freedom Summer* (1988); Mary Aiken Roths-child, *A Case of Black and White: Northern Volunteers and the Southern Freedom*

Summers, 1964–1965 (1982); Elizabeth Sutherland, ed., *Letters from Mississippi* (1965).

Jo Ann O. Robinson

FREEDOM VOTE CAMPAIGN. In November 1963, the Student Nonviolent Coordinating Committee* sponsored a protest vote within the Mississippi African-American community. According to Mississippi law, voters who claimed illegal exclusion from registration were permitted to cast ballots which would be set aside until they could appeal their exclusion. With the assistance of Allard Lowenstein and numerous northern white student volunteers, more than 80,000 African Americans cast ballots in the Freedom Vote Campaign. Since regular polling stations were intimidating, the Freedom Vote Campaign provided African Americans with an opportunity to vote for civil rights candidates in their own communities.

SELECTED BIBLIOGRAPHY
Clayborne Carson, *In Struggle: SNCC and the Black Awakening of the 1960s* (1981); James Forman, *The Making of Black Revolutionaries* (1972); Lawrence Guyot and Mike Thelwell, "The Politics of Necessity and Survival in Mississippi," *Freedomways* 6 (Spring 1966) 120–32; Margaret Long, "The Mississippi Freedom Vote," *New South* 18 (December 1963), 10–13; August Meier and Elliott Rudwick, *CORE: A Study in the Civil Rights Movement, 1942–1968* (1973).

Donald Cunnigen

FRIENDS ASSOCIATION OF PHILADELPHIA AND ITS VICINITY FOR THE RELIEF OF COLORED FREEDMEN (1863–1869). Organized in November 1863, this organization (also known as the Friends Freedmen's Relief Association and the Friends Colored Relief Association of Philadelphia) was one of two Quaker freedmen's aid societies in Philadelphia. Among its officers were Richard Cadbury, Thomas Scattergood, Benjamin Coats, and Charles Rhoads. Its purpose was "to relieve the wants, provide for the instruction and protect the rights of the freedmen." The association did its work mainly in Virginia and North Carolina, where, for example, it opened stores. It began with funds of $53,000, some of which was donated by English Quakers. By 1867 the association had spent $210,500 in support of its activities.

SELECTED BIBLIOGRAPHY
Julius H. Parelee, "Freedmen's Aid Societies, 1861–1871," U.S. Department of the Interior, Office of Education, *Bulletin* 38 (1916), 268–300; Henry Lee Swint, *The Northern Teacher in the South, 1862–1870* (1967).

Judith N. Kerr

FRIENDS OF NEGRO FREEDOM. Founded in Washington, D.C., in May 1920 by A. Philip Randolph* and Chandler Owen, the friends organized the "Garvey Must Go" campaign to eliminate the Universal Negro Improvement Association* led by Jamaican-born Marcus Garvey.*

GLIMPSES AT THE FREEDMEN'S BUREAU—ISSUING RATIONS TO THE OLD AND SICK.—FROM A SKETCH BY OUR SPECIAL ARTIST, JAS. E. TAYLOR.

Impoverished freedmen were assisted after emancipation by the Freedmen's Bureau and the Friends' Association for the Relief of Colored Freedmen. (Library of Congress.)

The organization, made up of black conservatives, moderates, and radicals all linked by their fear of Garveyism, in January 1923 wrote an open letter to United States Attorney General Harry M. Daugherty urging Garvey's deportation as an "undesirable alien."

SELECTED BIBLIOGRAPHY

Tony Martin, *Race First: The Ideological and Organizational Struggles of Marcus Garvey and the Universal Negro Improvement Association* (1976).

Quintard Taylor

FULLER, META VAUX WARRICK (9 June 1877, Philadelphia, Pa.–18 March 1968, Framingham, Mass.). One of America's first African-American women studio sculptors, Fuller attended Philadelphia public schools and received her art education at J. Liberty Tadd's, the Pennsylvania Museum School (1895–1898), and the Pennsylvania Academy of the Fine Arts (1906). Between 1899 and 1902, Fuller studied in Paris, where in 1902 she became a protégée of Auguste Rodin. Although Fuller's work predates the Harlem Renaissance,* she was active during that period. In 1917 she produced two antilynching sculptures, one of which depicted Mary Turner, whose case Walter F. White* investigated for the NAACP.* Her *Ethiopia Awakening* (1921) was a compelling representation of the Harlem Renaissance's spirit. Meta Fuller was still working at the time of the civil rights movement of the 1960s. She produced sculpture that symbolized that era as well: *The Crucifixion*, her reaction to the murder of four girls in the bombing of the Sixteenth Street Baptist Church in Birmingham, Alabama, on 15 September 1963; and *The Good Samaritan*, dedicated to the clergy who had gone south to Alabama to join Martin Luther King, Jr.'s* march across Selma's Edmund Pettus Bridge on Sunday, 9 March 1965. During a career that spanned more than sixty years, Fuller portrayed the dignity and human rights struggle of African Americans realistically, chronicled historical events, and, occasionally, created a silent protest against racial injustice.

SELECTED BIBLIOGRAPHY

Crisis (January 1918), 133, (January 1919), 135, (November 1919), 350, (April 1920), 337; Judith N. Kerr, "God-Given Work, The Life and Times of Sculptor Meta Vaux Warrick Fuller, 1877–1968," (Ph.D. diss., University of Massachusetts, 1986); William Francis O'Donnell, "Meta Vaux Warrick, Sculptor of Horrors," *The World Today* 13 (November 1907), 1139–45; James A. Porter, *Modern Negro Art* (1943).

Judith N. Kerr

FULLER, S. BACON (4 June 1905, Monroe, La.–24 October 1988, Blue Island, Ill.). A Chicago African-American businessman, Fuller, in 1935, established Fuller's Products Company with twenty-five dollars and built a multimillion dollar national sales corporation by 1960. In spite of having only a sixth grade education, Fuller was the "godfather" of many other black businesses. His holdings included the *Pittsburgh Courier** and *New York Age** newspapers, a department store and theater, and farming and beef cattle investments. He was the first black member of the National Association of Manufacturers (NAM). At a December 1963 NAM convention, Fuller infuriated black leaders when he stated that blacks should show more initiative in raising their economic level. In response blacks boycotted his enterprises, which nearly led to his bankruptcy.

SELECTED BIBLIOGRAPHY
"S. Bacon Fuller," *Jet*, 7 November 1988; *New York Times*, 7 December 1963, 16 January 1965, 28 October, 7 November 1988; *Who's Who in America, 1974–1975* (1975).

Wali Rashash Kharif

FULLILOVE v. KLUTZNICK, 448 U.S. 448 (1980). Race-conscious programs to remedy the effects of past discrimination have been extremely controversial. *Fullilove v. Klutznick* presented the Supreme Court with the congressional application of a race-conscious policy to the granting of contracts for state or local public works projects funded by the Public Works Employment Act of 1977. State or local governments receiving federal construction grants were required to set aside at least 10 percent of the funds to purchase goods or services from minority business enterprises. By a vote of six to three, the Supreme Court upheld the constitutionality of this minority "set-aside." The controversial nature of such programs was evident in that the six justices who voted to uphold the legislation could not produce a majority opinion. Three believed that the legislation was supported by several of Congress's powers. For the other three justices, class-based remedies were justified because discrimination against blacks had been class based. However, when the City of Richmond, Virginia, adopted a minority set-aside patterned after the one upheld in *Fullilove*, another divided Court held that a city had no such authority. The latter decisions reflected President Ronald Reagan's appointments to the Court.

SELECTED BIBLIOGRAPHY
City of Richmond v. J. A. Croson Co., 109 S Ct. 706 (1989); Comment, "*Fullilove* and the Minority Set Aside: In Search of an Affirmative Action Rationale," *Emory Law Journal* 29 (1980), 1127–82; Peter Kilgore, "Racial Preferences in the Federal Grant Programs: Is There a Basis for Challenge after Fullilove v. Klutznick?" *Labor Law Journal* 32 (1981), 306–14.

Patricia A. Behlar

G

GALAMISON, MILTON A. (25 January 1923, Philadelphia, Pa.–9 March 1988, New York City). An African-American Presbyterian minister in Brooklyn, New York, Galamison waged a campaign for full school desegregation through the use of black student boycotts and strikes. As chairman of the City Wide Committee for Integrated Schools, Galamison spearheaded the 1964 boycott of New York City schools and played a vital role four years later in a teachers' strike for equity and racial equality. For Galamison, the public school boycott was an effective "form of civil disobedience" against social injustice.

SELECTED BIBLIOGRAPHY
Kenneth B. Clark, *Dark Ghetto* (1965); August Meier and Elliott Rudwick, eds., *Black Protest in the Sixties* (1970); Benjamin Muse, *The American Negro Revolution: From Nonviolence to Black Power, 1963–1967* (1968).

LeRoy T. Williams

GARNER v. LOUISIANA, 368 U.S. 157 (1961). In the spring of 1960, several African-American college students in Baton Rouge, Louisiana, held a sit-in at drugstore and bus terminal lunch counters that were reserved for white customers. They were arrested and convicted of disturbing the peace. The United States Supreme Court overturned the students' convictions, stating that there was no evidence that they had violated Louisiana law by their peaceful sit-in at the lunch counters. The Court found that the students' peaceful protest did not fall within the state's own interpretation of its statute relating to disturbance of the peace and noted that the Louisiana legislature had, after the students' arrest, attempted to modify the statute to fit the actions of the sit-in participants. Garner and the other protesters had violated the custom of segregated lunch counters, but their activities could not be considered to be a violation of Louisiana law. The students' convictions had been a misapplication of the disturbing the peace statute and had deprived them of their right to due process under the Fourteenth Amendment.* This case struck a blow at the ability of states to prosecute African Americans for violating the custom of segregation and for peacefully protesting for their civil rights.

SELECTED BIBLIOGRAPHY

Derrick A. Bell, Jr., *Race, Racism and American Law* (1980); Loren Miller, *The Petitioners: The Story of the Supreme Court of the United States and the Negro* (1966); Aldon D. Morris, *The Origins of the Civil Rights Movement: Black Communities Organizing for Change* (1984); George Rossman, ed., "Review of Recent Supreme Court Decisions," *American Bar Association Journal* 48 (1962), 169.

Steve Sadowsky

GARVEY, MARCUS MOSIAH (17 August 1887, St. Ann's Bay, Jamaica– 10 June 1940, London, England). A Pan-African nationalist and founder of the Universal Negro Improvement Association* (UNIA), Garvey was born in rural Jamaica. After about seven years of schooling, he became an apprentice printer, became disillusioned after participating in an unsuccessful printers' strike that made him skeptical of trade unions, and migrated to England in about 1911. He enrolled briefly at Birbeck College, where he came into contact with African intellectuals who ignited in him a desire to study and disseminate information about Africa and Africans.

Returning to Jamaica in 1914, he launched the Universal Negro Improvement and Conservation Association and African Communities League. Its main aim was "to draw the peoples of the race together," and one of its earliest goals was to develop a trade school for the poor and unskilled patterned after Tuskegee Institute* in Alabama.

Garvey arrived in the United States on 23 March 1916 and immediately launched a year-long speaking tour of thirty-eight states. His message was well received, and he organized the first branch of UNIA in the United States in June 1917. He began publishing the *Negro World*,* which promoted his African nationalist ideas, and made Liberty Hall in New York City the official headquarters of the UNIA.

During 1919, Garvey's popularity soared as he tried to initiate a Back-to-Africa Movement. He presided over a UNIA with dozens of chapters and thousands of followers in the United States and around the world. The UNIA stressed the need for real economic opportunities and the uniting of persons of African descent for their collective betterment. In 1919 Garvey's UNIA purchased three ships and developed the Black Star Steamship Line.* In August 1920, at a UNIA convention, he was unanimously elected the provisional president of Africa. Garvey sought to work with the Liberian government to settle followers in Africa.

Marcus Garvey. (Negro Almanac Collection, Amistad Research Center, Tulane University, New Orleans.)

In 1925 Garvey was convicted on a mail fraud charge and sentenced to a five-year prison term. He had served half of the sentence when President Calvin Coolidge commuted the rest of his prison term and had him deported. Garvey returned to Jamaica to a hero's welcome from the Jamaican underclasses. Beginning in July 1932, he published *The New Jamaican* and *The Black Man's Magazine*. He also launched a development program aimed at raising millions of dollars for new job opportunities for the poor.

On 26 March 1935, Garvey sailed for England where he resided for the rest of his life. He continued speaking out on civil rights of Africans and the ideals of the Pan-African Movement.* He died on 10 June 1940 in London with unfulfilled aspirations, but his ideas and writings inspired many of the leaders and spokespersons of the civil rights era.

SELECTED BIBLIOGRAPHY

David E. Cronon, *Black Moses: The Story of Marcus Garvey and the Universal Negro Improvement Association* (1955); Elton C. Fax, *Garvey: The Story of a Pioneer Black Nationalist* (1972); Amy Jacques Garvey, ed., *Philosophy and Opinions of Marcus Garvey* (1969); Robert A. Hill, ed., *The Marcus Garvey and Universal Negro Improvement Association Papers*, 7 vols. (1983–1990); Judith Stein, *The World of Marcus*

Garvey: Race and Class in Modern Society (1986); Tony Martin, *Race First: The Ideological and Organizational Struggles of Marcus Garvey* (1976).

                                                                    Glenn O. Phillips

GASTON COUNTY v. UNITED STATES, 395 U.S. 285 (1969). Among the devices used by southern states to disfranchise blacks was the literacy test. Gaston County, North Carolina, had utilized such a test. When Gaston County came under the coverage of the Voting Rights Act of 1965,* however, its literacy test, like that of other covered states and subdivisions of states, was suspended. The county, under the terms of the Voting Rights Act, sought to have the ban on its literacy test lifted by obtaining a declaratory judgment from the District Court for the District of Columbia that no "test or device" had been used during the previous five years for the purpose or effect of denying the right to vote based upon race. In an opinion by Judge J. Skelly Wright,* the district court denied Gaston County's petition on grounds that the majority of its voting-age blacks had attended inferior, segregated schools; therefore, even a fairly administered literacy test would have a discriminatory effect. The Supreme Court affirmed the decision for "substantially the reasons given by the majority of the District Court." The decision meant that the literacy tests of other areas under the Voting Rights Act would remain suspended, since they too had had segregated schools.

SELECTED BIBLIOGRAPHY

Richard Claude, *The Supreme Court and the Electoral Process* (1970); Owen M. Fiss, "*Gaston County v. United States*: Fruition of the Freezing Principle," *Supreme Court Review* (1969), 379–445; *Washington Post*, 3 June 1969.

                                                                    Patricia A. Behlar

GENERAL EDUCATION BOARD. John D. Rockefeller, with an initial one-million-dollar gift, founded this organization in 1902. By the time of its final grant in 1960, the General Education Board (GEB) had appropriated almost $325 million to aid education. Approximately 20 percent of GEB funds went toward the development of African-American industrial and agricultural education in the South. Credited with helping to establish southern high schools through support of African-American training schools, the GEB is criticized for following an accommodationist policy that expanded educational programs modeled on the Hampton-Tuskegee industrial training curriculum and thus perpetuated racially segregated and unequal school systems.

SELECTED BIBLIOGRAPHY

James D. Anderson, "Northern Foundations and the Shaping of Southern Black Rural Education, 1902–1935," *History of Education Quarterly* (Winter 1978), 371–96; Raymond B. Fosdick, *Adventure in Giving* (1962); Waldemar A. Nielsen, *The Big Foundations* (1972); J. M. Stephen Peeps, "Northern Philanthropy and the

Emergence of Black Higher Education—Do-Gooders, Compromise, or Co-conspirators?" *The Journal of Negro Education* 50 (Summer 1981), 251–69.

Janice M. Leone

GIBSON v. FLORIDA LEGISLATIVE INVESTIGATION COMMITTEE,

372 U.S. 539 (1963). Following *Brown v. Board of Education,** the Florida Legislative Investigation Committee attempted to obtain the membership rosters of the state branches of the NAACP.* At a public hearing in 1958, Father Theodore R. Gibson, president of the Miami chapter, declined to turn over the records for fear of exposing NAACP members to the danger of racist retaliation. The committee claimed that it needed to uncover the identity of NAACP followers as part of its probe into Communist influence on race relations. The Florida Supreme Court ordered Gibson to consult his files before answering questions about the presence of alleged Communists in his group, but it did not require him actually to hand over the lists to the committee. Gibson refused, and in March 1963, the U.S. Supreme Court upheld his decision. Speaking for a majority of five, Justice Arthur Goldberg declared that the investigation committee had not shown a direct connection between the NAACP and subversive activities and could not infringe upon the group's right to privacy and the free association of its members. This opinion stymied further efforts to investigate the NAACP and raised the standard of protection for members of legitimate organizations investigated by legislative committees.

SELECTED BIBLIOGRAPHY

Harry Kalven Jr., *The Negro and the First Amendment* (1965); Paul L. Murphy, *The Constitution in Crisis Times* (1972); Wilson Record, *Race and Radicalism: The NAACP and the Communist Party in Conflict* (1964).

Steven F. Lawson

GILES v. HARRIS, 189 U.S. 475 (1903).

Alabama's 1901 constitution embodied various devices, including the good character requirement and understanding and literacy tests, designed to disenfranchise blacks. Jackson W. Giles, a black citizen of Montgomery, was denied the right to register, so he sought a federal court order compelling local election officials to register qualified blacks. He alleged that various provisions of the state constitution violated the Fourteenth* and Fifteenth Amendments.* The district court held that it did not have jurisdiction. Upon appeal, the Supreme Court held that federal courts could hear the case. However, on the curious grounds that if, as alleged, Alabama's registration scheme was a fraud upon the Constitution, an order to register Giles would make the Court a party to that fraud by adding another voter to a fraudulent registration list. The Court refused to order Giles's registration. Further, the Court took a narrow view of the judiciary's enforcement power; short of supervising elections in Alabama, the Court could envisage no means of enforcing political rights. It concluded that those suffering from political wrongs should turn to the political branches, not to the judiciary, for relief.

SELECTED BIBLIOGRAPHY

Richard Claude, *The Supreme Court and the Electoral Process* (1970); Donald R. Matthews and James Prothro, *Negroes and the New Southern Politics* (1966).

Earlean M. McCarrick

GILES v. TEASLEY, 193 U.S. 146 (1904). After the Supreme Court in 1903 refused in *Giles v. Harris** to order local officials to register Jackson W. Giles, a black citizen of Montgomery, Giles sued voting registrars in state court. He sought monetary damages and a court order compelling his registration, alleging that the state constitution's voting requirements, by design and administration, violated the Fifteenth Amendment.* The lower state court dismissed the suit. Giles next appealed to the Alabama Supreme Court. The highest state court avoided the national constitutional question and, in a Catch–22 process of reasoning, denied relief: If the challenged state constitutional provisions were in conflict with the national constitution, they were invalid and registrars appointed under those provisions were not authorized to register anyone. If, on the other hand, the provisions were valid, the registrars had acted within their authority. Upon appeal, the U.S. Supreme Court held that it had no authority to hear the case. Because it could review only federal questions decided by state courts and because the state court had not ruled on the national constitution issue, the Supreme Court could not review the decision. As in Giles's earlier suit, the Supreme Court afforded no remedy for Fifteenth Amendment violations.

SELECTED BIBLIOGRAPHY

Derrick A. Bell, Jr., *Race, Racism and American Law* (1980); Richard Claude, *The Supreme Court and the Electoral Process* (1970).

Earlean M. McCarrick

GIOVANNI, NIKKI (7 June 1943, Knoxville, Tenn.–   ). Educated at Fisk University,* where she was an honors graduate in history, and at the University of Pennsylvania, where she pursued postgraduate studies in social work, Giovanni abandoned plans for a social work career in order to pursue one in writing and teaching. She has taught creative writing and black studies at Rutgers, in New Jersey, Queens College of the City University of New York, and elsewhere. She emerged in the late 1960s as one of the most popular of the "New Black Poets" and was a leader of the black oral poetry movement. Her works include *Black Feeling, Black Talk/Black Judgement* (1970), *Re-Creation* (1970), *Gemini: An Extended Autobiographical Statement on My First Twenty-Five Years of Being a Black Poet* (1976), and *My House* (1972). Among her works for children, *Ego Tripping and Other Poems for Young People* (1973) remains popular.

Central to Giovanni's poetry is her political activism and militancy. Some of her early poems crackle with the intensity of defiance and black pride, others are gently satirical, personal, and introspective. In her later work some of her revolutionary fire fades and she shows a greater concern with the nature of poetry itself. Her collaborative works with James Baldwin* and Margaret Walker Alexander,* *A Dialogue* (1972) and *A Poetic Equation* (1974) respectively, received critical acclaim. Her awards include an honorary doctorate from Wilberforce University in Wilberforce, Ohio.

SELECTED BIBLIOGRAPHY

Mari Evans, ed., *Black Women Writers (1950–1980): A Critical Evaluation* (1984); Harry A. Ploski and James Williams, *The Afro-American* (1983); *Time*, 17 January 1972.

Maghan Keita

GOD'S TROMBONES. Acclaimed as "one of the most beautiful volumes of verse ever produced by a black poet," it ranks as one of James Weldon Johnson's* greatest and most lasting contributions to African-American and American poetry. Breaking out of the confines of the dialect tradition, these seven free-verse renditions authentically capture and preserve the spirit, idiom, and rhythm of the Negro folk sermon with powerful folk imagery, beauty, and originality. Johnson's 1927 work was a pioneering effort and a major influence on later Harlem Renaissance* poets. *God's Trombones* provided a model of excellence for the creation of a new Negro language and poetry.

SELECTED BIBLIOGRAPHY

Stephen Bronz, *Roots of Negro Racial Consciousness: The 1920s: Three Harlem Renaissance Authors* (1964); Eugenia W. Collier, "James Weldon Johnson: Mirror of Change," *Phylon* 21 (Winter 1960), 351–59; Robert Fleming, *James Weldon Johnson* (1987); Hugh M. Gloster, "James Weldon Johnson," in *Negro Voices in American Fiction* (1948); Richard Long, "A Weapon of My Song: The Poetry of James Weldon Johnson," *Phylon* 32 (December 1971), 374–82.

Jacquelyn Jackson

GOMILLION, CHARLES G. (1 April 1900, Johnston, S.C.–). After he graduated from Georgia's Paine College in 1928, Gomillion accepted a faculty appointment at Tuskegee Institute* to teach history. He spent the 1933–1934 academic year at Fisk University* studying sociology under E. Franklin Frazier,* after which he returned to Tuskegee and taught sociology. Gomillion devoted much time after 1934 working for civic improvement. Tuskegee blacks enjoyed few public services. Frustrated by the unresponsiveness of the local government to black requests for better streets, sanitation, and to the whole range of black concerns, Gomillion turned to political action. Believing that the ballot was the ultimate solution to African-American problems, he succeeded after some years of effort in registering to vote and he encouraged others of his race to do the same. By the early 1940s enough blacks had registered to influence the outcome of close political contests. In 1941 Gomillion organized the Tuskegee Civic Association to support black interests—such as better public services and equal educational opportunities—and to promote what he called a color-blind civic democracy. His leadership of the Tuskegee Civic Association carried with it leadership of the entire local black community. Employing a gradualist approach, he worked indefatigably over the next quarter of a century to improve the living and working conditions for his race and to establish a solid base for harmonious race relations. He made great strides. In the late 1950s he challenged the state legislature's racial gerrymander of Tuskegee's boundaries, which was a blatant move to dilute the effect of the black vote in the town. He was upheld in the Supreme Court's *Gomillion v. Lightfoot** decision in 1960. This victory notwithstanding, Gomillion came under attack from many younger blacks who were impatient with his gradualist approach and his unwillingness to engage whites in direct action* confrontations. The younger generation, many of whom were students at Tuskegee, turned to sit-ins, protest marches, and other similar strategies for gaining rights and privileges long denied them. Disappointed in his goal of achieving racial equality and shared political power without confrontation and bloodshed, Gomillion resigned his positions of leadership and retired in the early 1970s to Washington, D.C.

SELECTED BIBLIOGRAPHY

Loren Miller, *The Petitioners: The Story of the Supreme Court of the United States and the Negro* (1966); Robert J. Norrell, *Reaping the Whirlwind: The Civil Rights Movement in Tuskegee* (1985).

Charles D. Lowery

GOMILLION v. LIGHTFOOT, 364 U.S. 339 (1960). In May 1957 the Alabama legislature redrew the municipal boundaries of Tuskegee to place most of its four hundred black voters outside the city limits, assuring political control by the white minority. The action changed the city map from a four-sided figure to one with twenty-eight sides. Disfranchised black residents led by Charles G. Gomillion* sued Mayor Philip Lightfoot and the city of Tuskegee, contending that the gerrymander sought to deny black citizens their rights guaranteed by the Fourteenth* and Fifteenth Amendments.* The lower federal courts would not reverse the legislature, which they held had full power to set municipal boundaries regardless of the motives or consequences. In *Gomillion v. Lightfoot*, the Supreme Court reversed the lower courts, holding that the Tuskegee gerrymander was not merely political, but was "solely concerned" with segregating black citizens by "fencing" them from town. The action "despoiled" them exclusively "of their theretofore enjoyed voting rights" for the Fifteenth Amendment banned both "sophisticated" and "simple-minded" discrimination. The Supreme Court ordered review by the trial court, which nullified the offending statute in February 1961. This first instance of federal judicial involvement in state redistricting not only proscribed racial gerrymandering, but was also precedent for later one-man, one-vote decisions that affected legislative apportionment throughout the nation.

SELECTED BIBLIOGRAPHY

Paul L. Murphy, *The Constitution in Crisis Times, 1918–1969* (1972); Robert J. Norrell, *Reaping the Whirlwind: The Civil Rights Movement in Tuskegee* (1985); Martin Shapiro, *Law and Politics in the Supreme Court: New Approaches to Political Jurisprudence* (1964); Bernard Taper, *Gomillion versus Lightfoot: The Tuskegee Gerrymander Case* (1962).

James B. Potts

GONG LUM v. RICE, 275 U.S. 78 (1927). This 1927 U.S. Supreme Court decision permitted the state of Mississippi to classify Chinese Americans as "blacks" for the purpose of maintaining racially segregated schools. In 1924, Martha Gong Lum, a daughter of a prosperous Chinese grocer, was refused admittance to a white school. The Gong Lums sued and won at the circuit court level by arguing that Martha was not "a member of the colored races." The school trustees appealed to the Mississippi Supreme Court, which stated that "Chinese are not white and must fall under the heading, colored races." On appeal to the U.S. Supreme Court, plaintiff lawyers argued that their client's equal protection under the laws was denied because white children were separated and protected from the danger of associating with Negroes, but Chinese were not. Speaking for the Court, Chief Justice William Howard Taft affirmed the decision of the Mississippi Supreme Court.

SELECTED BIBLIOGRAPHY

James W. Loewen, *The Mississippi Chinese: Between Black and White* (1971); Robert Seto Quan, *Lotus among the Magnolias: The Mississippi Chinese* (1982); "Recent Decisions," *California Law Review* 16 (1928), 346–47.

Malik Simba

GOODMAN, ANDREW (23 November 1943, New York, N.Y.–21 June 1964, near Philadelphia, Miss.). A civil rights activist from a liberal Jewish background, Goodman was a junior at Queens College in New York, majoring in anthropology, when he became a volunteer for the Council of Federated Organizations'* (COFO) Freedom Summer of 1964* in Mississippi. He met James Earl Chaney* and Michael Henry Schwerner* at the COFO training session for summer volunteers at Western College for Women in Oxford, Ohio. On 21 June 1964, Goodman, along with Chaney and Schwerner, was arrested in Philadelphia, Mississippi, released from jail, abducted by Klansmen, and shot. Their bodies were found on 4 August 1964 and retrieved from an earthen dam. On 9 August

1964, Goodman was buried in Mount Judah Cemetery in Brooklyn, New York.

SELECTED BIBLIOGRAPHY

Seth Cagin and Philip Dray, *We Are Not Afraid: The Story of Goodman, Schwerner and Chaney and the Civil Rights Campaign for Mississippi* (1988); William Bradford Huie, *Three Lives for Mississippi* (1964, 1965, 1968); Jonathan Kaufman, *Broken Alliance: The Turbulent Times between Blacks and Jews in America* (1988); *New York Times*, 6 August 1964; Juan Williams, *Eyes on the Prize: America's Civil Rights Years, 1954–1965* (1987).

Barbara L. Green

GOSS v. BOARD OF EDUCATION OF KNOXVILLE, 373 U.S. 683 (1963). In the early 1960s, in response to federal mandates stemming from *Brown v. Board of Education** (1954), the school boards of Knoxville and Davidson County, Tennessee, promulgated desegregation plans which included a provision for a student to transfer from a desegregated school to one in which the student would be in the racial majority. Parents of African-American schoolchildren in the affected districts sued to block the implementation of the transfer provisions, charging that the provisions were designed to perpetuate racial segregation by allowing students to transfer from integrated to segregated schools. The Supreme Court found for the plaintiffs and voided the school transfer plans because their effect would be to perpetuate the segregation of the school systems.

SELECTED BIBLIOGRAPHY

Richard Bardolph, ed., *The Civil Rights Record: Black Americans and the Law, 1849–1970* (1970); Loren Miller, *The Petitioners: The Story of the Supreme Court of the United States and the Negro* (1966); George Rossman, ed., "Review of Recent Supreme Court Decisions," *American Bar Association Journal* 49 (1963), 1123–24; Mark V. Tushnet, *The NAACP's Legal Strategy against Segregated Education, 1925–1950* (1987).

Steve Sadowsky

GRAHAM, FRANK PORTER (14 October 1886, Fayetteville, N.C.–16 February 1972, Chapel Hill, N.C.). A history professor, college president, and social activist, Graham received an A.B. degree at the University of North Carolina in 1909 and a M.A. from Columbia University in 1916. Graham also studied at the Brookings Institute, the London School of Economics, and the University of Chicago where he completed courses for the doctorate but chose not to write a dissertation. A recognized leader of southern white liberals, Graham served as the first chairperson of the Southern Conference for Human Welfare* (1938–1948). This University of North Carolina president was one of two Southerners appointed by President Harry S. Truman to the first President's Committee on Civil Rights. In 1947 this committee issued the report *To Secure These*

*Rights,** which called for a sweeping transformation of race relations in the United States.

SELECTED BIBLIOGRAPHY

Warren Ashby, *Frank Porter Graham: A Southern Liberal* (1980); David R. Goldfield, *Black, White, and Southern: Race Relations and Southern Culture, 1940 to the Present* (1990); Thomas Krueger, *And Promises to Keep: The Southern Conference for Human Welfare, 1938–1948* (1969); Morton Sosna, *In Search of the Silent South: Southern Liberals and the Race Issue* (1977).

Barbara L. Green

GRANDFATHER CLAUSE. The grandfather clause was one post-Reconstruction device instituted by southern state legislatures to formalize restrictions on black voting already established through violence and intimidation. Unlike residence requirements, the poll tax,* literacy tests, and the white primary*—all used to deny the vote to blacks—grandfather clauses enabled those whites who would otherwise be disqualified to register and vote. The Louisiana constitution of 1898, for example, provided that males entitled to vote prior to 1867, and their sons and grandsons, were exempt from educational and property restrictions. In 1915 the Supreme Court ruled in *Guinn v. United States** that such clauses were an evasion of the Fifteenth Amendment.*

SELECTED BIBLIOGRAPHY

Alfred H. Kelly and Winfred A. Harbison, *The American Constitution: Its Origins and Development* (1970); V. O. Key, Jr., *Southern Politics in State and Nation* (1949); J. Morgan Kousser, *The Shaping of Southern Politics: Suffrage Restriction and the Establishment of the One-Party South, 1880–1910* (1974); Paul Lewinson, *Race, Class and Party: A History of Negro Suffrage and White Politics in the South* (1932).

Allen Kifer

GRANGER, LESTER B. (16 September 1896, Newport News, Va.–9 January 1976, New Orleans, La.). Granger's career in the Urban League Movement spanned the difficult years of the Great Depression, World War I, and the Joseph McCarthy era of the 1950s. He graduated from Dartmouth in 1918 and also attended New York University and the New York School of Social Work. After a tour as a lieutenant of artillery during World War I, Granger took the post of industrial secretary with the Newark League. He left the Urban League Movement in 1922 to become director of extension at the New Jersey state vocational school at Bordentown. Before becoming executive director of the National Urban League* in 1941, Granger served as educational secretary from 1934 to 1938 and assistant executive secretary from 1940 to 1941. From 1938 to 1940, he worked for the Welfare Council of New York City. By the 1950s, criticism of Granger's conservatism was mounting. Nevertheless, he had led the Urban League in pursuing more militant goals in civil rights. The league joined in pressuring the federal government to deny funding to any public or private housing development that practiced discrimination. Granger played an active role in the desegregation of the armed forces, and he worked to organize black workers and to fight discrimination within the ranks of organized labor.

SELECTED BIBLIOGRAPHY
Jesse Thomas Moore, Jr., *A Search for Equality: The National Urban League, 1910–1961* (1981); Guichard Parris and Lester Brooks, *Blacks in the City: A History of the National Urban League* (1971); *Who Was Who in America* (1976).

                                                                 Arvarh E. Strickland

GREAT MIGRATION. Eighty thousand black Southerners moved to the North, mostly to cities, in the two decades after 1870, a small number in comparison to the migration from Europe and northern farms. The northern movement of blacks quickened significantly, however, as southern repression increased by the turn of the century. During World War I, the economic boom produced a genuine Great Migration, marked by an exodus of more than 500,000 blacks, and in the next decade nearly 750,000 streamed northward. Slowed by the Great Depression, the Great Migration received fresh impetus from World War II and continued in the decades after 1940. The result was dramatic: In 1910, 75 percent of the nation's blacks lived in rural areas, and nine-tenths were in the South; in 1960, more than three-fourths lived in cities, mostly outside the South. Blacks had been transformed into a predominantly northern-based proletariat. Several factors precipitated the Great Migration. Racism—"de debil in de White Man"—evidenced in disfranchisement, injustice, and segregation; and serious economic problems, including a decline in cotton prices (1913–1915) that increased the burdens of sharecropping and tenancy, disposed blacks to flee to the North. Floods in the Mississippi Valley in 1915 and the destructive march of the boll weevil (1914–1917) spread destitution. Meanwhile, demands for war material from the Allies and then from American forces coupled with a decline in immigration generated opportunities for skilled and unskilled workers, often underscored by free transportation and wages as high as four dollars a day. Newspaper reports, particularly in the *Chicago Defender,** and letters emphasizing good wages and less severe discrimination in the North were especially attractive to younger blacks. The Great Migration produced competition for jobs and housing with whites that greatly altered northern life for blacks. Dramatic events like the East St. Louis race riot* (1917) and the Chicago race riot* in 1919 punctuated long-term economic trends that reduced blacks to the fringe of the industrial economy. The urban ghetto, attended by slumlords, overcrowding, disease, and inadequate education, emerged.

SELECTED BIBLIOGRAPHY
James R. Grossman, *Land of Hope, Chicago, Black Southerners, and the Great Migration* (1989); Florette Henri, *Black Migration: Movement North, 1900–1920* (1975);

Nicholas Lemann, *Promised Land: The Great Black Migration and How It Changed America* (1991); Gilbert Osofsky, *Harlem, the Making of a Ghetto, Negro New York, 1890–1930* (1963); Elliott Rudwick, *Race Riot at East St. Louis, July 2, 1917* (1964); Allan H. Spear, *Black Chicago: The Making of a Negro Ghetto, 1890–1920* (1967).

James B. Potts

GREEN, PAUL ELIOT (17 March 1894, Lillington, N.C.–4 May 1981, Chapel Hill, N.C.). Green attended the University of North Carolina and later taught philosophy there, when he became associated with a group that taught students to produce plays about regions of the South. In the 1920s, Green drew upon his knowledge of southern problems, particularly the plight of oppressed blacks, to champion civil rights. His plays *White Dresses* (1923) and *In Abraham's Bosom* (1926) depict failed efforts by southern blacks to better their lot. He wrote seven Broadway plays, collaborated with black novelist Richard Wright* on *Native Son,** and wrote the 1963 film script *Black Like Me*, the story of a white man who experienced racial prejudice after changing the color of his skin. He is also known for his fifteen "symphonic outdoor dramas" of the 1950s and 1960s which included folksongs, dance, drama, and music of the local community.

SELECTED BIBLIOGRAPHY

Stanley Hochman, ed., *McGraw-Hill Encyclopedia of World Drama* (1984); Obituary, *Newsweek*, 18 May 1981; *New York Times*, 6 May 1981.

Thomas D. Cockrell

GREEN *v.* SCHOOL BOARD OF NEW KENT COUNTY, VIRGINIA, 391 U.S. 430 (1968). New Kent County is a rural county in eastern Virginia, whose population of 4,500 in 1960 was divided evenly between blacks and whites. No distinct pattern of residential segregation existed. The county maintained two schools, a traditionally white school in the eastern part of the county and an all-black school in the west. In 1968 the U.S. Supreme Court took up the question of the constitutionality of the county's freedom-of-choice plan for school desegregation. Of the county's 1,300 school children, 740 were black and 550 were white. In the three years the plan had been in effect, no whites had attended the black school, and, although 115 blacks had attended the predominantly white school, 85 percent of the black students still attended the all-black facility. In a unanimous opinion by William J. Brennan, the court rejected the freedom-of-choice plan. Brennan's opinion stressed the local school board's long defiance of the Court's *Brown v. Board of Education** decision, the meager results of the freedom-of-choice plan, and the burden it placed on black parents. *Green* represented a milestone among school desegregation cases. The opinion went beyond a simple prohibition of segregation to place a clear duty on local school boards to take affirmative measures to abolish dual school systems.

SELECTED BIBLIOGRAPHY
"The Supreme Court, 1967 Term," *Harvard Law Review* 82 (1968), 111–18; J. Harvie Wilkinson III, *From Brown to Bakke: The Supreme Court and School Integration, 1954–1978* (1979); Raymond Wolters, *The Burden of Brown: Thirty Years of School Desegregation* (1984); Rowland Young, "Review of Recent Supreme Court Decisions," *American Bar Association Journal* 54 (1968), 912–13.

Jeff Broadwater

GREENE, PERCY (7 September 1898, Jackson, Miss.–6 April 1977, Jackson, Miss.). After serving during World War I in England and France, and graduation from Jackson State College, Greene studied law, but he was determined to be a journalist. His first publication, *The Colored Veteran* (1927), addressed the problem of the denial of blacks to membership in veterans' organizations. He founded the *Jackson Advocate** in 1939 and served as editor until his death in 1977. Greene organized the Mississippi Negro Democrat Association in 1946 in an effort to give blacks a voice in the Democratic party. During the civil rights movement of the 1950s and 1960s, he became something of a paradox, receiving criticism from both white segregationists and the NAACP.* Although he spoke strongly for black political rights, he also advocated moderation regarding integration, which brought chastisement from the NAACP leadership. His reputation was marred in the 1960s by his acceptance of contributions from Mississippi's segregationist Sovereignty Commission.

SELECTED BIBLIOGRAPHY
Jackson Advocate (1950–1977); Henry Lewis Suggs, ed., *The Black Press in the South, 1865–1979* (1983); *Who's Who among Black Americans* (1978).

Thomas D. Cockrell

GREENSBORO (NORTH CAROLINA) SIT-IN. On 1 February 1960, Ezell Blair, Jr., Franklin McCain, Joseph McNeil, and David Richmond, all African-American students at North Carolina Agricultural and Technical College, staged a sit-in at the Woolworth Store lunch counter in Greensboro, North Carolina. Although these were not the first sit-ins in North Carolina (there was a network of sit-ins between 1957 and 1960), this was the opening gambit of an unequalled student protest movement that shook the South to its foundations. On the evening of 1 February, fifty students met and created the Student Executive Committee for Justice. On 2 February, the original four protestors were joined by African-American students from A&T and Bennett College and by white students from Women's College. Soon more than three hundred demonstrators were protesting by sit-ins at all the city's downtown lunch counters. Sixteen hundred students decided at a mass meeting on 5 February to halt all demonstrations when asked by city leaders for time to negotiate the crisis. However, when no compromise was evident, the

Woolworth sit-in, Greensboro, N.C., 2 February 1960. (Photo by Jack Moebes/Greensboro News & Record.)

sit-ins resumed on 1 April, and the first arrests of forty-five demonstrators occurred on 21 April. Subsequent sit-ins and economic boycotts forced the city's business and political leaders to reopen lunch counters on a desegregated basis by July 1960.

SELECTED BIBLIOGRAPHY

William Chafe, *Civilities and Civil Rights* (1980); Aldon D. Morris, *The Origins of the Civil Rights Movement: Black Communities Organizing for Change* (1984); Harvard Sitkoff, *The Struggle for Black Equality: 1954–1980* (1981).

Aingred G. Dunston

GREENVILLE DELTA DEMOCRAT-TIMES. The *Greenville* (Mississippi) *Delta Democrat-Times* was established in 1938 by the merger of that city's *Greenville Delta Star* and *Daily Democrat-Times*. Hodding Carter II,* editor and publisher of the *Delta Star*, assumed the same duties at the *Delta Democrat-Times*. A Louisianan by birth but educated in Maine and New York, Carter became one of the South's most noted advocates of racial justice. Greenville, in the heart of the overwhelmingly black Mississippi Delta, seemed an unlikely place for such a journalist and newspaper. Yet, the Delta's confidence in the fixity of its caste system combined with the region's affinity for good writing allowed Carter—despite many threats—to produce the virtually unthinkable: a white-edited newspaper in the Deep South that promoted the cause of black civil rights. Carter won a Pulitzer Prize for his editorial writing, and he served as a model of journalistic courage throughout the South. Several editors drew strength from his example, as did other southern whites who sought to promote racial tolerance and goodwill. After Carter's death in 1972, his son Hodding Carter III continued the editorial policies of the *Delta Democrat-Times* before going to Washington, D.C., to work in the Carter administration. Subsequent editors of the newspaper have been less activist than the Carters, yet its niche in the cause of civil rights is secure.

SELECTED BIBLIOGRAPHY

Hodding Carter II, *So the Heffners Left McComb* (1965); *Greenville Delta Democrat-Times* (1938–   ); Charles Reagan Wilson and William Ferris, eds., *The Encyclopedia of Southern Culture* (1989).

Allen Dennis

GREGORY, RICHARD CLAXTON "DICK" (12 October 1932, St. Louis, Mo.–   ). From his achievement as an outstanding athlete at Southern Illinois University in 1953 to his inclusion in *Who's Who in America* (1968), Richard Claxton "Dick" Gregory achieved national recognition in the 1960s as a comedian, popular lecturer, and civil rights activist. By the 1970s he was being referred to as a noted political analyst. In the 1980s he became the guru of good health. His electric personality focused national attention on the student efforts to register African-American voters in Mississippi (Freedom Summer of 1964),* and he aided in the food, clothing, and book drives that funded the young activists. In June 1964 when three civil rights workers were murdered in Mississippi, Gregory offered a substantial reward for any information that would lead to arrests. He publicly accused the Federal Bureau of Investigation of "lying and hiding" in its attempts to uncover the truth. In his efforts to promote peaceful change, he was shot during the Watts race riot in Los Angeles (in 1965) and spent several periods in jail, the most publicized of which was in Birmingham, Alabama, in 1963. Gregory has authored and coauthored nine books including his autobiography (*Nigger*, 1964) and his view of the assassination of Martin Luther King, Jr.* (*Code Name Zorro*, 1977).

SELECTED BIBLIOGRAPHY

Joanne Grant, ed., *Black Protest* (1968); Stephen B. Oates, *Let the Trumpet Sound: The Life of Martin Luther King, Jr.* (1982); Edward Peeks, *Long Struggle for Black Power* (1971); Harry A. Ploski and James Williams, eds., *The Negro Almanac: A Reference Work on the African American*, 5th ed. (1989).

Aingred G. Dunston

Comedian Dick Gregory arrested for marching in Birmingham, May 1963. (Archives Collection, Birmingham Public Library. Courtesy *Birmingham News*.)

GRIFFIN, JOHN HOWARD (16 June 1920, Dallas, Tex.–9 September 1980, Fort Worth, Tex.). A white Texan, Griffin journeyed through the South in 1959 disguised as a black man and wrote about his experiences in *Black Like Me*, which established a unique double perspective of racism. As the first white to experience the reality of darkened pigment, he lost his personal identity and was transformed into a cultural stereotype. Facing death threats and hate stares, he pursued the ideals of brotherhood and justice. He did not speak for blacks but became a bridge across the racial divide. The integrity of his witness was read by millions worldwide and heard by thousands on his lecture tours during the 1960s and 1970s. Throughout his life he articulated the universal patterns of prejudice he had experienced as a black, as a member of the *Defense Passive* in France during World War II, and during his years of blindness (1946–1957). In these diverse contests, Griffin realized the condition of the other—that individual perceived as intrinsically inferior. He learned to think human and to understand the essential oneness of humankind.

His work reveals both a highly refined artistic temperament (as writer, photographer, and musicologist) and a spiritual dimension that transcends politics or sociology.

SELECTED BIBLIOGRAPHY
John Howard Griffin, *Black Like Me* (1961); John Howard Griffin, *A Time to Be Human* (1977).

                                                                     Robert Bonazzi

GRIFFIN v. PRINCE EDWARD SCHOOL BOARD, 377 U.S. 218 (1964). This case originated in 1951 as one of the cases eventually decided in *Brown v. Board of Education** (1954 and 1955). Virginia's Prince Edward County's public schools remained open but segregated until 1959, when federal courts ordered the county to proceed with desegregation. In response, the school board ordered the closing of all public schools. State funds, through tuition grants, supported the Prince Edward Academy, a private school newly opened only to white students. After years of continued litigation, the U.S. Supreme Court ruled in 1964 that the school board was in violation of the equal protection clause of the Fourteenth Amendment.* Speaking for the Court, and referring back to the language of the 1955 decision, Justice Hugo Black observed that Prince Edward had displayed "entirely too much deliberation and not enough speed" in moving against segregation in its schools. Under court order, the county resumed taxes for public schools and reopened the schools in 1964, although in the early years of desegregation few white students attended.

SELECTED BIBLIOGRAPHY
James T. Ely, *The Crisis of Conservative Virginia: The Byrd Organization and the Politics of Massive Resistance* (1976); Bob (Robert Collins) Smith, *They Closed Their Schools: Prince Edward County, Virginia, 1951–1964* (1965); Raymond Wolters, *The Burden of Brown: Thirty Years of School Desegregation* (1984).

                                                                  Peter Wallenstein

GRIGGS v. DUKE POWER COMPANY, 401 U.S. 424 (1971). Although the Civil Rights Act of 1964* opened some new doors of opportunity, many employers found new ways to exclude blacks from better paying jobs. This, contended Willie S. Griggs and his fellow black employees, was the case at Duke Power Company in North Carolina. Requirements for certain jobs included an educational component or standardized general intelligence test for placement or transfer. In a class action, blacks sued the company. They lost in district court but were affirmed in part by the court holding "that residual discrimination arising from past employment practices was" not "insulated from remedial action" at the appellate level. The U.S. Supreme Court unanimously held for the plaintiffs. It affirmed the prohibitions of the Civil Rights Act against requiring "a high school education or passing a standardized general intelligence test as a condition of employment or transfer" when neither could be "shown to be significantly related to successful job performance," when both requirements disqualified blacks at a substantially "higher rate than whites," and when the jobs "in question" had formerly been "filled by whites only due to long standing preference." This decision was a significant gain for civil rights.

SELECTED BIBLIOGRAPHY
Derrick A. Bell, Jr., *Race, Racism and American Law* (1980); Robert L. Gill, "Justice for Black Americans 200 Years after Independence: The Afro-American before the Burger Court, 1969–1976," *Negro Educational Review* 27 (July 1976) 271–317; Rowland L. Young, "Supreme Court Report," *American Bar Association Journal* 57 (1971), 609.

LeRoy T. Williams

GRIMKE, ANGELINA WELD (27 February 1880, Boston, Mass.–10 June 1958, New York, N.Y.). Trained as a teacher, Grimke was educated at various schools, including Carleton Academy in Northfield, Minnesota; Cushing Academy in Ashburnham, Massachusetts; Girls' Latin School in Boston; and the Boston Normal School of Gymnastics. Her teaching experience included work at Dunbar High School, Washington, D.C., between 1916 and the 1930s. She wrote the first successful drama created by a black and interpreted on stage by black actors. Produced in 1916 by the Drama Committee of the NAACP* in Washington, D.C., Grimke's *Rachel*, a play in three acts dealing with the lynching of a girl's father, addressed one of the leading concerns of the NAACP at that time. The program announcement made evident Grimke's and the NAACP's expectation of the play: "This is the first attempt to use the stage for race propaganda in order to enlighten the American people relative to the lamentable condition of ten millions of colored citizens in this free republic." In the 1920s, during the peak of the Harlem Renaissance,* Grimke contributed poetry and short stories to various magazines.

SELECTED BIBLIOGRAPHY
John Hope Franklin and Alfred A. Moss, Jr., *From Slavery to Freedom: A History of Negro Americans* (1988); Gloria T. Hull, *Color, Sex, and Poetry: Three Women Writers of the Harlem Renaissance* (1987); Gloria T. Hull, Patricia Bell Scott, and Barbara Smith, eds., *All the Women Are White, All the Blacks Are Men, but Some of Us Are Brave: Black Women's Studies* (1982).

Linda Reed

GRIMKE, ARCHIBALD (17 August 1849, Caneacres Plantation, S.C.–25 February 1930, Washington, D.C.). Emancipated from slavery by the Civil War, Grimke graduated in 1870 from Lincoln University in Pennsylvania and in 1874 from Harvard Law School with some financial assistance from his aunts, the abolitionists Sarah Grimke and Angelina

Weld Grimke.* Coeditor of *The Hub* (1883–1886) and a practicing attorney, in the early 1880s Grimke was a leader of the "Boston radicals," blacks who vigorously opposed racial discrimination. For the next forty years he fought segregation and disfranchisement with lawsuits, pamphlets, newspaper articles, and petitions to presidents from William McKinley to Woodrow Wilson. A lifelong Republican who urged blacks to vote independently, Grimke was appointed consul to Santo Domingo (1894–1898). After moving to Washington, D.C., in the early 1900s, he played a moderating political role among black leaders, maintaining contacts with Booker T. Washington* even as he supported the Niagara Movement* and the NAACP.* He was president of the American Negro Academy (1903–1906) which published many of his later essays. While president of the Washington branch of the NAACP (1913–1925), he helped prevent the passage of bills designed to segregate the Civil Service. In 1919 Grimke won the NAACP's fifth Spingarn Medal* "for service to race and country."

SELECTED BIBLIOGRAPHY
Rayford W. Logan and Michael R. Winston, eds., *Dictionary of American Negro Biography* (1982); Archibald H. Grimke, "The Shame of America, or the Negro's Case against the Republic," American Negro Academy, no. 21 (1924); Archibald H. Grimke Papers, Moorland-Spingarn Research Center, Howard University, Washington, D.C.; Rayford W. Logan, *The Betrayal of the Negro* (1965); August Meier, *Negro Thought in America, 1880–1915: Racial Ideologies in the Age of Booker T. Washington* (1963).

Francille Rusan Wilson

GRIMKE, FRANCIS JAMES (4 November 1850, Charleston, S.C.–11 October 1937, Washington, D.C.). The son of Nancy Weston, a slave, and her master, Henry Grimke, he graduated from Lincoln University in Pennsylvania in 1870. With the moral and financial support of his famous aunts, the abolitionist sisters Sarah and Angelina Weld Grimke,* Francis continued his education at Princeton Theological Seminary, graduating in 1878. For the next two generations he served as minister at Washington's Fifteenth Street Presbyterian Church, and he became a leading advocate of civil rights for blacks. Known as the "Black Puritan," Grimke rejected Booker T. Washington's* accommodationism and, as a well-known lecturer, essayist, and president of the capital's chapter of the NAACP,* he urged blacks to look beyond mere economic survival to full social and civil equality.

SELECTED BIBLIOGRAPHY
Gerda Lerner, *The Grimke Sisters of South Carolina: Rebels against Slavery* (1967); August Meier, *Negro Thought in America, 1880–1915: Racial Ideologies in the Age of*

Booker T. Washington (1963); Carter G. Woodson, ed., *The Works of Francis J. Grimke*, 4 vols. (1942).

James Marten

GROVEY v. TOWNSEND, 295 U.S. 45 (1935). In Harris County, Texas, black resident R. R. Grovey attempted to vote in the Democratic party primary in 1934. His vote was refused by white party official Albert Townsend. Grovey filed suit against Townsend but lost at both the district and appellate levels. The U.S. Supreme Court decided the case on 1 April 1935. The question before the court was whether or not Grovey's rights under the Fourteenth* and Fifteenth Amendments* had been violated. The court concluded that the Democratic party was "a private organization" and so, too, was Townsend a private citizen. Therefore, the party and Townsend were "not subject to limitations imposed on state action" under the constitutional amendments in question. "We find no ground," stated the Court, "for holding" that discrimination has occurred. It would be almost a decade later before the Supreme Court reversed its view of the political party as a private organization.

SELECTED BIBLIOGRAPHY
Richard Bardolph, ed., *The Civil Rights Record: Black Americans and the Law 1849–1970* (1970); Derrick A. Bell, Jr., *Race, Racism and American Law* (1980); Alfred H. Kelly and Winfred A. Harbison, *The American Constitution* (1970); "Recent Decisions," *Columbia Law Review* 35 (1935), 607–8.

LeRoy T. Williams

GUINN v. UNITED STATES, 238 U.S. 347 (1915). This case involved a grandfather clause* in Oklahoma. In 1910 the state adopted an amendment to its constitution exempting or "grandfathering" from its literacy test all people "who, on January 1, 1866 or who at that time resided in some foreign nation, and their lineal descendants." The government argued and the Court agreed that this amendment recreated the exact situation the Fifteenth Amendment* sought to prevent. The NAACP* filed an amicus curiae brief on behalf of the United States. This case was the first of the long line of successful constitutional cases supported by the NAACP.

SELECTED BIBLIOGRAPHY
Charles Flint Kellogg, *NAACP: A History of the National Association for the Advancement of Colored People* (1967); Melvin I. Urofsky, *A March of Liberty: A Constitutional History of the United States* (1987).

Kenneth W. Goings

H

HAAS, FRANCIS J. (18 March 1889, Racine, Wis.–29 August 1953, Grand Rapids, Mich.). A priest of the archdiocese of Milwaukee, Haas received a Ph.D. in sociology from the Catholic University of America in 1922 and, assigned to Washington, D.C., in 1931, served on several of President Franklin D. Roosevelt's labor relations boards and agencies. Appointed by Roosevelt to chair the reconstituted Fair Employment Practice Committee* (FEPC) in May 1943, he investigated charges of discrimination in various wartime industries, including the nationwide railway system, and spent three days in Detroit, Michigan, to report on the causes of racial violence there. Named bishop of Grand Rapids, Michigan, he resigned from the FEPC after serving only four months. In 1946, he was appointed to President Harry S. Truman's Committee on Civil Rights and was a signer of that committee's influential report, *To Secure These Rights,** in 1947.

SELECTED BIBLIOGRAPHY
Thomas E. Blantz, "Francis J. Haas: Priest and Government Servant," *Catholic Historical Review* 57 (January 1972), 571–92; Thomas E. Blantz, *A Priest in Public Service: Francis J. Haas and the New Deal* (1982); Franklyn Kennedy, "Bishop Haas," *The Salesianum* 39 (January 1944), 7–14; Constance Randall, "A Bio-Bibliography of Bishop Francis J. Haas" (Master's thesis, Catholic University of America, 1955).

Thomas E. Blantz

HALE v. KENTUCKY, 303 U.S. 613 (1938). In this case the Supreme Court, in a unanimous decision, struck down an earlier murder conviction and death sentence on the grounds that the plaintiff's civil rights had been violated. In an earlier 1936 trial in McCracken County, Joe Hale, an African American, had been convicted by an all-white jury, and his conviction was upheld by the Kentucky Court of Appeals. Hale argued that blacks were "systematic[ally] and arbitrar[ily] exclud[ed]" from the jury. In a county in which forty thousand whites resided, there also were eight thousand people of "African descent." At least seven thousand black were eligible for jury service. Yet no blacks had been members of any McCracken County jury within the past fifty years. The *Hale* decision was one in a series of cases in which the Supreme Court consistently opposed jury discrimination in the lower courts, the earliest of which was *Strauder v. West Virginia** in 1880 and the most recent of which was *Norris v. Alabama** in 1935. Hale was represented by NAACP* counsel, including Charles H. Houston* and Thurgood Marshall.* This case shows that the NAACP was concerned about jury discrimination before it focused its attention on public school integration in the 1940s and 1950s.

SELECTED BIBLIOGRAPHY

John R. Gillespie, "The Constitution and the All-White Jury," *Kentucky Law Journal* 39 (1950–1951), 65–78; *Louisville Courier-Journal*, 31 January, 11 April 1938; *New York Times*, 12 August 1938; Harry A. Ploski and James Williams, eds., *The Negro Almanac: A Reference Work on the African American*, 5th ed. (1989).

Lawrence H. Williams

HALEY, ALEX PALMER (11 August 1921, Ithaca, N.Y.– 10 February 1992, Seattle, Wash.). Since 1976 Alex Haley had been one of the most familiar names in contemporary American literature. He studied two years at North Carolina's Elizabeth City Teacher's College preparing to become a teacher before opting for a military career. Upon retiring from the military in 1959, he worked as a free-lance writer. His 1962 *Playboy Magazine* interview of Black Muslim* spokesman Malcolm X* became the genesis of a book, *The Autobiography of Malcolm X* (1965), which Haley largely wrote. Passionately written, the book familiarized Americans with both men—Malcolm X as a committed, but angry, race leader and Alex Haley as an emerging literary talent. Haley's greatest literary achievement was the 1976 publication of his historical novel entitled *Roots: The Saga of an American Family.** The book grew out of childhood stories told to Haley by his grandmother about the family's West African beginnings and its history through slavery and freedom in the American South. Despite reviewers' criticisms of the factual errors found in *Roots*, the book quickly became a best-seller and achieved even greater acclaim the next year when it was serialized on network television in a remarkably successful miniseries. However transitory their effect, the dramatizations impacted U.S. race relations by raising the consciousness of white America and sensitizing it to the African-American historical experience. Perhaps of greater long-term significance, Haley's work unleashed an energy in the black community that helped to "spur black identity and hence black pride."

SELECTED BIBLIOGRAPHY
Robert Bain, Joseph M. Flora, and Louis D. Rubin, Jr., eds., *Southern Writers: A Biographical Dictionary* (1979); David Gerber, "Haley's *Roots* and Our Own: An Inquiry into the Nature of a Popular Phenomenon," *Journal of Ethnic Studies* 3 (1977), 87–111; Alex Haley, "Roots: A Black American's Search for His Ancestral African," *Ebony* 31 (August 1976) 100–102, 104, 106–7; Alex Haley, *Roots: The Saga of an American Family* (1976); Charles Moritz, ed., "Alex Haley," in *Current Biography Yearbook* (1977); "Why 'Roots' Hit Home," *Time*, 14 February 1977, 68–72, 75.

Robert L. Jenkins

HALL v. DECUIR, 95 U.S. 485 (1878). In a Louisiana state court, Josephine DeCuir won a judgment of $1,000 against the master of a steamboat who refused her passage because of her race. An 1869 state law forbade common carriers to discriminate on grounds of race and permitted recovery of damages. The master claimed that the statute was an unconstitutional encroachment upon the federal interstate commerce power, since he operated from New Orleans to Vicksburg, although DeCuir's destination was in Louisiana. Chief Justice Morrison Waite, for the Court, agreed that the law placed a burden on interstate commerce. Steamboats and railroads often cross state lines, and local regulations that varied from place to place were invalid, a conclusion supported by some pre–Civil War precedents. Waite noted that, if the public interest required legislation on such a subject, it would have to be federal legislation, yet the case occurred in a period when the Court was also weakening federal protection for civil rights. The applicability of state antidiscrimination laws to interstate carriers returned to the Court in 1963, this time in relation to the hiring of airline pilots. By then the reasoning in the *DeCuir* case clearly seemed archaic, and the Colorado law in question prevailed.

SELECTED BIBLIOGRAPHY
Charles Fairman, *Reconstruction and Reunion, 1864–1888* (1987); C. Peter Magrath, *Morrison R. Waite: The Triumph of Character* (1963).

James E. Sefton

HAMBURG, SOUTH CAROLINA, RACE RIOT (1876). On 4 July 1876, Hamburg's Negro militia company, under the command of "Doc" Adams, was marching down the main street of town and failed to permit the passage of the carriage to two local whites. Following a complaint, Adams refused to apologize for the incident or to appear in court on 7 July. The refusal resulted in a demand by General Matthew C. Butler, counsel for the complainants, that the militia give up its weapons. Local whites armed themselves, and others from nearby Augusta, Georgia, arrived in Hamburg with a cannon. Adams and his militiamen gathered at their armory. Refusing to surrender the guns stored there, the militia

"The Bloody Shirt Reformed" (Hamburg, S.C., massacre). (Negro Almanac Collection, Amistad Research Center, Tulane University, New Orleans.)

fired from the windows but were finally routed from the armory. Five militiamen were captured, disarmed, and later singly executed by the white mob. A grand jury bound over the accused whites for trial, but the case was postponed at the insistence of the state's attorney general, who advised Governor Daniel H. Chamberlain that the white community's prevailing sentiments would only lead to further trouble. Chamberlain requested and received federal troops to restore order in Hamburg, but Butler and other whites were never brought to justice.

SELECTED BIBLIOGRAPHY

George C. Rable, *But There Was No Peace: The Role of Violence in the Politics of Reconstruction* (1984); Otis A. Singletary, *Negro Militia and Reconstruction* (1957); Alfred B. Williams, *Hampton and His Red Shirts: South Carolina's Deliverance in 1876* (1935, reprint, 1970).

Thaddeus M. Smith

HAMER, FANNIE LOU (6 October 1917, Montgomery County, Miss.– 14 March 1977, Mound Bayou, Miss.). She became an active member of the Student Nonviolent Coordinating Committee* (SNCC) in Ruleville, Mississippi, in 1962 and immediately met opposition when she attempted to register to vote. She was fired from her plantation job. In 1963 she became a field secretary for SNCC and a registered voter. Hamer

Elect
INFORMED

SINCERE

CAPABLE

MRS.
Fannie Lou HAMER

STATE SENATOR
District 11 – Post No. 2
BOLIVAR AND SUNFLOWER COUNTIES

NOVEMBER 2, 1971

Fannie Lou Hamer campaign poster, Mississippi, 1971. (Tougaloo College Civil Rights Archives, Jackson, Mississippi.)

then worked with voter registration drives and with programs designed to assist economically deprived black families in Mississippi. She knew poverty firsthand, being the youngest of twenty siblings whose parents seldom were able to provide adequate food and clothing. She was instrumental in starting the Delta Ministry,* an extensive community development program, in 1963. Next she took part in the founding of the Mississippi Freedom Democratic party* and was a chosen member of its delegation to the Democratic national convention which challenged the seating of the regular all-white Mississippi delegation. She made a famous address to the convention, which was televised to the nation. In 1965 Hamer, Victoria Gray, and Annie Devine unsuccessfully challenged the seating of the regular Mississippi representatives before the U.S. House of Representatives, and they became the first three black women ever to sit, albeit temporarily, on the floor of the House. Hamer remained active in civic affairs in Mississippi for the remainder of her life, being selected a delegate to the National Democratic convention in 1968. She founded the Freedom Farms Corporation (FFC), a nonprofit venture designed to help needy families raise food and livestock. The FFC also provided social services, minority business opportunities, scholarships, and grants for education.

SELECTED BIBLIOGRAPHY

Jerry DeMuth, "Tired of Being Sick and Tired," *Nation* 198 (1 June 1964), 548–51; The Fannie Lou Hamer Papers, available on microfilm from the Amistad Research Center, New Orleans, Louisiana; Phyl Garland, "Builders of a New South," *Ebony* 21 (August 1966), 27–30; Joyce A. Ladner, "Fannie Lou Hamer: In Memoriam," *Black Enterprise* 7 (May 1977), 56; P. Marshall, "Hunger Has No Color Line," *Vogue* 155 (June 1970), 126–27; Eleanor Holmes Norton, "Woman Who Changed the South: Memory of Fannie Lou Hamer," *MS* 5 (July 1977), 51.

Linda Reed

HAMILTON v. ALABAMA, 376 U.S. 650 (1964). In a hearing for a writ of habeas corpus, Mary Hamilton, an African-American citizen of Alabama, refused to answer questions on cross-examination when she was addressed on a first-name basis. It was not uncommon in Alabama courts for attorneys and judges to address a black witness as "boy" or to refer to the accused as "this nigger." Offended by the demeaning courtroom etiquette, Hamilton refused to respond to questions unless she was addressed by the polite title "Miss Hamilton" rather than the disrespectful "Mary." She was fined and jailed for contempt. Denied a rehearing by the Alabama Supreme Court, she appealed to the U.S. Supreme Court. It responded to her writ of certiorari by reversing the contempt conviction. The decision was a small but significant step forward for blacks in their struggle for equality before the law.

SELECTED BIBLIOGRAPHY
Richard Bardolph, ed., *The Civil Rights Record: Black Americans and the Law, 1849–1970* (1970); Thomas L. Emerson, David Haber, and Norman Dorsen, *Political and Civil Rights in the United States*, vol. 2 (1967); George C. Longshore, "Case Notes," *Alabama Law Review* 14 (1962), 431–38.

Charles D. Lowery

HAMPTON CONFERENCE. The First and Second Hampton Negro Conferences were part of a series of gatherings, commencing in the 1890s and lasting well into the turn of the century, which considered the plight of African Americans in the post-Reconstruction era. The Second Hampton Negro Conference of 1894 proved to be the more important of the two in terms of giving impetus and notoriety to the work of Booker T. Washington.* The Hampton Conference, as well as the earlier Tuskegee Conferences, served as inspiration for W.E.B. Du Bois* and the development of the Atlanta University Conference for the Study of Negro Problems.*

SELECTED BIBLIOGRAPHY
W.E.B. Du Bois, *The Autobiography of W.E.B. Du Bois* (1968; Louis R. Harlan, ed., *The Booker T. Washington Papers* (1972–1977); Mabel M. Smythe, ed., *The Black American Reference Book* (1976).

Maghan Keita

HAMPTON INSTITUTE. The Hampton Normal and Agricultural Institute was started on 1 April 1868. Founded by General Samuel C. Armstrong and the American Missionary Association,* its initial purpose was to train young black students to teach and lead their people. Using a system of "practical education" that combined academic classes with manual labor, it produced hundreds of teachers for the black educational system of the South. The training of these teachers was designed to help blacks adjust to a subordinate role in the politics and economy of the post–Civil War South. The "Hampton Idea," as the school's philosophy was called, which was supported by the nation's leading philanthropists, businessmen, and politicians, was seen as a national solution to the "Negro problem." Booker T. Washington* helped popularize this idea.

SELECTED BIBLIOGRAPHY
James D. Anderson, *The Education of Blacks in the South, 1860–1935* (1988); M. F. Armstrong and Helen W. Ludlow, *Hampton and Its Students* (1874, reprint 1971); Thomas Jesse Jones, ed., *Negro Education* (1969); Robert C. Morris, *Reading, 'Riting, and Reconstruction* (1981); Booker T. Washington, *The Story of the Negro: The Rise of the Race from Slavery* (1909, reprint 1969).

Robert A. Bellinger

HANSBERRY v. LEE, 311 U.S. 32 (1940). In 1937 Carl Hansberry, a black real estate agent, purchased a building in the Hyde Park section of Chicago, an area that had always been restricted to whites. Hansberry, the father of Lorraine Hansberry, the author of *Raisin in the Sun*, diligently attempted to resist the threats and vandalism from white neighbors who tried to force him to move and sell his property to a white. Finally the Kenwood Improvement Association (KIA) forced Hansberry to seek legal assistance. The KIA relied on a restrictive covenant prohibiting the purchase of any home in the area by African Americans. In 1940 the Hansberry family hired Earl B. Dickerson, a black civil rights lawyer, to challenge the restrictive covenant law that barred African Americans from living in certain areas of the city. Dickerson pointed out to the U.S. Supreme Court that the law legalizing restrictive covenants stipulated that 85 percent of the residents in a neighborhood had to agree to exclude people of color. Dickerson found that fewer than 85 percent of the Hyde Park residents had signed the contract to keep out minorities. Therefore, the contract was not binding. The court concurred—the immediate result was the opening of thirty blocks of Southside Chicago to African-American families. Although the case did not argue that restrictive covenants were unlawful, it did mark the beginning of their end across the nation.

SELECTED BIBLIOGRAPHY
Earl B. Dickerson Papers, Chicago Historical Society, Chicago, Illinois; Edward R. Moran, "Notes and Comments," *Cornell Law Quarterly* 26 (1941); Geraldine R. Segal, *Blacks in the Law* (1983); Vibert L. White, "Developing the 'School' of Civil Rights Lawyers: From the New Deal to the New Frontier" (Ph.D. diss., Ohio State University, 1988).

Vibert L. White

HARLAN, JOHN MARSHALL (1 June 1833, Boyle County, Ky.–14 October 1911, Washington, D.C.). Born into a proslavery family, John Marshall Harlan nevertheless became the first Supreme Court justice to take a significant stand against post–Civil War racial discrimination. Joining the Democratic party in the 1850s, Harlan served in the federal army during the Civil War and opposed Lincoln's reelection in 1864. He converted to the Republican party in the late 1860s, was appointed to the Supreme Court in 1877 by President Rutherford B. Hayes, and served on the Court until his death in 1911.

Branded as somewhat eccentric in his lifetime, Harlan has emerged in recent revisionist writing as an articulate spokesman for the most basic rights of citizenship. His eloquent dissent in *Plessy v. Ferguson** (1896), in which he asserted that the Constitution is "color-blind," became a seminal source for desegregation arguments in the 1950s and 1960s. In this famous opinion, Harlan prophetically warned that the Court's ruling (upholding the doctrine of separate but equal)* would "prove to be quite as pernicious as the decision . . . in the *Dred Scott* case."

Harlan wrote more opinions (1,161) than any other justice in the

John Marshall Harlan. (Library of Congress.)

Court's history, and more dissenting opinions than any before him. Combining a belief in a powerful national government with an awareness of human needs, he spoke positively for civil rights in an era when there were few echoes.

SELECTED BIBLIOGRAPHY

Loren P. Beth, "Justice Harlan and the Uses of Dissent," *American Political Science Review* 49 (December 1955), 1085–1104; Albert P. Blaustein and Roy M. Mersky, *The First One Hundred Justices: Statistical Studies on the Supreme Court of the United States* (1978); Louis Filler, "John M. Harlan," in Leon Friedman and Fred L. Israel, eds., *The Justices of the United States Supreme Court 1789–1969: Their Lives and Major Opinions*, vol. 2 (1969).

Allen Dennis

HARLEM RACE RIOT (1935). On 19 March 1935, a boy was caught stealing from a Harlem department store. Rumors flew that the police had killed the boy, and several groups protested on the street corner that evening. A rock thrown through the store window began the riot. Thousands eventually joined the crowd, breaking windows and looting. Police arrested seventy-five people, mostly black, and fifty-seven civilians and seven policemen were injured that night. Over six hundred store windows were broken. The riot arose out of the intense hardship of the Great Depression, intensified in black communities by racial discrimination. Blacks in Harlem were more often unemployed than whites and had fewer opportunities for mobility. Crowding and mortality rates were higher, and both private and public programs routinely served Harlem less well than other city neighborhoods. When the rumor of police brutality spread, Harlemites could well believe it; it fit their perception of race relations. Nor did there seem to be anything they could do to counter this discrimination effectively. Resentment at white racism, and at unrelenting hardship, made Harlemites riot. In the aftermath of the riot, many government programs improved their records on race, and several private organizations took black grievances more seriously.

SELECTED BIBLIOGRAPHY

Dominic J. Capeci, Jr., *The Harlem Riot of 1943* (1977); Cheryl Greenberg, *"Or Does It Explode?" Black Harlem in the Great Depression* (1991); Claude McKay, "Harlem Runs Wild," *Nation* 140 (3 April 1935), 382–83; Mayor's Commission on Conditions in Harlem, "The Negro in Harlem: A Report on Social and Economic Conditions Responsible for the Outbreak of March 19, 1935" (Report, 1935), Mayor LaGuardia Papers, box 2550; New York City Police Department, Sixth Division, "Memo to Police Commissioner: Report of the Disorder" (20 March 1935), Mayor LaGuardia Papers, box 41, Municipal Archives, New York City.

Cheryl Greenberg

HARLEM RACE RIOT (1943). On 1 August 1943 Harlem erupted in a second riot. Before peace returned to New York City's best-known black community twelve hours later, the disorder officially recorded 6 deaths, 185 injuries, and $225,000 worth of property damage. It came amid war, on the heels of several other racial upheavals and, surprisingly, in the municipality of liberal mayor Fiorello H. La Guardia. Like other major outbreaks in Mobile, Alabama, Beaumont, Texas, Los Angeles, California, and elsewhere, it revealed perennial racial conflict over job discrimination, abject living conditions, and police-community strain. Unlike them, it occurred more for reasons of unfulfilled democratic tenets, black soldier mistreatment, and previous outbursts. Harlemites seethed as city authorities committed several racial affronts, such as permitting segregated WAVE (Women Accepted for Volunteer Emergency Service) units use of public facilities. They were troubled further because whites assaulted community residents training in southern military camps and, during the nation's worst riot of late June, killed twenty-five blacks in the Detroit race riot (1943).* Hence the confrontation between a white

242   HARLEM RACE RIOT (1964)

patrolman and a black private in Harlem drew together longstanding and war-related grievances, which sparked violence. Rather than interracial combat between large numbers of both races, blacks fought white police and destroyed and looted white-owned stores in a protest that resembled both earlier and later commodity riots; for example, the Harlem race riot in 1935* and the Watts race riot in 1965.* And, despite La Guardia's even-handed quelling of the disturbance, it signalled increasing black awareness and future militancy in the face of failed civil rights initiatives.

SELECTED BIBLIOGRAPHY

John Morton Blum, *V Was for Victory: Politics and American Culture During World War II* (1976); Dominic J. Capeci, Jr., *The Harlem Riot of 1943* (1977); Kenneth B. Clark, "Group Violence: A Preliminary Study of the Attitudinal Pattern of Its Acceptance and Rejection: A Study of the 1943 Harlem Riot," *Journal of Social Psychology* 19 (May 1944), 319–37; Kenneth B. Clark and James Barker, "The Zoot Effect in Personality: A Race Riot Participant," *Journal of Abnormal and Social Psychology* 40 (1945), 143–48; Harold Orlansky, *The Harlem Riot: A Study in Mass Frustration* (1943).

                                                          Dominic J. Capeci, Jr.

HARLEM RACE RIOT (1964). When an off-duty policeman shot a fifteen-year-old black male on 16 July 1964, the long-simmering anger in Harlem against what was perceived as police brutality rushed to the surface. The long-held demand for a civilian police review board intensified. A Congress of Racial Equality* (CORE) protest meeting on 18 July turned into a march on the local police station. Police arrested the leaders and tried to disperse the protestors. Matters quickly escalated, and Central Harlem exploded. Protestors threw firebombs, bricks, and various kinds of other missiles all that night, and the police responded with gunfire. For the next four nights, there was widespread looting and violence. The acting mayor fanned the discord when he blamed the violence on communist instigators. Organizer of the 1963 March on Washington* Bayard Rustin* and CORE national director James Farmer* were on the scene trying to negotiate a settlement, and Roy Wilkins* of the NAACP,* A. Philip Randolph,* and President Lyndon B. Johnson all called for calm. But the established civil rights leaders were helpless in the face of the unleashed black rage over years of discrimination. The Harlem riot was the first of many such major 1960s disturbances that occurred in the urban areas of the North. It began as a protest against unfair police treatment, but its deeper causes were the white-imposed overcrowding and horrible living conditions of ghetto life.

SELECTED BIBLIOGRAPHY

"Civil Rights: The White House Meeting," *Newsweek*, 3 August 1964; *New York Times*, July 1964; Fred C. Shapiro and James W. Sullivan, *Race Riots, New York,*

1964 (1964); Arthur I. Waskow, *From Race Riot to Sit-In, 1919 and the 1960s: A Study in the Connections between Conflict and Violence* (1966).

John F. Marszalek

HARLEM RENAISSANCE. The Harlem Renaissance was a literary movement that took place in Harlem during the 1920s and 1930s when poets, fiction writers, and playwrights expressed pride in their race and in the colorful mosaic of African-American life while, at the same time, revealing the hardships visited upon African Americans. After Jean Toomer's* *Cane* (1923), which captured southern life, the renaissance writers aimed largely at capturing the dignity and beauty possessed by a newly urbanized people. Elevator operators, domestic workers, numbers runners, bootleggers, jazz and blues musicians, as well as the emerging small, black middle class, were their subjects. Langston Hughes's* "Harlem Sweeties" revels in the beauty of black women; Claude McKay's* *Harlem Dancer* (1917) describes a prostitute whose "self was not in that strange place." The African-Americans' struggle for their heritage was reflected in Hughes's "The Negro Speaks of Rivers" and racist violence in McKay's "If We Must Die."* Tragedy dramatically unfolded in Hughes's "A Dream Deferred" and through a man's "passing" in James Weldon Johnson's* *The Autobiography of an Ex-Colored Man** (1927).

The Harlem Renaissance writers were eclectic. They held differing views and lived diverse lifestyles. McKay and Hughes were socialists; Zora Neale Hurston,* Wallace Thurman, and Rudolf Fisher were freewheeling Bohemians. Older than the others, James Weldon Johnson and Jessie Redmond Fauset* remained fairly middle class in their perspectives. Jean Toomer never wrote a book after *Cane*. Sadly, he became preoccupied with denying his black identity. Hurston, an outspoken woman, challenged domineering patrons as well as some of the conventions established during the renaissance. Hurston held a deep appreciation for black southern language and folklore. Most renaissance writers rejected dialect because of past misrepresentations. Hurston's career suffered especially after her publication of *Their Eyes Were Watching God* (1978), which drew on dialect and feminism.

Writers developed strong ties with black and white promoters, patrons, and publishers. Some supporters were deeply involved in the movement itself; others were not. Critics argue that there was too much dependence on white patrons who unduly influenced the movement. Yet, white publishers would never have published black writers had not there been active advocates and a white market. The openness of the Roaring Twenties, greater exposure to black culture through vaudeville and minstrel shows, and new anthropological perspectives, which defined non-European cultures as "primitive" but not inferior, created greater acceptance for black culture among whites. Problematically, many whites came to Harlem in search of stereotypical images of the "primitive" and the "exotic."

Grounded in the fluidity and contradictions of post–Civil War African-American life, the Harlem Renaissance captured what Alain Leroy Locke* termed the "New Negro." From the crowded segregated cities of the South and the North, dynamic forces breathed life into blues, jazz, and literature. Writers gleaned the diverse experiences of discrimination, racist violence, and poverty, on the one hand, and those associated with urban culture, a burgeoning black intelligentsia, and an increasingly vocal group of political activists, on the other. The Harlem Renaissance provided literary roots for generations of black writers and became the rich cultural reservoir of the civil rights movement.

SELECTED BIBLIOGRAPHY
Arna Bontemps, ed., *The Harlem Renaissance Remembered* (1972); Amritjit Singh, William S. Silver, and Stanley Brodwin, eds., *The Harlem Renaissance: Revaluations* (1989); Jean Wagner, *Black Poets of the United States from Paul Laurence Dunbar to Langston Hughes* (1973); Cary D. Wintz, *Black Culture and the Harlem Renaissance* (1988).

Lisa Brock

HARLEM SUITCASE THEATRE. One of the independent community-based theaters founded during the Great Depression, this theater was established in 1937 by the noted writer Langston Hughes* and Louis Thompson under the auspices of the leftist International Workers Order and the New Theatre League. During its brief and turbulent two years of existence, it staged several of Hughes's satirical skits and his well-received *Don't You Want to Be Free?*, the theater's inaugural stage production and its concluding production two years later.

SELECTED BIBLIOGRAPHY
James V. Hatch, ed., *Black Theater, U.S.A.: 1847–1974* (1974); Lindsay Patterson, ed., *Anthology of the American Negro in the Theatre* (1967); Arnold Rampersad, *The Life of Langston Hughes*, vol. 1, *1920–1941: I, Too, Sing America* (1986).

Malik Simba

HARMON FOUNDATION. The Harmon Foundation was created in 1922 by the noted philanthropist William E. Harmon to promote and honor black achievement in the arts. Under its auspices, black artists and writers, among them Countee Cullen,* Langston Hughes,* and Laura Wheeler Waring, have been recognized since the 1920s. The Harmon Foundation was instrumental in establishing an art gallery at Howard University* in 1930 and established the Harmon Gallery in New York City for the showing of black art.

SELECTED BIBLIOGRAPHY
Peter M. Bergman, *The Chronological History of the Negro in America* (1969); Harry

A. Ploski and James Williams, eds., *The Negro Almanac: A Reference Work on the African American*, 5th ed. (1989).

Allen Dennis

HARMON v. TYLER, 273 U.S. 668 (1927). During the first half of the twentieth century, it was not uncommon for both northern and southern cities to adopt ordinances that prohibited blacks from residing in pre-dominantly white neighborhoods. In the 1920s the city of New Orleans, Louisiana, adopted a municipal code that forbade public authorities from issuing a building permit for the construction of a residence for black occupancy in a white community without the written consent of a ma-jority of the persons living in the community. Another section of the code applied the same restrictions to white citizens seeking residency in a black community. The provisions of the code, however, did not deter Benjamin Harmon, a black man, from seeking a building permit for a white residential area. After being denied his permit, Harmon brought suit against the city in federal court. The Supreme Court, after hearing the case on appeal, invalidated the New Orleans ordinance. Citing *Buchanan v. Warley,** a 1917 case involving a similar statute, the Court held that the ordinance violated the Fourteenth Amendment* by denying both whites and blacks the right to acquire and use property. The Court's decision, however, did little or nothing to prevent discrim-ination in residential housing. Until the landmark case *Shelley v. Kraemer** (1948), state courts enforced restrictive deeds and contracts that prohib-ited the sale of property to blacks.

SELECTED BIBLIOGRAPHY

Derrick A. Bell, Jr., *Race, Racism and American Law*, 2d ed. (1980); *New York Times*, 22 May 1927; Joel Williamson, *The Crucible of Race: Black-White Relations in the American South Since Emancipation* (1984).

Phillip A. Gibbs

HARPER v. VIRGINIA BOARD OF ELECTIONS, 383 U.S. 663 (1966). The Twenty-fourth Amendment (1964) banned the poll tax* as a con-dition of voting in federal elections. Annie E. Harper, a retired domestic, was one of many black Southerners who brought cases in the federal courts seeking a decision that would apply such a ban to poll taxes in state elections. Harper's case originated in Virginia, where poll taxes had restricted the electorate since 1902. In a six-to-three decision in March 1966, which relied on the Fourteenth Amendment's* equal pro-tection clause, the Supreme court overruled *Breedlove v. Suttles** (1937) and overturned a lower court decision in striking down a requirement in the Virginia state constitution that prospective voters must have paid poll taxes for the previous three years or forfeit the privilege of voting. In Virginia, whose political leaders preferred to leave controversial ini-tiatives to the federal courts, an effort to undo the poll tax requirement had failed in the previous session of the legislature. By the time the court made its ruling, lower federal courts had recently outlawed the poll tax as a requirement for voting in Texas and Alabama, and it had remained in effect only in Mississippi and Virginia. The decision culminated a series of significant changes in the electoral and legislative environments in Virginia and other southern states.

SELECTED BIBLIOGRAPHY

American Civil Liberties Union Papers, Princeton University, Princeton, N.J.; Philip B. Knight and Gerhard Casper, eds., *Landmark Briefs and Arguments of the Supreme Court of the United States: Constitutional Law* 62 (1975): 833–1087; *Washington Post*, 9 March 1965, and 25 March 1966.

Peter Wallenstein

HARRIS, ABRAM LINCOLN (17 January 1899, Richmond, Va.–16 November 1963, Chicago, Ill.). This African American received his B.S. from Virginia Union University, his M.A. from the University of Pittsburgh, and his Ph.D. in economics from Columbia University. His dissertation was published in 1931 as *The Black Worker* (with Sterling Spero). Except for a brief stint as executive secretary of the Minneapolis Urban League, Harris remained in academe, teaching at West Virginia State College (1924–1925), Howard University* (1927–1946), and the University of Chicago (1946–1963). He served on the Consumer Advisory Board of the National Recovery Administration, and was a Fellow of the John Simon Guggenheim Foundation. He was married to Callie McGuinn (1925), then to Phedorah Wynn (1946). In his early years Harris devoted his political and scholarly efforts to developing economic programs based on an interracial working-class alliance and critiquing alternative strategies. After the 1930s he retreated from activism to study different economic philosophies. He eventually embraced the classical liberalism of John Stuart Mill. Throughout his life he was concerned with the problems of race and the political implications of various programs of social reform.

SELECTED BIBLIOGRAPHY

Chicago Tribune, 17 November 1963; William Darity, Jr., "Abram Harris: An Odyssey from Howard to Chicago," *Review of Black Political Economy* 15 (Winter 1987), 4–40; William Darity, Jr., "Introduction," in William Darity, Jr., ed., *Race, Radicalism and Reform: Selected Papers of Abram Harris* (1989); Abram Harris, *Economics and Social Reform* (1958); Abram Harris, *The Negro as Capitalist* (1936); *New York Times*, 17 November 1963; Rayford W. Logan and Michael R. Wiston, eds., *Dictionary of American Negro Biography* (1982).

Cheryl Greenberg

HARRIS, PATRICIA ROBERTS (31 May 1924, Mattoon, Ill.–23 March 1985, Washington, D.C.). The daughter of a railroad dining car waiter and a teacher and a graduate of Howard University* and George Wash-

Patricia Harris, Secretary of HEW under President Carter. (Negro Almanac Collection, Amistad Research Center, Tulane University, New Orleans.)

ington University law school, Harris was appointed ambassador to Luxembourg by President Lyndon B. Johnson, the first black woman to hold that diplomatic rank. Under President Jimmy Carter she became the first black woman to hold a cabinet position, serving as secretary of both Housing and Urban Development and Health, Education, and Welfare. Described as "tough, abrasive and irascible," she was a powerful advocate for minorities and the poor.

SELECTED BIBLIOGRAPHY

Dictionary of Black Culture; Charles Moritz, ed., *Current Biography Yearbook* (1985); Obituary, *New York Times*, 24 March 1985.

Bernard Donahoe

HASTIE, WILLIAM HENRY (17 November 1904, Knoxville, Tenn.–14 April 1976, Philadelphia, Pa.). With the exception of Supreme Court Justice Thurgood Marshall,* William Henry Hastie was probably the century's best-known black lawyer. In 1925 he graduated from Amherst College and went on to law school, where he received a bachelor of law degree from Harvard in 1930 and a doctorate in jurisprudence in 1933. After a brief stint practicing law, he joined the faculty of Howard College's* law school in 1930 and became its dean in 1939. Hastie became active in the NAACP* and the New Negro Alliance.* His involvement in civil rights cases soon earned him a reputation as a talented lawyer even when decisions went against him. Notably he aided the attempt of Thomas R. Hocutt* to enter the University of North Carolina, argued cases involving salary equalization in North Carolina and Maryland, and fought employment discrimination. His public service career began in November 1933, when Secretary Harold L. Ickes* recruited him to work for the Department of the Interior as an assistant solicitor. This, in turn, led to his appointment to the district court of the Virgin Islands in March 1937 and a position in the War Department in 1940. After two years, Hastie resigned the position in protest of the continuing segregation and discrimination policies in the U.S. military. By 1946, however, he was back in public service and the governorship of the Virgin Islands. In 1949 President Harry S. Truman elevated him to the United States Court of Appeals for the Third Judicial Circuit, a post he held until 1971.

SELECTED BIBLIOGRAPHY

Phillip McGuire, *He, Too, Spoke for Democracy: Judge Hastie, World War II, and the Black Soldier* (1988); Gilbert Ware, *William Hastie: Grace under Pressure* (1984); *Who Was Who in America* (1981).

Gary B. Mills

HATCHER, RICHARD GORDON (10 July 1933, Michigan City, Ind.–). An African-American lawyer and the first black mayor of a major U.S. city, Hatcher was mayor of Gary, Indiana, from 1967 to 1988. Winning his first election by a slim margin in a campaign marred by racism and a corrupt Democratic machine, Hatcher ran as a reform candidate. His victory symbolized to black America the phrase: "From protest to politics." In 1972 Hatcher cochaired the first National Black Political Convention in Gary. Its purpose was "unification of black people." He is president of the National Black Political Council and a member of delegate selection and executive committees of the National Democratic Committee.

SELECTED BIBLIOGRAPHY

Current Biography (1972); *Who's Who among Black Americans, 1990–1991* (1990); *Who's Who in American Politics, 1989–1990* (1989).

Nancy E. Fitch

HAYDEN, ROBERT E. (4 August 1913, Detroit, Mich.–25 February 1980, Detroit, Mich.). Robert Hayden became a consultant in poetry to the Library of Congress in the 1970s. It was a fitting tribute to a man whose poetry, though not often consciously black, nonetheless dealt with major themes in African-American life during the 1960s. He is best known for his poems on Frederick Douglass* and Malcolm X.* Hayden, born in the North, taught at Fisk University* for twenty-three years. While there, he influenced a number of black writers, among them Julius Bernard Lester.* He symbolized the best of the early civil rights movement in his belief that good art spoke from one's experience and should not be tainted with ideological notions of color. Many of the later followers of the Black Aesthetic movement would reject that belief, viewing black art as political. Hayden, however, held to his views. His best-known poetry appeared in the late 1960s and early 1970s. In 1969, he accepted a professorship at the University of Michigan, where he remained until his death in 1980.

SELECTED BIBLIOGRAPHY

Michael R. Brown, "Homage to Robert Hayden, 1913–1980," *Commentary*, September 1980; Robert Hayden, *Words in Mourning Time* (1975); *New York Times*, 27 February 1980, II, 5:1.

Charles T. Pete Banner-Haley

HAYES, ROLAND (3 June 1887, Curryville, Ga.–31 December 1976, Boston, Mass.). An African-American tenor of classical and Negro spiritual music, Hayes was noted for his introduction and interpretation of indigenous "Aframerican" religious folk songs to concertgoers around the world. His outstanding talent and perseverance during the 1920s and 1930s provided opportunities for other black concert and operatic artists. Hayes attended Fisk University's* preparatory school and studied music privately in the United States and Europe. Through his research, he came to the realization that liberty and freedom were realities for American slaves and that "The Negro has his God-given music to bring to the sum total of good in the world."

SELECTED BIBLIOGRAPHY

Current Biography (1942); John Lovell, Jr., *Black Song: The Forge and the Flame. The Story of How the Afro-American Spiritual Was Hammered Out* (1986); Edgar A. Toppin, *A Biographical History of Blacks in America since 1528* (1971).

Nancy E. Fitch

HAYNES, GEORGE EDMUND (11 May 1880, Pine Bluff, Ark.–8 January 1960, New York, N.Y.). A pioneering sociologist whose writings chronicled the creation of a black industrial working class, Haynes was also an influential social reformer. Like W.E.B. Du Bois,* an early mentor, Haynes was editor of the Fisk University* *Herald* and class valedictorian (1903). After receiving a M.A. from Yale University (1905) and studying at the University of Chicago, Haynes became the first black to graduate from the New York School of Philanthropy (1910) and to earn a Ph.D. from Columbia University (1912). In 1910 Haynes and Mrs. William Baldwin, a wealthy philanthropist, cofounded the National Urban League,* and Haynes served as its executive secretary from 1910 to 1917. At the same time, Haynes became professor of sociology at Fisk where he established an undergraduate program to train black social workers. Haynes's own academic success convinced Columbia and other major universities to participate in the league's Urban Fellows Program which granted scholarships to black graduate students. Urban Fellows became

executives of Urban League branches, established Atlanta University's*
and Howard University's* schools of social work, and included influential social scientists in their own right, such as Abram Lincoln Harris,*
and Ira De A. Reid.* In 1918 Haynes was appointed director of the
Division of Negro Economics in the Department of Labor and used a
staff of black professionals to coordinate black defense workers during
World War I. From 1921 until his retirement in 1947, Haynes was the
first executive secretary of the Department of Race Relations of the Federal Council of Churches. He developed the concept of the interracial
clinic to deal with post–World War II racial tensions, and he introduced
Race Relations Sunday exchanges between black and white congregations (1923) and National Brotherhood Month (1940). Haynes conducted
surveys for the YMCA in Africa in 1930 and 1947 and taught at City
College of New York from 1950 to 1959.

SELECTED BIBLIOGRAPHY

George E. Haynes, *Africa, Continent of the Future* (1982); George E. Haynes,
The Negro at Work during the World War and Reconstruction (1921); George E.
Haynes, *The Negro at Work in New York City* (1912); George E. Haynes, *The
Trend of the Races* (1929); Rayford W. Logan and Michael R. Winston, eds.,
Dictionary of American Negro Biography (1982); Daniel Perlman, "Stirring the
White Conscience: The Life of George E. Haynes" (Ph.D. diss., New York
University, 1972); Nancy Weiss, *The National Urban League* (1974); Francille
Wilson, "The Segregated Scholars: Black Labor Historians, 1895–1950" (Ph.D.
diss., University of Pennsylvania, 1988).

                                                                     Francille Rusan Wilson

HEAD START. Head Start is a federal preschool compensatory program
for economically deprived families. It was developed as a part of the
Community Action Program established by the 1964 Economic Opportunity Act that authorized the War on Poverty* program. The first Head
Start program, in the summer of 1965, was an eight-week national demonstration project for the fifty states and territories. To help deprived
preschool children achieve their potential, Title II of the Economic Opportunity Act was amended in 1966 to include a year-round program in
social, educational, mental, and physical health services. The local community provided 10 percent and later 20 percent of the program costs;
Congress provided the larger percentage of costs. Funds were granted
directly to the local nonprofit community group or community action
agency from the United States Department of Education and later the
Department of Health and Human Services. Programs were organized
to meet the community needs and to involve low-income parents, usually as teacher aids and council members.

The Mississippi civil rights movement and Head Start's integration
requirements caused one of the most heated controversies during the
early years. Civil rights activists organized the Child Development

Mississippi Head Start children, mid-1960s. (Tougaloo College Civil Rights Archives, Jackson, Mississippi.)

Group of Mississippi. This group submitted an application through Mary Holmes Junior College on behalf of the low-income families in some of Mississippi's poorest counties. The group was in the news because of the involvement of civil rights workers, unclear guidelines, and fiscal irregularities. The controversy subsided with the organization of the Mississippi Action for Progress as an alternative local Head Start program in Mississippi.

Nationally, Head Start is representative of the best response to the injustices that Americans tried to alleviate during the civil rights movement. More than any other social program, it has provided the means for upward mobility, has encouraged self-advancement, and has fostered self-help in low-income families.

SELECTED BIBLIOGRAPHY

Polly Greenberg, *The Devil Has Slippery Shoes, A Biased Biography of the Child Development Group of Mississippi* (1969); Constance Holden, "Head Start Enters Adulthood," *Science* 247 (23 March 1990), 1400–1402; "Learning from Head Start's Efforts," *Insight* 6 (10 December 1990), 44–46; Robert K. Leik and Mary Anne Chalkley, "Parent Involvement: What Is It That Works?" *Children Today* (May-June 1990), 34–37; Edward Zigler and Jeanette Valentine, eds., *Project Head Start: A Legacy of the War on Poverty* (1979).

Alferdteen Harrison and Lavaree Jones

HEART OF ATLANTA MOTEL, INC. v. UNITED STATES, 379 U.S. 241 (1964). Within hours after the signing of the Civil Rights Act of 1964,* the manager of the Heart of Atlanta Motel filed suit in federal court attacking the constitutionality of the public accommodations section of this act. Prior to the passage of the Civil Rights Act, this motel, like similar establishments across the South, had refused to rent rooms to African Americans. The suit contended that the Civil Rights Act of 1964 exceeded the powers of Congress to regulate interstate commerce, violated the rights of business owners to choose their customers and operate their businesses as they desired, and subjugated owners to "involuntary servitude." Attorneys for the government countered that the commerce clause in the Constitution allowed Congress to remove restraints on interstate commerce such as the discriminatory policies of motels, that the Fifteenth Amendment allowed reasonable regulation of property, and that references to "involuntary servitude" were "frivolous." On 14 December 1964 the U.S. Supreme Court upheld the constitutionality of the public accommodations section of the 1964 Civil Rights Act. The decision was based on the commerce clause and the equal protection clause of the Fourteenth Amendment.* By upholding the constitutionality of the 1964 Civil Rights Act, the Supreme Court legally ensured the desegregation of public accommodations.

SELECTED BIBLIOGRAPHY

Atlanta Constitution, 15 December 1964; Derrick A. Bell, Jr., ed., *Civil Rights: Leading Cases* (1980); *Race Relations Law Reporter* 9 (1964), 908–11, 1650–68; George Rossman, ed., "Review of Recent Supreme Court Decisions," *American Bar Association Journal* 51 (1965), 268.

David A. Harmon

HENDERSON v. U.S. INTERSTATE COMMERCE COMMISSION AND SOUTHERN RAILWAY, 339 U.S. 816 (1950). Although this decision dealt a stinging blow to segregation in interstate transit, its impact proved to be limited because it fell short of overturning the basic tenets of *Plessy v. Ferguson.** Elmer W. Henderson filed his complaint in 1942 after he was repeatedly denied service in the dining car of the Southern Railway. That incident occurred because white passengers continued to occupy the two tables in the black section, which was separated from the rest of the car by a curtain. After lower courts determined that the railway's revised rules met the separate but equal holding of *Plessy,* Henderson appealed to the Supreme Court. In an unprecedented move, the Justice Department intervened to argue against the constitutionality of *Plessy.* Eschewing that question, a unanimous Court held that Henderson had been denied equal access in violation of the Interstate Commerce Act and that the use of partitions, curtains, and signs emphasized "the artificiality of a difference in treatment." In amicus briefs for *McLaurin v. Oklahoma State Regents** and *Sweatt v. Painter,** segregation cases decided on the same day as *Henderson*, the Justice Department reiterated its argument against *Plessy*. But in all three decisions, the Court addressed only the question of equality and avoided the legal issue of racial separation established in *Plessy*.

SELECTED BIBLIOGRAPHY

Catherine A. Barnes, *Journey from Jim Crow: The Desegregation of Southern Transit* (1983); Richard Kluger, *Simple Justice: The History of Brown versus Board of Education and Black America's Struggle for Equality* (1976); Laughlin McDonald, *Racial Equality* (1977); Paul L. Murphy, *The Constitution in Crisis Times, 1918–1969* (1972).

Jack E. Davis

HENRY, AARON (2 July 1922, Dublin, Miss.–   ). A black businessman, civil rights and political leader, who was educated at Xavier University in New Orleans, Louisiana, Henry has been at the center of the drive for racial justice for black Mississippians for nearly three decades. Upon graduation from Xavier in 1960, he established a pharmacy in Clarksdale. The racial inequities faced by that Delta town's large black population prompted him and other local leaders to organize the Coahoma County branch of the NAACP.* The state organization soon recognized his leadership abilities and elected him in 1960 as president of the state branches, an office which he held into the 1990s. A board member of numerous civil and human rights groups and governmental agencies, Henry is clearly one of the country's most well-known and respected civil rights activists. His involvement in the civil rights struggle has been active and direct. In 1961 he participated in the violence-plagued activities of the Freedom Riders,* courageous black and white college students who protested against segregated interstate bus terminal facilities. He was arrested with the riders when they arrived in Jackson to challenge Mississippi's stand. Henry was a close friend of Martin Luther King, Jr.,* and Mississippi's charismatic leaders Medgar W. Evers* and James Charles Evers,* and he marched with them in many of their demonstrations.

Henry directed much of his reform energy in his home county of Coahoma, where blacks enjoyed few of the advantages of real citizenship. During the 1960s, Henry launched an aggressive campaign of demonstrations, economic boycotts, and voter registration to help eliminate white intransigence. In response, he was arrested and convicted of spurious moral charges, and his home and business were repeatedly firebombed and vandalized. Despite constant threats on his life, he remained committed to the nonviolent change of Mississippi's racial order. He also worked for change through the Council of Federated Organizations* (COFO), a coalition of the nation's four major civil rights groups operating in the state. As its president, he directed the Freedom Summer of 1964* project when hundreds of mostly white college students came to Mississippi to participate in a massive voter registration drive and educational effort. A founding father of the biracial Mississippi Freedom Democratic party,* he served as its chairman when it successfully unseated the regulars at the 1968 Democratic national convention. A member of the Mississippi legislature in 1992, he remains an active participant in all aspects of Mississippi life and a living reminder of the turbulent 1960s.

SELECTED BIBLIOGRAPHY

T. H. Barker, "Interview with Aaron Henry," Lyndon Baines Johnson Oral History Collection, University of Texas, Austin; George A. Sewell and Margaret L. Dwight, *Mississippi Black History Makers* (1977); James W. Silver, *Mississippi, the Closed Society* (1966); Robert Penn Warren, *Who Speaks for the Negro* (1965).

Robert L. Jenkins

HERNDON, ANGELO (6 May 1913, Wyoming, Ohio–   ). The son of a miner and a domestic servant with a childhood marked by poverty, emotional religion, and entry into the mines at age thirteen upon the death of his father, Herndon worked in the Communist party* from 1930 for the Scottsboro Trials,* for unemployed councils for the relief and the unionization of miners (Alabama and Tennessee), and for striking longshoremen (New Orleans). On 30 June 1932, with demands for relief, he led a march of about a thousand unemployed blacks and whites on the Fulton County, Georgia, courthouse. Arrested and tried, like the Atlanta Six earlier, for "attempting to incite an insurrection," he became the focal point of a racial cause célèbre of the 1930s. Although young white reformers (C. Vann Woodward), southern moderates (Will W. Alexander), and major organizations (the NAACP* and the American Civil Liberties Union*) opposed his conviction, the effective defense of both Herndon and the cause of black rights in and out of court came mainly from radical black attorney William L. Patterson, the International Labor Defense, and the Communist party. In 1937 the U.S. Supreme Court invalidated the Georgia statute (which was nevertheless invoked against Stokely Carmichael* in 1966). After World War II, Herndon abandoned the Communist party and public activities for a chosen life of obscurity as a salesman in the Midwest.

SELECTED BIBLIOGRAPHY

Charles Crowe, *Slavery, Race and American Scholarship* (1988); Angelo Herndon, *Let Me Live* (1937); Charles H. Martin, *The Angelo Herndon Case and Southern Justice* (1976).

Charles Crowe

HERSKOVITS, MELVILLE JEAN (10 September 1895, Bellefontaine, Ohio–25 February 1963, Evanston, Ill.). A distinguished anthropologist and pioneer in African and African-American studies, Melville Herskovits, the son of Jewish immigrants, earned a B.A. degree in history

(1920) from the University of Chicago and an M.S. (1921) and Ph.D. (1923) in anthropology from Columbia University. In 1927 Herskovits began a thirty-six-year career at Northwestern University. He played a key role in establishing African and African-American studies as acceptable scholarly fields. His landmark work *The Myth of the Negro Past** (1941) describes a rich African heritage and debunks the myth that African Americans have no cultural past. Herskovits founded the first university program of African Studies in the United States at Northwestern. In 1970 Northwestern named its African library collection for him.

SELECTED BIBLIOGRAPHY

Sidney W. Mintz, "Introduction," in Melville J. Herskovits, *The Myth of the Negro Past* (1941); George E. Simpson, *Melville J. Herskovits* (1973); Earl E. Thorpe, *The Central Theme of Black History* (1969).

Barbara L. Green

HESBURGH, THEODORE M. (25 May 1917, Syracuse, N.Y.–). President of the University of Notre Dame from 1952 to 1987, a member of the Civil Rights Commission* from its creation in 1957 to 1972, and its chairman from 1969 to 1972, Hesburgh was an important influence in the American civil rights movement during these years. Deeply moved by the poignant testimony before the commission of black Americans being deprived of their right to vote, Hesburgh developed and acted upon the conviction that the commission was a kind of "national conscience." When President Richard M. Nixon named Hesburgh chairman of the commission in 1969, some observers thought that he regarded Hesburgh as a "pillar of the establishment, to be used by the White House for its own purposes." If so, this did not happen. Instead, Hesburgh publicly criticized the Nixon administration's civil rights policies, or what he perceived to be a lack of them. Testifying before the House Committee on Education and Labor in 1972, Hesburgh censured Nixon's proposed antibusing legislation in the guise of the Equal Opportunities Educational Act as failing to implement the Supreme Court's 1954 decision on desegregation, of failing to provide equal educational opportunities, and of succeeding to fractionalize further the nation along racial lines. Hesburgh's testimony against the proposed legislation aroused the Nixon administration to force his resignation as chairman and as a member of the commission. Nixon's abrupt dismissal of Hesburgh allowed the president to weaken the Civil Rights Commission's influence with the public and Congress and to remove it from the front pages where Hesburgh had put it for some years.

SELECTED BIBLIOGRAPHY

Charlotte A. Ames, comp., *Theodore M. Hesburgh, A Bio-Bibliography* (1989); Dorothy Gilliam, "The Hesburgh Years: Civil Rights," *Notre Dame Magazine* 1 (June 1972), 23–25; John C. Lungren, *Hesburgh of Notre Dame* (1987).

Vincent P. DeSantis

HIGHLANDER FOLK SCHOOL. Myles Horton and Don West co-founded a school in 1932 in Monteagle, Tennessee, to serve as a community folk school in the Danish tradition. Horton remained as its director until 1970; Septima Clark served as director of education. Until the 1950s the school worked primarily with trade unions; after that time, its focus shifted to the civil rights struggle. In the early 1970s Highlander turned to local problems of poverty and political powerlessness. Highlander served as a training center and meeting place for southern union and civil rights leaders, and sought to empower community members to organize on behalf of their own concerns. Its residential workshops, whose agendas were set by the students, included voter education, literacy, racial integration, cooperatives, union organizing, training in nonviolence, and civil rights strategies. Tremendously successful in its goal to develop leadership within oppressed communities, Highlander was frequently harassed by agents of the state and federal government. Surveillance by the Federal Bureau of Investigation, investigations by the Internal Revenue Service, criticism and investigation by state officials, the revocation of Highlander's charter in 1962, the confiscation of its property (Highlander returned under a new name and moved first to Knoxville, then to New Market, Tennessee, in 1971) and occasional attacks by the Ku Klux Klan failed to deter Highlander staff members from continuing their programs.

SELECTED BIBLIOGRAPHY

Frank Adams, *Unearthing Seeds of Fire: The Idea of Highlander* (1975); John Glen, *Highlander: No Ordinary School* (1988); Aimee Horton, *The Highlander Folk School: A History of Its Major Programs, 1932–1961* (1989); C. Alvin Hughes, "A New Agenda for the South: The Role and Influence of Highlander Folk School 1953–1961," *Phylon* 46 (September 1985), 242–50.

Cheryl Greenberg

HIGH POINT, NORTH CAROLINA, SIT-IN. On Thursday, 11 February 1960, twenty-six black teenagers from William Penn High School sat down at the downtown Highpoint Woolworth segregated lunch counter. Unprepared for this direct assault, Woolworth promptly closed the lunch counter and later announced the closing of the store. Fear of similar protests by black youth caused several other stores in the vicinity to close their doors as well. This grass-roots movement, strongly encouraged and supported by black adults in the community, set the tone for achieving equality. Despite abusive and violent attempts by whites to curtail the demonstrations, the sit-in movement was a success. By mid-1960, lunch counters were integrated. This victory set the stage for the successful integration of other facilities and was one method blacks used to pursue parity throughout the social, economic, and political arena in High Point.

SELECTED BIBLIOGRAPHY

Charlotte Observer, 16, 17 February 1960; Wanda Ann Hendricks, interview with Attorney Sammie Chess, 1222 Montlieu Avenue, High Point, N.C. 27262 (July 30, 1990); *High Point Enterprise*, February 1960, 25 January 1985; Martin Oppenheimer, *The Sit-In Movement of 1960* (1989).

Wanda Ann Hendricks

HILL, OLIVER W. (1 May 1907, Richmond, Va.–   ). An African American educated at Howard University,* Hill was the first black elected to public office in Richmond, Virginia, since Reconstruction. His 1949 election resulted from a single-shot voting by blacks and some whites who believed that the 40,000 black population deserved some representation on the city council. In a poll of voters, Hill was voted as the second most effective member of the nine-member council. However, in a 1951 reelection bid, he was defeated by forty-four votes. He returned to his legal practice and became active in NAACP* school suits. He defended seven Martinsville, Virginia, blacks who were convicted of rape and later electrocuted. Hill was strongly supported for an appointive vacancy on the council, but his refusal to compromise his stance on civil rights resulted in his failure to gain the position. Blacks were angered, and the controversy helped to destroy the improved relationship between the races initiated by Hill's election. Subsequently he served as a member of the President's Commission on Government Contracts and as an assistant to the commissioner of the Federal Housing Authority. Between 1940 and 1961, Hill served as chairman of the Virginia Legal Commission of the NAACP.

SELECTED BIBLIOGRAPHY

"Lily White Council," *New Republic* 124 (April 1951), 7; *Who's Who among Black Americans 1975–1976*, vol. 1 (1976), 293.

William Cash

HILL v. TEXAS, 316 U.S. 400 (1942). Henry Hill was charged by a Dallas County, Texas, grand jury with rape. His attorneys challenged the indictment on "the grounds that Negroes had been excluded from the jury." Hill was convicted by an all-white jury, and the verdict was sustained by the Texas Court of Criminal Appeals. When the case reached the U.S. Supreme Court, Hill's attorneys presented poll tax* receipts to show that there were "duly qualified blacks" in the county for jury service. They also provided evidence of the number of black males, aged twenty-five and over, who had formal schooling, including higher education, but were denied participation as jurors. The defense also made use of the testimony of elected officials to contend that "no Negro had been on the grand jury list for sixteen or more years." The Supreme Court reversed Texas.

SELECTED BIBLIOGRAPHY
Derrick A. Bell, Jr., *Race, Racism and American Law* (1980); Marvin E. Frankel and Gary Naftalis, *The Grand Jury* (1975); Joseph Tussman, ed., *The Supreme Court on Racial Discrimination* (1963).

LeRoy T. Williams

HIMES, CHESTER BOMAR (29 July 1909, Jefferson City, Mo.–12 November 1984, Moraira, Spain). An expatriate African-American master of quick-action prose packed with social protest and caustic visions of civil rights, Chester Himes flailed out early against the shackles restraining blacks and went from the Ohio State University (1926–1928) to the Ohio State Penitentiary (1928–1935) for a $53,000 armed robbery. He depicted raw racism in several early novels: *If He Hollers Let Him Go* (1945) depicts prejudice in a Los Angeles shipyard, and *Lonely Crusade* (1947) probes a black man's fears in America. He gained popular American notice with his Harlem stories, such as *Cotton Comes to Harlem* (1965), which features black detectives Coffin Ed Johnson and Grave Digger Jones.

SELECTED BIBLIOGRAPHY
Chester B. Himes, *My Life of Absurdity: The Later Years; The Autobiography of Chester Himes* (1976); Chester B. Himes, *The Quality of Hurt; The Early Years: The Autobiography of Chester Himes* (1972).

Thomas J. Davis

HOBSON v. HANSEN, 265 F. Supp. 902 (D.D.C. 1967). This case was part of civil rights activist Julius Hobson's broader attack on de facto segregation* in the public schools of Washington, D.C. Although Congress would later make the school board elective, a three-judge district court upheld the constitutionality of congressional legislation empowering the judges of the district court to appoint board members. Far more controversial was the next phase of the litigation—determining whether the operation of the public schools, with their system of ability grouping (track system), unconstitutionally discriminated against black children by segregating them into the lower tracks. In *Hobson v. Hansen*, Circuit Judge J. Skelly Wright,* sitting by designation as a district judge, concluded that the board of education had deprived black children of equal educational opportunity with white children. He did not hold that ability grouping was unconstitutional but rather that the Washington, D.C., track system failed to provide remedial and compensatory education to those in the lowest tracks, many of whom had not had the advantage of kindergarten in their neighborhood schools, which put them at a disadvantage when they were tested for placement. Critics of the decision believed it would result in increased white flight to the suburbs.

SELECTED BIBLIOGRAPHY

Alexander M. Bickel, "Skelly Wright's Sweeping Decision," *New Republic* (8 July 1967), 11–12; Robert L. Carter, "The Law and Racial Equality in Education," *Journal of Negro Education* 37 (Summer 1968), 204–11; Aaron Cohodes, "Who Can Perform What the Courts Promise?" *Nation's Schools* 80 (August 1967), 31; John N. Drowatzky, "Tracking and Ability Grouping in Education," *Journal of Law and Education* 10 (January 1981), 43–59; Carl F. Hansen, *Danger in Washington: The Story of My Twenty Years in the Public Schools of the Nation's Capital* (1968); Arthur Selwyn Miller, A *"Capacity for Outrage": The Judicial Odyssey of J. Skelly Wright* (1984).

Patricia A. Behlar

HOCUTT, THOMAS R. (dates unavailable). Thomas Hocutt, an African American, applied for admission to the University of North Carolina College of Pharmacy in 1933 but was rejected because of his race. Receiving legal representation from the national NAACP* in the person of William Henry Hastie,* he petitioned for admission. His legal appeal failed, however, partly because the president of the North Carolina College for Negroes reportedly would not supply him with the necessary credentials to support his eligibility. Although Hocutt lost, the judge declared that North Carolina had an obligation to provide "substantially equal" educational facilities for black residents. NAACP strategy thereafter was to contest segregation first in the schools.

SELECTED BIBLIOGRAPHY

Lerone Bennett, Jr., *Before the Mayflower. A History of the Negro in America, 1619–1964* (1981); John Hope Franklin and Alfred A. Moss, Jr., *From Slavery to Freedom: A History of Negro Americans* (1988); Harvard Sitkoff, A *New Deal for Blacks: The Emergence of Civil Rights as a National Issue, The Depression Decade* (1978).

Nancy E. Fitch

HOLLINS v. STATE OF OKLAHOMA, 295 U.S. 394 (1935). This U.S. Supreme Court case involved the reversal of a rape conviction, based on the denial of the defendant's equal protection under the law. In 1931, Jess Hollins was convicted by an all-white jury of raping a white woman in Sapulpa, Oklahoma. Before his scheduled execution, attorneys for the NAACP* appealed on the basis of the exclusion of African-American jurors. African Americans were excluded historically from jury duty in the county solely on the basis of their race or color. The reversal was a per curiam decision based on the previous decision in the famous Scottsboro Trials* of *Norris v. Alabama* (1935).

SELECTED BIBLIOGRAPHY

Mary D. Brite, "Kentucky's Scottsboro Case," *Crisis* (April 1936); Marvin E. Frankel and Gary P. Naftalis, *The Grand Jury* (1975); Richard Kluger, *Simple Justice:*

The History of Brown v. Board of Education and Black America's Struggle for Equality (1976).

                                                                              Donald Cunnigen

HOLMES v. ATLANTA, 350 U.S. 879 (1955). This suit challenged the right of a municipality to maintain segregated golf courses. On 19 July 1951 the manager of a municipally owned golf course in Atlanta, Georgia, refused to admit African-American citizens. After city officials failed to respond to petitions requesting the desegregation of Atlanta's golf courses, these citizens filed suit in district court. The district court upheld the city's right to maintain segregated golf courses. According to the court, local ordinances requiring segregation in the use of park and recreational facilities were not in conflict with the Fourteenth Amendment.* Since the city of Atlanta provided no golfing facilities for its African-American citizens, the decision allowed time for city officials to provide separate but equal* facilities. The United States Court of Appeals for the Fifth Judicial Circuit* concurred with this decision. On 7 November 1955 the U.S. Supreme Court reversed the decision of the lower courts by ruling that Atlanta could not deny the use of municipally owned golf courses to citizens on the basis of race or color. For the first time the Brown v. Board of Education decision, declaring segregated schools to be illegal, was extended to include other public facilities.

SELECTED BIBLIOGRAPHY

Atlanta Constitution, 8 November, 24 December 1955; Richard Bardolph, ed., The Civil Rights Record: Black Americans and the Law, 1849–1970 (1970); Race Relations Law Reporter, vol. 1 (1957), 14, 146–51.

                                                                              David A. Harmon

HOLMES v. DANNER, 191 F. Supp. 394 (M.D. Ga., 1961). This decision represented a victory for opponents of segregated higher education. A U.S. district court found that the University of Georgia had denied admission to Hamilton Holmes and Charlayne Hunter solely on the basis "of their race and color." Academically qualified applicants, the plaintiffs sued the university in September 1960. In January 1961, they became the institution's first black students under a temporary injunction of the district court. Violent campus demonstrations followed, prompting the university's decision to suspend Holmes and Hunter. The court immediately revoked the suspensions and enjoined state officials from invoking an appropriations statute requiring the cessation of funds to all-white institutions that admitted blacks. After grudgingly calling for compliance with the federal court orders, Governor Ernest Vandiver convened a special legislative session to amend the appropriations law, which the court had declared unconstitutional. The Holmes case was one of the South's numerous battles with the United States Court of Appeals for the Fifth Judicial Circuit* over the issue of federal interposition in higher education. Unlike some southern states, which tried to circumvent court orders by closing schools or by executing new legislation, Georgia resigned itself to desegregation.

SELECTED BIBLIOGRAPHY

Numan V. Bartley, *The Rise of Massive Resistance: Race and Politics in the South during the 1950s* (1969); David R. Goldfield, *Black, White, and Southern: Race Relations and Southern Culture, 1940 to the Present* (1990); Frank T. Read and Lucy S. McGough, *Let Them Be Judged: The Judicial Integration of the Deep South* (1978); "Retreat in Georgia," *Newsweek* (30 January 1961).

Jack E. Davis

HOOKS, BENJAMIN LAWSON (31 January 1925, Memphis, Tenn.–). Hooks became executive director of the NAACP* in 1977 making revitalization of the troubled organization his major objective. Prior to his selection, he enjoyed a varied background. He grew up in a relatively elite family of Memphis blacks. He was ordained a Baptist minister but became interested in the law. After military service in World War II, he enrolled in De Paul University, in Chicago, Illinois, where he earned a J.D. degree in 1948. He returned to Memphis to help change the segregated judicial system and became active in the civil rights sit-ins of the 1950s and 1960s. He gained enough support to become assistant public defender of Shelby County in 1961. Unsuccessful political races failed to weaken his determination. In 1965 Governor Frank Clement appointed Hooks to fill a vacancy as a Shelby County criminal court judge. The first black in the system, he won election to a full term the following year. He also remained an active minister in the 1950s and 1960s, serving as pastor of the Middle Baptist Church in Memphis and the Greater New Mount Moriah Baptist Church in Detroit, Michigan, where he held bimonthly services. Leaving the ministry for government service, Hooks called the church his first love and said he would "always go back to preaching." Fulfilling a 1968 campaign pledge, President Richard M. Nixon appointed Hooks to the Federal Communications Commission in 1972, making him the first black to serve on that agency.

SELECTED BIBLIOGRAPHY

Current Biography (1978); "Jimmy's Debt to Blacks—and Others," *Time*, 22 November 1976; "Judge Hook Finally Gets the Job," *Broadcasting*, 17 April 1972; *Who's Who among Black Americans* (1988).

Thomas D. Cockrell

HOPE, JOHN (2 June 1868, Augusta, Ga.–20 February 1936, Atlanta, Ga.). The son of a former slave, Fanny (Mary Francis), and a prosperous Scottish-born businessman, the light-skinned John Hope attended Worcester Academy in Massachusetts and Brown University, where he distinguished himself as a class orator (1894). As a teacher, a college president (Morehouse College,* Atlanta University*), and a member of numerous committees and commissions, Hope never wavered from his commitment to racial equality. "If we are not striving for equality," he said in 1896 following Booker T. Washington's* Atlanta Exposition Speech,* "in heaven's name for what are we living?" Hope served on the Advisory Board of the NAACP,* the Executive Committee of the National Urban League,* and as a YMCA field representative on the treatment of black troops in France (1918–1919).

SELECTED BIBLIOGRAPHY
Rayford W. Logan and Michael R. Winston, eds., *Dictionary of American Negro Biography* (1982); Ridgely Torrence, *The Story of John Hope* (1948).

Loren Schweninger

HORIZON: A JOURNAL OF THE COLOR LINE. Published in Washington, D.C., between 1907 and 1910, *Horizon* was edited and owned by W.E.B. Du Bois,* Freeman Murray, and Lafayette M. Henshaw. The unofficial organ of the Niagara Movement,* it advocated voting rights for blacks and females and the redistribution of wealth. The editorials challenged Booker T. Washington,* Jim Crow* laws, white immigration, and representative government in the South. *Horizon* failed to attract blacks to the Niagara Movement and, after becoming a bimonthly in 1909, it ceased publication.

SELECTED BIBLIOGRAPHY
August Meier, *Negro Thought in America 1880–1915: Racial Ideologies in the Age of Booker T. Washington* (1963); Elliott Rudwick, *W.E.B. DuBois: Propagandist of the Negro Protest* (1969).

Jessie M. Carter

HOSE, SAM (d. 1899, Palmetto, Ga.). An African-American agricultural worker employed by plantation owner Alfred Cranford near Palmetto, Georgia, Sam Hose was burned at the stake by white Georgians for his self-defense killing of Cranford in April 1899. This lynching was the capstone of a series of racial incidents in Georgia between 1898 and 1899. African-American soldiers mobilized for participation in the Spanish-American War were encamped in Georgia and Florida. The resulting racial friction spilled over into Georgia's communities after the troops departed. In Palmetto in March 1899, several local African Americans were lynched as supposed arsonists or assassins. Sam Hose and Lige Strickland, an African-American minister, were similarly accused. Hose was burned and dismembered. Strickland was tortured in the hopes of eliciting a confession that he had directed Hose to kill Cranford. The brutality of these two lynchings drew protests from African Americans and from some Northern whites such as Julia Ward Howe. Former Georgia Governor William J. Northern defended the South and justified its use of violence. President William McKinley contended, as other presidents would after him, that lynching was a local matter outside federal jurisdiction. This lynching took on an international dimension because of the United States' imperial venture in the Philippines following the Spanish-American War. Emilo Aguinaldo, nationalist leader of the Philippine resistance, noted how democracy was restricted to "whites only" whether it involved due process in the United States or building a nation-state for newly liberated peoples of color across the Pacific.

SELECTED BIBLIOGRAPHY

Atlanta Journal (1898–1899); *Boston Evening Transcript* (March–May 1899); Benjamin Brawley, *A Social History of the American Negro* (1921); W.E.B. Du Bois, *Dusk of Dawn* (1968); Herbert Shapiro, *White Violence and Black Response from Reconstruction to Montgomery* (1988).

Gregory Mixon

HOUSTON, CHARLES H. (3 September 1895, Washington, D.C.–20 April 1950, Washington, D.C.). Known as "The First Mr. Civil Rights," Houston graduated from Dunbar High School in Washington, D.C., earned a Phi Beta Kappa key from Amherst College, in Amherst, Massachusetts, and received the LL.B. and J.D. degrees from Harvard University Law School. As a professor of law and later the dean of Howard University* Law School, and as chief counsel for the NAACP* Legal Defense and Educational Fund,* Houston led the vanguard of African-American lawyers, including U.S. Supreme Court Associate Justice Thurgood Marshall,* who developed and utilized legal techniques that eventually led to the 1954 overthrow of the 1896 separate but equal* doctrine.

SELECTED BIBLIOGRAPHY

Richard Kluger, *Simple Justice: The History of Brown v. Board of Education and Black America's Struggle for Equality* (1976); Genna Rae McNeil, *Groundwork: Charles Hamilton Houston and the Struggle for Civil Rights* (1983); Loren Miller, *The Petitioners: The Story of the Supreme Court of the United States and the Negro* (1966); Geraldine R. Segal, *In Any Fight Some Fall* (1975).

Phillip McGuire

HOUSTON INFORMER. Founded by Houston businessmen Clifton F. Richardson in 1919, the *Informer* was purchased in 1930 by Carter W. Wesley, a prominent attorney who combined it with several other newspapers and developed it into one of the largest African-American newspaper chains in the United States with papers in Texas, Louisiana, and Alabama. Wesley managed the *Informer* chain until his death in 1969. Under his leadership the *Informer* supported such landmark civil rights cases as *Smith v. Allwright** (1944) and *Sweatt v. Painter** (1950) by providing extensive publicity in the African-American community and by soliciting funds to support the cases. Wesley was also personally involved in both cases; he provided legal opinions and donated money to support them.

SELECTED BIBLIOGRAPHY
Nancy Ruth Bessent, "The Publisher: A Biography of Carter W. Wesley" (Ph.D. diss., University of Texas, 1981); *Dallas Express* (13 April 1940, 8 April 1944, 14 April 1956); Steven F. Lawson, *Black Ballots: Voting Rights in the South, 1944–1969* (1976); J. William Snorgrass, "America's Ten Oldest Black Newspapers," *Negro History Bulletin* 36 (January-March 1983), 11–14; Roland E. Wolseley, *The Black Press, U.S.A.* (1990).

W. Marvin Dulaney

HOUSTON RACE RIOT (1917). Bitterness among black soldiers returned from Europe after World War I, systematic abridgement of black voting rights in Texas, oppressive conditions, resentment, frustration and anger at assaults upon black soldiers, and the arrest of a black woman caused men of the Third Battalion, Twenty-fourth Infantry, U.S. Army, stationed in Houston, Texas, to mutiny against their white officers, secure arms and munitions, march upon and riot in the city for three hours on 23 August 1917, and leave fifteen whites and four black soldiers dead and many others seriously wounded. In one of the longest courts-martial in military history, 118 men were charged with disobedience to orders, aggravated assault, mutiny, or murder. One hundred men were found guilty of at least one charge and only seven were acquitted. Eighty-two men were found guilty of all charges, and twenty-nine were given death sentences, although only thirteen were secretly hanged in April 1918. Fifty-three were sentenced to prison for life, and twenty-eight received prison terms of from two to fifteen years. One man was judged incompetent to stand trial, and all charges against him were dropped. The Houston riot stimulated the establishment of a NAACP* branch in Houston and prodded the national headquarters to undertake an extensive educational campaign and to seek to secure pardons for the condemned men. Most had been paroled by the early 1930s.

SELECTED BIBLIOGRAPHY
Robert H. Brisbane, *The Black Vanguard: Origins of the Negro Social Revolution, 1900–1960* (1970); Chandler Davidson, *Biracial Politics: Conflict and Coalition in the Metropolitan South* (1972); Robert V. Haynes, *A Night of Violence: The Houston Riot of 1917* (1976).

Lee E. Williams II

HOWARD, OLIVER OTIS (8 November 1830, Leeds, Maine–26 October 1909, Burlington, Vt.). A graduate of Bowdoin College, in Brunswick, Maine, in 1850 and the United States Military Academy, in West Point, New York, in 1854, Howard lost an arm and was awarded a Medal of Honor for his service during the Civil War. He fought in most of the major battles in Virginia and participated in General William T. Sherman's famous marches through Georgia and the Carolinas. In the 1870s

Largest murder trial in the history of the United States—court-martial of 64 blacks of 24th Infantry for alleged killing of 17 people in Houston, Texas, 23 August 1917. (Negro Almanac Collection, Amistad Research Center, Tulane University, New Orleans.)

General Oliver O. Howard. (From the Collection of John F. Marszalek.)

and 1880s, he campaigned against Apache and Nez Percé Indians. He also served briefly as the superintendent of West Point as a result of the problems caused by the presence of black cadet Johnson C. Whittaker.* Howard retired from the army in 1894 and devoted the remainder of his life to promoting higher education (he helped found Lincoln Memorial University in Harrogate, Tennessee) and campaigning for Republican party candidates. Although he had not been an ardent prewar abolitionist, Howard's opposition to slavery and his deeply held Christian faith earned him the post of commissioner of the Bureau of Freedmen, Refugees, and Abandoned Lands (see Freedmen's Bureau). He personally believed that former slaves deserved land, education, and the franchise, but his own political naivete, along with the entrenched opposition of President Andrew Johnson and many Freedmen's Bureau officials, limited his effectiveness. He did succeed in promoting the elementary and secondary education of southern blacks through the bureau, however, and he was the principal founder of Howard University* in 1867, where he served as president from 1869 to 1873 and as trustee until three years before his death.

SELECTED BIBLIOGRAPHY
John A. Carpenter, *Sword and Olive Branch: Oliver Otis Howard* (1964); Oliver Otis Howard, *Autobiography of Oliver Otis Howard*, 2 vols. (1908); William S. McFeely, *Yankee Stepfather: General O. O. Howard and the Freedmen* (1968).

James Marten

HOWARD UNIVERSITY. Established in Washington, D.C., by a charter of the U.S. Congress on 2 March 1867, the main purpose of Howard University was to create "a college for the instruction of youth in the liberal arts and sciences." Its founders were a zealous group of "Radical Republicans," Congregationalists, and former Civil War army officers of whom the most prominent was General Oliver Otis Howard,* for whom the institution was named. Howard, a Civil War hero and devout Christian, was commissioner of the Bureau of Refugees, Freedman and Abandoned Lands (see Freedmen's Bureau). He became the institution's third president, from 1869 to 1873, and then served on its board of trustees. During the early years the coeducational institution consisted of normal, preparatory, collegiate, theological, medical, and law departments. More than half of the student population was black. Between 1874 and 1889, Howard University experienced significant academic and student body expansion, and departments of dentistry and pharmacology were added. During Mordecai W. Johnson's (1926–1959) tenure, Howard grew into an outstanding university matriculating many of the nation's outstanding African Americans. Between 1960 and 1967, James M. Nabit, a leading civil rights lawyer, was president. The faculty and student body played pivotal roles in the civil rights movement. From 1968 to 1989, James E. Cheek presided over the institution's further modernization and expansion, molding it into one of national stature with over two hundred degree programs on four campuses. The university operates its own hospital, radio and television stations, hotel, and publishing house as well as a wide range of academic institutes and centers focusing primarily on the study of issues affecting persons of African descent. In 1990, Franklyn G. Jenifer became the first alumnus president.

SELECTED BIBLIOGRAPHY
Walter Dyson, *Howard University, The Capstone of Negro Education, A History: 1867–1940* (1941); David S. Lamb, ed., *Howard University Medical Department, Washington, D.C.: A Historical Biographical and Statistical Souvenir* (1900); Rayford W.

Logan, *Howard University: The First Hundred Years, 1867–1967* (1969); Frederick
D. Wilkinson, ed., *Directory of Graduates, Howard University, 1870–1963* (1965).

Glenn O. Phillips

HUGHES, LANGSTON (1 February 1902, Joplin, Mo.–22 May 1967,
New York, N.Y.). As a columnist, anthologist, translator, playwright,
novelist, and poet, Langston Hughes was widely acclaimed among black
Americans for his inimitable renderings of black life and racial problems
with devastating humor. Throughout his long career, Hughes believed

Langston Hughes, 1942. (Library of Congress.)

that literature should be used as a weapon to attack social injustice—a philosophy that is amply illustrated in his prodigious body of poetry from *The Weary Blues* (1926) to *The Panther and the Lash* (1967). Well-known as a poet before he graduated from Lincoln University, in Pennsylvania, in 1928, Hughes devoted much of his writing during the 1930s to civil rights and other political issues. He was particularly interested in the infamous Scottsboro Trials* as an example of class struggle and racial oppression, and he wrote a proletarian play *Scottsboro Limited* (1931) to draw attention to the "legal lynching." In the 1940s, Hughes's "Simple" stories began appearing as a weekly column in the *Chicago Defender.** Simple, in the words of Arthur P. Davis, grew into "a nationally recognized character and symbol" of the wisdom, humor, and race consciousness of working-class blacks. Until his death, Hughes was one of America's most eloquent spokesmen for racial understanding and human rights.

SELECTED BIBLIOGRAPHY
Faith Berry, *Langston Hughes: Before and Beyond Harlem* (1983); Donald C. Dickinson, *A Bio-bibliography of Langston Hughes, 1902–1967* (1967); James A. Emanuel, *Langston Hughes* (1967); Jemi Onwuchekwa, *Langston Hughes: An Introduction to the Poetry* (1985); Arnold Rampersad, *The Life of Langston Hughes* (1986).

                                                                Jerry Ward

HUMPHREY, HUBERT HORATIO (27 May 1911, Wallace, S. Dak.–13 January 1978, Waverly, Minn.). An extraordinary populist orator, Humphrey was the most effective progressive congressman in American history. Believing in government's capacity to do good, he midwifed a host of social democratic programs that gestated a long time before delivery, including federal aid to education, health insurance, vocational training, food stamps, the Peace Corps, the Job Corps, and welfare. Like his idol Franklin D. Roosevelt, he transformed the political landscape permanently, but, unlike him, he was frustrated four times in seeking the presidency.

Among this welter of causes, the emphatic Humphrey chose civil rights as his defining issue. As mayor of Minneapolis, which had only a 1.6-percent black population in the late 1940s, he instituted the Mayor's Council on Human Relations and the nation's first municipal Fair Employment Practice Committee.* In 1948, at the Democratic party's national convention in Philadelphia, Humphrey delivered a barnburning speech calling for Harry S. Truman's undiluted civil rights agenda. That speech, which made him a national figure, won him a U.S. Senate seat in Republican Minnesota. In the Senate, Humphrey became best known as the most vocal civil rights advocate since Reconstruction. He advocated an antilynching bill, the use of a majority vote to cut off paralyzing filibusters, the removal of all voting impediments, and a civil rights commission to enforce state and federal laws, a proposal that bore fruit

Hubert Humphrey and Aaron Henry at Mississippi Rally, in 1967. (Tougaloo College Civil Rights Archives, Jackson, Mississippi.)

in the Civil Rights Act of 1957.* He also pressed his cause outside the Senate with the National Citizens' Council on Civil Rights and the fledging Americans for Democratic Action,* of which he was chosen permanent chairman.

By the mid-1950s, Humphrey was accepted into the political establishment as he learned to control his abrasive tongue and became friendly with Senate majority leader Lyndon B. Johnson. He became genuinely admired for his ebullient personality, his deep knowledge of most complicated government subjects, and his tact. In 1961, he was chosen as Senate majority whip, where one of his greatest triumphs was the passage of the Civil Rights Act of 1964.*

In 1964, Humphrey finally reached national office as Johnson's running mate. As vice president, he coordinated civil rights activities within the federal government and pushed for the Voting Rights Act of 1965.* Johnson ordered his dissenting vice president to toe the line on the growing Vietnam war, a move that destroyed Humphrey's presidential hopes, fractured the Democratic party, and sacrificed Johnson's Great Society programs for the dispossessed of all races.

SELECTED BIBLIOGRAPHY
Hubert H. Humphrey, *Beyond Civil Rights* (1964); Hubert H. Humphrey, *The Cause Is Mankind: A Liberal Program for America* (1964); Hubert H. Humphrey, *The Education of a Public Man: My Life and Politics* (1976); Hubert H. Humphrey, ed., *Integration vs. Segregation* (1964); Hubert H. Humphrey, *Moral Crisis: The Case for Civil Rights* (1964); Carl Solberg, *Hubert Humphrey: A Biography* (1984).

Bruce J. Dierenfield

HURD v. HODGE, 334 U.S. 24 (1948). This companion case to *Shelley v. Kraemer** (1948) involved the constitutionality of racially restrictive covenants. Such covenants were widely used to segregate neighborhoods, not just in the South but in other sections of the United States as well. In *Hurd* the Supreme Court reversed the enforcement of a racially restrictive neighborhood covenant in the District of Columbia. In *Shelley* the Court ruled that judicial enforcement of such covenants was a state action and thus forbidden under the Fourteenth Amendment.* In *Hurd* the Court did not address the due process question but instead cited the Civil Rights Act of 1866* which guaranteed the right of all citizens equally "to inherit, purchase, sell, hold and convey" real property. If *Hurd* and *Shelley* did not eradicate restrictive covenants, they did make important inroads on discriminatory housing practices.

SELECTED BIBLIOGRAPHY
Albert A. Dorskinde, "Notes and Comments," *Cornell Law Quarterly* 33 (1947), 293–300; Jack Greenberg, *Race Relations and American Law* (1959); Donald G. Nieman, *Promises to Keep: African-Americans and the Constitutional Order, 1776 to the Present* (1991); Clement E. Vose, *Caucasians Only: The Supreme Court, the NAACP, and the Restrictive Covenant Cases* (1959).

Charles D. Lowery

HURSTON, ZORA NEALE (7 January 1906, Eatonville, Fla.–28 January 1960, Fort Pierce, Fla.). Probably the most famous female African-American writer of the Harlem Renaissance,* Hurston was a renowned anthropologist, folklorist, and novelist. Her time at Howard University,* from 1919 to 1924, enhanced her interest in African-American folklore and saw the publication of her first short story. At Barnard (B.A., 1928), Hurston pioneered in the collection and collation of southern African-American folktales. Her work includes four published novels, many short stories and nonfiction articles, and editorial board service on the first issue of *Fire!*, an ill-fated magazine jointly organized by some younger members of the Harlem Renaissance. Boldly proclaiming her blackness, Hurston brought ordinary African Americans alive in her folklore and novels.

SELECTED BIBLIOGRAPHY
The Chelsea House Library of Literary Criticism, vol. 4 (1986); Robert E. Hemenway, *Zora Neale Hurston: A Literary Biography* (1977); Lillie P. Howard, "Zora Neale

Hurston," *Dictionary of Literary Biography*, vol. 51 (1987); Lillie P. Howard, *Zora Neale Hurston* (1980); Alice Walker, "Looking for Zora," in Carol Ascher, Louise DeSalvo, and Sara Riddick, eds., *Between Women: Biographers, Novelists, Critics, Teachers and Artists Write about Their Work on Women* (1984).

Brenda M. Brock

I

"I HAVE A DREAM." The most famous speech of Martin Luther King, Jr.'s,* civil rights career was delivered from the steps of the Lincoln Memorial before an integrated mass rally—the March on Washington* for jobs and freedom on 28 August 1963. Climaxing the wave of nonviolent resistance* protests that occurred throughout the summer of 1963, this speech was an act of creative lobbying designed to "inaugurate an era of racial integration and social justice on the national scale." Powerful, elegant, and symbolically significant, "I Have a Dream" ranks with King's "Letter from Birmingham Jail"* as the quintessential statement of the nonviolent protest philosophy. Scholars consider it to be one of the great American speeches of the twentieth century, a peroration worthy of such earlier notable American orators as Patrick Henry, Daniel Webster, and Abraham Lincoln. Echoes of Lincoln's "Gettysburg Address" resonate throughout the speech. King used emotionally charged language, vivid metaphors, and repetition of phrases to create a powerful cadence and rhythm which elicted a strong response from his audience. His audience was not just the 200,000 people assembled at the Lincoln Memorial, it included an entire nation, many of whom were watching on television, that needed to be awakened to the conditions of racial injustice in America. King moved his followers to continue to work for civil rights and to pursue the American Dream; he also reminded the nation of its default: Black people were yet to receive freedom and equality. As a result of this speech, King emerged as the major spokesman for the civil rights movement and the voice of the nation's moral conscience.

SELECTED BIBLIOGRAPHY
Karl W. Anatol and John R. Bittner, "Kennedy on King: the Rhetoric of Control,"

Communication Quarterly 16 (April 1968), 31–34; John Graham, ed., *Great American Speeches, 1898–1963, Texts and Studies* (1970); David L. Lewis, *King: A Biography* (1970); Philip C. Wander, "The John Birch and Martin Luther King Symbols in the Radical Right," *Western Journal of Speech Communication* 35 (Winter, 1971), 4–14; Harris Wofford, *Of Kennedys and Kings* (1980).

                                                                Jacquelyn Jackson

ICKES, HAROLD L. (15 March 1874, Blair County, Pa.–3 February 1952, Washington, D.C.). A former Bull Moose Progressive and civil liberties lawyer, Ickes was a powerful advocate of black equity during Franklin D. Roosevelt's New Deal. Chosen by Roosevelt to be Secretary of the Interior in 1933, a post he held until 1946, Ickes also headed the Public Works Administration (PWA). A former president of the Chicago branch of the NAACP,* Ickes assumed personal responsibility during the early 1930s as "watchdog" for black rights and black people's inclusion within the social and economic programs of the New Deal. Working closely with such black leaders as the NAACP's Walter Francis White* and economist Robert C. Weaver,* his chief race relations adviser after 1935, Ickes saw that blacks were appointed to Interior and PWA staff positions, established quotas for black workers on PWA projects, and ensured black involvement in low-income housing. He lobbied also for the appointment of William Henry Hastie* as federal judge to the Virgin Islands, addressed conventions of the NAACP and National Urban League,* and ordered eating facilities in the Interior Department to be integrated. His most public affirmation of civil rights involved securing the Lincoln Memorial for Marian Anderson's* celebrated concert following the refusal of the Daughters of the American Revolution to allow her to perform in their convention hall. His introduction of Anderson to a crowd of some 75,000 in 1939 was characterized by the *Journal of Negro Education** as a worthy "rival" to "Lincoln's Gettysburg Address." A committed proponent of New Deal reforms and their importance to black people, Ickes was one of the twentieth century's foremost white racial liberals whose ideas influenced younger liberals of the 1950s and 1960s.

SELECTED BIBLIOGRAPHY

John B. Kirby, *Black Americans in the Roosevelt Era* (1980); Nancy J. Weiss, *Farewell to the Party of Lincoln* (1983); Graham White and John Maze, *Harold Ickes of the New Deal* (1985); Raymond Wolters, *Negroes and the Great Depression* (1970).

                                                                John B. Kirby

"IF WE MUST DIE." A poem in sonnet form by the Jamaican exponent of negritude, Claude McKay,* it was first published in the July 1919 issue of the *Liberator*, a New York–based journal edited by Max Eastman. McKay composed the poem in response to the Red Summer* of 1919, a time when the nation violently attempted to reassert the pre–World War I political and social status quo of unquestioning patriotism and second-

class African-American citizenship. "If We Must Die" calls for race solidarity and exhorts African Americans to armed self-defense. McKay
initially shared the sonnet with fellow black railway porters; even the
most jaded were profoundly moved. "If We Must Die" was reprinted
in newspapers, recited in churches, and became a rallying cry for positive
self-consciousness. It is a classic example of the New Negro movement.*

SELECTED BIBLIOGRAPHY
Wayne F. Cooper, *Claude McKay: Rebel Sojourner in Harlem Renaissance* (1987);
Wayne F. Cooper, *The Passion of Claude McKay: Selected Poetry and Prose, 1912–
1948* (1973); James Richard Giles, *Claude McKay* (1976); Claude McKay, *A Long
Way from Home* (1937).

                                                           Bernice F. Guillaume

INDIANAPOLIS FREEMAN. The *Indianapolis Freeman*, founded by Edward Elder Cooper, began publication in Indianapolis, Indiana, on 14
July 1888. The first black illustrated newspaper in the United States, it
provided realistic portrayals of black people. It regularly featured the
cartoons of Henry J. Lewis, who was probably the first black political
cartoonist in the United States. The paper was also unique in that it did
not use a boilerplate, but provided original writing by black authors. In
addition to the news, the paper provided nonpartisan political coverage,
articles on the history and literature of African Americans, and coverage
of the educational progress of the race. It was considered one of the
leading newspapers in the country at the turn of the century. It was
published until 1927.

SELECTED BIBLIOGRAPHY
Georgetta Merritt Campbell, *Extant Collections of Early Black Newspapers* (1981);
Martin E. Dann, *The Black Press, 1827–1890* (1971); George W. Gore, *Negro Jour-
nalism* (1922); John F. Marszalek and C. James Haug, "The *Freeman* and Its Ten
Greatest Blacks Contest: A People's Poll," *Mid-America* 67 (April-July 1985), 55–
68; I. G. Penn, *The Afro-American Press and Its Editors* (1891).

                                                           Robert A. Bellinger

INTERRACIAL REVIEW. Published from 1928 to 1971, the *Interracial
Review* was an outgrowth of the work of the Jesuit priest John LaFarge
(1880–1963), who urged the Catholic Church to see the African American
"not as a pitiful object of charity . . . but as a mighty factor for national
progress and . . . a unique contributor to the fullness of our religious
life." The biracial Layman's Union, which LaFarge organized, was the
forerunner of the Catholic Interracial Council,* founded in New York
City in 1936. By 1959 thirty-five such councils functioned in the United
States. The *Review*, which appeared sporadically before the founding of
the councils, served as their "clearinghouse for information" and as a
forum for continuing advocacy of racial justice and mutual respect.

SELECTED BIBLIOGRAPHY
Jay P. Dolan, *The American Catholic Experience* (1985); *Interracial Review* 1–40 (1928–1971); John LaFarge, *Interracial Justice* (1937; reprint 1978).

                                                          Jo Ann O. Robinson

J

JACKSON ADVOCATE. Percy Greene,* the founder of the *Jackson Advocate*, published this weekly, the oldest black-owned newspaper in Mississippi, from 1938 to 1977. Greene was a long-standing proponent of black voting rights, but his conservatism provoked frequent black protests in the 1960s. He criticized Martin Luther King, Jr.,* black-instigated violence, public demonstrations, modern-day "carpetbaggers" leading Mississippi voter registration drives, and federally forced integration; he continually expressed his fear of a white backlash. Greene urged "responsible" black leaders to work with like-minded whites for gradual black progress. In later years, black leaders accused him of having been paid by the Sovereignty Commission, the state's segregationist agency. After Greene's death, Charles Tisdale bought and published the *Advocate* and made it aggressive and at times strident in promoting black interests.

SELECTED BIBLIOGRAPHY

Jackson Advocate, 29 September 1962, 13 June, 4 July 1964, 14 August 1965; *Jackson Daily News*, 1 June 1982; Julius E. Thompson, *The Black Press in Mississippi, 1865–1986: A Directory* (1988).

Eric C. Clark

JACKSON, JESSE L. (8 October 1941, Greenville, S.C.–). A candidate for the Democratic party nomination for president in 1984 and 1988, he is a product of the 1960s civil rights movement. Following his student years at North Carolina Agricultural and Technical State University, in Greensboro, North Carolina, and his ordination as a Baptist minister, Jackson joined the Southern Christian Leadership Conference* (SCLC) during the Selma voting rights campaign. A year later he assisted Martin Luther King, Jr.,* in SCLC's Chicago open-housing campaign. Although the Chicago campaign was generally regarded as a failure, Jackson was given responsibility for SCLC's Operation Breadbasket, which utilized economic boycotts to promote the hiring of African Americans and to generate fair-share contracts for black business. In 1970 Jackson broke with the SCLC and formed People United to Save Humanity (Operation PUSH),* a "rainbow coalition" of blacks and whites dedicated to greater economic and political power for the impoverished. PUSH continued to target racially discriminatory corporations through economic boycotts, but Jackson in the mid-1970s expanded its role and his national visibility by speaking against violence, drug abuse, and pregnancy among teenagers. Always eager to challenge local and national politicians unresponsive to black concerns, in 1971 he unsuccessfully ran against Richard Daley for mayor of Chicago. One year later, at the National Democratic convention, Jackson and his supporters unseated the Daley-led Illinois delegation. Jackson now regularly promoted Democratic party reform and urged hundreds of blacks to run for state and local office and thousands of African Americans to register to vote. In 1983 Jackson helped elect Harold Washington the first black mayor of Chicago. The successful Chicago campaign and the growing sophistication of black voters prompted Jackson to enter the campaign for the Democratic nomination for president. His "rainbow coalition" campaign of political empowerment of poor people, a concept he first advanced in 1970, allowed him to garner the third highest number of party delegates at the national convention and gave him considerable influence on the party platform. Jackson ran again in 1988 and won nine state primaries. His calls for a Palestinian homeland and his campaign against South African apartheid increased his international stature, and the techniques he had developed over two decades as a negotiator also served him well when he arranged the release of an American airman shot down over Syria in 1983 and of forty-eight prisoners, including twenty-two Americans, from Cuban jails in 1984. In 1990 during the Persian Gulf Crisis, Jackson also arranged the release of forty-seven American hostages from Iraq.

SELECTED BIBLIOGRAPHY

Elizabeth Drew, *Election Journal: Political Events of 1987–1988* (1989); *Los Angeles Times*, 3 September 1990; Barbara Reynolds, *Jesse Jackson: America's David* (1985).
Quintard Taylor

JACKSON, JIMMIE LEE (December 1938, Marion, Ala.–26 February 1965, Selma, Ala.). The shooting and subsequent death of twenty-six-year-old Jimmie Lee Jackson made him a martyr of the civil rights movement and provoked the Selma to Montgomery March* of 1965. Alabama state troopers, under the direction of Colonel Al Lingo, routed an 18 February 1965 nighttime protest march for voter registration in Marion,

Alabama, headed by the Reverend C. T. Vivian. After shutting off the streetlights, the troopers began to beat the demonstrators and to chase them into nearby buildings. Several people followed Jackson, his mother, Viola Jackson, and his eighty-two-year-old grandfather, Cager Lee Jackson, into Mack's Cafe located near the movement headquarters in Zion's Chapel Methodist Church. When troopers hit his mother and grandfather, Jackson charged them, receiving several blows with billy clubs before he was shot in the stomach by a trooper identified only as Fowler. Transferred from Perry County Hospital to Good Samaritan in Selma, Jackson languished for eight days during which time Lingo arrested him for assault and battery with intent to kill. No charges were filed against the trooper. The quiet, young church deacon died on 26 February 1965. A laborer who cut pulpwood and farmed, Jackson had tried unsuccessfully many times to register to vote. It was during his funeral eulogy for Jackson that the Reverend James Bevel* of the Southern Christian Leadership Conference* suggested a protest march from Marion to Montgomery. The SCLC moved the starting point to Selma where Bloody Sunday had occurred on 7 March 1965.

SELECTED BIBLIOGRAPHY

Birmingham News, 19, 27 February 1965; Charles E. Fager, *Selma, 1965: The March That Changed the South* (1974); David J. Garrow, *Protest at Selma: Martin Luther King, Jr., and the Voting Rights Act of 1965* (1978); Jack Mendelsohn, *The Martyrs: Sixteen Who Gave Their Lives for Racial Justice* (1966).

Glenn T. Eskew

JACKSON, MAYNARD HOLBROOK, JR. (23 March 1938, Dallas, Tex.–
). A graduate of Morehouse College* and of North Carolina Central University Law School, Jackson was the first black to be elected mayor of Atlanta, Georgia, in 1973. With no prior political experience, he ran for the U.S. Senate against Herman Talmadge in 1968. He lost the election, but next year he won the office of vice mayor against a white candidate, winning 60 percent of the white vote. In a heated election with strong racial overtones, he became mayor in a runoff election with the incumbent Sam Massell, the city's first Jewish mayor. Jackson was reelected in 1977 and in 1989. As mayor, he helped to ensure to blacks and women economic and political opportunities which had long been denied them by a white business-political elite. His most significant accomplishment was securing for blacks a designated percentage of the construction contracts for the building of the new Atlanta airport.

SELECTED BIBLIOGRAPHY

Atlanta Constitution, 4, 17 October 1973; Henry Hampton and Steve Fayer, *Voices of Freedom: An Oral History of the Civil Rights Movement from the 1950s through the 1980s* (1990); Joint Committee for Political Studies and Johnson Publishing Co.,

Inc., *Black Profiles of Black Mayors in America* (1977); *New York Times*, 17, 18, 21 October 1973; *Washington Post*, 8 January 1974.

Dorothy A. Autrey

JAMES MEREDITH MARCH. *See* Meredith (James) March.

JEANES (ANNA T.) FUND. Named for Anna T. Jeanes, a Philadelphia Quaker, this fund was established in 1905 when Jeanes donated $200,000 for the benefit of African-American education in the South. In 1907 she set aside the bulk of her estate to improve African-American public schools through sponsorship of the "Jeanes Supervisors," industrial teachers who traveled among African-American schools to improve the teaching methods of local, untrained teachers. Until 1937, when the Jeanes Fund joined with other philanthropic endeavors to form the Southern Education Foundation, its focus remained the improvement of industrial education for African-American rural schools, the training of teachers for extension work, and the support of county agents for the improvement of rural homes and schools.

SELECTED BIBLIOGRAPHY

Benjamin Brawley, *Dr. Dillard of the Jeanes Fund* (1971); Raymond B. Fosdick, *Adventure in Giving* (1962); Mabel M. Smythe, ed., *The Black American Reference Book* (1976); Warren Weaver, *United States Philanthropic Foundations* (1967).

Janice M. Leone

JET. Modeled after the small news magazines that proliferated after World War II, *Jet* was the brainchild of *Ebony** publisher, John H. Johnson. In 1955 the magazine stunned the black world with a picture that showed the mutilated body of Emmett Louis Till* at his funeral. *Jet* widely covered the civil rights movement, chronicling the various incidents that happened to civil rights workers. It followed closely the growing stature of Martin Luther King, Jr.,* helping to familiarize the black community with his and other civil rights leaders' activities. Its breezy style and wide use of photographs to cover black activities and accomplishments in entertainment, business, sports, and politics made it an appealing magazine. To many black Americans it was and remains in 1991 their window to the world.

SELECTED BIBLIOGRAPHY

Taylor Branch, *Parting the Waters: America in the King Years, 1954–63* (1989); John H. Johnson, *Succeeding against All Odds* (1989); Juan Williams, *Eyes on the Prize, Episode 1* (1987).

Charles T. Pete Banner-Haley

JIM CROW. The term "Jim Crow" originated with the character in a popular minstrel show of the 1830s who did a song and dance routine to a song called "Jump, Jim Crow." As a historical term, it defines the practice of legal and extralegal racial discrimination against African Americans. When the Thirteenth Amendment* ended slavery at the close of the Civil War in 1865, Jim Crow laws and customs became a new means of ensuring white supremacy. Beginning in the 1870s, the nation's courts overturned the civil rights legislation of Reconstruction and, in 1896, replaced it with the legal doctrine of separate but equal.* Although local Jim Crow laws and customs varied, they all consistently promoted the systematic segregation, subordination, and dehumanization of African Americans.

SELECTED BIBLIOGRAPHY

Catherine A. Barnes, *Journey from Jim Crow: The Desegregation of Southern Transit* (1983); Leonard Williams Levy, *Jim Crow in Boston: The Origin of the Separate but Equal Doctrine* (1974); Neil R. McMillen, *Dark Journey: Black Mississippians in the Age of Jim Crow* (1989); John H. Stanfield, *Philanthropy and Jim Crow in American Social Science* (1985); C. Vann Woodward, *The Strange Career of Jim Crow* (1955).

Lillie Johnson Edwards

JOBS FOR NEGROES MOVEMENT. The Jobs for Negroes movement (1929–1941), or the "Don't Buy Where You Can't Work" movement,* constituted a wave of picket and boycott movements directed at businesses that excluded African Americans from equitable employment. The movement originated in Chicago in 1929 when an ex–prize fighter Big Bill Tate and A. C. O'Neal, editor of a local paper called the *Whip,* organized a boycott of white merchants who employed no blacks. The Jobs for Negroes campaigns spread across the country as a major form of African-American activism during the 1930s depression. Some of the well-known movements were the Future Outlook League in Cleveland, Ohio, the New Negro Alliance in Washington, D.C., the Colored Clerks Circle in St. Louis, Missouri, the Prophet Costonie in Baltimore, Maryland, and the *Sentinel* movement in Los Angeles, California. The most turbulent campaigns emerged in Harlem where a mystic Sufi Abdul Hamid, an Episcopalian minister John Johanson (the Citizens' League for Fair Play*), and the Harlem Labor Union competed in a cauldron of action boycotts that helped inflame the Harlem race riot (1935).* It was the young minister of the Abyssinian Baptist Church, Adam Clayton Powell, Jr.,* who caught the public's attention as his Citywide Coordinating Committee won "jobs for Negroes" in New York Edison Bell Telephone, the New York Bus Company, and the World Fair. Powell forged this movement into a political organization that catapulted him into a seat on the city council and in 1944 to a long congressional career. The activism of the boycott movements ended with full employment during World War II and did not appear again until 1955 with Martin Luther King, Jr.'s,* Montgomery bus boycott.*

SELECTED BIBLIOGRAPHY
Gary J. Hunter, " 'Don't Buy Where You Can't Work': Black Activism during
the Depression Years" (Ph.D. diss., University of Michigan, 1977); Henry
McGuinn, "The Courts and the Occupational Status of Negroes in Maryland,"
Social Forces 18 (1939), 256–68.

Gary J. Hunter

JOHNSON, CAMPBELL CARRINGTON (30 September 1895, Washington, D.C.–22 August 1968, Washington, D.C.). Johnson received a
B.S. degree from Howard University* in 1920 after financial difficulties
and service in World War I had delayed his education. He attained the
rank of first lieutenant and commanded the war's first battery of field
artillery composed of black troops. After completing law school in 1922,
he worked for social improvements in Washington's black community.
He was instructor of social sciences at Howard University (1932–1947),
and President Franklin D. Roosevelt appointed him executive assistant
to the director of Selective Service in 1940, where he remained until 1950.
President Harry S. Truman appointed him to the National Capitol Housing Authority, which he later served as vice chairman. He returned to
the Selective Service System in 1964 where he remained until his death.

SELECTED BIBLIOGRAPHY
Rayford W. Logan and Michael R. Winston, eds., *Dictionary of American Negro
Biography* (1982); *Who Was Who in America (1973); Who's Who in America* (1967).

Thomas D. Cockrell

JOHNSON, CHARLES S. (24 July 1893, Bristol, Va.–27 October 1956,
Louisville, Ky.). One of twentieth-century America's most respected
black educators, a sociologist by training, Johnson spent nearly a lifetime
studying and interpreting the nation's patterns of race relations. Even
before his graduation from the University of Chicago in 1917, his pen-
etrating analysis of America's changing black population trends established him as a leading social scientist. An eyewitness to several race
riots during the tumultuous Red Summer* of 1919, he investigated the
causes of Chicago's unrest for an official commission and for the Chicago
branch of the National Urban League.* His coauthorship of the league's
report, *The Negro in Chicago*, remains a landmark in social science research. In 1921 Johnson became the National Urban League's director
of research and investigations and continued his work on race relations.
His research, frequently published in the league's official magazine,
Opportunity,* which he founded and edited, clearly revealed that blacks
were being systematically excluded from sharing in the American dream.
In 1928 he became chairman of Fisk University's* Social Sciences Department, shaping its specialty in the field of race relations into one of
the nation's most respected. In 1947 he was selected as Fisk's first black
president. Enormous administrative responsibilities followed his ele-

vation, but he maintained a busy and prolific research and writing pace. Until his death, he remained a dedicated scholar committed to effecting better understanding between the races.

SELECTED BIBLIOGRAPHY

Ernest W. Burgess, Elmer A. Carter, and Clarence Faust, "Charles S. Johnson: Social Scientist, Editor, and Educational Statesman," *Phylon* 17 (Winter 1956), 317–25; Edwin R. Embree, *13 against the Odds* (1944); Patrick J. Gilpin, "Charles S. Johnson: An Intellectual Biography" (Ph.D. diss., Vanderbilt University, 1973); *New York Times*, 28 October 1956 (obituary); Joe M. Richardson, *A History of Fisk University, 1865–1946* (1980); Rayford W. Logan and Michael R. Winston, eds., *Dictionary of American Negro Biography* (1982), 347–48.

Robert L. Jenkins

JOHNSON, FRANK MINIS (30 October 1918, Delmar, Ala.–). President Dwight D. Eisenhower appointed this native Alabaman to the United States federal district court for Alabama's twenty-three southeastern counties on 22 October 1955. In 1979 President Jimmy Carter appointed him to United States Court of Appeals for the Fifth Judicial Circuit.* During his long tenure on the federal bench, Johnson handed down a series of decisions which brought about political and social changes that impacted not only on Alabama but also on the South and on the nation. He applied the 1954 U.S. Supreme Court *Brown v. Board of Education** desegregation decision to the Montgomery bus boycott* case, thus incidentally helping to launch the civil rights career of Martin Luther King, Jr.* He was part of the court that abolished the Alabama poll tax;* he ordered Alabama to reapportion its election districts; and he presided over the trial that convicted the murderers of Viola Liuzzo.* He ordered Alabama to integrate all of its school districts—the first statewide desegregation ruling. Throughout these years, his University of Alabama Law School classmate, Governor George C. Wallace, was a constant protagonist, but Johnson's decisions were so significant that many people came to call him the real governor of Alabama. Johnson refused all labels, insisting that his reverence for the law was his only guiding philosophy. According to a statement about Johnson attributed to Martin Luther King: "That is the man that I know in the United States who gives the meaning to the word justice."

SELECTED BIBLIOGRAPHY

"Interpreter in the Front Line," *Time* (May 12, 1967), 72–78; Robert F. Kennedy, Jr., *Judge Frank M. Johnson, Jr.* (1978); *New York Times*, 21 April 1975; *Who's Who in America*, 44th ed. (1986–1987); Tinsley F. Yarbrough, *Judge Frank Johnson and Human Rights in Alabama* (1981).

John F. Marszalek

JOHNSON, GEORGIA DOUGLAS (10 September 1877, Atlanta, Ga.– May 1966, Washington, D.C.). An African-American poet, playwright, biographer, educator, composer, and political appointee, Georgia Johnson graduated from Atlanta University's* Normal School in 1893, taught music in Marietta, Georgia, and attended the Oberlin Conservatory of Music, in Oberlin, Ohio, from 1902 to 1903. After her 1903 marriage to Henry Lincoln Johnson, creative writing became her métier. Renowned for her lyrical, frank, feminine tone and her use of the mixed-blood theme, Johnson was one of the first critically acclaimed female poets of color in the early twentieth century. Her works include *The Heart of a Woman and Other Poems* (1918), *Bronze: A Book of Verse* (1922), *An Autumn Love Cycle* (1928), and *Share My World: A Book of Poems* (1962). Johnson's plays, *Blue Blood* (1926) and *Plumes* (1927), won second and first prizes in *Opportunity** for their respective years. Other plays were published posthumously. She also wrote in collaboration with Gypsy Drago. Additional unpublished works include eight poems with songs and music, *Bridge to Brotherhood*; short stories, some written under the pseudonym of Paul Tremain; and *The Blue Cabinet, Being the Life of Henry Lincoln Johnson*, and *White Men's Children*. Johnson was appointed commissioner of conciliation in the Department of Labor by President Calvin Coolidge. Atlanta University bestowed a doctor of literature degree on Johnson in 1965.

SELECTED BIBLIOGRAPHY

Sterling A. Brown, Arthur P. Davis, and Ulysses S. Lee, eds., *The Negro Caravan* (1941); Countee Cullen, *Caroling Dusk* (1927); Trudier Harris and Thadious M. Davis, eds., *Afro-American Writers from the Harlem Renaissance to 1940* (1987); James V. Hatch, *Black Theater, U.S.A.* (1974); Gloria T. Hull, *Color, Sex, and Poetry* (1987); Ann Allen Shockley, *Afro-American Women Writers 1746–1933* (1988).

                                                                           Bernice F. Guillaume

JOHNSON, JAMES WELDON (17 June 1871, Jacksonville, Fla.–26 June 1938, Wiscasset, Maine). As a poet, critic, anthologist, and novelist, he contributed significantly to the development of twentieth-century African-American literature. As a diplomat, lawyer, and executive secretary of the NAACP,* Johnson left an indelible mark on sociopolitical history. Educated at Atlanta University* (A.B., 1894; A.M., 1904), he was admitted to the Florida bar in 1898. In 1900 he wrote "Lift Every Voice and Sing," which his brother John Rosamond set to music; the poem has a unique place in black life inasmuch as it was adopted as "The Negro National Anthem" in the 1930s. Johnson and his brother migrated to New York in 1902, where they worked as a songwriting team until Johnson was appointed United States consel to Venezuela in 1906 upon the recommendation of Booker T. Washington.* While in the diplomatic corps (1909–1912), Johnson published his only novel, *The Autobiography of an Ex-Colored Man** (1912), anonymously. The book did not become popular until it was reissued in 1927. In 1914 Johnson became an editor of *New York Age*,* and two years later Joel Spingarn offered him the position of field secretary for the NAACP. Johnson worked diligently in the South to increase the number of NAACP branches and members.

In 1917 he organized a silent protest march in New York against lynching and racial oppression, and in 1919 he made investigations of the race riots that had occurred during the Red Summer.* Serving as NAACP executive secretary from 1920 to 1936, Johnson maintained a fairly conservative posture as a key policymaker. He was quite visible, however, in his support of the Dyer antilynching bill (1921), of A. Philip Randolph's* labor organizing efforts, and of efforts to improve living and working conditions for blacks. Johnson resigned from the NAACP in 1930 to accept a chair in creative literature and writing at Fisk University.* This position gave him time for writing, teaching, and lecturing and relief from the pressures that aggravated his poor health. He remained at Fisk until his death in 1938. Johnson's literary activity during his NAACP years was substantial, and he was awarded the Spingarn Medal* in 1925 for distinguished achievement in writing, diplomacy, and public services. He published *Fifty Years and Other Poems* in 1917 and edited three books in quick succession: *The Book of American Negro Poetry* (1922), *The Book of American Negro Spirituals* (1925), and *The Second Book of Negro Spirituals* (1926). His second and third volumes of poetry were *God's Trombones:* *Seven Negro Sermons in Verse* (1927) and *Saint Peter Relates an Incident of the Resurrection Day* (1935). Johnson also wrote *Black Manhattan* (1930), an informal history of blacks in New York; *Along This Way* (1933), an urbane autobiography; and *Negro Americans: What Now?*, a thoughtful assessment of race relations.

SELECTED BIBLIOGRAPHY

Herbert Aptheker, "DuBois on James Weldon Johnson," *Journal of Negro History* 52 (July 1967), 224–27; Hugh Gloster, *Negro Voices in American Fiction* (1948); Eugene Levy, *James Weldon Johnson: Black Leader, Black Voice* (1973); Jean Wagner, *Black Poets of the United States* (1973).

Jerry Ward

JOHNSON, MORDECAI WYATT (12 January 1890, Paris, Tenn.–11 September 1976, Washington, D.C.). A leading educator, administrator, and champion of educational opportunities, Johnson was the first African-American president of Howard University.* His parents were Reverend Wyatt and Carolyn Freeman Johnson. He received his earliest education at the Academy of Roger Williams University in Nashville and at Howe Institute in Memphis, Tennessee. He graduated from Atlanta Baptist College (now Morehouse College*) in 1911 and then taught English, history, and economics there. He continued his studies at the University of Chicago, where he received his bachelor's degree in 1913. He assumed the pastorate of the First Baptist Church of Charleston, West Virginia, in 1916 and received a master's degree in theology from Harvard University's School of Divinity in 1922. Johnson, appointed president of Howard University in 1926, became a superb administrator and "one of the great platform orators of his day." His achievements included the ability to convince southern U.S. congressmen to increase and steadily expand the authorized annual federal appropriations to the university's capital expenditures. Between 1946 and 1960, Howard University received an average of over $1 million annually, in large measure the result of his persistent and skillful efforts.

SELECTED BIBLIOGRAPHY

Rayford W. Logan, *Howard University: The First Hundred Years 1867–1967* (1969).

Glenn O. Phillips

JOHNSON v. VIRGINIA, 373 U.S. 61 (1963). On 27 April 1962, Ford T. Johnson, Jr., was in traffic court in Richmond, Virginia, for driving with an expired tag. Regulations required that Johnson sit in the section set aside for blacks, but he sat in the white section. When he quietly refused to comply with an order to move to the black section, Johnson, a student at nearby Virginia Union University, was convicted of contempt of court. Now he, and the NAACP,* were in a position to challenge directly the constitutionality of segregated courtrooms. On appeal, the Virginia Supreme Court of Appeals ruled the conviction "plainly right." He took his case to the U.S. Supreme Court, which in April 1963 reversed the Virginia courts on Fourteenth Amendment* grounds. In a short, unsigned opinion, the Court asserted that "State-compelled segregation in a court of justice is a manifest violation" of "equal protection." By that time, Johnson was a Peace Corps worker in Ghana. He had secured a decision that desegregated southern courtrooms.

SELECTED BIBLIOGRAPHY

Loren Miller, *The Petitioners: The History of the Supreme Court of the United States and the Negro* (1966); *Richmond Afro-American*, 5, 12 May 1962, 11 May 1963; *Richmond Times-Dispatch*, 30 April 1963.

Peter Wallenstein

JOINT COMMITTEE ON NATIONAL RECOVERY. It became critical during the first one hundred days of the New Deal that someone champion the economic interests of blacks and press for their special needs. One attempt to do so was the establishment of the Joint Committee on National Recovery, formed during the summer of 1933 and initially supported by some twenty groups, the most important of which were the NAACP* and the Julius Rosenwald Foundation. Attorney John P. Davis* and economist Robert C. Weaver* represented the committee before congressional hearings involved with proposed New Deal legislation. Davis hoped that the committee would combine efforts of existing black and civil rights organizations in representing to the administration the concerns of black Americans and, at the same time, educating black communities to the importance of new federal programs. Unable, however, to sustain support from either the NAACP or Rosenwald, the Joint

Committee represented essentially the singular efforts of Davis; it had disappeared by 1935. As a result of his experience with the committee, however, Davis joined Ralph Bunche* and labor leader A. Philip Randolph* to create in 1935 the National Negro Congress.* The Joint Committee on National Recovery reflected the enormous significance of the changed relationship of the federal government to black people.

SELECTED BIBLIOGRAPHY

John B. Kirby, *Black Americans in the Roosevelt Era* (1980); Harvard Sitkoff, *A New Deal for Blacks: The Emergence of Civil Rights as a National Issue* (1978); Raymond Wolters, *Negroes and the Great Depression* (1970).

John B. Kirby

JONES, EUGENE KINCKLE (30 July 1885, Richmond, Va.–11 January 1954, New York, N.Y.). Much of the professional and personal career of Eugene K. Jones was reflected in the organizational history of the early National Urban League* (NUL). The son of a former slave and free black mother, Jones received a B.A. degree from Virginia Union University and an M.A. from Cornell. Shortly thereafter, he became the first field secretary of the National Urban League, which was organized in 1911. In 1917, he succeeded George Haynes* as executive secretary of the NUL, a post he held until 1941. During the 1920s the NUL began publishing *Opportunity,* which featured such talented black writers as Langston Hughes,* Countee Cullen,* and Claude McKay.* Under Jones's direction, the league assumed national prominence. Working with private foundations, corporate institutions, and governmental officials, Jones emphasized securing jobs for blacks within both the private and public sectors. During the New Deal era, he served as a race relations adviser to the Department of Commerce, working closely with black and white administration officials to ensure black participation in New Deal programs. Through the efforts of Lester B. Granger,* whom Jones had recruited, the NUL developed closer ties to organized labor. Although less publicly vocal than others in his affirmation of civil rights, Jones was a committed foe of race discrimination and segregation, and he made the NUL a strong organization supporting racial and economic justice.

SELECTED BIBLIOGRAPHY

Ralph J. Bunche, "Programs, Ideologies, Tactics, and Achievements of Negro Betterment and Interracial Organizations" (unpublished ms., Carnegie Study, 1940); Guichard Parris and Lester Brooks, *Black in the City: A History of the National Urban League* (1971); Nancy J. Weiss, *The National Urban League, 1910–1940* (1974).

John B. Kirby

JONES, LeROI (Amiri Baraka) (7 October 1934, Newark, N.J.–   ). Since the 1960s, LeRoi Jones has been a bellwether of changes in black political and artistic thought in the United States. After earning a B.A. (1954) at Howard University,* Jones established a brilliant career for himself as poet, essayist, and playwright. From the late 1950s to the early 1960s, his Bohemian writings were consistent with the integrationist thrust of the civil rights movement. The production of *Dutchman* (1964), a shockingly honest treatment of racial conflicts, and the publication of *Home* (1966), a collection of social essays, signaled Jones's shift to a nationalist stance. In the year the outcry for Black Power* created rifts among civil rights workers, Jones changed his name to Amiri Baraka. The anthology he coedited in 1968, *Black Fire*, was a telling record of how many young black writers and thinkers rejected the premises of integration in favor of black nationalist political development. In the 1970s Jones was a political activist in his hometown and on the national scene. As chairman of the Committee for a Unified Newark (1968–1975), Jones was instrumental in the election of Kenneth Gibson as the city's first black mayor. He was chairman of the National Black Political Convention (1972), a meeting in which those who wanted to work within traditional political systems could reach no agreement with the black separatists. Although Jones has not identified himself with a single political group in the early 1990s, his work reflects an intense Marxist critique of politics in a capitalist system.

SELECTED BIBLIOGRAPHY
Amiri Baraka, *The Autobiography of LeRoi Jones/Amiri Baraka* (1984); Kimberly W. Benston, *Baraka: The Renegade and the Mask* (1976); William J. Harris, *The Poetry and Poetics of Amiri Baraka* (1985); Theodore R. Hudson, *From LeRoi Jones to Amiri Baraka* (1973); Henry C. Lacey, *To Raise, Destroy, and Create: The Poetry, Drama, and Fiction of Imamu Amiri Baraka* (1981); Werner Sollors, *Amiri Baraka/LeRoi Jones: The Quest for a "Populist Modernism"* (1978).

Jerry Ward

JONES v. ALFRED H. MAYER CO., 392 U.S. 409 (1968). Although previous U.S. Supreme Court cases had outlawed segregation ordinances (*Buchanan v. Warley,** 1917) and racially restrictive covenants (*Shelley v. Kraemer,** 1948; *Barrows v. Jackson,** 1953), these decisions had limited impact on ending residential segregation. *Shelley* and *Barrows* permitted private discrimination if it was not enforced by state action. The *Jones* case, decided after Congress passed the Civil Rights Act of 1968* with a fair housing measure, outlawed racial discrimination in housing sales and rentals. The case originated in St. Louis County, Missouri, when the Alfred H. Mayer Company refused to sell a home to African-American Joseph Lee Jones. Both district and circuit courts rejected Jones's request for an injunction. His U.S. Supreme Court appeal received wide organizational support, including support from the NAACP,* the National Committee against Discrimination in Housing, and the Justice Department. In a controversial finding, Justice Potter Stewart's majority opinion found that the Civil Rights Act of 1866* "bars all racial discrimination, private as well as public, in the sale or rental of property, and that the statute, thus construed, is a valid exercise of the power of Congress to enforce the Thirteenth Amendment.*" Unlike earlier cases, the *Jones* decision more effectively reduced housing discrimination.

SELECTED BIBLIOGRAPHY

Lucius J. Barker and Twiley W. Barker, Jr., *Civil Liberties and the Constitution* (1986); Brian J. L. Berry, *The Open Housing Question: Race and Housing in Chicago, 1966–1976* (1979); Gerhard Casper, "Jones v. Mayer: Clio, Bemused and Confused Muse," *Supreme Court Review* (1968), 89–132; Robert F. Cushman with Susan P. Koniak, *Cases in Constitutional Law* (1989); R. F. Johnson, *Residential Segregation, the State and Constitutional Conflict in American Urban Areas* (1984); Sol Rabkin, *A Landmark Decision on Segregation in Housing: Jones v. Mayer* (n. d.).

James Borchert

JORDAN, BARBARA C. (1 February 1936, Houston, Tex.–). Graduating magna cum laude from Texas Southern University in 1956, Jordan received a law degree from Boston University three years later and soon thereafter became a member of the Texas and Massachusetts bars. Between 1959 and 1966, she served as an administrative assistant to the county judge of Harris County, Texas. On her third effort in a political race, she was elected to the Texas State Senate in 1966, becoming the first black woman to be elected to that body. By 1972, when she decided to run for the U.S. Congress, the Texas Senate had elected her president pro tempore. Elected U.S. Representative in 1972, Jordan joined sixteen black legislators, including the sole black senator, Edward Brooke* of Massachusetts, and three other black women. As part of the Congressional Black Caucus,* Jordan led the effort to extend the Voting Rights Act of 1965* in 1975. In 1976 the Democratic National Committee selected her to give one of the keynote addresses to the national Democratic convention, another first for a black woman. Jordan's eloquence and forceful speech swept the audience. She received a large number of honorary doctorates, including one from Harvard University in 1977 where she shared the same honor with renowned singer Marian Anderson.* She was chosen Democratic Woman of the Year of the Women's National Democratic Club, Woman of the Year in Politics in *Ladies Home Journal*, and "One of the 200 Faces of the Future," *Time Magazine*. Her appointment to President Jimmy Carter's Advisory Board on Ambassadorial Appointments marked her return to government service after she had resigned in 1976 to teach law at the University of Texas, in Austin.

SELECTED BIBLIOGRAPHY

John Hope Franklin and Alfred A. Moss, Jr., *From Slavery to Freedom: A History of Negro Americans* (1988); Barbara Jordan and Shelby Hearon, *Barbara Jordan: A Self-Portrait* (1979).

Linda Reed

JORDAN, VERNON EULION, JR. (15 August 1935, Atlanta, Ga.–). Jordan received a B.A. degree in political science from De Pauw University in 1957 and a J.D. degree from Howard University* in 1960. In 1961 he began a civil rights and public service career that spanned two decades. From 1961 to 1963 Jordan served as the field director for the Georgia branch of the NAACP.* Between 1964 and 1968 he directed the

President Gerald Ford with Vernon Jordan. (Negro Almanac Collection, Amistad Research Center, Tulane University, New Orleans.)

Voter Education Project* of the Southern Regional Council.* Jordan then worked for the Office of Economic Opportunity for two years before becoming the executive director of the United Negro College Fund* in 1970. In 1972 he succeeded the late Whitney Young* as executive director of the National Urban League,* which, under his leadership, increased its affiliates from 99 to 118, its budget from $40 million to $150 million, and its number of employees from 2,100 to 4,200. Jordan also launched a national voter registration drive and campaigns for a national full employment policy and a consumer-oriented national health system. On 29 May 1980, following an address to the Fort Wayne Urban League, Jordan was ambushed and shot. He recovered from his nearly fatal wound and resumed his post as head of the league until 31 December 1981. He is now in private law practice and partnership with the firm of Akin, Gump, Strauss, Hauer and Feld, in Washington, D.C.

SELECTED BIBLIOGRAPHY

Les Payne, "Vernon E. Jordan: In the Footsteps of Whitney Young," *Ebony* 27 (July 1972), 98; Harry A. Ploski and James Williams, eds., *The Negro Almanac: A Reference Work on the African American* (1989); Eleanora W. Schoenebaum, ed., *Political Profiles*, vol. 5 (1979).

Barbara L. Green

JOURNAL OF NEGRO EDUCATION. Created in 1932 at Howard University,* this journal reflected in part the growing number of African-American scholars in various disciplines during the early decades of the twentieth century. According to its first editor, Charles H. Thompson, Howard University professor of education, the journal was designed to stimulate the collection and dissemination of facts, to critique practices, and to investigate problems surrounding African-American education.

SELECTED BIBLIOGRAPHY

August Meier and Elliott Rudwick, eds., *Black History and the Historical Profession, 1915–1980* (1986); Mabel Smythe, ed., *The Black American Reference Book* (1976); Charles Thompson, "Why a Journal of Negro Education?" *Journal of Negro Education* 1 (April 1932), 1–4.

Janice M. Leone

THE JOURNAL OF NEGRO HISTORY. In order to seek and publish the records of black Americans, Carter Godwin Woodson* founded *The Journal of Negro History* in Washington, D.C., on 1 January 1916 and served as its editor until 3 April 1950. The journal was published by the Association for the Study of Afro-American Life and History.* Under Woodson's guidance, many black scholars were able to publish their work when the major historical journals discriminated against them. The *Journal* also represented an outlet for liberal white scholars whose ideas were rejected by the white historical establishment prior to 1950.

Woodson used the *Journal* to advance a positive image of blacks and to challenge a widely held view of racial inferiority. Articles published by Woodson and other scholars, for example, challenged the racist writings of U. B. Phillips and his followers and caused a historiographical shift from emphasis on the master's perspective to that of the slave. In the 1950s and 1960s, many articles on women's history and articles by women authors appeared in the *Journal*, something that did not regularly occur in other historical publications. On the *Journal*'s fiftieth anniversary in 1966, Benjamin Quarles* wrote: "[I]t is pluralistic, it is revolutionary, and it is purposeful." Arthur M. Schlesinger, Sr., hailed it as "an equal member of the family of American historical periodicals." Circulation reached two thousand that year. Due to the preservation of records by the *Journal* and Woodson's efforts to collect primary source material, contemporary scholars have invaluable material on which to draw for their studies. Since 1987, the *Journal* has experienced financial and staff difficulties, but it continues to provide significant scholarly contributions to the study of black life in America.

SELECTED BIBLIOGRAPHY
Editorial, *Journal of Negro History* 51 (April 1966), 75–97; Jacqueline Goggin, "Countering White Racist Scholarship: Carter G. Woodson and the *Journal of Negro History*," *Journal of Negro History* 68 (Fall 1983), 355–75; Rayford W. Logan and Michael R. Winston, eds., *Dictionary of American Negro Biography* (1982).

Thomas D. Cockrell

JOURNEY OF RECONCILIATION (1947). In one of the earliest non-violent, direct action* campaigns of the Congress of Racial Equality* (CORE), sixteen black and white men traveled by bus through the upper South to test new federal laws prohibiting segregated services in interstate transportation. Arrests stemming from an incident outside Chapel Hill, North Carolina, resulted in the trial and conviction of four of these riders: Bayard Rustin,* of the Fellowship of Reconciliation,* Andrew Johnson, a law student; Joe Felmet, a Worker's Defense League representative; and Igal Rodenko, a New York printer. The four men were sentenced to thirty days on a road gang, and all but Johnson served twenty-two days. This journey was a prototype for the more famous journeys of the CORE Freedom Riders* of 1961.

SELECTED BIBLIOGRAPHY
George Houser and Bayard Rustin, *We Challenged Jim Crow* (1947); August Meier and Elliott Rudwick, *CORE: A Study in the Civil Rights Movement, 1942–1968* (1973); James Peck, *Freedom Ride* (1962).

Jo Ann O. Robinson

JUBILEE SINGERS. The Fisk Jubilee Singers, led by George L. White, began a tour in October 1871 to raise "badly needed money" for financially strapped Fisk University.* Their initially mixed reception turned into an enthusiastic one after they abandoned the "white man's music" and replaced it with "slave songs." When the tour ended in May 1872, they had performed at the White House and had raised twenty thousand dollars. A European tour, 1873–1874, netted nearly fifty thousand dollars. During their campaigns, the black singers were often subject to indignities, but they continued to travel and popularize the spirituals. Within seven years, the Jubilee Singers had collected $150,000 and had saved Fisk from financial collapse.

SELECTED BIBLIOGRAPHY

J.B.T. Marsh, *The Story of the Jubilee Singers with Their Songs* (1876); Gustavus D. Pike, *The Jubilee Singers, and Their Campaign for Twenty Thousand Dollars* (1873); Joe M. Richardson, *A History of Fisk University, 1865–1946* (1980).

Maxine D. Jones

K

KATZENBACH v. McCLUNG, 379 U.S. 294 (1964). Title II of the Civil Rights Act of 1964* requires that patrons in places of public accommodation be afforded full and equal service without discrimination. Congress relied heavily on its power to regulate interstate commerce because of the extensive testimony heard regarding the effects of segregation on business and commerce and because of lingering doubts about its ability to regulate private actions. Ollie's Barbecue, owned by the McClung family for nearly thirty years, had a takeout service for blacks but would not seat blacks in the dining room. Its Birmingham, Alabama, location was well removed from interstate highways; its clientele largely was made up of local families and workers. Its only possible connection with interstate commerce was the rather tenuous one of having bought and served meat procured from a distributor who obtained it from out-of-state sources. However, the law established that circumstance as sufficient for jurisdiction, and the Court, speaking through Justice Tom C. Clark, upheld the statute. He noted that the commerce power was broad and sweeping, and that, in light of the testimony before Congress, legislative discretion in the choice of remedy should be honored. This case may represent an extreme departure from the principle of deciding constitutional issues narrowly in light of the facts of the case.

SELECTED BIBLIOGRAPHY

Robert F. Cushman, *Cases in Constitutional Law* (1979); Harry T. Quick, "Public Accommodations: A Justification of Title II of the Civil Rights Act of 1964," *Western Reserve Law Review* 16 (1965), 660–88; George Rossman, "Review of Recent Supreme Court Decisions," *American Bar Association Journal* 51 (1965), 268–69.

James E. Sefton

KATZENBACH v. MORGAN, 384 U.S. 641 (1966). The Voting Rights Act of 1965* provided for the suspension of literacy tests and other tests and devices in areas where there was reason to believe that such tests and devices discriminated against voters on account of race or color. Section 4(e) protected the right to vote of numerous New York City residents from Puerto Rico. This section "provides that no person who has completed the sixth grade in a public school, or an accredited private school, in Puerto Rico, in which the language of instruction was other than English, shall be disfranchised for inability to read or write English." The U.S. Supreme Court reversed a lower court ruling that challenged the authority of Congress to negate a New York English language literacy requirement for voting. It thus affirmed the constitutional authority of Congress to enact "appropriate legislation" to enforce the equal protection clause of the Fourteenth Amendment.*

SELECTED BIBLIOGRAPHY

Thomas I. Emerson, David Haber, and Norman Dorsen, *Political and Civil Rights in the United States*, vol. 2 (1967); William B. Lockhart, Yale Kamisar, and Jesse H. Choper, eds., *Cases and Materials on Constitutional Rights and Liberties*, 3d ed. (1970); Bernard Schwartz, ed., *Statutory History of the United States Civil Rights*, vol. 11 (1970).

Alfred Young

KENNEDY v. BRUCE, 298 F.2d 860 (5th Cir., 1962). Attorney General Robert F. Kennedy, determined to employ the full judicial power of the federal government in order to ensure African Americans of the right to vote, brought action against the registrar of voters in Wilcox County, Alabama. In that impoverished rural county, where blacks outnumbered whites by more than two to one, not a single one of the 6,085 black citizens of voting age was registered. By comparison, 112 percent of eligible whites were registered to vote. The registrar testified in district court that no blacks had been denied a request to register and vote. On appeal, the United States Court of Appeals for the Fifth Judicial Circuit* reversed the district court, saying that the disparity between the number of white and black voters was too great to accept the defendant's argument that no blacks had been refused the right to register. This case, together with the *United States v. Lynd* case a few months later involving a Mississippi county, gave federal officials the right to examine local voting and registration lists when there were reasonable grounds for assuming that certain voters were being discriminatorily denied their voting rights.

SELECTED BIBLIOGRAPHY

Jack Bass, *Unlikely Heroes* (1981); Harvey C. Couch, *A History of the Fifth Circuit,*

1891–1981 (1984); Frank T. Read and Lucy S. McGough, *Let Them Be Judged: The Judicial Integration of the Deep South* (1978).

Charles D. Lowery

KERNER COMMISSION (National Advisory Commission on Civil Disorders). At the height of the civil rights movement in 1964 and 1965, race riots erupted in urban ghettoes primarily outside the South. These uprisings demonstrated that civil rights laws alone would not achieve racial equality. Though black Northerners generally did not encounter official segregation and disfranchisement, they lacked real economic and political power. Crowded into slums, unable to find adequate jobs, treated harshly by the police, and lacking effective political representation, ghetto dwellers expressed their rage against white exploitation. From 1965 to 1968, approximately a half-million blacks in three hundred cities participated in these rebellions, leaving fifty thousand arrested, eight thousand injured, and more than $100 million in damaged property. On 27 July 1967, during another wave of summer violence, highlighted in Newark and Detroit (see Newark, New Jersey, race riot and Detroit race riot), President Lyndon Johnson created the National Advisory Commission on Civil Disorders, chaired by Governor Otto Kerner* of Illinois. On 1 March 1968, the eleven-member, bipartisan panel reported that the United States was "moving toward two societies, one black, one white—separate and unequal." The panel attributed the underlying causes of the riots to white racism; viewed the black uprisings as a form of political protest; and recommended a massive and costly governmental assault on unemployment, poor housing, and poverty. These suggestions largely went unheeded by the president, who was preoccupied by the Vietnam War, and by white officials, who were angered by violence and weary of expensive social welfare programs.

SELECTED BIBLIOGRAPHY

James Button, *Black Violence: Political Impact of the 1960s Riots* (1978); Joe R. Feagin and Harlan Hahn, *Ghetto Revolts* (1973); Michael Lipsky and David J. Olson, *Commission Politics: The Processing of Racial Crisis in America* (1977); National Advisory Commission on Civil Disorders, *Report* (1968); Anthony Platt, ed., *The Politics of Riot Commissions, 1917–1970* (1971).

Steven F. Lawson

KERNER, OTTO (15 August 1908, Chicago, Ill.–9 May 1976, Chicago, Ill.). An Illinois governor, Kerner is best remembered for his leadership of the president's National Advisory Commission on Civil Disorders,* the panel created by President Lyndon B. Johnson to investigate the racial disorders of the late 1960s. The commission's findings, published in 1968 and generally known as the Kerner Report, warned that the United States was becoming racially divided into two "separate but unequal" societies and urged policy changes to be made to reduce tensions between blacks and whites.

SELECTED BIBLIOGRAPHY
Current Biography (October 1961); Obituary, New York Times, 10 May 1976.

Quintard Taylor

KESTER, HOWARD ANDERSON (21 July 1904, Martinsville, Va.–12 July 1977, Asheville, N.C.). While attending Lynchburg College, Princeton Theological Seminary, and Vanderbilt University, he became a leader in the fledgling interracial activities of the intercollegiate Young Men's Christian Association (YMCA), the Student Volunteer Movement, and the Fellowship of Reconciliation.* In the 1920s he organized an interracial forum among college and seminary students in the Lynchburg, Virginia, area, agitated for the integration of the white YMCA conference center in western North Carolina, and was one of the first white students to attend Negro intercollegiate YMCA conferences in the South. From the late 1920s to the late 1930s, as a free-lance activist employed by the Fellowship of Reconciliation and Committee on Economic and Racial Justice, Kester promoted student interracialism, worked for the Southern Tenant Farmer's Union,* and investigated lynchings, riots, and alleged instances of black peonage* for the NAACP* and other groups. From the late 1930s to the mid-1950s, as secretary of the interracial, interdenominational Fellowship of Southern Churchmen* and as principal of Penn Normal Agricultural and Industrial School, a black institution in South Carolina, Kester labored to build a spirit of Christian fraternity that transcended racial or class distinctions.

SELECTED BIBLIOGRAPHY
John S. Bellamy, "If Christ Came to Dixie: The Southern Prophetic Vision of Howard Anderson Kester, 1904–1941" (master's thesis, University of Virginia, 1977); Anthony Dunbar, Against the Grain: Southern Radicals and Prophets, 1929–1959 (1981); John Egerton, A Mind to Stay Here: Profiles from the South (1970); Howard Anderson Kester Papers, Southern Historical Collection, University of North Carolina at Chapel Hill; Howard A. Kester, Revolt among the Sharecroppers (1936); Robert F. Martin, "A Prophet's Pilgrimage: The Religious Radicalism of Howard Anderson Kester, 1921–1941," Journal of Southern History 48 (November 1982), 511–30; Robert F. Martin, Howard Kester and the Struggle for Social Justice in the South, 1904–1977 (1991).

Robert F. Martin

KEYES v. SCHOOL DISTRICT NO. 1, DENVER, COLORADO, 413 U.S. 189 (1973). The Supreme Court in June 1973 decided its first case dealing with public school segregation outside of the South, and it held that discriminatory actions of school boards could lead to segregation,* even in states lacking a statutory or constitutional mandate for dual schooling. Sponsoring the suit filed by local blacks, the Legal Defense and Educational Fund* of the NAACP* charged the Denver school board with the deliberate intent to segregate its schools. School officials countered by arguing that social forces, not law, had created the school system's racial imbalance. In a landmark decision, a seven-to-one Supreme Court held that the school board had instituted segregation through "racially inspired" policies, including assigning minority faculty and staff to minority schools, utilizing mobile classrooms at overcrowded black schools, and gerrymandering student-attendance zones and school-site selections. Although the suit uncovered intentional segregation in only one part of the city, the court placed the burden on school authorities to prove that "segregative intent" had not influenced policy throughout the system. The *Keyes* decision facilitated victories against school segregation in other cities outside the South. But these victories, as in Denver, often led to forced busing, a remedy that proved to be controversial.

SELECTED BIBLIOGRAPHY

Paul R. Dimond, *Beyond Busing: Inside the Challenge to Urban Segregation* (1985); Jack Goodman, "Constitutional Law-School Desegregation—De Facto Hangs On," *North Carolina Law Review* 52 (1973), 431–32; Laurence R. Marcus and Benjamin D. Stickney, *Race and Education: The Unending Controversy* (1981); William D. Valente, *Law in the Schools* (1980); J. Harvie Wilkinson III, *From Brown to Bakke: The Supreme Court and School Integration, 1954–1978* (1979).

Jack E. Davis

KEYS v. CAROLINA COACH COMPANY, 64 M.C.C. 769 (1955). This case was decided by the Interstate Commerce Commission (ICC) on 7 November 1955. On 1 September 1953, Sarah Keys, an African American from New York City and a member of the Women's Army Corps stationed at Fort Dix, New Jersey, sued the Carolina Coach Company of Raleigh, North Carolina, which was a member of the National Trailways Bus System. Keys claimed that on 1 August 1952 she had purchased a joint-line ticket for transportation from Trenton, New Jersey, to Washington, North Carolina; but that upon arriving at Roanoke Rapids, North Carolina, she was refused further passage and was subjected by Carolina Coach employees to "false arrest and imprisonment solely because of her race and color." Keys had been sitting in the front half of the bus. Carolina Coach claimed that only white passengers could occupy front seats of the bus and that its company rules provided the company "full control and discretion as to the seating of passengers." The company's defense was based on the separate but equal* doctrine of the 1896 *Plessy v. Ferguson** decision. At question was section 216 of the Interstate Commerce Act which made it unlawful for any common carrier by motor vehicle "to subject any particular person . . . to any unjust discrimination or any undue or unreasonable prejudice or disadvantage in any respect whatsoever." Citing a precedent decision in a concurrent railroad case, the ICC declared separate but equal as no longer acceptable. Thus the ICC for the first time in its history rejected the separate but equal doctrine. Although the *Keys* ruling applied explicitly to seating on buses, implicitly it outlawed segregation in bus company terminals.

SELECTED BIBLIOGRAPHY

Catherine A. Barnes, *Journey from Jim Crow: The Desegregation of Southern Transit* (1983); *Columbia State* (Columbia, S.C.) newspaper, 16 July 1955; *New York Times*, 26 November 1955; *Pittsburgh Courier*, 3 December 1955.

Charles A. Risher

KILLENS, JOHN OLIVER (4 January 1916, Macon, Ga.–27 October 1987, Brooklyn, N.Y.). A founder of the Harlem Writers Guild (1952) and tutor to important African-American writers, John Oliver Killens was a commanding black voice in the literature of civil rights. He wrote and taught others to write in what he called "a crusade to decolonize the minds of black people." His first novel, *Youngblood* (1954), depicted blacks ready to fight and die for their rights in a small town in Georgia, a place not unlike his native Macon. His second novel, *And Then We Heard the Thunder* (1963), discussed racism in the American military. The protagonist, like Killens, was a law-school dropout who served as a commissioned officer in an all-black regiment during World War II. His later writing grew much more militant.

SELECTED BIBLIOGRAPHY

Obituary, *New York Times*, 29 October 1987; William H. Wiggins, Jr., "John Oliver Killens," in Thadious M. Davis and Trudier Harris, eds., *Afro-American Friction Writers after 1955* (1984).

Thomas J. Davis

KING, ALFRED DANIEL WILLIAMS (30 July 1930, Atlanta, Ga.–21 July 1969, Atlanta, Ga.). The younger brother of Martin Luther King, Jr.,* "A. D." assumed a support role in the civil rights movement. He graduated from Palmer Institute in Fedalia, North Carolina, earned a bachelor's degree from Morehouse College* in Atlanta, Georgia, and attended seminary at the Interdenominational Theological Center at Atlanta University.* After his home was bombed in Birmingham, Alabama, in May 1963, King led demonstrations calling the city "Bombingham." Moving to Louisville, Kentucky, in 1965, King became pastor at Zion Baptist Church and led a movement for an open-housing ordinance there in 1967. After his brother's assassination, he returned to Atlanta to assume the copastorate of Ebenezer Baptist Church. Although he was very active in the Southern Christian Leadership Conference,* he chose not to seek top administrative positions in the organization. He died in a swimming pool accident at his Atlanta home.

Bombed home of the Reverend A. D. King, Ensley, Alabama, 1963. (Archives Collection, Birmingham Public Library. Courtesy *Birmingham News*.)

SELECTED BIBLIOGRAPHY
Obituary, *Newsweek*, 4 August 1969; Obituary, *New York Times*, 22, 25 July 1969; Obituary, *Time*, 1 August 1969.

                                                        Thomas D. Cockrell

KING, CLENNON (1921, birthplace unknown–   ). Teacher, minister, and civil rights activist, King first burst into public notoriety in 1957 when students at Alcorn Agricultural and Mechanical College (now Alcorn State University), in Lorman, Mississippi, where King briefly taught history, protested a series of prosegregation newspaper articles he had written. In June 1958 he attempted to integrate the University of Mississippi summer session to begin work on a doctorate. State police arrested him, and a local judge briefly committed him to the state mental hospital. In 1960 he ran for the United States presidency on the Afro-American ticket, and in 1962 he unsuccessfully sought political asylum in Jamaica. While living in California, he was jailed for failing to support his family, but the state supreme court overturned the conviction. He is probably most famous for attempting to integrate Jimmy Carter's home Baptist church in Plains, Georgia, in the last days of the 1976 presidential campaign. His activity caused the church to drop its ban on black members, but eventually the congregation split and King never actually belonged anyway. He was found guilty of election violations when he ran for office in Georgia in the late 1970s, and he moved to Miami, Florida, where in the 1980s he founded the Holy King's Divine Mission to take in and feed the homeless. In 1982 he insisted that "America made an error in projecting Martin Luther King [Jr.*] as some kind of super man and Clennon King as some kind of super kook."

SELECTED BIBLIOGRAPHY

"A Feisty Preacher Finds a New Mission," *Newsweek* (8 February 1982); "I Speak as a Southern Negro," *American Mercury* 6 (January 1958), 23–33; *New York Times*, 1 November, 1 December 1976; "One Way to Kill a College," *Time* (18 March 1957); "The Plains Baptists," *Time* (17 October 1977); "Showdown in Plains," *Newsweek* (2 November 1976); "A Win for Carter in His Backyard," *Time* (22 November 1976).

John F. Marszalek

KING, CORETTA SCOTT (27 April 1929, Marion, Ala.–   ). Her mother, the former Bernice McMurray, and her father, Obadiah Scott, were hearty people who grew up in a world of harsh segregation, racial violence, and hard times but not in a climate of lost black pride and low

Charles Evers and Coretta Scott King at Woodville, Mississippi, political rally, 1971. (Charles H. Ramberg Collection, Mississippi Department of Archives and History.)

self-esteem. According to Coretta, she often wondered just "how far" her father "could have gone if he had had the opportunity" to get "a high school education." In a family of five, Coretta was described as determined, even aggressive, and "highly intelligent." She attended Lincoln High in Marion and then moved north to Antioch College in Yellow Springs, Ohio. Here, she excelled in music and received a scholarship to Boston's New England Conservatory of Music, where she met the Reverend Martin Luther King, Jr.* Coretta would later recall their first encounter and remark that Martin was "unlike any other" she had met and that, as he was "being prepared" for his journey, she was "being prepared to be his helpmate." They were married in June 1953. In the years that followed, four children were born. An extraordinary person in her own right and the wife of one of America's great leaders, Coretta's life from 1953 to 1968 was remarkable. She marched hand in hand with her husband and nurtured his faith in the dark days of anti–civil rights violence. In 1992 she is a major force behind the Martin Luther King, Jr., Center for Nonviolent Social Change in Atlanta, Georgia.

SELECTED BIBLIOGRAPHY

Coretta Scott King, *My Life with Martin Luther King, Jr.* (1969); Lynn Norment, "The King Family: Keepers of the Dream," *Ebony* (January 1987); Octavia Vivian, *Coretta: The Story of Mrs. Martin Luther King, Jr.* (1970).

LeRoy T. Williams

KING, MARTIN LUTHER, JR. (15 January 1929, Atlanta, Ga.–4 April 1968, Memphis, Tenn.). In December 1955 the twenty-six-year-old Martin Luther King, Jr., in his second year as pastor of the Dexter Avenue Baptist Church in Montgomery, Alabama, leapt from the relative obscurity of the southern black clergy into a meteoric career as the nation's preeminent civil rights leader. His achievements, which won for him the Nobel Peace Prize in 1964, ended when he was assassinated by a white sniper in Memphis, Tennessee, in 1968.

Son of the pastor of the prestigious Ebenezer Baptist Church, in Atlanta, Georgia, young "M. L." attended segregated Booker T. Washington High School and skipped the ninth and twelfth grades to enter Morehouse College* in 1944 at the age of fifteen. In 1947 he was ordained at his father's church, and he received his bachelor's degree from Morehouse the following year. From 1948 to 1951 he attended Crozer Theological Seminary in Pennsylvania, where he was valedictorian and president of the student body. In 1951 he began doctoral study in theology at Boston University (Ph.D., 1955). In Boston he met Coretta Scott, who had left rural Alabama to study voice at the New England Conservatory of Music.

In 1953 Martin and Coretta were married and in 1954, the year of the Supreme Court's school desegregation decision, the couple moved to

Fred Shuttlesworth, Ralph Abernathy, and Martin Luther King, Jr., during Birmingham Confrontation, 1963. (Archives Collections, Birmingham Public Library, Birmingham, Alabama.)

Montgomery, where King's predecessor at the Dexter church, the Reverend Vernon Johns, was a leader in the city's mobilizing community of civil rights activists. When seamstress Rosa Parks* sparked the Montgomery bus boycott* by refusing to give up her seat to a white passenger on 1 December 1955, King was drafted by the veteran leadership to lead the new Montgomery Improvement Association.* The drama of the boycott and King's eloquence drew national television coverage, and in 1956 a federal court ordered the buses desegregated. In 1958 King published *Stride toward Freedom,** a story of the Montgomery boycott, which explained his philosophy of nonviolent resistance* based on Christian brotherhood and love. In 1959 King moved to Atlanta to head the new Southern Christian Leadership Conference* and became copastor with his father at Ebenezer.

The sit-in movement of 1960 led to the formation, with King's encouragement, of the Student Nonviolent Coordinating Committee,* also headquartered in Atlanta, and also to King's first arrest and jailing which resulted in the now famous phone call from Senator John F. Kennedy to Coretta King. The failure of King's Albany, Georgia, sit-in,* during 1961–1962, led to revised nonviolent tactics which, in 1963, challenged segregation in Birmingham, Alabama. National revulsion at the televised brutality, led in the spring of 1963 by police chief Eugene "Bull" Connor, was reinforced in August 1963 by King's moving "I Have a Dream"* address before the Lincoln Memorial in Washington, D.C. This momentum, strengthened by President Kennedy's martyrdom in November and by President Lyndon B. Johnson's commitment, led to the Civil Rights Act of 1964.* A similar King-led protest against voting discrimination in Selma, Alabama, produced televised police violence and led to the Voting Rights Act of 1965.*

When the Watts race riot* of August 1965 was followed in 1966 by Stokely Carmichael's* Black Power* challenge to King's nonviolent leadership, and then by the massive Detroit race riot (1967)*, King shifted his operations increasingly to the North. His campaign in Chicago in 1966 against job discrimination, poor schools, and slum housing was opposed by Mayor Richard Daley's powerful city machine and was torn by violence from both white ethnic communities and black youth gangs. In 1967 King denounced the Vietnam War, and the FBI intensified its bizarre, secret program to destroy King by bugging his hotel rooms, leaking reports of his Communist associates and his philandering, and attempting through threats to break up his marriage and even to turn his morbid streak toward suicide. In 1968 King called for a Poor People's March on Washington* to demand withdrawal from Vietnam, but, before the march could occur, King was murdered on 4 April 1968 at a motel in Memphis, Tennessee, where he was supporting a strike by black sanitation workers.

The key to King's early leadership was his ability to mobilize a disciplined black peasantry in the South by appealing to their roots in the African-American church, while offering brotherhood rather than retribution to the white majority. By drawing televised attacks against nonviolent Negro protesters, King and his allies generated demands by nonsouthern whites that Congress reform the racist South. When King moved northward after 1965, the positive-sum goals of opening southern schools, restaurants, and ballot boxes were replaced by more difficult, zero-sum contests over jobs, promotions, and appointments. King's local victories in the North were few, but the legislative legacy of the congressional reforms of 1964 and 1965 has brought far-reaching change for minorities and women in educational and employment opportunity and electoral districting. Increasingly after 1965, the black social movement split, and King's original protest movement was deeply southern. His leadership radically altered the future for southern blacks, but King also profoundly changed the lives of southern whites, against their fierce resistance.

As King's vision and social agenda, after 1965, expanded beyond black rights toward economic justice, international peace, and human rights, his constituency broadened on the left, but resentment intensified on the right. Like Abraham Lincoln, King was assassinated and martyred in a turbulent and polarized republic. The collective memory of his cause and his courage has eased the pain that divided the nation during his life.

SELECTED BIBLIOGRAPHY
Taylor Branch, *Parting the Waters: America in the King Years, 1954–63* (1988); Adam Fairclough, *To Redeem the Soul of America: The Southern Christian Leadership Conference and Martin Luther King, Jr.* (1987); David J. Garrow, *Bearing the Cross: Martin Luther King and the Southern Christian Leadership Conference* (1986); David Levering Lewis, *King: A Critical Biography* (1970); Stephen B. Oates, *Let the Trumpet Sound: The Life of Martin Luther King, Jr.* (1982).

Hugh Davis Graham

KING, R. EDWIN, JR. (20 September 1936, Vicksburg, Miss.–). A sociologist at the University of Mississippi Medical Center in Jackson, King received a B.A. in sociology at Millsaps College in 1958, and a B.D. from Boston University School of Theology in 1961 followed by a master's degree in social theology in 1963. Active in the civil rights movement, he was arrested in Montgomery, Alabama, in 1960 and in Jackson, Mississippi, in 1963. King and his wife Jeanette worked closely with John R. Salter, Jr. and Medgar W. Evers* in the Jackson Movement campaign of 1962 and 1963, and King helped establish the Mississippi Civil Liberties Union. While serving as chaplain at primarily black Tougaloo College* in Jackson in the 1960s, he initiated attempts by students to attend white churches and led efforts to integrate Jackson's cultural events. King, a native white Mississippian, served as chairperson of the delegation of the Mississippi Freedom Democratic Party* to the Democratic national convention in 1964. He remained active in civil rights causes throughout the 1970s.

SELECTED BIBLIOGRAPHY
Clarice T. Campbell and Oscar Allan Rogers, Jr., *Mississippi: The View from Tougaloo* (1979); John R. Salter, Jr., *Jackson, Mississippi: An American Chronicle of Struggle and Schism* (1978).

Thomas D. Cockrell

KNIGHTS OF PETER CLAVER. This Roman Catholic, African-American fraternal and mutual aid order is one of the most visible aspects of Roman Catholicism's black laity. Named after St. Peter Claver (1581–1654), a Jesuit missionary who dedicated himself to the slaves of Carthagena, West Indies, it was founded on 7 November 1909 in Mobile, Alabama, by four priests of St. Joseph's Society of the Sacred Heart and three laymen. Five divisions involving male members, as well as female and minor auxiliaries, total 100,000 persons in more than twenty-five states. The Knights support parish and community activities, youth development, civic improvement, and scholarships for college-bound youths. These activities are achieved through recreational, insurance, and internal scholarship programs. An important link between the Knights and the larger African-American community is found in the Knights' scholarship program at Xavier University of Louisiana, the only historically black, Catholic institution of higher education in the United States. Additionally, the Knights contribute to the National Urban League,* the NAACP,* and the Southern Christian Leadership Conference.* Religious activities include collaborative presence at masses and participation in regalia at religious ceremonies.

SELECTED BIBLIOGRAPHY

The Claverite 70 (June 1989), *passim*; John W. Donohue, "Of Many Things," *America* 158 (February 1988), 1; Robert R. MacDonald, John R. Kemp, and Edward F. Haas, eds., *Louisiana's Black Heritage* (1979); Stephen J. Ochs, *Desegregating the Altar: The Josephites and the Struggle for Black Priests, 1871–1960* (1990); Charles B. Rousseve, *The Negro in Louisiana* (1937).

Bernice F. Guillaume

KNIGHTS OF PYTHIAS. Founded in Washington, D.C., in 1864, as a secret order for white men, the Pythians rejected a charter application from Philadelphia blacks in 1869. Some black men were still initiated into the mysteries of the order, allegedly because they infiltrated lodges by "passing as whites." By 1880 blacks organized themselves into the Supreme Council of the Knights of Pythias. Attempts to prevent their use of the insignia and the name of the order continued, however, resulting in at least one court case, which occurred in Tennessee in 1911. By the 1930s, black Pythian lodges were found throughout America.

SELECTED BIBLIOGRAPHY

James R. Carnahan, *Pythian Knighthood: Its History and Literature* (1889); W.E.B. Du Bois, ed., *Economic Cooperation among Negro Americans* (1907); E. Franklin Frazier, *The Black Bourgeoisie* (1957); E. A. Williams, *History and Manual of the Colored Knights of Pythias* (1917).

Betty L. Plummer

KNOXVILLE RIOT (1968). The urban riots of the mid-1960s, in particular the Detroit race riot (1967),* heightened tensions between the African-American and white communities. Tennessee was one of the states that instituted riot training for National Guard units. Black leaders in that state charged that "Task Force Bravo," a training exercise to test the mobility of the guard in riot or other emergency situations in the four largest cities of Tennessee, further exacerbated race relations. State officials denied such accusations, and on 8 March troops began the training exercise in the four cities. In an unrelated incident, but in this highly emotionally charged setting, a security officer at Knoxville College on 10 March 1968 stopped a car with out-of-state license plates at 2 A.M.

on the campus of this predominantly black college. A Knoxville student was arrested and charged with public intoxication, along with a Chicago man, who was booked for criminal trespass. Some fifty to seventy-five students rioted in protest over the arrest of the two men. A white taxicab driver responded to a call on the campus that morning and later radioed the police for aid. He died as a result of gunshot wounds, and his body and his destroyed vehicle were reported found on 11 March 1968. The riot subsided soon thereafter.

SELECTED BIBLIOGRAPHY

New York Times, 1, 3, 8, 10, 11 March 1968.

Robert A. Calvert

KOWALIGA INDUSTRIAL COMMUNITY. The Kowaliga Industrial Community was founded in 1896 by William E. Benson* to stop black migration to the North by creating a self-sufficient black community in Alabama which combined farming with year-round industrial employment. He bought tracts of land, subdivided some of it into small farms with affordable housing, and established a saw mill, shingle mill, turpentine plant, and plantation store. Education at the Kowaliga School followed the principles espoused by Booker T. Washington.* Incorporated as the Dixie Industrial Company in 1900 and dependent on the generosity of white northern philanthropists and shareholders, the community was in financial difficulties by the time of Benson's death in 1915 and soon ceased to exist.

SELECTED BIBLIOGRAPHY

William Benson, "Kowaliga: A Community with a Purpose," *Charities* 15 (7 October 1905), 22–24; W.E.B. DuBois, ed., *Economic Cooperation among Negro Americans* (1907); Louis R. Harlan, ed., *The Booker T. Washington Papers* (1972–1981); Elliott Rudwick, *W.E.B. DuBois: Voice of the Black Protest Movement* (1982).

Carole Shelton

L

LAKE MOHONK CONFERENCE. In the spring of 1890 and 1891 the first and second Mohonk conferences were held at Lake Mohonk, New York. They were organized by the Quaker philanthropist Albert K. Smiley at the suggestion of former President Rutherford B. Hayes to discuss the "negro question." Invitations were sent to several hundred representative men and women throughout the country; however, to ensure the attendance of southern whites, "Smiley decided not to invite any colored people." More than one hundred whites were in attendance. Topics discussed at these conferences included industrial education, the Negro ministry, the Negro family, and public education for the Negro. This was one of the many attempts made during these years to deal with the period's racial situation.

SELECTED BIBLIOGRAPHY

James D. Anderson, *The Education of Blacks in the South 1860–1935* (1988); Isabel C. Barrows, eds., *First Mohonk Conference on the Negro Question* and *Second Mohonk Conference on the Negro Question* (1969, reprint); *New York Times*, 2, 3, 6 June 1891.

Robert A. Bellinger

LANE v. WILSON, 307 U.S. 266 (1939). Following the U.S. Supreme Court's invalidation of Oklahoma's grandfather clause* (*Guinn v. United States,** 1915), the Oklahoma legislature enacted a law in 1916 which provided that all citizens qualified to vote in 1916 who failed to register between 30 April and 11 May 1916 would remain forever disfranchised, except eligible voters in 1914. The effect was that white citizens who were on the voting list in 1914 by virtue of the state's grandfather clause were entitled to vote, whereas African Americans, who had been kept from voting by the clause, would remain disfranchised unless they registered during a limited twelve-day period. Robert Lane, an African American, was qualified to vote in 1916, but he failed to register during the required time. Denied the right to register in October 1934, he sued, claiming discriminatory treatment resulting from the 1916 statute. The Supreme Court found the procedural requirements for voting discriminatory and invalidated the 1916 legislation. The case's significance lay in the sharp comments of Justice Felix Frankfurter who, in delivering the majority opinion, wrote that the "[Fifteenth] Amendment* nullifies sophisticated as well as simple-minded modes of discrimination. It hits onerous procedural requirements which effectively handicap exercise of the franchise by the colored race although the abstract right to vote may remain unrestricted by race."

SELECTED BIBLIOGRAPHY

John Hope Franklin, *From Slavery to Freedom*, 5th ed. (1980); Loren Miller, *The Petitioners: The Story of the Supreme Court of the United States and the Negro* (1966); "Recent Cases," *University of Chicago Law Review* 6 (1939), 296–301; "Recent Cases," *University of Pennsylvania Law Review* 87 (1939), 348–49.

Alfred Young

LANGSTON, JOHN MERCER (14 December 1829, Louisa Court House, Va.–15 November 1897, Washington, D.C.). A representative figure in the nineteenth-century phase of the civil rights struggle, Langston received his B.A. (1849) and M.A. (1852) from Oberlin College, in Oberlin, Ohio. Admitted to the Ohio bar in 1854, he was an active abolitionist. In 1864 he became president of the National Equal Rights League, a forerunner of the Niagara Movement* and the NAACP.* He served as an inspector general in the Freedmen's Bureau* (1868–1869) where he championed educational and employment rights for newly freed slaves.

John Mercer Langston, Congressman from Virginia. (Negro Almanac Collection, Amistad Research Center, Tulane University, New Orleans.)

During the remainder of his life, Langston played significant roles as an educator, diplomat, and politician. He served as dean of the Law School (1870–1873) and as vice president and acting president of Howard University* (1873–1875). From 1877 to 1885, he was minister resident to Haiti and chargé d'affaires to the Dominican Republic. For two years (1885–1887), he was president of the Virginia Normal and Collegiate Institute. Elected to the House of Representatives from Virginia in 1888, he was much concerned with the harassment of black voters in the South, and, as a congressman, he called for vigorous enforcement of the Fourteenth Amendment.*

SELECTED BIBLIOGRAPHY
William F. Cheek and Amiee L. Cheek, *John Mercer Langston and the Fight for Black Freedom, 1829–65* (1989); John Mercer Langston, *From the Virginia Plantation to the Nation's Capitol* (1894; reprint 1969); Rayford Logan, *Howard University: The First One Hundred Years, 1867–1967* (1969).

Jerry Ward

LARSEN, NELLA (13 April 1891, Chicago, Ill.–30 March 1964, New York, N.Y.). Best known for her two novels *Quicksand* (1928) and *Passing* (1930), Larsen, the product of an interracial background, poignantly portrayed the marginal existence of African-American women in American culture. Her books reflect her own experiences. After spending one year at the high school affiliated with Fisk University* in Nashville, Tennessee, Larsen spent several years at the University of Copenhagen; subsequently, she received a degree from New York's Lincoln Training School for Nurses in 1915. Prior to undertaking writing, Larsen pursued careers in nursing and library science. In 1928 the Harmon Foundation* recognized her work with a bronze medal. In 1930 she was the first African-American woman to receive a Guggenheim Fellowship for Creative Writing.

SELECTED BIBLIOGRAPHY
Thadious M. Davis, "Nella Larsen," *Dictionary of Literary Biography*, vol. 51 (1987); Thadious M. Davis, "Nella Larsen's Harlem Aesthetic" in Amritjit Singh, William S. Shiver, and Stanley Brodwin, eds., *Harlem Renaissance: Revaluations*, 1989; Cheryl A. Wall, *American Women Writers: A Critical Reference Guide from Colonial Times to the Present*, vol. 2 (1980); Mary Helen Washington, "Nella Larsen: Mystery Woman of the Harlem Renaissance," *Ms* 9 (December 1980), 44–50.

Brenda M. Brock

LASSITER v. NORTHAMPTON ELECTION BOARD, 360 U.S. 45 (1959). Until Congress barred literacy tests as a qualification for voting in the Voting Rights Act of 1965* and its subsequent extensions, they were common. In some states the tests disfranchised blacks only when coupled with such devices as a grandfather clause,* which typically exempted those individuals eligible to vote on 1 January 1867 and their descendants. The Court invalidated the grandfather clause in 1915 in *Guinn v. United States*,* but it approved nondiscriminatory literacy tests. When Louise Lassiter attempted to register to vote but was rejected because she refused to take a literacy test, she challenged the requirement on Fourteenth* and Seventeenth Amendment grounds. Although North Carolina's constitution contained a grandfather clause, its applicable 1957 statute did not. The Court, therefore, simply asked whether a literacy test equally applicable to all violated the Constitution. A unanimous Court, referring to *Guinn*, upheld the test. Noting the power conferred upon states in Article I, Section 2 and in the Seventeenth Amendment, which provided that "the Electors in each State shall have the Qualifications requisite for Electors of the most numerous Branch of the State Legislature," the Court concluded that a nondiscriminatory literacy test was a reasonable means of promoting intelligent use of the ballot.

SELECTED BIBLIOGRAPHY

Richard Claude, *The Supreme Court and the Electoral Process* (1970); Jack Greenberg, *Race Relations and American Law* (1959); George Rossman, ed., "Review of Recent Supreme Court Decisions," *American Bar Association Journal* 45 (1959), 964.

Earlean M. McCarrick

LAWSON, JAMES M., JR. (22 September 1928, Uniontown, Pa.–). A clergyman, pacifist, and leader of nonviolent protest* movements, Lawson gained prominence in the 1960s. Educated at Baldwin-Wallace College, in Berea, Ohio, and Boston University, Lawson helped organize the earliest sit-in demonstrations (November 1959) while he was a divinity student at Vanderbilt University, in Nashville, Tennessee. His dismissal in 1960 by the university chancellor caused a much-publicized crisis of conscience among the faculty of the divinity school. Lawson worked actively for the Student Nonviolent Coordinating Committee* before he accepted a pastorate in Memphis, Tennessee. In 1968 he turned the Memphis garbage collectors' strike into an occasion for focusing national attention on glaring instances of social injustice. Despite the tragic death of Martin Luther King, Jr.,* in this effort, these Lawson-inspired confrontations gained civil rights and economic opportunities for African Americans.

SELECTED BIBLIOGRAPHY

Paul K. Conkin, *Gone with the Ivy: A Biography of Vanderbilt University* (1985); *New York Times*, 8 April 1968; David M. Tucker, *Black Pastors and Leaders: Memphis, 1819–1972* (1975); *Who's Who among Black Americans*, 2d ed., 1977–1978, vol. 1 (1978).

James R. Chumney

LEAGUE OF REVOLUTIONARY BLACK WORKERS. Inspired by radical elements in the civil rights movement, some African-American members of the United Auto Workers (UAW) in Detroit, Michigan, formed

DRUM, FRUM, and ELRUM (i.e., the Dodge, Ford, and Eldon Avenue Revolutionary Movements, respectively) in the late 1960s. The now defunct league was created to coordinate the efforts of DRUM, FRUM, and ELRUM and to unite "the people" in their revolutionary struggle. Although the league remained in the UAW, the official viewpoint was that "the labor movement as represented by United Mine Workers, Steel Workers, UAW, AFL-CIO, etc. are all the antithesis of the freedom of black people, in particular, and the world in general."

SELECTED BIBLIOGRAPHY

James A. Geschwender, *Class, Race, and Worker Insurgency: The League of Revolutionary Black Workers* (1977); "League of Revolutionary Black Workers General Policy Statement, Labor History and League's Labor Program," *Inner City Voice*, 3 February 1971.

                                                                    Clarence Hooker

LEE, HERBERT (1 January 1912, Amite County, Miss.–25 September 1961, Liberty, Miss.). An Amite County, Mississippi, farmer, Lee was one of the first blacks who attempted to register to vote as part of the Student Nonviolent Coordinating Committee's* first voter registration effort in Mississippi. He was also active in the local chapter of the NAACP.* He was shot and killed, on 25 September 1961, by State Representative E. H. Hurst in Liberty, Mississippi. Hurst, who claimed he shot Lee in self-defense, was acquitted of the crime by a local jury. A witness to the murder, Lewis Allen, later testified to a Justice Department official that Lee had not assaulted Hurst. Allen was killed three years later, allegedly as a result of his testimony.

SELECTED BIBLIOGRAPHY

Seth Cagin and Philip Dray, *We Are Not Afraid: The Story of Goodman, Schwerner, and Chaney and the Civil Rights Campaign for Mississippi* (1988); Henry Hampton and Steve Fayer, *Voices of Freedom: An Oral History of the Civil Rights Movement from the 1950s through the 1980s* (1990); Doug McAdam, *Freedom Summer* (1988); Bob Moses, "Mississippi: 1961–1962," *Liberation* (January 1970); Howard Zinn, *SNCC: The New Abolitionists* (1964).

                                                                    Betsy Sakariassen Nash

LEE v. MACON COUNTY BOARD OF EDUCATION, 267 F. Supp. 458 (M.D. Ala., 1967). This case brought about the desegregation of Alabama public schools which, nine years after *Brown v. Board of Education,* * were nearly all still segregated. In January 1963, Detroit Lee and other black parents in Tuskegee, Alabama, the county seat of Macon County, sued the County Board of Education seeking an end to biracial schools. A federal district court in Alabama (see Frank M. Johnson) directed the board to admit thirteen blacks to the all-white Tuskegee High School in September 1963. The county board attempted to comply, but Governor George C. Wallace and the State Board of Education overruled its actions, first postponing the school's opening and then allowing the school to open only when forced to do so by federal court injunction. In January 1964, Wallace and the board closed Tuskegee High, returned the blacks to the all-black high school in the town, and permitted whites to transfer to segregated white schools in the county. The plaintiffs in the case then sought an injunction to compel the governor and the board to end segregation in all Alabama public schools, maintaining that they, not the local boards, were responsible for operating the schools in the state. The federal district court declined the request and only ordered the desegregation of the schools of Macon County. But in 1967, after Wallace and the board intervened with court-ordered desegregation in the other counties, it ordered Alabama to end its dual system of education. It also forbade state funding for private segregated institutions. The Supreme Court upheld the lower court ruling in 1970.

SELECTED BIBLIOGRAPHY

Robert F. Kennedy, Jr., *Judge Frank M. Johnson—A Biography* (1978); Tinsley E. Yarbrough, *Judge Frank Johnson and Human Rights in Alabama* (1981).

Dorothy A. Autrey

LEE v. MISSISSIPPI, 332 U.S. 742 (1948). On 19 January 1948, the United States Supreme Court reversed the conviction of Albert Lee, a seventeen-year-old black Mississippian, on a charge of assault with intent to ravish. Lee had earlier been convicted by the Hinds County Circuit Court, and his conviction had been upheld by the Mississippi Supreme Court.

In his appeals to both the Mississippi Supreme Court and the U.S. Supreme Court, Lee argued that the only basis for his conviction was his confession, which he claimed had been "extorted . . . by threats, force, duress, fear and physical violence." Vague eyewitness testimony, maintained Lee, was the only other evidence against him.

Complicating the case was the fact that Lee also said he had not confessed at all. The Mississippi Supreme Court ruled that Lee could not say that his confession had been coerced and then claim not to have confessed. But the U.S. Supreme Court, in an opinion written by Justice Frank Murphy, ruled that a confession had been made and that the confession had been extorted. The case is a significant one in the body of judicial precedents dealing with confessions.

SELECTED BIBLIOGRAPHY

Cases Argued and Decided in the Supreme Court of Mississippi, vol. 201; *Jackson Clarion-Ledger*, 14 April 1947; Harry A. Ploski and James Williams, eds., *The Negro Almanac: A Reference Work on the African American* (1989); Otis H. Stephens, *The Supreme Court and Confessions of Guilt* (1973).

Allen Dennis

LEGAL DEFENSE AND EDUCATIONAL FUND. The NAACP Legal Defense and Educational Fund, Inc., was created in 1939 as a tax-exempt corporation to direct the NAACP's* civil rights litigation and educational programs. Operating independently of the founding organization with an initial staff of two, the fund had grown by the early 1970s to employ some four hundred cooperating attorneys—black and white—on more than six hundred cases annually. Since its inception, the fund has fought for social justice for blacks in the areas of education, employment, administration of justice, voting rights, and housing. Its accomplishments include victories in such landmark civil rights cases as *Sweatt v. Painter** (1950) and *Brown v. Board of Education** (1954).

SELECTED BIBLIOGRAPHY

NAACP Legal Defense and Educational Fund, *30 Years of Building American Justice* (1970); Warren D. St. James, *Triumphs of a Pressure Group, 1909–1980* (1980); Mark V. Tushnet, *The NAACP's Legal Strategy against Segregated Education, 1925–1950* (1987).

Robert A. Calvert

LESTER, JULIUS BERNARD (27 January 1939, St. Louis, Mo.–). A Jewish African-American writer, educator, and folk singer, Lester has been both eloquent supporter and astute critic of Black Power* politics. He received a B.A. from Fisk University* in 1960. He was a volunteer for the Student Nonviolent Coordinating Committee's* (SNCC) Freedom Summer of 1964* in Mississippi where he sang at freedom rallies and organized music workshops. He has visited Sweden, Cuba, and Hanoi for SNCC. His late-1960s weekly radio show on WBAI in New York provided a platform for black political views. In 1983 Lester became a Jew; currently, he is a professor of Judaic/Near Eastern Studies at the University of Massachusetts, Amherst.

SELECTED BIBLIOGRAPHY

Julius Lester, *All Is Well* (1976); Julius Lester, *Look Out Whitey, Black Power's Gon' Get Your Mama* (1968); Julius Lester, *Lovesong: Becoming a Jew* (1988); Julius Lester, *To Be a Slave* (1968).

Linda G. Ford and Ira Glunts

"LETTER FROM BIRMINGHAM JAIL." During the violent, tension-filled days of the civil rights movement of the 1960s, the Reverend Martin Luther King, Jr.,* was often called an outside agitator as he carried the campaign for equality across the American South. After his arrest for leading a protest march in Birmingham, Alabama, King responded on 16 April 1963 from his jail cell to a letter from eight local Christian and Jewish clergymen chiding blacks for "unwise and untimely" activities. These ministers told King to "wait" patiently for justice and equality to come to Birmingham. Writing with a smuggled pen on a variety of surfaces including toilet paper and the margins of the *Birmingham News*, he told his critics why he was in Birmingham, outlined the existing injustices, and explained the tenets of nonviolent protest for social change. To the request for patience, King told of the agony of explaining

"King Remembered": Martin Luther King, Jr. in the Birmingham jail. (© Flip Schulke, Schulke Archives, Miami, Florida.)

to young black children why they were denied access to the city's amusement parks and how adult black men were saddled with the commonly used names of "nigger," "boy," and "John." If they understood what it meant to live at a "tiptoe stance" in a racist society and the overwhelming feeling of "nobodiness" experienced by most blacks, King challenged the ministers, they would not ask him to wait. King's lawyers smuggled the long letter out of the jail and the American Friends Service Committee published it, after which it appeared in magazines and newspapers all over the nation. Along with the "I Have a Dream"* speech, it stands as the most significant statement of the modern nonviolent civil rights movement.

SELECTED BIBLIOGRAPHY
James A. Colaiaco, "The American Dream Unfulfilled, Martin Luther King, Jr. and the 'Letter from Birmingham Jail,' " *Phylon* 45 (March 1984), 1–18; Richard P. Fulkerson, "The Public Letter as a Rhetorical Form: Structure, Logic and Style in King's 'Letter from Birmingham Jail' " *Quarterly Journal of Speech* 65 (April 1979), 121–36; C. Eric Lincoln, ed., *Martin Luther King, Jr.* (1970); Wesley T. Mott, "The Rhetoric of Martin Luther King, Jr.: Letter from Birmingham Jail," *Phylon* 36 (December 1975), 411–12; Stephen B. Oates, *Let the Trumpet Sound, The Life of Martin Luther King* (1982); Melinda Snow, "Martin Luther King's 'Letter from Birmingham Jail' as Pauline Epistle," *Quarterly Journal of Speech* 71 (August 1985), 318–34.

LeRoy T. Williams

LEVITT AND SONS, INCORPORATED v. DIVISION AGAINST DIS-CRIMINATION, STATE OF NEW JERSEY, WILLIE JAMES AND FRANKLIN TODD, 363 U.S. 418 (1959). In May 1954, during the same month the U.S. Supreme Court handed down its decision in *Brown v. Board of Education,*** Abraham Levitt and Sons, Inc., began to purchase farmland in Willingboro Township, New Jersey. Already a nationally known pioneer of suburban housing developments (Levittown, New York, 12,000 houses and Levittown, Pennsylvania, 17,300 houses), Levitt maintained a policy of not selling to Americans of African descent. The New Jersey Conference of NAACP* branches immediately lobbied the state legislature to expand a state law that already prohibited discrimination in employment, public accommodations, and local schools to include publicly assisted housing. The amended statute was enacted in 1957. In June 1978 Levitt announced that his project would be an all-white community and denied sale to two black men, Willie James, an officer from nearby Fort Dix, and Franklin Todd, an engineer at RCA. James and Todd filed a complaint with the state Division against Discrimination. While the division was investigating these complaints, Levitt initiated a suit to stop the terms of the new state law, arguing that the law contained no effective enforcement provisions and that, if the law was applicable to him, it was an "unconstitutional" restriction of a federal program (FHA Mortgage Insurance) by a state law. These claims were rejected by the appellate and supreme courts of New Jersey and in 1959 by the U.S. Supreme Court, thus ending the use of FHA mortgage insurance to perpetuate residential segregation.

SELECTED BIBLIOGRAPHY
Gary J. Hunter, *Up South: The Civil Rights Movement in Southern New Jersey 1940–1973* (1990).

Gary J. Hunter

LEWIS, JOHN (21 February 1940, Pike County, Ala.–   ). While attending the American Baptist Theological Seminary, Lewis became an early protest leader in the Nashville Student Movement.* He remained,

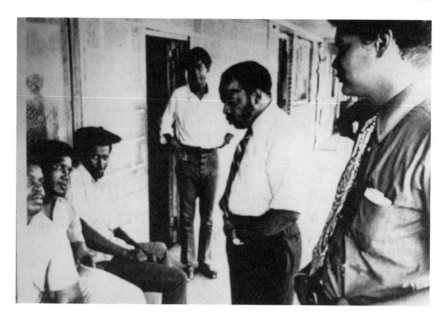

John Lewis (*center*) and Julian Bond (*right*) visit with penitentiary inmates. (Negro Almanac Collection, Amistad Research Center, Tulane University, New Orleans.)

throughout his civil rights career, an ardent supporter of Martin Luther King, Jr.'s* leadership and philosophy of nonviolent direct action,* and he went on to play a vital role in the establishment of the Student Nonviolent Coordinating Committee* (SNCC). He participated in 1961 with the Freedom Riders* and during the 1963 March on Washington.* As Chairperson of SNCC (1963–1966), Lewis delivered that organization's condemnation of American racism and segregation. He demonstrated with King in the civil rights protest at Selma, Alabama. In 1991 he is a U.S. congressman from Georgia.

SELECTED BIBLIOGRAPHY
Clayborne Carson, *In Struggle: SNCC and the Black Awakening of the 1960s* (1981); David J. Garrow, *Bearing the Cross: Martin Luther King, Jr. and the Southern Christian Leadership Conference* (1986); Paul Good, "Odyssey of a Man—And a Movement," *New York Times Magazine* (25 June 1967); Donald R. Matthews and James W. Prothro, *Negroes and the New Southern Politics* (1966); Allen Matusow, "From Civil Rights to Black Power: The Case of SNCC, 1960–1966," in Barton J. Bernstein and Allen Matusow, eds., *Twentieth-Century America: Recent Interpretations* (1969); Howard Zinn, *SNCC: The New Abolitionists* (1964).

Marshall Hyatt

LEWIS, WILLIAM HENRY (20 November 1868, Berkeley, Va.–January 1949, Boston, Mass.). Born the son of former slaves, William Henry Lewis attended Virginia Normal and Industrial Institute before he attended Amherst College, in Amherst, Massachusetts, where he played on the football team and became the first black person to be named All-American. In 1892 he received his B.A. from Amherst College and was elected class orator. He went on to Harvard Law School, where he was the first black person to play on the Harvard football team. In 1899 he was elected to the Cambridge city council and in 1902 to the Massachusetts legislature. From 1903 to 1906 he was assistant U.S. attorney general for the Boston area. He was also the head of the Naturalization Bureau for New England (1907), assistant U.S. attorney for New England (1907–1911), and assistant U.S. attorney general of the United States (1911–1913), the highest appointed black official up to that time. He was one of the first blacks admitted to membership in the American Bar Association. From 1913 to 1949 Lewis had a private practice and earned a reputation as "one of Boston's leading criminal lawyers."

SELECTED BIBLIOGRAPHY

Walter Christmas, ed., *Negroes In Public Affairs and Government*, vol. 1 (1966); Louis R. Harlan, *Booker T. Washington, The Wizard of Tuskegee, 1901–1915* (1983); Harold Wade, Jr., *Black Men of Amherst* (1976).

                                                                Robert A. Bellinger

LITTLE, MALCOLM. *See* Malcolm X.

LITTLE ROCK DESEGREGATION CRISIS. In September 1957, Orval Faubus of Arkansas became the first southern governor to attract worldwide attention by resisting court-ordered school desegregation. Faubus, an Ozark populist reformer who had appointed blacks to party office and who had presided over the quiet integration of state colleges in the state, turned against desegregation to ward off attacks from segregationist opponents as he sought reelection to an unprecedented third term. Expressing fear of mob violence, Faubus joined forces with a group of Little Rock citizens to obtain a state court injunction to prevent the integration of Central High School under a plan worked out between the federal court and the local school board. When the injunction was set aside by a federal court order, Faubus called out the National Guard to prevent nine black students from entering the school. Despite President Dwight D. Eisenhower's direct attempts to persuade Faubus to desist, the governor continued his defiance, keeping the troops in place and refusing to recognize the jurisdiction of a federal court over a state governor. In response to a renewed order from the federal court, a mob formed outside the school, attacked black reporters on the scene, and threatened the nine students. As the crowd grew—there were soon thousands of angry protesters in the streets of Little Rock—over the next days, Mayor Woodrow Mann sought Eisenhower's intervention. Although far from enthusiastic about court-ordered school desegregation

Integration of Central High, Little Rock. (Negro Almanac Collection, Amistad Research Center, Tulane University, New Orleans.)

and no advocate of federal supremacy, Eisenhower was angered by what he saw as Faubus's irresponsible behavior and reluctantly concluded that his administration would have to take action. Federal marshals, who would be used by subsequent administrations to enforce desegregation orders, had not yet been trained for such a task, and Eisenhower was uneasy about using the Arkansas Guard. The president ordered General Maxwell Taylor to send in a thousand highly disciplined troops of the 101st Airborne and simultaneously nationalized the Arkansas Guard to remove them from the governor's control. As soon as order had been established and the federal court order carried out, Eisenhower replaced the airborne troops with units from the Arkansas National Guard, who remained on duty in Little Rock until the end of that school year.

SELECTED BIBLIOGRAPHY
Stephen E. Ambrose, *Eisenhower: The President* (1984); Jack Bass and Walter DeVries, *The Transformation of Southern Politics: Social Change and Political Consequence since 1945* (1976); Daisy Bates, *The Long Shadow at Little Rock: A Memoir* (1962); Dwight D. Eisenhower Presidential Papers, Dwight D. Eisenhower Library, Abilene, Kansas; Tony A. Freyer, *The Little Rock Crisis: A Constitutional Interpretation* (1984).

                                                                    Allen Kifer

LIUZZO, VIOLA FAUVER GREGG (11 April 1925, California, Pa.–25 March 1965, Lowndes County, Ala.). Viola Liuzzo grew up in Tennessee and Georgia. After an earlier marriage and the birth of two daughters, she married Anthony J. Liuzzo, an official with a Teamsters union local, and they had three children. She worked as a medical laboratory assistant in Detroit, Michigan, hospitals. After watching on television the "bloody Sunday" clash in Selma, Alabama, she drove alone to Selma. A week later she drove to Montgomery for the last leg of the march. After the march she and LeRoy Moton, a young black man, ferried marchers back to Selma. On a return trip to Montgomery, four Ku Klux Klansmen pulled beside Liuzzo's car on highway 80 and fatally shot her in the head; Moton escaped uninjured.

The Klansmen were acquitted in her death in state court in 1965; however, the testimony of Gary Thomas Rowe, Jr., an FBI informant, helped convict William Orville Eaton, Eugene Thomas, and Collie LeRoy Wilkins, Jr., in 1966 of violating Liuzzo's civil rights. In 1978 the three charged that Rowe had fired the fatal shot, and he was indicted for murder. Federal courts ruled that he could not be tried, and a Justice Department inquiry found "no credible evidence" that Rowe had fired the shot. In 1983 a federal court rejected the Liuzzo family's two million dollar negligence suit against the FBI in Liuzzo's death.

SELECTED BIBLIOGRAPHY

Charles E. Fager, *Selma, 1965: The March That Changed the South* (1974); Jack Mendelsohn, *The Martyrs: Sixteen Who Gave Their Lives for Racial Justice* (1966); Southern Poverty Law Center, *Free at Last* (1989).

Charles W. Eagles

LOCKE, ALAIN LEROY (13 September 1885, Philadelphia, Pa.–9 June 1954, New York, N.Y.). Locke, who graduated magna cum laude from Harvard in 1907, was the first black man to be selected a Rhodes scholar. His triumph was tarnished when he was denied admission to five Oxford colleges before Hertford College accepted him. Three years at Hertford were followed by another year at the University of Berlin. He took a teaching position at Howard University* in 1912 and continued his studies; eventually, he received a Ph.D. from Harvard in 1924. Locke became a popular and outstanding teacher at Howard, but he was fired in 1925 in the midst of student and faculty unrest. When students, alumni, and the public protested his dismissal, he was not only reappointed to the faculty but he became a personal advisor to Mordecai Wyatt Johnson,* the school's first black president. The new administration placed greater emphasis on black life and problems and helped make the school the major African-American educational institution and a leader in the civil rights struggle. This change was a reflection of what Locke called the New Negro movement*—the development of black pride as a necessary prerequisite to the civil rights movement. His work in adult education led him to be elected president of the American Association for Adult Education in 1945, making him the first black national-level president of a predominantly white educational association. An immensely productive scholar, Alain Locke well represents the Harlem Renaissance,* which he personally described as "an artistic awakening of racial self-consciousness and a collective self-renewal for black people." Not only was he its chief philosopher and art critic, but he also played a significant part in helping others advance in their own careers. Among his most important works are *The New Negro* (1925), *The Negro in America* (1933), *The Negro in Art: A Pictorial Record of the Negro Artist and the Negro Theme in Art* (1940), and numerous other books and articles. At his death, he was working on *The Negro in American Culture* (completed by Margaret Just Butcher and published in 1956).

SELECTED BIBLIOGRAPHY

Laverne Gyant, "Contributors to Adult Education: Booker T. Washington, George Washington Carver, Alain L. Locke, and Ambrose Caliver," *Journal of Black Studies* 19 (September 1988), 97–110; Rayford W. Logan and Michael R. Winston, eds., *Dictionary of American Negro Biography* (1982); Wilhelmena S. Robinson, *Historical Negro Biographies* (1969); Jeffrey C. Stewart, *The Critical Temper of Alain Locke: A Selection of His Essays on Art and Culture* (1983).

                                                              Gary B. Mills

LOCKWOOD, LEWIS C. (birth and death information unknown). Soon after the start of the Civil War, the American Missionary Association* (AMA), a nonsectarian organization founded in 1846 and dominated by white abolitionists, contacted General Benjamin Franklin Butler* at Fortress Monroe, Virginia, about the status of the "contrabands." Butler said he intended to let the former slaves live in freedom. Consequently, the AMA sent the Reverend Lewis C. Lockwood as the first missionary to freed people. He conferred with the freedmen at Fortress Monroe, established schools, and organized church meetings. He also wrote back to the AMA for clothing, supplies, and additional missionaries. All this activity took place near the site where the first blacks had arrived in British America in 1619. The one-room school, under the direction of Mary S. Peake, a local black woman, was at first conducted in the former home of ex-President John Tyler. It is usually considered the cradle of the later famous Hampton Institute.* Lockwood remained in the area for thirteen months and enrolled 7,000 students in the day and night schools and 5,000 students in the Sunday Bible study. "This is not a day of small things," he surmised, "but already a day of great things."

SELECTED BIBLIOGRAPHY

Lewis C. Lockwood, *Mary S. Peake, The Colored Teacher at Fortress Monroe* (1864; reprint, 1969); James M. McPherson, *The Struggle for Equality: Abolitionists and the Negro in the Civil War and Reconstruction* (1964); Benjamin Quarles, *The Negro in the Civil War* (1953).

                                                           John F. Marszalek

LOGAN, RAYFORD WHITTINGHAM (7 January 1897, Washington, D.C.–4 November 1982, Washington, D.C.). An activist and historian of civil rights at home and human rights abroad, particularly in the

Caribbean basin and Africa, Rayford W. Logan as a scholar and public servant was a fact finder and investigator of racial injustice. A Phi Beta Kappa graduate of Williams College (B.A., 1917; M.A., 1929) and Harvard University (M.A., 1932; Ph.D., 1936), Logan was a pioneer in what he continued to prefer calling "Negro history." He taught as a history professor at Virginia Union University (1925–1930), Atlanta University* (1933–1938), and Howard University* (1938–1965; emeritus, 1965–1982); and he served as a consultant to the U.S. State Department and the NAACP.*

SELECTED BIBLIOGRAPHY
Obituary, *New York Times*, 6 November 1982; James A. Page and Jae Min Roh, comps., *Selected Black American, African, and Caribbean Authors: A Bio-Bibliography* (1985).

Thomas J. Davis

LOMAX, LOUIS E. (16 August 1922, Valdosta, Ga.–31 July 1970, Santa Rosa, N.M.). A prolific black writer, Lomax was a contemporary interpreter of the civil rights movement. A 1942 graduate of Paine College, in Augusta, Georgia, and the recipient of master's degrees from American University (1944), in Washington, D.C., and Yale University (1947), in New Haven, Connecticut, Lomax worked as a newspaperman from 1941 to 1958. He became a free-lance writer and briefly (1964 to 1968) worked as a broadcast news commentator. In the fall of 1969, he joined the faculty of Hofstra University, in Hempstead, New York. Lomax's first major book, *The Reluctant African*, won the Annisfied-Wolf Award in 1960, but he is probably best known for his *The Negro Revolt* (1962), an early analysis of the civil rights movement. He was a strong believer in equal rights, but he told college administrators that they should not give in to unreasonable black student demands or treat blacks preferentially. At the same time, he defended rebellious young people as being correct about society's deficiencies. He also denounced moderation as being irrelevant in the face of the long travails of the black masses. At the time of his death, Lomax was working on a three-volume history of black Americans. In addition to the books listed above, Lomax wrote *When the Word Is Given: A Report on Elijah Muhammad, Malcolm X, and the Black Muslim World* (1963); *Mississippi Eyewitness: The Three Civil Rights Workers, How They Were Murdered* (1964); *Thailand, The War That Is, The War That Will Be* (1967); *To Kill a Blackman* (1969).

SELECTED BIBLIOGRAPHY
Eric Foner, ed., *America's Black Past: A Reader in Afro-American History* (1970); Obituary, *New York Times*, 1 August 1970.

John F. Marszalek

LOMBARD v. LOUISIANA, 373 U.S. 267 (1963). Only public education was directly affected by *Brown v. Board of Education*.* Numerous state and local segregation laws governing aspects of public accommodations were left intact. Civil rights activists, believing such laws were immoral and unconstitutional, practiced civil disobedience and peacefully violated them, thus subjecting themselves to criminal prosecution for trespass, disorderly conduct, or criminal mischief. The situation which gave rise to *Lombard v. Louisiana* was slightly different from other sit-in cases, inasmuch as no state law or local ordinance required the management of McCrory Five and Ten Cent Store to deny service at its lunch counter to blacks. Both the mayor and the superintendent of police, however, had made recent public statements condemning sit-ins and stating that they would not be tolerated. The Supreme Court reversed the convictions that had been obtained under Louisiana's criminal mischief statute. Writing for the majority, Chief Justice Earl Warren denied that there had been merely private discrimination. Although no law required management to deny integrated service, the state could not "achieve the same result by an official command which has at least as much coercive effect as an ordinance." There had been "state action" prohibited by the equal protection clause of the Fourteenth Amendment.*

SELECTED BIBLIOGRAPHY

Abe Fortas, *Concerning Dissent and Civil Disobedience* (1968); Note, "State Action—Sit-Ins—Municipal Ordinances and Statements by Municipal Officials," *Arkansas Law Review* 18 (1964), 118–20; Louis H. Pollak, "The Supreme Court: 1962 Term," *Harvard Law Review* 77 (1963), 127–31.

                                                                Patricia A. Behlar

LONG HOT SUMMER, 1966. In 1966 the cry of "Burn, Baby, Burn" and the violent destruction of white business property in the ghettos reflected an outburst of suppressed black anger and pride. In March a recurrence of violence in the Watts race riot* in the Los Angeles area left two dead and caused further property damage. In Chicago, Illinois, three nights of rioting, 12–15 July, left two dead and over 400 people arrested. Violence continued when marchers for desegregation, led by Martin Luther King, Jr.,* in the Chicago suburb of Cicero, were stoned by a white mob of nearly 4,000. As black rage spread to Dayton, Ohio, Milwaukee, Wisconsin, Detroit, Michigan, San Francisco, California, and Cleveland, Ohio, President Lyndon B. Johnson called out the National Guard. On 18 July the black area of Hough in Cleveland exploded. Six days of rioting left 4 dead, 50 injured, and 164 persons arrested; property damage was widespread. On 9 August, Detroit's Kercheval area continued this pattern with three days of rioting. The long hot summer of 1966 reflected a paradoxical change in the pursuit of social change in America, from nonviolent resistance* and a multiracial civil rights movement to one of Black Power.*

SELECTED BIBLIOGRAPHY

Issac Balbus, *The Dialectics of Legal Repression* (1982); *Kerner Commission Report of the National Advisory Commission on Civil Disorders* (1968); J. Paul Mitchell, ed.,

Race Riots in Black and White (1970); Harvard Sitkoff, *The Struggle for Black Equality, 1954–1980* (1981).

Malik Simba

LONGVIEW RACE RIOT (1919). This riot, in a small northeast Texas town, sprang from the lynching of a black man in June 1919 for the alleged raping of a white woman. A local black schoolteacher, Samuel L. Jones, reported in the *Chicago Defender** that the white woman despaired the loss of her black lover. Whites also had become annoyed at Dr. C. P. Davis, who formed the Negro Business Men's League to prevent the exploitation of black cotton farmers in the area. Such black unity alarmed whites who decided to teach blacks a lesson by attacking the author of the *Defender* story. A white mob came to get Jones, who sought refuge in Davis's home where the physician and members of the Negro Business Men's League used their weapons to protect him. In the gun battle, several whites were wounded. The retreating whites then set fire to black homes and businesses, including Dr. Davis's office. During the melee, a black school principal was flogged and several prominent blacks were run out of town. Texas Rangers arrived on 12 July 1919 to restore order.

SELECTED BIBLIOGRAPHY

Robert H. Brisbane, *The Black Vanguard: Origins of the Negro Social Revolution, 1900–1960* (1970); John Hope Franklin and Alfred A. Moss, Jr., *From Slavery to Freedom: A History of Negro Americans*, 6th ed. (1988); William M. Tuttle, Jr., "Violence in a 'Heathen' Land: The Longview Race Riot of 1919," *Phylon* 33 (1972), 324–33; Arthur I. Waskow, *From Race Riot to Sit-In: 1919 and the 1960s: A Study in the Connections between Conflict and Violence* (1966).

Lee E. Williams II

LOUIS, JOE (13 May 1914, Chambers County, Ala.–12 April 1981, Las Vegas, Nev.). Born Joe Louis Barrow in a sharecropper's cabin in rural Alabama, Louis lost his father to a mental breakdown when he was two years old. In 1916 his mother married Pat Brooks who in 1926 moved the family to Detroit, Michigan, for economic betterment. Young Joe, a quiet child with a speech impediment, learned how to box for self-protection in his tough neighborhood. His first amateur fight saw him knocked down several times, but the next time he climbed into the ring he won the 1933 Detroit Golden Gloves Light Heavyweight Championship. He turned professional under black managers and quickly rose to the top of the heavyweight class. In 1935 he defeated Primo Carnera and Max Baer, but in 1936 the German champion, Max Schmeling, knocked him out. In 1936 he defeated James J. Braddock for the world heavyweight championship, and in one of the most famous battles in ring history he demolished Schmeling in the first round of their 1938 rematch. He took on all comers, spent World War II in the U.S. Army Special Services, and retired in 1949 having defended his title twenty-five times and holding the championship a record number of years. His later comeback attempt was a failure.

Joe Louis was the first universally admired black athlete. To African Americans, he represented black success in the white world; to whites, he was the nonthreatening symbol of American patriotism. When he defeated Schmeling, the American public saw it as a victory of American democracy over German Nazism. His World War II activities further buttressed his patriotic reputation. Though he was hardly the paragon of virtue he was made out to be and though he always remained silent on race relations, Joe Louis is a major figure in the civil rights movement. He opened doors for later black athletes and helped make possible black successes in American society as a whole. Sports writer Jimmy Cannon's famous line perhaps summarized Joe Louis's image in the American mind most succinctly: "He is a credit to his race—the human race."

SELECTED BIBLIOGRAPHY

Lenwood G. Davis, *Joe Louis: A Bibliography of Articles, Books . . .* (1983); Chris Mead, *Champion-Joe Louis, Black Hero in White America* (1985), condensed in *Sports Illustrated*, 16, 23 September 1985; Barney Nagler, *Brown Bomber* (1972).

John F. Marszalek

LOUISVILLE, NEW ORLEANS, AND TEXAS RAILWAY COMPANY v. MISSISSIPPI, 133 U.S. 587 (1890). In March 1888 Mississippi became the second southern state to enact legislation requiring all railroads doing business in the state, except for street railways, to segregate passengers by race. The law mandated that carriers had to provide separate passenger cars for each race, or to provide separate facilities in each car. The Louisville, New Orleans, and Texas Railroad challenged the law in the state's courts, claiming that the new law was burdensome to railroads and that it interfered with interstate commerce. The state supreme court upheld the law in 1889, and the case was appealed directly to the U.S. Supreme Court. On 3 March 1890 the highest court rendered its decision in favor of the state of Mississippi. The majority opinion written by Justice David Brewer declared that the state may compel a railway "to provide separate cars or compartments . . . equal in accommodations . . . to be used separately by individuals of both races," but it reserved judgment as to whether the state could require individuals to use separate facilities. The court would render that judgment six years later in the *Plessy v. Ferguson** case. This 1890 case, however, did send a legal signal to the southern states. By 1891 six other states had also enacted separate coach laws.

SELECTED BIBLIOGRAPHY
Charles A. Lofgren, *The Plessy Case: A Legal-Historical Interpretation* (1987); Catherine A. Barnes, *Journey from Jim Crow: The Desegregation of Southern Transit* (1983).

Larry T. Balsamo

LOVING v. VIRGINIA, 388 U.S. 1 (1967). Richard Perry Loving was white; Mildred Delores Jester was not; therefore, Virginia law prohibited their marriage. They went to Washington, D.C., in June 1958 to be married, and then they lived together in Caroline County, Virginia. Convicted in January 1959 of violating the state's antimiscegenation law, they were given the minimum sentence the law permitted, one year each in jail (though the law required the penitentiary), such sentence to be suspended if they left the state for twenty-five years. They moved to Washington, D.C., but in 1963 they initiated a challenge to the constitutionality of the law that had led to their banishment. In March 1966, the Virginia Supreme Court of Appeals upheld the statute and the conviction (206 Va. 924), but, in June 1967, the U.S. Supreme Court unanimously ruled that the Fourteenth Amendment's* equal protection and due process provisions denied any state the authority to use racial classifiers to determine which citizens could intermarry. Such statutes fell in the sixteen states where they were still on the books.

SELECTED BIBLIOGRAPHY
American Civil Liberties Union Papers, Princeton University; Simeon Booker, "The Couple That Rocked the Courts," *Ebony* 22 (September 1967), 78–84; "The Crime of Being Married," *Life Magazine* 60 (18 March 1966), 85–91; Bernard Schwartz, *Super Chief: Earl Warren and His Supreme Court—A Judicial Biography* (1983); Walter Wadlington, "The *Loving* Case: Virginia's Anti-Miscegenation Statute in Historical Perspective," *Virginia Law Review* 52 (1966), 1189–1223.

Peter Wallenstein

LOWERY, JOSEPH E. (6 October 1921, Huntsville, Ala.–   ). This United Methodist minister was a pioneer of the modern civil rights movement, perhaps most significantly in his role as one of the several cofounders, along with Martin Luther King, Jr.,* of the Southern Christian Leadership Conference* (SCLC). He served as a vice president of the SCLC in its earliest years, was chairman of the board from 1967 to 1977, and has served as president since then. Lowery began his ministerial career in 1952 at the Warren Street United Methodist Church in Mobile, Alabama. From 1964 to 1968 he pastored St. Paul United Methodist Church in Birmingham, Alabama, and in 1968 he began his longest assignment when he became pastor at the Central United Methodist Church in Atlanta, Georgia. He led civil rights activities in Mobile, in Nashville, Tennessee, and in Birmingham, and he was part of the historic *Sullivan v. New York Times* libel decision. He has also led antiapartheid efforts against South Africa. Despite these significant activities, Lowery has

Joseph Lowery. (© Flip Schulke, Schulke Archives, Miami, Florida.)

been overshadowed by more famous civil rights advocates. Even after King's death and Ralph Abernathy's* retirement, Lowery's ascension to head the SCLC did not make his name a household word. Even the most thorough account of the SCLC during the days of Martin Luther King mentions him only in passing.

SELECTED BIBLIOGRAPHY

Adam Fairclough, *To Redeem the Soul of America: The Southern Christian Leadership Conference and Martin Luther King, Jr.* (1987); Ron Harris, "Dr. Joseph Lowery, The Man Who's Reviving SCLC," *Ebony* 35 (November 1979), 53–56; *Who's Who in America*, 44th ed. (1986–1987).

John F. Marszalek

LOWNDES COUNTY FREEDOM ORGANIZATION. The Lowndes County Freedom Organization (LCFO) was created during the early spring of 1965 in Lowndes County, Alabama, by members of the Student Nonviolent Coordinating Committee* (SNCC) in an effort to counteract the political domination of the white supremacist state Democratic party. Pointing to the 1964 failure of the Mississippi Freedom Democratic party,* SNCC activist Stokely Carmichael* argued that the time had come for an independent black political party. Lowndes County, whose population of 15,000 included 12,000 blacks, none of whom were registered to vote at the beginning of 1965, was a promising starting point for such an independent movement. The LCFO became the first political organization in the civil rights movement to be identified with the symbol of the black panther. Chosen as a contrast to the Democratic party's symbol, the white rooster, the panther was viewed by LCFO members as a representation of the power and determination of its organization and would later be inherited as the symbol of the Black Panther* movement in Oakland, California. The LCFO proved its strength in an 8 May 1965 local election when 900 of 2,000 registered blacks in Lowndes County risked their personal safety and followed LCFO instructions to "Vote the panther, then go home." The LCFO was significant to the civil rights movement because it defined the growing differences between SNCC and the Southern Christian Leadership Conference.* The latter had urged Lowndes County blacks to remain in the Democratic party. LCFO also furthered the development of independent black political activity.

SELECTED BIBLIOGRAPHY

Adam Fairclough, *To Redeem the Soul of America: The Southern Christian Leadership Conference and Martin Luther King, Jr.* (1987); Raymond L. Hall, *Black Separatism in the United States* (1978); Henry Hampton and Steve Fayer, *Voices of Freedom: An Oral History of the Civil Rights Movement from the 1950s through the 1980s* (1990); Edward Peeks, *The Long Struggle for Black Power* (1971); Emily Stoper, *The Student*

Blacks waiting to vote in Lowndesboro precinct, Alabama, November 1966. (Photo by Les Jordan, Jr., Carl and Ann Braden Collection. State Historical Society of Wisconsin.)

Nonviolent Coordinating Committee: The Growth of Radicalism in a Civil Rights Organization (1989).

JoAnn D. Carpenter

LUCY, AUTHERINE JUANITA (5 October 1929, Marengo County, Ala.–). A tenant farmer's daughter and the youngest of ten children, Lucy had earned an undergraduate degree from Miles College, a black Methodist institution in Birmingham, Alabama, in 1952. For the next four years she taught high school English and Sunday school in Birmingham. In March, April, and September 1956 national attention centered on her when the University of Alabama at Tuscaloosa, after a three-year court fight, admitted her as its first black student. Twenty-six-year-old Lucy sought a graduate degree in library science. The disruption at the school caused by mob violence of white segregationists, some from outside the Tuscaloosa area, compelled the university's board of trustees to expel Lucy for her own safety and because she accused the university of conspiring with the white mob against her. Lucy's bravery and courage came at a time when blacks, as exemplified in the two-month-old Montgomery bus boycott,* had come to understand that they could meet the challenge of segregationists.

SELECTED BIBLIOGRAPHY
John Hope Franklin and Alfred A. Moss, Jr., *From Slavery to Freedom: A History of Negro Americans* (1988); Gilbert Osofsky, *The Burden of Race: A Documentary History of Negro-White Relations in America* (1967); Harry A. Ploski and James Williams, eds., *The Negro Almanac: A Reference Work on the Afro American* (1989); *The Progressive* 48 (July 1984), 15–19.

Linda Reed

LUCY v. ADAMS, 134 F. Supp. 235 (W.D. Ala., 1955). Autherine Juanita Lucy* and Polly Myers applied for admission to the University of Alabama in 1952. They were eminently qualified, both having performed well at a segregated college. They completed their registration by mail and enrolled for the fall term. They had arranged for classes and had received dormitory assignments in advance. School officials turned them away when they arrived on campus. After dealing with the school for more than a year, the women sued. A federal judge ruled in their favor. The university could not deny them admission because of their race. The university successfully appealed this decision. Attorneys for Lucy then carried the case to the U.S. Supreme Court. That winter, the university reluctantly admitted Autherine Lucy. It denied enrollment to Myers, however, because of her marital status and alleged misconduct. Violence followed. Throngs of students and townspeople staged riots by burning crosses to protest the admission of a Negro. University officials dismissed Lucy temporarily, supposedly for her own safety. The board of trustees later expelled her for allegedly making accusations about the university's racial policy. The state legislature supported this action and threatened to stop appropriations to Negro colleges and to discontinue its out-of-state tuition program for minority students.

SELECTED BIBLIOGRAPHY
Thomas I. Emerson, David Haber, and Norman Dorsen, *Political and Civil Rights in the United States* (1967); "Free Choice Plan Is Likely to Come before Alabama Legislature in May," *Southern School News* (April 1957); *New York Times*, February 1956; Raymond Walters, *The Burden of Brown: Thirty Years of School Desegregation* (1984).

Stephen Middleton

LYNCH, JOHN ROY (10 September 1847, Vidalia, La.–2 November 1939, Chicago, Ill.). Mississippi Reconstruction black politician, Republican party leader, businessman, army officer, and lawyer, Lynch was a leading figure in black America during the late nineteenth and early twentieth centuries. Born to an Irish immigrant and his slave wife, he lived in slavery until 1863. Appointed a justice of the peace in 1869, he was also almost immediately elected to the Mississippi House of Representatives and in 1872 became its speaker. That same year he was elected for the first of his three terms to the U.S. House of Representatives. His

John R. Lynch. (Courtesy Mississippi Department of Archives and History.)

staunch support for the Civil Rights Act of 1875* was his major accomplishment. He was also the first black man to be a keynote speaker at a national political convention (1884). He held several governmental and army posts in Republican administrations, was active in real estate and law in Mississippi, Washington, and Chicago, and published a revisionist book and two articles on Reconstruction in *The Journal of Negro History.** Upon his death he was buried at the Arlington National Cemetery with full military honors.

SELECTED BIBLIOGRAPHY

Rayford W. Logan and Michael R. Winston, eds., *Dictionary of American Negro Biography* (1982); John R. Lynch, *The Facts of Reconstruction* (1918); John R. Lynch, "More about the Historical Errors of James Ford Rhodes," *Journal of Negro History* 3 (April 1918), 139–57; John R. Lynch, *Reminiscences of an Active Life* (1970); John R. Lynch, "Some Historical Errors of James Ford Rhodes," *Journal of Negro History* 2 (October 1917), 345–68; James A. McLaughlin, "John R. Lynch" (Ph.D. diss., Ball State University, 1981); George A. Sewall, *Mississippi Black History Makers* (1977).

John F. Marszalek

LYNCHING. In this extralegal practice, members of a mob, using some form of injury or execution, punish an individual for allegedly breaking some law or local custom. The origin of the term can be traced to revolutionary Virginia where an American colonel, Charles Lynch, established an extralegal court and punished suspected criminals and Tories. In time, "lynching" became a popular means for social control on the southern and western frontiers.

Throughout the history of lynching, a variety of methods have been employed: floggings, brandings with acid, tarring and feathering, hangings, burnings, and dragging behind automobiles. From Reconstruction to the middle of the twentieth century, lynching was primarily used to intimidate, degrade, and control black people in the southern and border states. Increasingly during this period the use of the term lynching became associated with mob action resulting in death. The most reliable statistics, gathered by the Tuskegee Institute,* show that from 1882 to 1968 at least 4,743 deaths by lynching occurred (nearly three-fourths were black), mostly in the South. In the ten years from 1 January 1918 through 1927, at least thirty-nine blacks were burned alive. White Southerners perpetuated the myth that lynching was necessary to protect white women from assaults by black men. In fact, less than 30 percent of the recorded lynchings of blacks related to this particular crime. Organizations such as the Association of Southern Women to Prevent Lynching* (ASWPL), founded in 1930, fought lynching at the local level. The NAACP* lobbied unsuccessfully to obtain a federal antilynching bill. After 1921 the number of reported lynchings declined, possibly as a result of the attention focused on the practice. Finally, the Civil Rights Act of 1968* authorized the federal government to intervene if citizens were being deprived of their constitutional rights, whether or not death resulted.

SELECTED BIBLIOGRAPHY

James Elbert Cutler, *Lynch-Law: An Investigation into the History of Lynching in the United States* (1905); Neil R. McMillen, *Dark Journey: Black Mississippians in the Age of Jim Crow* (1989); Walter White, *Rope and Faggot: A Biography of Judge Lynch* (1929); Robert L. Zangrando, *The NAACP Crusade against Lynching, 1909–1950* (1980).

Horace D. Nash

LYONS v. OKLAHOMA, 332 U.S. 596 (1944). This case originated in Oklahoma in 1940 when the police arrested W. D. Lyons, a black man, for allegedly murdering Elmer Rogers, a white man, and his family. Lyons was an unsettled twenty-two-year-old whom the police regularly suspected for most area crimes. After a ten-hour interrogation, which included a beating, Lyons confessed. After he was convicted and sent to prison, he admitted having committed the crime on two separate occasions. His attorneys appealed his conviction, and the Supreme Court ruled that the police had coerced Lyons's confession. Because he had confessed voluntarily on two successive occasions, however, the Court approved those confessions, holding that the first confession did not control the later ones. Satisfied that it had protected Lyons's civil rights, the Court upheld his conviction.

SELECTED BIBLIOGRAPHY

"Recent Cases," *George Washington Law Review* 13 (1944) 109–111; Paul G. Kauper, *Constitutional Law* (1966); Otis H. Stephens, *The Supreme Court and Confessions of Guilt* (1973).

Stephen Middleton

M

McDEW, CHARLES (23 June 1938, Massillon, Ohio–). As a student at South Carolina State College, McDew organized some four hundred students in lunch counter demonstrations in Orangeburg, South Carolina. He was active on the Freedom Ride Coordinating Committee and served as Student Nonviolent Coordinating Committee* (SNCC) chairman. He participated in the 1961 protests in McComb, Mississippi, over the murder of Herbert Lee* and the arrest of Brenda Travis. In 1962 he was arrested along with Bob Zellner in Baton Rouge, Louisiana, on criminal anarchy charges. Subsequently, the charges were dropped. Much of McDew's expertise was used by SNCC to raise funds in the northern states. In June 1963 he was replaced as SNCC chairman by John Lewis.*

SELECTED BIBLIOGRAPHY

Clayborne Carson, *In Struggle: SNCC and the Black Awakening of the 1960s* (1981); James Forman, *The Making of Black Revolutionaries* (1985); Howard Zinn, *SNCC: The New Abolitionists* (1964).

Ray Branch

McDONALD v. KEY, 224 F.2d 608 (1955). One technique used by some southern states to discourage, harass, and defeat black candidates for public office was the racial identification requirement; it was particularly popular in the "massive resistance" period following the Supreme Court's 1954 invalidation of racial segregation in public education. Oklahoma had such a requirement: Its constitution defined "Negro" as a person of African descent; all others were considered "white." Statutory law required blacks to be racially identified on ballots; all others were presumed white and were racially unidentified. A. B. McDonald, a black aspirant for United States Senator, sued members of the state election board for placing Negro after his name on the ballot, alleging that the statutory requirement violated the equal protection clause of the Fourteenth Amendment.* The federal district court dismissed his complaint, holding that the designation of race was descriptive, not discriminatory. The Court of Appeals for the Tenth Circuit reversed this decision. The appellate court held that the requirement that candidates of only one race be identified while candidates of other races were racially unidentified discriminated against blacks and therefore violated the equal protection clause. The board members appealed to the Supreme Court which refused to hear the case.

SELECTED BIBLIOGRAPHY

Richard Claude, *The Supreme Court and the Electoral Process* (1970); Jack Greenberg, *Race Relations and American Law* (1959).

Earlean M. McCarrick

McGILL, RALPH (5 February 1898, Soddy, Tenn.–3 February 1969, Atlanta, Ga.). A southern liberal, this editor and publisher of the *Atlanta Constitution* was a loyal critic of the South, especially of its racial mores. He entered Vanderbilt University, in Nashville, Tennessee, in 1917 for a year, left for a brief stint in the United States Marine Corps, and returned to the university in 1919. He promised to be a typical student— an athlete, fraternity member, and newspaper staffer—but his activism, outspokenness, and love of practical jokes resulted in his expulsion in April 1921. He then began his journalistic career with the *Nashville Banner*. In 1929 he left the *Banner* to become assistant sports editor of the *Atlanta Constitution*, then its associate editor in 1938, editor in 1942, and publisher in 1960. Paralleling his career was an impressive record of community service including numerous volunteer positions in support of education, Brotherhood Week, and other social causes. Although best known for his support of civil rights in the 1960s, McGill actually advocated minority rights in the 1930s, 1940s, and 1950s, before it was fashionable to do so. His early views were more liberal than those of most people, but he did accept the doctrine of separate but equal.* Although most white Southerners considered him a "flaming liberal," by his own admission McGill could never be a crusader because he could always see both sides of the issue even while criticizing one or the other. The best phrase to describe him would be the one others have applied to him: "the conscience of the South." Ralph McGill received numerous honors for his achievements, including a Pulitzer Prize for editorial writing (1958), the Medal of Freedom (1964), and at least nineteen honorary degrees. In addition to his other types of writing, he authored *The South and the Southerner*.

Ralph McGill. (Special Collections Department, Robert W. Woodruff Library, Emory University.)

SELECTED BIBLIOGRAPHY
Cal M. Logue, *Ralph McGill: Editor and Publisher* (1969); Ralph McGill, *The South and the Southerner* (1959, 1963); Harold Martin, *Ralph McGill, Reporter* (1973).
                                                                                   Gary B. Mills

McKAY, CLAUDE (15 September 1889, Sunny Ville, Jamaica–22 May 1948, Chicago, Ill.). One of the best-known writers of the Harlem Renaissance,* McKay migrated from Jamaica to the United States in 1912 and studied agriculture at Tuskegee Institute* for several months and Kansas State College for two years (1912–1914). Abandoning his studies for a writing career in New York, McKay published his first volume of American poetry, *Harlem Shadows*, in 1922. This acclaimed book was followed by the novels *Home to Harlem* (1928), *Banjo* (1929), and *Banana Bottom* (1933); a collection of short stories, *Gingertown* (1932); his autobiography, *A Long Way from Home* (1937); a study of black urban culture, *Harlem: Negro Metropolis* (1940); and a posthumous collection, *The Selected Poems of Claude McKay* (1953). McKay did not become an American citizen until 1940. Viewing American racial problems from a West Indian perspective, McKay wrote poems reflecting nostalgia for his homeland, interest in the African continent and in the phenomenon of the city, and ambivalence about race in the United States. His main contribution to discourse about civil rights is to be located in such poems as "If We Must Die,"* "America," "White House," "Baptism," and "The Lynching"—models of the militant statement—and in his poems, essays, and reviews for Max Eastman's leftist magazine *The Liberator*.

SELECTED BIBLIOGRAPHY

Stephen H. Bronz, *Roots of Negro Racial Consciousness* (1964); Arthur P. Davis, *From the Dark Tower: Afro-American Writers, 1900 to 1960* (1974); James R. Giles, *Claude McKay* (1976).

Jerry Ward

McKISSICK, FLOYD B. (9 March 1922, Asheville, N.C.–28 April 1991, Durham, N.C.). A black lawyer, judge, civil rights activist, businessman, and minister, McKissick's leadership role in the 1960s national civil rights movement capstoned nearly a lifetime of opposition to racial barriers. Educated at Atlanta's Morehouse College* and North Carolina College, he desegregated the University of North Carolina Law School in 1951 and became its first black graduate. Establishing a law practice in Durham, he joined with black college students in 1960 when they launched the sit-in movement to protest segregated eating facilities. Their demonstrations dramatically escalated civil rights activities in North Carolina, and McKissick played an integral role in the effort. A longtime advisor to the state NAACP* youth groups, he concentrated much of his civil rights and legal activities on their behalf. Especially notable was his work in organizing and defending student demonstrators seeking to desegregate Durham's public accommodations.

McKissick gained national prominence as a civil rights activist through his association with the Congress of Racial Equality* (CORE). In 1947, as a young army veteran, he had participated in CORE's earliest freedom rides, and when CORE established a Durham chapter in 1962, McKissick was named director. Under his leadership, Durham's branch flourished. His role in planning and organizing the massive demonstrations and negotiations of North Carolina's "Freedom Highways" campaign helped desegregate a major motel chain and gave him considerable influence in the national organization as well. In 1963, CORE named him national chairman, a titular leadership post that came in response to the demands of more militant elements for a shift in emphasis in the civil rights program and a larger black-led role in the group's governing structure. Afterward, McKissick moved closer to the increasingly influential militant camp, which proved advantageous to his aspirations. In 1966, he replaced James Farmer* as national director.

By then, much of his race relations and civil rights philosophy had changed perceptibly. Disillusioned over a lack of substantive change in

Sandy Vanocur and Floyd McKissick at a black housing project. (Negro Almanac Collection, Amistad Research Center, Tulane University, New Orleans.)

America's racial order, he became an exponent of Black Power.* Although its meaning was unclear, the slogan frightened conservative whites, many of whom abandoned the organization, and concerned moderate black leaders. McKissick and CORE embraced it and were branded as militants. Thereafter, McKissick increasingly directed CORE's attention to persistent black ghetto problems, but little of consequence was achieved. Nevertheless, he helped focus national concern on an area heretofore neglected in the general thrust of civil rights activism. In 1968, McKissick left CORE to launch his ambitious, but unsuccessful, Soul City model town and industrial project in rural North Carolina. At his death in April 1991 he was serving as pastor of Soul City's First Baptist Church and capping a long legal career as a recent appointee to a North Carolina judgeship.

SELECTED BIBLIOGRAPHY

James Farmer, *Lay Bare the Heart: An Autobiography of the Civil Rights Movement* (1985); Floyd McKissick, *Three-Fifths of a Man* (1969); August Meier and Elliott Rudwick, *CORE: A Study in the Civil Rights Movement, 1942–1968* (1973); Charles Moritz, ed., *Current Biography Yearbook* (1968); Obituary, *New York Times*, 30 April 1991; Fred C. Shapiro, "The Successor to Floyd McKissick May Not Be So Reasonable," *New York Times Magazine* (1 October 1967); "Soul City," *Newsweek* (14 August 1972).

Robert L. Jenkins

McLAUGHLIN v. STATE OF FLORIDA, 379 U.S. 184 (1964). This U.S. Supreme Court case involved the reversal of a lower court conviction of an unmarried interracial couple, Dewey McLaughlin and Connie Hoffman, also known as Connie Gonzalez, who occupied the same room in the nighttime. Florida law subjected unmarried interracial couples to a different standard of punishment than unmarried same-race couples. The conviction was reversed on eleven points of constitutional law. Five points were of primary significance to civil rights: (1) The defendants were convicted unfairly by a Florida statute that denied equal protection under the law to unmarried interracial couples; (2) the Florida statute did not adhere to the central purpose of the equal protection clause which was to eliminate discrimination emanating from state official sources; (3) the Florida statute had racial classifications that were not relevant to any constitutionally acceptable legislative purpose; (4) the Florida court was not sensitive to policies of equal protection where state power used racial classifications in criminal statutes; and (5) an invidious form of discrimination was maintained through Florida's legal treatment of the same quality offense by different people in a different manner.

SELECTED BIBLIOGRAPHY

Derrick A. Bell, Jr., *Race, Racism and American Law* (1980); Thomas I. Emerson, David Haber, and Norman Dorsen, *Political and Civil Rights in the United States* (1967); Loren Miller, *The Petitioners: The Story of the Supreme Court of the United States and the Negro* (1966); *New York Times*, 28 April, 8 December, 1964; George Rossman, ed., "Review of Recent Supreme Court Decisions," *American Bar Association Journal* 51 (1965), 270.

Donald Cunnigen

McLAURIN v. OKLAHOMA STATE REGENTS, 339 U.S. 637 (1950). When he was almost seventy years old, George McLaurin decided he wanted to earn a doctorate in education. The University of Oklahoma admitted him but made him sit in the hallway at the classroom door, study inconspicuously on the library balcony, and eat in sequestration. He finally gained a classroom seat, but it was set apart and marked "reserved for colored." A unanimous Supreme Court, in an opinion by Chief Justice Fred Vinson, had little difficulty in finding that this treatment constituted a denial of equal protection under the Fourteenth Amendment.* Once admitted, students may not be treated differently based on race. Like all cases of this type, the basic issue was the extent to which race may be used as an acceptable classification of persons for legal purposes. In a companion case, Vinson made it clear that the Court would maintain its tradition of deciding constitutional issues as narrowly as possible and only in the context of the specific facts presented by the case at hand. For that reason, the *McLaurin* case did not occasion a full-scale review of the separate but equal* doctrine, although it did serve as an obvious stepping-stone to the 1954 decision that outlawed segregation (see *Brown v. Board of Education*).

SELECTED BIBLIOGRAPHY

Richard Kluger, *Simple Justice: The History of Brown v. Board of Education and Black America's Struggle for Equality* (1975); Irving Lefberg, "Chief Justice Vinson and the Politics of Desegregation," *Emory Law Journal* 24 (1975), 243–312; Mark V. Tushnet, *The NAACP's Legal Strategy Against Segregated Education, 1925–1950* (1987); Melvin I. Urofsky, *A March of Liberty* (1988).

James E. Sefton

MALCOLM X (Malcolm Little; also used adopted religious name, El-Hajj Malik El-Shabazz) (19 May 1925, Omaha, Nebr.–21 February 1965, New York, N.Y.). One of the so-called black militants of the civil rights movement, he was the voice of the northern big city ghettoes. While blacks fought segregation in the South, he kept the frustration of their northern brethren in view.

Born the son of a Baptist preacher and Marcus Garvey* organizer, Malcolm Little experienced first-hand the brutality of American racism. Antiblack hate groups burned his house in Lansing, Michigan, and murdered his father. Welfare agencies broke up his family; his mother was committed to a mental institution; and he found himself in a detention home run by a paternalistic but racist white couple. He quit school after the eighth grade and drifted to Boston and eventually to Harlem, where he became involved in drugs, gambling, and prostitution. Returning to Boston, he was arrested for burglary and was sentenced to ten years in prison.

During the six and a half years he spent in prison, he used his time to discover the Lost-Found Nation of Islam (Black Muslims*). When he left prison in 1952 he replaced his "slave name" of Little with an X, and he became actively involved as a Muslim recruiter. In 1954 he became minister of Harlem's Temple Number 7. He became famous quickly, rivaling Muslim leader Elijah Muhammad (see Elijah Poole) in public notoriety. He organized mosques all over the country and in 1961 began *Muhammad Speaks,** the order's official newspaper. In 1958 he married Betty X Shabazz, with whom he had six children.

A major crisis came in 1963 when Malcolm X, already a symbol of unyielding black hatred for whites, said that President John F. Kennedy's assassination was a matter of "the chickens coming home to roost." (White society hatred, developed to suppress blacks, had reached out to cut down the president.) Elijah Muhammad, who for several years had begun to suspect his ever more successful lieutenant, suspended Malcolm for his remark. Malcolm resigned from the Black Muslims on 12 March 1964.

Malcolm X. (Negro Almanac Collection, Amistad Research Center, Tulane University, New Orleans.)

This split, like his years in prison, he used to further his education. He left for Mecca in April 1964 and toured the Middle East where he met nonblacks who were not racists. As a result, he tempered his antiwhite rhetoric. He now blamed racism on Western culture and founded the Organization of Afro-American Unity* to unify blacks and to cooperate with sympathetic whites to arrest its scourge. He made another trip to Africa, but he remained too controversial to gain a broad following either among blacks or whites.

On 14 February 1965 unknown assailants firebombed his house, and on 21 February 1965 he was gunned down during a speech in New York. Three Black Muslims were found guilty of the crime, but scholars still dispute the validity of their convictions.

Malcolm X had few concrete accomplishments, but his legacy is important, nonetheless. To white America, he was a teacher of hate, the symbol of black pride: the refusal to apologize for one's blackness or to beg for what was inherently due any human being. He helped push a civil rights movement he did not support to take a more radical stance.

SELECTED BIBLIOGRAPHY
George Breitman, ed., *By Any Means Necessary* (1970); George Breitman, ed., *Malcolm X Speaks* (1965); James H. Cone, *Martin and Malcolm: A Dream or a Nightmare* (1991); Rayford W. Logan and Michael R. Winston, eds., *Dictionary of American Negro Biography* (1982); Peter Goldman, "Malcolm X: Witness for the Prosecution," in John Hope Franklin and August Meier, eds., *Black Leaders of the Twentieth Century* (1982); *Dictionary of American Biography*, Supplement 7 (1981); Malcolm X, *The Autobiography of Malcolm X* (1965).

John F. Marszalek

MANSFIELD, TEXAS, SCHOOL INTEGRATION CRISIS (1956).

Mansfield, seventeen miles southeast of Fort Worth, compelled its fifty-eight black students in 1956 either to attend a segregated elementary school, which had no indoor toilets, or to ride public buses to Fort Worth in order to attend high school. A federal court ordered it to allow blacks to attend its neighborhood public school, the first school district in Texas to be so ordered. Hundreds daily ringed the white school, preventing black enrollment. The mob took over the town, as the mayor and others left the community. Governor Allan Shivers dispatched Texas Rangers to uphold segregation, and President Dwight D. Eisenhower did not interfere in the election year. In this and many other communities throughout the South and Southwest, the implementation of the 1954 *Brown v. Board of Education* decision was postponed for years.

SELECTED BIBLIOGRAPHY
Robert Burk, *The Eisenhower Administration and the Civil Rights Movement* (1984); George N. Green, *The Establishment in Texas Politics: The Primitive Years, 1938–1957* (1979); John Howard Griffin and Theodore Freedman, "Mansfield, Texas: A Report of the Crisis Situation Resulting from Efforts to Desegregate the School System," Anti-Defamation League; *Texas Observer*, 5, 12 September 1956.

George N. Green

MARCH AGAINST FEAR. *See* Meredith March.

MARCH ON WASHINGTON. In 1963 A. Philip Randolph,* who headed the March on Washington Movement* in 1941, began to plan a second march. He involved Martin Luther King, Jr.,* Roy Wilkins* of the NAACP,* James Farmer* of the Congress of Racial Equality,* Whitney Moore Young, Jr.,* of the National Urban League,* and John Lewis* of the Student Nonviolent Coordinating Committee,* together with four whites—Mathew Ahmann, Eugene Carson Blake,* Rabbi Joachim Prinz, and Walter P. Reuther*—for the organizing committee. Bayard Rustin* was the person most responsible for the planning and efficient organizing of the demonstration. On 28 August 1963, over 200,000 people took part in the March on Washington, a peaceful demonstration of 170,000 black Americans and 30,000 white Americans. While they

March on Washington, D.C., 1963. (Negro Almanac Collection, Amistad Research Center, Tulane University, New Orleans.)

marched they sang the anthem of the civil rights movement, "We Shall Overcome,"* and carried banners and placards that called for decent housing and "Jobs and Freedom." The marchers assembled first on the grounds of the Washington Monument, where a distinguished group of white and black stars entertained them. Joan Baez sang the anthem of the movement, and Mahalia Jackson stirred the crowd with her powerful rendition of Negro spirituals. President John F. Kennedy endorsed the march although he feared that violence might erupt and embarrass the administration. The march was also endorsed by several leading members of the Senate, including Hubert H. Humphrey,* Jacob Javits, and George Aiken. The one great blow to the organizers was the failure of the executive council of the American Federation of Labor and Congress of Industrial Organizations to join. The program consisted mainly of speeches, and the list of speakers was long. After nine distinguished speakers had raised their voices against injustice, King rose to the strains of the "Battle Hymn of the Republic." The crowd and the millions watching on television at home listened with a new expectancy. "I have a dream," he said, "that one day this nation will rise up and live out the true meaning of its creed: 'We hold these truths to be self-evident, that all men are created equal.' " He dreamed of brotherhood in Georgia and an end to oppression in Mississippi (see "I Have a Dream"). The press proclaimed the march a success. President Kennedy was pleased that the predicted violence and vandalism did not occur. The civil rights leaders were satisfied with their efforts and knew that 28 August 1963 had been a day never to be forgotten.

SELECTED BIBLIOGRAPHY
Clayborne Carson, *In Struggle: SNCC and the Black Awakening of the 1960s* (1981); Thomas Gentile, *March on Washington: August 28, 1963* (1983); David L. Lewis, *King: A Critical Biography* (1970); Benjamin Muse, *The American Negro Revolution: From Nonviolence to Black Power, 1963–1967* (1968); Stephen B. Oates, *Let the Trumpet Sound: The Life of Martin Luther King, Jr.* (1982).

Arvarh E. Strickland

MARCH ON WASHINGTON MOVEMENT. This movement came as a response to employment discrimination at the beginning of World War II. The idea for a march came in 1941 during a meeting of civil rights groups in Chicago. A. Philip Randolph* liked the idea, and, two weeks later, he began planning for a nationwide mass demonstration to protest against discrimination in defense industries. In May 1941, Randolph issued a "Call to Negro America to March on Washington for Jobs and Equal Participation in National Defense on July 1, 1941." Black organizations and the black press rallied to the cause. Local groups formed branches of the March on Washington Movement throughout the country. By June, estimates of the number expected to participate were as high as 100,000. At this point, the Roosevelt administration could no longer ignore the movement. When other efforts to have Randolph and the other leaders call off the march failed, President Franklin D. Roosevelt agreed to issue Executive Order 8802,* which declared it national policy "to encourage full participation in the national defense program by all citizens of the United States, regardless of race, creed, color or national origin." The president also established the Fair Employment Practice Committee* to oversee the policy.

SELECTED BIBLIOGRAPHY
Herbert Garfinkel, *When Negroes March: The March on Washington Movement in the Organizational Politics for FEPC* (1959); Harvard Sitkoff, *A New Deal for Blacks: The Emergence of Civil Rights as a National Issue* (1978).

Arvarh E. Strickland

MARGOLD, NATHAN ROSS (21 July 1899, Jassy, Rumania–16 December 1947, Washington, D.C.). Born the son of immigrants to the United States, in 1919 Margold earned an associate degree from the College of New York and in 1923 an LL.B. cum laude from Harvard University Law School. In 1924 he was admitted into the New York Bar Association and went on to practice successfully as a private attorney. He was also a law professor at Harvard, the legal adviser for Indian affairs at the Brookings Institute, and a special assistant to the United States attorney general. The most distinguished part of his career, however, related to his service from 1930 to 1933 as special counsel to the NAACP.* After the stock market crash in 1929, the NAACP hired Margold to develop an agenda for improving African-American rights. He prepared a detailed book-length study that called for an attack on school segregation and the separate but equal* clause created by the United States Supreme Court in its 1896 *Plessy v. Ferguson** decision, the legal foundation of segregation in the United States. The Margold Report argued for an attack on segregation based on the fact that underfunded black southern schools were not equal. The Margold Report became the bible of the NAACP's legal campaign as well as the premier document of its Legal Defense and Educational Fund* organization.

SELECTED BIBLIOGRAPHY
Jonathan Kaufman, *Broken Alliance* (1988); Genna Rae McNeil, *Groundwork* (1983); National Association for the Advancement of Colored People Papers, Library of Congress, Washington, D.C.; Vibert L. White, "Developing the 'School' of Civil Rights Lawyers: From the New Deal to the New Frontier" (Ph.D. diss., Ohio State University, 1988).

Vibert L. White

MARSHALL, BURKE (1 October 1922, Plainfield, N.J.–). A veteran of World War II, he was a practicing attorney in Washington, D.C., until he became Assistant Attorney General of the United States in charge of the Civil Rights Division, 1961–1965. While serving in this post during the Kennedy and Johnson administrations, he directed the federal government's efforts to integrate the University of Mississippi in 1962 and served as a negotiator between Birmingham, Alabama, city officials and civil rights leaders during the 1963 desegregation campaign. Marshall also assisted in drafting the Civil Rights Act of 1964.* He became a familiar figure because of television's coverage of his front-line integration activities. In 1976 he was named chairman of the National Advisory Commission on Selective Service. He is, in 1992, a Professor of Law at Yale University.

SELECTED BIBLIOGRAPHY
Taylor Branch, *Parting the Waters: America in the King Years, 1954–63* (1988); Carl M. Brauer, *John F. Kennedy and the Second Reconstruction* (1977); Joseph Goldstein, Burke Marshall, and Jack Schwartz, eds., *The My Lai Massacre and Its Cover-Up: Beyond the Reach of Law* (1976); Burke Marshall, *Federalism and Civil Rights* (1964).

Quintard Taylor

MARSHALL, THURGOOD (2 July 1908, Baltimore, Md.–). Lawyer, federal judge, solicitor general, and United States Supreme Court justice, Marshall has played a major role in the civil rights movement of the

Autherine Lucy, Thurgood Marshall, and Arthur Shores at the federal building in Birmingham, March 1956. (Archives and Special Collections, University of Alabama. Courtesy *Birmingham News*.)

twentieth century. It is no exaggeration to title him "the lawyer of civil rights."

Marshall was born in the year that the Springfield, Illinois, race riot* caused the birth of the NAACP.* His father was chief steward for a number of important white social clubs, and his mother taught in a segregated black elementary school in Baltimore. His parents' example of racial pride, dignity, and learning helped mold his personality. In 1926 he began college studies at the all-black Lincoln University in Pennsylvania, holding odd jobs to defray expenses. He graduated in 1930 cum laude and entered Howard University* Law School. At Howard he met Charles H. Houston,* his later mentor, the school's assistant dean and later the NAACP's legal counsel. Marshall graduated in 1933 at the head of his class and for the next five years he practiced law in Baltimore and served as that city's NAACP chief counsel. In 1938, after two years of service as Houston's assistant at the NAACP legal office, Marshall became chief counsel himself. In 1939, the NAACP formed the Legal Defense and Educational Fund* as a separate entity, and Marshall was its first director.

It was in this capacity for the next twenty-two years that Marshall made his most profound impact on civil rights. He travelled all over the South and also argued before the Supreme Court in a variety of civil rights cases. Seldom combative, he usually stated his carefully prepared arguments in a calm, temperate voice. Without doubt, his most famous case was *Brown v. Board of Education** (1954) which resulted in the overthrow of the nineteenth-century *Plessy v. Ferguson** (1896) constitutional underpinning for segregation.

Marshall continued his civil rights litigation until President John F. Kennedy nominated him to the Second Circuit Court of Appeals on 23 September 1961. Despite determined southern opposition, the Senate finally confirmed him on 11 September 1962.

For the next four years, Marshall wrote over one hundred opinions on a variety of subjects, but his civil rights and criminal law opinions stand out. On 13 July 1965 President Lyndon B. Johnson nominated him to be solicitor general, and this time Johnson's political acumen prevented a repetition of the earlier opposition. As the nation's first black solicitor general, Marshall argued a wide variety of legal issues and gained experience and more respect.

On 13 June 1967, President Johnson nominated Marshall to the Supreme Court. Once again southern senators unsuccessfully fought his nomination. On 1 September 1967 he took his seat as the nation's first and, until the 1991 confirmation of Clarence Thomas, the only black Supreme Court justice. Since that time, Marshall has been a consistent member of the court's so-called liberal wing, continuing his lifetime support of individual rights. The presidency of Ronald Reagan proved to be a particularly difficult time for him, and in 1987 he told a television interviewer that Reagan had the worst presidential record on civil rights since Woodrow Wilson. Because of age and health considerations, and because he felt increasingly isolated on a conservative court, he resigned on 27 June 1991 after writing a strong dissent against a conservative majority decision in *Payne v. Tennessee*.

SELECTED BIBLIOGRAPHY

Richard L. Acayo, "Marshall's Legacy: A Lawyer Who Changed America," *Time* 138 (July 8, 1991), 24–25; John P. MacKenzie, "Thurgood Marshall," in Leon Friedman and Fred L. Israel, eds., *The Justices of the United States Supreme Court 1789–1969* (1969); "Marshall Resigns," *Editorials on File* 22 (June 16–30, 1991), 684–95; "Mr. Justice Marshall," *Newsweek* June 26, 1967, 34–36; *Who's Who in America*, 44th ed. (1986–1987).

John F. Marszalek

MASON, LUCY RANDOLPH (26 July 1882, Clarens, Va.–6 May 1959, Atlanta, Ga.). "Miss Lucy," as she came to be known, was a social worker and union organizer for the Congress of Industrial Organizations (CIO). She was born the daughter of an Episcopalian priest and the heir of numerous American founding fathers. She began her career in 1914 as industrial secretary of the Richmond Young Women's Christian Association and eventually became its general secretary. In 1931 she toured the South on behalf of women and child labor reform and wrote a pamphlet entitled *Standards for Workers in Southern Industry*. From 1931 to 1937 she was general secretary of the National Consumers League. From 1937 to 1941 she was at the height of her influence as southeastern public relations officer for the CIO. In this position, she utilized her southern roots and, less so, the threat of legal action or the intervention of her friend, Eleanor Roosevelt,* to help bring unions and labor reform to all parts of the South. Overcoming her own racial views, she matter-of-factly tried to organize both blacks and whites into single unions, thus causing at least a small chink in the wall of segregation.

SELECTED BIBLIOGRAPHY

Atlanta Constitution, 7, 9 May 1959; L. Lader, "Lady and the Sheriff," *New Republic* 118 (5 January 1948), 17–19; Lucy Randolph Mason, *To Win These Rights, A Personal Story of the CIO in the South* (1952); *New York Times*, 8 May 1959; *Dictionary of American Biography*, Supplement 6 (1980); John A. Salmond, *Miss Lucy of the CIO: The Life and Times of Lucy Randolph Mason, 1882–1959* (1988).

John F. Marszalek

MAVERICK, MAURY (23 October 1895, San Antonio, Tex.–7 June 1954, San Antonio, Tex.). As a member of the U.S. House of Representatives from 1935 to 1939, Maverick gained a national reputation for his uncompromising defense of civil liberties and civil rights. He battled to prevent passage of bills abridging freedom of speech, and he was the only Southerner to support the Gavigan antilynching bill. Maverick was defeated for reelection in 1938 and was then elected mayor of San Antonio. His popularity was eroded by his insistence on allowing the Communist party* to meet in the city auditorium and attempting to protect the Communists from rioters.

SELECTED BIBLIOGRAPHY

Richard B. Henderson, *Maury Maverick: A Political Biography* (1970); Maury Maverick Papers, University of Texas, Austin.

Bernard Donahoe

MAYOR AND CITY COUNCIL OF BALTIMORE CITY v. DAWSON, 350 U.S. 877 (1955). Robert M. Dawson instituted suit in federal district court challenging racially segregated public beaches, arguing that compulsory segregation violated the equal protection clause of the Fourteenth Amendment.* The district judge dismissed the suit. Although the Supreme Court's 1954 *Brown v. Board of Education** opinion specifically invalidated segregation only in education, it clearly called into question the constitutionality of compulsory segregation in any area. The district judge in *Dawson*, however, relied on pre-*Brown* Supreme Court and lower court decisions upholding segregation. The Court of Appeals for the Fourth Circuit reversed the district court, relying not only on *Brown* and its companion case of *Bolling v. Sharpe*,* outlawing educational segregation in Washington, D.C., but also on earlier Supreme Court opinions prohibiting racial discrimination in interstate commerce, within schools, and in the sale of property. The U.S. Supreme Court's opinion in its entirety was: "The motion to affirm is granted and the judgment is affirmed." That is, it simply upheld the court of appeals without comment. By 1955, the Supreme Court found it unnecessary to explain any further than it had done in *Brown* why states could not require segregation; in subsequent cases, it similarly invalidated state-required segregation in other public facilities with little or no discussion.

SELECTED BIBLIOGRAPHY

Albert P. Blaustein and Clarence Clyde Ferguson, Jr., *Desegregation and the Law: The Meaning and Effect of the School Segregation Cases* (1962); Albert P. Blaustein and Robert L. Zangrando, *Civil Rights and the American Negro: A Documentary History* (1968); Jack Greenberg, *Race Relations and American Law* (1959); C. Herman Pritchett, *Constitutional Civil Liberties* (1984).

Earlean M. McCarrick

MAYS, BENJAMIN ELIJAH (1 August 1894, Epworth, S.C.–28 March 1984, Atlanta, Ga.). As a minister and educator and the sixth president (1940–1967) of Atlanta's Morehouse College,* Mays's life developed naturally from several influences in his early life. Witnessing a lynch party intimidate his father made him a lifelong and eloquent foe of American racism. His early thirst for education and sense of calling to the Baptist ministry (ordained, 1921) further shaped his professional career. Interspersed with his graduations from Bates College, in Lewiston, Maine (B.A., 1920) and the University of Chicago Divinity School (M.A., 1925; Ph.D., 1935), he and Joseph W. Nicholson published *The Negro's Church* (1933), the first sociological study of African-American religion. From the deanship (1934–1940) of Howard University* School of Religion through his administration of Morehouse, Mays rose to become one of the most respected prophetic voices against segregation in the American black community; his articles and speeches often received nationwide black press coverage. He gave major addresses at over 250 colleges and received twenty-eight honorary doctorates. He became a ministerial model for the young Martin Luther King, Jr.,* who, by Mays's example, became convinced that one could combine a keen intellect with religious fervor and a prophetic consciousness. After King rose to leadership in the civil rights movement, Mays remained an unofficial senior advisor, and he delivered the eulogy at King's funeral. In 1970 he was elected the first African-American president of the Atlanta school board.

SELECTED BIBLIOGRAPHY

Benjamin E. Mays, *Born to Rebel:An Autobiography* (1971); Benjamin E. Mays,

Disturbed about Man (1969); Benjamin E. Mays, *The Negro's God* (1938); Obituary, *Time*, 9 April 1984; Henry J. Young, *Major Black Religious Leaders since 1940* (1979).

Andrew M. Manis

MEMPHIS RACE RIOT (1866). Immediately after the Civil War, there was continual friction between the city's predominantly Irish police force and the black Union soldiers stationed there who were waiting to be mustered out of federal service. The police force was well armed but poorly disciplined, and the city's government was both corrupt and inefficient. The local press and the white populace were hostile to and uneasy with the presence of large numbers of armed and indifferently disciplined black troops in the community. Restless black soldiers were widely accused of committing acts of violence and theft. The riot began on 1 May 1866 when police attempted to arrest a black driver involved in a traffic accident with a white teamster. A group of black soldiers intervened. Gunfire swept the streets of Memphis. White civilians from the surrounding area soon joined with the police in attacking black neighborhoods in the southern part of the city. Fighting came to an end on 4 May 1866 after the intervention of regular U.S. troops. A congressional committee blamed the riot on the city's poor government and the police. Forty-eight people died, two of them white. Dozens were injured. Four black churches, twelve black schools, and ninety-one black dwellings were destroyed.

SELECTED BIBLIOGRAPHY
Eric Foner, *Reconstruction: America's Unfinished Revolution, 1863–1877* (1988); Jack D. L. Holmes, "The Underlying Causes of the Memphis Race Riot of 1866," *Tennessee Historical Quarterly* 17 (September 1958), 195–223; Bobby L. Lovett, "Memphis Riots: White Reaction to Blacks in Memphis, May 1865–July 1866," *Tennessee Historical Quarterly* 38 (Spring 1979), 9–33; George C. Rable, *But There Was No Peace: The Role of Violence in the Politics of Reconstruction* (1984); James Gilbert Ryan, "The Memphis Riots of 1866: Terror in a Black Community during Reconstruction," *Journal of Negro History* 62 (July 1977), 243–58.

Larry T. Balsamo

MENARD, JOHN WILLIS (3 April 1838, Kaskaskia, Ill.–8 October 1893, Washington, D.C.). Educated in Sparta, Illinois, and at Iberia College in Ohio, he became the first African American to be elected to Congress. During the Civil War, he was a clerk in the Department of the Interior. Following the war, Menard moved to New Orleans, Louisiana, and became active in Republican party politics, winning the party's nomination in 1868 to fill the unexpired term of one James Mann who died in August of that year. A bizarre three-way contest for the seat developed when Caleb S. Hunt challenged Menard's election and Simon Jones, a Republican, contested the right of the deceased James Mann to have held the seat. The case was referred to the committee on elections where it was decided it was "too early" to admit an African American to the United States Congress. Hence, Menard may be credited as the first African American *elected* but not the first to serve in the House of Representatives. In 1869, after the Fortieth Congress refused to seat Menard, he was appointed inspector of customs of New Orleans and, later, commissioner of streets. In addition to his political activities, Menard was editor of a newspaper, *The Free South*, which was later renamed *The Radical Standard*. Both these papers carried on an unceasing campaign for black civil rights.

SELECTED BIBLIOGRAPHY

Philip S. Foner, ed., *The Voice of Black America: Major Speeches by Negroes in the United States, 1797–1971* (1972); Philip S. Foner and George E. Walker, eds., *Proceedings of the Black National and State Conventions, 1865–1900*, vol. 1 (1986).

George E. Walker

MEREDITH, JAMES HOWARD (25 June 1933, Kosciusko, Miss.–   ). An African-American civil rights activist in the 1960s and currently a conservative Republican, James Meredith received his early education in Mississippi and in Jacksonville, Florida. He attended Jackson State College from 1960 to 1962. He won a major civil rights victory when he became the first black to gain admission to the University of Mississippi. Although federal troops were sent to protect his right to attend the university, Meredith's presence was continuously opposed by students and state officials. Despite such opposition, Meredith succeeded in earning his B.A. He continued his education at the University of Ibadan in Nigeria, West Africa, from 1964 to 1965 and at Columbia University where he earned his J.D. in 1968. Following publication in 1966 of his autobiography, entitled *Three Years in Mississippi*, Meredith was shot and wounded as he and others carried out a civil rights march there (see Meredith March). Before he was shot, Meredith had told an interviewer that blacks would not achieve their civil rights objectives through non-violent means. If blacks wanted their rightful place in America, he later insisted, they would have to struggle aggressively for it. Meredith, however, began to change from being a militant civil rights activist to a moderate one in the late 1960s. He became, for example, a stockbroker and then an investor. Meredith's new entrepreneurship was viewed by some as an attempt on his part to establish a model for black entrepreneurs. Others, however, viewed it as an abandonment of the civil rights movement. Despite these views, Meredith's positions on civil rights continued to be moderate ones until the 1980s. He became a Republican candidate for the U.S. Congress in 1972, but he did not abandon his attack on racial injustices. By the 1980s, however, Meredith had become a bona fide conservative Republican. During the 1988 presidential election he called on blacks to support the Republican party, asserting that only through that party would blacks be treated as full citizens. He declared in 1988 that "the greatest enemy" of African Americans were the liberal whites and their black counterparts. He also strongly opposed divestment in South Africa. In 1989, Meredith became the first professional black to serve on the staff of North Carolina Senator Jesse Helms, an extreme conservative who opposed making the birthday of Martin Luther King, Jr.,* a national holiday and voted against civil rights bills.

SELECTED BIBLIOGRAPHY

Contemporary Authors (1979); James H. Meredith, *Three Years in Mississippi* (1966); *Washington Times*, 7 September 1988; "White House Camp-In," *Newsweek*, 18 April 1966.

Amos J. Beyan

MEREDITH MARCH. In the early afternoon of 5 June 1966, James Meredith* began a solitary, inspirational "March against Fear." When he was wounded by a sniper's bullet one day after beginning his trek from Memphis, Tennessee, to Jackson, Mississippi, civil rights leaders rallied to his cause. After much haggling and mutual suspicion among the members of the leadership core and after Meredith permitted them to continue in his name, the march resumed, led by Martin Luther King, Jr.,* Stokely Carmichael,* and Floyd McKissick.* What had begun as

The James Meredith March against Fear. (© Flip Schulke, Schulke Archives, Miami, Florida.)

one man's protest against racism became a major media event, highlighted by arrests, by public displays of white prejudice, and by the charisma of King. Aware of King's mass appeal, Carmichael took advantage of his presence to popularize his new slogan, Black Power.* On 25 June, Meredith rejoined the march, which arrived in Jackson the following day. The march itself accomplished little in terms of concrete legislation. As the first major demonstration to occur after passage of the Voting Rights Act of 1965,* it signaled the onset of a new, more militant phase of the movement which would find success elusive in the waning years of civil rights activism.

SELECTED BIBLIOGRAPHY

Paul Good, "The Meredith March," *New South* (Summer 1966), 216; Joyce Ladner, "What Black Power Means to Negroes in Mississippi," in August Meier, ed., *The Transformation of Activism* (1970); Neil R. McMillen, "Black Enfranchisement in Mississippi: Federal Enforcement and Black Protest in the 1960s," *Journal of Southern History* (August 1977), 351–72; Harvard Sitkoff, *The Struggle for Black Equality, 1954–1980* (1981); Milton Viorst, *Fire in the Streets: America in the 1960s* (1979); Nancy J. Weiss, "Creative Tensions in the Leadership of the Civil Rights Movement," in Charles W. Eagles, ed., *The Civil Rights Movement in America* (1986).

Marshall Hyatt

MEREDITH v. FAIR, 305 F.2d 343 (5th Cir., 1962). The decision of the United States Court of Appeals for the Fifth Judicial Circuit* in New Orleans, Louisiana, on 25 June 1962 to force the admission of James Meredith,* a black Mississippian, to the University of Mississippi marked the first desegregation of a public school in the state. Twice rejected in 1961 by university authorities, Meredith had filed a complaint with the district court on 31 May 1961 charging racial bias. Rejecting the charge, the court ruled that Meredith was denied admission not because of his race but because he had failed to fulfill admission requirements. On appeal from Meredith, the Fifth Judicial Circuit Court reversed the district court's ruling. By a 2 to 1 decision, the circuit court's three-judge panel held that Meredith had indeed been denied admission solely because of his race and that Mississippi was maintaining a policy of segregating state schools. The circuit court instructed the district court to issue an injunction commanding the university officials to refrain from activities barring Meredith's admission to the school. The decision initiated a bitter struggle between the federal government and Mississippi authorities over Meredith's admission to the University of Mississippi. In 1963 it took a federalized Mississippi National Guard to ensure Meredith's admission over the continued opposition of state officials and a violent mob.

SELECTED BIBLIOGRAPHY
Russell H. Barrett, *Integration at Ole Miss* (1965); Walter Lord, *The Past That Would Not Die* (1965); William J. Kupense, Jr., "Note," *Cornell Law Quarterly* 48 (1963), 743–53; James M. Meredith, *Three Years in Mississippi* (1966); Lester A. Sobel, ed., *Civil Rights, 1960–1966* (1967).

                                                                    Amm Saifuddin Khaled

MERRICK, JOHN (1859, Clinton, N.C.–6 August 1919, Durham, N.C.). Born a slave, Merrick worked at menial jobs in his youth, but by 1881 he had begun to display his natural talent for business. He joined a barber, John Wright, in a partnership; by 1896, he owned five barber-shops, two for blacks and three for whites, in Durham, North Carolina. Some of his customers included James B. Duke and William Jennings Bryan. He persuaded the Duke family to fund Lincoln Hospital in 1901, which became one of the leading black hospitals in the South. One of his greatest accomplishments was the founding of the North Carolina Mutual Life Insurance Company* in 1898 with over $16 million of insurance in force by 1919.

He accompanied Booker T. Washington* on his South Carolina tour in 1910, and he shared the black spokesman's economic ideology. Among Merrick's other contributions to the business community were banks, real estate, and drugstores.

SELECTED BIBLIOGRAPHY
Russell J. Adams, *Great Negroes: Past and Present* (1969); William J. Kennedy, *The North Carolina Mutual Story* (1970); Alain Locke, ed., *The New Negro: An Interpretation* (1925); Rayford W. Logan and Michael R. Winston, eds., *Dictionary of American Negro Biography* (1982).

                                                                    Thomas D. Cockrell

THE MESSENGER. Edited in New York City by A. Philip Randolph* and Chandler Owen and billed as the "Only Radical Newspaper in America," *The Messenger* first appeared in November 1917. It endorsed black labor unions, women's suffrage, the Russian Revolution, and socialism. It attacked World War I, capitalism, Garveyism, and on occasion, the NAACP.* The Old Negro, the editors charged, as represented by W.E.B. Du Bois,* Kelly Miller,* and James Weldon Johnson,* were stooges of the white establishment. The magazine's black contributors included Eugene Kinckle Jones,* George S. Schuyler,* and T. Thomas Fortune.* By the 1920s *The Messenger* opposed the brutality of Bolshevism and included columns on music, theater, sports, and college life. The newspaper was a victim of financial reverses; the last issue appeared in 1928, endorsing Alfred E. Smith for president, proclaiming, "A Catholic President and a mixed cabinet of Jews, theists, Negroes and Indians would be an excellent thing for the soul of America." *The Messenger* remains an indispensable source for the study of the Harlem Renaissance's* compelling vitality.

SELECTED BIBLIOGRAPHY

Jervis Anderson, *A. Philip Randolph: A Biographical Portrait* (1973); William H. Harris, *Keeping the Faith: A. Philip Randolph, Milton P. Webster, and the Brotherhood of Sleeping Car Porters, 1925–1937* (1977); Theodore Kornweibel, *No Crystal Star: Black Life and the Messenger, 1917–1928* (1975).

Richard W. Resh

MICHAUX, SOLOMON LIGHTFOOT (7 November 1884, Buckroe, Va.–29 October 1968, Washington, D.C.). It was Michaux's natural talents, fervor, and kindness, rather than his education, that led him to the pinnacle of his ministry. He had a true gift for attracting and holding audiences. In the words of E. Franklin Frazier,* the sermons of this "Happy Am I Prophet" consisted "chiefly of tirades against sin, rowdy women, slot machines, whiskey, beer, and gamblers." His early career was undistinguished until he established the Church of God Movement in Newport News, Virginia, complete with local radio broadcasts. In 1928 he built a Church of God in the nation's capital where his radio—and later television—broadcasts went national. By 1934 his broadcasts were carried by more than fifty radio stations, allowing him to reach an estimated audience of 25,000,000. He also published a popular monthly paper called *Happy News*, issued a songbook (*Spiritual Happiness-Making Songs*), and organized a group of religious singers for public appearances. His "Happy News Cafe" fed thousands at a penny a meal, and his Mayfair Mansion was one of the largest black housing developments in the country. His popularity peaked in the mid-1930s and began a slow decline into the early 1940s. By mid-decade he had faded away to mere local popularity. While some black leaders criticized his style and methods, Michaux helped to call the attention of whites to problems of blacks, especially because of his close contacts with high government officials who considered him to be a spokesman for black religious groups.

SELECTED BIBLIOGRAPHY

E. Franklin Frazier, *The Negro Church in America* (1964); Constance McLaughlin Green, *The Secret City: A History of Race Relations in the Nation's Capital* (1967); Rayford W. Logan and Michael R. Winston, eds., *Dictionary of American Negro Biography* (1982); J. Gordon Melton, *Biographical Dictionary of American Cult and Sect Leaders* (1986).

Gary B. Mills

MILHOLLAND, JOHN E. (20 May 1860, Lewis, N.Y.–29 June 1925, New York, N.Y.). A wealthy, white, New York businessman who became an advocate of anti-imperialist and racial causes, Milholland began his career as a newspaperman and later became a manufacturer of pneumatic tube equipment. In 1903 he formed the interracial Constitution League for the purposes of establishing the rights of blacks through legal test cases. Founder of the New York Republican State Club, he was one of the leading critics of the government's handling of the 1906 Brownsville, Texas, affray.* An early supporter of the Tuskegee Institute* movement, he broke with Booker T. Washington* over Washington's accommodationist views. In 1909 he was active in the founding of the NAACP.*

SELECTED BIBLIOGRAPHY

Charles Flint Kellogg, *NAACP: A History of the National Association for the Advancement of Colored People* (1967); August Meier, *Negro Thought in America, 1880–1915: Racial Ideologies in the Age of Booker T. Washington* (1963); Obituary, *New York Times*, 1 July 1925.

                                                                                      Ray Branch

MILLER, KELLY (18 July 1863, Winnsboro, S.C.–29 December 1939, Washington, D.C.). An African-American administrator and scholar, Miller received his early education at Fairfield Institute in Winnsboro. Following his studies there, he enrolled at Howard University* where he earned his undergraduate degree in 1886. Miller did advanced studies at Johns Hopkins University, in Baltimore, Maryland, but financial reasons prevented him from graduating. After leaving Johns Hopkins, Miller taught at a high school in Washington, D.C., until he was offered teaching and administrative positions at Howard University in 1890. As a dean of the College of Arts and Sciences at Howard, he redesigned the curriculum to address the problems faced by blacks. During his deanship, student enrollment increased. Although he was an integrationist, Miller was also an admirer of such radical black nationalists as Nat Turner, David Walker, Denmark Vesey, and Toussaint L'Ouverture.

SELECTED BIBLIOGRAPHY

Horace M. Bond, *Black American Scholars: A Study of Their Beginnings* (1972); Kelly Miller, *An Appeal to Conscience: America's Code of a Caste, A Disgrace to Democracy* (1918); Kelly Miller, *Out of the House of Bondage* (1914); Wilson J. Moses, *The Golden Age of Black Nationalism, 1850–1925* (1978); Earl E. Thorpe, *The Mind of the Negro: An Intellectual History of Afro-Americans* (1970).

                                                                                      Amos J. Beyan

MILLIKEN v. BRADLEY, 418 U.S. 717 (1974). In most northern cities, statutory school segregation had never existed or it had long been done away with by the 1970s. Yet despite the absence of forced segregation, the school systems in metropolitan cities remained divided along racial lines. The inner cities, for the most part, were predominantly black, while the suburbs were almost entirely white. Black organizations like the NAACP* found this situation intolerable. As long as racial imbalance continued in urban schools, they argued, blacks would receive an inferior education. In *Swann v. Charlotte-Mecklenburg Board of Education** (1971), the Supreme Court seemed to agree, maintaining that cities must bus students out of their neighborhoods if this was necessary to achieve integration. In *Milliken*, however, the Court rejected five to four a plan to integrate Detroit's schools with those of the outlying suburban areas. Writing for the majority, Chief Justice Warren Burger stated that there was no evidence that the suburban districts had operated segregated schools. The Court, he concluded, could not impose a busing plan on all school districts in order to remedy segregation in one district. The Court's ruling came in the wake of angry protests in Boston, Denver, and Pontiac, Michigan. Many white parents denounced what they saw as the destruction of the neighborhood school. This public opposition, together with the Court's moderate stance, slowed the process of metropolitan integration.

SELECTED BIBLIOGRAPHY

Derrick A. Bell, Jr., *Race, Racism and American Law*, 2d ed. (1980); Vincent Blasi, ed., *The Burger Court: The Counter-Revolution That Wasn't* (1983); Paul R. Dimond, *Beyond Busing: Inside the Challenge to Urban Segregation* (1985); J. Harvie Wilkinson III, *From Brown to Bakke: The Supreme Court and School Integration, 1954–1978* (1979); Rowland L. Young, "Supreme Court Report," *American Bar Association Journal* 60 (1974), 1261–62.

Phillip A. Gibbs

MILLS v. BOARD OF EDUCATION OF ANNE ARUNDEL COUNTY, 30 F. Supp. 245 (D. Md., 1939). Walter Mills, principal of a black school, challenged the constitutionality of a Maryland statute prescribing differing minimum salaries for white and black teachers in the state's segregated schools. He argued that the statute, on its face and in its application, violated the equal protection clause of the Fourteenth Amendment.* The statutory minimum annual salary was $1250 for white teachers and $765 for black teachers. Mills's initial suit against the state board of education was dismissed because, among other reasons, he had failed to include the county board as a defendant. He then instituted this suit against the county board. The federal district court found it unnecessary to determine whether the statute was unconstitutional on its face, noting that the statute did not necessarily require lower salaries for blacks. The court, however, held that its application was discriminatory and therefore unconstitutional: *no* black teacher in Anne Arundel county received as high a salary as *any* white teacher, and the actual salaries of white teachers were twice as high as that of black teachers. It ordered a cessation of salary discrimination based on race. The court, however, refused Mills's request to order the board not to pay black teachers less than white teachers.

SELECTED BIBLIOGRAPHY
Jack Greenberg, *Race Relations and American Law* (1959); Richard Kluger, *Simple Justice: The History of Brown v. Board of Education and Black America's Struggle for Equality* (1976); "Recent Cases," *Harvard Law Review* 53 (1940), 669–71.

                                                                    Earlean M. McCarrick

MISSISSIPPI FREEDOM DEMOCRATIC PARTY. The Mississippi Freedom Democratic party (MFDP) was organized during the summer of 1964 by members of the Student Nonviolent Coordinating Committee* and other participants of the Freedom Summer of 1964* project. The party was designed to challenge the power of the state Democratic party which, in June, had included in its platform a clause rejecting civil rights and opposing the national party's commitment to that cause. Charging that the state regulars were disloyal to the national party, the MFDP attempted in August 1964 to secure delegate representation at the national Democratic convention being held in Atlantic City, New Jersey. Hubert H. Humphrey* and Walter Mondale, working to preserve what was supposed to be an effortless renomination for Lyndon B. Johnson at the convention, proposed a compromise calling for Mississippi regulars to be seated if they swore loyalty to the national party and providing for the creation of two "at large" seats to be filled by members of the MFDP. The compromise failed when all but three of the party regulars walked out of the convention while the entire MFDP delegation, led by grass-roots activist, Fannie Lou Hamer,* was removed from the convention floor when they attempted to take the seats of the party regulars. The struggle of the MFDP promoted greater interest among many civil rights activists for the creation of a stronger independent black organization within the movement.

SELECTED BIBLIOGRAPHY
Adam Fairclough, *To Redeem the Soul of America: The Southern Christian Leadership Conference and Martin Luther King, Jr.* (1987); David J. Garrow, *Bearing the Cross: Martin Luther King, Jr. and the Southern Christian Leadership Conference* (1986); Henry Hampton and Steve Fayer, *Voices of Freedom: An Oral History of the Civil Rights Movement from the 1950s through the 1980s* (1990); Kenneth O'Reilly, *Racial Matters: The FBI's Secret File on Black America, 1960–1972* (1989); Juan Williams, *Eyes on the Prize: America's Civil Rights Years, 1954–1965* (1987).

                                                                    JoAnn D. Carpenter

MISSOURI ex rel. GAINES v. CANADA, 305 U.S. 337 (1938). Missouri denied Lloyd Gaines, a graduate of Lincoln University, in Jefferson, Missouri, admission to the University of Missouri law school solely because of his race. Since Missouri had no law school for blacks, based allegedly on a lack of demand, the state paid tuition at law schools in Kansas, Nebraska, Iowa, or Illinois that would accept nonresident blacks. Chief Justice Charles Evans Hughes found this practice to be a denial of equal protection of the laws. He noted that Gaines had a right to admission to the university in the absence of "other and proper provision for his legal training within the state." Demand was a legitimate basis for state policy, but, where a service was in fact provided, substantial equality of treatment was mandatory. The case is less a desegregation case than it is a further interpretation of the separate but equal* rule in specific circumstances. However, it also marks the first of a fifteen-year series of cases that concluded with *Brown v. Board of Education** in 1954.

SELECTED BIBLIOGRAPHY

Daniel T. Kelleher, "The Case of Lloyd Lionel Gaines: The Demise of the 'Separate-but-Equal' Doctrine," *Journal of Negro History* 56 (October 1971), 262–71; Richard Kluger, *Simple Justice: The History of Brown v. Board of Education and Black America's Struggle for Equality* (1976); Bernard H. Nelson, *The Fourteenth Amendment and the Negro since 1920* (1967); Mark V. Tushnet, *The NAACP's Legal Strategy Against Segregated Education, 1925–1950* (1987).

James E. Sefton

MITCHELL, ARTHUR W. (22 December 1883, Chambers County, Ala.–May 9, 1968, Petersburg, Va.). His election to the U.S. House of Representatives in 1934 marked a significant turning point in twentieth-century black politics. Running as a New Deal Democrat, Mitchell defeated black Republican Oscar DePriest* (elected in 1928), which symbolized the enormous impact of Franklin D. Roosevelt's New Deal on black political life. The son of ex-slaves and raised in rural Alabama, Mitchell worked as office boy for Booker T. Washington.* Imbued with Washington's philosophy, he studied at Talledega College and Snow Hill Normal and Industrial Institute, and, in 1908, he founded his own school, Armstrong Agricultural College. Following service in World War I, he migrated to Chicago, where he became involved in real estate and law, joined the Republican party, and in 1928 served on the staff of Herbert Hoover's presidential campaign. Unable to break into DePriest's Republican organization, disillusioned with Hoover's depression policies, and inspired by the New Deal, Mitchell became a Democrat in 1934. Backed by local Democrats, he narrowly defeated DePriest and, during his eight years in Congress, distinguished himself primarily as a loyal Roosevelt supporter. His most celebrated civil rights effort came with his lawsuit against the Pullman Company for refusing him accommodations in the white section of the railway car. As a result of his legal action, the U.S. Supreme Court overturned the segregation policies of the Interstate Commerce Commission (see *Mitchell v. United States*). Mitchell's support of other civil rights issues, such as antilynching legislation, was less forceful, and during the 1930s he was often criticized by such black leaders as Walter White* of the NAACP.* He retired from Congress in 1942.

SELECTED BIBLIOGRAPHY
Christopher Robert Reed, "A Study of Black Politics and Protest in Depression-Decade Chicago: 1930–1939" (Ph.D. diss., Kent State University, 1982); Nancy J. Weiss, *Farewell to the Party of Lincoln* (1983); Robert L. Zangrando, *The NAACP Crusade against Lynching, 1909–1950* (1980).

John B. Kirby

MITCHELL, HARRY LELAND (H. L.) (14 June 1906, near Halls, Tenn.–1989, Montgomery, Ala.). An agricultural day laborer as a boy and a sharecropper in his early teens, Mitchell understood well the problems of the rural poor. By the time he had graduated from high school he had become an atheist, evolutionist, and socialist. In 1932, after hearing a speech by Norman Thomas, he joined the Socialist party and organized a local in Tyronza, Arkansas. Two years later, with Thomas's encouragement, he and Henry Clay East helped a small interracial band of sharecroppers around Tyronza to organize the Southern Tenant Farmers' Union* (STFU). Throughout the remainder of the decade, the STFU, with Mitchell as secretary, attracted national attention to the plight of the South's croppers and tenants.

In the mid-1940s a remnant of the faction-ridden STFU became the National Farm Labor Union, later the National Agricultural Workers' Union, with Mitchell as president. From 1948 to 1960 Mitchell directed the union's activities and lobbied in Washington, D.C., on behalf of black, Hispanic, and white farmers and farm laborers in the South and West. In 1960, after the union was absorbed by the Amalgamated Meat Cutters and Butcher Workmen of North America, he became an organizer for an affiliate of the Amalgamated Meat Cutters and worked among food and agricultural laborers in the South. Mitchell was sometimes frustrated by what he considered the conservatism, bigotry, and narrowly economic aims of the labor establishment. Consequently, in 1969 he helped organize the Southern Mutual Help Association which undertook educational, health, and housing projects among the black and white rural poor of Louisiana. Following his retirement in 1973, Mitchell devoted his remaining years to perpetuating the memory of the pioneering interracial work of the Southern Tenant Farmers' Union.

SELECTED BIBLIOGRAPHY
Donald H. Grubbs, *Cry from the Cotton: The Southern Tenant Farmers' Union and the New Deal* (1971); H. L. Mitchell, *Mean Things Happening in This Land: The Life and Times of H. L. Mitchell, Co-Founder of the Southern Tenant Farmers' Union* (1979); H. L. Mitchell, *Roll the Union On: A Pictorial History of the Southern Tenant Farmers' Union, as Told by Its Co-Founder, H. L. Mitchell* (1987).

Robert F. Martin

MITCHELL, JOHN R., JR. (11 July 1863, Richmond, Va.–3 December 1929, Richmond, Va.). Mitchell took over management of the struggling *Richmond Planet* in 1884 and made it into a major black newspaper. The

Planet forthrightly battled the rising tide of late-nineteenth-century segregation, discrimination, and lynching, taking a more militant position
than most black newspapers. When Richmond's streetcars were segregated in 1904, Mitchell led the boycott that bankrupted the transportation
company. His life was frequently threatened because of his paper's
strong stands, but he fearlessly stood up to the threats. His close connections with the Republican party did not prevent his newspaper from
criticizing the GOP when he thought it appropriate, for example over
the issue of American imperialism. But he remained in the party all his
life. He served on the Richmond City Council from 1888–1896, attended
several national Republican conventions, and in 1921 he unsuccessfully
ran for governor on an all-black ticket. He founded the Mechanics Savings Bank in 1902 and later became the first black member of the American Bankers' Association. When he died in 1929, his son Roscoe briefly
succeeded him at the *Planet*, but the paper was sold in 1938.

SELECTED BIBLIOGRAPHY

Ann F. Alexander, "Black Protest in the New South: John Mitchell, Jr., and the
Richmond Planet," Ph.D. diss., Duke University, 1973; Willard B. Gatewood, Jr.,
"A Negro Editor on Imperialism: John Mitchell, 1898–1901," *Journalism Quarterly*
49 (1972): 43–50, 60; Rayford W. Logan and Michael R. Winston, eds., *Dictionary
of American Negro Biography* (1982); Henry Lewis Suggs, ed., *The Black Press in
the South, 1865–1979* (1983).

John F. Marszalek

MITCHELL v. UNITED STATES, 313 U.S. 80 (1941). Early challenges to
segregation in interstate travel failed, but civil rights lawyers began to
achieve some success on the eve of World War II. In 1937 U.S. Representative Arthur W. Mitchell* boarded a train in Chicago en route to
Hot Springs, Arkansas. He obtained first-class accommodations on a
nonsegregated basis. When he reached Arkansas, the conductor ordered
him to move to a segregated car so that the company could comply with
a local segregation law. Mitchell objected but ultimately complied to
avoid arrest. He filed charges against the railroad company before the
Interstate Commerce Commission (ICC). When the ICC dismissed the
complaint, he sought damages in court. Mitchell appealed to the Supreme Court after a district court ruled for the ICC. The Court ruled in
his favor, holding "that separate coach laws of the several states do not
apply to interstate commerce." Most southern states ignored the ruling,
however, and segregation prevailed in interstate travel into the 1960s.

SELECTED BIBLIOGRAPHY

Catherine A. Barnes, *Journey from Jim Crow: The Desegregation of Southern Transit*
(1983); Derrick A. Bell, Jr., *Race, Racism and American Law* (1980); Scott D. Breck-
inridge, Jr., "Effect of Mitchell v. United States on the Duty of the Common
Carrier in Kentucky Toward the Negro Passenger," *Kentucky Law Journal*, 30

(1942), 247–50; "Recent Cases," *George Washington Law Review* 10 (1941), 229–31; "Recent Decisions," *Michigan Law Review* 39 (1941), 1414–17.

Stephen Middleton

MONTGOMERY BUS BOYCOTT. Sparked by the arrest of Rosa Parks* for refusing to relinquish her seat to a white man and move to the back of a Montgomery, Alabama, city bus, as was mandated by that city's segregation ordinance, the 381-day bus boycott began in December 1955 and continued without interruption until 21 December 1956. At that time the U.S. Supreme Court upheld an earlier three-judge federal court decision which ruled that segregation on a common carrier violated the due process and equal protection of the law clauses of the Fourteenth Amendment* (see *Browder v. Gayle*). Beyond integrating the Montgomery buses, this precedent-setting decision allowed the nascent civil rights movement to adopt the Fourteenth Amendment as a formidable weapon against all forms of segregation.* The boycott also brought Martin Luther King, Jr.,* into a position of national visibility as a civil rights spokesperson. His leadership of the boycott began when he was elected president of the newly established Montgomery Improvement Association,* which organized and coordinated the protest. This visibility gave King a platform from which he could articulate his philosophy of nonviolent direct action* and keep it in the forefront of civil rights tactics and ideology. The boycott's success motivated many similarly fashioned protests throughout the South. Victory in Montgomery was achieved because of the strong grass-roots organizing efforts of such individuals as E. D. Nixon,* Ralph Abernathy,* and Fred L. Shuttlesworth* and the support of such advisors as Bayard Rustin* and Stanley Levison. Additionally, the NAACP* provided valuable legal support and handled the case as it went through the judicial process. As a direct and enduring legacy of the boycott, King in 1957 established the Southern Christian Leadership Conference,* intended to organize black clergymen "to assert their human dignity through nonviolent protest against segregation."

SELECTED BIBLIOGRAPHY

Taylor Branch, *Parting the Waters: America in the King Years: 1954–63* (1988); Adam Fairclough, *To Redeem the Soul of America: The Southern Christian Leadership Conference and Martin Luther King, Jr.* (1987); David J. Garrow, *Bearing the Cross: Martin Luther King, Jr. and the Southern Christian Leadership Conference* (1986); Martin Luther King, Jr., *Stride toward Freedom: The Montgomery Story* (1958); Aldon D. Morris, *The Origins of the Civil Rights Movement: Black Communities Organizing for Change* (1984); Jo Ann Gibson Robinson, *The Montgomery Bus Boycott and the Women Who Started It: The Memoir of Jo Ann Gibson Robinson* (1987); Norman A. Walton, "The Walking City, A History of the Montgomery Boycott—Part I," *Negro History Bulletin* 20 (October 1956), 17–21; Norman A. Walton, "The Walking City, A History of the Montgomery Boycott—Part II," *Negro History Bulletin* 20 (November 1956), 27–33; Norman A. Walton, "The Walking City, A History of the Montgomery Boycott—Part III," *Negro History Bulletin* 20 (February 1957), 102–4; Norman A. Walton, "The Walking City, A History of the Montgomery Boycott—Part IV," *Negro History Bulletin* 20 (April 1957), 147–52, 166.

Marshall Hyatt

MONTGOMERY IMPROVEMENT ASSOCIATION. When African Americans in Alabama's capital decided, at a mass meeting on the evening of 5 December 1955, to continue the one-day-old Montgomery bus boycott* of the city's segregated buses, they formed this organization to lead and coordinate the boycott. Martin Luther King, Jr.,* was elected president, and leaders of the black churches and civic organizations in the city made up its thirty-five-member executive board. Its finance and transportation committees created a free transportation system for the tens of thousands of black people in Montgomery who were affected by the boycott. The Montgomery Improvement Association (MIA) provided this service without interruption for the duration of the year-long boycott, despite acts of intimidation and attempts by the city and state to close down the operation. It held weekly meetings and published *The MIA Newsletter* to keep people informed of developments. After failing to get the city to agree to limited desegregation of the buses, the MIA filed suit in federal court on 1 February 1956, challenging the constitutionality of the bus segregation ordinances. On 13 November 1956, the U.S. Supreme Court upheld the lower court's ruling that the segregation of Montgomery's buses was unconstitutional (see *Browder v. Gayle*). After the boycott, the MIA continued to serve the black people of Montgomery in the civil rights movement it had helped initiate, and it became an affiliated member of the Southern Christian Leadership Conference.*

SELECTED BIBLIOGRAPHY

Taylor Branch, *Parting the Waters: America in the King Years, 1954–63* (1988); David J. Garrow, *Bearing the Cross: Martin Luther King, Jr. and the Southern Christian Leadership Conference* (1986); Aldon D. Morris, *The Origins of the Civil Rights Movement: Black Communities Organizing for Change* (1984); Martin Luther King, Jr., *Stride toward Freedom: The Montgomery Story* (1958); Jo Ann Gibson Robinson, *The Montgomery Bus Boycott and the Women Who Started It* (1987); Lamont H. Yeakey, "The Montgomery, Alabama, Bus Boycott, 1955–56," (Ph.D. diss., Columbia University, 1979).

Gloria Waite

MOODY, ANNE (15 September 1940, Centreville, Miss.–   ). Civil rights activist, writer, and lecturer, Anne Moody attended Natchez Junior College and received a bachelor's degree from Tougaloo College.* While a student, she and two other young blacks were among the first sit-in demonstrators at a Jackson, Mississippi, Woolworth's lunch counter. Later she was jailed on several occasions for her participation in marches and demonstrations. She continued to recruit high school and college students, and she conducted workshops on self-protection tactics. In 1963 Moody expanded her activities by going to work for the Congress of Racial Equality* in Canton, Mississippi. Having earned a national reputation, Moody became a civil rights coordinator at Cornell University (1964–1965). She has described her involvement in the civil rights movement in her *Coming of Age in Mississippi* (1968) which received several awards, including the American Library Association's "Best Book of the Year Award."

SELECTED BIBLIOGRAPHY

Marianna W. Davis, ed., *Contributions of Black Women to America*, vol. 2 (1982); Gerda Lerner, ed., *Black Women in White America, A Documentary History* (1972); Anne Moody, *Coming of Age in Mississippi* (1968); George A. Sewell, *Mississippi Black History Makers* (1977).

Betty L. Plummer

MOORE, AMZIE (23 September 1911, border of Carroll and Grenada Counties, Miss.–1 February 1982, Mound Bayou, Miss.). An African-American businessman and civil rights activist in the 1950–1960 decade of mass protestations, Moore was more interested in overthrowing segregationist regimes in Mississippi than in desegregation. He concentrated on voter registration and is credited with helping move Bolivar County, Mississippi, into the civil rights era. Elected president of the Cleveland, Mississippi, NAACP* in 1955 and a founder of the Delta's Regional Council of Negro Leadership, Moore persuaded Robert Moses,* working for the Student Nonviolent Coordinating Committee* (SNCC), that voter registration should be its focus for Mississippi and that local youth along with SNCC volunteers should be used in the effort.

SELECTED BIBLIOGRAPHY

Bolivar Commercial, 2 February 1982; Taylor Branch, *Parting the Waters: America in the King Years, 1954–63* (1988); Clayborne Carson, *In Struggle: SNCC and the Black Awakening of the 1960s* (1981); Charles W. Eagles, ed., *The Civil Rights Movement in America* (1986); *New York Times*, 7 February 1982.

Nancy E. Fitch

MOORE, HARRY T. (18 November 1905, Mims, Fla.–25 December 1951, Mims, Fla.). Florida coordinator of the NAACP,* he attacked racism along a variety of fronts. A former schoolteacher, he led the challenge against unequal salaries for black educators. Following the outlawing of the white primary* by the U.S. Supreme Court in 1944, he formed the Florida Progressive Voters League, which succeeded in tripling the enrollment of registered black voters. Moore was also involved in protesting the convictions of three black men for the rape of a white woman in Groveland, Florida, in July 1949. Two years later, after the U.S. Supreme Court ordered a new trial, Sheriff Willis McCall of Lake County shot and killed one unarmed prisoner and wounded another in his custody. Moore called for the sheriff's suspension. A month after the shooting on Christmas Day 1951, a bomb shattered Moore's house, killing the NAACP leader and his wife. Though members of the Ku Klux Klan were suspected of the crime, the assailants were never brought to trial. In 1955 Governor LeRoy Collins reopened the case and commuted the death sentence of the surviving prisoner.

SELECTED BIBLIOGRAPHY

Gloster Current, "Martyr for a Cause," *Crisis* 59 (February 1952), 72–81, 133–34; Steven F. Lawson, *Black Ballots: Voting Rights in the South, 1944–1969* (1976); Steven F. Lawson, David R. Colburn, and Darryl Paulson, "Groveland: Florida's Little Scottsboro," *Florida Historical Quarterly* 65 (July 1986), 1–26.

Steven F. Lawson

MOORE v. DEMPSEY, 261 U.S. 86 (1923). This 1923 U.S. Supreme Court decision upheld the constitutional right of fair trial and due process of law. In 1919, responding to the exploitation of black sharecroppers and tenant farmers by white merchant/planters, Robert L. Hill, a black veteran of World War I, organized in Arkansas the self-help Farmers Progressive Household Union of America. Its aim was to "advance the interests of the Negro." Fearing the worst, a white deputy and assistant approached a mass church meeting of the union; gunfire erupted which left the deputy wounded and his assistant seriously wounded. A subsequent race riot unofficially left nearly two hundred blacks dead. The surviving members of the union were rounded up and tried for murder. Upon a howling mob's insistence, the jury quickly sentenced twelve to death and sixty-seven to lengthy prison sentences. Attorneys for the NAACP* won appeals for the convicted on the grounds that the racist hysteria of the moment led to a trial in name only. The Supreme Court agreed with this assessment and overturned the convictions.

SELECTED BIBLIOGRAPHY

Richard Kluger, *Simple Justice: The History of Brown v. Board of Education and Black America's Struggle for Equality* (1976); Loren Miller, *The Petitioners: The Story of the Supreme Court of the United States and the Negro* (1966).

Malik Simba

MOORE, WILLIAM L. (28 April 1927, Binghamton, N.Y.–23 April 1963, Etowah County, Ala.). William Moore planned in 1963 to walk from Chattanooga, Tennessee, to Jackson, Mississippi, and deliver a letter protesting the state of race relations to Governor Ross Barnett. The Baltimore postmaster had been raised in Mississippi, but he deplored in his communication to Barnett the state's reputation as "the most backward and most bigoted in the land." Moore specifically objected to segregated public accommodations in the South. The thirty-five-year-old white man, pushing a cart with his possessions before him, began the solitary journey on 21 April. Heading south, with signs reading "Eat at Joe's—Both Black and White" and "Equal Rights for All" attached to him, Moore crossed into Alabama. He recorded in his diary a white woman's encouragement and the "nigger lover" taunts of others. Moore pushed on, sleeping one night in a school bus. In Etowah County, as he walked along a remote stretch of U.S. Highway 11, he was shot and killed on the evening of 23 September. Both President John F. Kennedy and Governor George Wallace, unusual allies, condemned the crime. Two individuals were questioned, but the murder went unpunished. Moore's undelivered letter to Governor Barnett was opened and read. In writing to Mississippi's governor, William Moore reasoned that "the white man cannot be truly free himself until all men have their rights."

SELECTED BIBLIOGRAPHY

Taylor Branch, *Parting the Waters: America in the King Years, 1954–63* (1988); *Gadsden* (Alabama) *Times*, 24 April 1973; *Montgomery Advertiser*, 24–26 April 1963.

William Warren Rogers, Jr.

MOREHOUSE COLLEGE. Established in 1867 as Augusta Institute, Morehouse College moved to Atlanta, Georgia, in 1879 where it became known as the Atlanta Baptist Seminary. In 1897 the name was changed to the Atlanta Baptist College. Throughout these years there was repeated debate over the issue of white versus black control of the institution, but it was not until John Hope* became president in 1906 that a black man first held that post. Through the influence of Booker T. Washington,* Hope was able to raise badly needed funds for the school, but his action temporarily alienated W.E.B. Du Bois.* In 1913 the school's name was changed to Morehouse College in honor of the secretary of the American Baptist Home Mission Society. The college grew and in 1929 joined with Spelman College and Atlanta University* in a successful cooperative venture that continues to the present day. In 1935 Benjamin Mays* ascended to the presidency and, like John Hope, put his mark on the school. Mays was also a major national black figure. Morehouse is perhaps most often remembered as the alma mater of Martin Luther King, Jr.,* but it also produced many black professionals, businessmen, and other important civil rights leaders. Morehouse students also played an active role in the 1960s desegregation struggles in Atlanta.

SELECTED BIBLIOGRAPHY

Benjamin Brawley, *History of Morehouse College* (1917); Addie Louis Joyner Butlar, *The Distinctive Black College: Talladega, Tuskegee and Morehouse* (1977); Benjamin E. Mays, *Born to Rebel, An Autobiography* (1971).

John F. Marszalek

MORGAN, CHARLES, JR. (11 March 1930, Cincinnati, Ohio–   ). A native of Kentucky, Morgan was educated at the University of Alabama and practiced law in Birmingham from 1955 to 1963. On 16 September

1963, the day after a bomb killed four black girls in the Sixteenth Street Baptist Church, Morgan told the Young Men's Business Club, "We all did it. Every last one of us is condemned for that crime. . . . Birmingham is not a dying city. It is dead." Within weeks he left Birmingham. From 1964 to 1972, Morgan directed the southern regional office of the American Civil Liberties Union* (ACLU) and later (1972–1976) headed the ACLU's Washington, D.C., office. Having established the one man–one vote doctrine in *Reynolds v. Sims,* Morgan attacked institutional racism. He defeated racial discrimination on juries (*White v. Crook, Bailey v. Wharton,* and *Whitus v. Georgia**) and segregation in Alabama prisons (*Lee v. Washington*). In 1966 he represented Julian Bond,* who had been denied a seat in the Georgia legislature after speaking against the war in Vietnam. A historian of the ACLU has called Morgan "the only other charismatic figure in ACLU history besides Roger Baldwin."

SELECTED BIBLIOGRAPHY

Charles Morgan, Jr., *One Man, One Voice* (1979); Charles Morgan, Jr., *A Time to Speak* (1964); Fred Powledge, "Profiles (Charles Morgan, Jr.)," *The New Yorker,* 25 October 1969; Samuel Walker, *In Defense of American Liberties: A History of the ACLU* (1990).

Charles W. Eagles

MORGAN v. VIRGINIA, 328 U.S. 373 (1946). Irene Morgan climbed aboard a Richmond, Virginia, Greyhound bus on 14 July 1944 in Gloucester County, Virginia. She had a ticket to Baltimore, Maryland, the destination of the bus. A short while later, the bus driver ordered her and another African-American woman to move two rows back to the last row so that four of six white passengers who were standing could be seated. A Virginia state law dating from 1930 required seating segregation by rows, and it required the bus driver to take the action he did. When Morgan chose to remain in her seat, she was forcibly removed and subsequently convicted of violating the law and resisting arrest. On appeal, the Virginia Supreme Court of Appeals unanimously sustained the segregation statute and its application to her (184 Va. 24). By a seven-to-one margin, however, the U.S. Supreme Court invalidated the law as it applied to interstate passengers. The state's police power under the Tenth Amendment might require segregation among intrastate passengers, but, according to the new interpretation of the Interstate Commerce Clause, it could not also reach interstate passengers. The court had issued its ruling, but only after two more decades would such segregation requirements—in intrastate and interstate travel alike—finally fall, particularly in the Deep South.

SELECTED BIBLIOGRAPHY

Catherine A. Barnes, *Journey from Jim Crow: The Desegregation of Southern Transit* (1983); Gilbert Ware, *William Hastie: Grace under Pressure* (1984).

Peter Wallenstein

MORIAL, ERNEST N. ("Dutch") (9 October 1929, New Orleans, La.–
23 December 1989, New Orleans, La.). Upon receiving his undergraduate education from Xavier University of New Orleans in 1951, Morial
was among the first black students to enroll in law school at Louisiana
State University (LSU). Accelerating his studies, he became the LSU
law school's first black graduate in 1954. Together with his law partner
Alexander Pierre Tureaud,* he hammered away at the walls of segregation and discrimination that made New Orleans a divided city.
As attorneys for the Legal Defense and Educational Fund* of the
NAACP,* they filed suits that brought an end to segregation in New
Orleans schools, places of public entertainment, municipal facilities,
buses, and taxicabs. Morial was president of the New Orleans branch
of the NAACP from 1963 to 1965. He became the first black to serve
as assistant U.S. attorney in the state of Louisiana (1965 to 1967). In
1967 he won a seat in the Louisiana House of Representatives, becoming the first black to sit in the legislature since the end of the
nineteenth century. He held the seat from 1968 to 1970, when Governor
John McKeithen appointed him to fill an unexpired term on the Orleans
Parish Juvenile Court in 1970. The first black to sit on that bench, he
was also the first of his race to win election to the state's Fourth Circuit
Court of Appeals, where he served from 1973 to 1977. In 1977 he
emerged victorious from a hotly contested mayoral race to become the
first black mayor of New Orleans. Morial's assertiveness endeared him
to thousands of ordinary black people throughout Louisiana, who took
vicarious pleasure in witnessing him stand up to white symbols of
power. As a champion of the poor and dispossessed of all races, he
used his intellect, courage, and skills as an attorney to broaden the
boundaries of freedom for all people. When his election as mayor
catapulted him into greater national prominence and the presidency
of the U.S. Conference of Mayors, he used that office to marshal
support for the continuation of General Revenue Sharing programs,
Community Services Block Grants, and other federal programs designed to enable financially strapped cities to provide services for the
poor.

SELECTED BIBLIOGRAPHY

Arnold R. Hirsch, *Dutch Morial: Old Creole in the New South*, working paper no.
4, College of Urban and Public Affairs, University of New Orleans (1990); Arnold
R. Hirsch, "Simply a Matter of Black and White: The Transformation of Racial
Politics in Twentieth Century New Orleans" (unpublished manuscript, 1989);
Ernest N. Morial, Mayor, City of New Orleans, no date (short political biography
in author's possession); Ernest Nathan Morial Papers, Amistad Research Center,
Tulane University, New Orleans, Louisiana; Ernest N. Morial and Marion Barry,
Jr., *Rebuilding America's Cities: A Policy Analysis of the U.S. Conference of Mayors*
(1986); *New Orleans Times-Picayune*, 25 December 1989.

Joe Louis Caldwell

MORRILL ACT (1890). The Morrill-McComas bill, or second Morrill Act (1890), led to the formation of the "Colleges of 1890," a collection of institutions of higher education for black Southerners that paralleled the colleges for whites from which blacks were excluded. In all, seventeen states—the former Confederate states plus Maryland, Delaware, West Virginia, Kentucky, Missouri, and Oklahoma—established separate institutions. Some of those schools had actually been set up before 1890; others reflected a direct response to the 1890 act, which thus inaugurated some benefits for black citizens. An amendment to the Morrill-Wade Act of 1862, the 1890 act offered substantially increased funding for each state, but it also required that, if any state's land-grant school barred the admission of black students, then the money go to a separate school for blacks. Over the past one hundred years, the black land-grant schools have provided employment and education for large numbers of black Southerners. And yet they have, as a rule, been highly underfunded. In a direct analogy to the way in which southern states allocated state funds to local governments for elementary schools, these federal funds were distributed on the basis of population, and then southern states supplied their white land-grant schools with most of the federal money and most of the state money as well.

SELECTED BIBLIOGRAPHY

Edward Danforth Eddy, *Colleges for Our Land and Time: The Land-Grant Idea in American Education* (1957); Jean L. Preer, *Lawyers v. Educators: Black Colleges and Desegregation in Public Higher Education* (1982); William Elton Trueheart, "The Consequences of Federal and State Resource Allocation and Development Policies for Traditionally Black Land-Grant Institutions: 1862–1954" (Ed.D. diss., Harvard University, 1979).

Peter Wallenstein

MORROW, EVERETTE FREDERIC (20 April 1909, Hackensack, N.J.–). From 1955 to 1961, in his position as administrative officer for special projects for President Dwight D. Eisenhower, Morrow was the first black appointed to a president's executive staff. This was one of several important positions he held in his career as public servant, businessman, and civil rights activist. Morrow graduated from Bowdoin College, in Brunswick, Maine, in 1930 and later from Rutgers University Law School, in New Brunswick, New Jersey. After college he worked for the National Urban League* and subsequently for the NAACP.* A major in the U.S. Army during World War II, he agitated for the rights of blacks in a segregated and discriminatory armed forces. In 1949 he was the first black writer hired by CBS in its Public Affairs Department, and he left that position in 1952 to serve on President Eisenhower's election campaign staff. As White House aide in the Eisenhower White House, he was not always successful in influencing administration racial policies; yet his voice was one of reason in the tension-filled days of the early civil rights movement. Morrow held a number of subsequent jobs, the most important of which was vice president for the Bank of America. He retired in 1975.

SELECTED BIBLIOGRAPHY
Robert Frederick Burk, *The Eisenhower Administration and Black Civil Rights* (1981); "E. Frederic Morrow—Whatever Happened To," *Ebony* 38 (December 1982), 120; E. Frederic Morrow, *Black Man in the White House: A Diary of the Eisenhower Years* (1963); E. Frederic Morrow, *Forty Years a Guinea Pig* (1980).

Dorothy A. Autrey

MOSES, ROBERT (23 January 1935, Harlem, N.Y.–   ). A shy, soft-spoken individual, Robert Moses was the driving force behind the Student Nonviolent Coordinating Committee* (SNCC). Born and raised in Harlem, Moses was quickly recognized as a gifted youth, and he distinguished himself by mastering the Chinese philosophy of Lao-tzu. While he was a Harvard graduate student, majoring in philosophy and teaching grade school, he heard of the civil rights movement in the South. Armed with a knowledge of French existentialist Albert Camus, a renewed interest in Eastern religions, and an interest in pacifist thought, Moses left his studies and immersed himself in the movement. The newly formed SNCC found in Moses a leader of rare courage and strong principles. In many respects, Robert Moses was the embodiment of the early SNCC belief in a "Beloved Community." He endured numerous beatings and jailings. He was also a masterful strategist who backed the move to involve white students in the Voter Registration Drive of 1964 (see Freedom Summer of 1964). Moses gave SNCC a vision and methods of operation, especially the idea of participatory democracy. Frustrated and saddened over the organization's later shift to Black Power,* Moses left it. He traveled to Africa and then returned to Harvard to pursue his doctorate in philosophy.

SELECTED BIBLIOGRAPHY
Taylor Branch, *Parting the Waters: America in the King Years, 1954–63* (1988); Clayborne Carson, *In Struggle: SNCC and the Black Awakening of the 1960s* (1981); James Forman, *The Making of Black Revolutionaries* (1985); Robert Weisbrot, *Freedom Bound: A History of America's Civil Rights Movement* (1990); Howard Zinn, *SNCC: The New Abolitionists* (1964).

Charles T. Pete Banner-Haley

MOTLEY, CONSTANCE BAKER (14 September 1921, New Haven, Conn.–   ). Born in Connecticut of recently emigrated West Indian parents, she studied law at Columbia University. While still a law student,

Constance Baker Motley at swearing-in ceremony. (Negro Almanac Collection, Amistad Research Center, Tulane University, New Orleans.)

she began to work for the Legal Defense and Educational Fund* of the NAACP.* Upon graduating, she went to work full-time for the fund, which, at that time, was fully engaged in an assault on the dual school system. As a black female lawyer, she faced many professional obstacles, but she was undeterred by the challenge. She gained widespread recognition for her defense of civil rights. In 1948, soon after finishing law school, she made her first trip to Mississippi, where she argued a wage equalization case for black teachers. Before she left the organization in 1964, Motley successfully argued nine NAACP cases before the Supreme Court, including Autherine Lucy's* suit for admission to the University of Alabama and James Meredith's* case for admission to the University of Mississippi. In 1964 she entered politics and won a seat in the New York Senate, thereby becoming the first African-American female to ever sit in that state's upper chamber. The following year she won election to the position of Manhattan borough president. In 1966 President Lyndon B. Johnson appointed her to the U.S. District Court for Southern New York, making her the nation's first black woman federal judge. In

1982 she became chief judge and served in that capacity until 1986 when she assumed the status of senior judge.

SELECTED BIBLIOGRAPHY

Jack Bass, *Unlikely Heroes* (1981); *The Negro Almanac* (1971); *New York Times,* 11 September 1963; *Who's Who in Colored America,* 7th ed. (1950).

Charles D. Lowery

MOTON, ROBERT RUSSA (26 August 1867, Rice, Va.–31 May 1940, Capahoosie, Va.). An African-American intellectual and administrator, Moton studied at Hampton Institute* and earned his M.A. degree at Harvard University. He also studied at Wilberforce University, Oberlin College, William and Mary College, and Howard University* and received a Litt.D. from Lincoln University in Pennsylvania. Moton was associated with Hampton Institute until he was appointed to replace Booker T. Washington* as the chief administrator of Tuskegee Institute* in 1915. He played a significant role in forming the National Negro Finance Corporation, and in the early 1920s he was among the sponsors of the National Urban League,* an organization founded in 1911 to address the problems of urban black dwellers. He also served on a

R. R. Moton. (Arthur P. Bedou Photographs, Xavier University Archives, New Orleans.)

committee established by the federal government to deal with discrimination against black troops during World War I. Moton was instrumental in the appointment of Emmett Jay Scott,* a former Booker T. Washington aide, as a special assistant to the secretary of war during World War I. Moton was sent to France by President Woodrow Wilson to investigate the grievances and allegations brought against African-American troops by their white officers. Although the main objective of his mission was to appease the black troops in France, Moton was able to bring black grievances to the attention of President Wilson.

SELECTED BIBLIOGRAPHY

Wilson J. Moses, *The Golden Age of Black Nationalism, 1850–1925* (1978); Robert R. Moton, *Finding a Way Out: An Autobiography* (1921); Robert R. Moton, *What the Negro Thinks* (1929).

Amos J. Beyan

MOUND BAYOU. Founded in the Mississippi Delta (Bolivar County) in 1887 by the freedmen Isaiah T. Montgomery and Benjamin T. Green, this town was conceived as a refuge from white supremacy—a nationalist utopia, built, governed, and occupied exclusively by blacks. A cotton center sustained and surrounded by a larger black agricultural colony of small black landowners and sharecroppers, it was the most celebrated of the several all-black towns formed in the United States during a period of mounting white racism and reflexive black separatism. The community briefly flourished through the entrepreneurial skills and energy of its first citizens (Montgomery and Charles Banks), the endorsement of Booker T. Washington,* and the patronage of such northern philanthropists as Andrew Carnegie. In its heyday, on the eve of World War I, this town of eight hundred inhabitants boasted a bank, a cotton seed oil mill, public and parochial schools, a newspaper, a depot, a telephone exchange and utilities company, and numerous businesses offering "nearly every necessity of the retail and supply trade." Although town leaders valiantly struggled to make it a model of black capitalism, self-help, and group consciousness, it declined rapidly after World War I. Victimized by a modernizing economy, heavy rural-to-urban migration, increased consumer mobility, and a racial system designed to keep African Americans economically dependent on whites, Mound Bayou was described in 1940 by a sympathetic traveler as "more dead than alive." And so it remains in the early 1990s.

SELECTED BIBLIOGRAPHY

Norman Crockett, *The Black Towns* (1979); Janet Sharp Hermann, *Pursuit of a Dream* (1981); Neil R. McMillen, *Dark Journey: Black Mississippians in the Age of Jim Crow* (1989).

Neil R. McMillen

MOYNIHAN REPORT (1965). Assistant secretary of labor and director of the Office of Policy Planning and Research in 1963, Daniel Patrick Moynihan authored *The Negro Family: The Case for National Action*, popularly known as the Moynihan Report. The report had been classified "For Official Use Only" until it became the basis for President Lyndon B. Johnson's address at Howard University's* commencement on 4 June 1965. The report argued that the deterioration of the black family was rooted in slavery and Reconstruction which had forced black society into a matriarchal structure with "often reversed roles of husband and wife." The deteriorated state of the African-American family was viewed as the fundamental source of weakness of the black community, resulting in a cycle of (1) matriarchy, (2) poor school achievement, (3) higher rates of delinquency, (4) alienation of men, (5) higher drug addiction, (6) and welfare dependency and poverty. The report ended by stating, "The policy of the U.S. is to bring Negro Americans to full and equal sharing in responsibilities and rewards of citizenship. To this end, the programs of the Federal government bearing on this objective shall be designed to have the effect, directly or indirectly, of enhancing the stability and resources of the Negro family." Widely discussed in the media, the controversial report was viewed by many as an attack on the black family and as a threat to the integrity of the social sciences and the autonomy of social agencies.

SELECTED BIBLIOGRAPHY
Herbert G. Gutman, *The Black Family in Slavery and Freedom, 1750–1925* (1976); Daniel Patrick Moynihan, *The Negro Family: The Case for National Action* (1965); Lee Rainwater and William L. Yancey, *The Moynihan Report and the Politics of Controversy* (1967).

                                                                        Clarence Hooker

MUHAMMAD, ELIJAH. *See* Poole, Elijah.

MUHAMMAD SPEAKS. This newspaper was the national organ of the Nation of Islam from 1960 to 1975. Created by Elijah Muhammad (see Elijah Poole), the paper served as the chief propaganda voice of the movement. It was initially headed by Malcolm X* of Muhammad's New York Temple. Under his direction *Muhammad Speaks* evolved from a monthly to a weekly paper. During the 1970s the Nation of Islam claimed that the organ had the largest circulation of any black newspaper in the United States. In fact, in 1975 it had 500,000 readers located not only in the United States but also in the West Indies, Central and South America, and Europe. *Muhammad Speaks* reported on social, religious, and political issues that affected black people throughout the world. But foremost, it was the Nation of Islam's voice to the world and represented the philosophies of Elijah Muhammad.

SELECTED BIBLIOGRAPHY

Peter Goldman, *The Death and Life of Malcolm X* (1979); C. Eric Lincoln, *The Black Muslims in America* (1963); Malcolm X, *The Autobiography of Malcolm X* (1965).

Vibert L. White

MUHAMMAD, WALLACE D. (Imam Warith Deen Muhammad) (30 October 1933, Chicago, Ill.–). Son of Elijah Muhammad (see Elijah Poole) and Clara Muhammad, Wallace Muhammad became the spiritual leader of the Black Muslims* on the death of his father in 1975. An orthodox Muslim, he stood as leader against various separatist splinter movements and brought the Nation of Islam into conformity with world Islam, beginning the "decultification" of the sect by lifting the ban on white membership, making certain internal reforms, releasing financial information about the nation, and even changing its name to the American Muslim Mission. This trend was traceable as far back as 1960 when, as minister of the Philadelphia temple, Muhammad helped to launch a fund drive for a NAACP* regional executive, a clear reversal of previous Black Muslim practices.

SELECTED BIBLIOGRAPHY

C. Eric Lincoln, *The Black Muslims in America* (1961); C. Eric Lincoln, *Race Religion, and the Continuing American Dilemma* (1984); *New York Times*, 17 June 1975.

Ray Branch

MUIR v. LOUISVILLE PARK THEATRICAL ASSOCIATION, 347 U.S. 971 (1954). This case extended the principle of the unconstitutionality of racial segregation to public facilities which are leased to nonpublic entities. James W. Muir, a black resident of Louisville, Kentucky, was refused the purchase of a ticket to a production in a city-owned amphitheater which had been leased to a nonprofit theatrical association. Muir brought suit claiming that the equal protection clause of the Fourteenth Amendment* prohibits racial segregation in publicly owned facilities. The lower courts rejected the claim on the grounds that, although the city owned the facility, it was leased to a nonpublic entity to which the Fourteenth Amendment did not apply. In the landmark *Brown v. Board of Education* school desegregation case of 1954, the Supreme Court ruled that racial segregation in public education violates the equal protection clause of the Fourteenth Amendment. Through a series of unanimous opinions, the Court summarily extended this principle to all public facilities. In *Muir*, the Supreme Court vacated the lower court decision and in a terse unanimous opinion ordered that its ruling in *Brown* be applied to publicly owned facilities whether operated by a public body or leased to a nonpublic entity.

SELECTED BIBLIOGRAPHY

Henry J. Abraham, *Freedom and the Court, Civil Rights and Liberties in the United States* (1988); Derrick A. Bell, Jr., *Race, Racism and American Law* (1980).

Frederick G. Slabach

MURRAY, ANNA PAULINE (Pauli) (20 November 1910, Baltimore, Md.–1 July 1985, Pittsburgh, Pa.). The daughter of William Henry and Agnes Georgianna Fitzgerald Murray, she was orphaned at an early age and reared by her grandmother and aunts in Durham, North Carolina. She is remembered principally as the first black woman Episcopal priest (ordained in 1977) and as a cofounder of the National Organization for Women, but her remarkably varied career included the law, academics, and creative writing as well. After graduating from Hunter College, in New York, she unsuccessfully attempted to desegregate the University of North Carolina School of Law in 1938. During several years of civil rights activism, she was arrested for refusing to sit at the back of a bus in Virginia in 1940 and for organizing sit-ins in Washington, D.C. Law degrees subsequently earned at Howard University* and the University of California, Berkeley, prepared her for stints as deputy attorney general of California in 1946, attorney for the American Jewish Congress, 1946–1947, and a private law practice in New York City, 1956–1960. She later taught at the University of Ghana, Benedict College, Brandeis University, and Boston University. Her writings include a volume of poetry, *Dark Testament, and Other Poems* (1970) and two autobiographical books, *Proud Shoes: The Story of an American Family* (1956) and *Song in a Weary Throat: An American Pilgrimage* (1987), which document her unusual life and family background.

SELECTED BIBLIOGRAPHY

Pauli Murray, *Song in a Weary Throat: An American Pilgrimage* (1987); Obituary, *New York Times*, 4 July 1985.

Brenda M. Eagles

MUSTE, ABRAHAM JOHN (8 January 1885, Zierkzee, the Netherlands–11 February 1967, New York, N.Y.). Clergyman, labor organizer, civil liberties advocate, and preeminent leader of the American peace movement, he championed racial justice. In the 1930s he fought union racism. During World War II he encouraged conscientious objectors' struggles against segregation in federal prisons and civilian public service camps. As executive secretary of the Fellowship of Reconciliation* (FOR), he authorized the founding of the Congress of Racial Equality* (CORE) and allocated staff and money for its early projects. An essay he wrote in 1943, "What the Bible Teaches about Freedom," was distributed widely in African-American churches and organizations.

Through FOR and, after 1953, the War Resisters League, Muste mentored numerous civil rights activists, including Bayard Rustin* and James M. Lawson, Jr.* He prodded Martin Luther King, Jr.,* to take a bolder stand against war. Conversely, he urged peace advocates to attack racism. He was a key advisor in the Albany, Georgia, sit-in,* sparked when an interracial "Quebec to Guantanamo" peace team was arrested in 1963. Muste worked fervently to unite the peace and civil rights movements against the war in Vietnam. He died in February 1967 but would have been gratified that half a million antiwar demonstrators attended the 15 April rally he had helped plan, which featured as principal speaker Martin Luther King, Jr.

SELECTED BIBLIOGRAPHY

Barbara Deming, *Prison Notes* (1966); Nat Hentoff, *Peace Agitator: The Story of A. J. Muste* (1963); A. J. Muste, "Rifle Squads or the Beloved Community," *Liberation* (May 1964), 1–6; A. J. Muste, "What the Bible Teaches about Freedom" (pamphlet, 1943); Jo Ann Ooiman Robinson, *Abraham Went Out: A Biography of A. J. Muste* (1981).

Jo Ann O. Robinson

THE MYTH OF THE NEGRO PAST. This path-breaking 1941 monograph, written by anthropologist Melville J. Herskovits (1895–1963), was aimed at disproving the myth that people of African descent had no past. Sophisticated institutions had existed in Africa, and blacks in the Americas had evolved distinct cultures. Herskovits charted Africanisms within African-American communities, and by so doing, stimulated heated debates concerning cultural primacy in African-American life. This book, connected with African independence and civil rights movements, challenged the supremacist notion that European culture singularly triumphs when in contact with non-Western societies. It served as one engine to African-American and African diaspora studies.

SELECTED BIBLIOGRAPHY

W.E.B. Du Bois, "Review of *The Myth of the Negro Past* by Melville J. Herskovits," *Annals of the American Academy* 222 (1942), 226–27; Melville J. Herskovits, *The Myth of the Negro Past*, with new introduction by Sidney Mintz (1990); W. Jackson, "Melville J. Herskovits and the Search for Afro-American Culture," in G. W. Stocking, Jr., ed., *Malinowski, Rivers, Benedict and Others* (1986); George E. Simpson, *Melville J. Herskovits* (1973).

Lisa Brock

N

NAACP. *See* National Association for the Advancement of Colored People.

NAACP v. ALABAMA, 377 U.S. 288 (1964). The last of four cases brought by the Alabama branch of the NAACP* before the U.S. Supreme Court (1958–1964), this case was an attempt to prevent Alabama from ousting the organization from the state. In June 1956, Alabama's attorney general sued the NAACP to bar it from the state charging that it had not registered as an out-of-state corporation. Meanwhile, the Alabama circuit court ordered the group to submit its membership lists and numerous other records or incur a $100,000 fine. In *NAACP v. Alabama* (1958), a unanimous Supreme Court ruled that this Alabama requirement violated NAACP members' rights to freedom of association. It vacated the fine and ordered the Alabama court to try the case on its merits. The court refused to do so, forcing the NAACP to return to the Supreme Court two additional times (1959, 1961) before the Alabama court ruled on the original charges. In 1962, it permanently banned the NAACP from doing business in the state. A unanimous Supreme Court in 1964 overturned this decision, ruling that the "freedom of individuals to associate for the collective advocacy of ideas" was a fundamental constitutional right. The Court ordered Alabama to qualify the NAACP as a legal organization.

SELECTED BIBLIOGRAPHY

Richard Bardolph, ed., *The Civil Rights Record: Black Americans and the Law, 1849–1970* (1970); Taylor Branch, *Parting the Waters: America in the King Years, 1954–63* (1988); "Case Comments," *University of Pennsylvania Law Review* 112 (1963), 148; Ann Fagan Ginger, *The Law, the Supreme Court and the People's Right* (1974); Loren

President John Kennedy greets an NAACP delegation at the White House, 1962. (Negro Almanac Collection, Amistad Research Center, Tulane University, New Orleans.)

Miller, *The Petitioners: The Story of the Supreme Court of the United States and the Negro* (1966).

Dorothy A. Autrey

NAACP v. ST. LOUIS–SAN FRANCISCO RAILROAD, 297 I.C.C. 335 (1955). Jim Crow* practices in interstate public transportation suffered a major defeat with this decision. For the first time, the Interstate Commerce Commission (ICC) rejected the separate but equal doctrine* of *Plessy v. Ferguson** and banned racial segregation on trains and in waiting rooms serving interstate travelers. The NAACP* argued its case against fifteen southern railway companies before a hearing of the ICC in July 1954. With evidence compiled over a three-year period and assistance from the Justice Department as amicus curiae, the NAACP demonstrated the existence of Jim Crow policies on all but one of the defendant railways. Building on the recent decision in *Brown v. Board of Education,** the ICC determined that segregated facilities subjected "Negro passengers to undue and unreasonable disadvantages" in violation of the Interstate Commerce Act. It then ordered that discriminatory policies be "removed" by 10 January 1956. In the companion case of *Keys v. Carolina Coach Company,** the ICC extended its order to buses and terminals; however, the decisions did not cover railway station restaurants or intrastate travel. As a result, many southern states managed to circumvent the rulings until the ICC issued a new decree in 1961 that abolished segregation in any facility that jointly served interstate and intrastate passengers.

SELECTED BIBLIOGRAPHY
Catherine A. Barnes, *Journey from Jim Crow: The Desegregation of Southern Transit* (1983); Minnie Finch, *The NAACP: Its Fight for Justice* (1981); *New York Times*, 26, 27 November 1955; Robert W. Steele, "Recent Decisions," *Michigan Law Review* 54 (1956), 1175–77.

Jack E. Davis

NASHVILLE SIT-INS. On 12 February 1960, about forty college students, primarily from Fisk University* and the American Baptist Theological Seminary, staged a sit-in at Woolworth's lunch counter with the intention of integrating eating establishments in Nashville, Tennessee. Well-organized and counseled by Vanderbilt University theology student James M. Lawson, Jr.,* to use passive resistance or the Gandhi method, they sat quietly at the counter. Their numbers increased daily; white hecklers harassed them, and hundreds were arrested. A city biracial committee was formed; by May, the downtown lunch counters began integrating. These sit-ins and others contributed to the formation of the Student Nonviolent Coordinating Committee.*

SELECTED BIBLIOGRAPHY
Kenneth B. Clark, "The Civil Rights Movement: Momentum and Organization," *Daedalus* 95 (Winter 1966), 239–67; *Knoxville News Sentinel*, 15 March 1960; Ruth Searles and J. Allen Williams, Jr., "Negro College Students' Participation in Sit-Ins," *Social Forces* 40 (March 1962), 215–20; Harvard Sitkoff, *The Struggle for Black Equality, 1954–1980* (1981).

Jane F. Lancaster

NASHVILLE STUDENT MOVEMENT. Under the leadership of James M. Lawson, Jr.,* Diane Nash, and John Lewis,* the Nashville Student Movement, in Nashville, Tennessee, was one of the largest and best organized student groups to conduct nonviolent sit-ins during the early 1960s. Noted for its careful, disciplined protests, preceded by workshops on nonviolent philosophy and tactics and tests of prospective targets, the group met with a fair degree of success in desegregating some Nashville public accommodations and calling attention to instances of discrimination throughout the city. As an organization, it played a pivotal role in the Shaw University retreat out of which the Student Nonviolent Coordinating Committee* emerged in 1960.

SELECTED BIBLIOGRAPHY
Taylor Branch, *Parting the Waters: America in the King Years 1954–63* (1988); Clayborne Carson, *In Struggle: SNCC and the Black Awakening in the 1960s* (1981); David J. Garrow, *Bearing the Cross: Martin Luther King, Jr., and the Southern Christian Leadership Conference* (1986); Harvard Sitkoff, *The Struggle for Black Equality, 1954–*

1980 (1981); Charles U. Smith, "The Sit-ins and the New Negro Student," *Journal of Intergroup Relations* 2 (Summer 1961), 223–29; Milton Viorst, *Fire in the Streets: America in the 1960s* (1979).

Marshall Hyatt

NATIONAL ADVISORY COMMISSION ON CIVIL DISORDERS. *See* Kerner Commission.

NATIONAL ASSOCIATION FOR THE ADVANCEMENT OF COL-ORED PEOPLE. Shocked by the violence directed against black people in the Springfield, Illinois, race riots* in 1908, William English Walling, a reporter who had covered the riots, Mary White Ovington,* a New York social worker and third-generation abolitionist, and Henry Moskowitz, another social worker, called for a conference on the so-called Negro problem to be held on Abraham Lincoln's birthday in 1909. Quick to join this group were other "neo-abolitionists," such as Oswald Garrison Villard,* the grandson of William Lloyd Garrison; members of the Niagara Movement,* including W.E.B. Du Bois,* and a prominent group of progressives, including Jane Addams, John Dewey, Ida Wells Barnett,* and William Dean Howells. In 1910 the National Association for the Advancement of Colored People (NAACP) was formally founded with Moorfield Storey,* a distinguished Boston attorney, as the first president.

The founding of the NAACP was a clear rejection by northern white and black progressives of Booker T. Washington's* accommodationist approach. Instead of accommodation, the NAACP strategy was to use publicity, protest, and legal redress to fight for equality and justice for African Americans. The first national publicity campaign was directed against lynching.* Indeed, when the NAACP was founded, lynchings were still averaging about seventy a year. By 1940 the number had dropped to four a year. In large part the reduction was due to the creation of public awareness through the publication of *Thirty Years of Lynching in the United States, 1889–1918** as well as pamphlets and speakers on the subject. Although their efforts were directed toward reducing the number of lynchings, the NAACP was never able to secure a federal antilynching bill.

The most important work of the association has been its legal approach to the redress of racial grievances. The NAACP, first through organizationally retained lawyers, then through its legal bureau, and now finally through the NAACP Legal Defense and Educational Fund,* is partially or wholly responsible for striking down the grandfather clause,* restrictive covenants by city ordinance, white primaries,* all-white juries, and public facility segregation (most notably school segregation).

Because of its legal approach to the redress of racial grievances, the NAACP has always been acutely sensitive to and aware of nominations to the Supreme Court. The NAACP's first successful national campaign was a lobbying/publicity campaign directed against the Supreme Court nomination of John J. Parker in 1930. The NAACP, along with the American Federation of Labor and later Senate Democrats and progressive Senate Republicans, was able to defeat this nomination. The NAACP has also been successful in helping to defeat the Supreme Court nominations of Judge Clement F. Haynesworth (1969), Judge G. Harrold Carswell (1970), and Judge Robert H. Bork (1986).

Other successful publicity campaigns were the "Don't Buy Where You Can't Work" movement* in the 1940s and, perhaps most important, the 1963 March on Washington* to help gain passage of what became the Civil Rights Act of 1964.* The desegregation of the United States is in a large measure due to the efforts of the NAACP and surely will be one of its most enduring legacies.

SELECTED BIBLIOGRAPHY

Kenneth W. Goings, *The NAACP Comes of Age: The Defeat of Judge John J. Parker* (1990); Charles F. Kellogg, *NAACP: A History of the National Association for the Advancement of Colored People* (1967); James M. McPherson, *The Abolitionist Legacy: From Reconstruction to the NAACP* (1975).

Kenneth W. Goings

NATIONAL ASSOCIATION FOR THE PROMOTION OF LABOR UNIONISM AMONG NEGROES.

Founded in 1919 by A. Philip Randolph* and Chandler Owen, socialist editors of *The Messenger*,* this group encouraged blacks to join with whites in a united, interracial, class-based labor movement. Located in New York, its advisory board members included such prominent white socialists as Morris Hilquit and Rose Schneiderman. Short-lived, the association disbanded in the early 1920s. Still, it remains one of the earliest and most significant interracial attempts to combine all workers into the organized labor movement and thus improve the general condition of the entire working class.

SELECTED BIBLIOGRAPHY

Philip S. Foner and Ronald L. Lewis, eds., *The Black Worker: A Documentary History from Colonial Times to the Present*, vol. V; *The Black Worker from 1900 to 1919* (1980); Charles L. Franklin, *The Negro Labor Unionist of New York* (1936); "The Negro and the American Federation of Labor" and "Our Reason for Being," *Messenger* 8 (August 1919), 10–12; Sterling D. Spero and Abraham L. Harris, *The Black Worker: The Negro and the Labor Movement* (1974).

Robert Cvornyek

NATIONAL ASSOCIATION OF COLORED WOMEN.

Founded in 1896 in Washington, D.C., the National Association of Colored Women (NACW) united the National League of Colored Women, the National

Federation of Afro-American Women, and over one hundred other clubs. In the preamble to its constitution, the organizers stated their intention "to furnish evidence of the moral, mental and material progress made by people of color through the efforts of our women." Ten years after its founding, the association had grown considerably and was addressing issues crucial to the progress of the race, such as lynching,* the convict lease system, and education. During World War I, the association boasted a membership of 300,000 with departments concentrating on suffrage, education, rural life conditions, motherhood, health conditions, and lynching. Among the special projects undertaken by the NACW was an agreement to assist the Frederick Douglass Memorial and Historical Association in restoring Douglass's home in Anacostia, in Washington, D.C. In 1916 the women pledged to clear the home of all indebtedness and to restore it to its former beauty in order that black youth might visit a historical site associated with a great black leader.

SELECTED BIBLIOGRAPHY

Elizabeth L. Davis, *Lifting as They Climb: The National Association of Colored Women* (1933); Gerda A. Lerner, ed., *Black Women in White America: A Documentary History* (1972); J. L. Nichols and William H. Crogman, *Progress of a Race* (1929); Mary Church Terrell, *A Colored Woman in a White World* (1940).

Betty L. Plummer

NATIONAL BAPTIST CONVENTION, USA. Founded in 1895 with headquarters in Nashville, Tennessee, in response to inferior racial treatment received by African-American Baptists working within and for the white Southern and Northern Baptist Conventions, the new all-black convention sent missionaries to West Africa, established five independent black Baptist colleges, and began a publishing board. Since 1924 the National Baptists and the Southern Baptists have operated jointly the American Baptist Seminary (now College) in Nashville. In the 1960s, a number of its students, including John Lewis,* were leaders in the civil rights movement. The National Baptist Convention has become the largest African-American denomination in the world, with eight million members in 1984. But in 1915, there was a split and the National Baptist Convention of America was organized. In 1961, another split (in part related to civil rights issues) established the Progressive National Baptist Convention. This second split resulted from the opposition of National Baptist Convention President Joseph H. Jackson to Martin Luther King, Jr.s,* social activism. In 1982, Theodore J. Jemison, a former civil rights leader, became convention president. As a sign of a new civil rights commitment, Jesse Jackson* and Benjamin Hooks,* the NAACP executive director, participated in the June 1989 dedication of the convention's new headquarters in Nashville.

SELECTED BIBLIOGRAPHY

Adam Fairclough, *To Redeem the Soul of America: The Southern Christian Leadership Conference and Martin Luther King, Jr.* (1987); Miles M. Fisher, *Short History of the Baptist Denomination* (1933); Joseph H. Jackson, "National Baptist Philosophy of Civil Rights," in Milton C. Sernett, ed., *Afro-American Religious History: A Documentary Witness* (1985); Emmanuel L. McCall, *Black Church Life-Styles* (1986); James M. McPherson, *The Abolitionist Legacy: From Reconstruction to the NAACP* (1975); Charles L. Sanders, "$10 Million Headquarters Signals New Course for National Baptist Convention, U.S.A., Inc.," *Ebony* (October 1989).

Lawrence H. Williams

NATIONAL BROTHERHOOD WORKERS OF AMERICA. Established in 1919, the National Brotherhood Workers of America (NBWA) reflected the move toward independent black unions following World War I. Under the leadership of T. J. Pree and R. T. Simms, the NBWA planned to organize and federate all African-American workers and thus counteract the discriminatory policies of unions affiliated with the American Federation of Labor. Membership remained concentrated in Virginia's Tidewater area, but, at its peak, the brotherhood attracted thousands of workers in twelve states and the District of Columbia. The short-lived NBWA collapsed in 1921, but not before it addressed squarely the issue of racial discrimination in the organized labor movement and offered black workers an alternative means of fighting employers and challenging white-controlled unions for economic justice.

SELECTED BIBLIOGRAPHY

Philip S. Foner, *Organized Labor and the Black Worker, 1619–1981* (1982); Philip S. Foner and Ronald L. Lewis, eds., *The Black Worker: A Documentary History from Colonial Times to the Present,* vol. V; *The Black Worker from 1900 to 1919* (1980); "The National Brotherhood Association," *Messenger* 8 (August 1919), 7; "Report of Resolutions Committee of the National Brotherhood Workers of America," *Messenger* 11 (December 1919), 16–19; Sterling D. Spero and Abraham L. Harris, *The Black Worker: The Negro and the Labor Movement* (1974).

Robert Cvornyek

NATIONAL CATHOLIC CONFERENCE FOR INTERRACIAL JUSTICE. Founded in 1960, in Washington, D.C., as the successor to the Catholic Interracial Council* (which was itself founded in 1934), the conference is a nonprofit organization historically focused on generating concern for interracial justice in the white community and fostering black-white dialogue and common action. Early accomplishments included cochairing the 1963 March on Washington,* mobilizing Catholics to join the 1965 Selma to Montgomery March,* and calling for federal legislation against civil rights violence in the South. It has also promoted integrated Catholic education and greater sensitivity to minority concerns within inner-city Catholic schools. In the 1990s, with the growing numbers of Hispanic, Asian-American, and Native American Catholics, the conference has broadened its agenda to creating a multiracially and multiculturally inclusive Catholic church in the United States.

SELECTED BIBLIOGRAPHY

John Hope Franklin, *From Slavery to Freedom: A History of Negro Americans*, 5th ed. (1980); National Catholic Conference for Interracial Justice, *A Future without Racism* and *Still Building Bridges between Races and Cultures* (pamphlets published by NCCIJ, 3033 Fourth Street, N.E., Washington, D.C.).

Andrew M. Manis

NATIONAL COMMITTEE TO ABOLISH THE POLL TAX. In 1938, encouraged by President Franklin D. Roosevelt, progressive Southerners formed the Southern Conference for Human Welfare* to seek ways of extending economic and political democracy to their region. Two of its members, Joseph Gelders and Virginia Foster Durr* of Alabama, headed

The National Committee to Abolish the Poll Tax helped black women to vote for the first time, on 13 February 1946, in Fulton County, Georgia. (Special Collections, Pullen Library, Georgia State University.)

a Civil Rights Committee to persuade Congress to repeal the poll tax*
in the eight southern states that had imposed it. In 1941, they chartered
a separate National Committee to Abolish the Poll Tax, consisting of
labor, liberal, and civil rights groups. Actively cooperating with the
NAACP,* the anti–poll tax federation nevertheless stressed that impoverished southern whites would benefit more than disfranchised blacks
from abolition of the suffrage burden. Headquartered in Washington,
D.C., the committee lobbied for several bills that won House approval
but failed in the Senate. Although the organization collapsed in 1948, it
succeeded in turning public opinion in the South against the poll tax.
By the mid–1950s Georgia, South Carolina, and Tennessee had abolished
their restrictions, and Alabama had reduced its required payment. In
1964, the ratification of the Twenty-fourth Amendment removed the poll
tax requirement in national elections, and two years later, in *Harper v.
Virginia State Board of Elections*,* the U.S. Supreme Court eliminated it
in state and local elections.

SELECTED BIBLIOGRAPHY

Virginia Durr, *Outside the Magic Circle* (1985); Thomas A. Krueger, *And Promises
to Keep: The Southern Conference for Human Welfare, 1938–1948* (1967); Steven F.
Lawson, *Black Ballots: Voting Rights in the South, 1944–1969* (1976); Frederic D.
Ogden, *The Poll Tax in the South* (1958).

Steven F. Lawson

NATIONAL CONFERENCE OF NEGRO YOUTH. The National Conference of Negro Youth grew out of its New Deal umbrella organization,
the National Youth Administration, a Works Progress Administration
subsidiary. Mary Mcleod Bethune* was the moving spirit behind the
conference. As the unofficial head of President Franklin D. Roosevelt's
Black Cabinet,* she utilized government facilities and goodwill to promote a series of conferences focused on the problems of black Americans.
One of the most notable of these conferences was a three-day affair held
in Washington, D.C., in 1937. An important aim was the enhancement
of federal programs for black Americans. Other concerns were increased
economic opportunities for blacks, an upgrading of educational and
recreational facilities for black youth, better housing and health care,
and equal protection under the law. Eleanor Roosevelt* addressed the
conference, along with several members of her husband's cabinet. The
National Conference of Negro Youth, and the other Washington conferences, garnered unprecedented national publicity for the plight of
black Americans. By reiterating the litany of demands articulated by the
NAACP,* the National Urban League,* and the National Negro Congress,* this effort gave impetus to the civil rights movement.

SELECTED BIBLIOGRAPHY

Ralph J. Bunche, *The Political Status of the Negro in the Age of FDR*, edited with
an introduction by Dewey W. Grantham (1973); Joyce B. Ross, "Mary Mcleod

Bethune and the National Youth Administration: A Case Study of Power Relationships in the Black Cabinet of Franklin D. Roosevelt," *Journal of Negro History*
60 (January 1975), 1–29; Harvard Sitkoff, *A New Deal for Blacks: The Emergence of
Civil Rights as a National Issue, vol. 1, The Depression Decade* (1978); Charles H.
Wesley, *International Library of Afro-American Life and History: The Quest for Equality*
(1976).

Joe Louis Caldwell

NATIONAL COUNCIL OF NEGRO WOMEN. Educator Mary McLeod
Bethune* founded the National Council of Negro Women (NCNW) in
New York City in December 1935 and served as its president until her
retirement in 1949. Bethune united the major national African-American
women's associations into the NCNW, focusing activities on racial discrimination, the enhancement of better international relationships, and
national liberal causes. The NCNW served as a clearinghouse for federal
legislation affecting women and children, sponsored an archives, and
published a quarterly, *Aframerican Woman's Journal*. As president of the
NCNW, Bethune strengthened the organization by establishing chapters
in major cities and, with a generous donation from Marshall Field III,
was able to purchase a permanent headquarters building in Washington,
D.C.

SELECTED BIBLIOGRAPHY
Franklin Fosdick, "War among the Women," *Negro Digest* 8 (February 1950), 21–
25; Stanley S. Jacobs, "The Story of Mary Bethune," *This Month* (March 1947),
110–13; Edward T. James and Janet Wilson James, eds., *Notable American Women*
(1971).

Janice M. Leone

NATIONAL EQUAL RIGHTS LEAGUE. This name refers to two different political organizations. One of these stemmed from a series of
national Negro conventions held between 1830 and 1864. The October
1864 convention created a National Equal Rights League to promote the
civil rights of African Americans. John Mercer Langston* was chosen as
its first president. A second National Equal Rights League was the brainchild of Monroe Trotter* of Boston. Concerned with the accommodationism of Booker T. Washington* and estranged from W.E.B. Du Bois,*
Trotter's organization sought to prevent William Howard Taft's election
to the presidency in 1908. The organization foundered and dissolved
because Trotter's brand of direct action* was too peripheral to the mainstream tactics of the emerging NAACP.*

SELECTED BIBLIOGRAPHY
Howard H. Bell, ed., *Minutes of the Proceedings of the National Negro Conventions,
1830–1964* (1969); Robert H. Brisbane, *The Black Vanguard: Origins of the Negro
Social Revolution, 1900–1960* (1970); Stephen Fox, *The Guardian of Boston: William*

Monroe Trotter (1970); Vincent Harding, *There Is a River: The Black Struggle for Freedom in America* (1981).

Malik Simba

NATIONAL FREEDMEN'S RELIEF ASSOCIATION. Urged on by leaders of the American Missionary Association,* opponents of slavery in New York City established the National Freedmen's Relief Association on 22 February 1862. The organization sought to aid ex-slaves on the South Carolina Sea Islands by providing instructors for schools, direction for the cultivation of plantations, and supplies. In 1863 the association joined similar groups to advocate organization of what would become the Freedmen's Bureau.* The association in 1865 cooperated with other societies to support black schools across the South through the American Freedmen's Aid Commission, which expanded into the American Freedmen's Union Commission from 1866 to 1868.

SELECTED BIBLIOGRAPHY
Robert C. Morris, *Reading, 'Riting, and Reconstruction: The Education of Freedmen in the South, 1861–1870* (1981); Willie Lee Rose, *Rehearsal for Reconstruction: The Port Royal Experiment* (1964).

Alwyn Barr

NATIONAL MEDICAL ASSOCIATION. Founded in Atlanta, Georgia, in 1895 by a group of black men attending the Cotton States and International Exposition, the National Medical Association (NMA) was designed as a national organization for black physicians, dentists, and pharmacists. Specifically, its purpose was to unite "men and women of African descent who are legally and honorably engaged in the cognate professions of medicine, surgery, pharmacy and dentistry." Since its inception, members of the NMA have struggled to end any discrimination and segregation directed toward health care professionals and discrimination in health care facilities. During World War II the NMA opposed the construction of segregated Veterans Administration hospitals. In 1945 representatives from the NMA and other black groups met with the director of the Veterans Administration to discuss policies for the complete integration of the veteran hospital system. At the same time, the NMA opposed federal funding for segregated hospitals for the general population. It was especially critical of the Hill-Burton Hospital Construction Act (1946) with its separate but equal* clause which allowed for further creation of Jim Crow* hospitals at government expense. During the civil rights crusade of the 1960s and 1970s, the NMA intensified its campaign to end segregation in hospital facilities and demanded that black physicians and surgeons be allowed privileges in all hospitals.

SELECTED BIBLIOGRAPHY
Benjamin F. Mays, "The Diamond Jubilee of the National Medical Association," *Journal of the National Medical Association* 62 (November 1970), 408–10; Herbert

M. Morais, *The History of the Negro in Medicine* (1967); Charles E. Odegaard, *Minorities in Medicine* (1977); Dietrich C. Reitzes, *Negroes and Medicine* (1958).

Betty L. Plummer

NATIONAL NEGRO BUSINESS LEAGUE. The idea for such an organization may have come from W.E.B. Du Bois,* but Booker T. Washington* created it in 1900 in Boston. It sought to achieve racial economic independence in an increasingly commercial age. The first annual meeting drew 300 delegates, representing business and the professions. In 1915, 3,000 delegates from 300 chapters attended its convention. Total membership, in thirty-six states and West Africa, ranged from 5,000 to 40,000. Life memberships at $25 each reached nearly 100 by 1915, and two philanthropists—Julius Rosenwald* and Andrew Carnegie—contributed generously. Many local chapters existed only on paper, however, and others were torn by internecine personal disputes. Washington resolutely staffed the league with his conservative loyalists. Lynching,* segregation, and race riots incurred only oblique condemnation. Instead, the league concentrated on self-help, race loyalty, and material success. Offering encouragement and commercial instruction, the league remained, until Washington's death, an integral part of the Tuskegee Machine, a resolute opponent of the more radical black organizations. In the 1930s, it emphasized interracial cooperation because black "progress will tend to strengthen the whole structure of American business." During World War II, the league promoted victory gardens, thrift, and the easing of racial tensions.

SELECTED BIBLIOGRAPHY
Louis R. Harlan, "Booker T. Washington and the National Negro Business League," in William G. Shade and Roy C. Herrenkohl, eds., *Seven on Black: Reflections on the Negro Experience in America* (1969); August Meier, *Negro Thought in America, 1880–1915: Racial Ideologies in the Age of Booker T. Washington* (1963).

Richard W. Resh

NATIONAL NEGRO CONGRESS. The National Negro Congress (NNC), although it never established itself as a mass movement, was a noble attempt at racial solidarity. The call to membership was made to all African Americans and their organizations, churches, unions, and political groups. The NNC urged unionization of African-American women workers, desegregation of public accommodations and schools, and protection of migrant workers. It lobbied for antilynching legislation and against fascism. Its first president, A. Philip Randolph,* cautioned against Communist party* infiltration in the first meeting held in Chicago, Illinois, in 1936. By 1940, the NNC was a Communist-controlled group, and remained under Federal Bureau of Investigation surveillance until the 1950s.

SELECTED BIBLIOGRAPHY
Robert L. Allen, *Reluctant Reformers* (1974); Scholarly Resources Microfilm, "FBI Files," 1986; Monroe Work, ed., *Negro Year Book: 1937–1938* (1937).

Aingred G. Dunston

NATIONAL URBAN LEAGUE. Officials of this organization consider it the most versatile of the groups founded for the advancement of black Americans. The seventieth anniversary *Journal,* published in 1980, summed up the role of the league as being "a provider of direct services; a research institution; a laboratory in which human development programs are conceived and implemented; an advocate for civil rights, equity and justice; a catalytic force that unites diverse people in pursuit of unselfish goals; a dreamer and a doer." In October 1911, three organizations, which had been formed between 1905 and 1910 to help black migrants adjust to urban life, merged to form the National Urban League. At first, the league was primarily a New York organization, but the founders intended that it become a national movement. The first directors, George Haynes* and Eugene Kinckle Jones,* led in developing programs and structures applicable to cities throughout the country. The mass migration of black workers to northern cities during World War I accelerated the league's growth. Soon, there were branches in most industrial cities. Throughout its history, the league has participated in efforts to end discrimination within the ranks of organized labor and in federal programs. Lester B. Granger,* who became executive director in 1941, worked to foster the integration of the armed forces. From 1923 to 1948, the league published the magazine *Opportunity** which published articles on black life and served as a medium of expression for black writers and artists. After Whitney M. Young, Jr.,* became executive director in 1961, the league became an active participant in the civil rights movement. League branches were established in many southern cities. In 1968, in response to the Black Power* movement and to the urban violence of the 1960s, the league concentrated more of its resources on helping the underclass in black communities. Young called these efforts to aid high school dropouts, to launch voter registration drives, to promote community health, and to start neighborhood improvement programs the league's "New Thrust" approach. The league's work in civil rights and in community improvement has continued under Young's successors, Vernon E. Jordan, Jr.,* and John Jacob.

SELECTED BIBLIOGRAPHY
Jesse Thomas Moore, Jr., *A Search for Equality: The National Urban League, 1910–1961* (1981); National Urban League, *70th Anniversary* (1980); Guichard Parris and Lester Brooks, *Blacks in the City: A History of the National Urban League* (1971); Arvarh E. Strickland, *History of the Chicago Urban League* (1966); Nancy J. Weiss,

The National Urban League, 1910–1940 (1974); Nancy J. Weiss, *Whitney M. Young, Jr., and the Struggle for Civil Rights* (1990).

Arvarh E. Strickland

NATION OF ISLAM. *See* Black Muslims.

NATIVE SON. Chosen as a Book of the Month Club selection when it was published in 1940, *Native Son* gave American readers "a terrible picture of reality which they could see and feel and yet not destroy." Richard Wright* created a searing indictment of institutionalized racism in his novel, for he believed society could not continue to ignore the probable results of its having created the conditions for an underclass in its urban ghettoes. The novel challenged, and continues to challenge, readers regardless of their attitudes about civil rights. It exposes in graphic episodes the deep resentments bred by what Margaret Walker Alexander* has aptly termed "the psychic wound of racism." Through his archetypal hero Bigger Thomas, Wright shows how the poverty and ignorance born of rigid segregation and discrimination can erupt in violence. As a fictional treatment of the sociology of racism, *Native Son* remains unsurpassed as a portrayal of what happens in America's inner cities. *Native Son* provided a prophetic vision of the hatreds unleashed in the urban riots of the 1960s.

SELECTED BIBLIOGRAPHY

Richard Abcarian, ed., *Richard Wright's Native Son: A Critical Handbook* (1970); Houston A. Baker, Jr., ed., *Twentieth-Century Interpretations of Native Son* (1972); Katherine Fishburn, *Richard Wright's Hero* (1977); Joyce Ann Joyce, *Richard Wright's Art of Tragedy* (1986); Richard Macksey and Frank E. Moorer, eds., *Richard Wright: A Collection of Critical Essays* (1984); Margaret Walker, *Richard Wright, Daemonic Genius, A Portrait of the Man, A Critical Look at His Works* (1988).

Jerry Ward

NEAL, CLAUDE (date and place of birth unknown–27 October 1934, Greenwood, Fla.). This twenty-three-year-old, illiterate, black man was lynched in Greenwood, in Jackson County, Florida, on 27 October 1934 for the alleged murder and rape of a young white woman. He was arrested on circumstantial evidence and placed in concealed confinement in Brewton, Alabama. Some men from Jackson County easily abducted Neal and returned him to Florida, where Neal was castrated, forced to eat his penis and testicles, and "horribly mutilated." Walter F. White* of the NAACP* called Neal's lynching "one of the most bestial crimes ever committed by a mob." Neal's lynching received widespread media and newspaper coverage, which White utilized to garner support for a proposed federal antilynching bill.

SELECTED BIBLIOGRAPHY
Walter T. Howard, "Vigilante Justice: Extra-Legal Executions in Florida, 1930–1940" (Ph.D. diss., Florida State University, 1987); Lynching File, Florida State Archives, Tallahassee; James R. McGovern, *Anatomy of a Lynching: The Killing of Claude Neal* (1982); James R. McGovern and Walter T. Howard, "Private Justice and National Concern: The Lynching of Claude Neal," *The Historian* 43 (August 1981), 546–59; National Association for the Advancement of Colored People, *The Lynching of Claude Neal* (1934).

Maxine D. Jones

NEAL v. DELAWARE, 103 U.S. 370 (1880). William Neal was a black man accused of rape in a Delaware court. At his trial Neal's defense attorney moved to dismiss the all-white jury because blacks were systematically and completely excluded from juries in the state. The trial court refused to consider the motion, and Neal was convicted and sentenced to death. In reviewing the trial court's action, the chief justice of Delaware's highest appeals court admitted that blacks were and had always been excluded from juries but explained the phenomenon with the observation that "the great body of black men residing in this State are utterly unqualified by want of intelligence, experience or moral integrity, to sit on juries." When Neal appealed his conviction to the U.S. Supreme Court, the state attorney general also admitted that the state purposefully had excluded blacks from juries.

Justice John Marshall Harlan,* writing for the majority of the Court, declared that the state's open admission of the exclusion of blacks from juries presented a prima facie case of denial "of that equality of protection which has been secured by the Constitution and laws of the United States." He explained that, while the Court would generally presume that states were acting within the dictates of the Fourteenth* and Fifteenth Amendments,* the Delaware chief justice's "violent presumption" that all blacks were "utterly disqualified" for jury service, without further inquiry, denied Neal his constitutional rights. The Supreme Court reversed Neal's conviction and instructed the new trial court to grant him a hearing on his motions challenging the all-white jury.

Although the Supreme Court decision guaranteed Neal a hearing, it in no way guaranteed that blacks would serve on future juries. It only prevented states from recognizing the total exclusion of blacks from juries and cavalierly refusing to consider, even cursorily, the possibility of racial discrimination.

SELECTED BIBLIOGRAPHY
Charles Fairman, *History of the Supreme Court of the United States, Vol. 7, Reconstruction and Reunion 1864–1888 Part II* (1986); Loren Miller, *The Petitioners: The Story of the Supreme Court of the United States and the Negro* (1966); Harvey B.

Rubenstein, "The Case of the 'Violent Presumption': Another Delaware Controversy That Shaped the Constitution," *Delaware Lawyer* 6 (1988), 46.

Kenneth DeVille

NEARING, SCOTT (6 August 1883, Morris Run, Pa.–23 August 1983, Harborside, Vt.). A socialist and pacifist dedicated to civil liberties, Nearing thought society should "provide a good life for all." He attended the University of Pennsylvania (Ph.D. in Economics, 1909), served on child labor committees, and gained notoriety by getting fired from teaching positions at the University of Pennsylvania (1915) and Toledo University (1917) because of his antiwar views. Later, Nearing taught at the Rand School, was a socialist candidate for Congress, and then a farmer. He wrote two books on racism: *Black America* (1924), urging black workers to join whites in a worker's party, and the novel *Free Born* (1932), the violent tale of a black laborer leading a Pennsylvania coal strike.

SELECTED BIBLIOGRAPHY

Scott Nearing, *The Making of a Radical: A Political Autobiography* (1972); Stephen J. Whitfield, *Scott Nearing: Apostle of American Radicalism* (1974).

Linda G. Ford

NEGRO AMERICAN LABOR COUNCIL. Organized in May 1960 as a gathering of black and white trade unionists, unhappy with AFL-CIO inaction against racial discrimination in the labor movement, the council was formed to promote increased black membership in labor unions and black advancement within union administrations. The council's most notable accomplishment was its leadership in organizing the 1963 March on Washington.* Council President A. Philip Randolph* was already planning an Emancipation March to Washington for Jobs, which had aroused little interest. Martin Luther King, Jr.,* heard of Randolph's fading proposal and decided to adopt the idea and expand the scope of the march. Forty thousand union members participated under the council's auspices. The Negro American Labor Council was replaced in 1972 by the Coalition of Black Trade Unionists,* which has continued to seek greater black participation in organized labor.

SELECTED BIBLIOGRAPHY

Adam Fairclough, *To Redeem the Soul of America: The Southern Christian Leadership Conference and Martin Luther King, Jr.* (1987); Philip S. Foner and Ronald L. Lewis, eds., *Black Workers: A Documentary History from Colonial Times to the Present* (1989).

Randall L. Patton

THE NEGRO ARTISAN. Edited by W.E.B. Du Bois* in 1902, this first comprehensive study of black workers exhaustively documented the exclusionary practices of labor unions and the growing frustration of black skilled workers. Arguably the best study in the series of the Atlanta University Conference for the Study of Negro Problems,* *The Negro*

Artisan also provided Du Bois with the empirical data that underlined his growing opposition to industrial education. The monograph, which was reprinted in 1912, combined a historical narrative with surveys of artisans, employer attitudes, training schools, and union practices. It established the standard approach in black labor history for the next fifty years.

SELECTED BIBLIOGRAPHY

Herbert Apetheker, ed., *The Correspondence of W.E.B. Du Bois*, vol. 1 (1973); W.E.B. Du Bois, ed., *The Negro Artisan* 7 (Atlanta, 1902); W.E.B. Du Bois and Augustus Dill, eds., *The Negro American Artisan* 14 (Atlanta, 1912); Francille Rusan Wilson, "The Segregated Scholars: Black Labor Historians, 1895–1950" (Ph.D. diss., University of Pennsylvania, 1988), 77–92; Elliot Rudwick, "W.E.B. Du Bois as a Sociologist," in James Blackwell and Morris Janowitz, eds., *Black Sociologists: Historical and Contemporary Perspectives* (1975).

Francille Rusan Wilson

NEGRO HISTORY BULLETIN. Carter G. Woodson* founded this magazine in October 1937 under the auspices of the Association for the Study of Afro-American Life and History* (ASALH) and served as its managing editor. The initial subscription of $1.00 a year targeted an audience which professional or scholarly publications would not ordinarily reach. Combining scholarly and popular topics, the *Bulletin* early enjoyed a large circulation, which reached 5,000 in 1966 and 7,500 in 1984. The publication provided an invaluable service to black school children by promoting black culture and history and filling gaps in textbooks which often neglected black contributions to America's past. During the 1980s the *Bulletin* failed to meet scheduled publication dates due to a lack of staffing resulting from financial difficulties experienced by the ASALH.

SELECTED BIBLIOGRAPHY

Rayford W. Logan and Michael R. Winston, eds., *Dictionary of American Negro Biography* (1982); Publication Information, *Negro History Bulletin* 1 (October 1937), 47 (July–December 1984).

Thomas D. Cockrell

NEGRO HISTORY WEEK. Negro History Week was first commemorated during the second week of February 1926 to highlight the outstanding accomplishments of African Americans and to call attention to their history. The concept was most vigorously promoted by Carter G. Woodson,* the initiator of the observance. This week was selected to coincide with the birthdates of Frederick Douglass* and Abraham Lincoln. This week-long activity's primary purpose, according to Woodson, was "to stage dramatizations and other exercises in order to demonstrate the role of the Negro in the past and secure for the race the same considerations in the curriculum that we give others." During the peak years of the civil rights era and to the mid–1970s, an increasing demand was made by a wide cross-section of the African-American community to extend the celebration period. This led to expanding the observance to all four weeks of February, which then became Black History Month.

SELECTED BIBLIOGRAPHY

Albert N. D. Brooks, "Proud American Day," Association for the Study of Negro Life and History, Washington, D.C. (1956); Nerissa L. Milton, "Negro History Week, 1958," Association for the Study of Negro Life and History, Washington, D.C. (1958); Edgar A. Toppin, "Carter Woodson Began Black History Week," *Washington Afro-American*, 8 February 1975.

Glenn O. Phillips

NEGRO NEWSPAPER PUBLISHERS' ASSOCIATION. Established in 1940, the association is currently known as the National Newspaper Publishers' Association. It met the need of African-American publishers to establish a relationship between the black press and black business. It improved its members' advertising capabilities and unified their editorial stance on all African-American issues. It was instrumental in breaking the color barrier in the Congressional Press Galleries in 1947, and two of its members further broke social barriers when they traveled with President Harry S. Truman in 1948. Presently, the association gives annual awards and maintains a hall of fame.

SELECTED BIBLIOGRAPHY

Encyclopedia of Associations (1990); Lawrence D. Hogan, *A Black National News Service: The Associated Negro Press and Claude Barnett, 1919–1945* (1984).

Jessie M. Carter

NEGRO PEOPLE'S THEATER. This Harlem-based theatrical company was the first of many independent theater groups established in the 1930s. The founders, Rose McClendon, Dick Campbell, and Muriel Rahn, sought to create a cultural platform in which real drama about black life, with black actors, devoid of denigrating stereotypes, could be performed. The company presented its version of Clifford Odets's *Waiting for Lefty* in 1935 and, in conjunction with the New Theater League, presented Odets's *Remember*, a play about a black family on relief, during the same year. These were the only productions of this theater company.

SELECTED BIBLIOGRAPHY

Malcolm Goldstein, *The Political Stage: American Drama and Theater of the Great Depression* (1974); Errol Hill, ed., *The Theater of Black Americans* (1980); Loften Mitchell, *Black Drama: The Story of the American Negro in the Theater* (1967).

Malik Simba

NEGRO SPIRITUAL. An oral record and classic folk expression of African Americans, the Negro spiritual became a major source of communication for African Americans who refused to reconcile themselves to slavery. The Negro spiritual, first sung on southern plantations, was probably shaped by a mixture of African musical influences, hymns sung in white churches, and music by white composers. It is a vehicle for understanding African-American slave experiences, which provided a medium of black communication that mitigated the debilitating effects of slavery. The Negro spiritual also indicated that slavery was not a closed institution; that the process of dehumanization was not complete; that African Americans were able to maintain their essential humanity; and that African Americans were aesthetically and morally equal to whites. Furthermore, the Negro spiritual represented the sorrow, escape, relief, and rebellious nature of the African American. From its beginning in American musical culture, the Negro spiritual has contained some persistent themes that have helped to explain the African-American ethos in antebellum as well as in postbellum America. The following major ideas permeated these songs: the obtaining of physical freedom in the secular world; death and resurrection in celestial happiness; freedom from white oppression; despair intertwined with confidence and joy; and the notion that African Americans were God's chosen people. Early in its history, the Negro spiritual was denigrated and maligned. As African Americans allegedly had made no worthwhile contributions to shaping American culture, the Negro spirituals were viewed with contempt. It was through the efforts of the famed Jubilee Singers* of Fisk University that the Negro spiritual was rescued from obscurity. This group, organized around 1875, popularized this music and enhanced its acceptance throughout the world.

SELECTED BIBLIOGRAPHY

James H. Cone, *The Spirituals and the Blues: An Interpretation* (1972); Miles Mark Fisher, *Negro Slave Songs in the United States* (1953); James Weldon Johnson and Rosamund Johnson, *The Book of American Negro Spirituals* (1926); Lawrence W. Levine, *Black Culture and Black Consciousness: Afro-American Folk Thought from Slavery to Freedom* (1977); Alain Locke, "The Negro Spirituals," in Alain Locke, ed., *The New Negro* (1925); J.B.T. Marsh, *The Story of the Jubilee Singers: With Their Songs* (1881).

Phillip McGuire

THE NEGRO WORKER. This pamphlet, written by Abram Lincoln Harris* for the National Committee for Labor Action, addressed the problems African Americans were having in the "entire labor movement." Depicting the problem as one of vital concern, the essay provided statistics for the number of African-American workers involved in the unions, which amounted to 45,000 in affiliated and 11,000 in independent unions. It listed twenty-six unions with racial bars, including the names of eleven American Federation of Labor and thirteen unaffiliated unions. It further claimed that, in 1930, nine federated and ten unaffiliated unions had provisions in their constitutions barring blacks from membership.

SELECTED BIBLIOGRAPHY
Abram L. Harris, *The Negro Worker* (1930); Ray Marshall, *The Negro Worker* (1967).
Jessie M. Carter

NEGRO WORKERS COUNCILS. With the New Deal passage of Section 7a of the 1933 Wagner Act, which gave workers the right to organize and bargain collectively, the National Urban League* urged African-American workers, through Negro workers councils, to "seek union membership and maintain it, even when their presence was undesired by white officers or members of local unions." This new militancy by the National Urban League contrasted with its previous cooperation with the racially exclusionist American Federation of Labor. This change reflected a growing realization by league officials that the new unions, in particular the Congress of Industrial Organizations, were organizing African-American workers without discrimination.

SELECTED BIBLIOGRAPHY
Horace R. Cayton and George S. Mitchell, *Black Workers and the New Unions* (1939); Philip S. Foner, *Organized Labor and the Black Worker, 1619–1973* (1974); F. Ray Marshall, *The Negro and Organized Labor* (1965).
Malik Simba

NEGRO WORLD. Published from 1919 to 1933 by Marcus Garvey* as the official organ for the Universal Negro Improvement Association* and editorialized as "a newspaper devoted solely to the interests of the Negro race," the paper repeated Garvey's nationalist aims and reflected his strong personality. His message—that black people are beautiful, are overwhelmed by white oppression, and should rid themselves of self-hatred—was as uncompromisingly adamant as that found in any other major African-American newspaper of the period. Along with promoting his shipping line, the editorials criticized men like W.E.B. Du Bois* for being the intellectual pawns of whites.

SELECTED BIBLIOGRAPHY
Nathan Irvin Huggins, *Harlem Renaissance* (1971); Amy Jacques-Garvey, *Philosophy & Opinions of Marcus Garvey* (1971).
Jessie M. Carter

NEW ENGLAND FREEDMAN'S AID SOCIETY. An outgrowth of the Boston Educational Commission, this organization, begun on 7 February 1862, was the first among many nonsectarian freedman's aid societies. Its goal, according to its secretary J. H. Chapin, was "to pave the way for a good free school system at the South open alike to all races and colors." Consequently, it sent its first group of teachers to Port Royal, South Carolina, in March 1862. In 1865 the society affiliated with the American Freedman's Aid Commission, a coalition of nondenominational societies in the Northeast and Midwest. It was also instrumental in the establishment of the Freedmen's Bureau* in March 1865. By January 1871, however, its work decreased because of the rise of southern public education and black self-help. It gave up all normal school work in 1874, with the exception of two schools in Virginia and Georgia.

SELECTED BIBLIOGRAPHY

Ronald Butchart, *Northern Schools, Southern Blacks and Reconstruction, Freedmen's Education, 1862–1875* (1980); Robert C. Morris, *Reading, 'Riting and Reconstruction: The Education of Freedmen in the South, 1861–1871* (1981); Julius H. Parmelee, "Freedmen's Aid Societies, 1861–1871," U.S. Department of the Interior, Office of Education, *Bulletin*, no. 38 (1916), 268–300; Willie Lee Rose, *Rehearsal for Reconstruction: The Port Royal Experiment* (1964); Henry Lee Swint, *The Northern Teacher in the South, 1862–1870* (1967).

Judith N. Kerr

NEW NEGRO ALLIANCE. The New Negro Alliance began in Washington, D.C., during the summer of 1933 as a picketing and boycott movement directed at businesses and chain stores operating in African-American neighborhoods without black workers. Organized by Frank Thorne, William Henry Hastie,* and Beford Lawson, the alliance was one of several dozen Jobs for Negroes movement* campaigns launched in black neighborhoods in cities across the nation during the depression of the 1930s. Picketing had to be suspended when the Kauffman Five and Dime and the Sanitary Drug Store in Washington, D.C. secured a temporary court injunction contending that the pickets were "unlawful assemblies that restrained trade, endangered lives of pedestrians that could result in violent riots." While William Hastie (later the first African American appointed to the federal bench) appealed the injunction, the alliance organized neighborhoods in support of a civil rights law, set up a community school to train clerks and managers, and established several citywide recreational programs. By 1938, when the U.S. Supreme Court agreed that African Americans did have the right to use pickets to address racial discrimination, the New Negro Alliance had established itself as a vital community institution in Washington, D.C., that would last until the 1950s.

SELECTED BIBLIOGRAPHY

Gary J. Hunter, " 'Don't Buy Where You Can't Work': Black Activisim during the Depression Years" (Ph.D. diss., University of Michigan, 1977); *Baltimore Afro-American*, 27 January 1934.

Gary J. Hunter

NEW NEGRO MOVEMENT. This post–World War I movement merged two streams of African-American consciousness: social and civil equality and cultural identity. Black intellectuals and artists broke with the nineteenth century's social and intellectual tradition of accommodation and attempted to build a new concept of race and to define a culture rooted in Africa, not Europe. Militant African Americans announced that they would use physical action in self-defense to achieve equality, and artists exploited the beauty and richness of blackness. Alain Locke's* The New Negro (1920) showcased the affirmation of the artistic self-consciousness of the Negro's human and cultural worth, the sense of an urgent need for self-assertion and militancy, and the belief in a culturally enriched past in America and Africa.

SELECTED BIBLIOGRAPHY

Nathan Irvin Huggins, The Harlem Renaissance (1971); David L. Lewis, When Harlem Was in Vogue (1979); Wilson J. Moses, The Golden Age of Black Nationalism, 1850–1925 (1978); Gary D. Wintz, Black Culture and the Harlem Renaissance (1988).

Thaddeus M. Smith

NEW ORLEANS RACE RIOT (1866). By summer 1866, portents of political conflict in Louisiana were unmistakable. Unionist Governor James Madison Wells was moving closer to the so-called Radical Republicans* of both races who were centered in New Orleans. Wells had taken the unusual step, with Radical support, of calling the 1864 constitutional convention back in session. The convention was to meet on 30 July 1866 in New Orleans. The convention and its main goal, black suffrage, were both bitterly opposed by the Democrat-controlled state legislature, the Democratic mayor of New Orleans who promised to arrest the delegates, and the city's Democratic press. Delegates convened about noon on the appointed day. At the same time several hundred blacks marching in support of the convention were set upon by a large crowd of police and white civilians near the convention site. Amidst shooting and wild disorder, the white mob pursued the marchers to the nearby Mechanics' Institute, where they forced entry and proceeded to beat, stab, and shoot delegates and their supporters. In mid-afternoon federal troops arrived and brought order. The day of violence was less a riot than a police-led massacre with distinct political overtones. Of the thirty-six dead, all but one was a black or white Republican.

SELECTED BIBLIOGRAPHY

Joseph G. Dawson, Army Generals and Reconstruction: Louisiana: 1862–1877 (1982); George C. Rable, But There Was No Peace: The Role of Violence in the Politics of Reconstruction (1984); Joe Gray Taylor, Louisiana Reconstructed, 1863–1877 (1974); Ted Tunnell, Crucible of Reconstruction: War, Radicalism, and Race in Louisiana, 1862–1877 (1984); Gilles Vandal, The New Orleans Riot of 1866: Anatomy of a Tragedy (1983).

Larry T. Balsamo

NEW ORLEANS RACE RIOT (1874). See Battle of September 14th (or Canal Street) 1874.

NEW ORLEANS RACE RIOT (1900). The New Orleans race riot of 1900 started on 23 July and lasted until 28 July. Race relations were especially tense that summer as poor whites were being displaced from their jobs by African-American migrants from rural areas and African Americans were resentful of increasing restrictions as segregation was more strictly enforced. The violence began when Robert Charles, a member of the International Migration Society who had been outraged by the story of the 1899 lynching and mutilation of Sam Hose* in Georgia, scuffled with a police officer. They exchanged pistol shots, and both were wounded. Charles killed two pursuing police officers. Before he died in a hail of bullets on 27 July, he had killed seven whites including three police officers, wounded eight whites seriously including three additional police officers, and wounded an additional twelve whites slightly. During this time, a white mob which had broken into roving gangs randomly attacked African Americans, killing eight, severely injuring twenty-one, and beating approximately fifty others. The mob also burned the best African-American school in Louisiana. Five whites were hospitalized. In all probability only Mayor Paul Capdeville's swift action in deputizing 1,500 special police and deploying state militia troops prevented more extremes in white violence.

SELECTED BIBLIOGRAPHY

William Ivy Hair, *Carnival of Fury: Robert Charles and the New Orleans Race Riot of 1900* (1976); Dale A. Somers, "Black and White in New Orleans: A Study in Urban Race Relations, 1865–1900," *Journal of Southern History* 40 (February 1974), 19–42; Daphne Spain, "Race Relations and Residential Segregation in New Orleans: Two Centuries of Paradox," *Annals of the American Academy of Political and Social Science* 441 (January 1979), 82–96.

                                                                             Lorenzo Crowell

NEW ORLEANS TRIBUNE (*La Tribune de la Nouvelle-Orleans*). The *New Orleans Tribune* was the first African-American daily newspaper in the United States. With a bilingual format, the *Tribune* was published from 21 July 1864 to 27 April 1868, with intermittent revivals between 1868 and 1871. It supplanted an earlier Afro-Creole newspaper, *L'Union*, and paralleled the biracial publication, *Louisianan*. The *Tribune*'s founder and publisher was Louis Charles Roudanez, M.D. (1823–1890), a Louisiana free Creole. Editors included Paul Trevigne and Jean-Charles Houzeau, a Belgian scientist who actively participated in liberation causes in Europe and the United States. The *Tribune* uncompromisingly supported universal suffrage and counseled against blind loyalty to the Republican party. This position, along with counter-Reconstruction impulses, contributed to factionalism in the African-American community and in the newspaper's management. Nonetheless the *Tribune* remains an important document of African-American political consciousness during the immediate postbellum era.

SELECTED BIBLIOGRAPHY
John W. Blassingame, *Black New Orleans, 1860–1880* (1973); Rodolphe Lucien Desdunes, *Our People and Our History* (1911; reprint 1973); Jean-Charles Houzeau, *My Passage at the New Orleans Tribune* (1870; reprint 1984); Robert R. MacDonald, John R. Kemp, and Edward F. Haas, eds., *Louisiana's Black Heritage* (1979).

Bernice F. Guillaume

NEW YORK AGE. T. Thomas Fortune* and Jerome B. Peterson founded the *New York Age* in 1886. Fortune used the paper to promote political awareness among black readers, and he urged blacks to place race before party. Under his aggressive leadership, the *New York Age* championed the civil rights of blacks, bemoaned the stereotypical black characters depicted on New York stages, and sounded a clarion call for black Southerners to migrate north. During his tenure, Fortune's temperamental nature and his excessive drinking caused inconsistencies in the *New York Age*'s editorials. However, his radical posture on the question of race shaped the paper's protest image. Financial ties to Booker T. Washington* did not prevent Fortune from denouncing President Theodore Roosevelt, Washington's political ally, for his role in the infamous Brownsville, Texas, affray.* Fortune launched a blistering attack against Roosevelt in the *New York Age*. When Fortune, after suffering a physical and mental breakdown, sold his share of the *New York Age* in 1907, the heyday of its role in the forefront of civil rights protest journalism had passed.

SELECTED BIBLIOGRAPHY
John Hope Franklin and Alfred A. Moss, Jr., *From Slavery to Freedom: A History of Negro Americans* (1988); August Meier, *Negro Thought in America, 1880–1915: Racial Ideologies in the Age of Booker T. Washington* (1963); Gilbert Osofsky, *Harlem: The Making of a Ghetto Negro New York, 1890–1930* (1963); Emma Lou Thornbrough, "More Light on Booker T. Washington and the *New York Age*," *Journal of Negro History* 43 (1958), 30–49; Emma Lou Thornbrough, *T. Thomas Fortune: Militant Journalist* (1972).

Joe Louis Caldwell

NEWARK, NEW JERSEY, RACE RIOT (1967). This riot was one of the most destructive of the many civil disturbances that swept American cities during the "long, hot summers" of the late 1960s. Newark was a city of over 400,000, the thirtieth largest metropolitan area in the United States. It had serious social and economic problems. "White flight" during the 1950s and early 1960s had transformed it from a majority white to a majority black city. The city's tax base also shrank as white businesses fled the inner city, and city revenues could not keep pace with increased social needs. Inadequate educational opportunities, combined with racial discrimination, had a ripple effect on the city's economy; by 1967, over 24,000 adult black males were unemployed. The white community, despite its minority status, maintained control over the city's government. Complaints of police brutality escalated but were generally brushed aside. Black anger at this indifference erupted into a riot. The riot began on 12 July, when police beat a black cab driver after arresting him. Protesters gathered at the police station near the Hayes Homes housing project. A firebomb hit the wall of the station house. Police charged out of the building, clubbing everyone within reach and triggering a four-day riot. Angry protesters looted local businesses. The 1,300-man Newark police force was augmented by 475 state troopers and over 4,000 National Guardsmen. The Guardsmen often fired on suspected looters or snipers, killing twenty-one blacks, most of them bystanders, including two children. Two whites, a policeman, and a fireman, were killed. The riot caused over ten million dollars in property damage.

SELECTED BIBLIOGRAPHY

Jules Archer, *Riot! A History of Mob Action in the United States* (1974); Tom Hayden, *Rebellion in Newark* (1976); Andrew Kopkind, "White on Black: the Riot Commission and the Rhetoric of Reform," in Anthony Platt, ed., *The Politics of Riot Commissions, 1917–1970* (1971); *Report of the National Advisory Commission on Civil Disorders* (1968).

                                                                    Randall L. Patton

NEWTON, HUEY P. (17 February 1942, Monroe, La.–22 August 1989, New Orleans, La.). Capitalizing on the growing militancy in urban black communities, Huey P. Newton, a former college student, cofounded the Black Panthers* with Bobby Seale* in October 1966. Newton, Seale, and Eldridge Cleaver,* whose prison writings titled *Soul on Ice* became a national best-seller, embraced Marxism-Leninism as they led the paramilitary organization through much of the late 1960s. However, Newton himself emerged as the principal symbol of the party when in October 1967 he was arrested for the murder of an Oakland, California, policeman. His case, becoming a cause célèbre among black and leftist groups, prompted a "Free Huey" campaign across the nation. Panther membership in the San Francisco Bay area soared from sixty to several hundred, and new chapters sprang up across the United States. Newton was convicted of voluntary manslaughter in July 1968, but two years later the California Supreme Court overturned the conviction and he was released from prison. Nevertheless the fortunes of the party declined considerably during the years of his imprisonment. In 1970 Eldridge Cleaver led a faction out of the party, which was targeted by the Federal Bureau of Investigation, which mounted a national campaign to disrupt Black Panther activities. Membership declined from 2,000 in 1968 to less than 1,000 before being further reduced by the schism with Eldridge Cleaver. By the early 1970s, Newton shifted the party's focus to voter registration campaigns and free health clinics. Newton's personal fortunes also declined. In and out of jail on a series of criminal charges, including the murder of a teenage prostitute, he was killed in August 1989 outside an Oakland "crack" house, allegedly by a drug dealer whom he had robbed.

SELECTED BIBLIOGRAPHY
Current Biography, February 1973; Obituary, *New York Times*, 23 August 1989; Bobby Seale, *Seize the Time*, 1970.

Quintard Taylor

NIAGARA MOVEMENT. Founded in 1905 on the Canadian side of Niagara Falls and organized under the leadership of W.E.B. Du Bois,* this short-lived movement was the principal forerunner of the NAACP.* In its declaration of principles, "radical" organizers drew up a plan for aggressive action and demanded among other things: manhood suffrage, equal economic opportunities, equal educational opportunities, a healthier environment, an end to segregation, and full civil rights. At the same time, the organizers acknowledged that African Americans had duties to fulfill—a duty to vote, to work, to obey the laws, to respect the rights of others, to be clean and orderly, and to respect themselves as well as others.

SELECTED BIBLIOGRAPHY
Herbert Aptheker, ed., *A Documentary History of the Negro People in the United States*, vol. 2 (1951); Francis L. Broderick and August Meier, eds., *Negro Protest Thought in the Twentieth Century* (1965); S. P. Fullinwider, *The Mind and Mood of Black America* (1969); Rayford W. Logan, *The Betrayal of the Negro* (1954).

Betty L. Plummer

NINETY-NINTH PURSUIT SQUADRON. For black Americans during World War II, this unit symbolized both achievement and inequality. Because of black insistence, the War Department in September 1940 established the Civilian Pilot Training Program at Tuskegee, Alabama (see Tuskegee Airmen). The entirely black squadron, organized in October 1942 and commanded by Col. Benjamin O. Davis, Jr., was sent to the Mediterranean theater in April 1943. The maligned and undermanned unit gained combat experience over Sicily and Italy; at Anzio in January 1944 it downed eighteen enemy planes. This performance earned the squadron two Distinguished Unit Citations and prompted the Air Corps command to employ additional black pilots in combat. The 450 pilots of the all-black 332nd Fighter Group, which included the Ninety-Ninth, ultimately flew thousands of sorties in Europe. In more than 200 missions over Germany in 1945, no allied bomber fell to enemy fighters when escorted by Tuskegee airmen, of whose number eighty-five won the Distinguished Flying Cross during the war.

SELECTED BIBLIOGRAPHY
Charles E. Francis, *The Tuskegee Airmen: The Story of the Negro in the U.S. Air Force* (1955); Bernard C. Nalty, *Strength for the Flight: A History of Black Americans in the Military* (1986); Alan M. Osur, *Blacks in the Army Air Forces during World War II* (1977); Robert A. Rose, *The Lonely Eagles: The Story of America's Black Air Force in World War II* (1946).

James B. Potts

NIXON, EDGAR DANIEL (12 July 1899, Montgomery, Ala.–25 February 1987, Montgomery, Ala.). Commonly regarded by Alabamians as the father of the civil rights movement, through five decades E. D. Nixon led the struggle for civil rights in that state. During the 1920s and 1930s he advanced the cause for black justice in the Brotherhood of Sleeping Car Porters and Maids* as the founder and president of the state's branch of that organization. In 1944 as president of the Voters League of Montgomery, he led a march to the court house to demand the vote for blacks. During the 1950s he took an active role in desegregating Alabama's public schools. In the 1960s and 1970s he worked for various civil rights acts and affirmative action* programs. However, it was his participation in the Brotherhood of Sleeping Car Porters Union between 1928 and 1964 and in the Montgomery Improvement Association* that gave him the nickname "Mr. Civil Rights."

In 1928 E. D. Nixon joined the Brotherhood of Sleeping Car Porters. He soon assumed a leadership role in that organization, and became the leading advocate in Alabama for black justice and equality. At the same time, he became the president of the Alabama NAACP.* When Rosa Parks* was arrested in December 1955 for refusing to move to the rear of a Montgomery city bus, Nixon bailed her out of jail and was one of the leading figures in the Montgomery bus boycott.* He helped to create the Montgomery Improvement Association (MIA), which launched the civil rights career of Martin Luther King, Jr.* Nixon called the meeting of Montgomery's major black leaders at the Dexter Avenue Church, where King was minister, to discuss the formation of a civil rights campaign. It was at this meeting that the young King was chosen spokesman of the movement. Unfortunately, after the great victory in the bus campaign, Nixon and King had a major disagreement and parted company.

SELECTED BIBLIOGRAPHY
Richard Blake Dent, "The Man behind the Movement: E. D. Nixon Remembers," *Tusk* (4 February 1982); "E. D. Nixon," *Economic Spirit* (July 1979), 4; "A Fierce Black Eye," *Montgomery Advertiser*, 17 November 1981; Rheta Grimsley Johnson, "The End of One Man's Struggle," *The Commercial Appeal*, Viewpoint, 4 March 1987; Lynn Lanier, "E. D. Nixon: Leader of the Times," *Alabama Journal* (Montgomery, Alabama), 17 May 1974; "Profile of Dr. E. D. Nixon," *The Montgomery-Tuskegee Times*, 23–29 August 1979, Archives of History at the Levi Watkins Learning Center at Alabama State University, Montgomery, Alabama; *South*

Central Regional Report, Montgomery, Alabama, vol. 8, no. 4; Peggy Wilhide, "Bus Boycott Leader Feels Forgotten Now," Montgomery Advertiser, 5 December 1985.

Vibert L. White

NIXON v. CONDON, 286 U.S. 73 (1932). Together with Nixon v. Herndon* (1927), Grovey v. Townsend* (1935), and Smith v. Allwright* (1944), this was one of four Supreme Court cases brought by black Texans, supported by the NAACP,* that overturned the Democratic white primary* laws. In 1923, the Texas legislature provided that "in no event shall a negro be eligible to participate in a Democratic party election." Challenged by Dr. L. A. Nixon, a black El Paso physician, the Court declared the Texas law a "direct infringement of the Fourteenth" Amendment* in Nixon v. Herndon. The Texas legislature's response was to delegate voter qualifications for primary elections to the party's executive committee, which promptly excluded blacks from the Democratic primary.

Urban black Texans immediately challenged the exclusion. The NAACP championed El Paso blacks, and, in Nixon v. Condon, the Supreme Court held the Texas law unconstitutional by a slender five-to-four majority. Relying upon the Fourteenth Amendment, the Court majority decreed that the Executive Committee acted as state agent under the statute and violated black rights by eliminating them from the primary. "A narrow and incomplete victory," the decision left the door open, and the state essentially returned to the pre–1923 policy; the Democratic party controlled its membership. In a party convention, white Democrats barred blacks. Not until 1944, after another decade of struggle, was the white primary abrogated.

SELECTED BIBLIOGRAPHY

J. Alston Atkins, The Texas Negro and His Political Rights: A History of the Fight of Negroes to Enter the Democratic Primaries of Texas (1932); Conrey Bryson, Dr. Lawrence A. Nixon and the White Primary (1974); Bruce A. Glasrud, "Blacks and Texas Politics during the Twenties," Red River Valley Historical Review 7 (Spring 1982), 39–53; Darlene Clark Hine, Black Victory: The Rise and Fall of the White Primary in Texas (1979); Walter Lindsey, "Black Houstonians Challenge the White Democratic Primary, 1921–1944" (master's thesis, University of Houston, 1969); Samuel Paschal Wilson, "The White Primary Laws in Texas from 1923–1953" (master's thesis, Southwest Texas State University, 1971).

Bruce A. Glasrud

NIXON v. HERNDON, 273 U.S. 536 (1927). In 1923 the Texas legislature passed a law barring African Americans from its primary elections. The law stated that "in no event shall a Negro be eligible to participate in a Democratic Party primary election held in the state of Texas." The Democratic party in El Paso enforced this statute in 1924, when it created the white primary.* In a one-party state, whoever won the primary automatically won the election. This practice rendered the regular election moot. Nixon brought suit when an El Paso registrar denied him suffrage solely because of his race. His attorneys argued that the Fifteenth Amendment* provided him immunity from racial discrimination. The Supreme Court agreed and held unconstitutional the Texas white primary law. It ruled that the Fifteenth Amendment protected eligible black citizens from discrimination at the polls. Congress had adopted the Civil War amendments, the Court asserted, to "protect the blacks from discrimination against them." Although the *Nixon* case outlawed the white primary, southern states adopted new strategies to disenfranchise blacks.

SELECTED BIBLIOGRAPHY
Derrick A. Bell, Jr., *Race, Racism and American Law* (1980); Conrey Bryson, *Dr. Lawrence A. Nixon and the White Primary* (1974); Darlene Clark Hine, *Black Victory: The Rise and Fall of the White Primary in Texas* (1979); "Notes and Comments," *Marquette Law Review* 11 (1927), 259–60; "Recent Cases," *Nebraska Law Bulletin* 6 (1928), 212–14.

Stephen Middleton

NONVIOLENT RESISTANCE. Nonviolent resistance is a method of social change that employs such instruments as strikes, sit-ins, boycotts, fasts, and civil disobedience. The use of these means by religious dissenters, abolitionists, advocates for women's rights, and labor union organizers is a significant theme in United States history. *The Essay on Civil Disobedience* by Henry David Thoreau (1849) is a seminal statement of nonviolent resistance theory. Mohandas K. Gandhi drew on Thoreau in fashioning the movement that forced Great Britain from India in 1947. Civil rights advocates in the United States drew on Gandhi. "It may be through the Negroes that the unadulterated message of non-violence will be delivered to the world," Gandhi told Dr. Howard Thurman in 1936. Adaptations of Gandhi's *Satyagraha* (soul force) characterized the March on Washington Movement* of A. Philip Randolph* and, until the era of Black Power,* the methods of the Congress of Racial Equality* and the Student Nonviolent Coordinating Committee.*

Faith in nonviolent resistance sustained Martin Luther King, Jr.,* and remained the hallmark of the Southern Christian Leadership Conference* which he founded. "Christ showed us the way," he averred, "and Mahatma Gandhi showed us it would work." He insisted that nonviolent resistance was "the only morally and practically sound method open to oppressed people in their struggle for freedom" and that it was the key to lasting and profound change. Its "transforming power," he declared, "can lift a whole community to new horizons of fair play, goodwill and justice."

SELECTED BIBLIOGRAPHY
Joan V. Bondurant, *Conquest of Violence, the Gandhian Philosophy of Conflict* (1965); Severyn T. Bruyn and Paula M. Rayman, eds., *Nonviolent Action and Social Change*

(1979); Robert Cooney and Helen Michalowski, *The Power of the People, Active Non-Violence in the United States* (1977); August Meier, Elliott Rudwick, and Francis L. Broderick, eds., *Black Protest Thought in the Twentieth Century* (1980); Gene Sharp, *The Politics of Nonviolent Action* (1973); Mulford Q. Sibley, ed., *The Quiet Battle, Writings on the Theory and Practice of Non-Violent Resistance* (1963).

Jo Ann O. Robinson

NORFOLK JOURNAL AND GUIDE. Originally called the *Gideon Safe Guide*, then the *Lodge Journal and Guide*, this newspaper began in 1900 as the official newspaper of the Supreme Lodge Knights of Gideon. P. B. Young* purchased it in 1910 and eventually adopted the motto "Build Up, Don't Tear Down" in espousing the accommodationist philosophy of Booker T. Washington.* Its circulation grew steadily, reaching its peak in the post–World War II years and becoming one of the nation's major black newspapers. It consistently took a conservative position on race relations, reflecting its editor-publisher's viewpoint. It remained cautious during the civil rights years, much to the dismay of more activist African Americans. In 1992 it is still being published although its importance is greatly reduced.

SELECTED BIBLIOGRAPHY

Henry Lewis Suggs, *P. B. Young, Newspaperman: Race, Politics and Journalism in the New South 1910–1962* (1988); Henry Lewis Suggs, ed., *The Black Press in the South, 1865–1979* (1983).

John F. Marszalek

NORRIS v. ALABAMA, 294 U.S. 587 (1935). In 1932 the Supreme Court reversed the first rape convictions of Clarence Norris and the eight other "Scottsboro Boys" (see Scottsboro Trials) due to deprivation of their constitutional right to counsel. The state of Alabama retried the defendants and convicted them again. Norris appealed his second conviction on the ground that blacks had been deliberately excluded from the jury. The Supreme Court agreed. Chief Justice Charles Evans Hughes noted that no blacks had served on juries in the counties in question for many decades, even though qualified blacks were available to serve. State law did not overtly discriminate, but local officials had evolved their own customary ways of avoiding blacks. The Court found that the exclusion had been systematic and racially motivated, and it was thus a violation of the equal protection clause of the Fourteenth Amendment.* The ruling was not surprising, since it had precedents going back even to the 1880s, a period when the Court showed concern for the impartial administration of justice, if not for civil rights generally. Following various retrials and appeals, Norris escaped and vanished. He surfaced many years later in Michigan and returned to Alabama upon extradition to receive a ceremonious pardon from Governor George Wallace.

SELECTED BIBLIOGRAPHY
J. F. Barbour, Jr. "Note and Comment," *Mississippi Law Journal* 8 (1935), 196–204; Dan T. Carter, *Scottsboro* (1969); Robert F. Cushman, *Cases in Constitutional Law* (1979).

James E. Sefton

NORTH CAROLINA MUTUAL LIFE INSURANCE COMPANY. Chartered in 1899, the North Carolina Mutual Life Insurance Company, an industrial insurer with a philanthropic impulse, has played a pivotal role in the economic, political, and social lives of black North Carolinians throughout this century. The genius behind this pioneering black business was John Merrick,* an ex-slave who, along with Dr. Aaron McDuffie and a grocer named Charles Clinton Spaulding, gave leadership to the company. Expanding rapidly, it was doing business in twelve states and the District of Columbia by 1915. In keeping with the tenor of the times, the leadership of the company touted the principle of black self-help during the first fifty years of its existence. The influence of Booker T. Washington* was unmistakable. Never aloof from the everyday affairs of the black community, Merrick and his colleagues were involved in the civil rights struggles in North Carolina both publicly and behind the scene. C. C. Spaulding lobbied the legislature strenuously for better funding for black colleges in North Carolina. During the 1930s he threw the resources of the company, and his personal prestige, behind the fight for equalization of pay for black teachers in the state. At first his support of the NAACP* was cautious, but in time he became a staunch supporter. Spaulding died in 1952, having husbanded the company through good times and bad. He meshed entrepreneurialism with a social philosophy oriented toward race pride. North Carolina Mutual was what he and his colleagues made it—a monument to black enterprise, a landmark of the new South, and a testament to the twin desires of black economic progress and equal rights for all peoples. Today it is one of the three largest, black-owned insurance companies in America.

SELECTED BIBLIOGRAPHY
John Hope Franklin and Alfred A. Moss, Jr., *From Slavery to Freedom: A History of Negro Americans*, 6th ed. (1988); August Meier, *Negro Thought in America: 1880–1915: Racial Ideologies in the Age of Booker T. Washington* (1963); Walter B. Weare, *Black Business in the New South: A Social History of the North Carolina Mutual Life Insurance Company* (1973).

Joe Louis Caldwell

NORTHERN STUDENT MOVEMENT. Founded in New Haven, Connecticut, during the spring of 1961 by a Yale University student, Peter Countryman, the Northern Student Movement (NSM) initially consisted of northern, white college students eager to join the burgeoning civil rights movement. These students entered the northern ghettos in 1962 with the simple goal of tutoring disadvantaged inner-city blacks. By 1965, NSM's inner-city experience had resulted in dramatic changes. Led by William Strickland, a black activist who succeeded Countryman as NSM's executive director in 1963, NSM had evolved into a primarily black organization concerned with mobilizing northern black communities. Its strategy involved using tutorials to gain community trust, recruiting a core of indigenous leaders, and then expanding to broader inner-city dilemmas, such as poverty, substandard housing, unemployment, poor education, police brutality, and welfare rights. Ultimately, NSM members hoped to ignite an independent, black political movement capable of empowering inner-city blacks and mounting a direct challenge to existing racist institutions. NSM amassed sixty-five campus affiliates nationwide, and it established community action projects in Boston, Chicago, Detroit, Hartford, New York, and Philadelphia. NSM members created a Freedom Library in Philadelphia, waged rent strikes in Harlem, confronted police brutality in Detroit, and helped coordinate public school boycotts in Boston, Chicago, and New York.

SELECTED BIBLIOGRAPHY

Students for a Democratic Society Papers, 1958–1970, series 2A, National Office (Fall 1962–August 1965), reel 9, "Related Groups no. 113"; *The Northern Student Movement, 1962–1965*, n.d., Glen Rock, N.J., Microfilming Corporation of America (1977).

Mark E. Medina

NORTON, ELEANOR HOLMES (13 June 1937, Washington, D.C.–). The eldest of three girls born to working-class parents, Eleanor Holmes Norton was educated at segregated public schools in Washington, D.C., and earned her high school diploma from the district's only college preparatory school for blacks—Dunbar High School. She graduated from Antioch College, in Yellow Springs, Ohio, in 1960 and received her M.A. from Yale Graduate School in New Haven, Connecticut, in 1963, and her LL.B. from Yale Law School in 1964. Her specialty in civil liberties led to an appointment as assistant legal director of the American Civil Liberties Union,* a post she held from 1965 to 1970. In chairing the New York City Commission on Human Rights (1970–1977) and the Equal Employment Opportunity Commission* (EEOC) (1977–1981)—the only woman to chair the latter—she revitalized both agencies. By spearheading its 1978 reorganization, she brought the EEOC into the forefront as the lead agency in the enforcement of equal employment opportunity. Between 1982 and 1990, Norton was a faculty member of the Georgetown University Law Center, when she took a leave of absence to seek political office. Despite a last-second discovery that her husband had not filed their local income taxes for seven years, she won the nonvoting-delegate seat from the District of Columbia to the U.S. House of Representatives in the 1990 election. Described as "One of the Most Powerful Women in Washington" by the *Washingtonian Magazine* in 1989, Norton has received honorary doctorates from more than fifty universities. From 1982 to 1988 she served as a board member of the Yale Corporation.

SELECTED BIBLIOGRAPHY

"America's 100 Most Important Women," *Ladies Home Journal* (November 1988), 47–48, 223; Ed Gordon, "Dialogue with Eleanor Holmes Norton," *Emerge* (August, 1990), 11–12; Richette Haywood, "A Black Woman's Place Is in the . . . House of Representatives: Eleanor Holmes Norton Takes D.C. Seat," *Ebony* 46 (January 1991), 104–6; Brian Lanker, *I Dream a World* (1989); Leslie Milk, "100 Most Powerful Women," *Washingtonian Magazine* (September 1989), 132–35.

Jennifer J. Beaumont

NOT WITHOUT LAUGHTER. An incisive and convincing psychological study of interracial, intrafamilial relationships in a racially oppressive, small, Midwestern town, Langston Hughes's* first novel (1930) heralded a new spirit and direction in the canon of black literature—the advent of a racial consciousness committed to the affirmation, spirit, and rich heritage of the folk experience. In this novel, Hughes, an acclaimed innovative stylist, rejected the exoticism of the plantation tradition and the conservatism of his progenitors and adopted black folk materials and cultural tradition—the blues,* black idiom, folk laughter—to reveal the complexity of black life. Forging beyond the limitations of romanticism, Langston Hughes pioneered the rise of a realistic Negro literature.

SELECTED BIBLIOGRAPHY

James Emanuel, *Langston Hughes* (1967); Edward J. Mullen, ed., *Critical Essays on Langston Hughes* (1989); Thermon B. O'Daniel, ed., *Langston Hughes, Black Genius* (1971); Armstead Rampensad, *The Life of Langston Hughes* (1986); Amritjit Singh, *The Novels of the Harlem Renaissance* (1976).

Jacquelyn Jackson

O

ODUM, HOWARD WASHINGTON (24 May 1884, Bethlehem, Ga.–8 November 1954, Chapel Hill, N.C.). A white, southern sociologist dedicated to improving race relations in the region, Odum was chairman of the Commission on Interracial Cooperation* from 1937 to 1944. He was influential in developing the Southern Regional Council,* a major white, southern, liberal, civil rights group. He received his undergraduate degree from Emory College and his graduate education from the University of Mississippi, Clark University, and Columbia University. He held positions at the University of Georgia, Emory College, and the University of North Carolina. He founded the *Journal of Social Forces* and the Institute for Research in Social Sciences which explored civil rights issues.

SELECTED BIBLIOGRAPHY
Wayne Douglas Brazil, "Howard W. Odum, the Building Years 1884–1930" (Ph.D. diss., Harvard University, 1975); Howard W. Odum, *An American Epoch* (1930); Howard W. Odum, *Southern Regions of the United States* (1936); Rupert B. Vance and Katherine Jocher, "Howard W. Odum," *Social Forces* 33 (March 1955), 203–17.

Donald Cunnigen

OFFICE OF FEDERAL CONTRACT COMPLIANCE PROGRAMS. Created in the fall of 1965 by Labor Secretary W. Willard Wirtz, the Office of Federal Contract Compliance (OFCC) Programs was charged with enforcing nondiscrimination in employment by government contractors and in federally assisted construction programs. This was required by President Lyndon B. Johnson's Executive Order 11246* of September 1965, which designated the Labor Department as the principal agency for coordinating contract compliance under Title VI of the Civil Rights Act of 1964.* In early 1966 Wirtz appointed Edward K. Sylvester to head the OFCC, and under Sylvester the office developed a preaward program that compelled bidders on contracts of $1 million or more to first be reviewed and approved for compliance with the executive order. Following unsuccessful experiments with construction contracts in St. Louis, San Francisco, and Cleveland, the OFCC developed in Philadelphia a formula that required bidders to set numerical goals for minority employees. Builders complained that the minority goals required under Title VI enforcement amounted to racial quotas, which were banned by Title VII, and that the OFCC should place the onus of desegregation at the source of discrimination: the hiring-hall system required by labor union contracts. In November 1968, Comptroller-General Elmer Staats ruled that the Philadelphia Plan* illegally required contractors to set racial quotas in hiring. The OFCC's affirmative action* program was revived in 1969, however, by President Richard M. Nixon's secretary of labor, George P. Shultz. Its effect was to split the liberal Democratic coalition between civil rights groups and organized labor. In April 1970, the Third Circuit Court of Appeals upheld the Philadelphia Plan in a suit brought by Pennsylvania contractors. Shortly thereafter the Nixon administration expanded the goals-and-timetables requirements for minorities and women to apply to all federal contractors. These policies were continued under the Ford and Carter administrations. By the Reagan administration, the OFCC program had become sufficiently entrenched that the Labor Department, under Secretary William Brock, was able to defeat conservative attacks on its minority preferences led by Attorney General Edwin Meese.

SELECTED BIBLIOGRAPHY
Nelson A. Bruce and Mary Lou Christie, "Affirmative Action Requirements for the Construction Industry under Executive Order 11246," in David A. Corpus and Linda Rosenweig, eds., *The OFCC and Federal Contract Compliance* (1981); Hugh Davis Graham, *The Civil Rights Era* (1990).

                                                                                      Daniel Gomes

OFFICE OF MINORITY BUSINESS ENTERPRISE. On 5 March 1969, President Richard M. Nixon established, by executive order, the Office of Minority Business Enterprise (OMBE) within the Commerce Department. Attempting to ameliorate some of the causal conditions of racial turbulence, Nixon planned to use this office to spur black capitalism.* The OMBE was charged with coordinating all efforts to expand minority businesses. In October, the OMBE implemented Project Enterprise, which established the Minority Enterprise Small Business Investment Company. This company offered "venture capital and long term credit" to minority businesses but did not provide the "support necessary for the second stage of growth"; therefore, a high failure rate resulted among these businesses.

SELECTED BIBLIOGRAPHY

Theodore Cross, *The Black Power Imperative* (1984); Roy F. Lee, *The Setting for Black Business Development* (1972); Gerald Whittaker, ed., *Minority Business: The Second Stage of Growth* (1977).

Malik Simba

OPEN (OR FAIR) HOUSING ACT (1968). Part of the Civil Rights Act of 1968,* signed by President Lyndon B. Johnson on 11 April, this act was the last major civil rights legislation of the 1960s. The passage of open-housing legislation was a surprise, considering the declining enthusiasm for such a bill in Congress. The summers of urban violence since the Watts race riot* of 1965 had produced white "backlash" against civil rights protests and had reduced the likelihood of new legislation. An open-housing bill was originally sent to Congress by President Johnson in 1966. The House of Representatives passed it, but opposition from minority leader Everett Dirksen, a Republican from Illinois, and a filibuster by southern Democrats doomed the measure in the Senate. No action was taken during 1967, but early in 1968 a bill protecting civil rights workers was passed by the House and was amended in the Senate to include the dormant open-housing measure. Again a southern-led filibuster occurred, but cloture was voted after Dirksen switched sides and supported the bill. The Open Housing Act prohibited discrimination on the basis of race in 80 percent of all rental and sale housing. In a political compromise the law also expanded federal protection for civil rights workers, and an antiriot provision provided tougher criminal penalties for activities that caused civil disturbances. The Open Housing Act of 1968 had an ambiguous legacy; housing discrimination was made a national crime, but federal enforcement was hampered by small budgets and weak penalties.

SELECTED BIBLIOGRAPHY

Hugh Davis Graham, *The Civil Rights Era* (1990); U.S. Commission on Civil Rights, *The Federal Fair Housing Enforcement Effort* (1979).

William J. Thompson

OPPORTUNITY. The official publication of the National Urban League,* *Opportunity* first appeared in January 1923. Charles S. Johnson,* its first editor, intended it to be a factual presentation of employment opportunities for black urban residents and future migrants. Research properly conducted, he believed, would blunt prejudice, reduce discrimination, and encourage interracial cooperation. Articles covered a wide range of topics: child placement, health, the labor market, housing, history, and international affairs. The arts were also represented. Claude McKay,*

Langston Hughes,* Alain Locke,* and Countee Cullen* made their appearances at a time when few white magazines would publish any African-American authors. In 1928, Elmer A. Carter assumed editorship, and *Opportunity* opened its pages to such prominent white writers as H. L. Mencken, Pearl Buck, and Clarence Darrow. During the Great Depression, the journal increasingly dealt with unemployment and supported the New Deal. An increasing financial burden to the Urban League, it ceased publication in 1949. Some 40 percent of its readership was white, and it never equaled the circulation of the NAACP's* *Crisis.* It has been criticized by some scholars for overemphasizing black success stories and underplaying racial violence; nevertheless, it is an important source for the study of African-American life.

SELECTED BIBLIOGRAPHY

Guichard Parris and Lester Brooks, *Blacks in the City: A History of the National Urban League* (1971); Nancy J. Weiss, *The National Urban League, 1910–1940* (1974).

Richard W. Resh

ORANGEBURG, SOUTH CAROLINA, MASSACRE (1968). This event was the climax of a struggle between black college students and local segregationists that went back to a failed attempt in 1963 to integrate local lunch counters. In 1967 a student chapter of the NAACP* was organized at South Carolina State College with John Stroman as its leader. The students tried with no success to get Harry Floyd to integrate his All Star Bowling Lanes, and on the night of 5 February 1968, Stroman led a group to the bowling alley. Some students got in, but the bowling alley was closed. The following night the students returned in larger numbers and Student Nonviolent Coordinating Committee* organizer Cleveland Sellers was also present. This time law officials were waiting. General disorder erupted and several students, including coeds, were beaten. On the state college campus the next day, a student grievance committee made plans for a march on city hall and a boycott of local businesses unless grievance demands were met. No agreements could be reached between students and city officials. The mood grew tense. Governor Robert E. McNair activated additional National Guardsmen to reinforce the highway patrolmen who were already on the scene. By the morning of 8 February, an eerie calm had settled over the state college campus, and acting President M. Maceo Nance instructed the students to stay on campus. That evening a group of students attempted to start a bonfire on the edge of the campus near the command post of the patrolmen. When a fencepost was thrown and struck an officer, the other patrolmen thought that the officer had been shot, and they opened fire. In a few seconds thirty students were shot, three of whom were killed. The press claimed that shots had been exchanged, but later investigation proved that no student had fired a single shot. Governor

McNair declared a state of emergency. Cleveland Sellers was arrested and found guilty of inciting a riot though his case was later remanded. Nine of the patrolmen involved were tried, but all were found "not guilty." Legal action did, however, later require Harry Floyd to desegregate his bowling alley.

SELECTED BIBLIOGRAPHY

Charlotte Observer 9, 10 February 1968; Jack Nelson and Jack Bass, *The Orangeburg Massacre* (1970); *Orangeburg Times and Democrat*, 7, 8, 9, 10 February 1968.

Charles A. Risher

ORGANIZATION OF AFRO-AMERICAN UNITY. The Organization of Afro-American Unity (OAAU) was established in 1965 by Black Muslim* leader Malcolm X* after his break with Elijah Muhammad (see Elijah Poole), the leader of the Nation of Islam. In the name of universal brotherhood of Islam, OAAU sought to make common cause with the Third World nations. In effect, Malcolm X moved from civil rights to human rights. His premature death at the hands of an assassin on 21 February 1965 halted OAAU's activities. Although Malcolm's sister, Ella Mae Collins, assumed leadership of the organization, it soon became inactive.

SELECTED BIBLIOGRAPHY

John H. Bracey, *Black Nationalism in America* (1970); Robert C. Twombly, *Blacks in White America since 1865: Issues and Interpretations* (1971); Malcolm X and Alex Haley, *The Autobiography of Malcolm X* (1965).

Amm Saifuddin Khaled

OVINGTON, MARY WHITE (11 April 1865, Brooklyn, N.Y.–15 July 1951, Auburndale, Mass.). The granddaughter of an abolitionist and the daughter of a pre–Civil War abolitionist, the wealthy, white Ovington attended the 1906 meeting of the Niagara Movement* as a reporter for the *New York Evening Post*. In 1909 she answered the call that went out for a conference to organize what became the NAACP* to protest "present evils" to blacks and to ask that a new struggle be initiated to ascertain civil and political liberty for all. In 1911 she wrote *Half a Man: The Status of the Negro in New York*.

Ovington's stand with the NAACP was all the more significant because the interracial organization had formed when Progressives paid little attention to the needs of blacks and when lynching* increased each year. Between 1910 and 1941, Ovington held important offices in the NAACP for longer periods than any of the organization's other officials. Having worked persistently for racial equality all of her life, the aging Ovington still understood that much more had to be done. Indeed, she died only three years before the *Brown v. Board of Education** decision of 1954.

SELECTED BIBLIOGRAPHY
W.E.B. Du Bois, *The Autobiography of W.E.B. Du Bois: A Soliloquy on Viewing My Life from the Last Decade of Its First Century* (1968); John Hope Franklin and Alfred A. Moss, Jr., *From Slavery to Freedom: A History of Negro Americans* 6th ed. (1988); B. Joyce Ross, *J. E. Spingarn and the Rise of the NAACP, 1911–1939* (1972).

Linda Reed

OWENS, JESSE (12 September 1913, Oakville, Ala.–31 March 1980, Tucson, Ariz.). With four gold medals emblazoned around his neck—three for individual feats, the other as part of a relay team—Jesse Owens was catapulted into instant fame during the 1936 Olympic games held in Berlin and attended by Adolph Hitler, chancellor of Germany. Owens was the tenth and last child of an impoverished southern sharecropper in northern Alabama who with millions of other African Americans migrated to the North for a better life. Cleveland, Ohio, became the Owenses' home, the place where Jesse encountered the complexities of northern racism and the institutions that educated and excited him about athletics and success. A white coach, whose background was poor Pennsylvania Irish, nurtured, tutored, and honed his talents. He enrolled at Ohio State University but never graduated. Shortly after his Olympic triumph, Jesse turned his energies in pursuit of the American Dream. He plunged into a myriad of investments, worked for public relations firms, lent his name to commercial products, crisscrossed the country delivering inspirational talks, stumped for Republican presidential candidates, attended Olympic games as a goodwill ambassador, managed black basketball and softball teams, worked for the Works Projects Administration, and professionally competed against other runners. His was a middle-class existence that was constantly forced to cope with the realities of racist practices. Toward the end of his life, his conservative approach to racial issues was criticized by Black Power* advocates, but Owens held steadfast to his ideas of patriotism, opportunity, and nonconfrontation.

SELECTED BIBLIOGRAPHY
William J. Baker, *Jesse Owens: An American Life* (1986); Jesse Owens, *Blackthink: My Life as Black Man and White Man* (1970).

Joseph Boskin

OXLEY, LAWRENCE AUGUSTUS (17 May 1887, Boston, Mass.–2 July 1973, Washington, D.C.). A veteran social worker, Oxley began his career as a teacher at Saint Augustine's College, in Raleigh, North Carolina. Subsequently, he developed social surveys of the black communities in Washington, D.C.; Louisville, Kentucky; Cincinnati, Ohio; Chicago, Illinois; North Carolina; and Little Rock, Arkansas. After serving as the Director of Negro Work for the North Carolina State Board of Charities and Public Welfare, Oxley became a member of Franklin D.

Roosevelt's Black Cabinet* as special assistant to the secretary of labor. Later, he was the director of special projects for the National Council of Senior Citizens.

SELECTED BIBLIOGRAPHY
Jet (19 July, 21 September 1973); Obituary, *Washington Post*, 5 July 1973; *Who's Who in Colored America, 1940* (1940).

Ray Branch

P

PACE v. ALABAMA, 106 U.S. 583 (1883). This miscegenation case challenged an Alabama law that dictated greater punishment for adultery between an interracial couple than between a same-race couple. Tony Pace, a black man, and Mary J. Cox, a white woman, were convicted under the law and received the minimum sentence of two years each at hard labor. An unmarried couple of the same race would have been fined $100, and could have served six months in prison. In a unanimous decision, the Supreme Court upheld the state law, claiming that it was not in violation of the equal protection clause of the Fourteenth Amendment* of the Constitution or civil rights legislation because it applied the same punishment to both offenders and therefore was not discriminatory. The Court said that equal protection guaranteed a person, regardless of race, the same punishment for the same offense. The rationale for the decision was that both blacks and whites who crossed racial barriers to engage in such acts were punished equally. The Alabama law and fifteen similar laws in other southern states were overturned in 1967, when the Supreme Court declared antimiscegenation laws invalid under the Fourteenth Amendment in the case *Loving v. Virginia.**

SELECTED BIBLIOGRAPHY

Richard Bardolph, ed., *The Civil Rights Record: Black Americans and the Law, 1849–1970* (1970); Derrick A. Bell, Jr., *Race, Racism, and American Law* (1980); Robert F. Cushman, *Cases in Constitutional Law*, 4th ed. (1975); Robert J. Sickels, *Race, Marriage and the Law* (1972).

Carol Wilson

PAN-AFRICAN MOVEMENT. This concept seeks to unite peoples of African ancestry around the world to help systematically emancipate their race from further socioeconomic and political discrimination and to restore the dignity of the African motherland. Pan-Africanism emerged as a coordinated international movement in the early twentieth century with plans to help liberate the continent of sub-Sahara Africa and Africans living abroad from colonialism and imperialism. The early dialogue was international in scope and included Africans, African Americans, and West Indians. One early organizer, Henry S. Williams, a Trinidadian lawyer, created the first All African Association in London in September 1897. He spearheaded the first Pan-African conference in London on 23–25 July 1900, which was attended by thirty-three delegates from Africa, the Caribbean, the United States, and Canada. The first follow-up conference in the United States was sponsored by Tuskegee Institute* in 1914. W.E.B. Du Bois* played a key role in "giving reality to the dream before its world-wide acceptance" in the post–World War I years. Seven Pan-African Congresses were held between 1919 and 1963, in Europe, the United States, and Africa. During the civil rights period, a large percentage of African Americans were strong supporters of the Pan-African movement.

SELECTED BIBLIOGRAPHY

Stokely Carmichael, *Stokely Speaks: Black Power Back to Pan Africanism* (1971); Imanuel Geiss, *The Pan-African Movement: A History of Pan Africanism in America* (1974); Robert A. Hill, ed., *Pan African Biography* (1987); Tony Martin, *The Pan African Connection: From Slavery, to Garvey and Beyond* (1984); George Padmore, *Pan-Africanism or Communism?* (1956).

Glenn O. Phillips

PARKS, ROSA (4 February 1913, Tuskegee, Ala.–). A black seamstress educated at Alabama State College in Montgomery, Rosa Parks became during the 1950s a simple but powerful symbol of black protest against segregation. Perhaps nowhere in the South was the color line more rigidly enforced than on Montgomery's city buses. On 1 December 1955 Rosa Parks boarded a city bus. Finding no vacancy in the black section, she took a seat toward the front. When she refused to move to the rear, she was arrested and jailed. Montgomery's black leaders rushed to her support. A year earlier they had received promises from the city commission and bus authority that changes would be made in the segregation of the city's buses. Nothing had happened, however, and black leaders decided that direct action* was necessary. Martin Luther King, Jr.,* E. D. Nixon,* and others rallied the black community and organized the Montgomery bus boycott.*

Rosa Parks. (© Flip Schulke, Schulke Archives, Miami, Florida.)

That boycott and its symbol, Rosa Parks, helped usher in the black revolt and catapulted Martin Luther King, Jr., and nonviolent direct action into national prominence.

SELECTED BIBLIOGRAPHY

Alabama Journal, 1 December 1973; Taylor Branch, *Parting the Waters: America in the King Years, 1954–63* (1988); Eric Foner, ed., *America's Black Past: A Reader in Afro-American History* (1970); George R. Metcalf, *Black Profiles* (1980); *Montgomery Advertiser,* 15 January, 2 December 1980; Jo Ann Gibson Robinson, *The Montgomery Bus Boycott and the Women Who Started It: The Memoir of Jo Ann Gibson*

Robinson, (1987); J. Mills Thornton III, "Challenge and Response in the Montgomery Bus Boycott of 1955–1956," *The Alabama Review* 33 (July 1980), 163–235.

Charles D. Lowery

PASADENA BOARD OF EDUCATION v. SPANGLER, 427 U.S. 424 (1976). This 1976 U.S. Supreme Court decision concerned resegregation of schools after desegregation. The problem arose in Pasadena, California, where segregation was found to be recurring because whites were moving out from the district and minorities, including blacks, were moving in. Busing was blamed for this situation. In 1970, a federal district court had ruled that there could be no school in the Pasadena district with a majority of minority students. The court authorized the school officials to make yearly readjustments in the racial composition of the schools. Reversing this decision in 1976, the Supreme Court ruled by a 6-to-2 vote that once desegregation was accomplished in the schools, court authority was not required to make annual readjustments. In Pasadena, the Court said, the changes in the racial composition of the schools had occurred because of normal human migration and not because of any official action. Justices Thurgood Marshall* and William Brennan, however, said that Pasadena schools had never been truly desegregated due to the noncooperation of the school authorities. The Pasadena problem of resegregation after desegregation was, in fact, representative of similar problems in many other districts throughout the nation.

SELECTED BIBLIOGRAPHY

Paul R. Dimond, *Beyond Busing: Inside the Challenge to Urban Segregation* (1985); Bruce E. Fein, *Significant Decisions of the Supreme Court, 1975–1976* (1977); "Court Turning Against Reverse Discrimination," *U.S. News and World Report* (12 July 1976); J. Harvie Wilkinson III, *From Brown to Bakke: The Supreme Court and School Integration, 1954–1978* (1979); Perry A. Zirkel, ed., *A Digest of Supreme Court Decisions Affecting Education* (1978).

Amm Saifuddin Khaled

PATTON v. MISSISSIPPI, 332 U.S. 463 (1947). This Supreme Court case involved a black petitioner named Eddie "Buster" Patton who was indicted by an all-white grand jury and was tried and convicted by an all-white petit jury in Lauderdale County, Mississippi. The NAACP* defense team, led by Thurgood Marshall,* argued that Patton had been denied his constitutional rights under the Fourteenth Amendment* because blacks had been systematically excluded from jury duty for at least the past thirty years. Mississippi, represented by its attorney general, argued that jurors were selected from voting lists and, since there were few or no black voters on the list, the state had not discriminated when it had selected an all-white jury. Justice Hugo Black, in a unanimous decision for the Court, declared that "when a jury selection plan whatever it is, operates in such a way as always to result in the complete and long-continued exclusion of any representative at all from a large group of Negroes, or any other racial group, indictments and verdicts returned against them by juries thus selected cannot stand." Black went on to note that Patton was not necessarily free, but if Mississippi were to indict and try him again, the juries would have to be more representative of the state's population.

SELECTED BIBLIOGRAPHY

Robert S. Harris, *The Quest for Equality: The Constitution, Congress and the Supreme Court* (1960); C. Herman Pritchett, *Civil Liberties and the Vinson Court* (1954); "Recent Cases," *George Washington Law Review* 16 (1948), 426–29.

Kenneth W. Goings

PAYNE, ETHEL L. (1912, Chicago, Ill.–28 May 1991, Washington, D.C.). Ethel L. Payne, often called "the first lady of the black press," became the first African-American woman to join the White House press corps in 1951. A journalism graduate of Northwestern University, Payne was working in Tokyo in 1949 and keeping a journal about discrimination against American black servicemen when journalists urged her to send her work to the *Chicago Defender*.* Her stories impressed John H. Sengstacke,* publisher and editor of the paper, who hired her as the Washington political correspondent.

Payne's persistence in raising civil-rights-related questions at the White House news conferences of Dwight D. Eisenhower prompted a presidential fit of temper in 1955. When she asked about his position on segregation, Eisenhower angrily retorted: "What makes you think I am going to give special favoritism to special interests? I am the president of all the people." Eisenhower became so irritated with her that he seldom called on her for questions for the remainder of his presidency. Payne had a special reputation for reporting on international affairs, having interviewed Chinese Premier Chou En-Lai and African dictator Idi Amin. She covered her first international conference in Bandung, Indonesia, in 1956 at a time when black newspapers were not covering international news.

Driven by a "great sense of indignation for people who couldn't defend themselves," Payne was not reserved about pushing civil and human rights issues into print or playing an active role in causes. She wrote about discrimination against African Americans in the armed forces and the federal government. She marched in civil rights demonstrations and campaigned through letters, petitions, and other means to secure the freedom of Nelson Mandela in South Africa.

SELECTED BIBLIOGRAPHY

New York Times, 29 April 1955; Ethel L. Payne, "Loneliness in the Capitol: The

Black National Correspondent," in Henry G. La Brie III, ed., *Perspectives of the Black Press: 1974* (1974); *Washington Post*, 27 April 1955 and 1 June 1991.

Danny Blair Moore

PEABODY EDUCATION FUND. The Peabody Education Fund was established in 1867 by merchant and banker George Peabody (1795–1869), a New Englander who made his fortune in Baltimore and London and was known for his widespread philanthropy in both the United States and Great Britain. Peabody's endowment of the education fund provided for "the promotion and encouragement of intellectual, moral, or industrial education among the young people of the more destitute portions of the Southern and Southwestern states of our Union." The fund supported education for both black and white students, primarily through aid in establishing and maintaining public schools and teachers' training schools. Over the years, the fifty-six trustees of the Peabody Fund, who included Presidents Grover Cleveland and Theodore Roosevelt, chose a policy of passive acceptance of racial segregation in education. The fund, the first of many established by northern philanthropists to aid southern and black education, distributed over $3,500,000 before liquidating in 1914. At that time, $350,000 of the principal was given to the Slater Fund,* devoted solely to the support of education for African Americans, and the rest was given to the Peabody Normal College, a white teachers' college in Nashville, Tennessee.

SELECTED BIBLIOGRAPHY

Henry Allen Bullock, *The History of Negro Education in the South from 1619 to the Present* (1967); George A. Dillingham, *The Foundation of the Peabody Tradition* (1989); John Hope Franklin and Alfred A. Moss, Jr., *From Slavery to Freedom: A History of Negro Americans*, 6th ed. (1988); Franklin Parker, *George Peabody: A Biography* (1971).

Suzanne Ellery Greene Chapelle

PEOPLE AGAINST RACISM. An all-white organization which evolved out of the Detroit, Michigan, branch of the Northern Student Movement (NSM),* People against Racism (PAR) was established in 1965 by white activist Frank Joyce as a response to two beliefs: Racism was fundamentally a white problem, and white activists should not be organizing in black communities. PAR's goal was to educate and organize white communities, to confront racist institutions, and to support the black movement, when possible and requested. By combining research, education, organization, and action with a historical analysis of American racism, PAR hoped to create a strong, antiracist faction within the white community. Although PAR disappeared in the early 1970s, its existence was important to both the civil rights movement and American society. By stressing that racism was a white problem, the group made it clear that apathetic white Americans were the problem nearly as much as outspoken racists. PAR also revealed the high level of commitment and dedication that would be required to produce meaningful change in the white community. PAR's ideas are still considered to be an advanced and sophisticated analysis of American racism.

SELECTED BIBLIOGRAPHY

"A Collection of Racist Myths" and "Repression in America: Law, Order, and the White Backlash," Kansas Collection, University of Kansas, Lawrence; Students for a Democratic Society Papers, 1958–1970, series 3, section VII (1965–1969), reel 31, "Related Groups-United States no. 167," Glen Rock, New Jersey, Microfilming Corporation of America (1977).

Mark E. Medina

PEOPLE UNITED TO SAVE HUMANITY (Operation PUSH). This Chicago-based, black economic rights organization was founded by Jesse Jackson* in 1971 after his break* with the Southern Christian Leadership Conference.* Worried that civil rights, unaccompanied by economic advancement, would be meaningless, PUSH leadership worked toward obtaining support from big business. Using massive boycotts of products and services, PUSH forced companies such as Coca-Cola, Seven-Up, Burger King, and Kentucky Fried Chicken to increase black employment as well as to deposit company funds in black banks. During the early 1980s, PUSH's boycott strategy indeed helped blacks come closer to their dream of equal employment opportunity.

SELECTED BIBLIOGRAPHY

John Martin Burke, *Civil Rights: A Current Guide to the People, Organization, and Events* (1974); Theodore Cross, *The Black Power Imperative: Racial Inequality and the Politics of Nonviolence* (1984).

Amm Saifuddin Khaled

PEPPER, CLAUDE DENSON (8 September 1900, Dudleyville, Ala.–30 May 1989, Washington, D.C.). Claude Pepper, the son of poor Alabama cotton farmers and heir to the state's populist tradition, rose to become the South's leading liberal Democratic congressman. Most of his proposals for government help for the powerless became law decades later. Pepper rose quickly in political life. He earned Phi Beta Kappa honors from the University of Alabama in 1921 and received his law degree from Harvard before moving to Florida to practice law. In 1929, Pepper was elected to the Florida legislature and staked out liberal positions on two controversial issues that marked his entire public life: senior citizen benefits and civil rights for blacks. He pushed through a popular bill exempting persons over sixty-five years of age from having to obtain a fishing license. But when he refused to censure the president's wife, Eleanor Roosevelt,* for inviting a black man to a White House tea, his constituents turned him out of office. Pepper reached the U.S. Senate in 1936 after highly publicized service as a state government attorney.

He was an unabashed New Deal liberal; he even went beyond Franklin D. Roosevelt's proposals to call for national health insurance, poll tax* repeal, and permanent federal agencies for public works and the arts. After World War II, Pepper's liberal crusade played poorly in Florida. His support for a permanent Fair Employment Practice Commission, his filibuster against the Taft-Hartley bill, and his opposition to the Truman aid package to Greece and Turkey conveyed to some constituents the impression that Pepper was nothing more than a "nigger-lover," a "Red Pepper," and a "wily, oily-tongued apologist" for northern union bosses. In 1950 Pepper was bounced from office. After his stunning defeat, Pepper practiced law until he won the new House seat for growing Dade County in 1962. He was one of the few Southerners to back John F. Kennedy's New Frontier and Lyndon B. Johnson's Great Society, including the medicare programs for the elderly of all colors and the epic Civil Rights Act of 1964* and the Voting Rights Act of 1965.* Later he gained fame as the chief defender of the elderly.

SELECTED BIBLIOGRAPHY
John Egerton, "Courtly Champion of America's Elderly," *New York Times Magazine* (29 November 1981), 125–31; Bill Keller, "I, Claude," *New Republic* 188 (7 March 1983), 16–18; Obituary, *New York Times*, 31 May 1989; Claude Denson Pepper and Hays Gorey, *Pepper: Eyewitness to a Century* (1987).

Bruce J. Dierenfield

PETERSON v. GREENVILLE, 373 U.S. 244 (1963). Ten African-American youths, including James Richard Peterson, entered the S. H. Kress store in Greenville, South Carolina, on 9 August 1960 and seated themselves at the lunch counter. The Greenville police arrested them, and a district court convicted them of trespass. On 21 May 1963 the U.S. Supreme Court threw out the conviction on the grounds that the Kress management had excluded the petitioners from the lunch counter solely because of their race. Such private actions abridging individual rights, however, would not have violated the equal protection clause of the Fourteenth Amendment* had the state not been involved. In this case, Chief Justice Earl Warren said that the city of Greenville, an agency of the state, had an ordinance requiring separation of the races in restaurants. The Court ruled that it was unconstitutional for a state or a community to require segregation in a business and that the state could not use the police power to enforce such segregation. The *Peterson* case was typical of a series of Supreme Court decisions outlawing segregation in privately owned businesses.

SELECTED BIBLIOGRAPHY
Alexander M. Bickel, "Civil Rights Boil-Up," *New Republic* (8 June 1963), 10–14; James E. Clayton, *The Making of Justice: The Supreme Court in Action* (1964); "In High Court—A Blanket Rule Against Segregation?" *U.S. News and World Report* (3 June 1963), 65; Milton R. Konvitz, *Expanding Liberties: Freedom's Gains in Postwar*

America (1966); George Rossman, ed., "Review of Recent Supreme Court Decisions," *American Bar Association Journal* 49 (1963), 1012.

Amm Saifuddin Khaled

PHELPS-STOKES FUND. The Phelps-Stokes Fund was established as a bequest from white philanthropist Caroline Phelps Stokes in 1911 for "the education of Negroes both in Africa and the United States, North American Indians and needy . . . white students" and for improved housing in New York City. The fund set up schools in Africa, endowed schools in the United States for black youth (at first supporting Booker T. Washington's* industrial training program), and conducted studies of African, African-American, and Native American education both here and in Africa. It established residences for black working women in New York and published works about black Americans and their accomplishments. A fund president conceived the idea for the United Negro College Fund.* Currently, the fund provides scholarships, develops educational programs that serve blacks and Native Americans, and examines the treatment of minorities in New York's state courts.

SELECTED BIBLIOGRAPHY

Edward Berman, "American Influence on African Education: The Role of the Phelps-Stokes Fund's Education Commission," *Comparative Education Review* 15 (June 1971), 132–45; *Educational Adaptations: Report of Ten Years Work of the Phelps-Stokes Fund, 1910–1920* (1920); Phelps-Stokes Fund Papers, Schomburg Center for Research in Black Culture, New York City; Anson Phelps Stokes, *Negro Status and Race Relations in the United States, 1911–1946* (1948); *Twenty Year Report of the Phelps-Stokes Fund, 1911–1931* (1932).

Cheryl Greenberg

PHILADELPHIA PLAN. Following a 1967 investigation of problems of compliance with Executive Order 11246* in construction trades in Philadelphia, Pennsylvania, the Labor Department, headed in 1969 by Secretary George F. Shultz, developed a plan for extending minority employment in that city. The Philadelphia Plan required that individuals bidding on contracts of $500,000 or more submit an acceptable affirmative action* program that outlined specific numerical goals for minority group employment. Contractors responded by claiming that such goals amounted to racial quotas, which were banned by Title VII of the Civil Rights Act of 1964.* In November 1968, Comptroller-General Elmer Staats ruled that the Philadelphia Plan illegally required contractors to set racial quotas, and the plan was suspended. Following hearings, which produced evidence of continuing discrimination by the Philadelphia construction unions, Assistant Secretary of Wage and Labor Standards Arthur Fletcher supervised the design of a revised plan. As a gesture toward the antiquota language of Title VII, the June 1969 plan now suggested a target range expressed as a percentage, rather than a numerical, goal. Under its provisions, prospective bidders were required to commit to a target range of minority (now defined as "Negro, Oriental, American Indian and Spanish Surnamed Americans") manpower utilization and a timetable for its accomplishment. In September Fletcher's implementation memorandum set five-year target ranges. In December 1969, the Nixon administration defeated an attempt by Congress to ban the plan. To revive the plan, Labor Secretary Shultz issued an order in February 1970 which required all bidders, not just construction contractors, to submit an affirmative action plan within 120 days of signing a contract. An acceptable program required an analysis of all major job categories to identify underutilization of minorities. In March 1970 a suit brought against the Philadelphia Plan by Pennsylvania contractors was dismissed in federal district court. The Third Circuit Court of Appeals upheld the plan in April 1971.

SELECTED BIBLIOGRAPHY
Hugh Davis Graham, *The Civil Rights Era* (1990); U.S. Congress, Senate, Committee on the Judiciary, Subcommittee on the Separation of Powers, *The Philadelphia Plan: Hearing before the Subcommittee on the Separation of Powers*, 91st Cong., 1st sess., 27–28 October 1969.

Nancy Diamond

PHYLON. Founded in 1940 by W.E.B. Du Bois,* *Phylon* emerged, almost immediately, as the preeminent journal of scholarly and intellectual thought in the African-American community. The editorial board was a virtual who's who of African-American intellectuals of the period. It included Horace Mann Bond, Rayford W. Logan,* Mercer Cook, and William S. Braithwaite.* *Phylon*'s stature was due, predominantly, to the fact that the journal was in many ways a personification of Du Bois's own intellectual rigor and scholarship. *Phylon* closely followed the research staked out in Du Bois's earlier Atlanta University* scholarly monographs on black history; yet, *Phylon* appealed to a much wider intellectual public, and that appeal placed it among the "best university journals in the nation."

SELECTED BIBLIOGRAPHY
Herbert Aptheker, ed., *The Correspondence of W.E.B. DuBois* (1968); Walter C. Daniel, *Black Journals of the United States* (1982); W.E.B. Du Bois, *The Autobiography of W.E.B. DuBois* (1968).

Maghan Keita

PINCHBACK, PINCKNEY BENTON STEWART (10 May 1837, Macon, Ga.–21 December 1921, Washington, D.C.). The son of Major William Pinchback by the newly manumitted, racially mixed Eliza Stewart, he was said to have been so light in appearance that he was often "mistaken for a white man." His education at Cincinnati came to an abrupt halt in 1849 when his father died without adequately providing for Eliza and her offspring; thus, at twelve years of age, Pinckney began to work on riverboats to help support his family. Entering Union service at New Orleans during the Civil War, he was placed in charge of recruiting black troops and was made a captain in the Louisiana Native Guards. He demanded that blacks be given political rights, and he protested the treatment of black troops. His outspokenness cost him promotions and compelled him to resign in September 1863. When he subsequently raised a cavalry company of free men of color, the Union army refused to muster it into service. He left Louisiana for Ohio in disappointment. Returning to New Orleans after the war, he became a delegate to the constitutional convention of 1867–1868, where his proposals for free public education and civil rights aided his election to the state senate in 1868. He continued to push such measures both in office and in the *New Orleans Louisianian*, which he founded in 1871. After the death of Lieutenant Governor Oscar J. Dunn in November 1871, the Senate elected Pinchback to the post. Forty-three days before his term ended, Governor Henry Clay Warmoth was impeached; and from 9 December 1872 until 13 January 1873, Pinchback served as the nation's first black governor. In 1872 he was elected to both the United States House of Representatives and to the United States Senate, but he was not allowed to take either seat when enemies within his own party conspired with Democrats against him. He was appointed to the state board of education in 1877, was elected a state constitutional convention delegate in 1879, and was appointed surveyor of customs at New Orleans. In 1893 he left Louisiana and eventually settled in Washington, D.C., where he remained active in politics and civil rights.

SELECTED BIBLIOGRAPHY

James Haskins, *Pinckney Benton Stewart Pinchback* (1973); Joe Gray Taylor, *Louisiana Reconstructed, 1863–1877* (1974); Rayford W. Logan and Michael R. Winston, eds., *Dictionary of American Negro Biography* (1982).

Gary B. Mills

PITTSBURGH COURIER. Founded in 1910 by Edwin N. Harleston, the *Pittsburgh Courier* quickly came under the editorship of Robert Vann,* an attorney, who with the help of Ira Lewis was eventually to make it one of the nation's leading black newspapers. At first, however, it struggled financially and mainly promoted Vann's career. By the 1920s the newspaper had a city and a national edition with approximately 55,000 circulation. It had also built its own printing plant. In the 1930s the paper helped convince blacks to switch from the Republican to the Democratic party. By 1937 it was the nation's leading black newspaper with around 150,000 subscribers all over the nation. Vann died in 1940, but during World War II the newspaper conducted an effective Double V for victory campaign: against the overseas enemy and against discrimination at home. It reached its circulation peak of 357,212 in 1947, but Ira Lewis died in 1948; and, during the civil rights struggle, white newspapers began to cover black news, so its circulation slid disastrously. The newspaper continues in business in 1992 as the *New Pittsburgh Courier*, but it is no longer the national force it once was.

SELECTED BIBLIOGRAPHY

Andrew Buni, *Robert L. Vann of the Pittsburgh Courier, Politics and Journalism* (1974); Nancy J. Weiss, *Farewell to the Party of Lincoln* (1983).

John F. Marszalek

PLESSY v. FERGUSON, 163 U.S. 537 (1896). The separate but equal* doctrine upheld by the Supreme Court in the 1896 *Plessy v. Ferguson* decision constituted a major legal barrier to equal rights for blacks for more than half a century. The decision was one of a long series of Court opinions beginning in the 1870s—the *Slaughter House Cases,** *United States v. Reese,** *United States v. Cruikshank,** the *Civil Rights Cases*—which eroded the rights and privileges gained by blacks during Reconstruction and guaranteed by the Fourteenth* and Fifteenth Amendments.* The *Plessy* principle, by rendering all but meaningless the Fourteenth Amendment's equal protection clause, provided the constitutional basis for a plethora of southern Jim Crow* laws that accompanied the reestablishment of white supremacy after 1876.

A Louisiana statute of 1890 required all railroad companies operating in the state to provide equal but separate accommodations for black and white passengers. Homer A. Plessy, an African American who often passed as white, was arrested for refusing to vacate a seat in a white compartment of a Louisiana train. He instituted action to restrain enforcement of the 1890 law on grounds that it was unconstitutional. Losing in the state courts, he appealed to the Supreme Court. In the *Civil Rights Cases* of 1883, the Court had said that the federal government could protect blacks from segregation and discrimination arising from state action but that private "invasion of individual rights" was not prohibited. In the *Plessy* decision, state action was at issue, however, and the Court seemingly ignored the distinction between private and state action it had delineated earlier. The Louisiana Jim Crow statute, said the Court, did not deprive African Americans of equal protection of the laws. The Fourteenth Amendment "could not have been intended to abolish distinctions based upon color," and laws permitting or even requiring separation of the races did not necessarily imply the inferiority of either race to the other. Such laws, continued the Court, were clearly authorized by the Constitution under the police power of the states. And although every exercise of the police power must be reasonable, there was nothing unreasonable in the Louisiana statute requiring the separation of the two races in public conveyances.

Registering a vigorous lone dissent, Justice John Marshall Harlan* insisted, "Our Constitution is color-blind, and neither knows nor tolerates classes among citizens." His prediction that "the judgment this day rendered will, in time, prove to be quite as pernicious as the decision made by this tribunal in the Dred Scott Case" was sound prophecy. With the *Plessy* decision, the separate but equal formula became the new constitutional orthodoxy that prevailed until 1954.

SELECTED BIBLIOGRAPHY
Catherine A. Barnes, *Journey from Jim Crow: The Desegregation of Southern Transit* (1983); Charles A. Lofgren, *The Plessy Case: A Legal-Historical Interpretation* (1987); Otto H. Olsen, *The Thin Disguise: Turning Points in Negro History, Plessy v. Ferguson, a Documentary Presentation* (1967); Mark V. Tushnet, *The NAACP's Legal Strategy against Segregated Education, 1925–1950* (1987); C. Vann Woodward, *The Strange Career of Jim Crow*, 2nd ed. (1974).

Charles D. Lowery

POLL TAX. Although the word "poll" in the phrase "poll tax" refers to the head of household upon whom this tax was levied, in the public perception the ancient tradition of the poll tax has become inextricably linked with voter qualifications. In the late nineteenth century many states sought to circumvent the Fifteenth Amendment* by denying the right to vote to those who had not paid the poll tax. Poor blacks, as well as many poor whites, were unable to pay the tax and were thus disfranchised. The Twenty-fourth Amendment, ratified in 1964, prohibited use of the poll tax in prescribing voter qualifications for federal elections.

SELECTED BIBLIOGRAPHY
J. Morgan Kousser, *The Shaping of Southern Politics: Suffrage Restriction and the Establishment of the One-Party South, 1880–1910* (1974); Paul Lewinson, *Race, Class, and Party: A History of Negro Suffrage and White Politics in the South* (1965).

Stephen Cresswell

POLLOCK v. WILLIAMS, 322 U.S. 4 (1944). This case was one of a series of important black peonage* cases in which the Supreme Court, between the years 1911 and 1944, helped to sustain the national antipeonage campaign then being waged by African Americans. The circumstances of the case closely parallel those of earlier important peonage cases, such as *Bailey v. Alabama** (1911), *United States v. Reynolds** (1914), and *Taylor v. Georgia** (1942). James Pollock was a black resident of Florida who accepted a cash advance from an employer and then failed to provide the promised services. His actions violated a Florida statute typical of laws passed by southern states after Reconstruction permitting the arrest of blacks for vagrancy, breach of labor contracts, and other crimes. The laws were used by southern planters and others to create a pool of cheap

Blacks waiting to register to vote in Fulton County, Georgia, May 1946, following Georgia's repeal of the poll tax. (Special Collections, Pullen Library, Georgia State University.)

black labor and to prevent indebted employees from leaving their service. The Florida trial court held that Pollock's breach of the labor contract into which he had entered was prima facie evidence of intent to defraud his employer. The Supreme Court reversed the lower court and ruled that the Florida statute violated the Thirteenth Amendment* and federal antipeonage laws. *Pollock* dealt a death blow to southern black peonage. A few prosecutions were filed by the Civil Rights Section, Justice Department* in the 1950s, but for all practical purposes black peonage disappeared after *Pollock*.

SELECTED BIBLIOGRAPHY

Pete Daniel, *The Shadow of Slavery: Peonage in the South, 1909–1969* (1972); Loren Miller, *The Petitioners: The Story of the Supreme Court of the United States and the Negro* (1966); Edgar Bronson Talman, "Review of the Recent Supreme Court Decisions," *American Bar Association Journal* 30 (1944), 297–99; Melvin I. Urofsky, *A March of Liberty: A Constitutional History of the United States* (1988).

Charles D. Lowery

POOLE, ELIJAH (Elijah Muhammad) (7 October 1897, Sandersville, Ga.–25 February 1975, Chicago, Ill.). The son of sharecroppers and former slaves, Elijah Poole, or Elijah Muhammad, rose to prominence as the spiritual leader of the Nation of Islam, commonly known as the Black Muslims.* By the 1960s he had become a powerful symbol of black nationalism, not only to his religious movement but also to the mushrooming secular Black Power* movement as well. At the time of his death in 1975, he had become a controversial figure for his militant racial views, such as derogating whites as incorrigible "blue-eyed devils," and his well-publicized feud with his former lieutenant, Malcolm X,* whose assassination in 1965 has been attributed to three of Poole's zealous followers.

Poole left Georgia for the North in 1923, settling finally in Detroit, Michigan, where he met W. D. Fard, who claimed to be "Allah," the self-annointed leader of the "Lost-Found Nation of Islam in the Wilderness of North America." After Fard's unexplained disappearance in 1934, Poole, who came now to be known as Elijah Muhammad the "Apostle" or "Prophet," assumed control of the fledgling Nation of Islam, a position he held officially or unofficially until his death. Under Muhammad's leadership, the Nation of Islam grew into a Chicago-based, religious-nationalistic organization whose national membership, located primarily in the urban North, ranged between 50,000 and 250,000. Muhammad preached his doctrines of racial separation, self-help, self-defense (a direct precursor to Black Power*), and racial dignity through his powerful speeches and through such written works as the Black Muslim weekly tabloid *Muhammad Speaks** and his *Message to the Black Man* (1965). As the contemporary civil rights movement peaked in the

1960s, Elijah Muhammad remained a controversial figure: suspect in the eyes of moderate integrationists and revered in the minds of militant Black Power advocates.

SELECTED BIBLIOGRAPHY

"Elijah Muhammad Dead; Black Muslim Leader, 77," *New York Times*, 26 February 1975; E. U. Essien-Udom, *Black Nationalism: A Search for an Identity in America* (1962); Raymond L. Hall, *Black Separatism in the United States* (1978); C. Eric Lincoln, *The Black Muslims in America* (1973); *Muhammad Speaks*, 1961–1975.

Irvin D. Solomon

POOR PEOPLE'S MARCH ON WASHINGTON (Poor People's Campaign). The last major demonstration planned by Martin Luther King, Jr.,* and the Southern Christian Leadership Conference,* this protest was designed "to force Americans to face the fact that America is a racist country" and that her racism had impoverished thousands. King argued that the right to vote and to eat in any establishment failed to affect living conditions. The poor needed something more. Among the demands of this campaign were full employment, a guaranteed annual income, and construction funds for low-cost housing. Since it was essential to make the federal government aware of the plight of the poor, King proposed a mule cart procession, involving thousands, which would begin around 22 April 1968 in Mississippi and terminate in Washington, D.C. There, the participants would construct a shantytown close to the federal buildings. He suggested that demonstrators might bring some shanties from Mississippi on flatbed trucks to further dramatize the poverty in America. His assassination temporarily halted preparations for the campaign, but Ralph Abernathy,* King's successor, vowed to lead the demonstrators to Washington as King had planned. Nine caravans (buses and cars) of people converged on Washington where they built a plywood shantytown—Resurrection City*—within walking distance of the White House. The campaign proved unsuccessful.

SELECTED BIBLIOGRAPHY

Jim Bishop, *The Days of Martin Luther King, Jr.* (1971); Charles E. Fager, *Uncertain Resurrection: The Poor People's Washington Campaign* (1969); Gerold Frank, *An American Death* (1972); David J. Garrow, *Bearing the Cross: Martin Luther King and the Southern Christian Leadership Conference* (1986); *The Negro Almanac* (1983).

Betty L. Plummer

PORTSMOUTH, VIRGINIA, SIT-INS (1960). The sit-in movement in Virginia began in February 1960. These demonstrations were part of a movement which had originated in Greensboro, North Carolina, and had spread quickly first to other North Carolina cities and then to Hampton, Norfolk, and Portsmouth, Virginia. Although students from Virginia State College, Hampton Institute,* and Norcom High School were among the participants, the movement was primarily an effort organized by the NAACP.* Students from Hampton Institute staged sit-ins at the W. F. Woolworth store in Hampton and a Hampton drugstore lunch counter. The sit-ins spread to the Norfolk-Portsmouth area when P. L. Artis sought to be served breakfast and later lunch at Bradshaw-Diehl's Department Store. At the same time eighteen blacks entered Rose's and took seats at the lunch counter, and thirty-eight blacks asked to be served at Norfolk's Woolworth counter. In each case the sit-ins were orderly, and no arrests were made. The following week about 150 black students demonstrated at Rose's in Portsmouth. The situation evolved into fist-fights between white and black youths. Later, when a crowd of some 3,000 assembled at the shopping center, twenty-seven persons, white and black, were arrested for various disturbances. As a result of these events, some establishments closed their lunch counters for the next several days. Eventually, court orders and voluntary action by some store owners permanently desegregated the facilities.

SELECTED BIBLIOGRAPHY

Norfolk Ledger Dispatch, 13, 15, 16 February 1960; *Virginia Pilot*, 17, 18 February 1960.

Charles A. Risher

POSTON, THEODORE "TED" ROOSEVELT AUGUSTUS MAJOR (4 July 1906, Hopkinsville, Ky.–11 January 1974, Brooklyn, N.Y.). Poston began his career with the family newspaper, *The Contender*, in Hopkinsville, Kentucky. In 1929 he went to work for Harlem's *Amsterdam News*,* becoming city editor in 1934 and taking an active part in the *News* strike of 1934. During World War II, he served as chief of the Negro News Desk in the Office of War Information. After the war, he was hired by the *New York Post*, and he became the first black columnist to work full time for a New York daily. Poston's byline ran in the *Post* for thirty-three years.

SELECTED BIBLIOGRAPHY

James Forman, *The Making of Black Revolutionaries* (1985); Obituary, *New York Times*, 12 January 1974; Roi Ottley, *New World A-Coming* (1943); Ted Poston, "My Most Humiliating Jim Crow Experience," *Negro Digest* 2 (April 1944), 55–56; Theressa Rush, Carol Myers, and Esther Arata, *Black American Writers Past and Present: A Biographical and Bibliographical Dictionary* (1975).

Ray Branch

POWELL, ADAM CLAYTON, JR. (29 November 1908, New Haven, Conn.–4 April 1972, Miami, Fla.). Easily the nation's most recognized African-American politician from the 1940s to the 1960s, Adam Clayton Powell, Jr., was heir to one of the nation's largest black congregations—the Abyssinian Baptist Church in New York City's Harlem. He grew up in the middle of what he would later call Black Power,* listening to his father and to the black nationalist Marcus Garvey.* Educated at Colgate

University, in Hamilton, New York (A.B., 1930), Columbia University, in New York (M.A., 1932), and Shaw University, in Raleigh, North Carolina (D.D., 1935), Powell succeeded his father as pastor in 1937 and became a force in city politics as he led demonstrations to force major employers in Harlem to hire blacks. He was elected in 1941 to the city council of New York and in 1945 to the U.S. House of Representatives, where he served for eleven successive terms. With characteristic panache, he broke the racial bars in congressional service facilities, pushed to admit black journalists to the press galleries, and pioneered the use of the power of the federal purse to punish segregation. He sought, for instance, to deny federal funds to any public project that discriminated. As chair of the House Committee on Education and Labor (1960–1967) he managed the enactment of numerous laws from minimum wage to antipoverty.

SELECTED BIBLIOGRAPHY

P. Allan Dionisopoulos, *Rebellion, Racism, and Representation: The Adam Clayton Powell Case and Its Antecedents* (1970); Charles V. Hamilton, *Adam Clayton Powell, Jr.: The Political Biography of an American Dilemma* (1991); James Haskins, *Adam Clayton Powell: Portrait of a Marching Black* (1974); Robert E. Jakoubek, *Adam Clayton Powell, Jr.* (1988); Adam Clayton Powell, *Adam by Adam; the Autobiography of Adam Clayton Powell, Jr.* (1971).

Thomas J. Davis

POWELL v. ALABAMA, 287 U.S. 45 (1932). In 1931 Ozie Powell and the eight other teenage "Scottsboro Boys" (see Scottsboro Trials) stood trial for the alleged rape of two white women, a capital offense. The trial judge somewhat casually appointed all members of the local bar as their counsel and invited anyone willing to help to do so. At trial the same day, all received death sentences, which (except for one juvenile) the state supreme court affirmed. This first of two appeals to the Supreme Court focused on the inadequacy of trial counsel, in violation of the Sixth Amendment and the due process clause of the Fourteenth Amendment.* Justice George Sutherland, for the seven-to-two majority, reversed the convictions. He combined sociological considerations with a historic review of due process back to the Magna Carta. Counsel was a necessary part of any hearing, and since the defendants were "young, ignorant, illiterate, surrounded by hostile sentiment, hauled back and forth under guard of soldiers" and charged with the community's most atrocious crime, effective counsel was vital. This case marked the first incorporation of any element of criminal due process from the Bill of Rights into the Fourteenth Amendment. Such incorporation seemed to be precluded by *Hurtado v. California* (1884), but "compelling circumstances" supported this exception. The subsequent retrials led to *Norris v. Alabama** (1935), another appeal on a different issue.

SELECTED BIBLIOGRAPHY
Dan T. Carter, *Scottsboro* (1969); Robert F. Cushman, *Cases in Constitutional Law* (1979); "Notes," *University of Pennsylvania Law Review* 81 (1933), 337–38; "Recent Decisions," *Columbia University Law Review* 32 (1932), 1430–31.

James E. Sefton

PRAYER PILGRIMAGE TO WASHINGTON (1957). The Prayer Pilgrimage was a mass rally held in Washington, D.C., to demonstrate support for the proposed Civil Rights Act of 1957.* The idea for the pilgrimage came out of a meeting of the Southern Christian Leadership Conference* in February 1957. Originally, the concept of the march had been to protest President Dwight D. Eisenhower's earlier failure to meet with a group of black leaders led by A. Philip Randolph.* Randolph, Martin Luther King, Jr.,* and Roy Wilkins* organized the protest. Held on 17 May, the third anniversary of the *Brown v. Board of Education** decision, the Prayer Pilgrimage drew a disappointing crowd of between 15,000 and 25,000; organizers had predicted a turnout of 50,000. Randolph presided. The crowd heard Mahalia Jackson sing and listened to speeches by Wilkins, Adam Clayton Powell, Jr.,* Mordecai Johnson,* Fred L. Shuttlesworth,* and others. Entertainers such as Sammy Davis, Jr., Ruby Dee, Sidney Poitier, and Harry Belafonte made appearances, as did baseball great Jackie Robinson.* King spoke last, and his speech, in which he repeatedly demanded "give us the ballot," drew the greatest response from the crowd. The event helped establish King's position as a national leader.

SELECTED BIBLIOGRAPHY
Taylor Branch, *Parting the Waters: America in the King Years, 1954–63* (1988); Adam Fairclough, *To Redeem the Soul of America: The Southern Christian Leadership Conference and Martin Luther King, Jr.* (1987); David J. Garrow, *Bearing the Cross: Martin Luther King and the Southern Christian Leadership Conference* (1986); David Levering Lewis, *King: A Critical Biography* (1970).

Michael S. Mayer

PRICE, J[OSEPH] C[HARLES] (10 February 1854, Elizabeth City, N.C.– 25 October 1893, Salisbury, N.C.). One of the most prominent African-American educators of his generation, Price's career was established after his graduation from Lincoln University in Pennsylvania in 1881, when the African Methodist Episcopal Zion Church enlisted him to embark on a speaking tour of England on behalf of a struggling denominational school named Zion Wesley Institute. Price raised nearly ten thousand dollars for Zion Wesley and was named president of the institute in 1882. He built the Salisbury, North Carolina, school into a four-year liberal arts institution named Livingstone College. Subsequent speaking tours established Price not only as a minister but also as an advocate of education and civil rights in the post–Reconstruction South.

In North Carolina, Price fought for a state-supported college for his race and pleaded for federal funds for education. Price received national attention in 1890 after he was elected president of the Afro-American League,* an organization founded by *New York Age** editor T. Thomas Fortune* for the legal protection of blacks. For the next three years, Price continued to address civil rights as a national concern, denouncing separate car laws and defending black suffrage. Price's promise as a national leader ended abruptly when he died of Bright's disease in 1893 at the age of thirty-nine.

SELECTED BIBLIOGRAPHY

Daniel W. Crofts, "The Blair Bill and the Elections Bill: The Congressional Aftermath to Reconstruction" (Ph.D. diss., Yale University, 1968); Lenwood Davis, "A History of Livingstone College, 1879–1957" (D.A. thesis, Carnegie-Mellon University, 1979); Frenise A. Logan, *The Negro in North Carolina 1876–1894* (1964); August Meier, *Negro Thought in America 1880–1915: Racial Ideologies in the Age of Booker T. Washington* (1963); William J. Walls, *Joseph Charles Price, Educator and Race Leader* (1943); Paul Yandle, "Joseph Charles Price and the Southern Problem" (master's thesis, Wake Forest University, 1990).

Paul D. Yandle

PRICE, LEONTYNE (10 February 1927, Laurel, Miss.–). "The prima donna absoluta," she earned a B.A. from Central State University in Ohio in 1948. She pursued additional voice training at the Julliard School in New York and with Florence Page Kimball in New York. Despite the reluctance of the American opera world to permit blacks to sing major roles at the leading opera houses, she dreamed of singing at the Metropolitan Opera. In 1959 she was offered that opportunity, but she refused the part of Aida, choosing to wait and make her debut in a role where race was insignificant. In 1961 when she sang the role of Leonora in *Il Trovatore* she became the first black woman to sing a major role on opening night at the Met.

SELECTED BIBLIOGRAPHY

John P. Davis, ed., *The American Negro Reference Book* (1966); Marianna W. Davis, ed., *Contributions of Black Women to America*, vol. 1, *The Arts, Media, Business, Law, Sports* (1982); Hugh Lee Lyon, *Leontyne Price: Highlights of a Prima Donna* (1973); William C. Matney, ed., *Who's Who among Black Americans* (1988); George A. Sewell, *Mississippi Black History Makers* (1977).

Betty L. Plummer

PROJECT C. *See* Birmingham Confrontation.

PUBLIC SCHOOL BUSING. Court-ordered busing to achieve racial desegregation of the public schools in areas where dual systems once existed resulted from the 1971 *Swann v. Charlotte-Mecklenburg Board of Education** decision, the national test case for busing. Busing, the Su-

Leontyne Price at Jackson, Mississippi, concert, 26 April 1970. (Charles H. Ramberg Collection; courtesy Mississippi Department of Archives and History.)

preme Court said in its unanimous but controversial ruling, was a legal remedial tool to fulfill the intent of the 1954 *Brown v. Board of Education** decision. Transporting students to ameliorate school-board-imposed segregation violated no one's constitutional rights, said the Court. "Every available technique," including massive crosstown busing and the redrawing of school districts, should be employed to correct persistent racial imbalances in the public schools. President Richard M. Nixon, who praised the ideal of the neighborhood school and predictably denounced busing because it challenged his administration's legal position on school desegregation issues, tried unsuccessfully to get Congress to pass legislation limiting busing. Such legislation was passed during the presidency of Gerald Ford.

In 1973–74 busing became a politically volatile topic outside the South when northern cities came under judicial scrutiny. In 1974 Boston became the center for northern urban opposition to the use of the school bus to integrate the city school system. The federal courts stood firm, however, and proponents of integration beat back a serious attempt to pass a constitutional amendment against court-ordered busing. As the Supreme Court became more conservative, however, it issued a series of decisions in the late 1970s and 1980s, which rejected busing as a means of integration. Many blacks were not entirely unhappy at this turn of events because it was their children, not those of white parents, that were usually bused. In 1992 the school bus is no longer an important civil rights vehicle; busing is widely viewed both by black leaders and white liberals as a failure, and urban schools remain de facto segregated.

SELECTED BIBLIOGRAPHY

Judith Bentley, *Busing the Continuous Controversy* (1982); Bernard R. Boxill, *Blacks and Social Justice* (1984); Paul R. Dimond, *Beyond Busing* (1985); Frye Gaillard, *The Dream Long Deferred* (1988); Edward Keynes, *The Courts vs. Congress* (1989); Bernard Schwartz, *Swann's War* (1986).

Jessie M. Carter

Q

QUARLES, BENJAMIN (23 January 1904, Boston, Mass.–). A renowned African-American historian, Quarles earned his B.A. at Shaw University, in Raleigh, North Carolina, and his M.A. and Ph.D. at the University of Wisconsin. He lectured at Shaw and Dillard Universities before moving to Morgan State University, a predominantly black institution in Maryland. At Morgan State, Quarles taught history and became the chairperson of the History Department. Quarles is well known for his many outstanding publications, including *Frederick Douglass* (1948), *The Negro in the Civil War* (1953), *The Negro in the American Revolutionary War* (1960), *The Negro in the Making of America* (1964), and *Allies for Freedom: Blacks and John Brown* (1974). Quarles provided concrete evidence in these works to support his main argument that blacks have always played a significant role in the development of America.

SELECTED BIBLIOGRAPHY

Directory of American Scholars, 8th ed. (1982); *Afro-American Encylcopedia* (1974).

Amos J. Beyan

R

RACE RELATIONS LAW REPORTER. This journal was started by the Vanderbilt University School of Law, in Nashville, Tennessee, in February 1956 with funding provided by the Fund for the Republic, Inc. In 1959 the Southern Education Reporting Service* took over management functions for the *Reporter*, but the law school continued to edit it. Originally a bimonthly, the journal became a quarterly in spring 1959. Over the years most of its support has come from the Ford Foundation. The *Reporter* aimed to "report the materials in all fields where the issue of race and color is presented as having legal consequence" by systematically compiling the primary documents in the field. It included the texts of decisions by the United States Supreme Court, lower federal courts, and state courts; federal and state legislation; administrative rules, regulations, and orders; opinions of state attorneys general; and a sampling of local ordinances. Editors provided case summaries and occasionally abridged and summarized documents. Lacking financial support, the *Reporter* ended publication in the winter of 1967 and was succeeded from May 1969 to March 1972 by the Vanderbilt Law School's briefer *Race Relations Law Survey*.

SELECTED BIBLIOGRAPHY
Race Relations Law Reporter; Southern School News.

Charles W. Eagles

RADICAL RECONSTRUCTION. This term, also called Military Reconstruction and Congressional Reconstruction, refers to the period from 1867 to 1876, when Congress asserted control over readmission of former Confederate states into the Union. Radical Reconstruction was initiated in 1867 with the passage of a series of Reconstruction Acts. The first act,

The first vote. (Library of Congress.)

passed on 2 March 1867, divided the conquered South into five military districts each under the control of a general appointed by the president. States were directed to convene constitutional conventions in which former slaves could participate and to frame new state constitutions providing for black citizenship and suffrage. Supplemental acts ensured implementation by instructing federal commanders to expedite elections, register voters, and convene constitutional conventions. Some historians argue that Radical Reconstruction is a misnomer. After all, former slaves were not distributed real property or other compensations which would have radically altered the distribution of wealth and influence in the South. Another group contends, however, that granting blacks suffrage (considering that in 1867 eighteen of twenty-five northern states refused blacks the vote) made Reconstruction radical. During the period, blacks became politically active in the South and gained valuable experience.

SELECTED BIBLIOGRAPHY

Avery Craven, *Reconstruction: The Ending of the Civil War* (1969); Robert Cruden, *The Negro in Reconstruction* (1969); W.E.B. Du Bois, *Black Reconstruction in America* (1935); Rembert W. Patrick, *The Reconstruction of the Nation* (1967); Hans L. Trefousse, *The Radical Republicans: Lincoln's Vanguard for Racial Justice* (1969).

Wali Rashash Kharif

RADICAL REPUBLICANS. The most advanced groups of Republicans, they advocated resistance to the slaveholders before the Civil War, emancipation during the conflict, and civil rights for the freedmen afterward. Never an organized faction, they differed among themselves on issues other than slavery and race. The radicals took an active part in the founding of the Republican party, its early struggles in Congress, and in opposing compromise during the secession crisis. Their relations with Abraham Lincoln were controversial; his end aims were similar to theirs, but he had a better sense of timing and angered them by moving too slowly against slavery. Yet he was able to make use of their pressure to move forward in spite of conservative opposition, so that emancipation became a fact before the war was over. At first the radicals greeted the accession of Andrew Johnson with pleasure, but when the new president unfolded his conservative program of Reconstruction, they became his most determined opponents. They were never able to frame Reconstruction measures exactly to their liking; nevertheless, their relentless pressure induced the majority of Congress to override his veto of the Civil Rights Bill, pass the Fourteenth Amendment,* and, with the Reconstruction Acts, inaugurate Congressional Reconstruction. And while they were unable to convict Johnson in the impeachment trial, they did succeed in passing the Fifteenth Amendment* which enfranchised blacks. During the 1870s their influence began to wane. Advancing age and death removed the most active; lessening interest in Reconstruction made it difficult to sustain the Republican governments in the South, and the disputed election of 1876 led to the compromise of the following year involving the inauguration of Rutherford B. Hayes in return, in part, for the removal of federal troops from the statehouses in the South, so that Reconstruction ended.

SELECTED BIBLIOGRAPHY

Hans L. Trefousse, *The Radical Republicans: Lincoln's Vanguard for Racial Justice* (1968); T. Harry Williams, *Lincoln and the Radicals* (1941).

Hans L. Trefousse

RAINEY, HOMER P. (19 January 1896, Clarksville, Tex.–19 December 1985, Boulder, Colo.). Rainey, who held degrees from Austin College and the University of Chicago, had a distinguished career in education when he was hired as president of the University of Texas in 1939. He soon alienated the ultraconservative board of regents, who complained that Rainey wanted to improve educational opportunities for blacks in Texas and that he favored equal rights in general. The regents fired him in 1944, largely because of his defense of academic freedom. African Americans, voting in Democratic primaries for the first time in 1946, overwhelmingly supported Rainey for governor, but he lost the runoff and left the state.

SELECTED BIBLIOGRAPHY
Alice Cox, "The Rainey Affair: A History of the Academic Freedom Controversy at the University of Texas, 1938–1946" (Ph.D. diss. University of Denver, 1970); George N. Green, *The Establishment in Texas Politics: The Primitive Years, 1938–1957* (1979); "Rainey, Homer P.," *Current Biography* (1946); Homer Rainey Biographical File, Barker Texas History Center, University of Texas at Austin; Homer Rainey Papers, University of Missouri Library, Columbia.

George N. Green

RAINEY, JULIAN D. (1889–30 March 1961, Boston, Mass.). A graduate of the City College of New York and the Suffolk Law School, in Boston, Massachusetts, Rainey was the first black to serve as corporation counsel for the city of Boston. He held this position from 1929 to 1932, when he left to become special assistant to the U.S. Attorney General, a position he held until 1944. Assistant to the Democratic national chairman, Rainey also functioned as a counsel for the NAACP.*

SELECTED BIBLIOGRAPHY
Obituary, *New York Times*, 1 April 1961.

Ray Branch

RANDOLPH, A. PHILIP (15 April 1889, Crescent City, Fla.–16 May 1979, New York, N.Y.). A leading African-American labor unionist and civil rights activist, Randolph received his high school education in Jacksonville, Florida, and his post–secondary education at City College of New York. While in New York, Randolph served as an elevator operator, a porter, and a waiter. In 1917 he and Chandler Owen launched a radical magazine, *The Messenger,** to address the social injustices blacks experienced. Randolph was arrested in Cleveland, Ohio, by federal marshals because he opposed black support for World War I. Randolph's short-term imprisonment did not deter him from his militant civil rights and union activities. He organized black porters into a union, founding the Brotherhood of Sleeping Car Porters and Maids* in 1925. Despite opposition to the newly founded union from other unions and the Pullman company, its membership and bargaining power continued to increase. In 1941 Randolph warned the administration of President Franklin D. Roosevelt that, if the discriminatory hiring practices of companies that received federal subsidies did not stop, he and some 50,000 blacks would march on Washington, D.C. This threat was a factor in President Roosevelt's promulgation in June 1941 of Executive Order 8802,* out of which grew the Fair Employment Practice Committee.* President Harry S. Truman established a similar committee in 1950. Randolph and Grant Reynolds of New York founded a movement against racism in the U.S. Army in 1947. Their movement influenced President Truman to give assurance in 1948 that racism in the army would be abolished. Randolph was among the prominent leaders of the 1963 March on Washington.* He remained active in the civil rights struggle until his death in 1979.

SELECTED BIBLIOGRAPHY

Jervis Anderson, *A. Philip Randolph: A Biographical Portrait* (1973); *Current Biography* (1951); Julius Jacobson, ed., *The Negro and the American Labor Movement* (1968); Thomas Palm, ed., *The Economics of Black America* (1972).

Amos J. Beyan

RANDOLPH INSTITUTE, A. PHILIP. Founded in 1965 by A. Philip Randolph* and Bayard Rustin,* the Randolph Institute serves as a bridge between the African-American community and organized labor. Part of the American Federation of Labor and Congress of Industrial Organizations, AFL-CIO, it seeks to represent the interests of each community to the other. In 1968 the institute established local affiliates; by 1990 there were approximately two hundred in thirty-seven states. There black union activists work on local civil rights, union, and community service issues including voter registration and get-out-the-vote drives, job training, union organizing, food banks, and winning community support for strikes or boycotts. The institute helped organize the Memphis, Tennessee, sanitation workers in 1968 and the Mississippi catfish workers in the 1980s. It promotes legislation of concern to African Americans or unionists generally, including civil rights, health care, and worker safety.

SELECTED BIBLIOGRAPHY

Norman Hill, "The APRI: Looking Back at 25 Years of Struggle" (Report, A. Philip Randolph Institute, 1990); Bayard Rustin, "The History of the A. Philip Randolph Institute," *Debate and Understanding* (Winter 1976), 29–35.

Cheryl Greenberg

RANSOM, FREEMAN B. (7 July 1884, Grenada, Miss.–6 August 1947, Indianapolis, Ind.). Nationally known attorney, civic worker, and general manager of the Madame C. J. Walker* Manufacturing Company, Ransom received a degree from the Law Department of Walden University in Nashville, Tennessee, and pursued further legal studies at Columbia University. He settled in Indianapolis in 1910 where he became one of its most respected residents. In 1940 he was voted Indianapolis's most outstanding citizen. Eulogized as one "who served unselfishly the cause of progress for his race," Ransom was a member of the Legal Committee and the Board of Directors of the Indianapolis NAACP.* He also served as vice president of the National Bar Association and of the National Negro Business League.*

SELECTED BIBLIOGRAPHY
Florence Murray, ed., *The Negro Handbook* (1949); Thomas Yenser, ed., *Who's Who in Colored America* (1937); "National Association for the Advancement of Colored People," *Crisis* 8 (September 1914), 237; *Chicago Defender*, 12 December, 1936; 23 August 1947.

Betty L. Plummer

RANSOM, REVERDY CASSIUS (4 January 1861, Flushing, Ohio–22 April 1959, Wilberforce, Ohio). Ransom was the African Methodist Episcopal (A.M.E.) Church's earliest proponent of the social gospel and an outspoken opponent of accommodationism. His traditional ministries were infused with social and political programs; he founded the Institutional Church and Social Settlement in 1900 in Chicago. Ransom denounced Booker T. Washington's* tactics at the 1899 meeting of the Afro-American Council* and gave a fiery address, "The Spirit of John Brown," at the Niagara Movement's* 1906 gathering at Harpers Ferry. Ransom was editor of the A.M.E. Church *Review* from 1912 to 1924. His 1918 write-in campaign sponsored by the United Civic League for the state legislature was an effective protest against Republican racial policies in Harlem. An acerbic advocate of a more educated ministry, Ransom was a mentor to young A.M.E. scholars such as R. R. Wright, Jr.,* Charles H. Wesley, and Monroe Work.* Ransom was elected forty-eighth Bishop of the African Methodist Episcopal Church in 1924.

SELECTED BIBLIOGRAPHY
Calvin Morris, *Reverdy C. Ransom* (1990); Reverdy C. Ransom, *The Pilgrimage of Harriet Ransom's Son* (1949); David Wills, "Reverdy Ransom, The Making of an A.M.E. Bishop," in Randall K. Burkett and Richard Newman, eds., *Black Apostles: Afro-American Clergy Confront the Twentieth Century* (1978).

Francille Rusan Wilson

RAUH, JOSEPH, JR. (3 January 1911, Cincinnati, Ohio–). Rauh, a lawyer noted for his tireless efforts behind the scenes of the civil rights movement, as well as for peace and union activism, worked with A. Philip Randolph* in drafting Executive Order 8802,* which created the Fair Employment Practice Committee* in 1941. In 1947, Rauh helped lead the fight to adopt a civil rights plank in the Democratic party platform, which caused Southerners to bolt from the convention. After 1964, Rauh fell out of favor with more militant blacks, particularly because of his role in attempting a compromise between the Mississippi Freedom Democratic party* and the Lyndon B. Johnson camp at the 1964 Democratic convention.

SELECTED BIBLIOGRAPHY
Thomas R. Brooks, *Walls Come Tumbling Down: A History of the Civil Rights Movement, 1940–1970* (1974); David J. Garrow, *Bearing the Cross: Martin Luther King,*

Jr., and the Southern Christian Leadership Conference (1986); Milton Viorst, *Fire in the Streets: America in the 1960's* (1979).

Carol Wilson

RED SUMMER (1919). Black writer and civil rights leader James Weldon Johnson* coined the phrase "Red Summer" to describe the wave of racial violence that swept through America between late spring and early fall 1919. As many as twenty-five incidents have been identified; the major confrontations occurred in Charleston, South Carolina (see Charleston race riot); Longview, Texas (see Longview race riot); Washington, D.C.; Chicago, Illinois [see Chicago race riot (1919)]; Knoxville, Tennessee (see Knoxville riot); Omaha, Nebraska; and Elaine, Arkansas (see Elaine, Arkansas, race riot). These episodes varied widely in nature and scale. The deadliest occurred in Chicago, where thirty-eight died during nearly a week of urban warfare, and in Arkansas, where white planters, responding to rumors of black insurrection, massacred over two hundred black sharecroppers. The racial violence of 1919 had precedents extending back to slavery days, but its particular intensity has been linked to the unrest of the immediate post–World War I years. The Red Summer coincided with the "red scare"—the wave of antiradicalism and xenophobia that followed the 1918 armistice—and analysts have seen in both a need to find an "inner enemy" to account for unsettling social change. White Northerners feared the rapid increase in the black population resulting from wartime migration; white Southerners resented the growing assertiveness of a people they had long dominated. Whites initiated most of the violence in 1919, but blacks fought back, presaging the more militant mood of the 1920s.

SELECTED BIBLIOGRAPHY
Richard C. Cortner, *A Mob Intent on Death: The NAACP and the Arkansas Riot Cases* (1988); William M. Tuttle, Jr., *Race Riot: Chicago in the Red Summer 1919* (1970); Arthur I. Waskow, *From Race Riot to Sit-In, 1919 and the 1960s: A Study in the Connections between Conflict and Violence* (1966).

Allan H. Spear

REEB, JAMES J. (1 January 1927, Wichita, Kan.–10 March 1965, Selma, Ala.). Reeb, a white Unitarian minister, was murdered during civil rights activities in Selma, Alabama. Attacked by club-wielding whites on 8 March 1965, Reeb died from massive head injuries in a Birmingham hospital two days later. Whereas the nation scarcely noticed the murder of a black activist eighteen days earlier, Reeb's death prompted a national outcry, including a presidential call to the bereaved family. Reeb's murder, among other such incidents in and around Selma, sparked a demand, particularly from the nation's religious leaders, for federal legislation against civil rights violence. Such legislation was passed in 1968 after the assassination of Martin Luther King, Jr.*

SELECTED BIBLIOGRAPHY
Michael R. Belknap, *Federal Law and Southern Order: Racial Violence and Constitutional Conflict in the Post-Brown South* (1987); Henry Hampton and Steve Fayer, *Voices of Freedom: An Oral History of the Civil Rights Movement from the 1950s through the 1980s* (1990); Jack Mendelsohn, *The Martyrs: Sixteen Who Gave Their Lives for Racial Justice* (1966); *New York Times*, 11–13 March 1965.

Andrew M. Manis

REID, IRA DE A. (2 July 1901, Clifton Forge, Va.–16 August 1968, Haverford, Pa.). Scholar, teacher, writer, activist, and son of a Baptist minister, Reid was raised in both Philadelphia and Georgia. A 1922 graduate of Morehouse College,* he studied sociology at the Universities of Chicago and Pittsburgh, and in 1939 he received a Ph.D. from Columbia. Supported in his studies by a National Urban League* (NUL) fellowship, Reid became industrial secretary of the New York Urban League in 1924 and later succeeded Charles S. Johnson* as NUL director of research and editor of *Opportunity*.* During the 1930s, Reid combined roles as sociologist, NUL official, and race relations adviser to the Roosevelt administration. From 1934 until 1946, he taught sociology at Atlanta University* and later headed the Department of Sociology and Anthropology at Haverford College. He also edited *Phylon*∗ (1943–1946) and wrote extensively on black economic and social life. His *Urban Negro Worker in the United States* (1938) was one of the first major studies on black labor conditions. Reid's expertise in black economics and his NUL experience led to his appointment in the late 1930s and early war years as a race relations adviser to the Social Security Board and the War Manpower Commission in the Roosevelt administration. Like many black activists and professionals of his time, Reid sought to provide a scientific basis for analyzing and assessing black American racial and class circumstances while working within and outside government for meaningful social programs that responded to those conditions. After World War II, he remained active both as a sociologist and public advocate for black rights and equal opportunity.

SELECTED BIBLIOGRAPHY
Current Biography, 1946; Harvard Sitkoff, *A New Deal for Blacks: The Emergence of Civil Rights as a National Issue* (1978); Nancy J. Weiss, *The National Urban League, 1910–1940* (1974); Raymond Wolters, *Negroes and the Great Depression* (1970).

John B. Kirby

REITMAN v. MULKEY, 387 U.S. 369 (1967). This was one of several 1960s cases concerning the issue of housing discrimination. Voters in California supported Proposition 14, which resulted in an amendment to the state constitution. The amendment prevented the state from interfering with the right of individuals to sell or lease property to whomever they chose. The California Supreme Court decided that the amendment violated the U.S. Constitution. The U.S. Supreme Court adjudicated two fair housing cases together: *Reitman v. Mulkey* and *Prendergast v. Snyder*. The Mulkeys, husband and wife, charged that they had been prevented from renting an apartment because of their race. Another black couple, the Prendergasts, sued their landlord for attempting to evict them, again because of race. The Supreme Court upheld the decision of the California court, five to four. Justice Byron R. White wrote the majority opinion, arguing that the state was a neutral party in housing matters. It did not have an obligation to enforce fair housing practices, but it could not be prevented from doing so. The California amendment, he claimed, had, in effect, legalized discrimination.

SELECTED BIBLIOGRAPHY

Derrick A. Bell, Jr., *Race, Racism and American Law* (1980); Rowland L. Young, "Review of Recent Supreme Court Decisions," *American Bar Association Journal* 53 (1967), 753–54.

Carol Wilson

REPUBLIC OF NEW AFRICA. Brothers Milton Henry (Gaidi Obadele) and Richard Henry (Imari Abubakari Obadele) led the founding in March 1968 of the Republic of New Africa (RNA) with Robert F. Williams,* who was living in exile in Cuba, as president. The RNA, which during the early 1970s claimed about 2,500 adherents, advocated African-American separatism in an independent country which was to include Louisiana, Mississippi, Alabama, Georgia, and South Carolina. African-American migration into these states was to provide a popular majority who would gain political control peacefully and then secede. If necessary, African Americans in northern cities would conduct an urban guerilla war. The RNA included a military arm, the Black Legion. In 1971 the RNA dedicated a Mississippi farm as its first sovereign territory. Significant RNA activity ended in August 1971 with a shoot-out between RNA members and FBI agents and local police in Jackson, in which one policeman died. Eleven RNA members were imprisoned.

SELECTED BIBLIOGRAPHY

Robert H. Brisbane, *Black Activism: Racial Revolution in the United States 1954–1970* (1974); Raymond L. Hall, *Black Separatism in the United States* (1978); *Jackson Clarion-Ledger*, Jan. 28, 1990.

Lorenzo Crowell

RESURRECTION CITY. During the spring of 1968, Dr. Martin Luther King, Jr.,* and his advisers mapped a strategy for a Poor People's March on Washington* to dramatize the need for the national government to better address the needs of the poor. After King's assassination in April, plans for the march continued under the direction of Ralph David Abernathy.*

Leaving Memphis, Tennessee, on 2 May, the marchers officially began the Poor People's Campaign* on 12 May in Washington, D.C., with a Mother's Day march and an address by Coretta Scott King,* King's widow. Construction of a temporary town to house the demonstrators began on 11–12 May near the Lincoln Memorial. Dubbed "Resurrection City" by the campaign's strategists and consisting chiefly of plywood and tarpaper shacks, Resurrection City was designed to epitomize the real living conditions of many poor blacks.

Bad weather during May turned the campsite into a quagmire, and tension increased between Resurrection City's inhabitants and District of Columbia authorities. On 24 June District police moved in to clear the area since the campaign's camping permit had expired. Abernathy and about three hundred others were arrested soon after when they marched on the Capitol to protest the razing of the city.

SELECTED BIBLIOGRAPHY

Peter M. Bergman, *The Chronological History of the Negro in America* (1969); Charles E. Fazer, *Uncertain Resurrection: The Poor People's Washington Campaign* (1969); David J. Garrow, *Bearing the Cross: Martin Luther King, Jr., and the Southern Christian Leadership Conference* (1986).

Allen Dennis

REUTHER, WALTER (1 September 1907, Effengham, Ill.–9 May 1970, Peliston, Md.). A leader in the United Auto Workers (UAW) from 1936 until his death in a plane crash in 1970, Reuther became the union's president in 1947. Trained as a tool and die maker, he moved to Detroit, Michigan, in 1927 and attended what is now Wayne State University as a prelaw student while working briefly at Briggs Manufacturing Company and Ford Motor Company from 1927 to 1932. From early 1933 to 1935 Reuther's activities included traveling in Europe and working as a tool and die maker at the Molotov Automobile Works in the Soviet Union. Soon after returning to Detroit in 1936, he was elected to the executive board of the UAW and became president of West Side Local 174. Leading the effort to organize automotive workers in Detroit, Reuther collided with Ford's infamous Service Bureau, and he and others were severely beaten. This so-called Battle of the Overpass catapulted Reuther to national prominence. He was elected president of the UAW in 1946 and took control of the executive board in 1947. Reuther's power in the UAW was never seriously challenged, and he became the third president of the Congress of Industrial Organizations in 1952. A powerful figure in labor and politics, Reuther was active in the civil rights movement. He participated in both the Selma to Montgomery March* and the March on Washington.*

SELECTED BIBLIOGRAPHY

John Barnard, *Walter Reuther and the Rise of the Auto Worker* (1983); Frank Cormier and William J. Eaton, *Reuther* (1970); Jean Gould and Loren Hickok, *Walter*

Reuther: Labor's Rugged Individualist (1972); Irving Howe and B. J. Widick, *The UAW and Walter Reuther* (1949).

Clarence Hooker

REVELS, HIRAM R. (27 September 1827, Fayetteville, N.C.–16 January 1901, Aberdeen, Miss.). In 1870 Mississippi elected Hiram R. Revels, a free-born black Natchez resident, to an unexpired term in the U.S. Senate. Educated in midwestern Quaker seminaries and at Knox College, in Galesburg, Illinois, Revels was the first of his race to sit in the U.S. Senate. An African Methodist Episcopal minister, he had spent most of his adulthood tending the spiritual needs of his people, so little politically constructive was expected of him as a senator. He refused to regard his election as a mere symbolic gesture, however. By nature unassuming and cautious, he supported amnesty for ex-Confederates and urged black moderation in the treatment of former slaveholders. He reminded white America of its debt to blacks for their loyalty during the Civil War and appealed eloquently to Republicans to protect black civil and political rights. Revels failed to convince colleagues that integrating the District

Senator Hiram Revels of Mississippi being sworn into office. (Courtesy Mississippi Department of Archives and History.)

of Columbia's schools would lessen racial prejudice, but he won white support and black acclaim for his efforts to integrate the work force in Baltimore's naval shipyard. He encouraged black elevation through education and, following his one-year Senate term, he became president of Alcorn State University in Lorman, Mississippi. Notwithstanding his controversial support for Mississippi Democrats after the overthrow of Republican rule, Revels remained for many late nineteenth-century blacks a symbol of their hopes and aspirations for full American citizenship.

SELECTED BIBLIOGRAPHY
Robert L. Jenkins, "The Senate Careers of Hiram R. Revels and Blanche K. Bruce" (master's thesis, Mississippi State University, 1976); John R. Lynch, *Reminiscences of an Active Life: The Autobiography of John Roy Lynch* (1970); George Sewell and Margaret L. Dwight, *Mississippi Black History Makers* (1977); Vernon L. Wharton, *The Negro in Mississippi* (1947).

Robert L. Jenkins

REVOLUTIONARY ACTION MOVEMENT. This Marxist-Leninist revolutionary organization of about fifty dedicated individuals, organized in 1963 by American exile Robert F. Williams,* intended to wage an urban guerrilla war against the U.S. establishment in the cause of African-American nationalism. Revolutionary Action Movement (RAM) adherents armed themselves heavily. After raids by the police in New York City and Philadelphia, RAM members were charged in 1967 with planning such terrorist acts as the assassinations of Roy Wilkins* of the NAACP* and Whitney Young* of the National Urban League* and poisoning the Philadelphia water supply. In 1968 the RAM collapsed under police pressure.

SELECTED BIBLIOGRAPHY
John H. Bracey, Jr., August Meir, and Elliott Rudwick, eds., *Black Nationalism in America* (1970); Robert H. Brisbane, *Black Activism: Racial Revolution in the United States 1954–1970* (1974).

Lorenzo Crowell

RICE v. ARNOLD, 340 U.S. 848 (1950). Joseph Rice, a black resident of the city of Miami, Florida, sued H. H. Arnold, the superintendent of the Miami Springs Country Club, because his use of the public golf course was restricted to Mondays whereas whites had use of the facilities the other six days. Rice sought Fourteenth Amendment* equal protection under the law compliance to use the golf course without day or hour restriction. The claim was denied. On appeal, the U.S. Supreme Court held, per curiam, that the judgment be vacated and remanded to the Supreme Court of Florida for reconsideration in light of the recent (1950) federal Supreme Court decisions of *Sweatt v. Painter** and *McLaurin v. Oklahoma State Regents.** The Florida Supreme Court concluded that neither case, involving glaring inequalities in segregated higher education, applied to the Rice appeal because the same public golf course facilities were used by both whites and blacks and because neither case voided the separate but equal doctrine of *Plessy v. Ferguson*.* Because appellant Rice had not properly raised the issue that the regulations failed to grant equal facilities and because he was inappropriately seeking to invalidate legally upheld segregation laws, the Florida Supreme Court affirmed their earlier decision and rejected Rice's petition. On reappeal, the Supreme Court denied certiorari because the Florida case was based on nonfederal issues. Justices Black and Douglas dissented.

SELECTED BIBLIOGRAPHY

"Rice v. Arnold," *Minnesota Law Review* 35 (1951), 399–41; "Rice v. Arnold," *Notre Dame Lawyer* 27 (1952), 270–73.

William A. Paquette

RICHMOND PLANET. See Mitchell, John R., Jr.

RICE v. ELMORE, 165 F.2d 387 (4th Cir., 1947). After the Supreme Court in 1944 overturned the Texas white primary* in *Smith v. Allwright,** South Carolina attempted to circumvent that decision. On 20 April 1944, the state legislature deleted all statutes relating to primaries on the assumption that without state sanction the Democratic primary became a private matter operating outside the scope of the Fifteenth Amendment's* ban against official suffrage discrimination. Represented by Thurgood Marshall,* the chief counsel of NAACP,* George Elmore challenged South Carolina's action. On 12 July 1947, Federal District Judge Julius Waties Waring,* an iconoclastic Charleston native who braved the enmity of his neighbors, ruled in favor of the plaintiff. He asserted that as long as the Democratic primary constituted the only real election in the state, blacks were entitled to participate in it. On appeal, Circuit Court Judge John J. Parker, whose nomination to the Supreme Court the NAACP had helped block in 1930, upheld the ruling. After the Supreme Court refused to grant review, further attempts to resurrect the white primary came to an end. In August 1948, 35,000 blacks voted in the South Carolina Democratic primary for the first time.

SELECTED BIBLIOGRAPHY

V. O. Key, *Southern Politics in State and Nation* (1949); Steven F. Lawson, *Black Ballots: Voting Rights in the South, 1944–1969* (1976); Henry Lee Moon, *Balance of Power* (1948); Tinsley E. Yarbrough, *A Passion for Justice: J. Waties Waring and Civil Rights* (1987).

Steven F. Lawson

RIVES, RICHARD TAYLOR (15 January 1895, Montgomery, Ala.–27 October 1982, Montgomery, Ala.). Educated in the public schools in Montgomery, Alabama, Rives attended Tulane University, in New Orleans, Louisiana, for one year (1911–1912) before financial considerations forced him to drop out of school and study law at a Montgomery law firm. Admitted to the Alabama bar in 1914, he rose in the esteem of fellow lawyers to become president of both the Montgomery and the Alabama bar associations. In 1951 he was appointed by President Harry S. Truman to the United States Court of Appeals for the Fifth Judicial Circuit* where he served until his retirement in 1966. During the last six years of his tenure he was chief judge. He spoke with the accent but not the language of segregation. On the Fifth Circuit he was a powerful voice for equal rights and justice for blacks. Together with fellow Fifth Circuit judges Elbert P. Tuttle,* John Minor Wisdom,* and John Robert Brown,* he helped to ensure the success of the civil rights movement by making the federal courts, and especially the Fifth, a powerful vehicle for social and political change. He was impatient with the delaying tactics employed by southern whites to postpone compliance with the decision in *Brown v. Board of Education,** and he continually reminded fellow Southerners that they must obey the law whether they liked it or not. He played a key role in implementing in the lower South the *Brown* decision calling for the desegregation of public schools. He also helped to expand *Brown*'s mandate for equality beyond education, joining in landmark decisions issued by the Fifth Circuit Court that swept away barriers of discrimination in jury selection, employment, and voting.

SELECTED BIBLIOGRAPHY

Jack Bass, *Unlikely Heroes* (1981); Harvey C. Couch, *A History of the Fifth Circuit, 1891–1981* (1984); J. W. Peltason, *Fifty-Eight Lonely Men: Southern Federal Judges and School Desegregation* (1961).

Charles D. Lowery

ROBESON, PAUL (9 April 1898, Princeton, N.J.–23 January 1976, New York, N.Y.). The son of William Drew Robeson and Maria Louisa Bustin, he received his elementary, secondary, and college education in the Garden State. In 1915 he won a scholarship to attend Rutgers University. While there, Robeson earned Phi Beta Kappa honors as a junior and was valedictorian of his class. In addition, he was the class debating champion, won thirteen varsity letters in four sports, and was a member of the Cap and Skull Honorary Society as well as the Glee Club, the last of which had race restrictions that barred him from traveling with the club. In 1919 Robeson entered Columbia Law School. Following his graduation in 1923, he briefly practiced law in New York City. From 1924 through the 1950s Robeson exhibited remarkable talent on the stage and in film as a concert singer and actor. During this period he performed in concerts throughout the United States and Europe, including the Soviet Union, and starred in over ten major musicals, movies, and plays, including *Porgy and Bess, Show Boat, Othello,* and *The Emperor Jones.* Robe-

Paul Robeson as "Emperor Jones." (Negro Almanac Collection, Amistad Research Center, Tulane University, New Orleans.)

son received the Donaldson Award for the best acting performance of the year and the Gold Medal Award granted by the American Academy of Arts and Sciences for the actor with the best diction.

Robeson was also a political activist. In 1946 he led a delegation of the American Crusade to End Lynching to see President Harry S. Truman to demand that he sponsor antilynching legislation. In 1949 he called for African Americans, if drafted, to resist. During the midst of the Cold War and the red scare, Robeson's name became synonymous with anti-American rhetoric and Communism. During the House Committee on Un-American Activities hearings in 1947, for example, Richard M. Nixon asked Adolphe Menjou how the government could identify Communists. Menjou said it was anyone who attended a Robeson concert or who purchased his record albums. In 1958 the government lifted the ban it had earlier imposed prohibiting Robeson from leaving the

United States. From this period until his death in 1976, he spent his time writing, traveling, and occasionally giving public lectures. By the end of the 1960s Robeson had become one of the most recognized Americans in the world. African leaders as well as European governments viewed and honored him as a great civil and human rights advocate. Robeson recorded his remarkable career in his autobiography entitled *Here I Stand*.

SELECTED BIBLIOGRAPHY
Martin Baunl Duberman, *Paul Robeson* (1988); Editors of *Freedomways, Paul Robeson: The Great Forerunner* (1985).

Vibert L. White

ROBINSON, JACKIE (31 January 1919, Cairo, Ga.–24 October 1972, Stamford, Conn.). A football, baseball, basketball, and track star at UCLA, Robinson gained national prominence in 1947 when he smashed major league baseball's color bar. Although blacks like Joe Louis* and Jesse Owens* were outstanding in boxing and track, organized baseball had been segregated since the 1880s. In 1945 the Brooklyn Dodgers purchased Robinson's contract from the black Kansas City Monarchs. After his brilliant season with their Montreal farm team, the Dodgers promoted him to the majors in 1947 when he was rookie of the year. Robinson survived merciless taunts from players and fans to become the league's most valuable player in 1949, a favorite of blacks and whites, and the first black in baseball's Hall of Fame in 1962. Larry Doby, Leroy "Satchel" Paige, and other talented blacks followed his path; the signing of Elijah "Pumpsie" Green by the Boston Red Sox in 1959 marked the final integration of all major league teams. Subsequent participation of blacks in tennis, football, and basketball was a precursor of the later civil rights revolutions.

SELECTED BIBLIOGRAPHY
Obituary, *New York Times*, 25 October 1972; Benjamin Rader, *American Sports: From the Age of Folk Games to the Age of Spectators* (1983); Jackie Robinson, *Baseball Has Done It* (1964); Jules Tygiel, *Baseball's Great Experiment: Jackie Robinson and His Legacy* (1983).

James B. Potts

ROCHESTER, NEW YORK, RACE RIOT (1964). Situated in Monroe County about 250 miles northwest of New York City, Rochester was considered to be a model city in terms of race relations. Out of a population of 318,611, African Americans numbered 35,000. City planners boasted of their efforts to improve the quality of housing and provide job opportunities for the black residents. Yet there were tensions, mostly centered on subtle forms of discrimination and police actions in the black community. One hot July evening, at a fund-raising street dance in the heavily black Genesee Street–Joseph Avenue District, two police arrested a seventeen-year-old black male on charges of public drunkenness. Remembering the brutal beating of a black teenager the year before and the widely publicized refusal to serve Richard Claxton (Dick) Gregory* and several black ministers at the Rochester airport in the spring, a crowd of 500 people began smashing windows. The police were reinforced and joined by the fire department, which turned high-pressure hoses on the crowd. By morning the black commercial district (fifty blocks) was in a shambles, and the city manager proclaimed a state of emergency. The next night rioting began again: 10,000 people were in the streets as gangs of white youths joined blacks in smashing shops and stores. The National Guard was called to quell the disturbances. Calm was finally restored on 26 July. Four died; 350 were injured, including 35 policemen; and 800, three-fourths of whom were black, were arrested.

SELECTED BIBLIOGRAPHY

"Civil Rights: The White House Meeting," *Newsweek* (3 August 1964); "Crisis in Race Relations," *U.S. News and World Report* (10 August 1964); *Rochester Democrat and Chronicle*, 26–27 July 1964.

Charles T. Pete Banner-Haley

ROCKEFELLER FOUNDATION. John D. Rockefeller established this largest of his four benevolent corporations with an initial contribution in 1909 of fifty million dollars worth of shares in Standard Oil Company of New Jersey. Reorganized in 1928, the foundation sponsored programs on health, medicine, natural and social sciences, arts, and humanities. Although most of Rockefeller's efforts for the improvement of African-American education were coordinated by the General Education Board,* beginning in the 1960s the foundation sponsored programs at selected colleges to improve the opportunities for economically deprived, talented high school students to study at the nation's universities. Foundation assets in the late 1980s totalled more than $1.5 billion.

SELECTED BIBLIOGRAPHY

Waldemar A. Nielsen, *The Big Foundations* (1972); Mabel M. Smythe, ed., *The Black American Reference Book* (1976); Warren Weaver, *United States Philanthropic Foundations* (1967).

Janice M. Leone

ROGERS v. ALABAMA, 192 U.S. 226 (1904). Dan Rogers was an Alabama black who had been indicted for murder. In the state trial court, Rogers's attorney moved to quash the indictment on the ground that the juror list from which grand jurors were selected systematically excluded blacks, in violation of the equal protection clause of the Fourteenth Amendment.* The motion also suggested that juror lists excluded nonvoters, among them blacks who had been wrongly disenfranchised by the Alabama constitution. The trial court overruled the motion and was upheld by the Alabama Supreme Court, which held that Rogers's two-page motion was too long under Alabama's code of civil procedure. In a unanimous decision, the U.S. Supreme Court overturned the decision of the state court. Delivering the Supreme Court's opinion, Oliver Wendell Holmes dismissed the state's procedural objections, although he did seem to suggest that the claimed suffrage restrictions were irrelevant to Rogers's case. Nevertheless, Holmes noted that prior decisions of the court had barred racial discrimination in grand jury selection and that Rogers had raised a legitimate constitutional issue which the lower courts should have addressed. The case was returned to the Alabama courts for further hearings on Rogers's original motion. Despite Holmes's unambiguous language, the question of racial discrimination in grand jury selection would bedevil the Supreme Court for years to come.

SELECTED BIBLIOGRAPHY

Romualdo P. Eclavea, "Construction and Application of Provisions of Jury Selection and Service Act of 1968," in Henry C. Lind, ed., 17 *American Law Reports, Federal* 590 (1973); Marvin E. Frankel and Gary P. Naftalis, *The Grand Jury* (1975); Richard D. Younger, *The People's Panel: The Grand Jury in the United States, 1634–1941* (1963).

Jeff Broadwater

ROOSEVELT, ELEANOR (11 October 1884, New York, N.Y.–7 November 1962, New York, N.Y.). Wife of President Franklin D. Roosevelt, she became known as a strong defender of racial justice and black equal opportunity. In the late 1920s, she became acquainted with the black educator Mary McLeod Bethune,* who remained her close friend and adviser on racial issues throughout her life. When the New Deal was launched in the early 1930s, Mrs. Roosevelt sought to link its social and economic programs to the special needs of black Americans. She was instrumental in the selection of Bethune to head the Negro Division of the National Youth Administration. Along with a handful of other racial liberals, Mrs. Roosevelt was a persistent advocate of greater black participation in the federal government and argued the federal government's obligation to black and other minority peoples to her husband and powerful New Deal officials such as Harry Hopkins and Frances Perkins. Frequently she used her ties to the presidency to gain administration support for such concerns as federal antilynching laws. Mrs. Roosevelt was especially close to NAACP* national secretary, Walter Francis White,* and in 1934 she arranged a meeting between White and her husband to discuss proposed antilynching legislation. Although no law came out of their conference, Mrs. Roosevelt continued to lobby for such legislation.

Her identification with such prominent black figures as White and Bethune, her entertaining of black groups at the White House, her participation in pro–civil rights organizations such as the Southern Conference for Human Welfare,* and, during the war, her advocacy of the rights of black workers, nurses, and servicemen won her the applause of friends and the condemnation of white racists. Her best-known championing of racial justice involved her resignation from the Daughters of the American Revolution in 1939 following their refusal to permit noted black singer Marian Anderson* to perform in Constitution Hall. Her support for Anderson won her the coveted NAACP Spingarn Medal* in 1939.

Although during the post–World War II years she sometimes hesitated in fully embracing the civil rights struggles and refused to advocate fundamental changes in American institutions, she remained until her death a close friend and supporter of black Americans. As her longtime friend Walter White wrote in 1945, Eleanor Roosevelt "gave to many Americans, particularly Negroes, hope and faith which enabled them to continue the struggle for full citizenship."

SELECTED BIBLIOGRAPHY

John B. Kirby, *Black Americans in the Roosevelt Era* (1980); Joseph P. Lash, *Eleanor and Franklin* (1971); Joseph P. Lash, *Eleanor: The Years Alone* (1972); Nancy J. Weiss, *Farewell to the Party of Lincoln* (1983); Joanna Schneider Zangrando and Robert L. Zangrando, "ER and Black Civil Rights," in Joan Hoff-Wilson and Marjorie Lightman, eds. *Without Precedent* (1984).

John B. Kirby

ROOTS. In 1976 Alex Palmer Haley* wrote *Roots: The Saga of an American Family*, a historical novel in which he traced six generations of his family lineage from eighteenth-century Africa. After twelve years of research, based on family stories he had heard while growing up in Tennessee, he discovered the name of his Gambian ancestor, Kunte Kinte. Haley's discovery of the tangible link between his family and its African ancestry recaptured and reaffirmed the African heritage of all African Americans and the richness of their African identity. In telling the personal history of his family, Haley brought to life the oppression and struggles of African Americans as well as their faith, hope, and triumphs. Transformed into the first television miniseries after its publication, *Roots* awakened the consciousness of the nation to the impact of racial discrimination in America.

SELECTED BIBLIOGRAPHY

Alex Haley, *Roots: The Saga of an American Family* (1976).

Lillie Johnson Edwards

ROPE AND FAGGOT: A BIOGRAPHY OF JUDGE LYNCH. Walter Francis White's* 1929 investigative study of mob lynching centers on the psychological, economic, political, religious, and sexual causes of the lynchings that occurred in the late nineteenth and early twentieth centuries. White explains that lynchings functioned as a solution to white America's "Negro problem" and helped to retain the status quo of antebellum race relations. Extralegal lynchings did not take place to protect white womanhood but to control African-American social, economic, and political progress. Mobocracy, he concludes, could only be checked by the federal government either by a law or by a constitutional amendment. White and other national antilynch law advocates used the study to change public opinion on extralegal lynchings.

SELECTED BIBLIOGRAPHY

Donald L. Grant, *The Anti-Lynching Movement: 1883–1932* (1975); Lynching Records, Tuskegee Institute Archives, Tuskegee, Alabama; George C. Rable, "The South and the Politics of Antilynching Legislation, 1929–1940," *Journal of Southern History* 51 (May 1985), 201–20; Walter White, *A Man Called White* (1948); Walter White, *Rope and Faggot: A Biography of Judge Lynch* (1929); Robert L. Zangrando, *The NAACP Crusade against Lynching, 1909–1950* (1980).

Thaddeus M. Smith

ROSE McCLENDON PLAYERS. Producer Dick Campbell and actress-singer Muriel Rahn founded this community theater group in the late 1930s. Campbell believed that Broadway would continue to reflect stereotypes of African-American life and to mistreat black actors. The group's goal, therefore, was to provide a supportive base for black playwrights, producers, and actors. In 1938 the community group was invited to use the auditorium of the 135th Street branch of the New York City Public Library. There they formed the Rose McClendon Workshop Theater in 1939. Among the productions that year were George Norford's *Joy Exceeding Glory*, about Father Divine (see George Baker); Abram Hill's *On Striver's Row*; and William Ashley's *Booker T. Washington*. The players thrived until World War II, when the group was disbanded. It was never revived. Its alumni included such notables as Canada Lee, Dooley Wilson, Christola Williams, George Norford, Margerie Strickland Green, Ossie Davis, and Ruby Dee.

SELECTED BIBLIOGRAPHY

James Haskins, *Black Theater in America* (1982); Lofton Mitchell, *Black Drama, The Story of the American Negro in the Theatre* (1967).

Judith N. Kerr

ROSENWALD, JULIUS (12 August 1862, Springfield, Ill.–6 January 1932, Ravinia, Ill.). A businessman and philanthropist who amassed his fortune through the Sears, Roebuck mail order firm, Rosenwald was a major contributor to African-American educational and social institutions. His gifts led to the construction of twenty-five YMCA buildings for black youth and over five thousand schools for black children in the rural South. A friend and supporter of Booker T. Washington,* he shared his philosophy of self-help, and his contributions were usually contingent upon additional funds from the local community. The Julius Rosenwald Fund,* established in 1917, carried on his philanthropic work until its dissolution in 1948.

SELECTED BIBLIOGRAPHY
Edwin R. Embree and Julia Waxman, *Investment in People: The Story of the Julius Rosenwald Fund* (1949); M. R. Werner, *Julius Rosenwald: The Life of a Practical Humanitarian* (1939).

Allan H. Spear

ROSENWALD (JULIUS) FUND. One of the several philanthropic educational funds founded in the early decades of the twentieth century, the fund was created in 1917 by Julius Rosenwald,* an Illinois native and president of Sears, Roebuck. Until its demise in 1948, the fund's program focused on enlarging opportunities for southern African Americans by making funds available for schoolhouse construction, educational programs at high schools and colleges, fellowships for career advancement, support for hospitals and health agencies, development of library services, and improvement of race relations. Rosenwald policy required matching funds from grant recipients for construction of "Rosenwald Schools" and resulted in African Americans contributing a significant portion of the total resources expended for southern schools.

SELECTED BIBLIOGRAPHY
James D. Anderson, *The Education of Blacks in the South, 1860–1935* (1988); Edwin R. Embree and Julia Waxman, *Investment in People: The Story of the Julius Rosenwald Fund* (1949); Mabel M. Smythe, ed., *The Black American Reference Book* (1976).

Janice M. Leone

RUFFIN, JOSEPHINE ST. PIERRE (31 August 1842, Boston, Mass.—13 March 1924, Boston, Mass.). Philanthropist, suffragist, and civil rights activist, Ruffin was educated in the public schools of Salem, Massachusetts, and, after 1855, when Boston ended segregation in its schools, at Bowdoin School in Boston. Ruffin's life was one of tireless philanthropic work and social activism on issues relating to civil rights, women's suffrage, and local welfare. She is perhaps best known for her involvement in the women's club movement, founding The Woman's Era* Club in 1894 and in 1895 organizing the first national conference of black women. Ruffin's aims were fourfold: to mobilize the energies and unlock the potential of black women, to press for social reforms, to facilitate black uplift, and to demonstrate to whites that blacks were worthy of equal rights. Under Ruffin's direction, women's groups played an important part in the civil rights movement by challenging all forms of social injustice to which women and blacks were subjected.

While never rejecting racial solidarity and self-help, Ruffin was a committed integrationist, as evidenced by her club's willingness to accept members regardless of race or gender, her membership in predominantly white women's clubs, and her opposition to segregated facilities, such as those at the Cotton States and International Exhibition in Atlanta in 1895. Through such positions she offered an alternative to the accommodationist philosophy of Booker T. Washington* and helped set in motion a process of interracial cooperation that continued into the twentieth century.

SELECTED BIBLIOGRAPHY

E. Flexner, *Century of Struggle: The Women's Rights Movement in the US* (1959); E. T. James, ed., *Notable American Women 1607–1950* (1971); J. W. Leonard, ed., *Woman's Who's Who of America: A Biographical Dictionary of Contemporary Women of the U.S. and Canada* (1914); Rayford W. Logan and M. R. Winston, eds., *Dictionary of American Negro Biography* (1982); W. J. Moses, *The Golden Age of Black Nationalism 1850–1925* (1978); A. H. Zophy and F. M. Karenik, eds., *Handbook of American Women's History* (1990).

Jeffrey Sainsbury

RUSSELL, DANIEL LINDSAY, JR. (7 August 1845, Winnabow Plantation, Brunswick County, N.C.–14 May 1908, Belville Plantation, Brunswick County, N.C.). Scion of two prominent Whig planter families in eastern North Carolina, Russell pursued a highly unorthodox political career from the Civil War into the twentieth century. After a brief stint at the University of North Carolina, an abortive career in the Confederate army, and two terms in the North Carolina General Assembly (1864–1866), Russell was admitted to the bar and elected as a Republican in 1868 to a six-year term as judge of the Superior Court of the Fourth Judicial Circuit. In that capacity he rendered an opinion in the 1873 Wilmington "opera house case" that anticipated *Plessy v. Ferguson** (1896). When a theater manager refused to seat a group of blacks, Judge Russell declared that no "public place" could deny a person admittance "only on account of color or race." Russell said the theater could "separate different classes of persons whose close association is not agreeable to each other," but the "accommodations given, the comfort, style, convenience" must be "the same as to all." Russell's political career culminated in his election to the governorship of North Carolina (1897–1901), in a fusion campaign of Populists and Republicans. During his term, the Democrats launched two furious white supremacy campaigns, incited the Wilmington race riot of 1898, enacted Jim Crow* legislation, and passed a suffrage amendment in 1900 that disfranchised blacks and poor whites.

SELECTED BIBLIOGRAPHY

Jeffrey J. Crow and Robert F. Durden, *Maverick Republican in the Old North State:*

A Political Biography of Daniel L. Russell (1977); Robert F. Durden, *Reconstruction Bonds and Twentieth-Century Politics: South Dakota v. North Carolina (1904)* (1962).
                                                                   Jeffrey J. Crow

RUSTIN, BAYARD (17 March 1912, West Chester, Pa.–24 August 1987, New York, N.Y.). Preeminent nonviolent strategist, Rustin helped shape and connect the civil rights and peace movements before he turned to coalition politics in later life. After five years in the Young Communist League, Rustin became an organizer for the Fellowship of Reconciliation* (1941) and simultaneously served as youth organizer for the March on Washington Movement.* He was significant in founding the Congress of Racial Equality,* served prison time as a conscientious objector (1942–1945), and worked on a chain gang following arrest in the 1947 Journey of Reconciliation.* In 1953 Rustin became executive secretary of the War Resisters League. Behind the scenes, he helped guide the Montgomery bus boycott* and launch and develop tactics for the Southern Christian Leadership Conference.* He spearheaded civil rights demonstrations at both national party conventions in 1960; was master planner for the 1963 March on Washington;* was a principal strategist behind the 1964 New York City public schools boycott; and was a leading author of the "Freedom Budget" alternative to Lyndon B. Johnson's War on Poverty. After 1964, while executive director of the A. Philip Randolph Institute,* Rustin advocated a change "From Protest to Politics" and broke with peace movement allies over U.S. foreign policy. A homosexual, he saw the emergence of the gay rights movement as an important extension of the civil rights movement. He declared shortly before his death: "The barometer of where one is on human rights questions is no longer the black community, it's the gay community. Because it is the community which is most easily mistreated."

SELECTED BIBLIOGRAPHY

Taylor Branch, *Parting the Waters: America in the King Years, 1954–63* (1989); George Chauncey and Lisa Kennedy, "Time on Two Crosses, an Interview with Bayard Rustin," *The Village Voice* (30 June 1987), 28–29; David J. Garrow, *Bearing the Cross: Martin Luther King, Jr. and the Southern Christian Leadership Conference* (1986); Bayard Rustin, *Down the Line* (1971); Bayard Rustin, *Strategies for Freedom* (1976).
                                                                   Jo Ann O. Robinson

S

SAM, ALFRED CHIEF (1879, Akyen Abuakwa District, Ghana, West Africa, date and place of death unknown). An African who became a pan-Africanist in the United States in 1913, Sam arrived in Ofuskee County, Oklahoma, in the summer of 1913. Immediately after his arrival, Sam told the blacks there to develop all-black towns in the state. (In the 1890s blacks had tried to make the Oklahoma Territory a black state.) The result of Sam's idea was the establishment of twenty-five predominantly black towns in Oklahoma. Later Sam founded the Akim Trading Company for the purpose of sending blacks to Africa. Despite opposition from other blacks, Sam was able to send sixty blacks to Ghana in 1914. His movement died when the British government stopped colonization.

SELECTED BIBLIOGRAPHY

William Bittle and Gilbert Geis, *The Longest Way Home* (1964); Wilson J. Moses, *The Golden Age of Black Nationalism, 1850–1925* (1978).

Amos J. Beyan

SCARBOROUGH, WILLIAM SANDERS (16 February 1852, Macon, Ga.–9 September 1926, Wilberforce, Ohio). Educator, political activist, and early champion of political and social equality for blacks, Scarborough was the first African-American to achieve scholarly distinction as a student of classical philology. Though born a slave, he learned to read and write as a child. In 1869 he entered Atlanta University,* where he was introduced to Latin and Greek. He continued his education at Oberlin College, from which he received the B.A. degree in 1875 and an M.A. in classics in 1878. In 1877 he was appointed professor of Latin and Greek at Wilberforce University, where he spent his academic career, teaching, writing, and filling various administrative offices, including that of the university president from 1908–1920. In 1881, he published a widely used textbook, *First Lessons in Greek*, which was followed by other scholarly monographs and articles in professional journals. In recognition of his substantial scholarly achievements, he was elected to membership in the American Philological Association in 1882, a rare honor at that time for one of his race.

Scarborough also worked to improve educational, political, and economic opportunities for blacks. Beginning in the late 1880s he published a number of controversial articles in national magazines, including *Forum* and *Arena*, calling for equality of opportunities for blacks. Challenging the Booker T. Washington* model of industrial education, he argued that classical studies should be open to everyone regardless of race. Blacks were no less able than whites, he asserted, to enjoy the fruits of a liberal education. Scarborough spoke at numerous educational meetings and political rallies concerned with racial problems. Active in the Republican party in Ohio, he played a major role in securing legislation abolishing legal segregation of blacks in the states' schools. He was president of the Afro-American League* of Ohio, which was established to advance black rights, and which challenged Jim Crow* railroad cars coming into the state from the South. To a remarkable degree, Scarborough combined the life of the scholar with that of the political activist. He did not think it was enough for educated blacks to be good scholars and professionals; they must also assume a leadership role in municipal and national affairs, acting together to fight racism wherever it existed.

SELECTED BIBLIOGRAPHY

Rayford W. Logan and Michael R. Winston, eds., *Dictionary of American Negro Biography* (1982); *New York Times*, September 12, 1926; W. J. Simmons, *Men of Mark* (1887); "Notes," *Journal of Negro History* 11 (October, 1926), 689–92; Francis P. Weisenburger, "William Sanders Scarborough: Scholarship, the Negro, Religion, and Politics," *Ohio History*, 72 (January, 1963), 25–50.

Charles D. Lowery

SCHNELL v. DAVIS, 336 U.S. 933 (1949). In 1944 the Supreme Court in *Smith v. Allwright** struck down a Texas law which allowed state political parties the right to determine their membership qualifications. According to the Court, the Democratic party, with the approval of the state, had used this provision to exclude blacks from voting. In response to the Court's decision, many southern states adopted other measures for eliminating black participation. In 1949 Alabama added the Boswell Amendment* to its constitution. This amendment required that prospective voters be able not only to read and write, but also to "understand and explain" any part of the United States Constitution to the satisfaction of a board of registrars. In Alabama, three whites, none of whom was trained in constitutional law, made up the board of registrars in each county. Few blacks, consequently, were allowed to vote. The federal district court which heard the case declared the Boswell Amendment an unconstitutional scheme designed to deny blacks their voting rights. Despite the lower court's decision, however, southern states found other ways to disenfranchise blacks, including poll taxes* and lengthy voter application forms.

SELECTED BIBLIOGRAPHY

Derrick A. Bell, Jr., *Race, Racism and American Law* (1980); Earl and Merle Black, *Politics and Society in the South* (1987); Dewey W. Grantham, *The Life and Death of the Solid South: A Political History* (1988); William C. Havard, ed., *The Changing Politics of the South* (1972); Steven F. Lawson, *Black Ballots: Voting Rights in the South, 1944–1969* (1976).

Phillip A. Gibbs

SCHUYLER, GEORGE S. (25 February 1895, Providence, R.I.–31 August 1977, New York, N.Y.). A maverick African-American writer who moved from socialism to conservatism, Schuyler was born in Providence, Rhode Island, and grew up in Syracuse, New York. In 1923 he began contributing to *The Messenger,** a radical journal edited by A. Philip Randolph.* At the height of the Harlem Renaissance,* he dismissed the notion of a unique African-American character: "Your American Negro is just plain American." Such views were anathema to Langston Hughes* and the New Negro movement.* By the 1930s, Schuyler had abandoned socialism, mocked the New Deal, and shared the iconoclastic views of his mentor, H. L. Mencken. As editor of the *Pittsburgh Courier,** a prominent black newspaper, he denounced the internment of Japanese Americans during World War II and Randolph's proposed March on Washington.* Later he criticized Martin Luther King, Jr.,* and rejected the teaching of black history as a separate discipline. The nation's military involvement in Vietnam cheered him, and when he died he was eulogized by the conservative *National Review.* Schuyler's longer works include *Black No More* (1931); *Adventures in Black and White* (1960); and an autobiography, *Black and Conservative* (1971). His views exasperated liberals, but he was a superb stylist and relished his role as a scoffer.

SELECTED BIBLIOGRAPHY

Nathan Irvin Huggins, *Harlem Renaissance* (1971); Michael Peplow, *George S. Schuyler* (1980).

Richard W. Resh

SCHWARE v. BOARD OF BAR EXAMINERS OF NEW MEXICO, 353 U.S. 232 (1957). In this decision, the Supreme Court continued the activist role established under the leadership of Chief Justice Earl Warren. A unanimous court held that the New Mexico bar had wrongfully denied Rudolph Schware the opportunity of candidacy to its association on the basis of his Communist background. The *Schware* suit was a response to the growing practice of states inquiring into the political affiliations of applicants to the practice of law. The New Mexico Board of Bar Examiners maintained that Schware lacked good moral character, a requisite for admission to its ranks. More than fifteen years earlier, he had been a member of the Communist party,* had used various aliases, and had been arrested but not prosecuted on several occasions. Overturning lower court rulings, the Supreme Court determined that past membership in the Communist party did not "raise substantial doubt about [Schware's] present good moral character" and that the board's actions had violated the due process clause of the Fourteenth Amendment.* Critics charged that the court's rulings in Schware and Konigsberg v. State Bar of California, a related case heard the same day, represented unwarranted intrusions into state affairs. Defenders welcomed the decisions as victories for the rights of individuals whose views conflicted with mainstream society.

SELECTED BIBLIOGRAPHY

Robert F. Cushman and Susan P. Koniak, Cases in Civil Liberties (1989); Paul L. Murphy, The Constitution in Crisis Times, 1918–1969 (1972); William H. Rehnquist, "The Bar Admission Cases: A Strange Judicial Aberration," American Bar Association Journal 44 (1958) 229–232; Elder Witt, The Supreme Court and Individual Right (1988).

Jack E. Davis

SCHWERNER, MICHAEL HENRY (6 November 1939, New York, N.Y.– 21 June 1964, Neshoba County, Miss.). Michael Schwerner grew up in New York City and in Westchester County. A 1961 graduate of Cornell University, he studied social work at Columbia University and worked as a social worker in Manhattan. He married Rita Levant in June 1962, and they joined the Congress of Racial Equality* (CORE) early in 1963. In January 1964 they became CORE field-workers in Meridian where they prepared for the Freedom Summer of 1964* in Mississippi. One of their closest coworkers there was James Earl Chaney.* In June the Schwerners and Chaney helped train workers for the Summer Project in Ohio where they met Andrew Goodman.* After they returned to Mississippi, Schwerner, Chaney, and Goodman went to Longdale on 21 June to visit a church that had been burned by the Ku Klux Klan because it was going to be used to house a freedom school. On their way back to Meridian, the three men were arrested. Late that evening they were released from the Neshoba jail only to be stopped again on a rural road where local whites shot them and buried them in a dam. After an intensive search, FBI agents uncovered the bodies on 4 August. In October 1967, seven whites were convicted in federal court of conspiring to deprive Schwerner, Chaney, and Goodman of their civil rights.

SELECTED BIBLIOGRAPHY
Michael R. Belknap, *Federal Law and Southern Order: Racial Violence and Constitutional Conflict in the Post-Brown South* (1987); Seth Cagin and Philip Dray, *We Are Not Afraid: The Story of Goodman, Schwerner, and Chaney and the Civil Rights Campaign for Mississippi* (1988); William Bradford Huie, *Three Lives for Mississippi* (1965).

Charles W. Eagles

SCOTT, EMMETT JAY (13 February 1873, Houston, Tex.–12 December 1957, Washington, D.C.). An African-American intellectual, journalist, and administrator, Scott received his early education in Houston. He enrolled at Wiley College, in Marshall, Texas, where he earned his M.A. in 1901. He was employed by the *Houston Post*, and he later became editor of the *Texas Freeman*, a newspaper that addressed the problems of blacks. Scott became Booker T. Washington's* special assistant at Tuskegee Institute,* and he served as secretary of that institute from 1912 to 1919. Scott was appointed by President Woodrow Wilson as a special assistant to the secretary of war during World War I. He served as business manager of Howard University* from 1919 to 1934. Scott's publications on blacks include *Tuskegee and Its People* (1910), *The History of the American Negro in the World War* (1919), *Negro Migration during the War* (1920), and, with Lyman B. Stowe, *Booker T. Washington, Builder of a Civilization* (1916).

SELECTED BIBLIOGRAPHY
Rayford W. Logan and Michael R. Winston, eds., *Dictionary of American Negro Biography* (1982).

Amos J. Beyan

SCOTTSBORO TRIALS. On 25 March 1931 nine black youths (aged twelve to nineteen) were arrested for the alleged rape of two white girls on a freight train in northern Alabama. Two weeks later in Scottsboro, the boys were tried and convicted, and eight were sentenced to die in the electric chair. Their number and age and the unseemly haste with which they were condemned aroused the concern of several civil rights organizations. In particular, the International Labor Defense (ILD) Committee, a Communist party* affiliate, assumed the defense of the "Scottsboro boys" in mid-1931 and prepared an appeal. The party, meanwhile, conducted an international propaganda campaign, including mass demonstrations, meetings, and petitions in the boys' behalf. In 1932, the Supreme Court in *Powell v. Alabama** overturned the convictions on grounds that the accused had not received proper counsel. In a second trial in 1933, in Decatur, Alabama—even though one of the alleged victims confessed that neither she nor her companion had been assaulted—the all-white jury returned a guilty verdict. On appeal by ILD lawyers, the Supreme Court in *Norris v. Alabama** (1935) set aside the conviction because the arbitrary exclusion of blacks from jury service violated the defendants' Fourteenth Amendment* rights. The Communist party subsequently invited to the defense team other civil liberties groups including the NAACP,* which dominated a newly formed Scottsboro Defense Committee (SDC). The SDC won the acquittal of four defendants in 1937 and laid the groundwork for the pardon of the others. The last "boy" was released on 9, June 1950, nineteen years and two months after his arrest.

SELECTED BIBLIOGRAPHY

Richard Bardolph, ed., *The Civil Rights Record: Black Americans and the Law, 1849–1970* (1970); Dan T. Carter, *Scottsboro: A Tragedy of the American South* (1969); Hugh T. Murray, "The Scottsboro Rape Cases, 1931–1932," in Bernard Sternsher, ed., *The Negro in Depression and War: Prelude to Revolution, 1930–1945* (1969); Wilson Record, *The Negro and the Communist Party* (1951).

James B. Potts

SCREWS v. UNITED STATES, 325 U.S. 91 (1945). In the 1940s, the Department of Justice resurrected dormant remnants of Reconstruction legislation protecting civil rights because there were no such contemporary laws. One section of the Civil Rights Act of 1866,* codified as Title 18, Section 242, provides punishment for "whoever, under color of law, . . . willfully" deprives an individual of national rights. Screws, a Georgia sheriff, was convicted for violating the Fourteenth Amendment* due process rights of a black prisoner whom he had beaten to death. He challenged the constitutionality of Section 242 insofar as it made due process deprivations a crime, arguing that the meaning of due process was so vague that he could not have known that his actions violated Section 242; since it is clear, however, that due process condemns vagueness in criminal statutes, Section 242 violated his due process rights. The Supreme Court upheld the constitutionality of Section 242 and its applicability to due process deprivations, thus authorizing federal prosecution of state officials for civil rights violations; it held that due process was understandable because "willfully" means intent to deprive a person of a specific constitutional right. It also held that "color of law" means "pretense" of law, rather than authorized by law. But it reversed Screws's conviction; the trial judge had misconstrued "willfully." Upon retrial, Screws was acquitted.

SELECTED BIBLIOGRAPHY

Derrick A. Bell, Jr., *Race, Racism and American Law* (1980); Robert Carr, *Federal Protection of Civil Rights: Quest for a Sword* (1947); Robert J. Harris, *The Quest for Equality: The Constitution, Congress and the Supreme Court* (1960).

Earlean M. McCarrick

SEALE, BOBBY (22 October 1936, Dallas, Tex.–). As cofounder and chairman of the Black Panther* party, Seale was instrumental in fashioning part of the militant political ideology which characterized the late

1960s civil rights movement. With his compatriot, Huey P. Newton,* he drafted the Ten Point Program, which became the constitution of the party, helped write and edit the *Black Panther* newspaper, and wrote a personal history of the Panthers: *Seize the Time: The Story of the Black Panther Party and Huey P. Newton* (1968). Seale was one of those put on trial in the Chicago Eight Conspiracy case for his protest activities during the 1968 Democratic national convention. He captured nationwide attention when Judge Julius Hoffman ordered him bound and gagged during the trial. Seale was later charged with murder in a Panther killing in New Haven, Connecticut, but he was acquitted after deliberations ended in a hung jury. During the course of his activist political career, he forced a runoff election against the incumbent mayor of Oakland, California. Seale's contributions to the movement were his ideological stance, powerful rhetoric, and symbolism as a victim of American oppression.

SELECTED BIBLIOGRAPHY

Earl Anthony, *Picking up the Gun: A Report on the Black Panthers* (1970); Philip S. Foner, ed., *The Black Panthers Speak* (1970); Gene Marine, *The Black Panthers* (1969); Bobby Seale, *A Lonely Rage* (1978); Bobby Seale, *Seize the Time: The Story of the Black Panther Party and Huey P. Newton* (1968); Gail Sheehy, *Panthermania: The Clash of Black against Black in One American City* (1971).

                                                                Marshall Hyatt

Selma to Montgomery March, 1965. (Alabama Department of Archives and History, Montgomery, Alabama.)

Rev. Jesse Jackson with other civil rights leaders on the twentieth anniversary of the Selma to Montgomery March. Shown (*front row, left to right*) are John Lewis, Jesse Jackson, and Joseph Lowery and his wife. (UPI/Bettmann.)

SELMA TO MONTGOMERY MARCH (1965). In 1965, following an unsuccessful voter registration drive by the Student Nonviolent Coordinating Committee* (SNCC) centered on Selma, Alabama, Martin Luther King, Jr.,* and the Southern Christian Leadership Conference* (SCLC) selected Selma to dramatize the need for a federal voter registration law. King and the Reverend Ralph Abernathy* led a mass march on 1 February which culminated in the arrest of 770 people. On 16 February Sheriff James G. "Bull" Clark punched a civil rights worker in the face while TV news cameras recorded the scene, and two days later in Marion, state troopers killed Jimmy Lee Jackson.* Demands arose for a march on the state capital. On Sunday, 7 March 1965, between 500 and 600 marchers led by Hosea Williams* and John Lewis* marched from Selma. After they crossed the Edmund Pettus Bridge at the edge of Selma, they were stopped by state troopers and a posse including men on horseback. The mounted men rode down the fleeing marchers, and TV cameras captured "Bloody Sunday" for the evening news. King called for a ministers' march on Tuesday, 9 March, but federal judge Frank M. Johnson* ordered the SCLC not to march. The Justice Department's Community Relations Service arranged a compromise whereby the marchers would cross the bridge and then be stopped. On Tuesday King led the marchers. At the prearranged point when the marchers stopped and prayed, the troopers opened the road. King ordered the marchers to return to Selma. Many were outraged at the apparent betrayal. White supremacists then attacked three white ministers in Selma and killed the Reverend James J. Reeb.* President Lyndon B. Johnson called Governor George Wallace to the White House for consultation. On 15 March the president, in an address to Congress and a national TV audience, announced that he would submit voter registration legislation. On 17 March Judge Johnson ruled in favor of the march. The president nationalized the Alabama National Guard and sent regular troops, FBI agents, and marshals to secure the route. On Sunday, 21 March, some eight thousand people set out from Selma. Three hundred camped by the road that evening while the rest returned to Selma. On Thursday, 25 March, some twenty-five thousand people assembled before the Alabama State Capitol where King and others spoke. Wallace's executive secretary accepted a petition while the governor peeked out of his office window. For safety the participants left Montgomery hurriedly. That night while Viola Liuzzo* was returning marchers to Selma, a Ku Klux Klansman shot and killed her. On 6 August President Johnson signed the Voting Rights Act of 1965.*

SELECTED BIBLIOGRAPHY

Thomas R. Brooks, *Walls Come Tumbling Down: A History of the Civil Rights Movement 1940–1970* (1974); David J. Garrow, *Protest at Selma: Martin Luther King, Jr., and the Voting Rights Act of 1965* (1978); Juan Williams, *Eyes on the Prize: America's Civil Rights Years, 1954–1965* (1987).

Lorenzo Crowell

SENGSTACKE, JOHN H. (25 November 1912, Savannah, Ga.–   ). John H. Sengstacke, publisher of the *Chicago Defender** and founder of the Negro Newspaper Publishers' Association* (NNPA), helped save the black press from being shut down for seditious libel during World War II. He joined the staff of the *Defender* in 1934 as the assistant to its founder and his uncle, Robert S. Abbott.* Shortly before the United States' entrance into the Second World War, he succeeded his uncle as publisher and editor.

Throughout the war period, the *Defender*, like other African-American publications, criticized the treatment of black servicemen and advocated the integration of the armed forces. When the federal government considered indicting black publishers for sedition in order to silence the black press, Sengstacke worked out a compromise with the Justice Department. According to the deal, black newspapers would tone down their criticism and be more cooperative with the war effort if black journalists were given access to government officials. Sengstacke, as president of the NNPA, also helped gain accreditation for Harry S. McAlpin, the first black White House correspondent.

SELECTED BIBLIOGRAPHY
St. Clair Drake and Horace R. Cayton, *Black Metropolis* (1945); G. James Fleming and Christian E. Burckell, *Who's Who in Colored America* (1950); Anna Rothe, ed., *Current Biography* (1949); Patrick S. Washburn, *A Question of Sedition: The Federal Government's Investigation of the Black Press During World War II* (1986).
Danny Blair Moore

SEPARATE BUT EQUAL. This legal doctrine was established as the law of the land by the Supreme Court in its *Plessy v. Ferguson** decision of 1896 and was overturned in its 1954 *Brown v. Board of Education** decision. In the *Plessy* decision, the Court declared that a Louisiana law requiring separation by race of passengers on a railroad was a "reasonable" exercise of the state's police power which did not violate the Fourteenth Amendment.* This doctrine provided the precedent for legal segregation ranging from rest rooms to schools until it was undermined in a series of cases brought by the NAACP* between 1938 and 1950. Usually the separate facilities provided for African Americans were definitely separate but rarely equal.

SELECTED BIBLIOGRAPHY
Albert P. Blaustein and Robert L. Zangrando, *Civil Rights and the American Negro: A Documentary History* (1968); Richard Kluger, *Simple Justice: The History of Brown v. Board of Education and Black America's Struggle for Equality* (1976); C. Vann Woodward, *The Strange Career of Jim Crow*, 2nd ed. (1974).
Lorenzo Crowell

SHELLEY v. KRAEMER, 334 U.S. 1 (1948). In the first of the four restrictive covenant cases (*McGhee v. Sipes, Hurd v. Hodge*,* and *Urciolo v. Hodge*) decided in 1948, the U.S. Supreme Court held racially restrictive property deeds unenforceable. Placed in deeds by developers or neighborhood organizations, restrictive covenants became a major device urban whites used to segregate African Americans (and others by race, national origin, and religion) from white neighborhoods. In St. Louis, where the *Shelley* case originated, covenants restricted more than five square miles. When the Shelleys, an African-American family, purchased a home covered by a covenant, the Kraemers, a white family, sought an injunction to block occupancy. The circuit court refused, but Missouri's Supreme Court reversed this decision. The NAACP* coordinated the work of lawyers George Vaughn (*Shelley*), Thurgood Marshall* (*McGhee*), and Charles H. Houston* (*Hurd* and *Urciolo*), whose briefs drew heavily on sociological data and theory. Chief Justice Frederick Vinson's unanimous opinion found racially restrictive covenants, voluntarily maintained, permissible, but state action to enforce them violated Fourteenth Amendment* "rights to acquire, enjoy, own and dispose of property." Although a major victory, *Shelley* failed to stop private housing discrimination or correct economic limitations. Neither the Federal Housing Administration nor the Public Housing Administration fully complied.

SELECTED BIBLIOGRAPHY

Tom C. Clark and Philip B. Perlman, *Prejudice and Property: An Historic Brief against Racial Covenants* (1948); Peter Irons, *The Courage of Their Convictions: Sixteen Americans Who Fought Their Way to the Supreme Court* (1988); Kenneth T. Jackson, "Federal Subsidy and the Suburban Dream, the First Quarter-Century of Government Involvement in the Housing Market," Columbia Historical Society *Records* 50 (1980), 421–51; Herman H. Long and Charles S. Johnson, *People vs. Property: Race Restrictive Covenants in Housing* (1947); B. T. McGraw and George B. Nesbitt, "Aftermath of *Shelley v. Kraemer* on Residential Restrictions by Race," *Land Economics* 29 (August 1953), 280–87; Clement E. Vose, *Caucasians Only: The Supreme Court, the NAACP, and the Restrictive Covenant Cases* (1959).

James Borchert

SHEPHERD v. FLORIDA, 341 U.S. 50 (1951). In 1949 Samuel Shepherd and Walter Irvin, both black men, were accused of raping a seventeen-year-old white girl at gunpoint. They were indicted by an all-white grand jury, convicted, and sentenced to death by an all-white trial jury. The NAACP,* in representing the defendants before the Supreme Court, argued that Shepherd and Irvin were denied their constitutional rights to due process because blacks had been systematically excluded from the jury. In addition, despite the sensational nature of the case and the fact that black citizens in the county had been forced to flee for their lives, the defendants were denied a change of venue. The Supreme Court reversed the convictions. Justice Robert Jackson, with Justice Felix Frankfurter concurring, declared that racial discrimination in the selection of a jury was a constitutional violation of due process and equal protection. And Jackson declared, "for the court to reverse these convictions upon the sole ground of jury selection is to stress the trivial and ignore the important. . . . I do not see, as a practical matter how any Negro on the jury would have dared to cause a disagreement of acquittal. The only chance these Negroes had of acquittal would have been in the courage and decency of some sturdy and forthright white person of sufficient standing to face and live down the odium among his white neighbors."

SELECTED BIBLIOGRAPHY

Robert J. Harris, *The Quests for Equality: The Constitution, Congress, and the Supreme Court* (1960); Herman Pritchett, *Civil Liberties and the Vinson Court* (1954); Rowland L. Young, "Review of Recent Supreme Court Decisions," *American Bar Association Journal* 37 (1951), 528.

Kenneth W. Goings

SHUTTLESWORTH, FRED L. (18 March 1922, Mt. Meigs, Ala.–   ). The leader of the Birmingham, Alabama, civil rights movement, he survived two bombings, a mob beating, and numerous jailings in his efforts to achieve racial equality. After he earned his A.B. degree at Selma University in 1951 and his B.S. degree from Alabama State College in 1952, Shuttlesworth returned to Birmingham as pastor of Bethel Baptist Church in 1953. He organized the Alabama Christian Movement for Human Rights* on 5 June 1956, and he served as president until 1969. A colleague of Martin Luther King, Jr.* and Ralph Abernathy,* Shuttlesworth joined them and others in forming the Southern Christian Leadership Conference* (SCLC), where he held the position of secretary from 1958 to 1970. King called Shuttlesworth "the most courageous civil rights fighter in the South." On Christmas night of 1956 the charismatic Shuttlesworth survived a bomb blast that destroyed his house. The next day he led a challenge to bus segregation. In 1957 a mob of whites beat him with whips and chains during an attempt to integrate an all-white public school. Shuttlesworth witnessed the Greensboro, North Carolina, sit-ins* in 1960 and helped the Congress of Racial Equality* (CORE) with the 1961 Freedom Rides.* Shuttlesworth asked King and the SCLC in 1962 to assist him in conducting mass demonstrations against segregation in Birmingham. After Albany, King agreed, and the SCLC prepared Project C. The Birmingham Confrontation* began on 3 April 1963 and ended with Shuttlesworth reaching a negotiated accord on 10 May 1963. During the interim, he was arrested on 6 and 12 April 1963 and hospitalized on 7 May 1963 after being slammed against a wall by water from fire hoses. The demonstrations in Birmingham led to the Civil Rights Act of 1964.* A veteran of the St. Augustine and Selma to Montgomery* campaigns, Shuttlesworth remained active in the movement after his move to Cincinnati, Ohio, in the early 1960s. He served on the boards of the Southern Conference Education Fund and CORE. In 1990, Shuttlesworth is pastor of the Greater New Light Baptist Church, which he organized in 1966, and is also director of the Shuttlesworth Housing Foundation which helps the poor buy homes.

SELECTED BIBLIOGRAPHY

Cincinnati Enquirer, 15 January 1989; Glenn T. Eskew, "The Alabama Christian Movement for Human Rights and the Birmingham Struggle for Civil Rights, 1956–1963," and Lewis W. Jones, "Fred L. Shuttlesworth, Indigenous Leader," in David J. Garrow, ed., Birmingham, Alabama, 1956–1963 (1989); Pittsburgh Courier, 14 February 1959; Who's Who among Black Americans (1977–1978).

Glenn T. Eskew

"THE SILENT SOUTH." The essay, "The Silent South," was written by George Washington Cable for inclusion in the September 1885 issue of *Century* magazine. Intended as a response to the racially conservative writings of Henry Grady of the *Atlanta Constitution*, it served as one of the most thoughtful criticisms of southern racial policy during the postbellum era. In the essay, Cable suggested that there was in the South a silent and conscientious majority of Southerners who supported a just and compassionate approach to race relations. Cable's frustration with the South's inability to progress racially and politically resulted in his eventual move to Northampton, Massachusetts, where he continued to analyze conditions in the South.

SELECTED BIBLIOGRAPHY

George W. Cable, "The Silent South," in *The Silent South with an Introductory Essay* (1969); Louis D. Rubin, Jr., *George W. Cable: The Life and Times of a Southern Heretic* (1969); Arlin Turner, ed., *Critical Essays on George W. Cable* (1980); C. Vann Woodward, *Origins of the New South, 1877–1913* (1951).

JoAnn D. Carpenter

SILVER, JAMES WESLEY (28 June 1907, Rochester, N.Y.–25 July 1988, Tampa, Fla.). James W. Silver began teaching history at the University of Mississippi in 1936. A popular professor, he quickly became a lightning rod for suspicious Mississippians who saw him as a dangerous radical. He survived a series of relatively minor inquisitions in the 1940s and 1950s, which presaged the firestorm surrounding the publication of his *Mississippi: The Closed Society* (1964). A scathing and meticulous indictment of Mississippi political and racial practices, the book drew copious amounts of praise and scorn. In the wake of this controversy, Silver joined the history faculty at Notre Dame in 1964 and in 1969 went to the University of South Florida. He retired in 1979. Silver was less an activist than an advocate of simple human rights. He often downplayed his role in the civil rights movement, calling himself a "paper radical" and a "quiet reformer." In his later writings, Silver faulted some black leaders for separatist thinking, seeing them as little better than the architects of white supremacy he had earlier excoriated.

SELECTED BIBLIOGRAPHY

James W. Silver, *Mississippi: The Closed Society* (1964); James W. Silver, *Running Scared: Silver in Mississippi* (1984); Obituary notice, *The Journal of Southern History* 54 (November 1988), 695–97.

Allen Dennis

SIMKINS v. CITY OF GREENSBORO, 149 F. Supp. 562 (M.D. N.C., 1957). This 1957 case grew out of a legal battle that had begun in December 1955 when George Simkins, Jr., a Greensboro, North Carolina, dentist and head of the local NAACP,* and a number of his colleagues were arrested and put on trial for attempting to play on the segregated Greensboro public golf course. The defendants were convicted, sentenced, and fined, although their sentences were later commuted. Simkins subsequently brought a federal discrimination suit against the city of Greensboro. Until 1949 the Gillespie Park Course had been an eighteen-hole public golf course restricted to whites and located on land leased by the city from the board of education. In an effort to comply with *Plessy v. Ferguson*,* the city also operated a nine-hole golf course for African Americans, known as Nacho Park Golf Course. After a group of black citizens applied for permission to play on the Gillespie course in 1949, the city and the board of education leased the entire course to the Gillespie Park Golf Club, which then operated as a private nonprofit corporation. Annual membership and green fees were established. In practice, however, white nonmembers were allowed to play on the course by paying only the green fees, while blacks who asked to play were denied such, always being told that they were not members. On 20 March 1957 in this *Simkins* case, the U.S. District Court ruled that the city of Greensboro and the city board of education could not avoid giving equal treatment to black citizens by leasing an entire golf course to a nonprofit corporation. In order for the golf course to remain open, it could not discriminate against any citizens of Greensboro on account of race. In reaction to this decision, the city closed both golf courses.

SELECTED BIBLIOGRAPHY

Richard Bardolph, ed., *The Civil Rights Record, Black Americans and the Law, 1849–1970* (1970); William H. Chafe, *Civilities and Civil Rights: Greensboro, North Carolina, and the Black Struggle for Freedom* (1980).

Charles A. Risher

SIMKINS v. MOSES H. CONE MEMORIAL HOSPITAL, 323 F.2d 959 (4th Cir., 1963). This was a landmark decision in the struggle against segregation. The Fourth Circuit Court of Appeals in November 1963 held that governmentally owned, operated, or subsidized hospitals practicing racial discrimination violated the due process clause of the Fifth Amendment and the equal protection clause of the Fourteenth Amendment.* Black physicians, dentists, and patients brought the suit in 1962 against two Greensboro, North Carolina, hospitals that practiced exclusionary policies based on race. The plaintiffs argued that, since the defendant hospitals received federal funds under the Hill-Burton Hospital Survey and Construction Act, they were subject to constitutional restraints against racial discrimination. The Justice Department intervened in support of the plaintiffs' contention that a provision of Hill-Burton permitting separate but equal facilities in recipient hospitals was unconstitutional. Reversing lower court decisions, a divided court of appeals ruled in favor of the plaintiffs. This decision became an important precedent in lawsuits dealing with the discriminatory policies of nongovernmental medical facilities. It and other related cases helped to establish the premise for Title VI of the Civil Rights Act of 1964* which prohibited racial discrimination in federally assisted programs and activities.

SELECTED BIBLIOGRAPHY

Derrick A. Bell Jr., *Race, Racism and American Law*, 2nd ed. (1980); William H. Chafe, *Civilities and Civil Rights: Greensboro, North Carolina, and the Black Struggle for Freedom* (1980); Loren Miller, *The Petitioners: The Story of the Supreme Court of the United States and the Negro* (1966); Stephen L. Wasby, Anthony A. D'Amato, and Rosemary Metrailer, *Desegregation from Brown to Alexander: An Exploration of Supreme Court Strategies* (1977).

Jack E. Davis

SINGLETON, BENJAMIN "PAP" (1809, Nashville, Tenn.–1892, St. Louis, Mo.). Born a slave, Singleton was sold south several times but always managed to return to Nashville. He finally escaped to Canada, but recrossed the border and settled in Detroit, Michigan. There, Singleton harbored other runaways. After the Civil War, he returned to Nashville where, by the 1870s, he had become involved in the millenarian movement. In 1874 he and several others established the Edgefield Real Estate and Homestead Association. Between 1877 and 1897, the association directed hundreds of landless and persecuted black Southerners to Kansas. Thus, by the time Singleton testified before the Senate committee on the exodus, he claimed to be the "father" of the millenarian exodus.

SELECTED BIBLIOGRAPHY

Walter L. Fleming, " 'Pap' Singleton, the Moses of the Colored Exodus," *American Journal of Sociology* 15 (July 1909), 61–82; Ray Garvin, "Benjamin or 'Pap' Singleton and his Followers," *Journal of Negro History* 33 (January 1948), 7–23; Nell Irvin Painter, *Exoduster: Black Migration to Kansas Following Reconstruction* (1977); U.S. Senate, *Report and Testimony of the Select Committee . . . to Investigate the Causes of the Removal of the Negro from the Southern States to the Northern States,* U.S. 46th Cong., 2nd Sess., Senate Report 693 (1880), 3:379–91.

Judith N. Kerr

SIPUEL v. BOARD OF REGENTS OF THE UNIVERSITY OF OKLAHOMA, 332 U.S. 631 (1948). The racially segregated University of Oklahoma School of Law denied Ada Lois Sipuel admission in 1946. Although Oklahoma had no law school accessible to blacks, it did provide tuition grants for African Americans to attend institutions outside the state and claimed that this practice satisfied the separate but equal* doctrine established in *Plessy v. Ferguson** (1896). Sipuel challenged the *Plessy* rule which Oklahoma courts subsequently upheld. The U.S. Supreme Court in January 1948 reversed the state courts and said that the plaintiff was entitled under the Fourteenth Amendment* to a legal education within the state of Oklahoma that was equal to that given whites. The state responded by opening a black law school. The ad hoc school offered a faculty of three white attorneys, three classrooms, and access to the law library at the capitol. Sipuel refused to attend. Only one student actually enrolled during the school's short history. Meanwhile, Sipuel returned to court, arguing that the new school did not satisfy the equal protection clause in the Fourteenth Amendment. The Supreme Court agreed and held that the resources of the new school were inadequate. Sipuel, admitted in 1949, graduated from the University of Oklahoma School of Law in 1951.

SELECTED BIBLIOGRAPHY

Derrick A. Bell, Jr., *Race, Racism and American Law* (1980); E. W. Broore, Jr., "Notes and Comments," *Boston University Law Review* 28 (1948), 240–42; Geoffrey R. Stone, *Constitutional Law* (1986); Mark V. Tushnet, *The NAACP's Legal Strategy against Segregated Education, 1925–1950* (1987).

Stephen Middleton

SISSLE, NOBLE (10 July 1889, Indianapolis, Ind.–17 December 1975, Tampa, Fla.). African-American orchestra leader and lyricist, Sissle was educated in the public schools in Indianapolis and in Cleveland, Ohio, where his family lived from 1909 to 1913. He attended DePauw University, in Greencastle, Indiana (1913) and Butler University, in Indianapolis (1914–1915). A protégé of black orchestra leader James Reese Europe,* Sissle toured with Europe from 1917 to 1919, first as a member of his dance orchestra, than, during World War I, as drum major of the 369th Infantry Regiment Band of which Europe was leader. In the fall of 1917, while stationed with the 15th New York Infantry in Spartanburg, South Carolina, Sissle almost precipitated a race riot when he went into a white hotel to purchase a newspaper and was assaulted by whites. Sissle was best known as pianist-composer Eubie Blake's lyricist partner. They toured the vaudeville circuit from 1919 to 1920. In 1921 they collaborated in the production of the Broadway production *Shuffle Along*, which began their career as writers of musicals. The partnership ended in 1927, after which Sissle formed his own orchestra (1928–1931). In 1937, he was one of the founders of the Negro Actor's Guild.

SELECTED BIBLIOGRAPHY

Rudi Blesh, *Combo USA* (1971); Robert Kimball and William Bolcom, *Reminiscing with Sissle and Blake* (1973); Obituary, *New York Times*, 18 December 1975.

Judith N. Kerr

SLATER FUND. Established in 1882 with a million dollar endowment by Connecticut industrialist John Fox Slater, the Slater Fund was dedicated to the elevation of black Southerners through education. Conservative white businessmen, churchmen, educators, and politicians, including former President Rutherford B. Hayes, were the charter members of the fund's board of trustees. They agreed that black students would reap the most benefits from training in the manual occupations. This special brand of education was endorsed by the major northern philanthropists who were interested in black education in the South. For the first twenty-nine years of its life, the Slater Fund gave the lion's share of its aid to black colleges offering industrial training. Tuskegee*

These Tuskegee Institute students benefited from the support the Slater, Peabody, and Phelps-Stokes funds provided for black educational institutions. (Arthur P. Bedou Photographs, Xavier University Archives, New Orleans.)

and Hampton Institutes* received the greatest portion of the appropriations. After 1911 the fund gave a significant amount of aid to county/parish training schools. Its aim was to increase the pool of trained black elementary schoolteachers in the rural South. Segregation was not an issue of concern for directors of the Slater Fund, most of whom endorsed separate schools. However, by filling the financial void of underfunded black schools and colleges in the South, the Slater Fund, unwittingly perhaps, helped lay the foundation for a middle-class, college-bred black leadership elite that worked with white allies in tearing down the walls of Jim Crow.*

SELECTED BIBLIOGRAPHY
Will W. Alexander, "The Slater and Jeanes Funds, an Educator's Approach to a Difficult Social Problem," Washington, D.C.: Trustees of the John F. Slater Fund, Occasional Papers, no. 286 (1948); Henry Allen Bullock, *A History of Negro Education in the South from 1619 to the Present* (1967); Jabez Lamar Monroe Curry Papers, Manuscript Division, Library of Congress; John E. Fisher, *The John F. Slater Fund: A Nineteenth Century Affirmative Action for Negro Education* (1986); Edward E. Redcay, *County Training Schools and Public Secondary Education for Negroes in the South* (1935).

Joe Lewis Caldwell

SLAUGHTERHOUSE CASES, 83 U.S. 36 (1873). Challenging a Louisiana statute that gave a twenty-five-year monopoly on the business of slaughtering cattle in New Orleans to one favored company, the rival butchers asserted that section one of the Fourteenth Amendment* protected their property rights. The law, they said, deprived them of the equal protection of the laws, took their property without due process, and abridged the privileges and immunities of citizenship. Justice Samuel Miller, writing for a five-to-four majority, rejected each of these claims. The equal protection clause prohibited only state laws that discriminated against blacks as a class; the due process clause had only procedural meaning rather than substantive; and the privileges and immunities protected against state intrusion were only those, largely undefined, that derived from federal citizenship. While the opinion thus recognized the intent of the equal protection clause, this first Supreme Court interpretation of the Fourteenth Amendment was so narrow that it left very little opportunity for protection of civil rights. The case marks the beginning of a ten-year period that culminated in the *Civil Rights Cases** (1883), during which the Court, through narrow interpretations of the Thirteenth* and Fourteenth Amendments, blunted most federal efforts to legislate on civil rights.

SELECTED BIBLIOGRAPHY

Charles Fairman, *Mr. Justice Miller and the Supreme Court, 1862–1890* (1939); Charles Fairman, *History of the Supreme Court of the United States, Vol. VII: Reconstruction and Reunion, 1864–1888, Part I* (1986); William Gillette, "Samuel Miller," in Leon Friedman and Fred L. Israel, eds., *The Justices of the United States Supreme Court, 1789–1969: Their Lives and Major Opinions* (1969); Robert C. Palmer, "The Parameters of Constitutional Reconstruction: Slaughter-House, Cruikshank, and the Fourteenth Amendment," *University of Illinois Law Review* (1984), 739–70; John A. Scott, "Justice Bradley's Evolving Concept of the Fourteenth Amendment from the Slaughterhouse Cases to the Civil Rights Cases," *Rutgers Law Review* 25 (1971), 552–69.

James E. Sefton

SMALLS, ROBERT (5 April 1839, Beaufort, S.C.–22 February 1915, Beaufort, S.C.). Born a slave in Beaufort, South Carolina, Robert Smalls became a Civil War hero after he abducted the *Planter*, a Confederate steamer, into Union lines in 1862. He became a major figure in South Carolina Republican politics during Reconstruction, championing black economic, political, and social rights. Smalls attended the 1867 Constitutional Convention, and he represented Beaufort County in the general assembly, the state senate, and in the United States Congress. Even though his congressional career ended in 1888, Smalls continued to wield considerable power and influence in local politics. He was appointed collector of customs for the Port of Beaufort in 1888.

SELECTED BIBLIOGRAPHY

Deborah Moore, "The King of Beaufort" (Master's thesis, Columbia University, 1968); Willie Lee Rose, *Rehearsal for Reconstruction: The Port Royal Experiment*

Congressman Robert Smalls (top). (Negro Almanac Collection, Amistad Research Center, Tulane University, New Orleans.)

(1964); Dorothy Sterling, *Captain of the Planter: The Story of Robert Smalls* (1958); Okon Edet Uya, *From Slavery to Public Service: Robert Smalls 1839–1915* (1971).

Maxine D. Jones

SMILEY, GLENN (19 April 1910, Loraine, Tex.–   ). Martin Luther King, Jr.,* once wrote: "I rode the first integrated bus in Montgomery with a white minister, and a native Southerner as my seatmate." That seatmate was Glenn Smiley, credited with guiding King in the transition from advocating nonviolent resistance* as a tactic to adopting it as a way of life. Smiley conducted nonviolence training workshops during the Montgomery campaign (1955–1956) and stumped the nation interpreting the protest. Staff member of the Fellowship of Reconciliation* from 1952 until 1967 (imprisoned 1944–1945 as a conscientious objector), Smiley cultivated nonviolence in Latin America during the years from 1967 to 1970. Appointed to the board of advisors of the New York State Institute on Nonviolence in 1987 and founder of the Martin Luther King Center for Nonviolence in Los Angeles, Smiley published a nonviolence training manual in 1990.

SELECTED BIBLIOGRAPHY

Taylor Branch, *Parting the Waters: America in the King Years, 1954–63* (1989); Vera Brittain, *The Rebel Passion* (1964); David J. Garrow, *Bearing the Cross: Martin Luther King, Jr. and the Southern Christian Leadership Conference* (1986); Aldon D. Morris, *The Origins of the Civil Rights Movement: Black Communities Organizing for Change* (1984); Juan Williams, *Eyes on the Prize: America's Civil Rights Years, 1954–1965* (1987).

Jo Ann O. Robinson

SMITH, FRANK ELLIS (21 February 1918, Sidon, Miss.–). After serving as an artillery officer in World War II, Smith returned to Greenwood to be the managing editor of the *Morning Star*. He was elected to the Mississippi state senate, worked in John Stennis's 1946 election campaign, and went to Washington, D.C., with Stennis. In 1950 Smith was elected to the U.S. House of Representatives, and in 1962 John F. Kennedy appointed him to the Tennessee Valley Authority (TVA) board. Smith condemned Mississippi's efforts to prevent the integration of the university, and he published his autobiography, *Congressman from Mississippi* (1964), to inspire white Southerners to integrate. He served as "confessor" to Mississippians who disagreed with their state's policies and aided exiles who made their views known and had to flee. He counseled state politicians who worked for integration, spoke to groups interested in furthering integration, and used his public role as a TVA director to argue for political and economic justice for blacks. He published his arguments for integration in *Look Away from Dixie* (1965). To provide biracial role models, Smith published a series of short biographies entitled *Mississippians All* (1968). Smith also served on the Southern Regional Council* and worked with their Voter Education Project* to register and encourage blacks to vote.

SELECTED BIBLIOGRAPHY

James W. Loewen and Charles Sallis, eds., *Mississippi: Conflict and Change* (1974); James W. Silver, *Mississippi: The Closed Society* (1963); Frank Smith, *Congressman from Mississippi* (1964); Frank Smith Papers, in the possession of Dennis J. Mitchell, Jackson State University.

Dennis J. Mitchell

SMITH, LAMAR (1892–13 August 1955, Brookhaven, Miss.). Lamar Smith was not a typical Lincoln County, Mississippi, black man; he owned land and wealth. His active participation in the civil rights movement also set him apart. Although warned to "stay out of white folks' politics," Smith organized black voters throughout the county. He was intensely involved in a county supervisor election during the summer of 1955. His activities figured prominently in the events of Saturday, August 13. While arguing with several whites, on the courthouse grounds in Brookhaven, Smith was shot and killed. Although at the time—10 A.M.—many blacks and whites were present, gaining a clear understanding of what had occurred proved difficult. Some witnesses mentioned a blood-spattered white man who sped away in a truck, but Sheriff Robert Case first reported "nobody knows nothing." Before the week had passed, however, three local white men were in custody. A coroner's jury concluded they had committed the crime. Yet, subsequently, due to a lack of evidence, the grand jury failed to return any indictments. District Attorney E. C. Barlow put the murder of the sixty-three-year-old black man in perspective when he attributed the death to "local politics."

SELECTED BIBLIOGRAPHY
Sara Bullard, ed., *Free at Last* (1989); *Jackson Clarion-Ledger*, 14, 15, 17, 19 August 1955; James W. Silver, *Mississippi: The Closed Society* (1963).

William Warren Rogers, Jr.

SMITH, LILLIAN (12 December 1887, Jasper, Fla.–28 September 1966, Clayton, Ga.). A southern writer and teacher, Lillian Smith devoted much of her talent and energy to exploring the causes and implications of white racism and being an advocate for black equality and racial understanding. Through the pages of *South Today*, which she coedited, Smith publicized the works of black writers, attacked the racial assumptions of popular novels like *Gone with the Wind*, and probed the historical sources of southern racism and segregation. She directly challenged Jim Crow* and often criticized fellow white liberals for not confronting the full terror of race separation and violence in the South. In 1944, she published *Strange Fruit*, a novel which looked at the tragic effects of a love affair between a white man and a black woman. Despite being banned in Boston and elsewhere for sexual and racial references, it became a national best-seller. *Killers of the Dream*, a collection of essays on the psychological and historical meaning of southern racism published in 1949, further enhanced Smith's stature as the South's foremost critic of racism. Because of her views, Smith was often harassed by state and local government officials and was attacked by the Ku Klux Klan. During the 1950s and 1960s, she celebrated the civil rights movement, giving special praise to the philosophy and tactics of Martin Luther King, Jr.,* and to the young black students who initiated sit-in protests in Georgia and elsewhere. A board member of the Congress of Racial Equality* (CORE), she resigned prior to her death in 1966 protesting what she felt was CORE's failure to maintain a commitment to integration and nonviolent resistance.* A courageous advocate of equality, Lillian Smith embodied the best of southern white race liberalism.

SELECTED BIBLIOGRAPHY

Louise Blackwell and Frances Clay, *Lillian Smith* (1971); John B. Kirby, *Black Americans in the Roosevelt Era* (1980); Morton Sosna, *In Search of the Silent South* (1977); Anne C. Loveland, *Lillian Smith, A Southerner Confronting the South: A Biography* (1986).

John B. Kirby

SMITH v. ALLWRIGHT, 321 U.S. 649 (1944). On 3 April 1944, the U.S. Supreme Court ruled that the white primaries* of the Texas Democratic party were unconstitutional because they denied African Americans the right to participate in the electoral process on the basis of race. NAACP* General Counsel Thurgood Marshall* and Dallas lawyer William J. Durham filed and argued the case for the plaintiff, Houston dentist Lonnie E. Smith. Smith was denied a ballot in the 1940 Harris County primary by election judge S. E. Allwright. To eliminate the Texas white primary, the Supreme Court had to reverse its 1935 *Grovey v. Townsend** decision, which had stated that Democratic party primaries were private affairs and not subject to state regulation. In 1941, however, the Supreme Court ruled in the *United States v. Classic** case that party primaries constituted state action because the state delegated to political parties the power to choose candidates to hold elective office. Using this ruling in the *Classic* case, the Supreme Court ruled that African Americans had as much right to participate in party primaries as in general elections and that the denial of their participation violated the Constitution. This landmark case won by the NAACP in Texas removed a major barrier that had prevented African Americans from participating in the electoral process in the South.

SELECTED BIBLIOGRAPHY

Darlene Clark Hine, *Black Victory: The Rise and Fall of the White Primary in Texas* (1979); Darlene Clark Hine, "The Elusive Ballot: The Black Struggle against the Texas Democratic White Primary, 1932–45," *Southwestern Historical Quarterly* 81 (April 1978), 371–92; Steven F. Lawson, *Black Ballots: Voting Rights in the South, 1944–1969* (1976); *New York Times*, 4 April 1944; Papers of the NAACP, Part 4: The Voting Rights Campaign, 1916–1950.

W. Marvin Dulaney

SMITH v. STATE OF TEXAS, 311 U.S. 128 (1940). This U.S. Supreme Court case helped define what constituted racial discrimination in the selection of grand juries as proscribed under the equal protection clause of the Fourteenth Amendment.* Edgar Smith, a black resident of Harris County, Texas, was convicted of rape in the state district court in 1938. His appeal, which reached the Supreme Court in November 1940, contended that his conviction had come under an indictment returned by a grand jury from which blacks had been systematically excluded—as indicated by their almost complete absence on such panels from 1931 to 1938. He had been denied, he argued, the equal protection of law. The court accepted Smith's argument, holding that it is not sufficient that state law merely promise equal protection, as did the Texas grand jury–selection statute; equal protection must actually be provided. The fact that, for example, only one black had served on Harris County grand juries in the four years between 1935 and 1938 indicated the existence of a pattern of discrimination by race in the selection of grand jury members. Regardless of whether that discrimination had been accomplished deliberately or innocently, the fact deprived Smith of the equal protection of the laws and so invalidated his conviction.

SELECTED BIBLIOGRAPHY

Richard Bardolph, ed., *The Civil Rights Record: Black Americans and the Law, 1849–1970* (1970); Thomas I. Emerson et al., *Political and Civil Rights in the United States* (1967); *New York Times*, 26 November 1940.

Robert A. Calvert

THE SOULS OF BLACK FOLK. In 1903 W.E.B. Du Bois,* scholar and intellectual, rose to national prominence as a political propagandist when he published an intensely personal manifesto of fourteen essays on the spiritual, cultural, and political significance of being black in America. Using the motif of a "veil" which had created for African Americans a "double-consciousness," Du Bois assessed the past, present, and future of American race relations.

In a national environment of increased racial violence, discrimination, disenfranchisement, and scientific racism, Du Bois offered a prophetic vision of black nationalism for the legal recognition of black human rights and the assertion of an African-American cultural identity. In doing so, Du Bois challenged and rejected the leadership and philosophy of Booker T. Washington,* not only in the one essay entitled "Of Mr. Booker T. Washington and Others," but in the entire book. In place of Washington's accommodationist policy of economic development, Du Bois confronted and challenged what he called the problem of the twentieth century: the color line.

SELECTED BIBLIOGRAPHY

Francis L. Broderick, *W.E.B. DuBois: Negro Leader in a Time of Crisis* (1959); W.E.B. Du Bois, *The Souls of Black Folk* (1903); Manning Marable, *W.E.B. DuBois: Black Radical Democrat* (1986); Arnold Rampersad, *The Art and Imagination of W.E.B. DuBois* (1976); Elliott M. Rudwick, *Propagandist of the Negro Protest* (1968).

Lillie Johnson Edwards

SOUTH CAROLINA ELECTRIC AND GAS COMPANY v. FLEMING, 351 U.S. 901 (1956). Although the Montgomery bus boycott* received enormous publicity, other cities staged similar demonstrations against segregation in transportation. The case involving the South Carolina Electric and Gas Company grew out of one of these protests. Sara Mae Fleming brought suit in 1955, alleging that a driver compelled her to change her seat under a state segregation law. The driver explained that his job required that he enforce the laws of the state, including segregation. A lower court upheld the statute, contending that what the "state statute complained of was valid under *Plessy v. Ferguson*."* Fleming appealed. Attorneys for the South Carolina Electric and Gas Company argued that the *Brown v. Board of Education** case applied only to education. If the court of appeals had accepted this interpretation, cities could legally have continued to enforce segregated public accommodations. But the court rejected the argument on the grounds that previous U.S. Supreme Court decisions had rendered segregation unconstitutional. The judges applied *Brown* to transportation, concluding that it left "no doubt that the separate but equal doctrine approved in *Plessy v. Ferguson* has been repudiated." The Supreme Court refused to hear the appeal of the defendant.

SELECTED BIBLIOGRAPHY

Chester J. Antieau, ed., *Federal Civil Rights Acts: Civil Practice* (1980); Catherine A. Barnes, *Journey from Jim Crow: The Desegregation of Southern Transit* (1983).

Stephen Middleton

SOUTH CAROLINA v. KATZENBACH, 383 U.S. 301 (1966). In a suit filed by the state of South Carolina, the Supreme Court upheld the constitutionality of key provisions of the Voting Rights Act of 1965,* legislation based upon Section Two of the Fifteenth Amendment,* authorizing Congress to enforce the amendment by appropriate legislation. The Court held that the coverage formula, bringing under coverage of the act states and subdivisions of states using "tests or devices" as prerequisites for voting and having less than 50 percent of their otherwise eligible voters registered and voting in the presidential election of 1964, was appropriate legislation. The suspension of literacy tests and other devices in covered jurisdictions, and the authorization of federal examiners to register voters, was also legal. In an even more controversial move, it upheld the requirement that covered states and subdivisions must preclear any changes in laws regarding voting and elections with either the attorney general or the Federal District Court for the District of Columbia before they could go into effect. In dissent, Justice Hugo L. Black asserted that the preclearance requirement violated principles of federalism. Significantly increasing the minority electorate and the number of minority elected officials, the Voting Rights Act of 1965 and the decision upholding its constitutionality revolutionized southern politics.

SELECTED BIBLIOGRAPHY
Alexander Bickel, "The Voting Rights Cases," *Supreme Court Review* (1966), 79–102; Richard Claude, *The Supreme Court and the Electoral Process* (1970); United States Commission on Civil Rights, *The Voting Rights Act: Unfulfilled Goals* (1981).
                                                              Patricia A. Behlar

SOUTH v. PETERS, 339 U.S. 276 (1950). This Supreme Court case involved a 1917 Georgia statute that established a county unit system, which gave sparsely populated rural counties a vote in primary elections disproportionately larger than the vote of more populous urban counties where much of the black population was located. Plaintiff Bernard South and other black residents of Atlanta argued that, because they resided in a large county, their vote had, in effect, only one-tenth the value it would have had in less populated counties. James Peters, chairman of the state Democratic party, defended the statute by arguing, and the Court agreed, that "federal courts consistently refuse to exercise their equity powers in cases posing political issues arising from a state's geographical distribution of electoral strengths among its political subdivisions." Justices William Douglas and Hugo Black dissented. Douglas wrote that "I suppose that if a state reduced the vote of Negroes, Catholics, or Jews so that each got only one-tenth of a vote, we would strike the law down. . . . The discrimination against citizens in the more populous counties of Georgia is plain." Although the county unit vote was upheld in this case, the Court would revisit this issue in *Baker v. Carr* and *Reynolds v. Sims,* ultimately deciding that even though it involved a political issue, federal courts had a duty to ensure the equity of votes.

SELECTED BIBLIOGRAPHY
Richard Claude, *The Supreme Court and the Electoral Process* (1970); Richard C. Cortner, *The Apportionment Cases* (1970).
                                                              Kenneth W. Goings

SOUTHERN BURLINGTON COUNTY NAACP, ETHEL LAWRENCE et al. v. MT. LAUREL TOWNSHIP, NEW JERSEY, 67 N.J. 151, 336 A.2d 713 (1975). In 1950 Mt. Laurel, New Jersey, was a sprawling twenty-two-square-mile township located fifteen miles northeast of Philadelphia with a population of only 2,817 people engaged almost exclusively in farming. About four hundred African Americans lived there, most of them descendants of pre-Civil War fugitive slaves. Most were people of modest means who worked largely as laborers on nearby farms. Over the next decade, Mt. Laurel experienced rapid suburban development. Small industries and commercial establishments arrived, and the population had quadrupled by 1970. In 1964 the township's council and zoning board adopted a general land use ordinance that prohibited the construction of multiunit apartments, attached townhouses, and mobile home parks. Furthermore, the ordinance mandated minimum house lot sizes of 9,375 to 20,000 square feet with homes having at least 1,100 square feet of living space. Developers were discouraged from selling or leasing to households with more than two children. The zoning code meant that only people of middle and upper income would be able to live in the township. Ethel Lawrence, a fourth-generation African-American resident of Mt. Laurel, pointed out that most black youth had to leave because they could not afford to purchase or rent housing in their hometown. In conjunction with the local branch of the NAACP,* she sued Mt. Laurel Township for using restrictive zoning ordinances to exclude from residency certain racial and socioeconomic groups. The superior and supreme courts of New Jersey agreed and found exclusionary zoning so pervasive that they ordered every region and municipality in the state to affirmatively provide housing for low- and moderate-income families.

SELECTED BIBLIOGRAPHY

Gary Hunter, *Up South: The Civil Rights Movement in Southern New Jersey 1940–1973* (1990); Derrick A. Bell, Jr., *Race, Racism and American Law* (1980).

Gary J. Hunter

SOUTHERN CHRISTIAN LEADERSHIP CONFERENCE. The Southern Christian Leadership Conference (SCLC) was established in 1957 in order to "coordinate local, nonviolent direct-action[*] protest movements" in the South. The key officers were ministers, mostly Baptist. The first executive director was Reverend Wyatt Tee Walker,* who, by 1963, headed a staff of fifty and supervised eighty-five affiliate groups. But the key leader, the essence of the SCLC, was Martin Luther King, Jr.* The organization shared his goal, inspired by Mohandas K. Gandhi, to achieve full equality for blacks through the use of mass nonviolent resistance* to win public sympathy and support and to apply "redemptive love" to heal America's troubled society.

The group's first action, in 1957, was a Prayer Pilgrimage to Washington,* led by King, which attracted 25,000 people. It was followed, in 1959, by a youth march on Washington, attended by 40,000. Mass marches were followed by dramatic, televised "sit-ins," used to publicize the wrongs of segregation, beginning with the Greensboro, North Carolina, sit-in* in 1960. The aim of the next series of SCLC campaigns was to fight segregation and to secure voting rights, as in the activities of the Freedom Riders,* the Albany, Georgia, sit-in,* the Birmingham Confrontation* with Commissioner Bull Connor, and the 1964 St. Augustine fight against segregation and the Ku Klux Klan. The SCLC brilliantly mobilized blacks, organizing and leading marches, filling up jails, and displaying to an international television audience the mindless violence of southern whites. In 1964, influenced by the SCLC–led mass protest movement, Congress finally passed the Civil Rights Act of 1964.* As

SCLC leadership during Birmingham Confrontation, 1963: the Reverends Martin Luther King, Jr., Fred Shuttlesworth, and Ralph Abernathy. (Archives Collection, Birmingham Public Library. Courtesy *Birmingham News*.)

Stephen B. Oates and Pat Watters have shown, the SCLC clashed with the Student Nonviolent Coordinating Committee* (SNCC) first in Selma, in 1965, over tactics and philosophy, with SNCC members feeling the SCLC took too much credit for local movements they had initiated. The SCLC also opposed their burgeoning black supremacy ideas as another form of tyranny. The violence in Selma, including killings, which occurred during the Selma to Montgomery March,* moved President Lyndon B. Johnson to urge the passage of the Voting Rights Act of 1965.* The SCLC quickly registered 85,000 new voters within four months.

After the 1964 and 1965 bills were passed, the SCLC turned to the problems of northern cities, such as segregation, job discrimination, and poverty. The Chicago Freedom Movement* and Operation Breadbasket in 1967 resulted in violent white resistance. Chicago's Mayor Richard J. Daley eventually promised to enforce city housing laws against discrimination, but clearly northern cities presented a huge challenge. Dr. King, by 1967, was speaking out against the Vietnam War, which did not help his popularity. In 1968 the SCLC organized the Poor People's March on

Washington* as a civil disobedience action. While taking time out from this campaign to support sanitation workers in Memphis, Tennessee, King was assassinated in April 1968. The campaign continued, but the movement had lost its articulation. Regrouping under the leadership of the Reverend Ralph David Abernathy,* the SCLC continued the struggle on the local level, fighting against the evils of race discrimination and poverty. Its political influence in the South, as well as its role in changing the national conscience, has been enormous.

SELECTED BIBLIOGRAPHY

Adam Fairclough, *To Redeem the Soul of America: The Southern Christian Leadership Conference and Martin Luther King, Jr.* (1987); David J. Garrow, *Bearing the Cross: Martin Luther King, Jr., and the Southern Christian Leadership Conference* (1986); David J. Garrow, ed., *We Shall Overcome: The Civil Rights Movement in the United States in the 1950s and 1960s* (1989); Martin Luther King, Jr., Papers, King Center for Nonviolent Change, Atlanta, Georgia; Stephen B. Oates, *Let the Trumpet Sound: The Life of Martin Luther King, Jr.* (1982); Pat Watters, *Down to Now: Reflections on the Civil Rights Movement* (1971).

Linda G. Ford

SOUTHERN COMMISSION ON THE STUDY OF LYNCHING. This commission was created in June 1930 in response to the "marked increase" in lynchings. It included some of the most prominent African Americans of the day: John Hope,* B. F. Hubert, Robert R. Moton,* and Monroe Work.* Its work was summarized in two reports, *Lynchings and What They Mean* and *The Mob Murder of S. S. Mincey.* The commission concluded that lynching would be eliminated when all Americans have "opportunities for development and are accorded fundamental human rights."

SELECTED BIBLIOGRAPHY

Arthur F. Roper, *The Tragedy of Lynching* (1933); Robert L. Zangrando, *The NAACP Crusade against Lynching, 1909–1950* (1980).

Maghan Keita

SOUTHERN CONFERENCE FOR HUMAN WELFARE. The Southern Conference for Human Welfare (SCHW) was formed in 1938 to promote civil liberties and to provide the South's answer to the National Emergency Council's *Report on the Economic Conditions of the South,* which labeled the region "the nation's No. 1 economic problem." Chaired in the early years by University of North Carolina President Frank Porter Graham,* the SCHW campaigned against the poll tax* and in favor of expanding the New Deal to attack southern poverty. The organization held interracial meetings and allied itself with the Congress of Industrial Organizations for a time. Following a "popular front" strategy, the conference did not exclude Communists from membership. This policy led to exaggerated charges of Communist influence within the organization, and the "red" label was a significant factor in the demise of the organization in 1948.

SELECTED BIBLIOGRAPHY

Thomas A. Krueger, *And Promises to Keep: the Southern Conference for Human Welfare, 1938–1948* (1967); Randall L. Patton, "Southern Liberals and the Emergence of a New South, 1938–1950" (Ph.D. diss., University of Georgia, 1990); Morton Sosna, *In Search of the Silent South: Southern Liberals and the Race Issue* (1977); Patricia Sullivan, "Gideon's Southern Soldiers: New Deal Politics and Civil Rights Reform, 1933–1948" (Ph.D. diss., Emory University, 1983).

Randall L. Patton

SOUTHERN EDUCATION BOARD. Formed in 1901, with a donation from banker George Foster Peabody, this organization promoted a tax-supported southern school system, with the long-term goal of solving complex problems arising from southern poverty, ignorance, and racial tension. By 1914 when the Southern Education Board went out of existence, annual expenditures for education in the South had quadrupled. Although board members considered their efforts successful, historians have criticized the board as a conservative organization that failed to challenge a growing white supremacy movement at the turn of the century. Instead, the board emphasized the education of southern whites to the detriment of southern African Americans, thus contributing to the growth of separate and unequal schools.

SELECTED BIBLIOGRAPHY

Charles W. Dabney, *Universal Education in the South* (1936); Raymond B. Fosdick, *Adventure in Giving* (1962); Louis R. Harlan, *Separate and Unequal* (1958); Louis R. Harlen, "The Southern Education Board and the Race Issue in Public Education," *Journal of Southern Education* 23 (May 1957), 189–202.

Janice M. Leone

SOUTHERN EDUCATION REPORTING SERVICE. The Southern Education Reporting Service (SERS) was started in the spring of 1954 by a group of southern editors and educators who wanted "to tell the story, factually and objectively, of what happened in southern education as a result of the Supreme Court's May 17 opinion." It was incorporated in Tennessee, located in Nashville, and funded primarily by the Ford Foundation. Executive directors included Edward D. Ball, Don Shoemaker, C. A. "Pete" McKnight, and Reed Sarrat. The board of directors included Frank Ahlgren, Virginius Dabney, Alexander Heard, Charles S. Johnson,* Thomas R. Waring, Luther H. Foster, John Siegenthaler, P. B. Young,* and John Popham. For the first decade its staff included, only briefly, one black. Its most important publications were the monthly *Southern School News,** a periodical "Statistical Summary of School Segregation-Desegregation in the Southern and Border States," and a quarterly *Race Relations Law Reporter.** SERS's library gathered information on race relations throughout the United States by clipping more than fifty newspapers and most news magazines and by collecting books, speeches, reports, and other documents. It made its collections available on microfilm as "Facts on Film." On 1 September 1969, SERS ceased to exist when the Race Relations Information Center began operation in Nashville.

SELECTED BIBLIOGRAPHY

Patrick J. Gilpin, "Charles S. Johnson and the Southern Education Reporting Service," *Journal of Negro History* 63 (July 1978), 197–208; *Race Relations Law Reporter; Southern Education Report; Southern School News.*

Charles W. Eagles

SOUTHERN HOMESTEAD ACT (1866). After emancipation, former slaves expected federal allocations of free land, implied in the Confiscation Act of 1862 and the Freedmen's Bureau Act of 1865. William T. Sherman's Special Order no. 15 actually settled some freedmen on "forfeited" and "abandoned" land in January 1865. But Congress failed to enact effective confiscation measures after President Andrew Johnson's amnesty proclamation in 1865 restored rebel property. The federal government came closest to fulfilling ex-slaves' hopes when the Southern Homestead Act of 1866 extended the original (1862) homestead measure to Alabama, Arkansas, Florida, Louisiana, and Mississippi. Initially, white Unionists and freedmen enjoyed exclusive access to eighty-acre grants. The inferior quality of the land and their lack of capital and equipment inhibited the freedmen. Only seven thousand claimed homesteads; only one thousand gained final title. The failure of the act and of land reform generally during Reconstruction condemned most black Southerners to living on white-owned land as tenants and sharecroppers, with the attendant cycle of poverty and despair.

SELECTED BIBLIOGRAPHY

James M. McPherson, *Ordeal by Fire: The Civil War and Reconstruction* (1982); David M. Potter, *Division and the Stresses of Reunion, 1845–1876* (1973); Willie Lee Rose, *Rehearsal for Reconstruction: The Port Royal Experiment* (1964); C. Vann Woodward, *Reunion and Reaction: The Compromise of 1877 and the End of Reconstruction* (1951).

James B. Potts

SOUTHERN NEGRO YOUTH CONGRESS. Organized in February 1937 at a convention in Richmond, Virginia, the congress's mission was to encourage young blacks to join trade unions. The congress joined forces with the National Negro Congress* in May 1937 to coordinate a wildcat strike by predominantly black tobacco workers in Richmond. After an eighteen-month campaign, the two organizations had organized seven local unions in the Richmond tobacco-processing industry representing several thousand black workers. The union locals were then turned over to the Congress of Industrial Organizations (CIO) for permanent jurisdiction. The Southern Negro Youth Congress was an important ally of the CIO in its efforts to organize black workers in the late 1930s. The congress did not exclude Communists from membership, and this policy led to the organization's demise after World War II.

SELECTED BIBLIOGRAPHY

Philip S. Foner, *Organized Labor and the Black Worker, 1619–1973* (1974); Nell I. Painter, ed., *The Narrative of Hosea Hudson: His Life as Negro Communist in the South* (1979).

Randall L. Patton

SOUTHERN POVERTY LAW CENTER. The Southern Poverty Law Center (SPLC) is a private, nonprofit, public interest, legal organization located in Montgomery, Alabama, founded in 1971 by Morris Dees and Joseph J. Levin, Jr., with Julian Bond* as the largely honorary president. The SPLC initially provided legal representation in individual and class action suits in cases dealing with racial discrimination such as the integration of the Montgomery YMCA and the reapportionment of the Alabama legislature. In 1974 the SPLC assisted in the successful defense of Joan Little, accused of murdering her jailer in North Carolina. After the 1981 lynching of David Donald, the SPLC successfully represented his mother in a civil suit which resulted in a seven-million-dollar liability judgment which bankrupted the United Klans of America. Success in the Donald case led the SPLC to institute a series of successful suits on behalf of victims of racist violence aimed at bankrupting the responsible racist organizations. The SPLC maintains an active publishing and information program including its Klanwatch Program.

SELECTED BIBLIOGRAPHY

Morris Dees with Steve Fiffer, *A Season for Justice: The Life and Times of Civil Rights Lawyer Morris Dees* (1991); John Egerton, "Poverty Palace: How the Southern Poverty Law Center Got Rich Fighting the Klan," *The Progressive* (July 1988); Robb London, "Sending a $12.5 Million Message to a Hate Group," *New York Times*, 26 October 1990.

Lorenzo Crowell

SOUTHERN REGIONAL COUNCIL. Formed in 1944, the Southern Regional Council (SRC) was a descendant of the Commission on Interracial Cooperation* and the brainchild of University of North Carolina sociologist Howard W. Odum.* Composed of black and white moderates, the council's original mission was to work within the system of racial separation in the South to make "separate but equal more equal" and to promote economic development in the region. In 1949, as a result of an internal debate, the SRC publicly announced its opposition to segregation. Though its membership dropped dramatically after that decision, the SRC survived. The council, still in existence, has since worked to promote racial integration, voter registration, and increased public awareness of southern social and economic problems.

SELECTED BIBLIOGRAPHY

Guy B. Johnson, "Southern Offensive," *Common Ground* 4 (Summer 1944), 87–93; Anne C. Loveland, *Lillian Smith: A Southerner Confronting the South : A Biography* (1986); Morton Sosna, *In Search of the Silent South: Southern Liberals and the Race Issue* (1977); Southern Regional Council Papers (microfilm edition, 1984).

Randall L. Patton

SOUTHERN SCHOOL NEWS. Published monthly by the Southern Education Reporting Service* from September 1954 to June 1965, the *Southern School News (SSN)* aimed to provide factual, objective, unbiased coverage of school segregation-desegregation in seventeen southern and border states and the District of Columbia. Drawing on correspondents who worked for newspapers across the South, each issue of *SSN* contained a major article on events in each state. It reached more than ten thousand educators, government officials, clergy, libraries, and interested layman in all fifty states and more than forty foreign countries. *SSN* staff and correspondents also produced several books, including *With All Deliberate Speed* (1957) and *Southern Schools: Progress and Problems* (1959). *SSN* won a number of awards. In 1956 the National Newspaper Publishers Association awarded it its Russworm Award for outstanding achievement, and in 1962 Texas Southern University gave *SSN* its "layman's citation for distinguished service in the public journals." In 1965 the board of the Southern Education Reporting Service decided that the Civil Rights Act of 1964* signaled the end of the transition from segregated to desegregated schools and ended publication of *SSN*. In the summer of 1965 *SSN* was replaced by the *Southern Education Report*, which concentrates on the education of socially and economically handicapped in the southern and border states.

SELECTED BIBLIOGRAPHY

Race Relations Law Reporter; Southern Education Report; Southern School News.

Charles W. Eagles

SOUTHERN TENANT FARMERS' UNION. In July 1934 two Socialists, Harry Leland Mitchell* and Henry Clay East, helped a small band of economically displaced black and white farmers around Tyronza, Arkansas, organize the Southern Tenant Farmers' Union (STFU). STFU leaders attempted to unite the disinherited of both races in Arkansas, Oklahoma, and Missouri in hopes of forcing more equitable treatment from the planters. They also tried to secure constructive changes in Agricultural Adjustment Administration policy. The strikes, protests, and propaganda of the union were never more than marginally successful. Although it eventually evolved into the National Farm Labor

Union, ideological, interracial, and personal strife had enervated the STFU by the early 1940s. During the mid-1930s, however, this union represented a rare and courageous attempt at economic and interracial solidarity.

SELECTED BIBLIOGRAPHY

Donald H. Grubbs, *Cry from the Cotton: The Southern Tenant Farmers' Union and the New Deal* (1971); Howard A. Kester, *Revolt among the Sharecroppers* (1936); H. L. Mitchell, *Mean Things Happening in This Land: The Life and Times of H. L. Mitchell, Co-founder of the Southern Tenant Farmers' Union* (1979); Southern Tenant Farmers' Union Papers, Southern Historical Collection, University of North Carolina at Chapel Hill.

Robert F. Martin

SPENCER, ANNE (8 February 1882, Henry County, Va.–27 July 1975, Lynchburg, Va.). An important African-American Harlem Renaissance* poet, her home in Lynchburg, Virginia, was a way station to the South for civil rights leaders and African-American artists of renown denied public accommodations in the region. James Weldon Johnson,* poet and, at the time, field secretary for the NAACP,* not only opened the way for publishing her work but also helped her organize a NAACP chapter in the city. Spencer graduated from Virginia Theological Seminary and College and was a librarian at segregated Dunbar High School, both in Lynchburg. She was instrumental in making library facilities and materials accessible to black residents.

SELECTED BIBLIOGRAPHY

J. Lee Greene, "Anne Spencer of Lynchburg," *Virginia Cavalcade* (Spring 1987), 178–82; J. Lee Greene, *Time's Unfading Garden: Anne Spencer's Life and Poetry* (1977).

Nancy E. Fitch

SPINGARN, ARTHUR BARNETT (28 March 1878, New York, N.Y.–1 December 1971, New York, N.Y.). A leading civil rights attorney and one of the founders of the NAACP,* Spingarn was involved in its operation for over half a century and was its president for twenty-six years (1940–1966). He was born into a socially prominent and wealthy New York family on 28 March 1878 to Elias and Sarah Barnett Spingarn. Spingarn received a bachelor's degree in 1897, a master's degree in 1899, and his law degree in 1900 from Columbia University. He gave thirty-five years as the volunteer chairman of the National Legal Defense Committee and served as vice president of the NAACP from 1911 to 1940. Additionally Spingarn won a number of important civil rights court cases for African Americans from the mid–1920s in northern cities and southern state courts. He also was instrumental in defeating many presidential federal judge nominees who opposed civil rights legislation. Spingarn was one of the leading bibliophiles and collectors of African and African-American works. In 1946 he incorporated his extensive personal collection of over five thousand books and pamphlets into the already impressive holdings at Howard University's* Negro Foundation Library, now called the Moorland-Spingarn Research Center.

SELECTED BIBLIOGRAPHY

"Arthur B. Spingarn" *Current Biography* 26 (June 1965), 34–35; Arthur Spingarn Papers, Manuscript Division, Moorland-Spingarn Research Center, Howard University, Washington, D.C.; Beverly Gray, "White Warrior," *Negro Digest* 41 (September 1962), 63–64.

Glenn O. Phillips

SPINGARN MEDAL. Established in 1913 by Joel E. Spingarn, the Spingarn Medal is awarded annually by the NAACP* to a man or woman of African descent for outstanding achievement. In offering the gold medal, which he endowed with a $20,000 bequest, Joel Spingarn hoped to promote cultural awareness and black pride by honoring people whose achievements helped to preserve or enrich the unique black cultural heritage. Spingarn thought that blacks were especially well endowed in the arts, but he did not stipulate that only black artists were eligible for the award. Indeed, the first recipient in 1915, Ernest E. Just, was a research biologist, and over the years those honored have come from the fields of law, religion, education, politics, and business along with the arts and sciences. Spingarn Medalists, which include such distinguished people as W.E.B. Du Bois,* James Weldon Johnson,* Mary McLeod Bethune,* Richard Wright,* A. Philip Randolph,* Thurgood Marshall,* Martin Luther King, Jr.,* Leontyne Price,* and Benjamin Mays,* constitute a veritable Who's Who of African Americans.

SELECTED BIBLIOGRAPHY

Harry A. Ploski and James Williams, eds., *The Negro Almanac: A Reference Work on the Afro-American* (1983); B. Joyce Ross, *J. E. Spingarn and the Rise of the NAACP, 1911–1939* (1972); Mabel M. Smythe, ed., *The Black American Reference Book* (1976).

Charles D. Lowery

SPRINGFIELD, ILLINOIS, RACE RIOT (1908). The migration of blacks into Illinois's urban areas at the turn of the century threatened white dominance of jobs and the ballot box. In July 1908, a white man discovered a young black vagrant named Joe James in his sixteen-year-old daughter's bedroom and in the scuffle was severely cut and later died. James was indicted for murder. Five weeks later another black man allegedly raped a white woman, and, though he protested his innocence, he was arrested and placed in jail along side James. A mob which quickly grew to four thousand people threatened the jail house. The sheriff, who had done nothing to disperse the crowd, now decided to move the prisoners, spiriting them away to the state prison in Bloomington. When the mob discovered it had no prisoners to punish, it went on a rampage against the community's blacks. Significant property damage was done;

numerous individuals were beaten and injured; and two blacks, both elderly males, were lynched. The state militia had to be called in to restore order. Thousands of terrified blacks left the city permanently; white residents even refused to sell them any food. The horror of the situation was only increased by the fact that Springfield was preparing to celebrate the centennial of the birth of its most famous citizen, Abraham Lincoln. On 12 February 1909, reformers, horrified by the disaster, met in Springfield and founded the NAACP.*

SELECTED BIBLIOGRAPHY

James L. Crouthamel, "The Springfield, Illinois Race Riot of 1908," *Journal of Negro History* 45 (July 1960), 164–81; *Illinois State Journal* (Springfield), July, August 1908; William E. Walling, "Race War in the North," *The Independent* 65 (3 September 1908), 529–34.

John F. Marszalek

SPRINGFIELD, MASSACHUSETTS, RACE RIOT (1965). A few weeks before the worst race riot of 1965 took place in the Watts community of Los Angeles, California, a racial incident caused several weeks of unrest in the rifle manufacturing city of Springfield, Massachusetts. While not as destructive to life and property as the Watts race riot,* the Springfield disturbance highlighted the serious racial discord that existed throughout the nation. The incident leading to the riot occurred in the early morning hours of 17 July when Springfield police attempted to break up a fight outside a black nightclub. According to the authorities, several hundred onlookers pelted police with rocks and bottles, forcing them to arrest eighteen people. Black witnesses charged the police with excessive force in making the arrests. Springfield blacks protested for the next several weeks. Led by the local branches of the Congress of Racial Equality* and the NAACP,* they marched on City Hall and picketed downtown stores, demanding an official investigation of the incident. Mayor Charles V. Ryan, Jr., called out the National Guard, but he also promised an official probe. The demands of blacks were not met, and the protests continued as the summer ended.

SELECTED BIBLIOGRAPHY

New York Times, 20, 22, 25 July, 11, 14, 15, 16, 17, 19, 22, 23, 24 August 1965; *Springfield Daily News,* 17, 21, 22 July 1965.

Dorothy A. Autrey

STATE ATHLETIC COMMISSION v. DORSEY, 359 U.S. 533 (1959). The decision in this case extended the principle of the unconstitutionality of racial segregation to public athletic contests. Joseph Dorsey, Jr., a black professional boxer, sought to compete against both black and white opponents. Louisiana law prohibited interracial contests. Dorsey sued to prohibit the Louisiana State Athletic Commission from enforcing this law on the grounds that it violated the equal protection clause of the Fourteenth Amendment.* In the landmark school desegregation case of *Brown v. Board of Education*,* the Supreme Court had ruled that classification based upon race in public education is inherently discriminatory and violates the equal protection clause of the Fourteenth Amendment. Through a series of unanimous opinions, the Supreme Court summarily had extended this principle to segregation in any public facilities or functions. In *Dorsey*, the Supreme Court affirmed the lower court decision which concluded that the Louisiana law violated the equal protection clause by requiring racial segregation in a publicly regulated activity.

SELECTED BIBLIOGRAPHY

Henry J. Abraham, *Freedom and the Court, Civil Rights and Liberties in the United States* (1988); Derrick A. Bell, Jr., *Race, Racism and American Law* (1980).

Frederick G. Slabach

STAUPERS, MABEL (27 February 1898, Barbados, West Indies–). While she was executive director (1934–1946) and president (1949–1951) of the National Association of Colored Graduate Nurses (NACGN), Staupers campaigned for the desegregation of the American nursing service. From 1945 to 1950, desegregation took place in the Army and Navy Nurse Corps, the American Nurses Association, most of the southern state nursing associations, and most of the formerly all-white nursing schools. As a result of these developments, Staupers believed that the NACGN was no longer necessary and helped disband it in 1951. The NAACP* awarded her its Spingarn Medal* in 1951.

SELECTED BIBLIOGRAPHY

Darlene Clark Hine, *Black Women in White: Racial Conflict and Cooperation in the Nursing Profession, 1890–1950* (1989); Darlene Clark Hine, "Mabel K. Staupers and the Integration of Black Nurses into the Armed Forces," in John Hope Franklin and August Meier, eds., *Black Leaders of the Twentieth Century* (1982); Mabel Keaton Staupers, *No Time for Prejudice: A Story of the Integration of Nurses in Nursing in the United States* (1961).

Gloria Waite

STEELE, CHARLES KENZIE (7 February 1914, Gary, W. Va.–19 August 1980, Tallahassee, Fla.). A graduate of Morehouse College* and an ordained minister, Steele was a leading civil rights activist, a charter member and first vice president of the Southern Christian Leadership Conference,* and a friend and confidant of Martin Luther King, Jr.* Steele pastored Baptist churches in Georgia and Alabama before assuming pastorship of the Bethel Baptist Church in Tallahassee, Florida, in 1951. In Tallahassee, as local president of the NAACP* and president of the Inter-Civic Council, Steele attacked segregation through nonviolent means. In 1956 he led the ultimately successful Tallahassee, Florida, bus boycott* against the City Transit Company.

SELECTED BIBLIOGRAPHY

Adam Fairclough, *To Redeem the Soul of America: The Southern Christian Leadership Conference and Martin Luther King, Jr.* (1987); David J. Garrow, *Bearing the Cross: Martin Luther King, Jr. and the Southern Christian Leadership Conference* (1986); Gregory B. Padgett, "C. K. Steele and the Tallahassee Bus Boycott" (master's thesis, Florida State University, 1977); Glenda A. Rabby, "Out of the Past: The Civil Rights Movement in Tallahassee, Florida" (Ph.D. diss., Florida State University, 1984); Charles U. Smith, ed., *The Civil Rights Movement in Florida and the United States* (1989); Charles U. Smith and Lewis M. Killian, *The Tallahassee Bus Protest* (1958).

Maxine D. Jones

STEVENS, THADDEUS (4 April 1792, Danville, Vt.–11 August 1868, Washington, D.C.). Thaddeus Stevens was born with a birth defect commonly known as clubfoot—a problem that is said to have affected his thinking as much as his life-style. It also channeled him into education and intellectual pursuits rather than physical ones. He graduated from Dartmouth College, in Hanover, New Hampshire, in 1814. His unpopularity among his peers there would be a problem that would follow him throughout his life. He spent 1815 teaching at Pennsylvania's York Academy while studying law. When the local bar association ruled that a year of full-time study was a prerequisite for taking the bar exam, he went to Maryland and passed the examination there. He established his law practice in Gettysburg in 1816, and he earned a reputation as a sly lawyer. One of his victories ironically came before the state supreme court, when he represented a slave owner against a slave claiming freedom as a result of six months' residence in Pennsylvania. He was also implicated in the death of a black woman, a murder that was never officially solved. Local voters apparently did not believe him guilty, however, for they elected and reelected him to state and national offices. Stevens served seven terms in the state legislature of Pennsylvania beginning in 1833. Moving to Lancaster in 1842, he was sent to Congress on the Whig ticket from 1849 to 1853 and from 1859 to 1868. Anti-Masonry and abolition were the two issues that Stevens rode to political prominence. Somewhat less passionately, he also promoted free public education and the equality of all men. His great ambitions were injured by his apparent concubinage with a free woman of color who kept his house. Stevens could be a ruthless and self-seeking politician. An ardent abolitionist, he was a humanitarian and one of the few politicians of his era who believed that equal rights should be granted to freedmen. As a key leader in the House during and after the Civil War, he helped pass much of the period's legislation. His mark is clearly visible on measures that supported the Union war effort, ranging from taxes to the Emancipation Proclamation.* He was a principal architect of military

Thaddeus Stevens. (Library of Congress.)

and Radical Reconstruction* plans and a major force behind the Thirteenth,* Fourteenth,* and Fifteenth Amendments,* which granted freedom to African Americans and laid the foundations for the twentieth-century civil rights movement. In spite of venality and personality quirks, Thaddeus Stevens, arguably, did more for American blacks than any other politician of his era.

SELECTED BIBLIOGRAPHY

Biographical Directory of the American Congress, 1774–1971 (1971); Fawn M. Brodie, *Thaddeus Stevens: Scourge of the South* (1959); Richard N. Current, *Old Thad Stevens: A Story of Ambition* (1942); Ralph Korngold, *Thaddeus Stevens: A Being Darkly Wise and Rudely Great* (1955).

Gary B. Mills

STILL, WILLIAM GRANT (11 May 1895, Woodville, Miss.–3 December 1978, Los Angeles, Calif.). The undisputed dean of African-American composers, Still grew up in Arkansas, earned a baccalaureate degree from Wilberforce University, and studied at Oberlin Conservatory of Music before embarking upon a career in popular music. Working especially with the violin, cello, and oboe, playing and orchestrating, he worked during the 1920s for such notable musicians as W. C. Handy, Paul Whiteman, Sophie Tucker, and Artie Shaw. After studying briefly at the New England Conservatory in the mid-1920s, he moved to New York and successfully made the difficult transition from popular to classical music. His fame as arranger, composer, and orchestrator grew quickly. In 1924, while he was doing the orchestration for various musical shows, his composition *Darker America* won a publication prize at the Eastman School of Music. Three years later he completed his first ballet, *La Guiablesse*, which was later performed in New York and Chicago. In 1926 he wrote *Levee Land* and in 1927 *From the Black Belt*, pioneering pieces that drew upon his racial heritage and experience. In 1930 he wrote *Afro-American Symphony*, his first major success. In this and in a companion piece, *Africa* (1930), Still employed his new black idiom, incorporating black musical influences—spirituals, blues, work songs, and jazz—into his compositions.

As a black, Still had no chance of becoming resident composer for a large symphony orchestra. Only his exceptional talent gained for him access to areas of music normally open only to whites. He was among the few blacks who managed to obtain regular employment on radio, occasional work in Hollywood, where he wrote the score for *Pennies from Heaven* and other movies, and in television, where in the 1960s he wrote music for such popular series as *Perry Mason* and *Gunsmoke*. He was a man of many firsts whose extraordinary talent helped lower the racial barriers in the area of serious music. For example, he was the first African American to compose a symphony performed by a major orchestra; the first of his race to conduct a major symphony orchestra in the United States; and the first black to have an opera produced by a major company in the United States. His music, though inspired by black culture and experience, was universal in appeal.

SELECTED BIBLIOGRAPHY

Tilford Brooks, *America's Black Musical Heritage* (1984); Robert Haas, ed., *William Grant Still and the Fusion of Cultures in American Music* (1972); James Haskins, *Black Music in America: A History Through Its People* (1987); Obituary, *New York Times*, December 6, 1978.

Charles D. Lowery

STOKES, CARL B. (21 June 1927, Cleveland, Ohio–). First African American to hold positions in all three branches of government, Stokes was reared in poverty. A high school dropout and a self-described street hustler, he enlisted in the army in July 1945. He then resumed his education, completed high school, and obtained a bachelor's degree from the University of Minnesota and a law degree from Cleveland's John Marshall School of Law. His election as the mayor of Cleveland in 1967 made him the first African-American mayor of a major American city. In offce he increased the number of African-American officeholders and opened the door for African-American entrepreneurs. He also served in the Ohio legislature and as a municipal court judge.

SELECTED BIBLIOGRAPHY

Carl B. Stokes, *Promises of Power, Then and Now* (1989); Kenneth G. Weinberg, *Black Victory, Carl Stokes and the Winning of Cleveland* (1968).

Lester S. Brooks

STOREY, MOORFIELD (19 March 1845, Roxbury, Mass.–24 October 1929, Lincoln, Mass.). Lawyer, author, reformer, and civil rights advocate, Storey combined a highly successful corporate practice with a commitment to racial equality that culminated in his becoming the first president of the NAACP.* Descended from New England Puritan stock, Storey's parents and grandparents moved in Boston Brahmin society. Graduating from Harvard College in 1866, Storey attended the law school of that institution briefly, before pursuing legal studies in a prominent Boston firm and being admitted to the bar in 1869.

In 1867 he went to Washington, D.C., to become Senator Charles Sumner's* personal secretary playing, at the same time, an active behind-the-scenes role in the impeachment proceedings of President Andrew Johnson. As a reformer, Storey crusaded against political corruption, and he led the Anti-Imperialist League in opposition to American involvement in the Philippine Islands. He also defended the rights of the American Indian. As a staunch supporter of the struggle of African Americans, he brought his enormous personal influence and legal talents to bear on behalf of the NAACP's most important cases before the Supreme Court.

SELECTED BIBLIOGRAPHY

Boston Transcript, 25 October 1929; *Dictionary of American Biography*, vol. 20 (1937); William B. Hixon, Jr., *Moorfield Storey and the Abolitionist Tradition* (1972).

George E. Walker

STRAUDER v. WEST VIRGINIA, 100 U.S. 303 (1880). In 1874 a Wheeling, West Virginia, jury found a black carpenter named Taylor Strauder guilty of murdering his wife. The jury was composed entirely of whites; in fact, state law limited jury service to whites. Strauder petitioned to have his case moved into a federal court on the grounds that he could not receive a fair trial under West Virginia law. Although the motion was denied by the county court, the U.S. Supreme Court agreed to review the case in 1879. In *Strauder* the Court ruled that West Virginia's statutory exclusion of blacks from juries was unconstitutional under the Fourteenth Amendment.* The Court also held that the removing of a case like Strauder's from a state to federal court for trial was a proper way of enforcing rights under the Fourteenth Amendment. The *Strauder* case, however, was far from being a great civil rights victory; handed down at the same time was *Virginia v. Rives** in which the court displayed unconcern with all-white juries if the state statutes did not specifically limit jury service to whites.

SELECTED BIBLIOGRAPHY

Stephen Cresswell, "The Case of Taylor Strauder," *West Virginia History* 44 (1983), 193–211; Benno C. Schmidt, "Juries, Jurisdiction, and Race Discrimination: The Lost Promise of *Strauder v. West Virginia*," *Texas Law Review* (1983), 1402–99.

                                                              Stephen Cresswell

STRIDE TOWARD FREEDOM. Subtitled *The Montgomery Story*, Martin Luther King, Jr.'s,* 1958 book depicted the use of collective mass action during the successful 1955–1956 Montgomery bus boycott.* A combination of autobiography, history, and philosophy, the study encompasses King's life, the protest tactic of nonviolent resistance,* race relations in Montgomery, community mobilization, and the virulent opposition. King wrote the account while preoccupied with his other duties as the civil rights conflict intensified after Montgomery. Reviewers either lauded or condemned the work depending upon their perspective of the civil rights struggle. Although scholars recently have pointed to some factual and textual problems, this remains an informative book remarkably rich in content.

SELECTED BIBLIOGRAPHY

Taylor Branch, *Parting the Waters: America in the King Years, 1954–63* (1988); Adam Fairclough, *To Redeem the Soul of America: The Southern Christian Leadership Conference and Martin Luther King, Jr.* (1987); David J. Garrow, *Bearing the Cross: Martin Luther King, Jr. and the Southern Christian Leadership Conference* (1986); David J. Garrow, ed., *The Walking City: The Montgomery Bus Boycott, 1955–1956* (1990); David Levering Lewis, *King: A Critical Biography* (1970); Stephen B. Oates, *Let the Trumpet Sound: The Life of Martin Luther King, Jr.* (1982).

                                                              Bruce A. Glasrud

STUDENT NONVIOLENT COORDINATING COMMITTEE. The Student Nonviolent Coordinating Committee (SNCC) resulted from the need to coordinate the widespread student protests following the

Four of the original sit-in group leaving Woolworth's, Greensboro, N.C., 1 February 1960. Following the Greensboro movement, SNCC was organized and carried the movement to other towns. (Photo by Jack Moebes/*Greensboro News & Record*.)

Greensboro, North Carolina, sit-in.* At a conference at Shaw University in Raleigh, North Carolina, in April 1960, over two hundred student delegates—after listening to Martin Luther King, Jr.,* and other civil rights leaders urge them to affiliate with the Southern Christian Leadership Conference* (SCLC), NAACP,* or some other similar group—established a Temporary Coordinating Committee to provide communications among the campuses and student groups. A few months later they organized as the Temporary Student Nonviolent Coordinating Committee, with Marion S. Barry,* a leader of the student movement in Nashville, Tennessee, as chairman. Robert Moses* left the SCLC to work for SNCC. At a conference in October, the delegates decided to drop the temporary from the organization's name. They also elected Charles McDew* to replace Barry as chairman. McDew served until 1963, when John Lewis* succeeded him. SNCC staff members and volunteers became involved with the Freedom Riders* in 1961 and in other forms of protest throughout the South. In 1961, James Forman,* a Chicago schoolteacher, became executive secretary and brought a measure of stability to the organization. When SNCC members could not agree on whether to concentrate on direct action* or to place primary emphasis on voter registration, they compromised by agreeing to do both. SNCC led voter registration drives in Mississippi and other southern states. As a part of the Council of Federated Organizations* (COFO), SNCC sponsored the Freedom Summer of 1964* project in Mississippi. Members also staged sit-ins at segregated lunch counters, wade-ins at segregated beaches, and pray-ins and kneel-ins at segregated churches. By late 1961 about fifty towns and cities in the South had experienced demonstrations. Over 70,000 white and black students had participated, and many of them had gone to jail. The demonstrations resulted in the desegregation of eating places in many southern and border cities. In 1966 SNCC members elected Stokley Carmichael* chairman, and he became a leader and interpreter of the Black Power* movement. Racial violence during the remaining years of the 1960s led to repression of student activities by law enforcement agencies and to the decline of SNCC.

SELECTED BIBLIOGRAPHY

Clayborne Carson, *In Struggle: SNCC and the Black Awakening of the 1960s* (1981); James Forman, *The Making of Black Revolutionaries* (1972); Howell Raines, *My Soul Is Rested: Movement Days in the Deep South Remembered* (1977); Cleveland Sellers, *The River of No Return: The Autobiography of a Black Militant and the Life and Death of SNCC* (1973).

Arvarh E. Strickland

SULLIVAN v. LITTLE HUNTING PARK, 396 U.S. 229 (1969). This case extended the application of the Civil Rights Act of 1866* to prohibit discrimination in access to community facilities conveyed incident to a sale or lease of property. Paul E. Sullivan, a white home owner in an unincorporated community known as Little Hunting Park in Virginia, rented his home to a black, T. R. Freeman, Jr., and assigned his membership in a community organization which operated recreation facilities for all community residents. The organization refused to admit Freeman; Sullivan and Freeman sued. The Supreme Court had ruled in *Jones v. Alfred H. Mayer Co.** (1968) that the Civil Rights Act of 1866 prohibited racial discrimination by private individuals in the sale or rental of housing. In *Sullivan,* the Supreme Court reasoned that the right to sell or lease property enunciated in *Jones* would be impaired if an owner could not also assign membership rights in a neighborhood recreational facility to a black, and ruled that such discrimination violated the Civil Rights Act of 1866. As a result of the *Jones* and *Sullivan* cases, the Supreme Court significantly expanded the protection of minorities to enter into a broad range of commercial transactions involving property.

SELECTED BIBLIOGRAPHY

Henry J. Abraham, *Freedom and the Court, Civil Rights and Liberties in the United States* (1988); Chester J. Antieau, *Federal Civil Rights Acts, Civil Practice* (1980);

Derrick A. Bell, Jr., *Race, Racism and American Law* (1980); Theodore Eisenberg, *Civil Rights Legislation* (1981).

Frederick G. Slabach

Charles Sumner. (Library of Congress.)

SUMNER, CHARLES (6 January 1811, Boston, Mass.–10 March 1874, Washington, D.C.). After graduating from Harvard Law School in 1833, working as a reporter for the United States Circuit Court, teaching for two years at his alma mater, and touring Europe extensively, Sumner began to practice law in Boston in 1840. An enthusiastic reformer, Sumner's hatred of slavery and of war led him to oppose the annexation of Texas and the Mexican War. Elected to the United States Senate as a Free Soiler in 1851, he fought against the enforcement of the 1850 fugitive slave law and the Kansas-Nebraska Act of 1854. His abolitionism and inflammatory rhetoric angered Southerners and Northerners alike; after his 1856 speech, "The Crime against Kansas," Congressman Preston Brooks of South Carolina beat Sumner severely and made the New England senator an abolitionist martyr. During the Civil War, Sumner pressured Abraham Lincoln to emancipate the slaves, and, after the war, he argued vehemently for an end to segregation and racial discrimination. He helped lead the congressional impeachment attempt against President Andrew Johnson, and from 1870 until his death in early 1874 he unsuccessfully tried to force through Congress a broad-based civil rights act that would have outlawed most forms of segregation and guaranteed equal economic and legal rights. The Civil Rights Act of 1875,* a watered-down version of Sumner's bill, was largely ignored in the South and in 1883 was ruled unconstitutional by the United States Supreme Court.

SELECTED BIBLIOGRAPHY
David Herbert Donald, *Charles Sumner and the Coming of the Civil War* (1960); and David Herbert Donald, *Charles Sumner and the Rights of Man* (1970); Edward Pierce, *Memoirs and Letters of Charles Sumner*, 4 vols. (1878–1893).

James Marten

SWANN v. CHARLOTTE-MECKLENBURG BOARD OF EDUCATION, 402 U.S. 1 (1971). This decision upheld the first extensive court-ordered use of busing to achieve desegregation. In 1965 only 2 percent of black students in the Charlotte-Mecklenburg school system, in North Carolina, attended school with whites. Black parents filed suit to establish the school district's affirmative obligation not merely to abolish its segregated system but also to create an integrated system. Judge J. Braxton Craven rejected the plaintiff's arguments, and the Fourth Circuit upheld his position a year later. The plaintiffs reopened *Swann* after the Supreme Court ruled, in *Green v. School Board of New Kent County, Virginia** (1968), that school districts had an "affirmative duty to take whatever steps" necessary to create a nonsegregated system. Judge James B. McMillan ruled that the school district did not meet the requirement established in *Green*. After the school district submitted several unsatisfactory desegregation plans, McMillan appointed a consultant to advise the court on how desegregation should be accomplished. The plan redrew school districts and bused about one thousand students solely for the purpose of desegregation. By a vote of four to two, the Fourth Circuit Court of Appeals upheld McMillan's use of busing in junior and senior high schools but overturned the extensive busing of elementary school children. The Supreme Court unanimously upheld McMillan's use of busing.

SELECTED BIBLIOGRAPHY
Owen M. Fiss, "The Charlotte-Mecklenburg Case—Its Significance for Northern School Desegregation," *University of Chicago Law Review* 38 (1971), 699–709; Frye

Gaillard, *The Dream Long Deferred* (1988); Robert I. Richter, "School Desegregation after *Swann*: A Theory of Government Responsibility," *University of Chicago Law Review* 39 (1972), 421–47; Bernard Schwartz, *Swann's Way* (1986); J. Harvie Wilkinson III, *From Brown to Bakke: The Supreme Court and School Integration, 1954–1978* (1979).

Michael S. Mayer

SWEATT v. PAINTER, 339 U.S. 629 (1950). On 5 June 1950, the U.S. Supreme Court ruled that the University of Texas Law School had to admit Heman Marion Sweatt, a postal worker from Houston, as a full-time student. In 1946 Sweatt applied for admission to the University of Texas Law School, but the Texas State Board of Regents denied him admission on the basis of a state law that required segregation in Texas schools. The *Sweatt* case was unique because in 1947 the regents also established a separate but equal* Negro law school on the campus of Texas College for Negroes in Houston to prevent any further challenges to segregated education in Texas. The regents were fully aware of the Supreme Court's decisions in the *Gaines* (see *Missouri ex rel. Gaines v. Canada*) (1938) and *Sipuel v. Board of Regents of the University of Oklahoma** (1948) cases requiring state-assisted graduate and professional schools to admit African-American students when no separate but equal institution existed for them. The regents attempted to circumvent these precedents by establishing a Negro law school in Houston almost overnight to prevent the integration of the University of Texas. Despite their effort, the Supreme Court ruled that the regents had denied Sweatt his individual rights under the equal protection clause because he would not have received as good an education at the hastily created Negro law school as he would have at the University of Texas with its prestigious faculty, larger library, and national accreditation. Thurgood Marshall* of the NAACP* and Dallas attorney William J. Durham won this landmark decision, which became one of the precedents for overturning the 1896 *Plessy v. Ferguson** decision.

SELECTED BIBLIOGRAPHY

Dallas Express, 18 May 1946, 17 June 1950, 14 April 1956; Richard Kluger, *Simple Justice: The History of Brown v. Board of Education and Black America's Struggle for Equality* (1976).

W. Marvin Dulaney

SWEET BRIAR INSTITUTE v. BUTTON, 280 F. Supp. 312 (1967). When southern institutions of higher education went into court in the 1950s and 1960s, as a rule it was in an effort to prevent desegregation. Sweet Briar College, a private school in Virginia, was different. As early as November 1963, the college's board of directors determined to explore the possibility of contravening a trust fund provision that restricted enrollment to "white girls and young women." Some months later,

Sweet Briar felt itself compelled to act—and, in the end, found itself empowered to act—as a consequence of the Civil Rights Act of 1964,* which barred federal aid to institutions of higher education that could not certify that they accepted students regardless of race. The school initiated legal action in both the state and federal courts. Eventually, in July 1967, the U.S. District Court for the Western District of Virginia ruled that judicial enforcement of the restriction would constitute "state action" in violation of the Fourteenth Amendment.* The previous year, the college had enrolled its first African-American student, Marshalyn Yeargin.

SELECTED BIBLIOGRAPHY

Richard Bardolph, ed., *The Civil Rights Record: Black Americans and the Law, 1849–1970* (1970); Richard Paul Chait, "The Desegregation of Higher Education: A Legal History" (Ph.D. diss., University of Wisconsin, 1972); *Richmond Times-Dispatch*, 31 August 1966.

Peter Wallenstein

SWEET, OSSIAN HAYES (1895, Barstow, Fla.–21 March 1960, Detroit, Mich.). An African-American physician and activist, Sweet was educated at Wilberforce University, in Ohio (B.S., 1917) and Howard University* (M.D., 1921). In 1926 Sweet purchased a home in a white neighborhood in Detroit, Michigan. An angry white mob attacked the house, and a shot rang out which killed one man. Police arrested Sweet, his wife, his brother, Henry, and nine other occupants of the house and charged them with murder. The case became a cause célèbre for the NAACP* which hired Clarence Darrow for the defense. In a trial presided over by future U.S. Supreme Court Justice Frank Murphy, the trial ended in a hung jury.

SELECTED BIBLIOGRAPHY

Clarence S. Darrow, *Attorney for the Damned* (1957); Clarence Darrow, *The Story of My Life* (1932); Sidney Fine, *Frank Murphy: The Detroit Years* (1966); Irving Stone, *Clarence Darrow for the Defense* (1941); B. J. Widick, *Detroit: City of Race and Class Violence* (1972).

Brenda M. Brock

SYMBIONESE LIBERATION ARMY. A Marxist, revolutionary group with a handful of members, the Symbionese Liberation Army (SLA) was founded in 1973 and led by Donald Defreeze. In Berkeley, California, on 5 February 1974, the SLA kidnapped Patricia Hearst, the nineteen-year-old scion of the Hearst newspaper family. The SLA demanded ransom in the form of food given to the poor. On 3 April Patricia denounced her father as a capitalist and announced that she had joined the SLA. She participated in a bank robbery for which she and other SLA members were convicted in 1976. Defreeze and five other SLA members died in a shoot-out with Los Angeles police on 17 May 1974.

The publicity from the Hearst kidnapping gave the SLA visibility without which it would have been little noted.

SELECTED BIBLIOGRAPHY

Nathan M. Adams, "The Rise and Fall of the S.L.A.," *Reader's Digest* (September 1974), 64–69; Vin McLellan and Paul Avery, *The Voices of the Guns: The Definitive and Dramatic Story of the Twenty-Two Month Career of the Symbionese Liberation Army—One of the Most Bizarre Chapters in the History of the American Left* (1977); "The Politics of Terror," *Time* (4 March 1974), 11–15; John F. Stacks, "Patricia Hearst," *1975 Britannica Book of the Year* (1975).

Lorenzo Crowell

T

TACONIC FOUNDATION. Located in New York City, the foundation was created in 1958 by Stephen and Audrey Currier as a vehicle for opening the doors of opportunity to all Americans. Under the leadership of the Curriers, the foundation made grants to nonprofit organizations and to private and public institutions. During the civil rights era, the foundation financed several programs aimed at improving the status of blacks. The most important of these programs was its Voter Education Project.* Established in 1962, the Voter Education Project distributed funds to major civil rights groups and local voters' leagues for voter registration drives. In addition, Taconic financed programs to improve southern race relations and to provide legal aid for minorities and the poor who could not afford an attorney. Taconic's most recent concerns have been with youth unemployment and urban housing.

SELECTED BIBLIOGRAPHY

Taylor Branch, *Parting the Waters: America in the King Years, 1954–63* (1988); David J. Garrow, *Bearing the Cross: Martin Luther King, Jr. and the Southern Christian Leadership Conference* (1986); Taconic Foundation, *Taconic Foundation: Twenty-Five Years* (1983).

Dorothy A. Autrey

TALLAHASSEE, FLORIDA, BUS BOYCOTT. The bus boycott was launched in May 1956 when Florida Agricultural and Mechanical University (FAMU) students Wilhemina Jakes and Carrie Patterson ignored the segregated seating policy of the City Transit Company and took the only remaining seats available in the white section of the bus. They were arrested for "inciting a riot." FAMU students then overwhelmingly agreed to boycott the bus company. Although it began as a student

Woman hitchhiking during Tallahassee, Florida, bus boycott. (© Flip Schulke, Schulke Archives, Miami, Florida.)

movement, the Reverend Charles K. Steele* and the Tallahassee Inter-Civic Council quickly assumed leadership of the boycott. By May 1958 the bus company had abolished its segregated seating policy.

SELECTED BIBLIOGRAPHY
Adam Fairclough, *To Redeem the Soul of America: The Southern Christian Leadership Conference and Martin Luther King, Jr.* (1987); David J. Garrow, *Bearing the Cross: Martin Luther King, Jr. and the Southern Christian Leadership Conference* (1986); Gregory B. Padgett, "C. K. Steele and the Tallahassee Bus Boycott" (master's thesis, Florida State University, 1977); Glenda A. Rabby, "Out of the Past: The Civil Rights Movement in Tallahassee, Florida" (Ph.D. diss., Florida State University, 1984); Charles U. Smith, ed., *The Civil Rights Movement in Florida and the United States* (1989); Charles U. Smith and Lewis M. Killian, *The Tallahassee Bus Protest* (1958).

                                                                            Maxine D. Jones

TALLAHASSEE, FLORIDA, JAIL-IN. On 20 February 1960, eleven Florida Agricultural and Mechanical University students, members of the Congress of Racial Equality,* were arrested after staging a second sit-in at the Woolworth's counter. Charged on 17 March with disturbing the peace and assembling unlawfully, they were sentenced to pay $300 in fines or serve sixty days in the Leon County jail. Eight of the students chose the jail sentence. This militant tactic attracted national attention, encouraged other young activists to "fill the jails for equal rights," and contributed to the integration of Tallahassee.

SELECTED BIBLIOGRAPHY
Kenneth B. Clark, "The Civil Rights Movement: Momentum and Organization," *Daedalus* 95 (Winter 1966), 239–67; Glenda A. Rabby, "Fighting for Civil Rights: The Tallahassee Story," *Research in Review* (June 1985), 10–12; Glenda A. Rabby, "Out of the Past: The Civil Rights Movement in Tallahassee, Florida" (Ph.D. diss., Florida State University, 1984); Ruth Searles and J. Allen Williams, Jr., "Negro College Students' Participation in Sit-Ins," *Social Forces* 40 (March 1962), 215–20; Harvard Sitkoff, *The Struggle for Black Equality, 1954–1980* (1981); Robert Melvin White, "The Tallahassee Sit-Ins and CORE: A Nonviolent Revolutionary Submovement" (Ph.D. diss., Florida State University, 1964).

Jane F. Lancaster

TALLAHASSEE, FLORIDA, SIT-INS. In January and February 1960, Patricia and Priscilla Stephens, both students and Congress of Racial Equality* members at Florida Agricultural and Mechanical University (FAMU), led several sit-ins at the Tallahassee Greyhound Bus terminal and the Woolworth lunch counter. On 20 February, the two women and eleven of their peers were arrested and charged with disturbing the peace and unlawful assembly. Eight of the students decided to serve sixty days in the local jail rather than pay $300 for their release. This was the first case of "jail-versus-bail" in the civil rights movement. More sit-ins were staged on 5 and 12 March with students from FAMU and white students from Florida State University. Two hundred forty students were arrested but only after the police used tear gas and the governor intervened. The movement then lost its momentum. Florida's Interracial Committee claimed that it would be in a weaker position to negotiate with Tallahassee officials if the sit-ins continued. Black leaders argued that further student agitation would influence whites to support the Democratic gubernatorial candidate, segregationist Farris Bryant. Finally, internal tension among black leaders over the direction of the movement hurt the campaign. The result was the first loss in the sit-in movement.

SELECTED BIBLIOGRAPHY
Martin Oppenheimer, *The Sit-In Movement of 1960* (1989); Southern Regional Council, *The Student Protest Movement* (1961).

Vibert L. White

TAMPA, FLORIDA, RACE RIOT (1967). During the early 1960s, many of Tampa's racial barriers had fallen without fanfare under the guidance of a biracial committee. However, discrimination persisted in subtle and powerful forms, especially with respect to the quality of housing, employment, and police protection. On Sunday, 11 June 1967, a major race riot erupted in the black section adjacent to the downtown business district. Triggered by a white policeman's fatal shooting of an unarmed black robbery suspect, rioting broke out in an area where over half of the families earned less than $3,000; the unemployment rate for black males was double that of whites; and 60 percent of the housing units were substandard. The riot lasted for four days and caused considerable property damage. No one was killed, though 16 people were injured and 111 were arrested. The riot ended after the city's Commission on Community Relations arranged for withdrawal of police and dispatched black youths wearing white helmets to patrol ghetto streets. With calm restored, business and civic leaders disbursed increased funds for recreational activities and job training programs. By the end of the decade, however, most of these projects had terminated, and many of the problems that had sparked the riot remained.

SELECTED BIBLIOGRAPHY

Gayle Everett Davis, "Riot in Tampa" (master's thesis, University of South Florida, 1976); Steven F. Lawson, "From Sit-In to Race Riot: Businessmen, Blacks, and the Pursuit of Racial Moderation in Tampa, 1960–1967," in Elizabeth Jacoway and David R. Colburn, eds., *Southern Businessmen and Desegregation* (1982); National Advisory Commission on Civil Disorders, *Report* (1968).

Steven F. Lawson

TANNER, BENJAMIN TUCKER (25 December 1835, Pittsburgh, Pa.– 15 January 1923, Philadelphia, Pa.). An editor and the eighteenth bishop of the African Methodist Episcopal (A.M.E.) Church, Tanner attended Avery College in Allegheny, Pennsylvania (1852–1857), working as a barber to pay his expenses. He studied at Western Theological Seminary (1858–1860) and was ordained a deacon and then an elder in the A.M.E. Church (1860). From 1868 to 1884 Tanner edited the *Christian Recorder*, the official organ of the A.M.E. Church, which emerged as an important newspaper whose columns focused on national political events as well as church affairs. In 1884 he launched the *A.M.E. Church Review*, a quarterly that soon became a leading periodical of African-American literary and intellectual thought. During the post-Reconstruction era, which witnessed a racially repressive climate in the United States, Tanner urged racial solidarity as the most effective means to combat racial injustice and prodded African Americans to support the black press and black businesses. For a brief period in 1901, he served as dean of Payne Theological Seminary of Wilberforce University, in Wilberforce, Ohio.

SELECTED BIBLIOGRAPHY

Christian Recorder (21 June 1888); August Meier, *Negro Thought in America, 1880–1915: Racial Ideologies in the Age of Booker T. Washington* (1963); *New York Times*,

16 January 1923; Charles Spencer Smith, *A History of the African Methodist Episcopal Church*(1922); Richard R. Wright, Jr., ed., *Encyclopedia of African Methodism* (1948).

George E. Walker

TAPPAN, LEWIS (23 May 1788, Northampton, Mass.–21 June 1873, Brooklyn, N.Y.). Lewis Tappan served as the leader of the evangelical wing of the nineteenth-century abolition movement. In the early 1830s, he formulated the chief strategies of the fledgling crusade to free American slaves: raising of funds, growth of local and state antislavery societies, and creation of reading materials designed for special audiences—children, churchwomen, businessmen. The antislavery program in which he and coworkers engaged consisted of these propositions: It should begin at once; it should take place on American, not foreign, soil; it should provide no compensation to slave owners. Without the New Yorker's expertise in finance, journalism, and organization, "immediate emancipation" would probably not have had the impact on northern society and national politics that it did.

Like most other abolitionists, Tappan and a brother had first adopted the colonization scheme. Then, William Lloyd Garrison convinced them that sending blacks to Africa stained its sponsors with sin and strengthened slavery at home. With Garrison and other reformers, the New York entrepreneurs founded the American Anti-Slavery Society, over which Arthur Tappan presided until 1840.

The abolitionist cause split apart on issues ranging from women's rights to the efficacy of reform partisanship. Though reluctant at first, the New York merchant eventually saw the value of political action. In 1843 he vainly tried to persuade the British government to recognize a Texas without slavery and to prevent its American annexation. With greater success, he helped to form the Liberty and Free Soil parties but always mistrusted politicians as guardians of pure principle.

Tappan's real influence lay in evangelical circles in which he urged separation from the sin of slaveholding. Out of his work to free the Amistad prisoners from 1839 to 1841, he fashioned the American Missionary Association.* This fast-growing agency united abolitionists in various evangelical faiths (but chiefly the Presbyterian and Congregational). As its chief supervisor, Tappan supported missions at home and abroad, most particularly in emancipated British Jamaica, Free Soil Kansas, and even slaveholding Kentucky where the Reverend John G. Fee was to found the future antiracist Berea College. In his declining years, Tappan helped the AMA to send to the South hundreds of Yankee teachers, male and female, black and white, for the instruction of the African Americans freed during and after the Civil War.

Far ahead of his time with regard to race relations, Tappan often spoke forcefully against the "spirit of caste," which he found displayed even in antislavery councils. Although Tappan's religious inspiration and his sternly paternalistic precepts for action might be regarded as outdated, he did more to further the cause of racial equality than all but a handful of his fellow white contemporaries.

SELECTED BIBLIOGRAPHY

Lawrence F. Friedman, *Gregarious Saints: Self and Community in American Abolitionism, 1830–1870* (1982); James Brewer Stewart, *Holy Warriors: The Abolitionists and American Slavery* (1976); Lewis Tappan, *The Life of Arthur Tappan* (1870); Bertram Wyatt-Brown, *Lewis Tappan and the Evangelical War against Slavery* (1969).

Bertram Wyatt-Brown

TAYLOR, HOBART, JR. (17 December 1920, Texarkana, Tex.–3 April 1981, Washington, D.C.). Hobart Taylor, Jr., son of a successful African-American businessman, grew up in Houston, Texas, and graduated from Prairie View State College in 1939. Two years later he earned a master's degree in economics from Howard University* and then received a law degree at the University of Michigan in 1943. Although he was an established lawyer in Wayne County, Michigan, where he worked as both a prosecuting attorney and corporate counsel, Hobart Taylor, Jr., gained national prominence during the administrations of John F. Kennedy and Lyndon B. Johnson. In February 1961, Vice President Johnson appointed Taylor to be the special counsel for the President's Committee on Equal Employment Opportunity (PCEEO), which Johnson chaired. Following an internal dispute over the future direction of the committee, Johnson in 1962 named Taylor to be its executive vice chairman, a job which Taylor held until 1965. When the PCEEO was replaced by the Equal Employment Opportunity Commission* in 1965, President Johnson appointed Taylor the director of the Export-Import Bank of the United States. In 1968 Taylor resigned to enter private law practice in Washington, D.C. In addition to his political successes, Taylor received achievement awards from the National Urban League* (1965) and the NAACP* (1975).

SELECTED BIBLIOGRAPHY

Hugh Davis Graham, *The Civil Rights Era* (1990); *Who's Who among Black Americans* (1976).

Dean K. Yates

TAYLOR v. ALABAMA, 335 U.S. 252 (1942). Samuel Taylor was a nineteen-year-old black accused of raping a fourteen-year-old white girl in Prichard, Alabama, on 12 April 1946. After his arrest, Taylor confessed. At his trial, he pled not guilty, but he did not testify. He was convicted and sentenced to the electric chair. The Alabama Supreme Court upheld the conviction, and Taylor's execution was set for 19 September 1947. One day before his scheduled execution, Taylor filed a petition with the Alabama Supreme Court in which he alleged that his confession had been coerced. Taylor's claims rested on his own statements and on those of three cellmates who said they had heard Taylor being beaten. No evidence of coercion had been presented during the trial or the appeal, and the Alabama court refused to grant Taylor any relief. The U.S. Supreme Court upheld the Alabama tribunal. Speaking for the majority, Harold H. Burton held that neither Alabama procedures nor the decision of the state supreme court violated the due process clause of the Fourteenth Amendment.* In a concurring opinion, Felix Frankfurter noted that Taylor might still obtain relief by seeking a writ of habeas corpus from the federal district court. Dissenting, Frank Murphy argued that Taylor was at least entitled to a full hearing on his claims. William O. Douglas and Wiley Rutledge joined in the dissent.

SELECTED BIBLIOGRAPHY

Mark Berger, *Taking the Fifth: The Supreme Court and the Privilege against Self-Incrimination* (1980); Yale Kamishar, *Police Interrogations and Confessions: Essays in Law and Policy* (1980); Leonard W. Levy, *Origins of the Fifth Amendment* (1968); Otis H. Stephens, Jr., *The Supreme Court and Confessions of Guilt* (1973).

Jeff Broadwater

TAYLOR v. GEORGIA, 315 U.S. 25 (1942). James Taylor, a black citizen of Georgia, was indicted and convicted in 1940 of accepting an advance money payment for work he did not subsequently perform. He stood convicted of violating a Georgia statute that made breach of a labor contract prima facie evidence of intent to defraud the employer. In a nearly identical 1911 case, *Bailey v. Alabama,** the Supreme Court had ruled that state statutes that make it a crime to fail to perform the terms of a labor contract after receiving a cash advance violated both the Thirteenth Amendment* and federal antipeonage laws. Despite this earlier ruling, Taylor was compelled to carry his case to the Supreme Court to secure justice. The Court was unanimous in reversing Taylor's conviction. The Georgia statute, it held, sanctioned coerced labor, which was prohibited by the Constitution and by federal antipeonage laws. Like a number of earlier rulings, *Taylor* struck a blow at forced labor statutes. It was not until 1944, however, in *Pollock v. Williams,** that the Supreme Court dealt the death blow to the black peonage* system.

SELECTED BIBLIOGRAPHY

Pete Daniel, *The Shadow of Slavery: Peonage in the South, 1909–1969* (1972); Loren Miller, *The Petitioners: The Story of the Supreme Court of the United States and the Negro* (1966); "Recent Cases,"*George Washington Law Review* 10 (1942), 748–50; Melvin I. Urofsky, *A March of Liberty: A Constitutional History of the United States* (1988).

Charles D. Lowery

TERRELL, MARY CHURCH (9 September 1863, Memphis, Tenn.–24 July 1954, Annapolis, Md.). An educator, writer, and lifelong activist against discrimination, Terrell received a B.A. and M.A. (1884, 1888) from Oberlin and then taught the classics in Washington, D.C. The first black woman to be on the District of Columbia Board of Education, she formed the Colored Women's League of D.C., served as president of the National Association of Colored Women* (1896–1901), and was a charter member of the NAACP.* As an activist, she worked for women's suffrage, workers' rights, and black achievement; against lynching,* discrimination, and black disenfranchisement. She was eloquent and powerful as a writer and orator; she reached out to both whites and blacks.

SELECTED BIBLIOGRAPHY

Gladys B. Shepperd, *Mary Church Terrell: Respectable Person* (1959); Mary Church Terrell, *A Colored Woman in a White World* (1940); Mary Church Terrell Papers, Howard University.

Linda G. Ford

TERRELL, ROBERT HERBERTON (27 November 1857, Charlottesville, Va.–20 December 1925, Washington, D.C.). Terrell attended public schools in Washington, D.C., and later graduated magna cum laude from Harvard College in June 1884. After teaching in Washington's public schools for five years, he attended Harvard University Law School and received an LL.B. in 1889 and an LL.M. in 1893. While in law school, he married Mary E. Church of Memphis (See Mary Church Terrell). His public career was varied. He worked as a clerk in the U.S. Treasury in 1889 and was elected to the Board of Trade in the 1890s. He enjoyed a successful law partnership with John R. Lynch,* former Mississippi congressman, from 1892 to 1898. After receiving an appointment as a municipal court judge in the District of Columbia from President William H. Taft in 1910, he served with distinction in that position until his death. While on the bench, he also served on the faculty of the Howard University* Law School. Living most of their lives in Washington, D.C., Terrell and his wife participated in numerous black community organizations. The city recognized his contributions by naming an elementary school in his honor.

SELECTED BIBLIOGRAPHY

Rayford W. Logan and Michael R. Winston, eds., *Dictionary of American Negro Biography* (1982); Obituary, *The Journal of Negro History* 11 (January 1926), 223–25; Mary Church Terrell, *A Colored Woman in a White World* (1940).

Thomas D. Cockrell

TERRY v. ADAMS, 345 U.S. 461 (1953). The Jaybird Democratic Association, organized in 1889 in Fort Bend County, Texas, restricted its membership to white citizens. Winners of the Jaybird's primary filed as candidates in the regular Democratic primary. With few exceptions, Jaybird candidates won every election. John Terry sought a declaratory judgment and injunction to permit black participation in the Jaybird primary. The federal district court ruled the Jaybird Association a political party and found for Terry. Defendants appealed and the United States Court of Appeals for the Fifth Judicial Circuit* reversed the decision. By writ of certiorari, the Supreme Court held the Jaybird "primary" in violation of the Fifteenth Amendment* and existing civil rights laws. Citing *United States v. Classic** (1941), extending federal power to state primary elections, and *Smith v. Allwright** (1944), condemning discrimination when the primary was the only effective means of choice, the court ruled that the state was obliged to protect its citizens' voting privileges and to guarantee voters access to all phases of the election process. Justices Hugo Black, William Douglas, and Harold Burton charged the state's election process with denying blacks political influence and participation. Justice Felix Frankfurter concurred, arguing that county officials participated in and condoned efforts to exclude blacks from voting. Justices Tom Clark and Stanley Reed and Chief Justice Fred Vinson concurred, claiming that the Jaybird organization was a political party that excluded blacks. Justice Sherman Minton dissented: Jaybird activities were not state actions and, therefore, not forbidden.

SELECTED BIBLIOGRAPHY

"Terry v. Adams," *American Bar Association Journal* 39 (1953), 822–23; "Terry v. Adams," *Alabama Law Review* 6 (1954), 291–95; "Terry v. Adams," *Harvard Law Review* 67 (1953), 104–5; "Terry v. Adams," *Texas Law Review* 32 (1953), 223–25; "Terry v. Adams," *Washington and Lee Law Review* 11 (1954), 60–65.

William A. Paquette

THEY SHALL NOT DIE. A play by John Wexley, loosely based on the Scottsboro Trials,* *They Shall Not Die* was performed in New York on 23 February 1934. The play revolves around black lynching,* Jim Crow* restrictions, white supremacy, and economic oppression of both blacks and whites. It exposes the racial fears, hatred, and ignorance behind the Scottsboro case. It was barred after its 26 February 1934 performance in Washington, D.C., and again in 1947 in Trenton, New Jersey. The play has, however, been hailed as a disturbing yet important statement of racial prejudice in American society.

SELECTED BIBLIOGRAPHY

Schomburg Center Clipping File, 1925–1974; John Wexley, *They Shall Not Die* (1934).

Jessie M. Carter

THIRTEENTH AMENDMENT. This 1865 measure capped a series of Civil War emancipation endeavors, including abolition of slavery in the District of Columbia and the territories, the Confiscation Act* of 1862,

GENERALS STEEDMAN AND FULLERTON CONFERRING WITH THE FREEDMEN IN THEIR CHURCH AT TRENT RIVER SETTLEMENT.—SKETCHED BY T. R. DAVIS.—[SEE PAGE 366.

General James B. Steedman and freedmen, *Harper's Weekly*, 9 June 1866. (Negro Almanac Collection, Amistad Research Center, Tulane University, New Orleans.)

and President Abraham Lincoln's Emancipation Proclamation,* which freed the slaves in areas still in rebellion after 1862. In addition, three border states (West Virginia, Maryland, and Missouri) and three occupied Confederate states (Arkansas, Louisiana, and Tennessee) ended slavery during the war. When the Civil War ended, the institution legally existed in two border states and parts of two others under Union control, but many Republicans, including Lincoln, questioned whether these wartime actions had peacetime legal force. In 1864, therefore, Congress initiated the Thirteenth Amendment, which banned slavery and involuntary servitude (except as punishment for crime) in the nation and its territories. The measure passed the Senate on 8 April 1864, but lacked the necessary two-thirds vote in the House until 31 January 1865 when it passed under strong administration pressure. By 18 December 1865 the requisite three-fourths of the states had completed ratification. Three Union states (New Jersey, Kentucky, and Delaware) withheld support, but eight former Confederate states ratified the amendment in the fall of 1865 as a condition of restoration under President Andrew Johnson's Reconstruction program.

SELECTED BIBLIOGRAPHY

Herman Belz, *Emancipation and Equal Rights: Politics and Constitutionalism in the Civil War Era* (1978); John H. Cox and LaWanda Cox, *Politics, Principle, and Prejudice, 1865–1866: Dilemma of Reconstruction America* (1963); James M. McPherson, *Ordeal by Fire: The Civil War and Reconstruction* (1982); David M. Potter, *Division and the Stresses of Reunion, 1845–1876* (1973).

James B. Potts

THIRTY YEARS OF LYNCHING IN THE UNITED STATES, 1889–1918. Written as a part of the NAACP* campaign to stop mob violence against black people in the United States, this work documented more than 2,500 lynchings during the time period covered. Additionally, researchers working on the project were able to demonstrate that the vast majority of lynchings were *not* due to rape accusations. Later this information was used to help support efforts in Congress to pass a federal antilynching law sponsored by Missouri Congressman L. C. Dyer. The act did not pass due to southern resistance and Republican party indifference.

SELECTED BIBLIOGRAPHY

NAACP, *Thirty Years of Lynching in the United States, 1889–1918* (1919); Robert L. Zangrando, *THE NAACP Crusade against Lynching 1909–1950* (1980).

Kenneth W. Goings

TILL, EMMETT LOUIS (25 July 1941, near Chicago, Ill.–28 August 1955, near Glendora, Miss.). Till was the only child of Louis Till and Mamie Bradley Till, who had migrated to Chicago from Missouri and Tallahatchie County, Mississippi, respectively. Till had completed the seventh grade when his mother sent him in August 1955 to Mississippi for a vacation wih relatives. Till and his cousin, Curtis Jones, stayed in Leflore County with Jones's grandfather, Mose Wright. In the evening of 24 August, Till and Jones went to Bryant's Grocery and Meat Market in Money. Mrs. Carolyn Bryant later claimed the black youth grabbed her at the waist and asked her for a date; and when he was pulled from the store by friends, Till allegedly said, "Bye, baby" and "wolf whistled." Late the following Saturday night, Roy Bryant and his half brother, J. W. Milam, took Till from Mose Wright's home, drove him to the Tallahatchie River, shot him in the head, tied a heavy cotton gin fan to his body, and threw him in the river. The body was found three days later. Till's murder and, especially, the pictures of his nearly unrecognizable body shocked black Americans. The acquittal on 23 September of Bryant and Milam on murder charges prompted demonstrations in many northern cities.

SELECTED BIBLIOGRAPHY
William Bradford Huie, *Wolf Whistle* (1959); Stephen J. Whitfield, *A Death in the Delta: The Story of Emmett Till* (1988); Juan Williams, *Eyes on the Prize: America's Civil Rights Years, 1954–1965* (1987).

Charles W. Eagles

TO SECURE THESE RIGHTS. President Harry S. Truman, at the instigation of the NAACP's* Walter Francis White,* appointed a special committee to investigate racial violence. In 1947 this interracial organization issued its report, *To Secure These Rights,* which became the Democrats' civil rights agenda for the next several decades. The agenda included the establishment of a permanent civil rights commission,* the abolition of the poll tax,* and an end to segregation in the armed forces. Based on the testimony of some forty witnesses and information from twenty-five federal agencies, the report summed up past progress in the area of race relations but also warned that full equality was far from a reality.

SELECTED BIBLIOGRAPHY
William C. Berman, *The Politics of Civil Rights in the Truman Administration* (1970); Alonzo L. Hamby, *Beyond the New Deal: Harry S. Truman and American Liberalism* (1973); President's Committee on Civil Rights, *To Secure These Rights: The Report of the President's Committee on Civil Rights* (1947).

Carol Wilson

TOLSON, MELVIN BEAUNORUS (6 February 1898, Moberly, Mo.–29 August 1966, Dallas Tex.). African-American educator and writer of poetry, drama, and fiction, Tolson was especially noted for his work, *Harlem Gallery,* published after his death, which chronicled Harlem's "double consciousness." Tolson attended Fisk University* and received his baccalaureate degree from Lincoln University, in Pennsylvania. He did graduate work at Columbia University, taught at Wiley and Langston

Colleges, and served four terms as mayor of historically black Langston, Oklahoma. He lectured for the NAACP* and said he was often a "facer of mobs." Tolson's themes were democracy, universal brotherhood, the developing Third World, and the U.S. race problem, which he saw as economic exploitation.

SELECTED BIBLIOGRAPHY

Book World, Washington Post, 14 October 1984; Mariann Russell, *Melvin B. Tolson's Harlem Gallery: A Literary Analysis* (1980).

Nancy E. Fitch

TONKINS v. CITY OF GREENSBORO, 171 F. Supp. 476 (M.D. N.C., 1959). Decided on 13 August 1959, this U.S. district court case involved a decision made on a supplemental complaint by Deloris Tonkins and her colleagues against the City of Greensboro, North Carolina. The original complaint, filed in 1958, had sought to enjoin the city from refusing to permit African-American citizens from using the Lindley Park Swimming Pool and from selling the pool for the sole purpose of denying these same citizens their constitutional rights. The original complaint had been dismissed, but the plaintiffs were allowed to file a supplemental complaint. One of the plaintiff's attorneys was Thurgood Marshall.* After the first dismissal, the city sold the pool at a public sale to the Greensboro Pool Corporation. The supplemental complaint by Tonkins sought to show that the sale was not bona fide in the sense that there was collusion between the city and the successful bidder regarding the future operation of the pool to the exclusion of nonwhites. The plaintiffs alleged that the Greensboro Pool Corporation would either default in its payments, be granted an extension of time to pay the annual installments, or that the city would repurchase the property at a subsequent foreclosure sale. These and other allegations were determined by the court to be unsupported theories and thus not sufficient evidence upon which to decide a legal issue. The plaintiffs' supplemental complaints were dismissed.

SELECTED BIBLIOGRAPHY

Richard Bardolph, ed., *The Civil Rights Record: Black Americans and the Law, 1849–1970* (1970); William H. Chafe, *Civilities and Civil Rights: Greensboro, North Carolina, and the Black Struggle for Freedom* (1980).

Charles A. Risher

TOOMER, JEAN (26 December 1894, Washington, D.C.–30 March 1967, Doylestown, Pa.). Poet, novelist, and short story writer, Jean Toomer was born in Washington, D.C., and attended the University of Wisconsin, the University of Chicago, and the City College of New York. Hailed by critics as the most promising and original voice of the Harlem Renaissance,* Toomer launched a modernist revolution in African-American writing that signaled "an awakening of black artistic expression." Boldly experimental in form, technique, language, and perception, *Cane* (1923), a collection of short fiction, poetry, and drama, presents an all-inclusive portrait of the black American experience: a fusion of past and present, pain and beauty, strength and failings. In this literary masterpiece, Jean Toomer established a precedent that liberated black writing.

SELECTED BIBLIOGRAPHY

Hurston Baker, "Journey towards Black Art: Jean Toomer's *Cane*," in Henry Louis Gates, Jr., ed., *Singers of Daybreak: Shades in Black American Literature* (1977); Brian Benson and Mable Dillard, *Jean Toomer* (1980); Charles Davis, "Jean Toomer and the South: Region and Race as Elements within Literary Imagination," in *Black Is the Color of the Cosmos: Essays on Afro-American Literature and Culture, 1942–1981* (1982); Cynthia E. Kerman, *The Lives of Jean Toomer: A Hunger for Wholeness* (1987); Darwin Turner, *In a Minor Cord* (1971).

Jacquelyn Jackson

TOUGALOO COLLEGE. Tougaloo College, established in 1869 by the American Missionary Association,* is one of the nation's oldest and most noted predominantly black private colleges. The campus is located approximately eight miles north of Jackson, Mississippi. Initially a private institution, Tougaloo was chartered by the state in 1871 and remained state related until 1892 when it once again became private. After becoming a state institution, its name became Tougaloo University; in 1916, the original designation was restored. Tougaloo has an excellent academic reputation among both black and white educators. It has served Mississippi and the South well, producing some of Mississippi's most prominent black educational and business leaders. It played a major role in Mississippi in the civil rights movement of the 1960s.

SELECTED BIBLIOGRAPHY

Clarice T. Campbell and Oscar Allan Rogers, Jr., *Mississippi: The View from Tougaloo* (1979); W. Augustus Low and Virgil A. Clift, eds., *Encyclopedia of Black America* (1981).

Allen Dennis

TOWNSEND, WILLARD SAXBY (4 December 1897, Cincinnati, Ohio–3 February 1957, Chicago, Ill.). Founder and president of the United Transport Service Employees (Redcaps), Townsend grew up in Cincinnati, Ohio, with his grandfather. After completing two years of high school he went to work as a Redcap and later served in an all-black stateside unit during World War I. Following the war Townsend completed his education in Canada and then returned to Chicago, where he turned his energy toward labor organization. He equated the unionization of black workers as a prerequisite for first-class citizenship. Later he sat on the executive board of the American Federation of Labor and Congress of Industrial Organizations as one of the two highest-ranking black officers in the hierarchy of American labor.

SELECTED BIBLIOGRAPHY
Richard Bardolph, *The Negro Vanguard* (1959); Obituary, *New York Times*, 5 February 1957.

                                                        Michael S. Downs

TRENT, WILLIAM JOHNSON, JR. (8 March 1910, Asheville, N.C.–
). The son of the fourth president of Livingstone College, in Salisbury,
North Carolina and a graduate of and later professor at that institution,
he was appointed a member of Franklin D. Roosevelt's Black Cabinet*
in 1934. He served as advisor on Negro affairs for the Department of
Interior (1938–1939) and as a race relations officer in the Federal Works
Agency (1934–1944). In 1944, Trent became the first executive director
of the newly formed United Negro College Fund*—an organization of
privately supported, generally church-related, African-American colleges. He served until 1963 when he became the top African-American
executive for Time, Incorporated.

SELECTED BIBLIOGRAPHY
David Bradley, *A History of the AME Zion Church* (1970); Editors of *Ebony*, *Negro Handbook* (1966), *Ebony Handbook* (1974); John Hope Franklin and August Meier, eds., *Black Leaders of the Twentieth Century* (1982); J. P. Guzman, ed., *Negro Year Book: 1947* (1947).

                                                        Aingred G. Dunston

TROTTER, (WILLIAM) MONROE (7 April 1872, Chillicothe, Ohio–7
April 1934, Boston, Mass.). Monroe Trotter inherited a militant civil
rights stance from his father, James Monroe Trotter (1842–1892), who
declared himself for "a great Principle, that for the attainment of which
we gladly peril our lives—Manhood and Equality." Monroe Trotter lived
his life in that vein. He showed brilliance at Harvard (A.B., 1895; M.A.,
1896), where he won election to the prestigious honor society Phi Beta
Kappa in his junior year—the first black the college so honored. He
employed his cutting intelligence in the *Boston Guardian*,* the newspaper
he began in 1902. Assailing what he considered to be the misguided
leadership of Booker T. Washington,* Trotter and his newspaper became
primary antagonists of what was called "the Tuskegee Machine." Invoking "the spirit of protest, of independence, of revolt," Trotter lam-
basted Washington's accommodationism for demeaning black political
rights and denigrating classical education. For a time Trotter allied himself with W.E.B. Du Bois,* notably in the Niagara Movement* of 1905.
Trotter founded the National Equal Rights League* (1908) which he
described, in contrast to the NAACP,* as "an organization of the colored
people and for the colored people and led by the colored people."

SELECTED BIBLIOGRAPHY
Stephen R. Fox, *The Guardian of Boston: William Monroe Trotter* (1970); Rayford

W. Logan and Michael R. Winston, eds., *The Dictionary of American Negro Biography* (1982).

Thomas J. Davis

TUCKER, ROSINA C. (4 November 1881, Washington, D.C.–3 March 1987, Washington, D.C.). A music teacher, civic worker, organizer for the Brotherhood of Sleeping Car Porters and Maids,* and president of a local chapter and international secretary treasurer of the Ladies Auxiliary of the Brotherhood of Sleeping Car Porters, Tucker attended M Street High School, but left in 1898 to marry James D. Corrothers, a literary figure and clergyman. Corrothers died in 1917, and in 1918 she married Berthea J. Tucker, a pullman porter. In 1928 she and other porters' wives formed the Ladies Auxiliary of the Brotherhood of Sleeping Car Porters. Believing that they could assist their husbands in the struggle against racism and unfair labor practices, Tucker and others held secret meetings (some at her home). They raised money and disseminated information about the union for A. Philip Randolph.*

SELECTED BIBLIOGRAPHY

Obituary, *Washington Post*, 5 March 1987; Jack Santino, *Miles of Smiles, Years of Struggle Stories of Black Pullman Porters* (1989); Rosina C. Tucker, *Life as I Have Lived It* (unpublished memoirs).

Betty L. Plummer

TUREAUD, ALEXANDER PIERRE (26 February 1899, New Orleans, La.–22 January 1972, New Orleans, La.). A civil rights attorney and legal counsel for the NAACP* in Louisiana, Tureaud was educated in the public schools of New Orleans and Washington, D.C. In 1922 he entered the Howard University* Law School and was graduated in 1925. On returning to New Orleans in 1926, he began his long years of association with the New Orleans Branch of the NAACP. After he spearheaded the ouster of the old leadership, the NAACP became the symbol of progressive action throughout Louisiana. He used the courts to transform the *Brown v. Board of Education** decision into reality for African Americans. Although his main efforts were made in the field of education, Tureaud also devoted time to securing voting rights and integration of public accommodations. From 1940 to 1943 he helped gain salary equalization for public schoolteachers in Orleans, Jefferson, East Baton Rouge, and Iberville parishes. *Hall v. Nagel* (1946) opened voter registration rolls to African Americans. In the 1950s he helped gain equal access to higher education and integrate the public schools. He filed *Garner v. Louisiana** in 1960, the first sit-in case decided by the U.S. Supreme Court.

SELECTED BIBLIOGRAPHY

Numan V. Bartley, *The Rise of Massive Resistance: Race and Politics in the South during the 1950s* (1969); Robert Carter and Thurgood Marshall, "The Meaning and Significance of the Supreme Court Decree," *Journal of Negro Education* 24

Alexander Pierre Tureaud. (Negro Almanac Collection, Amistad Research Center, Tulane University, New Orleans.)

(Summer 1955), 397–404; Morton Inger, *Politics and Reality in an American City: The New Orleans School Crisis of 1960* (1960); August Meier and Elliott Rudwick, *CORE: A Study in the Civil Rights Movement, 1942–1968* (1973); J. W. Peltason, *Fifty-Eight Lonely Men: Southern Federal Judges and School Desegregation* (1961); Frank T. Read and Lucy S. McGough, *Let Them Be Judged: The Judicial Integration of the Deep South* (1978); Barbara A. Worthy, "The Travail and Triumph of a Southern Black Civil Rights Lawyer: The Legal Career of Alexander Pierre Tureaud, 1899–1972" (Ph.D. diss., Tulane University, 1984).

Barbara A. Worthy

TUREAUD v. BOARD OF SUPERVISORS, 347 U.S. 971 (1954). This was the final decision arising out of a class action suit filed in 1953 by A. P. Tureaud,* who wished to pursue a combined six-year arts and sciences and law curriculum at Louisiana State University. Tureaud was denied admission because a similar course of study was offered at Southern University, a predominantly African-American institution. The suit contended that the Southern University course was not substantially equal to that offered by Louisiana State University. On 24 May 1954 the U.S. Supreme Court affirmed the judgment of the district court which had ordered Tureaud's admission to Louisiana State University.

SELECTED BIBLIOGRAPHY
Board of Supervisors Louisiana State University et al. v. Tureaud, 207 F.2d 807 (1953); *McLaurin v. Oklahoma*, 339 U.S. 637 (1950); Loren Miller, *The Petitioners: The Story of the Supreme Court of the United States and the Negro* (1966); *Missouri ex rel. Gaines v. Canada*, 305 U.S. 337 (1938); *Sweatt v. Painter*, 339 U.S. 629 (1950); *Tureaud v. Board of Supervisors Louisiana State University et al.*, 116 F. Supp. 248 (1953).
Barbara A. Worthy

TURNER, HENRY McNEAL (1 February 1834, Newberry Court House, S.C.–8 May 1915, Atlanta, Ga.). A bishop in the African Methodist Episcopal (A.M.E.) church, he was born a free person and served as a plantation laborer, porter, United States Army chaplain, political organizer, college chancellor, editor, emigrationist, black nationalist, preacher and minister, teacher, and political activist. The Civil War raised Turner's hopes, but Reconstruction put an end to his faith in white America's ability to trade its racism for equality and justice for all United States citizens. Expelled illegally from the Georgia legislature in 1868, he was reprimanded by the Republican party for organizing African-Americans to be members of the A.M.E. Church and the Republican party. In 1876,

Bishop Henry M. Turner. (Negro Almanac Collection, Amistad Research Center, Tulane University, New Orleans.)

he became the manager of the A.M.E. Book Concern. This position allowed Turner to voice the discontent he and the African-American rural class had about life in the United States. In 1880 he became an A.M.E. bishop. In the 1890s, black violence escalated and it led Turner and working-class African Americans to view emigration as the only alternative. Using his editorial control of the A.M.E. publication *Voice of Missions*, Turner diligently tried to facilitate African-American migration to Africa by demanding the first reparations to ex-slaves, a steamship company, and middle-class African-American financial support. He envisioned trade, guidance, independence, self-governance, and modernization for Africa. Turner combined religion and politics in an attempt to make African Americans full citizens. He was part of a century-old protest movement based in the African-American religious-political tradition that spanned the Atlantic Ocean linking the resistance to racism and colonialism.

SELECTED BIBLIOGRAPHY

Edwin S. Redkey, *Black Exodus, Black Nationalist, and Back-to-Africa Movements 1890–1910* (1969); Edwin S. Redkey, ed., *The Writings and Speeches of Henry McNeal Turner* (1971); George Shepperson and Thomas Price, *Independent African, John Chilembwe and the Origins, Setting, and Significance of the Nyasaland Native Rising of 1915* (1958); Clarence E. Walker, *A Rock in a Weary Land: The African Methodist Episcopal Church during the Civil War and Reconstruction* (1982); Gayraud S. Wilmore, *Black Religion and Black Radicalism, An Interpretation of the Religious History of Afro-American People* (1983).

Gregory Mixon

TURNER, JAMES MILTON (16 May 1840, St. Louis, Mo.–1 November 1915, Ardmore, Okla.). Born a slave but freed at an early age through purchase by his father, he attended Oberlin College, in Ohio, before the Civil War. After the war, he rose to prominence in Missouri as the major spokesman for the Equal Rights League. He taught school and organized black schools across the state during 1869–1870, while also getting out the black vote for Radical Republican* candidates. As a reward, President Ulysses Grant appointed Turner minister resident and consul general to Liberia in 1871, a post he held until 1878. Returning to Missouri politics but also involving himself in the interests of black residents of the Indian Territory, Turner continued to serve his race until debris from an explosion killed him.

SELECTED BIBLIOGRAPHY

Lawrence O. Christensen, "J. Milton Turner: An Appraisal," *Missouri Historical Review* 70 (October 1975), 1–19; Lawrence O. Christensen, "Schools for Blacks: J. Milton Turner in Reconstruction Missouri," *Missouri Historical Review* 76 (January 1982), 121–35; Gary R. Kremer, "Background to Apostacy: James Milton Turner and the Republican Party," *Missouri Historical Review* 71 (October 1976),

59–75; Gary R. Kremer, "A Biography of James Milton Turner" (Ph.D. diss., American University, 1978); Gary R. Kremer, "For Justice and a Fee: James Milton Turner and the Cherokee Freedmen," *Chronicles of Oklahoma* 58 (July 1981), 376–91; Gary R. Kremer, "The World of Make-Believe: James Milton Turner and Black Masonry," *Missouri Historical Review* 74 (October 1979), 50–71.

Lawrence O. Christensen

TUSKEGEE AIRMEN. The Tuskegee Airmen breached the color barrier in the U.S. Army Air Corps in 1941 and went on to compile a distinguished combat record during World War II, a record that served as an important source of pride for black Americans, who resented the dominant view of whites that blacks could not fight. In 1940 African Americans made up approximately 1.5 percent of the Regular Army and Navy. Although law and tradition guaranteed the existence of four black army regiments (see Buffalo Soldiers), Negroes had been totally excluded from the Air Corps. Civil rights leaders such as Walter F. White,* A. Philip Randolph,* William H. Hastie,* and others used America's preparation for and entry into the war to expand opportunities for their people and to attack Jim Crow* in the armed services. The racial barrier in the glamorous Air Corps fell in January 1941 when the War Department announced formation of a black aviation pursuit squadron. It was a Pyrrhic victory, however, because the black pilots were to be trained at separate facilities in Tuskegee rather than at the white airbase in nearby Montgomery.

Initially the Tuskegee Airmen, who numbered almost one thousand before war's end, were trained exclusively for difficult and dangerous pursuit flying. The first such unit to be organized, the 99th Pursuit Squadron,* was sent to the Mediterranean theater in April 1943. It was followed a year later by the 332nd Fighter Group. A black bomber group, the 477th, was organized in late 1943, but the overburdened training facility at Tuskegee was unable to train the bomber crews before the war was over. The "Black 99th" and the 332nd Fighter Group, commanded by Lieutenant Colonel Benjamin O. Davis, Jr., engaged in combat all over Europe, escorting bombers and flying other missions. Their record on escort duty was unparalleled. In more than two hundred missions in the European theater, not a single bomber escorted by the 99th was lost to enemy fighters. These all-black units were credited with destroying 111 enemy planes in the air and 150 others on the ground while flying a total of 15,533 sorties. The exceptional combat record of the Tuskegee Airmen, who during the war had been such a powerful symbol of armed forces segregation, contributed much to the ultimate demise of Jim Crow* in the military.

SELECTED BIBLIOGRAPHY

Richard M. Dalfiume, *Desegregation of the U.S. Armed Forces: Fighting on Two Fronts, 1939–1953* (1969); Jack D. Foner, *Blacks and the Military in American History:*

Benjamin O. Davis, Jr., commander of the 99th Pursuit Squadron (WWII). (Negro Almanac Collection, Amistad Research Center, Tulane University, New Orleans.)

A New Perspective (1974); Alan L. Gropman, *The Air Force Integrates, 1945–1964* (1985); Morris J. MacGregor, Jr., *Integration of the Armed Forces, 1940–1965* (1981); Robert A. Rose, *The Lonely Eagles: The Story of America's Black Air Force in World War II* (1946).

Charles D. Lowery

TUSKEGEE CIVIC ASSOCIATION. Organized in 1941 by black professors at Tuskegee Institute*—including President Charles G. Gomillion*—and by black employees at the Veterans Hospital in the town, this group fought for the rights of blacks in Macon County, Alabama, for more than twenty-five years. Blacks outnumbered whites more than three to one in Macon County, yet whites deprived them of basic constitutional rights, particularly the right to vote. Beginning in the 1940s, working chiefly through the courts, the association began to challenge disenfranchisement in the county. Its most important victory came in *Gomillion v. Lightfoot** (1960) when the U.S. Supreme Court declared unconstitutional an Alabama gerrymandering law that excluded nearly all black voters from Tuskegee's city limits. By the 1960s, largely as a result of the organization's efforts and federal law, Justice Department suits, and the work of other local civil rights groups, blacks had achieved full voting rights in the county. The association also acted to equalize city services for blacks and to desegregate the county's public schools.

SELECTED BIBLIOGRAPHY

Harry Holloway, *The Politics of the Southern Negro—From Exclusion to Big City Organization* (1969); Robert J. Norell, *Reaping the Whirlwind: The Civil Rights Movement in Tuskegee* (1985).

Dorothy A. Autrey

TUSKEGEE INSTITUTE. In 1880 a political deal was consummated between Lewis Adams, a black tinsmith, and two white Democrats from Macon County, Alabama: William F. Foster, who was a candidate for the state senate, and Arthur L. Brooks, who was running for a seat in the lower house. They promised to secure in exchange for Adams's deliverance of the black vote in Macon County, approval for a Negro normal school in Tuskegee. Both men were elected, and in 1881 they used their influence to pass a bill which secured an appropriation of $2,000 annually for Tuskegee. This act placed the proposed school under the control of a three-member board of commissioners. The board's search for someone to organize the school led them to Hampton Institute* and General Samuel C. Armstrong, who recommended his former pupil, Booker T. Washington.* Washington came to Tuskegee on 14 June 1888 and on 4 July he opened the doors of Tuskegee Negro Normal Institute. The school emphasized industrial education, but did not neglect academic subjects. Under Washington's conservative leadership, Tuskegee grew into one of the finest black schools in the country. Its students and faculty remained aloof from local, state, and national politics—the key to its survival in the white-controlled hill country of Macon County. Still, Washington lobbied against the disenfranchising clauses of Alabama's 1901 constitution and surreptitiously supported the *Giles v. Harris** suit of 1903, the first test case challenging the constitutionality of the Alabama suffrage law. The Supreme Court ruled against the plaintiff. A second Washington-supported suit, *Giles v. Teasley** in 1904, suffered the same fate. The *Bailey v. Alabama** black peonage* case, which received Washington's behind-the-scene support, resulted in the Su-

Tuskegee Institute. (Negro Almanac Collection, Amistad Research Center, Tulane University, New Orleans.)

preme Court's invalidating an Alabama contract labor law in 1911. When Booker T. Washington died in 1915, he was replaced by Robert Russa Moton,* Hampton Institute's commandant of cadets. Moton continued the school's apolitical policy and its tradition of industrial training. In 1930, during Moton's tenure, Tuskegee was rated a class "B" institution by the Southern Association of Colleges and Secondary Schools. Concern over the denial of the franchise to Alabama blacks did not die with Washington. Charles G. Gomillion,* a black South Carolinian trained at Paine's College in Georgia, came to Tuskegee to teach in 1928. In 1941, he changed the Tuskegee men's club into the Tuskegee Civic Association* and opened membership to women. Through this organization and the efforts of its founder, Tuskegee assumed a leading role in the civil rights struggle in Macon County.

SELECTED BIBLIOGRAPHY

Addie Louise Joyner Butler, *The Distinctive Black College: Talladega, Tuskegee, and Morehouse* (1977); Louis R. Harlan, *Booker T. Washington: The Making of a Black Leader, 1856–1901* (1972); Louis R. Harlan, *Booker T. Washington: The Wizard of Tuskegee, 1901–1915* (1983); Robert J. Norrell, *Reaping the Whirlwind: The Civil Rights Movement in Tuskegee* (1985).

                                                                    Joe Louis Caldwell

TUTTLE, ELBERT PARR (17 July 1897, Pasadena, Calif.–   ). Educated at Cornell University, where he earned both baccalaureate and law degrees, he practiced law in Atlanta, Georgia, and in Washington, D.C., from 1937 until 1955, when he was appointed to the United States Court of Appeals for the Fifth Judicial Circuit.* He served as chief judge of the Fifth Circuit from 1961 to 1967, when he retired. In 1981 he was reassigned to the Eleventh Circuit Court of Appeals. During the late 1950s and 1960s, Judge Tuttle provided vigorous leadership for a court which, more than any other appeals court in the country, bore the burden of civil rights litigation. He, together with colleagues John Minor Wisdom,* John Robert Brown,* and Richard Taylor Rives*—all of whom shared a strong commitment to racial justice—transformed the role of the federal judiciary in the Deep South by making the courts a major vehicle for social and political change. The judicial activism he promoted helped ensure the ultimate success of the civil rights revolution. Much of the Fifth's caseload after 1955 had to do with the desegregation of the public schools in the Deep South, but Tuttle and his colleagues expanded the mandate of *Brown v. Board of Education** for equality beyond education, issuing landmark decisions that swept away the barriers of discrimination in jury selection, voting, and employment. Tuttle led the court as it pioneered procedures, most notably the civil rights injunction, which transformed the Fourteenth Amendment's* neglected due process clause into a powerful instrument for racial justice.

SELECTED BIBLIOGRAPHY

Jack Bass, *Unlikely Heroes* (1981); Harvey C. Couch, *A History of the Fifth Circuit, 1891–1981* (1984); J. W. Peltason, *Fifty-Eight Lonely Men, Southern Federal Judges and School Desegregation* (1961).

Charles D. Lowery

U

UNCLE TOM'S CHILDREN. Awarded the best fiction prize in 1938 and critically acclaimed, Richard Wright's* novella firmly established his place as a major American writer and ushered in a powerful new voice and tradition in black literature. Direct, forceful, and starkly realistic, this seminal collection signaled something terrifyingly new: a refutation of the myths of the docile Negro. Its impact was resounding. In each story, the characters assert themselves, expressing racial hatred, stoic endurance, and at times mass action. *Uncle Tom's Children* sounded a warning that forced America's attention to the violent realities of race relations in the South and to the black person's determination to survive and reclaim his rightful place.

SELECTED BIBLIOGRAPHY

Edwin B. Burgum, "The Art of Richard Wright's Short Stories," *Quarterly Review of Literature* 1 (Spring 1944); Michael Fabre, *The Unfinished Quest of Richard Wright* (1973); James R. Giles, "Richard Wright's Successful Failure: A Look at *Uncle Tom's Children*," *Phylon* 34 (Fall 1973), 256–66; Edward Margolies, *The Art of Richard Wright* (1969).

Jacquelyn Jackson

UNION LEAGUE. Originating in the North during the Civil War, the Union League notion hitched a ride South in the political baggage of Union soldiers and so-called carpetbaggers. It proved to be an effective tool for raising the political consciousness of ex-slaves and sowing the seeds of Republicanism among them. Although some local Union Leagues existed in the South before 1867, by 1 January 1868, nearly all eligible black voters had become league members. Interracial groups like the ones established in Tennessee and North Carolina were the exceptions. Union League members attempted to push the nation toward true republicanism by insisting upon equality before the law, full participation by blacks in the political and economic life of the South, the promotion of black education, and the elimination of racial barriers to social intercourse. Union League success among blacks was the result not only of the skill and zeal of its organizers, but also of the fact that its platform was identical to black ideals and aspirations. A short-lived phenomenon, Union League radicalism had succumbed to Republican moderation by the end of 1868.

SELECTED BIBLIOGRAPHY

Avery Craven, *Reconstruction: The Ending of the Civil War* (1969); Michael W. Fitzgerald, *The Union League Movement in the Deep South: Politics and Agricultural Changes during Reconstruction* (1989); Eric Foner, *Reconstruction: America's Unfinished Revolution, 1863–1877* (1988).

Joe Louis Caldwell

UNITED COLORED SOCIALISTS OF AMERICA. In 1928 Frank P. Crosswaith, the leading African-American socialist spokesperson, the black "Eugene Debs," founded this organization in Harlem, New York, to recruit African Americans into the Socialist party. Eager to organize a socialist-based, black labor movement as well as achieve political and economic equality, the group attacked racism in organized labor, demanded more funding for education, and urged that blacks be allowed to serve on juries and be extended voting rights in all states. Black Harlemites Ethelred Brown, V. C. Gasper, Arther C. Parker, and Noah C. A. Walker led this group until 1934, when intraparty conflict split the local Socialist party.

SELECTED BIBLIOGRAPHY

Philip S. Foner, *American Socialism and Black Americans: From the Age of Jackson to World War II* (1977); Philip S. Foner, *Organized Labor and the Black Worker, 1619–1973* (1974); Mark Naison, *Communism in Harlem during the Depression* (1983).

Barbara L. Green

UNITED NEGRO COLLEGE FUND. In 1944 Frederick D. Patterson, the president of Tuskegee Institute,* met with fourteen presidents from a consortium of twenty-seven black colleges and universities and established the United Negro College Fund. Chartered in New York, the fund became the first cooperative fund-raising venture in the history of higher education. Initial funding for the organization came, in part, from the General Education Board* established by John D. Rockefeller and the Rosenwald Fund* founded by Julius Rosenwald,* president of Sears Roebuck. Today over forty traditional black colleges and universities benefit from the organization's financial support, public relations efforts, advocacy role, and overall self-help philosophy.

Early college classroom associated with United Negro College Fund. (Negro Almanac Collection, Amistad Research Center, Tulane University, New Orleans.)

SELECTED BIBLIOGRAPHY

Antoine Garibaldi, *Black Colleges and Universities: Challenges for the Future* (1984); John H. Johnson, "Biggest Fundraiser Ever for Black Education," *Ebony* 36 (April 1981), 146–47; Lea Williams, "The United Negro College Fund in Retrospect— A Search for Its True Meaning," *Journal of Negro Education* 46 (Fall 1980), 363– 72; Charles V. Willie and Ronald R. Edmonds, eds., *Black Colleges in America* (1978).

Barbara L. Green

UNITED STATES COURT OF APPEALS FOR THE FIFTH JUDICIAL CIRCUIT. During the decade bracketed by the *Brown v. Board of Education** decision of 1954 and the Voting Rights Act of 1965,* the Fifth Circuit Court, with headquarters in New Orleans, Louisiana, was a major legal battleground for the civil rights revolution. Because its jurisdiction included six states of the old Confederacy (Georgia, Florida, Alabama, Mississippi, Louisiana, and Texas), the Fifth had the heaviest civil rights caseload of any of the federal circuit courts. This load, together with the failure of the Supreme Court after *Brown* to provide direction to the lower courts, created the opportunity for the Fifth Circuit Court to blaze a new trail in civil rights law. This it did, making law as well as following it.

As a result of the vigorous and imaginative leadership of a small group of liberal judges unequivocally committed to justice and equality under the law, the Fifth became one of the most active instruments for social and political change in the recalcitrant American South. These liberal judges were Elbert P. Tuttle,* John Robert Brown,* John Minor Wisdom,* and Richard Taylor Rives.* By dominating three-judge panels that heard appeals from the seventeen district courts composing the circuit, these four jurists translated the Supreme Court's school desegregation decision into a broad mandate for justice and equality under the law. They vigorously worked to dismantle the dual school system. They led the Fifth Circuit Court to develop the civil rights injunction, which concentrated power in judges and thereby enabled them to restructure the school system. They led the court beyond education to issue landmark decisions striking down barriers of discrimination in employment, voting, and jury selection. As Judge Tuttle explained, "We started to enforce *Brown* in the lower courts and then expanded it from the schools to everything else, long ahead of the Supreme Court, by adopting the same principles as *Brown*." The strong civil rights record of the Fifth Circuit Court during a period of social upheaval provided assurance to civil rights activists that the federal courts could serve as effective instruments of peaceful change. After 1968, when President Richard Nixon, as a part of his "Southern Strategy," began to appoint strict constructionists to the federal bench, the Fifth began to backslide on school desegregation cases and ceased to offer judicial leadership in the area of civil rights.

SELECTED BIBLIOGRAPHY

Deborah J. Barrow and Thomas G. Walker, *A Court Divided: The Fifth Circuit Court of Appeals and the Politics of Judicial Reform* (1988); Jack Bass, *Unlikely Heroes* (1981); Harvey C. Couch, *A History of the Fifth Circuit, 1891–1981* (1984); J. W. Peltason, *Fifty-Eight Lonely Men: Southern Federal Judges and School Desegregation* (1961).

Charles D. Lowery

UNITED STATES ex rel. GOLDSBY v. HARPOLE, 263 F.2d 71 (5th Cir., 1959). Robert Lee Goldsby, a black resident of Carroll County, Mississippi, was indicted and convicted of the 1954 murder of a white couple. His jury was all white even though 57 percent of Carroll County was black. Jury duty in the state was confined to registered voters, and since there were no registered black voters in the county, there were no blacks eligible for jury duty. In what would become one of its landmark civil rights decisions, the United States Court of Appeals for the Fifth Judicial Circuit* reversed Goldsby's conviction on the ground that blacks had been systematically excluded from jury duty. The court remanded the case to Mississippi with instructions that Goldsby be retried speedily by a jury from which blacks were not excluded. Although Goldsby was subsequently retried, adjudged guilty, and executed, his trial affirmed the fundamental constitutional right of the accused to a jury selected without discrimination by race. *Goldsby* provided the important basis for a number of juror discrimination cases that came before the Fifth Circuit Court subsequently.

SELECTED BIBLIOGRAPHY

Jack Bass, *Unlikely Heroes* (1981); Harvey C. Couch, *A History of the Fifth Circuit, 1891–1981* (1984); Loren Miller, *The Petitioners: The Story of the Supreme Court of the United States and the Negro* (1966); Frank T. Read and Lucy S. McGough, *Let Them Be Judged: The Judicial Integration of the Deep South* (1978).

Charles D. Lowery

UNITED STATES v. ALABAMA, 171 F. Supp. 720 (M.D. Ala., 1959). To thwart the enforcement of the Civil Rights Act of 1957,* southern election officials sometimes resigned from office en masse, thereby leaving the U.S. Department of Justice without a proper party to sue. Shortly before a suit against an Alabama registrar was to begin, the offending official resigned. The Justice Department responded by amending its complaint to name as defendants the state of Alabama and the board of registrars. Holding that the resigned registrar could not be tried since he was no longer an official, and that the board of registrars and the state of Alabama were not suable, the lower courts dismissed the suit. The case was appealed, but before it reached the Supreme Court the Civil Rights Act of 1960* was enacted. Under the new law action could be brought against a state, making it a suable entity. The Supreme Court thereupon remanded the case for retrial under the new statute.

SELECTED BIBLIOGRAPHY

Richard Bardolph, ed., *The Civil Rights Record: Black Americans and the Law, 1849–1970* (1970); Jack Greenberg, *Race Relations and American Law* (1959); Charles V. Hamilton, *The Bench and the Ballot* (1973); Steven F. Lawson, *Black Ballots: Voting Rights in the South, 1944–1969* (1976).

Charles D. Lowery

UNITED STATES v. CLASSIC, 313 U.S. 299 (1941). Growing out of the federal government's prosecution of an election fraud case in New Orleans, Louisiana, *United States v. Classic* indirectly undermined the legal doctrine supporting the constitutionality of white primaries,* that is, primaries restricting participation to whites. The case did not involve racial discrimination but rather the criminal prosecution of five election commissioners for violating the Civil Rights Act of 1870 (see Enforcement Acts) by altering ballots in favor of one of the candidates seeking the Democratic nomination for a seat in the United States House of Representatives. Reversing a lower court decision that Congress lacked power to regulate primaries, the Supreme Court noted that primaries, which restricted voters' choices in the general election, were funded and regulated by the state. They were not private activities but rather a part of the electoral process. The Court held that Article I, Section 4 of the Constitution authorized Congress to regulate primaries to protect the people's constitutional right to elect their representatives. The Court's reasoning would later be extended to invalidate white primaries. If primaries were part of a state's electoral process, then the state was prohibited by the Fifteenth Amendment* from denying participation to blacks.

SELECTED BIBLIOGRAPHY

Theodore M. Berry, "*United States v. Classic*," *National Bar Journal* 1 (1941), 149–56; Richard Claude, *The Supreme Court and the Electoral Process* (1970); V. O. Key, Jr., *Southern Politics: In State and Nation* (1949); Note, "Primaries as Subjects of Congressional Regulation," *Brooklyn Law Review* 11 (1941), 90–97.

Patricia A. Behlar

UNITED STATES v. CRUIKSHANK, 92 U.S. 542 (1876). Heard by the U.S. Supreme Court on appeal from circuit court, this case resulted from the bloodiest violence of Reconstruction—the massacre of 280 African Americans in Colfax, Louisiana, on Easter Sunday in 1873. Federal prosecutors brought indictments against scores of whites under the Civil Rights Enforcement Act of 1870 (see Enforcement Acts). The Court quashed the indictments (and the sole three resulting convictions) for the failure to specify the defendants' racial intentions to deprive blacks of civil rights. Writing for the majority, Justice Joseph P. Bradley spelled out constitutional limits to congressional civil rights legislation. Bradley held that the Fourteenth Amendment* permitted federal laws against state action that denied rights but not against private actions; and while the Thirteenth* and Fifteenth Amendments* allowed federal acts against private denial of rights, they did so only on the specified bases of race, color, or previous conditions of servitude. *United States v. Cruikshank* was one of two major reversals of the federal protections of civil rights that the U.S. Supreme Court handed down on 27 March 1876. In it and *United States v. Reese** the court advanced the states' primary jurisdiction and affirmed limited federal power in civil rights.

SELECTED BIBLIOGRAPHY

Michael L. Benedict, "Preserving Federalism: Reconstruction and the Waite Court," *Supreme Court Review* (1978), 39–79; William Gillette, *Retreat from Reconstruction, 1869–1879* (1979); Robert Kaczorowski, *The Politics of Judicial Interpretation: The Federal Courts, Department of Justice and Civil Rights, 1866–1876* (1985); John Anthony Scott, "Justice Bradley's Evolving Concept of the Fourteenth Amendment from the Slaughterhouse Cases to the Civil Rights Cases," *Rutgers Law Review* 25 (1971) 552–69; Joe Gray Taylor, *Louisiana Reconstructed, 1863–1877*

(1974); Ted Tunnell, *Crucible of Reconstruction: War, Radicalism, and Race in Louisiana 1862–1877* (1984).

Thomas J. Davis

UNITED STATES v. GUEST, 383 U.S. 745 (1966). Defendant Herbert Guest, with five others, was indicted under 18 U.S.C., Section 241, for conspiracy to deprive black citizens in the vicinity of Athens, Georgia, of the free exercise and enjoyment of the rights secured to them by the Constitution and laws of the United States, viz., the right to use state facilities without discrimination on the basis of race, the right freely to engage in interstate travel, and the right to equal enjoyment of privately owned places of public accommodation. The defendants contended that the indictment was invalid because Section 241 protected only against interference with the exercise of the right to equal utilization of state facilities, which was not a right "secured" by the Fourteenth Amendment.* The district court dismissed the indictment on the ground that it did not involve national citizenship rights to which it deemed Section 241 solely applicable. The Supreme Court, upon appeal, ruled that it had no jurisdiction over that portion of the indictment dealing with interference with the right to use public accommodations. The Court did, however, claim jurisdiction over other parts of the indictment and reversed the lower court and remanded the case back for further adjudication.

SELECTED BIBLIOGRAPHY
John E. Moye, "Fourteenth Amendment Congressional Power to Legislate Against Private Discriminations: The Guest Case," *Cornell Law Quarterly* 52 (1967), 586–99; Harvard Sitkoff, *The Struggle for Black Equality, 1954–1980* (1981); C. Vann Woodward, *The Strange Career of Jim Crow*, 3rd rev. ed. (1974).

Michael S. Downs

UNITED STATES v. HARRIS, 106 U.S. 629 (1882). In 1876 R. G. Harris and nineteen other whites violently attacked four black suspects in the custody of a Tennessee deputy sheriff. A federal prosecution charged them with conspiracy to deprive their victims of the equal protection of the laws, in violation of the third Enforcement Act* (Ku Klux Act) of 1871. In addition to prohibiting the use of disguises on public or private property for purposes of intimidation, this act also punished attempts to prevent state authorities from according equal protection of the laws. Justice William Woods's opinion for the Supreme Court majority struck down the law as being broader than either the Thirteenth* or Fourteenth Amendments* would allow, and irrelevant to the Fifteenth.* The statute punished private actions of individuals, whereas the Fourteenth Amendment prohibited only discriminatory actions by states. In this case there had been no wrongful state action to correct. The doctrine of "state action" was a central pillar of the Court's reasoning in cases involving interpretation of the postwar amendments, and also the area of greatest criticism on the part of scholars. This case saw the first of several dissents by Justice John Marshall Harlan,* objecting to what he perceived as disregard for the legal rights of blacks.

SELECTED BIBLIOGRAPHY

Alfred Avins, "The Ku Klux Klan Act of 1871: Some Reflected Light on State Action and the Fourteenth Amendment," *St. Louis University Law Journal* 11 (1967), 331–73; Charles Fairman, *Reconstruction and Reunion, 1864–1888* (1987).

James E. Sefton

UNITED STATES v. JEFFERSON COUNTY BOARD OF EDUCATION, 372 F.2d 836 (5th Cir., 1966). This decision by the United States Court of Appeals for the Fifth Judicial Circuit* clarified the 1954 *Brown v. Board of Education** ruling by ordering compulsory integration to achieve a racially nondiscriminatory school system. The decision, which combined cases from the Northern Alabama and Western Louisiana U.S. district courts, ordered affirmative action* to eliminate the effects of de jure segregation and to achieve a shift to unitary, nonracial public school systems. The Civil Rights Act of 1964* had mandated that the United States Office of Education, Department of Health, Education and Welfare (HEW), establish guidelines for school integration. With the Jefferson County decree, the Fifth Circuit adopted the 1966 HEW guidelines as its uniform plan, which strengthened the government's ability to withhold federal funds, and thus forced recalcitrant districts to comply with the court-ordered integration. In effect, the opinion, written by Judge John Minor Wisdom,* invalidated for the Fifth Circuit the largely unsuccessful free choice method of school desegregation set forth by the *Briggs v. Elliot** decision of 1955. The NAACP* called the *Jefferson County* opinion the most significant since *Brown*. The U.S. Supreme Court would later uphold compulsory integration over free choice in its 1968 ruling in *Green v. School Board of New Kent County, Virginia.**

SELECTED BIBLIOGRAPHY

George R. Metcalf, *From Little Rock to Boston* (1983); "Recent Cases—Constitutional Law," *Harvard Law Review* 81 (1967), 474–79; Frank T. Spindel, "Constitutional Law," *Texas Law Review* 46 (1967), 266–74; Raymond Wolters, *The Burden of Brown: Thirty Years of School Desegregation* (1984).

Glenn T. Eskew

UNITED STATES v. LYND, 349 F.2d 785 (5th Cir., 1965). Soon after the passage of the Voting Rights Act of 1965,* federal authorities began to investigate the activities of Theron C. Lynd, a registrar of voters for Forrest County, Mississippi. Less than 3 percent of the county's black voting-age population was registered at that time. Acting under provisions of the new Voting Rights Act, federal officials asked Lynd for permission to examine the registration records. When he refused, they filed suit. Federal District Court Judge W. Harold Cox, a staunch segregationist, allowed the case to drag on for years, granting the defendants numerous postponements. Exasperated Justice Department officials asked the United States Court of Appeals for the Fifth Judicial Circuit* for relief. The appellate court responded with an injunction enjoining Lynd from continuing his discriminatory registration practices. This action was a sharp departure from standard appellant procedure. Ordinarily the appeals court only reviewed final decisions of district courts. In *Lynd*, Judge Cox had postponed action and had rendered no final decision. The Fifth blazed a new trail in legal procedure by issuing an injunction, pending appeal, that did more than preserve the status quo. The decision put recalcitrant district judges such as Cox on notice that attempts to delay justice by inaction or postponement would not be tolerated. The "injunction pending appeal" became a legal procedure widely employed by civil rights lawyers in voter registration and school desegregation cases.

SELECTED BIBLIOGRAPHY

Jack Bass, *Unlikely Heroes* (1981); Harvey C. Couch, *A History of the Fifth Circuit, 1891–1981* (1984); Frank T. Read and Lucy S. McGough, *Let Them Be Judged: The Judicial Integration of the Deep South* (1978).

Charles D. Lowery

UNITED STATES v. MONTGOMERY COUNTY SCHOOL BOARD, 395 U.S. 225 (1969). The public schools of Montgomery County, Alabama, had failed to desegregate by ten years after the 1954 *Brown v. Board of Education** decision in defiance of repeated federal court decisions that such actions were unconstitutional and despite court orders to expedite integration. The school board's failure forced the federal district court to order desegregation of faculty and staff on a three-to-two ratio of white to black faculty in each school to reflect the county's population and to fix the ratio of substitute, student, and night schoolteachers in the same ratio as the number of white to black teachers for the entire school system. In addition, the court required schools with fewer than twelve full-time teachers to have at least one teacher whose race was different from the faculty racial majority and required schools with more than twelve full-time teachers to have at least one teacher of a minority race for every six faculty and staff. The United States Court of Appeals for the Fifth Judicial Circuit* reversed the decision. On certiorari, the Supreme Court reversed the appeals court. Writing for a unanimous court, Justice Hugo Black held that the goal of faculty and staff desegregation was important to end the county's history of desegregation and that the district court's action was appropriate and necessary given the school board's intransigence.

SELECTED BIBLIOGRAPHY
Lino A. Graglia, *Disaster by Degree, the Supreme Court Decisions on Race and the Schools* (1976); E. Edmund Reutter, Jr., *The Supreme Court's Impact on Public Education* (1982); Roland L. Young, "Review of Recent Supreme Court Decisions—Schools," *American Bar Association Journal* 55 (1969), 876.

William A. Paquette

UNITED STATES v. NORTHWEST LOUISIANA RESTAURANT CLUB, 256 F. Supp. 151 (W.D. La. 1966). This and similar cases prohibited sham private organizations from utilizing the "private club" exemption of the antidiscrimination in public accommodations section of the Civil Rights Act of 1964.* The U.S. attorney general sued the Northwest Louisiana Restaurant Club to prohibit its member restaurants from refusing to serve blacks. The club's voting members consisted of approximately one hundred restaurant owners in Shreveport and Lake Charles, Louisiana. No-voting membership cards were routinely issued to any white customer who sought admission to a member restaurant. Blacks were denied membership cards and then were denied admission to the restaurants on the basis of nonmembership. Club officers admitted the club was formed for the express purpose of circumventing the 1964 Civil Rights Act by claiming the statutory exemption of a "private club." The court ruled that only bona fide private clubs, which based exclusive membership on some identifiable nonracial requirement or condition, could claim exemption from the public accommodation section of the 1964 Civil Rights Act. This decision and others like it prevented businesses providing public accommodations from circumventing the 1964 Civil Rights Act by forming sham private clubs which continued to operate on a racially discriminatory basis.

SELECTED BIBLIOGRAPHY
Henry J. Abraham, *Freedom and the Court, Civil Rights and Liberties in the United States* (1988); Chester J. Antieau, *Federal Civil Rights Act, Civil Practice* (1980); Derrick A. Bell, Jr., *Race, Racism and American Law* (1980); Theodore Eisenberg, *Civil Rights Legislation* (1981).

Frederick G. Slabach

UNITED STATES v. RAINES, 362 U.S. 17 (1960). Reversing a decision of Judge T. Hoyt Davis of the Middle District of Georgia, the Supreme Court upheld the constitutionality of the Civil Rights Act of 1957.* The legislation had authorized the attorney general to seek an injunction in federal court against persons who had deprived others of the right to vote based upon race. Although the defendants were public officials accused of voter discrimination, Judge Davis accepted their argument that, because the legislation did not refer to persons acting "under color of law," it unconstitutionally authorized the attorney general to act in cases in which there was only private discrimination and thus was beyond the reach of the Fifteenth Amendment.* In reversing Judge Davis, the Court noted that the defendants were indeed acting "under color of law" and could not challenge the law on the basis of how it might affect others. Moreover, Justice William Brennan stated that it was within the power of Congress to protect private constitutional rights. A contrary decision would have meant that victims of voter discrimination would have had to bear the financial burden of bringing suit themselves rather than relying upon the attorney general to defend their rights.

SELECTED BIBLIOGRAPHY
Richard Claude, *The Supreme Court and the Electoral Process* (1970); Note, "Civil Rights-Elections-Federal Injunction against Racial Discrimination," *Michigan Law Review* 58 (1960), 925–29; Donald S. Strong, *Negroes, Ballots and Judges: National Voting Rights Legislation in the Federal Courts* (1968).

Patricia A. Behlar

UNITED STATES v. REESE, 92 U.S. 214 (1876). This Supreme Court decision undercut the protection of the voting rights of African Americans. The case involved a Kentucky voting official who refused to count a black's vote, thus effectively denying suffrage. Federal prosecutors charged the official with violating the Civil Rights Enforcement Act of 1870 (see Enforcement Acts). The Court quashed the indictment, ruling that in providing penalties for obstructing any person's vote, Congress had overreached its constitutional powers. States held primary control of suffrage, the Court said. The Fifteenth Amendment* also conferred no right of suffrage but prohibited only the stipulated denial or abridgement of the right to vote on the basis of race, color, or previous condition of servitude. Thus, the Court ruled, Congress had no power for comprehensive proscriptions. And as neither the indictment against Reese nor the statute restricted itself to offenses based on "race, color, or previous condition of servitude," both the indictment and statute were unlawful. *United States v. Reese* was one of two major reversals of federal protections of civil rights handed down by the U.S. Supreme Court on 27 March 1876; the other was *United States v. Cruikshank.**

SELECTED BIBLIOGRAPHY
William Gillette, "Anatomy of a Failure: Federal Enforcement of the Right to Vote in the Border States during Reconstruction," in Richard L. Curry, ed., *Radicalism, Racism, and Party Realignment: The Border States during Reconstruction* (1969); William Gillette, *Retreat from Reconstruction, 1869–1879* (1979); Robert J. Harris, *The Quest for Equality: The Constitution, Congress and the Supreme Court* (1960); Everette Swinney, "Enforcing the Fifteenth Amendment, 1870–1877," *Journal of Southern History* 28 (May 1962), 202–18.

Thomas J. Davis

UNITED STATES v. REYNOLDS, 235 U.S. 133 (1914). This case involved the constitutionality under the Thirteenth Amendment* of an Alabama criminal-surety statute. The law provided that a convict who was unable to pay his fines and court costs could be confined to hard labor on a chain gang. Alternatively, he could be released into the custody of a surety who paid the convict's debt. Typically, the period of labor owed by the convict (usually black) to the surety far exceeded the convict's sentence to hard labor. In the case that generated *Reynolds*, a man convicted of petit larceny was fined fifty-eight dollars or sixty-eight days on a chain gang. Instead, a local farmer paid the fine, and the convict signed a contract that required him to work for over nine months to satisfy the debt. The U.S. Supreme Court found nothing objectionable with this part of the arrangement. The Thirteenth Amendment allowed involuntary servitude "as punishment for crime," and individuals were free to sell their labor for whatever price they chose.

The Alabama statute, however, provided that if the ex-convict broke his contract with the surety, he could be imprisoned again with an enhanced fine. A second surety could then pay the fine and employ the convict for an even longer period, "thus keeping him chained to an everturning wheel of servitude to discharge the obligation which he ha[d] incurred to his surety." The *Reynolds* majority reasoned that, though the ex-convict had a private contract with his surety, he worked under "the constant coercion and threat" of arrest if he broke his contract. This form of coercion, the Court found, "is as potent as it would have been had the law provided for the seizure and compulsory service of the convict." While the state could impose servitude "as punishment for crime," the ex-convict was being punished for breach of a labor contract. This arrangement, according to the Court, violated the Thirteenth Amendment prohibition against involuntary servitude and federal statutes prohibiting peonage (see also black peonage).

SELECTED BIBLIOGRAPHY

Alexander M. Bickel and Benno C. Schmidt, *History of the Supreme Court of the United States*, vol. 9, *The Judiciary and Responsible Government 1910–21* (1984); Pete Daniel, *The Shadow of Slavery: Peonage in the South, 1909–1969* (1972); Loren Miller, *The Petitioners: The Story of the Supreme Court of the United States and the Negro* (1966); Daniel A. Novak, *The Wheel of Servitude: Black Forced Servitude after Slavery* (1978).

Kenneth DeVille

UNITED STATES v. SCHOOL DISTRICT OF COOK COUNTY, 286 F. Supp. 786 (W.D. Ill. 1968). This is one of several cases holding that affirmative policies of school systems to preserve segregation, originally caused by housing patterns, transforms permissible de facto segregation* into unconstitutional de jure segregation. The U.S. attorney general sued to desegregate Illinois School District 151 in suburban Chicago. The school district contended that natural ethnic housing choices resulted in the system's segregation and that such neighborhood schools were permissible pursuant to the landmark Supreme Court case of *Brown* *v. Board of Education** (1954). The district court ruled that the school district affirmatively constructed school buildings, drew attendance zones, and assigned teachers by race to preserve racial segregation in violation of the Fourteenth Amendment* and the Civil Rights Act of 1964.* Many lower federal courts had interpreted *Brown* as ruling that mere failure to correct a de facto racial imbalance is not de jure segregation. Thus, neighborhood schools which merely recognized natural ethnic housing patterns were not unconstitutional. This and other cases like it looked not only at the formal laws of the state, but also at the policies and procedures of the school district to determine whether impermissible de jure segregation existed.

SELECTED BIBLIOGRAPHY

Derrick A. Bell, Jr., *Race, Racism and American Law* (1980); Paul R. Dimond, *Beyond Busing, Inside the Challenge to Urban Segregation* (1985); Note, "Demise of the Neighborhood School Plan," 55 *Cornell Law Review* 55 (1970), 594.

Frederick G. Slabach

UNITED STATES v. WALLACE, 218 F. Supp. 290 (N.D., Ala., 1963). This case grew out of efforts by the Department of Justice to prevent Governor George C. Wallace from interfering with the court-ordered desegregation of the University of Alabama. On 16 May 1963, a federal district court in Alabama had directed the university to admit two blacks during its summer session. Wallace publicly stated his intention to uphold his 1962 campaign pledge to oppose desegregation even if it required that he stand in the schoolhouse door. The Justice Department on 5 June requested and received a federal court injunction blocking the governor from carrying out his plan. But Wallace defied the injunction, and on 11 June he stood in the doorway of a university building barring Assistant Attorney General Nicholas Katzenbach from escorting the black students inside to register. Wallace's action was perhaps more a move to gain national attention than an attempt to impede the integration process in the state. Later that day, he vacated the university door and allowed the students to enter when ordered to do so by the commander of the federalized Alabama National Guard.

SELECTED BIBLIOGRAPHY

Michael R. Belknap, *Federal Law and Southern Order: Racial Violence and Constitutional Conflict in the Post-Brown South* (1987); Taylor Branch, *Parting the Waters— America in the King Years, 1954–63* (1988); Jody Carlson, *George C. Wallace and the Politics of Powerlessness—The Wallace Campaign for the Presidency, 1964–1970* (1981); Philip Crass, *The Wallace Factor* (1975); Donald S. Strong, "Alabama–Transition and Alienation," in William C. Havard, ed., *The Changing Politics of the South* (1972).

Dorothy A. Autrey

UNITED STATES v. WARD, 352 F.2d 329 (5th Cir., 1965). The decision in this case recognized the codification and expansion of the "freeze" principle developed by federal courts in voting rights cases prior to the passage of the Voting Rights Act of 1965.* The U.S. attorney general sued Katherine Ward, the registrar of voters of Madison Parish and the state of Louisiana, to stop discriminatory application of state registration requirements. The appeals court ordered a freeze on restrictive registration requirements for two years allowing all applicants to use the less restrictive methods applied to whites. After two years, the restrictive registration requirements could again be applied, but in a racially non-discriminatory manner. Immediately after the effective date of the 1965 Voting Rights Act, the court modified its ruling to extend the freeze to five years as authorized by the act. The federal courts developed the freeze principle because merely to apply restrictive voting prerequisites uniformly to blacks *and* whites would perpetuate the effect of past discrimination by locking onto voter rolls whites already registered without restrictive requirements and prohibiting most blacks from registering to vote because of the onerous prerequisites. Passage of the 1965 Voting Rights Act and the courts' application of the freeze principle attempted to treat all registrants equally.

SELECTED BIBLIOGRAPHY

Chester J. Antieau, *Federal Civil Rights Acts, Civil Practice* (1980); Jack Bass, *Unlikely Heroes* (1990); Derrick A. Bell, Jr., *Race, Racism and American Law* (1980).

Frederick G. Slabach

UNITED STEELWORKERS v. WEBER, 443 U.S. 193 (1979). The Supreme Court, in *United Steelworkers v. Weber*, upheld the legality of an affirmative action* training program in the skilled crafts over a challenge that it violated the Civil Rights Act of 1964* by reserving 50 percent of the positions in the program for blacks. Brian Weber, a white man, challenged the program, instituted voluntarily by a collective bargaining agreement, because he had been denied admission while blacks with less seniority had not. The Court based its decision on statutory interpretation, stating that the act's ban on discrimination in hiring and training was not intended to prohibit voluntary race-conscious programs having the same objective as the legislation—that is, the elimination of the last vestiges of job discrimination. The majority stressed that the program was temporary, until the percentage of blacks in skilled positions approximated their percentage in the local labor force, and that it cost no whites their jobs. But the dissenters considered the program a violation of the clear language of the act, which prohibited discrimination based upon race. Such race-conscious programs, called affirmative action by supporters and reverse discrimination by opponents, continued to be controversial throughout the decade of the 1980s.

SELECTED BIBLIOGRAPHY

Robert K. Fullinwider, *The Reverse Discrimination Controversy: A Moral and Legal Analysis* (1980); Edmund W. Kitch, "The Return of Color-Consciousness to the

Constitution: Weber, Dayton, and Columbus," *Supreme Court Review* (1979), 1–15; Terry Leap and Irving Kovarsky, "What Is the Impact of Weber on Collective Bargaining?" *Labor Law Journal* 31 (1980), 323–27.

Patricia A. Behlar

UNIVERSAL AFRICAN LEGION. One of the many uniformed auxiliary units to Marcus Garvey's* Universal Negro Improvement Association,* the African Legion's spit-and-polish military appearance and physical conditioning were intended to promote race pride and brotherhood. The unit, dressed in dark blue uniforms with narrow red trouser stripes, officers outfitted with dress sabres, appeared at public functions both on horseback and foot. The African Legion also frequently served as Garvey's personal bodyguard.

SELECTED BIBLIOGRAPHY

Edmund David Cronon, *Black Moses* (1955); Elton C. Fox, *Garvey* (1972); Tony Martin, *Marcus Garvey, Hero* (1983).

Michael S. Downs

UNIVERSAL NEGRO IMPROVEMENT ASSOCIATION (UNIA). Established in 1914 by Jamaican Marcus Garvey,* the Universal Negro Improvement Association (UNIA) became the prototype for future black nationalist organizations in the United States. The organization's aim was to improve the lives of African peoples and their descendants. In 1916 Garvey established a branch office (destined to become international headquarters) in New York City, and within months he enlisted a thousand members in Harlem. By 1919 the Universal Negro Improvement Association had thirty branch offices throughout the United States and claimed two million members. The UNIA operated as an independent nation. The organization's motto was: "One God! One Aim! One destiny!" It also adopted a flag with the colors red, black, and green; published *Negro World*,* a weekly newspaper; established "Liberty halls" (auditoriums) as meeting places; operated the Black Star Steamship Line,* a steamship company; and incorporated a Negro Factories Corporation. In addition, the UNIA organized the Black Cross Nurses, the African Orthodox Church, and paramilitary units such as the Universal African Legion,* the Universal Africa Motor Corps, and the Black Eagle Flying Corps. At the First International Convention in 1920, Garvey was elected provisional president of Africa and president general and administrator of the UNIA. A Declaration of Rights of the Negro Peoples of the World was drafted, and titles, such as Knight of the Nile, Earl of the Congo, Viscount of the Niger, and Baron of Zambesi, were created. Integrationists attacked the UNIA for its black nationalist and separatist ideas. These critics included Monroe Trotter,* W.E.B. Du Bois,* and prominent NAACP* members. The association's downfall, however, was Garvey's 1923 federal court conviction for selling Black Star Line

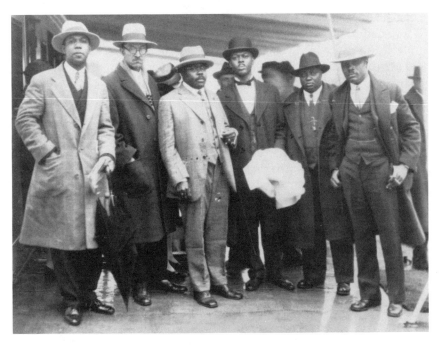

Marcus Garvey and UNIA associates at his deportation from the United States, 1927. (Arthur P. Bedou Photographs, Xavier University Archives, New Orleans.)

stock when the company was insolvent. He was fined $1,000 and sentenced to five years in prison. The UNIA never recovered; by 1930 it was defunct.

SELECTED BIBLIOGRAPHY

Adolph Edwards, *Marcus Garvey: 1887–1940* (1967); Robert A. Hill, ed., *The Marcus Garvey and Universal Negro Improvement Association Papers*, 7 vols. (1983–1990); Rupert Lewis, *Marcus Garvey: Anti-Colonial Champion* (1988).

Wali Rashash Kharif

UNIVERSITY OF CALIFORNIA REGENTS v. BAKKE, 438 U.S. 265 (1978). This popularly labelled "reverse discrimination" case led to a split decision by the U.S. Supreme Court. The University of California at Davis medical school twice rejected Alan Bakke's application for admission, leading him to file suit on the grounds that the school's affirmative action* policy denied him admission because he was white and in so doing violated his constitutional right to equal protection of the law. The medical school had mandated that sixteen seats be reserved for minority applicants in each class of one hundred students to ensure a diverse medical student body. Bakke contended that, had this affirmative action policy not been in operation, he would have gained admission to the school, since several minority applicants who were admitted allegedly had inferior qualifications. The Supreme Court voted 5 to 4 that no state university could establish a quota system setting aside a number of spots for minorities because that process would deny nonminorities fair access. To complicate matters, the Court added a second and different 5-to-4 opinion, arguing that a university policy could include race as one variable among others in its admissions criteria, if it was attempting to rectify past instances of discrimination which were not present in the Bakke case.

SELECTED BIBLIOGRAPHY

John Brigham, *Civil Liberties and American Democracy* (1984); Frank Brown, "Equal Educational Opportunity, the Law, and the Courts," *Urban Education* 11 (July 1976), 135–50; Reynolds Farley, "Trends in Racial Inequalities: Have the Gains of the 1960s Disappeared in the 1970s?" *American Sociological Review* 42 (April 1977), 189–208; Richard Kluger, *Simple Justice: The History of Brown v. Board of Education and Black America's Struggle for Equality* (1976); Finis Welch, "Affirmative Action and Its Enforcement," *American Economic Review* 71 (May 1981), 127–33; J. Harvie Wilkerson III, *From Brown to Bakke: The Supreme Court and School Integration, 1954–1978* (1979).

                                                                    Marshall Hyatt

UNIVERSITY OF MARYLAND v. MURRAY, 165 Md. 478 (1935). In 1935 Donald Gaines Murray, an African-American resident of Baltimore and a graduate of Amherst College, was refused admission to the University of Maryland School of Law in Baltimore. Murray sued. He was represented by Charles H. Houston,* special counsel for the NAACP,* and his assistant, Thurgood Marshall.* On 15 January 1936, the Maryland Court of Appeals affirmed a Baltimore City Court decision admitting Murray. The court of appeals ruled that the state's failure to provide a separate law school for black Marylanders violated the equal protection clause of the Fourteenth Amendment.* The court also ruled that Maryland's policy of providing $200 toward the cost of an out-of-state education when in-state facilities were not available to African Americans placed an undue hardship on Murray. The state's tuition scheme, said the court, "falls short of providing for students of the colored race facilities substantially equal to those furnished to the whites in the law school maintained in Baltimore." The state had a choice between opening a new law school for blacks or admitting Murray to the existing school. Since Murray was entitled to immediate relief, he had to be admitted. *Maryland v. Murray* was one of many landmark cases handled by the NAACP in the decades before *Brown v. Board of Education*★ that helped erase the color line. The case, along with the similar *Missouri ex rel. Gaines v. Canada*★ case three years later, closed off an avenue (the out-of-state tuition grant) by which some states hoped to preserve segregated education without building separate facilities for blacks.

SELECTED BIBLIOGRAPHY
"The Admission of Negroes to the University of Maryland," *School and Society* 46 (11 September 1937); *Baltimore Evening Sun*, 22 April 1935; Richard Bardolph, ed., *The Civil Rights Record: Black Americans and the Law, 1849–1970* (1970); Mark V. Tushnet, *The NAACP's Legal Strategy against Segregated Education, 1925–1950* (1987).
Stephen P. Labash

UP FROM SLAVERY. Booker T. Washington's* autobiography, written in 1901, recounts his life from childhood as a slave in Franklin County, Virginia, through the early days of freedom, his struggle for literacy and then a higher education at Hampton Institute,* and the founding of the Tuskegee Institute* and the National Negro Business League.* It contains an account of and the text of the Atlanta Exposition Speech* of 1895 as well as commentary on the philosophy underlying his national program. A nationwide best-seller, which has been translated into many languages, the narrative has been praised by literary critics and hailed as an account of human triumph over adversity.

SELECTED BIBLIOGRAPHY
Louis R. Harlan, *Booker T. Washington: The Wizard of Tuskegee, 1901–1915* (1983); Booker T. Washington, *Up from Slavery* (1901).
Suzanne Ellery Greene Chapelle

V

VANCE, RUPERT BAYLESS (15 March 1899, Plummerville, Ark.–25 August 1975, Chapel Hill, N.C.). The best known and most widely cited sociologist in the South, Vance, a native of Arkansas, received his education at Henderson-Brown College, Vanderbilt, and the University of North Carolina, where he later served as Kenan Professor of Sociology. His first book, *Human Factors in Cotton Culture* (1929), described tenancy as a social humiliation greater than slavery. His research on sharecropping later influenced the formation of New Deal land-tenure programs. Vance was one of the founders of the Southern Sociological Society (1935) and helped set the policy that the organization would meet only in hotels open to its black members. He and Howard Washington Odum* developed the thesis of "regional sociology."

SELECTED BIBLIOGRAPHY

Obituary, *New York Times*, 26 August 1975; John Shelton Reed and Daniel Joseph Singal, eds., *Regionalism and the South: Selected Papers of Rupert Vance* (1982).

Ray Branch

VANN, ROBERT (27 August 1879, Hertford County, N.C. –24 October 1940, Philadelphia, Pa.). Throughout the 1920s Robert Vann, editor of the *Pittsburgh Courier*,* was the head of the "colored division" of the Republican party, which sought to gain patronage and rights for African Americans. Seeing little prospect for himself as a Republican leader, he defected to the Democratic party. In his newspaper during the 1932 elections, he told his readers that it was time to turn Lincoln's portrait to the wall. In many black homes there was a picture of the Great Emancipator and most African Americans continued to vote Republican because of Lincoln. While Vann's now famous editorial did not have a great impact on the 1932 election, by 1934 and 1936 many African Americans had abandoned the Republican party for the Democratic party. This set into motion a process that would greatly aid the Democratic party, its candidates, and the black leaders themselves. In other ways, Vann used the *Courier*, the largest-selling Negro newspaper in the United States, to champion the political, economic, and social interests of his race and to champion racial equality. During the New Deal he served as a special adviser to the U.S. attorney general and as a member of Franklin D. Roosevelt's Black Cabinet,* which advised the president on various matters affecting the African-American community.

SELECTED BIBLIOGRAPHY

Andrew A. Buni, *Robert L. Vann of the Pittsburgh Courier: Politics and Black Journalism* (1974); Harvard Sitkoff, *A New Deal for Blacks: The Emergence of Civil Rights as a National Issue*, vol. 1, *The Depression Decade* (1978); Nancy J. Weiss, *Farewell to the Party of Lincoln* (1983).

Charles T. Pete Banner-Haley

VILLARD, OSWALD GARRISON (13 March 1872, Wiesbaden, Germany–1 October 1949, New York, N.Y.). Born to railroad and newspaper wealth, the grandson of famed abolitionist William Lloyd Garrison, Villard took seriously his family's passion for social justice. After earning two Harvard degrees in history by 1896, Villard embraced virtually every liberal cause, particularly black civil rights and pacifism. He was particularly well equipped to pursue liberal causes because of his impeccable pedigree, his social connections, and his ownership of the *New York Evening Post* and *The Nation*, which he turned into a muckraking journal. On Lincoln's birthday in 1909, Villard joined Mary White Ovington,* William English Walling, and others to protest the recent Springfield, Illinois, race riot* and to create the interracial National Association for the Advancement of Colored People* (NAACP). Under Villard's chairmanship, the NAACP gathered data on racial crimes and established a legal defense arm to take discrimination cases to court. The NAACP quickly became and would remain the most important civil rights organization in American history, but Villard withdrew from the organization's leadership when the fiery black editor of the NAACP's the *Crisis*,* W.E.B. Du Bois,* challenged him. Despite this conflict, Villard worked tirelessly to remove racial discrimination. Villard never moderated his invariably unpopular beliefs, and this "aristocrat of liberalism" paid a price for his convictions. His editorials against World War I and the American invasion of Siberia scandalized subscribers and forced the sale of the *Post* and *The Nation*. Villard himself was vilified as a Bolshevik traitor, and his family suffered social ostracism.

SELECTED BIBLIOGRAPHY

Flint Kellogg, "Villard and the NAACP,* *The Nation* 81 (14 February 1959), 137–40; Mary White Ovington, *How the National Association for the Advancement of*

Colored People Began (1914); Oswald Garrison Villard, *Fighting Years: Memoirs of a Liberal Editor* (1939); Michael Wreszin, *Oswald Garrison Villard: Pacifist at War* (1965).

Bruce J. Dierenfield

VIRGINIA SCHOOL CLOSING EXPERIMENT. In 1956 in response to the *Brown v. Board of Education** decision, the Virginia General Assembly passed a law which provided for the closing of any school or schools ordered integrated by the federal courts. In 1959 the Virginia Supreme Court declared this law unconstitutional. In response, the Virginia Assembly repealed the state's compulsory school attendance laws. With school attendance now a matter of local choice, several school boards closed their schools. In cities such as Norfolk, Charlottesville, and Front Royal, local citizens sought to accommodate the needs of students through private education. These efforts, however, were an inadequate substitute for public schooling. Many white parents and businessmen, consequently, came to believe that public education was more important than maintaining segregation. This shift in public opinion, together with a series of federal court orders, forced the opening of integrated schools in most of the cities and counties which previously had been closed. By 1962, only Prince Edward County schools remained closed. With tuition grants from the Virginia Assembly and tax credits from the board of supervisors, white citizens opened a private school system in the county. In *Griffin v. Prince Edward School Board** (1964), the Supreme Court struck down the county's system of subsidization of private white schools. In the fall of that same year, Prince Edward County schools reopened.

SELECTED BIBLIOGRAPHY

Earl Black and Merle Black, *Politics and Society in the South* (1987); Robbins L. Gates, *The Making of Massive Resistance: Virginia's Politics of Public School Desegregation, 1954–1956* (1964); Dewey W. Grantham, *The Life and Death of the Solid South: A Political History* (1988); J. Harvie Wilkinson III, *From Brown to Bakke: The Supreme Court and School Integration, 1954–1978* (1979).

Phillip A. Gibbs

VIRGINIA v. RIVES, 100 U.S. 545 (1880). On 1 March 1880 the U.S. Supreme Court handed down a trio of decisions dealing with black jury rights. In *Strauder v. West Virginia,** the Court overturned a state law that limited jury service to whites; in *Ex parte Virginia,** the court went so far as to approve the indictment and arrest of a state judge who had excluded blacks from juries. The third case, *Virginia v. Rives,* was not a victory for American blacks. In this case, two black citizens of Virginia were charged with murdering a white man. When an all-white jury pool was summoned, the defendants asked that a new pool including black citizens be ordered. The state court denied the defendants' petition, pointing out that the jury had been summoned according to Virginia's jury law, which did not exclude blacks. The Supreme Court upheld the action of the state court, since Virginia's law did not bar blacks from the jury box. Black jury service in the South became a rarity, as state leaders passed laws allowing black jury service, then appointed state officials who would not choose blacks for the jury panels.

SELECTED BIBLIOGRAPHY
Stephen Cresswell, "The Case of Taylor Strauder," *West Virginia History* 44 (Spring 1983), 193–211; Benno C. Schmidt, "Juries, Jurisdiction, and Race Discrimination: The Lost Promise of *Strauder v. West Virginia*," *Texas Law Review* (1983), 1402–99.

Stephen Cresswell

VOICE OF THE NEGRO. Edited in Atlanta by John Wesley Edward Brown and later in Chicago by Jesse Max Barber, this monthly journal first appeared in January 1904. Topics included church life, lynching,* family values, business, politics, and international affairs. In September 1905 the editors endorsed the Niagara Movement,* precursor of the NAACP,* and applauded demands for an unfettered press, which Booker T. Washington* had attempted to subvert to his accommodationist views. After the brutal Atlanta race riot (1906),* in which Brown was badly injured, the magazine found a new home in Chicago. Circulation, once 12,000, dropped off, and in October 1907 the last issue, a skimpy thirty pages, was published. An important primary source, *Voice of the Negro* reflected competing African American ideologies in the early twentieth century. It was the first substantial journal edited by southern blacks for a national audience.

SELECTED BIBLIOGRAPHY
Louis R. Harlan, ed., *The Booker T. Washington Papers* (1972–1979); August Meier, *Negro Thought in America 1880–1915: Racial Ideologies in the Age of Booker T. Washington* (1963); Alfred A. Moss, Jr., *The American Negro Academy: Voice of the Talented Tenth* (1981).

Richard W. Resh

VOTER EDUCATION PROJECT. In 1960 and 1961, as the sit-ins and activities of the Freedom Riders* began to meet with success in desegregating lunch counters and interstate travel facilities, black civil rights leaders sought new goals for their movement. In September 1961, following months of debate and wrangling, the Congress of Racial Equality* (CORE), the Student Nonviolent Coordinating Committee* (SNCC), the National Urban League,* and the NAACP* joined together to launch the Voter Education Project (VEP). The project had the full blessing of the Kennedy administration, which was willing to provide federal protection for civil rights workers engaged in registering voters, but not for protestors participating in direct action* activities. Scheduled to last for two and one-half years and financed by $870,000 in grants from the

Taconic Foundation* and other northern foundations, VEP got under way in April 1962. The campaign targeted southern blacks in the rural black belt and Mississippi Delta regions, where white election officials had manipulated literacy tests and complex registration forms to prevent even literate blacks from voting. At the beginning of the project, only about 25 percent of voting-age southern blacks were registered; in Mississippi the figure stood at 5 percent.

Student activists working for CORE, SNCC, or one of the other organizations canvassed blacks throughout the rural South, conducted literacy and citizenship clinics, and encouraged blacks to register and vote. In Mississippi SNCC workers led by Robert Moses* encountered determined opposition from inveterate white racists. There and elsewhere student volunteers were threatened, jailed, beaten, bombed, and killed, but they persisted in their efforts. Attorney General Robert Kennedy assisted them by enlarging the Civil Rights Section, Justice Department* and directing it to begin wholesale prosecution of voting rights cases. The results of the VEP were mixed. The percentage of southern adult blacks who were registered to vote rose from 25 to 40 percent between 1962 and 1964, but the educational and political process was laborious, difficult, and dangerous. The frustrations and dangers involved in the voter registration campaign ultimately contributed to the passage of the Civil Rights Act of 1964* and the Voting Rights Act of 1965.*

SELECTED BIBLIOGRAPHY

Taylor Branch, *Parting the Waters: America in the King Years, 1954–63* (1988); David J. Garrow, *Bearing the Cross: Martin Luther King, Jr., and the Southern Christian Leadership Conference* (1968); Donald G. Nieman, *Promises to Keep: African-Americans and the Constitutional Order, 1776 to the Present* (1991); Harvard Sitkoff, *The Struggle for Black Equality, 1954–1980* (1981).

                                                                        Charles D. Lowery

VOTING RIGHTS ACT OF 1965. In 1964 the Lyndon B. Johnson administration began to plan voting rights legislation, and the president called for legislation in his 1965 State of the Union address. Meanwhile, Martin Luther King, Jr.,'s* voting rights campaign in Selma, Alabama, prompted the administration to act more quickly. In a 15 March address to Congress at the height of the Selma demonstrations that climaxed with the Selma to Montgomery March,* the president employed the phrase "we shall overcome" to call for voting rights legislation. On 25 May, the Senate invoked cloture and the next day passed (78–18) the bill. Six weeks later the House of Representatives also passed (333–85) a voting rights bill. A conference quickly approved a bill very similar to the administration's proposal, and Congress easily approved it early in August. On 6 August the president signed it.

The main provisions of the Voting Rights Act, first, outlawed educational requirements for voting in states or counties where less than half of the voting age population had been registered on 1 November 1964 or voted in the 1964 presidential election and, second, empowered the attorney general to have the Civil Service Commission assign federal registrars to enroll voters. Other parts of the bill required a federal district court in Washington, D.C., to approve all changes in voting procedures in the affected jurisdictions for the next ten years and permitted the court to lift the provisions when a state proved it had not discriminated for ten years.

Implementation began on 10 August when, at the direction of Attorney General Nicholas Katzenbach, federal registrars began registering voters in nine southern counties. By the end of 1965, federal examiners had registered nearly eighty thousand new voters. Many of the affected southern states attempted to use a variety of devices—gerrymandering, at-large elections, more appointive offices, higher qualifications for candidates—to dilute or negate the effect of black voters.

Largely as a result of enforcement of the Voting Rights Act, black registration soared in the South. In Mississippi, for example, black registrants went from 28,500 in 1964 to 251,000 in 1968. The percentage of voting-age blacks registered to vote in the South grew from 43 percent in 1964 to 62 percent in 1968. The larger number of black voters produced more black officeholders and white officials more receptive to black constituents.

In 1966 the U.S. Supreme Court upheld the Voting Rights Act in *South Carolina v. Katzenbach** and *Katzenbach v. Morgan.** Congress renewed the Voting Rights Act in 1970, 1975, and 1982.

SELECTED BIBLIOGRAPHY

David J. Garrow, *Protest at Selma: Martin Luther King, Jr., and the Voting Rights Act of 1965* (1978); Steven F. Lawson, *Black Ballots: Voting Rights in the South, 1944–1969* (1976); Frank R. Parker, *Black Votes Counts: Political Empowerment in Mississippi after 1965* (1990).

Charles W. Eagles

W

WAGNER-GAVAGAN ANTILYNCHING BILL (1940). In their continuing fight against mob violence directed toward black Americans, the NAACP* supported the Wagner-Gavagan antilynching bill, the third such major bill to come before the Congress. In 1921 the NAACP had supported the Dyer antilynching bill and, although it passed the House, the bill was defeated in the Senate by a combination of southern resistance and Republican indifference. In 1935 the NAACP supported the Costigan-Wagner Antilynching Bill.* In its support the NAACP released a pamphlet on the Claude Neal* lynching, which had taken place in 1934. The pamphlet detailed Neal's castration, his mutilation with hot irons, and finally his lynching. Although it aroused some passion in Congress and around the nation, the Costigan-Wagner bill met the same fate as the Dyer bill: southern resistance and Republican indifference in the Senate. Again, in 1940, the NAACP supported a bill, this time the Wagner-Gavagan bill. The bill would ensure that, if the state did not take actions against the perpetrators of lynchings, the federal government would intervene. The bill received widespread support in the North. However, President Franklin D. Roosevelt gave the bill only lukewarm support. Southern resistance this time, teamed up with Democratic indifference, meant a defeat for the bill.

SELECTED BIBLIOGRAPHY

Charles F. Kellogg, *NAACP: A History of the National Association for the Advancement of Colored People* (1967); Robert L. Zangrando, *The NAACP Crusade against Lynching, 1909–1950* (1980).

Kenneth W. Goings

WALKER, ALICE (9 February 1944, Eatonton, Ga.–). Since 1968 this poet, novelist, essayist, editor, biographer, social activist, and "womanist" has won critical acclaim as a major American writer and has been awarded both the Pulitzer Prize and the American Book Award for *The Color Purple* and honored with numerous other fellowships and awards. As a student in the 1960s at Spelman College, in Atlanta, Georgia, where she was actively involved in the civil rights movement, and later at Sarah Lawrence College, in Bronxville, New York (B.A., 1965), she came to poetic maturity in the climate of civil rights activism. This period was vital to Walker's personal and artistic growth, for it allowed her to find her artistic, spiritual, and political identity: a commitment to and strong identification with the South and the whole survival of her people. Alice Walker's insistence that the writer be actively involved and politically committed gives her works a depth of understanding of the human condition and of the spiritual significance of the black experience.

SELECTED BIBLIOGRAPHY

Harold Bloom, ed., *Alice Walker* (1989); Elliott Butler-Evans, "History and Genealogy in Alice Walker's *The Third Life of Grange Copeland*," in *Race, Gender and Desire* (1989); Klaus Enssler, "Collective Experience and Individual Responsibility in Alice Walker's *The Third Life of Grange Copeland*," in *Afro-American Novel since 1960* (1982); Trudier Harris, "Folklore in the Fiction of Alice Walker: A Perpetuation of Historical and Literary Tradition," *Black American Literature Forum* 2 (Spring 1977), 3–8; Mary Helen Washington, "Black Women: Myth and Image Maker," *Black World* 23 (August, 1974), 10–18.

Jacquelyn Jackson

WALKER, MADAME C. J. (23 December 1867, Delta, La.–25 May 1919, Irvington, N.Y.). Sarah Breedlove was born to sharecroppers in 1867. She was orphaned at six, married at fourteen, and widowed at twenty with one daughter, A'Leila. In 1905, working as a washerwoman in St. Louis, Missouri, she created hair growers and straighteners for African Americans. She then moved to Denver, Colorado, where she married newspaperman Charles Walker and established a mail-order business which flourished. Calling herself Madame C. J. Walker, she established an office in Pittsburgh, Pennsylvania, and in Indianapolis, Indiana. She founded labs and training schools for "Walker agents" who sold her products across the United States. She employed over 3,000 people, mostly women, and supported philanthropic and educational efforts. She founded scholarships for women at Tuskegee Institute* and elsewhere, and she supported the NAACP* and black philanthropies. In 1914 she moved to New York. In 1917 she built Villa Lewaro on the Hudson River, designed by black architect Vertner Tandy. Her house in Harlem, the "Dark Tower," became after her death a meeting place for black and white artists and intellectuals, presided over by her daughter. She died in Irvington in 1919, leaving the bulk of her million-dollar estate to her daughter, with generous bequests to several educational and philanthropic causes.

SELECTED BIBLIOGRAPHY

Crisis 18 (July 1919), 131; Walter Fisher, "Madame C. J. Walker," in *Notable American Women* (1971), 533–35; *Dictionary of American Biography* (1936); Rayford W. Logan, and Michael R. Winston, *Dictionary of American Negro Biography* (1982); Obituary, *New York Times*, 26 May 1919, 15.

Cheryl Greenberg

WALKER, MARGARET. *See* Alexander, Margaret Walker.

WALKER v. CITY OF BIRMINGHAM, 388 U.S. 307 (1967). In this decision, a divided U.S. Supreme Court ruled that injunctions against protests were to be challenged in the courts and not defied in the streets. The case stemmed from the arrests of Martin Luther King, Jr.,* A. D. King,* Ralph Abernathy,* and Wyatt Tee Walker* in Birmingham, Alabama, on Good Friday, 12 April 1963. Unlike the Albany, Georgia, sit-ins,* in which Martin Luther King had obeyed a federal court injunction that prohibited marches— and by doing so ended the protests and lost the creative tension necessary for reform—in Birmingham, he violated state circuit Judge William A. Jenkins's ex parte temporary injunction against "unlawful street parades, unlawful processions, unlawful demonstrations, unlawful boycotts, unlawful trespasses, and unlawful picketing or other like unlawful conduct." This marked a turning point in King's life. Henceforth he decided to violate unjust laws and risk arrest. While incarcerated, King wrote "Letter from Birmingham Jail,"* and President John F. Kennedy intervened on his behalf. Disobeying the injunction, the Birmingham Confrontation* continued as the Southern Christian Leadership Conference* led the demonstrations that ultimately forced the federal government to support the movement. As a result, the Kennedy administration proposed the civil rights bill of 1963. Sustaining the Alabama Supreme Court ruling in *Walker v. City of Birmingham,** the U.S. Supreme Court diminished greatly the constitutional protection afforded protestors under the Bill of Rights. Five of the justices ruled that petitioners must appeal the issuance of the injunction and not a contempt conviction. Thus until properly challenged, a court injunction remained the law. Chief Justice Earl Warren and Justices William J. Brennan, William O. Douglas, and Abe Fortas dissented, arguing that the delay created by the appeals process against a clearly unconstitutional injunction violated the petitioners' First Amendment rights. The Walker ruling was immediately used to stifle student protest, and it ushered in a new era of law and order.

SELECTED BIBLIOGRAPHY
The American University Law Review 17 (1967), 113–19; David J. Garrow, Bearing the Cross: Martin Luther King, Jr. and the Southern Christian Leadership Conference (1986); "The Supreme Court, 1966 Term—Civil Rights," Harvard Law Review 81 (1967), 141–46; Alan F. Westin and Barry Mahoney, The Trial of Martin Luther King (1974).

Glenn T. Eskew

WALKER, WYATT TEE (16 August 1929, Brockton, Mass.–). As first permanent executive director of the Southern Christian Leadership Conference* (SCLC), Walker assumed the task of turning the new movement, based on nonviolent resistance,* which was under the leadership of Martin Luther King, Jr.,* into a prominent, permanent civil rights organization. During his tenure (1960–1964), Walker developed an effective civil rights bureaucracy and hired a talented staff, including Walter Fauntroy, who became director of the Washington, D.C., bureau. After graduating from Virginia Union University with B.S. and M.Div. degrees, Walker had pastored the historic Gillfield Baptist Church in Petersburg, Virginia, had served as the chairman of the local NAACP* and Virginia director of the Congress of Racial Equality,* and had been an SCLC board member. Under Walker's no-nonsense direction, the SCLC became one of the leading civil rights organizations of the 1960s. However, Walker's greatest asset also proved to be a liability. His heavy-handed leadership caused staff tensions and morale problems. After a series of impasses, Walker resigned to help publish a black history series for the Negro History Library. In 1975 he received the D.Min. degree from Colgate Rochester School of Divinity and published "Somebody's Calling My Name": Black Sacred Music and Social Change.

SELECTED BIBLIOGRAPHY
Lerone Bennett, Jr., What Manner of Man: A Biography of Martin Luther King, Jr. (1976); Adam Fairclough, To Redeem the Soul of America: The Southern Christian Leadership Conference and Martin Luther King, Jr. (1987); David J. Garrow, Bearing the Cross: Martin Luther King, Jr., and the Southern Christian Leadership Conference (1986); David Levering Lewis, King: A Critical Biography (1970); Willie C. Matney, ed., Who's Who among Black Americans, 1977–1978, 2d ed. (1978); Stephen B. Oates, Let the Trumpet Sound: The Life of Martin Luther King, Jr. (1982).

Lawrence H. Williams

WALTERS, ALEXANDER (1 August 1858, Bardstown, Ky.–2 February 1917, New York, N.Y.). Twenty-fourth bishop of the African Methodist Episcopal (A.M.E.) Zion Church, Walters, the sixth of eight children, was born of slave parents. He studied at private schools, including a church theological seminary, and he graduated in 1875 as valedictorian of his class. Licensed to preach in 1877, he pastored a number of churches, including the famed Mother A.M.E. Zion Church in New York

City. Rising rapidly in church ranks, he became one of the leaders of his denomination, contributing much to the administration of its affairs and to the extension of its bounds.

The widespread lynchings and other racially repressive acts directed against his people in the South prompted Bishop Walters to sign the call for the formation of the Afro-American League* in 1889. In 1898 the league was merged with the Afro-American Council* under his presidency. Later, Walters joined the Niagara Movement,* which had been organized by W.E.B. Du Bois* in 1905 to fight racial segregation and disenfranchisement. He also helped to found the National Negro Committee in 1909, which, a year later, changed its name to the National Association for the Advancement of Colored People.*

SELECTED BIBLIOGRAPHY
New York Age (11 October 1890); William Jacob Walls, The African Methodist Episcopal Zion Church, Reality of the Black Church (1974); Alexander Walters, My Life and Work (1917); Carter G. Woodson, Negro Orators and Their Orations (1925).

George E. Walker

WAR ON POVERTY. In January 1964 President Lyndon B. Johnson announced that his administration "declares unconditional war on poverty." The Economic Opportunity Act, followed by other legislation, created such programs as the Community Action Programs (CAP), Operation Head Start,* the Job Corps, and Volunteers in Service to America (VISTA) to conduct a multifront assault on poverty entrenched amid plenty in America. To win this war, Johnson appointed Sargent Shriver to head the Office of Economic Opportunity. President Johnson linked the abolition of poverty with the civil rights movement to provide the full benefits of citizenship to African Americans. The war on poverty, which helped millions, expanded the scope and changed the nature of federal spending on social welfare, but it failed to eliminate poverty.

SELECTED BIBLIOGRAPHY
Roger Friedland, "Class Power and Social Control: The War on Poverty," Politics and Society 6 (1976), 459–89; Sar A. Levitan and Robert Taggart, The Promise of Greatness (1976); Allen J. Matusow, The Unraveling of America: A History of Liberalism in the 1960s (1984); Charles Murray, "The War on Poverty, 1965–1980," The Wilson Quarterly 8 (Autumn 1984), 95–136; John E. Schwarz, America's Hidden Success: A Reassessment of Twenty Years of Public Policy (1983).

Lorenzo Crowell

WARD v. REGENTS OF THE UNIVERSITY SYSTEM OF GEORGIA, 2 R.R.L.R. 369, 599 (1957). In 1950 Horace Ward, an African American, was denied admission to the law school of the University of Georgia. After unsuccessful appeals to the law school and the board of regents, Ward sought an injunction in 1952 to prevent the regents from denying his admission on the basis of race. The case was continued when Ward was drafted into the armed forces; it was not taken up again until December 1956. University officials urged that Ward had not been denied admission for racial reasons but because he had failed to file for readmission for later school terms as required by school regulations. Besides, he was presently a student at the Northwestern University Law School. In February 1957 the court declared itself unable to rule on Ward's claim. He had not made any new application since 1950, so the board of regents had thus been unable to review his qualifications and make an admission decision. Ward had further refused to submit character references as required by new board regulations promulgated in 1952. Finally, he had become a law student at Northwestern, thus abandoning his application for admission to the Georgia law school as a first-year student. Ward then asked the Court to retain jurisdiction because he planned to seek admission to the Georgia law school as a transfer student. In March 1957, the Court denied the motion insisting it had already declared its lack of jurisdiction. Since Ward now planned to reapply, this fact indicated that his position in the original motion in refusing to reapply had indeed been proper reason for the Court to dismiss his case. There was no longer an issue over which the Court had jurisdiction. Ward, therefore, was kept out of the Georgia law school on administrative procedural grounds; the true segregation reasons did not have to be utilized.

SELECTED BIBLIOGRAPHY
Jack Greenberg, *Race Relations and American Law* (1959).

John F. Marszalek

WARD v. TEXAS, 316 U.S. 547 (1942). This U.S. Supreme Court case helped clarify the conditions under which a confession becomes involuntary and its admission into evidence becomes a violation of the due process clause of the Fourteenth Amendment.* On the basis of his confession alone, William Ward, a black house servant residing in Titus County, Texas, was convicted in state district court of the murder without malice of Levi Brown, an elderly white man, and sentenced to three years' confinement in the state penitentiary in January 1941. In May 1942 Ward's appeal reached the Supreme Court. An uneducated man, Ward had been arrested at night without a warrant, driven for three days from county to county under continuous interrogation, jailed more than one hundred miles from home, and warned of alleged threats of mob violence against him. He finally said that although he was innocent, he would make any statement desired of him. The Court ruled that ample precedent had established the involuntary character of confessions elicited from ignorant persons who are subjected to protracted questioning, or held incommunicado, or threatened with mob violence, or taken at night to isolated places for interrogation, and that on any one of these grounds Ward's conviction was reversible.

SELECTED BIBLIOGRAPHY

Jack Greenberg, *Race Relations and American Law* (1959); *New York Times*, 2 June 1942; "Recent Decisions," *Virginia Law Review* 29 (1942), 115–16.

Robert A. Calvert

WARING, J. WATIES (27 July 1880, Charleston, S.C.–11 January 1968, New York, N.Y.). An eighth-generation Charlestonian, Waring stands with Richard Taylor Rives,* Frank M. Johnson,* and a few other contemporary southern federal judges who spoke the accent but not the language of segregation. After earning a baccalaureate degree from the College of Charleston in 1900, he studied law on his own, passed the state bar exam, and joined a prominent Charleston law firm. His practice flourished. As an assistant U.S. attorney during Woodrow Wilson's presidency he developed expertise in federal litigation, and in 1942 Franklin D. Roosevelt appointed him to the position of U.S. District Judge for the Eastern District of South Carolina. During his controversial tenure on the federal bench, Waring ended such racially discriminatory practices within his court as white-only jury lists; ruled in favor of equal pay for the state's black and white teachers; and struck down the political basis of white supremacy in South Carolina by ruling, in *Rice v. Elmore** (1947), that the white primary* was unconstitutional. The *Rice* ruling was a major victory for blacks whose Fifteenth Amendment* rights had effectively been thwarted by the white primary. When South Carolina Democratic party officials subsequently tried to get around the ruling by organizing the party by counties into private clubs open only to white Democrats, Judge Waring was incensed. In *Brown v. Baskin* (1948), he issued an injunction on the grounds that the party's actions were "a clear and flagrant evasion of the law." He went on to admonish Democratic officials that his court would not tolerate "further evasions, subterfuges or attempts to get around" the law.

Waring was as great an enemy of segregated schools as he was of the white primary. He encouraged NAACP* officials such as Thurgood Marshall* to make a direct frontal assault on the separate but equal* doctrine in the public schools. When fellow jurists on a three-judge panel upheld the state's segregated school system, Waring vigorously dissented, saying that "Segregation is *per se* inequality." Waring's controversial rulings, together with his numerous public speeches and statements from the bench criticizing southern bigotry, alienated and isolated him from South Carolina's white society. In 1952 he retired from the bench and lived out his life as an "exile" in New York City. Upon his death in 1968, journalist Carl Rowan wrote that "the judge's indestructible monument is the army of Americans who walk a bit more proudly because of the courage he had in interpreting the rules of justice."

SELECTED BIBLIOGRAPHY

Derrick A. Bell, Jr., *Race, Racism and American Law* (1980); J. W. Peltason, *Fifty-Eight Lonely Men: Southern Federal Judges and School Desegregation* (1961); Mark V. Tushnet, *The NAACP's Legal Strategy against Segregated Education, 1925–1950* (1987); Tinsley E. Yarbrough, *A Passion for Justice: J. Waties Waring and Civil Rights* (1987).

Charles D. Lowery

WASHINGTON BEE. See Chase, W. Calvin.

WASHINGTON, BOOKER TALIAFERRO (5 April 1856, Franklin County, Va.–14 November 1915, Tuskegee, Ala.). Educator, founder, and first president of Tuskegee Normal School (Tuskegee Institute*), he was, after the death of Frederick Douglass* in 1895, the most famous black man in America and indisputably the spokesman for his race until his own death in 1915.

Born of a slave mother and white father, Washington received only an informal education before entering Hampton Institute.* There he came under the influence of General Samuel C. Armstrong, who became his mentor and guiding light. There, too, he caught the spirit of helping blacks to help themselves, a spirit which remained with him for the rest of his life. After graduating from Hampton in 1875, Washington taught school for three years and then enrolled at Wayland Seminary in Washington, D.C. Unimpressed by its liberal arts emphasis, he became convinced that Hampton had the best solution for blacks who were taking their first steps as free citizens.

In 1881 Washington was offered the principalship of a normal school to be founded at Tuskegee, Alabama. He shrewdly nurtured the support of the white Alabamians for his school, which he modeled after Hampton. By investing power in the trustees, he kept his school free from direct state intervention. He also relied on sources outside of the state for financial support. During his first year he had an average of thirty-seven students and three faculty members. By 1915 Tuskegee had 1,500 students, 180 faculty—many of them distinguished such as George Washington Carver—and an endowment of $2,000,000.

As early as 1884, Washington indicated his acceptance of the separate but equal* doctrine. When he announced it before the Cotton States and International Exhibition in Atlanta in 1895, he became famous. Frederick Douglass, long the voice of black Americans, had just died. Southern Populists had raised the question of black voting in recent elections. All eyes were on Washington, the one black man who had been invited by southern whites to give an address. When Washington announced, "In

Booker T. Washington, 1908. (Arthur P. Bedou Photographs, Xavier University Archives, New Orleans.)

all things that are purely social we can be as separate as the fingers, yet one as the hand in all things essential to mutual progress," the applause from all sections was deafening. Praise for the speech, which was universal, included praise from later critics, such as T. Thomas Fortune* and W.E.B. Du Bois.* By his stance Washington traded away hard-won civil rights for the promise of economic gain. Popular among whites, his position became increasingly controversial among blacks. Du Bois soon referred to the speech as the "Atlanta Compromise." For the next twelve years, however, Washington was the unchallenged black spokesman. No African American was appointed to federal office without his consent or recommendation. His bases of power were the "Tuskegee Machine," a large network of influential blacks with whom he kept in touch, and the National Negro Business League,* which he controlled from its founding in 1900. His dinner with President Theodore Roosevelt in 1901 raised a storm of protest in the South, but it only gained him further national fame.

At the apogee of his popularity, Washington wrote his own story, *Up from Slavery** (1901), which has become one of the classic American autobiographies and established him as an international figure. Washington remained the undisputed spokesman of his race until the Brownsville, Texas, affray* of 1906. Washington feared the loss of his influence over federal appointments and offered little protest to President Roosevelt's action against the black soldiers involved in the incident. He had always placed his trust in white authority figures and could not reverse his practice at this time. Black voices of protest, heretofore known as the Niagara Movement,* reached a crescendo at Washington's failure, and they soon found a more effective voice in the NAACP.*

Washington fought segregation and discriminatory practices by secretly financing court cases and by writing articles. Some cases were successful, particularly *Rogers vs. Alabama** (1904) and *Bailey v. Alabama** (1911), which struck down Alabama black peonage* laws. Washington also fought a long but losing battle for equality in black public education in the South.

SELECTED BIBLIOGRAPHY

W.E.B. Du Bois, *Dusk of Dawn* (1941); Louis R. Harlan, *Booker T. Washington*, 2 vols. (1972, 1983); *The Booker T. Washington Papers*, 14 vols. (1972–1989); Hugh Hawkins, *Booker T. Washington and His Critics* (1962); Samuel R. Spencer, Jr., *Booker T. Washington* (1955); Booker T. Washington, *Up from Slavery* (1901).

James G. Smart

WASHINGTON (COLORED) AMERICAN. This paper, edited and owned by Edward E. Cooper and published during the years from 1893 to 1904, received sustained financial support from Booker T. Washington.* It espoused a philosophy for African Americans that encouraged economic development, self-help, racial solidarity, civil rights, and political enfranchisement. Washington secretly subsidized the paper to use as a weapon against those who criticized him. He used it to send out Tuskegee Institute* news releases, paying for the cost of their printing. The paper also received advertisements from friends of Washington, and Republican party campaign patronage was distributed through Washington to the paper.

SELECTED BIBLIOGRAPHY

Frederick Detweiler, *The Negro Press in the United States* (1922); August Meier, *Negro Thought in America 1880–1915: Racial Ideologies in the Age of Booker T. Washington* (1963).

Jessie M. Carter

WASHINGTON, D.C., RACE RIOT (1919). In late June and early July of 1919, rumors, fanned by a sensationalist press and general antiblack attitudes, spread throughout the city that white women were under attack by black males. This alleged violence included something as trivial as a black man's accidentally bumping into a white woman. On Friday, 18 July, two black men jostled a white woman, the wife of a sailor. This incident set off a riot which saw sailors and marines, quickly joined by other whites, attacking blacks almost at the very door of the White House. The violence spread into black neighborhoods, and some blacks tried to fight back. The NAACP* and the U.S. Congress bemoaned the rioting, and preparations were begun to bring in federal troops to put down the violence. Blacks grew increasingly frightened and began to arm themselves; there were sporadic attacks on men in uniform. Monday night, 21 July, was a horrible night of white-on-black and black-on-white violence. President Woodrow Wilson called in the secretary of war and made arrangements to call up additional troops. Meanwhile the NAACP worked to calm matters and protect the besieged black citizens. On Tuesday all this activity paid dividends; the level of rioting lessened considerably. On Wednesday morning Secretary of War Newton D. Baker announced that matters were under control. In the aftermath of the riot, there were calls for a stronger police force. Black leaders wanted, instead, a neutral police. The riots showed the depth of the antiblack feeling that existed in the nation's capital and demonstrated that blacks were willing and able to fight back when they found themselves unprotected by the legal authorities.

SELECTED BIBLIOGRAPHY

Joseph Boskin, ed., *Urban Racial Violence in the Twentieth Century*, 2d ed. (1976); Robert T. Kerlin, *The Voice of the Negro, 1919* (1920); *Washington Post*, June and July 1919; Arthur I. Waskow, *From Race Riot to Sit-In, 1919 and the 1960s: A Study in the Connections between Conflict and Violence* (1966).

John F. Marszalek

WASHINGTON, FORRESTER (24 September 1887, Salem, Mass.–24 August 1963, New York, N.Y.). Born in Massachusetts and educated at Tufts, Harvard, and Columbia universities, Washington's career reflected some of the important changes in the twentieth-century black American experience. In 1917, Washington earned his M.A. degree in social work from Columbia while assuming a role in the growth of the National Urban League* (NUL). Executive secretary of the Detroit Urban League prior to World War I, he was later a league organizer in Michigan and Illinois. During the 1920s, he maintained his NUL ties while serving both local and national government in various capacities. In 1927, he became head of the Atlanta University* School of Social Work where he came in contact with Will W. Alexander* of the Commission on Interracial Cooperation.* Due in part to Alexander, Washington joined the Roosevelt administration in 1934 as a race relations adviser to the Federal Emergency Relief Administration and as a participant in an informal group of white and black New Dealers who sought the inclusion of blacks in the New Deal's social and economic programs. Washington left government service after six months because he believed that the Roosevelt administration's policies failed to address the root causes of black economic and social inequality. Although a political moderate, he called for an expanded federal involvement to ensure jobs for skilled and unskilled black workers. Fearful of black dependency on federal relief and welfare, a notion later expressed by more radical critics in the 1960s and 1970s, Washington returned to Atlanta where he felt he could be "of the most service to the needy of my race."

SELECTED BIBLIOGRAPHY

Allen Kifer, "The Negro under the New Deal, 1933–1941," (Ph.D. diss., University of Wisconsin, 1961); John B. Kirby, *Black Americans in the Roosevelt Era* (1980); Charles R. Lawrence, "Negro Organizations in Crisis: Depression, New Deal, World War II" (Ph.D. diss., Columbia University, 1953); Arvarh E. Strickland, *History of the Chicago Urban League* (1966).

John B. Kirby

WATSON v. CITY OF MEMPHIS, 373 U.S. 526 (1963). I. A. Watson, Jr., and other black residents of Memphis, Tennessee, sought declaratory and injunctive relief from the continued segregation of municipal parks and other city-owned recreational facilities. Two-thirds of the sixty-one city playgrounds, thirty of fifty-six recreational areas, eight of twelve community centers, and five of seven golf courses were reserved for whites; the remainder were set aside for black use. While acknowledging that continued segregation of the Memphis municipal facilities was unconstitutional since the *Brown v. Board of Education** decision in 1954, the Tennessee courts agreed to allow Memphis a six-month extension to submit a desegregation plan. On certiorari, Justice Arthur Goldberg, writing for a unanimous Supreme Court, reversed the Tennessee decision. City claims that a proposed slower desegregation process would avert race conflicts, would promote peace, and would enable planning for potential problems were inadequate justifications for invoking the 1955 *Brown** decision, which allowed a "step by step" desegregation of schools to facilitate a smooth transition in a complex environment. With the zoo, art gallery, and boating areas desegregated without incident, constitutional rights under the Fourteenth Amendment* could not be denied simply out of fear of their exercise.

SELECTED BIBLIOGRAPHY

Richard Bardolph, ed., *The Civil Rights Record: Black Americans and the Law, 1849–1970* (1970); George Rossman, "Review of Recent Supreme Court Cases—Segregation," *American Bar Association Journal* 49 (1963), 1124; David A. Strauss, "The Myth of Colorblindness," *Supreme Court Review Annual, 1986* (1986), 99–134.

William A. Paquette

WATTS RACE RIOT (1965). Watts, a small neighborhood in south-central Los Angeles, California, has become symbolic for a series of massive African-American urban uprisings that occurred in the mid-1960s. In terms of magnitude, the Newark, New Jersey, race riot* and the Detroit race riot,* both of which occurred in 1967, were greater in intensity, but the sudden explosion that took place in Los Angeles between 11 and 16 August 1965 remains the significant episode precisely because it was not supposed to have happened in America's paradise city. The oppressive quality of black life, visible in many eastern and midwestern cities by thickly compacted housing projects in deteriorating neighborhoods with poor-quality schools, high unemployment, low-paying jobs, and law enforcement bias, was obscured in Los Angeles by an urban horizontal spread, stuccoed houses with grass lawns, a freeway system that bypassed the section, and the state's self-image of fulfilling the American Dream.

Similar to other urban protests of the period, the event in Watts began inauspiciously during a heat wave with the arrest by white officers of two black men for a minor vehicle violation. Within minutes, however, the police car was surrounded, and reinforcements were subsequently attacked with stones and bottles. The riot then spread to virtually the entire south-central region of the city. After several days of skirmishes between the residents and police and fire departments, the area came under total control of the community, whose people proceeded to loot and firebomb those businesses and professional groups long known for their exploitative practices. Surveys taken after the riot pointed to a high

National Guardsmen fighting one of the dozens of major fires set during the 1965 Watts riot. (UPI/Bettmann.)

degree of resident participation, paralleling that of the other riots as well, and indicating the development of a nationwide ghetto urban consciousness. Approximately 15 percent of the inhabitants (teenagers and older) were active at some point during the week; an additional 35 to 40 percent looked on as lively spectators. Significantly, all of the actions took place *within* the perimeters of the black community.

The riot eventually ended as hundreds of law enforcement personnel from throughout the state and the National Guard surrounded the area. Thirty-four people were killed, mostly blacks, and property damage was estimated at from thirty-five to forty million dollars. The revolt fused a powerful identity within the black community, but the factors that caused the uprising nonetheless persisted.

SELECTED BIBLIOGRAPHY

Kenneth B. Clark, *Dark Ghetto: Dilemmas of Social Power* (1965); Robert Conot, *Rivers of Blood, Years of Darkness* (1967); Hugh Davis Graham and Ted Robert Gurr, *The History of Violence in America* (1969); U.S. Riot Commission, *Report of the National Advisory Commission on Civil Disorders* (1968).

Joseph Boskin

WATTS v. INDIANA, 338 U.S. 49 (1949). On 12 November 1947, Robert A. Watts, a black man, was arrested and held for an alleged criminal assault that had occurred earlier that day. Later that same day, a woman's body was found in the vicinity of Watts's alleged crime. Taken to the Indiana State Police headquarters and kept there for several days in solitary confinement, Watts was interrogated by from six to eight officers in relays for eight or nine hours a day for six days. He confessed. He had not been given a prompt preliminary hearing, had been without friendly or professional aid, had not been advised of his constitutional rights, and had not been given proper food or rest. Watts was convicted, and his appeals were rejected by the Indiana courts. He appealed on a writ of certiorari to the United States Supreme Court. Justice Felix Frankfurter, joined by Justices Frank Murphy and Wiley Rutledge, wrote the majority opinion. The Court held that, in a murder trial in a state court, the use of a confession obtained by relentless police interrogation violated due process under the Fourteenth Amendment,* a decision which allowed the federal courts to restrict severely the states in their administration of criminal justice. Concurring opinions were written by Justices Hugo Black, William O. Douglas, and Robert Jackson. Chief Justice Fred Vinson and Justices Stanley Reed and Harold Burton dissented without comment. Petitioner Watts was represented by attorney Thurgood Marshall.*

SELECTED BIBLIOGRAPHY

William V. Batchelder, "Notes and Comments," *Journal of Criminal Law* 40 (1950), 671–72; "Recent Decisions," *Syracuse Law Review* 1 (1949), 313–15.

William A. Paquette

"WE SHALL OVERCOME." The anthem, slogan, and philosophy of the 1960s civil rights movement, and certainly the best known of the freedom songs, "We Shall Overcome" was based on an old black church hymn. It began as a labor song in the 1940s, spreading from black tobacco workers in South Carolina to the Highlander Folk School* in Tennessee. There future Student Nonviolent Coordinating Committee* activists learned a version whose words and music were copyrighted in 1960 by Zelphia Horton, Frank Hamilton, Guy Carawan, and Pete Seeger. In the early 1960s—first at Nashville, Tennessee, and then at Raleigh, North Carolina—black student demonstrators participating in the sit-in movement ritualized the song with spirited resolve and emotion as a serious and resonant affirmation of their goals. It was an oath of mutual determination and courage. From that spirit, this song became the theme song of the 1963 March on Washington* and the concluding song of all black sit-ins, marches, demonstrations, church meetings, and racial confrontations throughout the South and later the North. A moving and majestic song, "We Shall Overcome" was "the 'Marseillaise' of the movement."

SELECTED BIBLIOGRAPHY

Frank Adams with Myles Horton, *Unearthing Seeds of Fire: The Idea of Highlander* (1975); Taylor Branch, *Parting the Waters: America in the King Years, 1954–63* (1988); Guy Carawan and Candie Carawan, compilers, *Songs of the Southern Freedom Movement: We Shall Overcome!* (1963); Josh Dunson, *Freedom in the Air: Song Movements of the 1960s* (1965); Mary King, *Freedom Journey* (1987); Pete Seeger and Robert S. Reiser, *Everyone Knows Freedom: The Civil Rights Movement in Words, Pictures and Song* (1990).

Jacquelyn Jackson

WEAVER, ROBERT C. (29 December 1907, Washington, D.C.–   ). Raised by middle-class parents in Washington, D.C., Weaver was taught the value of an education and racial self-respect. He earned a scholarship to Harvard, where he came to know black students Ralph Bunche* and William H. Hastie* who remained his friends and allies throughout his career. After graduating cum laude, he earned his Ph.D. in economics from Harvard. At the start of the New Deal, Weaver joined a Harvard colleague, John P. Davis,* in establishing the Joint Committee on National Recovery* which represented black concerns before Congress and the Roosevelt administration. In 1933 Clark H. Foreman,* race relations adviser to Secretary of Interior Harold L. Ickes,* selected Weaver as his assistant. Two years later he succeeded Foreman, and in 1937 he assumed a similar position with the U.S. Housing Authority. During World War II, Weaver worked for a number of government agencies, principally as an expert on black labor and racial issues. From the 1930s on, Weaver's public and professional career focused on black employment, housing, and urban conditions and on the need for more enlightened public and private responses to these circumstances. With Mary McLeod Bethune,* he was a key figure in the Roosevelt administration's Black Cabinet,* and he encouraged black involvement in the federal government. A prolific scholar, his two most important works are *Negro Labor* (1946) and *The Negro Ghetto* (1948).

Weaver left the Roosevelt administration during World War II but returned to government service in 1961 as an administrator for the U.S. Housing and Finance Agency during the Kennedy years. In 1966 he became the first black to head a federal cabinet post when Lyndon B. Johnson appointed him Secretary of Housing and Urban Development. Following the Johnson years, Weaver served for two years as president of Baruch College, in New York City.

SELECTED BIBLIOGRAPHY
John B. Kirby, *Black Americans in the Roosevelt Era* (1980); Nancy J. Weiss, *Farewell to the Party of Lincoln* (1983); Raymond Wolters, *Negroes and the Great Depression* (1970).

John B. Kirby

WESTERN FREEDMEN'S AID COMMISSION. The Western Freedmen's Aid Commission evolved from the Cincinnati Contraband Relief Association (1862), one of the earliest private societies committed to providing for future freedmen. A group dominated by evangelical clergymen withdrew from the latter and organized the commission when their proposal to expand the association's efforts to include educating the freedmen met with opposition. Following the Civil War the commission entered into a close association with the American Methodist Association and maintained its own identity until 1870, when it merged with the Methodist organization.

SELECTED BIBLIOGRAPHY
G. K. Eggleston, "The Works of Relief Societies during the Civil War," *Journal of Negro History* 14 (July 1929), 272–99; Joseph E. Holliday, "Freedmen's Aid Societies in Cincinnati, 1862–1870," *Cincinnati Historical Society Bulletin* 22 (July 1964), 169–85.

Michael S. Downs

WHARTON, CLIFFTON REGINALD (13 September 1926, Boston, Mass.–). Son of the first African-American career diplomat, Wharton entered Harvard at the age of sixteen and graduated with a B.A. in history in 1947 and went on to earn an M.A. at Johns Hopkins in 1948. He worked five years at the American Institute of International Social Development before entering the University of Chicago where he earned M.A. and Ph.D. degrees in economics. Wharton became the first African American to head a major, predominantly white, university when he was appointed president of Michigan State University in 1970. Eight years later he became the first black chancellor of the State University of New York, the largest university complex in the United States. In

Unemployed freedmen such as these stevedores at the Jacksonville, Florida, docks benefited from the help of the Western Freedmen's Aid Commission. (Negro Almanac Collection, Amistad Research Center, Tulane University.)

1987 Wharton assumed the presidency of Teachers' Insurance and Annuity Association (TIAA), the nation's largest independent pension fund.

SELECTED BIBLIOGRAPHY

Detroit News Sunday Magazine, 14 December 1969; "A New Boss Takes Over at Michigan State," *Ebony*, July 1970, February 1987.

Clarence Hooker

WHAT THE NEGRO THINKS. Robert Russa Moton,* Booker T. Washington's* successor at the Tuskegee Institute* and longtime president of the National Negro Business League,* wrote *What the Negro Thinks* in 1928. In it, he addressed white America, citing black advances in education, business, and income and summarized the many forms of discrimination that had made blacks "the most underprivileged group in American Life." Moton struck a conciliatory posture, chiding rather than condemning society. Like his mentor, Washington, he appealed to decency and fair play from the more educated and progressive whites, especially in the South. Segregation, increasingly unacceptable to more radical blacks, might continue "if [it were] equitable and voluntary following the natural lines of social cleavage . . . and [was] the most favorable condition for the development of [black] latent capacities." *What the Negro Thinks* showed practically none of the New Negro movement's* greater militancy. The work reveals the depth of white racism that existed in the 1920s, and it remains a disturbing document.

SELECTED BIBLIOGRAPHY

August Meier, "Booker T. Washington and the Rise of the NAACP," in August Meier and Elliott Rudwick, *Along the Color Line* (1976); August Meier, *Negro Thought in America, 1880–1915: Racial Ideologies in the Age of Booker T. Washington* (1963).

Richard W. Resh

WHEELER, JOHN W. (1847, Lexington, Ky.–5 January 1912, St. Louis, Mo.). A freeborn African American, Wheeler made his contribution to civil rights by representing the interests of his race as a St. Louis politician and newspaper publisher from the 1870s until 1911. A Republican stalwart, Wheeler mobilized black votes for the party but always made it clear that he expected protection of black rights and patronage in return. As publisher of the *St. Louis Palladium*, he consistently echoed the racial philosophy of Booker T. Washington,* while preaching a doctrine of racial solidarity. It is through extant copies of his newspaper (1903–1907) that researchers have an excellent window into the black life of St. Louis.

SELECTED BIBLIOGRAPHY

Lawrence O. Christensen, "The Racial Views of John W. Wheeler," *Missouri Historical Review* 67 (July 1973), 535–47; *St. Louis Palladium*, 10 January 1903–5

October 1907, copies available on microfilm, State Historical Society of Missouri, Columbia, Missouri.

Lawrence O. Christensen

WHITE HOUSE CONFERENCE "TO FULFILL THESE RIGHTS." In June 1965, with most of the legal barriers to racial equality tumbling, President Lyndon B. Johnson proposed a White House Conference on Civil Rights to find affirmative ways to combat the remaining social and economic problems hampering blacks. Scheduled for the fall, it was postponed when a controversial agenda item, based on a report written by Assistant Secretary of Labor Daniel Patrick Moynihan on the pathology of the black family, nearly wrecked the effort. After the subject was scrapped at the insistence of black leaders and a planning session was held in November, Johnson appointed Ben Heineman, a railway executive, to ensure that the conference came off smoothly. The planners drew up a detailed document, "To Fulfill These Rights," and carefully selected the 2,500 participants from across the nation. The militant Student Nonviolent Coordinating Committee* boycotted the proceedings in protest of Johnson's domestic and foreign policies. On 1 and 2 June 1966, the delegates hotly debated the topics of housing, welfare, education, and the administration of justice, but they were not permitted to change the specific contents of the report drawn up in advance. Increasingly stung by criticism from black activists, upset by urban race riots, and preoccupied with the Vietnam War, the president did not give the conference report high priority; nevertheless, several of the recommendations did become the basis for the Civil Rights Act of 1968.*

SELECTED BIBLIOGRAPHY

Steven F. Lawson, *In Pursuit of Power: Southern Blacks and Electoral Politics, 1965–1982* (1985); Harry McPherson, *A Political Education* (1972); Lee Rainwater and William L. Yancey, *The Moynihan Report and the Politics of Controversy* (1967).

Steven F. Lawson

WHITE PRIMARY. The white primary was one of several devices used by southern states to disenfranchise blacks after Reconstruction. Across the South, where impotent Republican parties gave Democrats a monopoly, the white primary excluded blacks from the only elections that mattered, the Democratic primaries. It was justified by the argument that political parties and primaries were private institutions. The first suit that challenged the white primary was brought in Texas in 1923. It was not until 1944, however, after years of litigation and evasive action by legislatures, that the Supreme Court ruled in *Smith v. Allwright** that a primary was an election and, therefore, the white primary violated the Fifteenth Amendment.*

SELECTED BIBLIOGRAPHY
Alfred H. Kelly and Winfred A. Harbison, *The American Constitution: Its Origins and Development* (1970); V. O. Key, Jr., *Southern Politics in State and Nation* (1949); Paul Lewinson, *Race, Class and Party: A History of Negro Suffrage and White Politics in the South* (1932).

Allen Kifer

WHITE v. REGESTER, 412 U.S. 755 (1973). In this case, the U.S. Supreme Court explained how the reapportionment requirements enunciated in *Baker v. Carr* and *Reynolds v. Sims* applied to state legislative districts. This line of cases held that federal congressional districting schemes should produce as close to one-person, one-vote representation as possible. Where precise mathematical equality was not reached, the state was required to provide an acceptable policy justification to explain the discrepancy.

The Texas 1970 reapportionment plan for its state legislative districts provided 150 representatives to be selected from 90 single and multi-member districts. While the ideal representative district would contain 74,645 persons, the actual apportionment varied from 71,597 in the smallest district to 78,943 in the largest district. Consequently, the smallest district was overrepresented 5.8 percent, and the largest district was underrepresented 4.1 percent. The average district deviated from the ideal by 1.8 percent.

The federal district court found the Texas plan unconstitutional under the equal protection clause of the Fourteenth Amendment* because the population was not perfectly apportioned and the court "could discover no acceptable state policy to support the deviation." The U.S. Supreme Court reversed the decision. The majority opinion explained "that state reapportionment statutes are not subject to the same strict standards applicable to reapportionment of congressional seats." The fact that the largest and smallest districts varied from one another by 9.9 percent when compared to the ideal was not sufficient to defeat the plan. Deviations of this size did not even require the state to provide policy justification for the discrepancy as would be required in the designation of federal congressional districts. While the Court implied that larger disparities might require rationalization, the decision provided states with significant latitude in constructing districts for state elections.

SELECTED BIBLIOGRAPHY
Bruce Adams, "A Model State Reapportionment Process: The Continuing Quest for 'Fair and Effective Representation,' " *Harvard Journal on Legislation* 14 (1977), 825–904; Bernard Grofman, Arend Lijphart, Robert McKay, and Howard Scarrow, eds., *Representation and Redistricting Issues* (1981).

Kenneth DeVille

WHITE v. TEXAS, 309 U.S. 631 (1940). This case originated in Livingston, Texas, in 1937 when a white female reported that a black man had raped her. Police in Livingston corralled sixteen black men. The police chief noticed that Robert White, an uneducated farmhand, did not eat well and appeared withdrawn. He decided White committed the crime. On the sixth night of interrogation, White confessed at 3:30 A.M. An all-white jury convicted him, and the court sentenced him to death. Appellant courts affirmed his conviction. Ultimately, the U.S. Supreme Court overturned the conviction under the coerced confession rule. Justice William Douglas explained, "Due process of law, preserved for all by our Constitution, commands that no such practice as that disclosed by this record shall send any accused to his death."

SELECTED BIBLIOGRAPHY

William D. Good, "Burden of Admissability of Confessions [Federal]," *Journal of Criminal Law and Criminology* 31 (1941), 598–600; Jack Greenberg, *Race Relations and American Law* (1959).

                                                                                   Stephen Middleton

WHITE, WALTER FRANCIS (1 July 1893, Atlanta, Ga.–21 March 1955, New York, N.Y.). Reared in a middle-class, African-American family, White graduated from Atlanta University* in 1916. Two years later, the NAACP* appointed him assistant executive secretary at its national headquarters in New York City. Until his fatal coronary thirty-seven years later, he, the NAACP, and the civil rights movement were inseparable. White investigated forty-one lynchings* and eight race riots. His widely publicized findings fueled the association's campaign for federal antilynching legislation from 1918 to the 1950s. His book, *Rope and Faggot: A Biography of Judge Lynch** (1929), became a standard. He achieved further recognition through the Harlem Renaissance,* when he published two novels, *The Fire in the Flint** (1924) and *Flight* (1926), and worked unselfishly to promote the careers of young African-American authors, performers, and artists.

In 1931 White became the executive secretary of the NAACP. He placed the association at the center of an emerging civil rights coalition of civil libertarian, labor, ethnic, church, and women's groups—a coalition with close ties to the New Deal. During the presidential campaign of 1948, the Truman administration embraced the coalition's agenda: antilynching and anti–poll tax* legislation, military desegregation, and a Fair Employment Practice Committee.* White and his associates had made interracial justice a fixture on the national landscape.

Walter White possessed a world vision. He attended the 1921 Pan-African Congress in London and Paris, campaigned for an end to American domination in Haiti, and championed economic development throughout the Caribbean. As a war correspondent, he visited England, North Africa, and Italy in 1944 and the South Pacific in 1945 to monitor the treatment accorded black troops. Serving as advisor to the American delegation to the United Nations, in April 1945 at San Francisco and in autumn 1948 at Paris, White urged the decolonization of Italy's former territories in Africa.

Three of White's six books appeared in the last decade of his life: *A Rising Wind* (1945), *A Man Called White* (his autobiography, 1948), and *How Far the Promised Land?* (published posthumously in 1955). His influence declined after 1949. Cold War hysteria and the conservative posture of the Eisenhower presidential years diverted public attention from civil rights. Still, White remained head of the NAACP, wrote his weekly newspaper columns, hosted a public affairs radio show in New York City, and maintained an exhausting speaking schedule. Nonetheless, a series of NAACP Supreme Court victories from 1944 to 1955 allowed Thurgood Marshall's* reputation to eclipse White's; by the end of 1955, the public had found a new hero in Martin Luther King, Jr.*

SELECTED BIBLIOGRAPHY

Poppy Cannon, *A Gentle Knight: My Husband, Walter White* (1956); Edward E. Waldron, *Walter White and the Harlem Renaissance* (1978); Robert L. Zangrando, *The NAACP Crusade against Lynching, 1909–1950* (1980).

Robert L. Zangrando

WHITTAKER, JOHNSON C. (23 August 1858, Camden, S.C.–14 January 1931, Orangeburg, S.C.). Born a slave on the plantation of the senior James Chesnut, he attended the then integrated University of South Carolina (1874–1876). He was admitted to the United States Military Academy, at West Point, in 1876. Briefly a roommate of the first black West Point graduate, Henry Ossian Flipper,* Whittaker was ostracized by white cadets for his race. On the morning of 6 April 1880, he was found unconscious and bleeding, the result, he said, of the visit of three masked men. Authorities decided he had actually mutilated himself to escape the upcoming June examinations. To clear himself, he demanded a court of inquiry and later a court martial, both of which found him guilty. The U.S. Army judge advocate general reversed the decision, but military authorities separated him from the academy in March 1882 for alleged deficiencies in the June 1880 examination. Whittaker later became a lawyer and a school principal in South Carolina and Oklahoma. His courtroom battles were among the most sensational and widely publicized trials in American history; in them was exemplified the depth of prejudice against black Americans in the post–Civil War era.

SELECTED BIBLIOGRAPHY

John F. Marszalek, "A Black Cadet at West Point," *American Heritage* 12 (August 1971), 30–37, 104–6; John F. Marszalek, *Court Martial: A Black Man in America* (1972).

John F. Marszalek

Faculty of the Colored Normal, Industrial, Agricultural, and Mechanical College of South Carolina, including Johnson C. Whittaker (far right). (From the Collection of John F. Marszalek.)

WHITUS v. GEORGIA, 385 U.S. 545 (1967). Petitioners Phil Whitus and Leon Davis, both convicted of a crime, filed a writ of certiorari with the United States Supreme Court charging racial discrimination in the grand and petit jury selection process in Mitchell County, Georgia. They sought redress under the equal protection clause of the Fourteenth Amendment.* In 1962 on certiorari, the Supreme Court in *Whitus v. Balkcom* vacated an earlier judgment and remanded the case to district court for reconsideration. *Whitus v. Georgia* was a reappeal. Prior to 1965 Georgia county commissioners used white tax-return sheets for white taxpayers and yellow ones for blacks to compile the jury list. Although blacks constituted 45 percent of Mitchell County's population, none had ever been chosen for jury duty. After 1965, tax returns were still segregated, but commissioners selected jurors whom they knew personally. In 1966, of the 2,004 black males in the county, only three of thirty-three prospective grand jurors were black. One was selected to serve with eighteen whites. Of the ninety chosen for petit jury selection, seven were black; however, none of them was selected. Justice Thomas Clark wrote a unanimous Supreme Court opinion which reversed earlier decisions and confirmed racial discrimination when Georgia could offer no explanation for the disparity between the number of blacks on the tax lists and those called. The Supreme Court did not order that petitioners be set free, but rather that they be properly retried.

SELECTED BIBLIOGRAPHY

Derrick A. Bell, Jr., *Race, Racism and American Law* (1980); George Rossman and Rowland L. Young, "Review of Recent Supreme Court Decisions—Juries," *American Bar Association Journal* 53 (1967), 361.

William A. Paquette

WILDER, LAWRENCE DOUGLAS (31 January 1931, Richmond, Va.–). P.B.S. Pinchback* served as acting governor of Louisiana for six weeks in 1872–1873, but he had been elected only to the state senate. William H. Hastie* served as governor in the late 1940s, but that was an appointive post and in the Virgin Islands. Thus, until 1989, when L. Douglas Wilder won the election in Virginia, no African American had ever won a popular election to be the governor of any state. That he did so by only the slenderest of margins masked the fact that, in a state fully 80 percent white, a substantial majority of his support came from white voters. Wilder had earned his undergraduate degree from Virginia Union University in 1951 and his law degree (J.D.) at Howard University* in 1959. In between, he had been awarded a Bronze Star in the Korean War. After a decade of law practice in Richmond, he ran for a seat in the state senate in 1969. The first black candidate to win election to that body in the twentieth century, he won reelection in 1973, 1977, and 1981; by 1976, he had gained the first of three committee chairmanships. Then, in 1985, elected to the office of lieutenant governor, he became the first successful black candidate in a statewide popular election for any legislative or executive post in a southern state since the 1870s. That victory, followed by his gubernatorial win four years later, epitomized the transformation of southern life that the civil rights movement had fostered.

SELECTED BIBLIOGRAPHY

Donald P. Baker, *Wilder: Hold Fast to Dreams, A Biography of L. Douglas Wilder* (1989); Margaret Edds, *Claiming the Dream: The Victorious Campaign of Douglas Wilder of Virginia* (1990); Dwayne Yancey, *When Hell Froze Over: The Untold Story of Doug Wilder, a Black Politician's Rise to Power in the South* (1988).

Peter Wallenstein

WILKINS, ROY (30 August 1901, St. Louis, Mo.–9 September 1981, New York, N.Y.). An African-American civil rights activist, Wilkins served as executive director of the NAACP* from 1955 until his retirement in 1977. He strongly opposed violence and rejected the concepts of Black Power* and black nationalism. He also opposed student demands for all-black departments on college campuses as a "return to segregation and Jim Crow."* Wilkins graduated from the University of

Roy Wilkins with President Lyndon B. Johnson. (Negro Almanac Collection, Amistad Research Center, Tulane University, New Orleans.)

Minnesota in 1923 with a degree in sociology. He also was a talented journalist, having served as night editor of the university newspaper, Minnesota *Daily*, and editor of the St. Paul *Appeal*, a black weekly. After graduation he worked as a newspaperman with the *Kansas City Call*, in Kansas City, Missouri. Life in Kansas City introduced him to rigid segregation. Wilkins was active in the St. Paul and Kansas City chapters of the NAACP. He later became assistant secretary under Walter Francis White,* and from 1931 to 1934 he took investigative assignments in the Deep South which placed his life in jeopardy. When W.E.B. Du Bois,* editor of *Crisis*,* left the NAACP in 1934, the versatile Wilkins replaced him. He jointly held the assistant secretary and editor positions until 1949. Following the death of White in 1955, Wilkins became executive secretary of the NAACP, only the third black to hold that position. Wilkins was a strong proponent of desegregation, protection of voting rights, and equality in jobs, housing, and public accommodations. He participated in the 1963 March on Washington,* the Selma to Montgomery March* (1965), and the Meredith March* (1966), among others. His judgment and opinions were often solicited by American presidents. Wilkins's tenure as NAACP executive secretary (executive director) parallels significant gains in black civil rights: school desegregation, federal antilynching, fair housing, and voting rights legislation.

SELECTED BIBLIOGRAPHY
Joan M. Burke, *Civil Rights: A Current Guide to the People, Organizations, and Events* (1974); Elton C. Fax, *Contemporary Black Leaders* (1970); Edgar A. Toppin, *A Biographical History of Blacks in America since 1528* (1971); Roy Wilkins, *Standing Fast: The Autobiography of Roy Wilkins* (1982).

Wali Rashash Kharif

WILLIAMS, AUBREY (23 August 1890, Springville, Ala.–3 March 1965, Washington, D.C.). Born in Alabama and educated as a social worker at the University of Cincinnati, Williams became head of the University of Wisconsin Conference of Social Work in 1922. Ten years later he joined the staff of the American Public Welfare Association where he worked on behalf of impoverished blacks and whites in Mississippi. In 1933, Harry Hopkins selected Williams to head the southwestern district for the Federal Emergency Relief Administration. In 1935 he was appointed first head of the National Youth Administration (NYA) where he remained until 1943 when the agency was closed by Congress.

Under Williams, the NYA created the Division of Negro Affairs, led by Mary McLeod Bethune.* Working with Bethune, Williams saw to it that blacks were hired to fill NYA supervisory positions at national and state levels and that NYA educational funds went to black students and institutions. Increasingly militant in the cause of civil rights, Williams was a major influence during the 1930s in fostering greater racial understanding among New Deal liberals. He had a particularly strong impact on the racial ideas of Eleanor Roosevelt.* Unlike some white interracialists, his commitment to race equality increased during and after the war years. In 1947 he became president of the Southern Conference Educational Fund (SCEF), one of the few organizations during the Cold War era that opposed segregation and discrimination in the South. Because of his activities, Williams was often branded a "Communist sympathizer" by racist white politicians. Undaunted, he supported the emerging southern civil rights movement and the leadership of Martin Luther King, Jr.,* during the 1950s and 1960s.

SELECTED BIBLIOGRAPHY
Irwin Kilbaner, "The Southern Conference Educational Fund: A History" (Ph.D. diss., University of Wisconsin, 1971); Thomas A. Krueger, *And Promises to Keep* (1967); John Salmond, *A Southern Rebel* (1983); Morton Sosna, *In Search of the Silent South* (1977).

John B. Kirby

WILLIAMS, GEORGE WASHINGTON (16 October 1849, Bedford Springs, Pa.–2 August 1891, Blackpool, England). From his humble upbringing in the backwoods of western Pennsylvania, Williams became a soldier, theologian, journalist, lawyer, politician, and scholar. He was the first historian committed to a serious, scientific investigation of

African and African-American history. His life epitomized the African-American struggle for individual and community achievement. Following five years of military service, Williams graduated from Howard University's* Theological Department in 1874 and became the minister of Baptist churches in Boston, the District of Columbia, and Cincinnati. He served as editor and columnist for two newspapers between 1875 and 1878. He studied law in 1878, entered Ohio politics in 1879, and frequently traveled in Europe and Africa from 1884 until his death in England in 1891. In all his careers, Williams was committed to the study of African-American history. A prodigious researcher and prolific writer of books, speeches, newspaper columns, pamphlets, and articles, Williams's illumination of African-American history has earned him the title, "Grandfather of Afro-American History."

SELECTED BIBLIOGRAPHY

John Hope Franklin, *George Washington Williams: A Biography* (1985); John Hope Franklin, *George Washington Williams: The Massachusetts Year* (1983); George Washington Williams, *History of the Negro Race in America from 1619 to 1880*, 2 vols. (1883); George Washington Williams, *A History of the Negro Troops in the War of the Rebellion, 1861–1865* (1887).

Lillie Johnson Edwards

WILLIAMS, HOSEA LORENZO (5 January 1926, Attapulgus, Ga.–   ). The son of blind African-American parents, Williams survived a troubled, violent youth and military service in World War II. Educated at Morris Brown College and Atlanta University,* both in Atlanta, Georgia, he was employed by the U.S. Department of Agriculture as a research chemist in Savannah. By 1961 he was a controversial activist in the local NAACP* chapter. In 1963 Williams moved to Atlanta to join the staff of Martin Luther King, Jr.,* at the Southern Christian Leadership Conference.* Because of his ability to organize and embolden constituencies at the grass roots with his fiery rhetoric and forceful personality, and because of his supervision of voter registration efforts in the South, he was arrested on 124 occasions. He led marchers who were brutally assaulted by state troopers near the Edmund Pettus Bridge outside Selma, Alabama, on 7 March 1965 (see Selma to Montgomery March). Williams was elected to the Georgia General Assembly in 1974. He publicly endorsed Ronald Reagan for U.S. President in 1980; he was elected to the Atlanta City Council in 1985; he led a march in Forsyth County, which resulted in a violent confrontation with the Ku Klux Klan in 1987; and he lost a bid to become mayor of Atlanta in 1989.

SELECTED BIBLIOGRAPHY

Atlanta Journal, 24 May 1981; Joan M. Burke, *Civil Rights: A Current Guide to the People, Organizations, and Events* (1974); John D'Emilio, ed., *The Civil Rights Strug-*

gle: Leaders in Profile (1979); William C. Matney, ed., *Who's Who among Black Americans* (1990).

Robert Fikes, Jr.

WILLIAMS, ROBERT F. (1925, Monroe, N.C.–   ). A United States Marine veteran, Williams became president of the Union County, North Carolina, NAACP* in 1956. An advocate of armed self-defense, he recruited and drilled his membership. Faced with an unequal county judicial system, he began to urge using violence against violence. The national NAACP suspended him for this call. Falsely accused of kidnapping a white couple, Williams and his wife fled to Cuba in 1961. From there he published a monthly newsletter, *The Crusader*, and became chairman of the Revolutionary Action Movement,* a small militant group of college-educated youth. In 1969 he returned to the United States but charges were not dropped until 1976.

SELECTED BIBLIOGRAPHY

James Forman, *The Making of Black Revolutionaries* (1985); James A. Geschwender, ed., *The Black Revolt* (1971).

Ray Branch

WILLIAMS v. MISSISSIPPI, 170 U.S. 213 (1897). In the late nineteenth century, political leaders in Mississippi tried to find a way to circumvent black voting without violating the Fifteenth Amendment.* The result was the state's constitution of 1890, soon widely imitated across the South. The new constitution and subsequent statutes provided that the would-be voter must have paid a poll tax* for at least the previous two years. Further, a voter had to be literate or else show his ability to interpret a section of the state constitution when it was read to him. White registration officials had full power to decide whether a black applicant's performance on the literacy or understanding test was sufficient. *Williams v. Mississippi* was the Supreme Court's first major ruling on the constitutionality of the legal devices used to effect black disenfranchisement in the late nineteenth century. The Court ruled that, because the Mississippi constitution did not mention race and because the poll tax and literacy test on their face applied equally to blacks and whites, Mississippi's constitution and statutes were not in conflict with the Fifteenth Amendment. The Court's decision made it clear that the Fifteenth Amendment would be a dead letter in the South for many years to come.

SELECTED BIBLIOGRAPHY

Richard Bardolph, ed., *The Civil Rights Record: Black Americans and the Law, 1849–*

1970 (1970); John Braeman, *Before the Civil Rights Revolution: The Old Court and Individual Rights* (1988).

Stephen Cresswell

WILLIS AND KENNEDY v. PICKRICK RESTAURANT, 243 F. Supp. 179 (N.D. Ga. 1964). After three African-American citizens were refused service at a restaurant in Atlanta, Georgia, they filed suit seeking an injunction restraining the Pickrick Restaurant from violating the provisions of the Civil Rights Act of 1964.* Deeming the case one of "general public importance," Attorney General Robert F. Kennedy, under Section 204 of the Civil Rights Act, intervened in the case on the side of the plaintiffs. Lester Maddox, the owner of Pickrick Corporation, contended that the Civil Rights Act of 1964 was unconstitutional. When the constitutionality of the act was upheld in *Heart of Atlanta Motel, Inc. v. United States*,* the Court ordered Maddox to desegregate his restaurant. He closed the restaurant for a brief period of time and then reopened it as the Lester Maddox Cafeteria. On 5 February 1965 the Court found Lester Maddox bound by the original court order to desegregate. He was found guilty of civic contempt for refusing to serve African-American customers. Future contempt charges would result in a $200 fine per day from the date the court order was entered. Choosing not to desegregate, Lester Maddox closed his establishment. This case showed that the judicial system and the federal government were willing to intervene to uphold the provisions of the Civil Rights Act of 1964.

SELECTED BIBLIOGRAPHY

Atlanta Constitution, 6 February 1965; Bruce Galphin, *The Riddle of Lester Maddox* (1968); Lester Maddox, *Speaking Out: The Autobiography of Lester Maddox* (1975); *Race Relations Law Reporter* 9 (1964), 912–18, 1434–38; *Race Relations Law Reporter* 10 (1965), 353–58.

David A. Harmon

WILSON, BUTLER ROLAND (22 July 1860, Greensboro, Ga.–31 October 1939, Boston, Mass.). Lawyer and civil rights leader, Wilson was educated in the public schools of his small hometown near Atlanta and at Atlanta University,* where he excelled in public speaking. In 1881 he moved to Boston and enrolled in the Boston University School of Law. He became a close friend of Harvard University Law School's second black graduate, Archibald Grimke.* Together they edited the local black newspaper, *The Hub*, during the mid-1880s. After graduating from law school in 1884, Wilson established a successful private criminal law practice in Boston. He soon was involved with Grimke as joint counsel for an African American who had been denied admission to a local skating rink because of his race. They won their discrimination suit in the lower court only to have it lost by dismissal in the higher court. This defeat intensified Wilson's life-long mission to protect and extend the civil rights of blacks. In 1893 he initiated action that resulted in the passage of a Massachusetts statute enlarging these rights by giving blacks access to public facilities and businesses that had previously been closed to them.

A vocal member of the Boston "radicals," which included Grimke and Monroe Trotter,* Wilson was a sharp critic of the accommodationist philosophy espoused by Booker T. Washington.* He was one of the originators of the Niagara Movement* and a founder of the Boston branch of the NAACP,* which he served first as executive secretary and then as president from its founding in 1912 until a few short years before his death. As the leader of this organization his voice could be heard far beyond Boston as he denounced racial discrimination of every type and championed the civil rights of blacks. In 1912 Wilson was one of the first two African Americans to gain admission to the American Bar Association.

SELECTED BIBLIOGRAPHY

Clarence G. Contee, "Butler R. Wilson and the Boston NAACP Branch," *The Crisis* 81 (December 1974), 346–48; John Daniels, *In Freedom's Birthplace* (1941); Stephen R. Fox, *The Guardian of Boston, William Monroe Trotter* (1970).

Charles D. Lowery

WINSTON-SALEM (N.C.) SIT-IN. Carl Matthews, Jr., "beat the students to the punch" and sat-in at the S. H. Kress Company lunch counter on 8 February 1960. Sit-ins had been planned by Winston-Salem State University students. Within hours, twenty-five students had joined Matthews who stated that he wanted "to test the authority of the All-American City." By 9 February lunch counter sit-ins were being staged all over the city. Mass meetings in the African-American community began on the evening of 12 February. By April all the city's lunch counters were closed and did not reopen on a desegregated basis until 25 May 1960.

SELECTED BIBLIOGRAPHY

Aingred G. Dunston, "Black Struggle for Equality in Winston-Salem, North Carolina: 1947–1977" (Ph.D. diss., Duke University, 1981); Aldon D. Morris, *Origins of the Civil Rights Movement: Black Communities Organizing for Change* (1984).

Aingred G. Dunston

WISDOM, JOHN MINOR (17 May 1905, New Orleans, La.–). Born into a prominent New Orleans family, Wisdom was educated at Washington and Lee University (A.B. 1925) and Tulane University (LL.B. 1929). After graduating first in his law class, he established a successful private practice in his home town, specializing in trusts and estates and teaching part time at the Tulane law school. Convinced that the South would never enjoy a robust, democratic political and social order without a two-party system, he devoted much time in the 1940s and 1950s trying to organize a viable Republican party in Louisiana. This effort brought him into association with like-minded men such as Elbert P. Tuttle* of Georgia and attracted the attention of national Republican leaders. In 1957 President Dwight D. Eisenhower appointed him to the U.S. Fifth Circuit Court of Appeals.*

Widely read in the fields of history, literature, and political philosophy, Wisdom was the intellectual leader of the Fifth Circuit Court. He quickly aligned himself with the court's liberal integrationist bloc, which included his old friend Elbert P. Tuttle, Richard T. Rives,* and John Robert Brown.* These four men, irrevocably committed to justice and equality for all under the law, made the Fifth Circuit Court one of the most effective instruments for social change in the embattled South of the 1950s and 1960s. With Wisdom providing much of the intellectual context, the Court blazed a new trail in civil rights law. It translated the Supreme Court's 1954 *Brown v. Board of Education** decision into a broad mandate not just to dismantle the dual school system, but also to strike down barriers of discrimination in voting, employment, and jury selection. Many of the landmark civil rights decisions handed down by the Appeals Court bear Wisdom's strong imprint—careful craftsmanship, intellectual vigor, scholarly opinions rich in historical and legal analyses. In the area of race relations law, Wisdom was the voice of the Fifth Circuit Court of Appeals, and that voice resonated throughout the South and the nation.

SELECTED BIBLIOGRAPHY

Deborah J. Barrow and Thomas G. Walker, *A Court Divided: The Fifth Circuit Court of Appeals and the Politics of Judicial Reform* (1988); Jack Bass, *Unlikely Heroes* (1981); Harvey C. Couch, *A History of the Fifth Circuit, 1891–1981* (1984); Frank T. Read and Lucy S. McGough, *Let Them Be Judged: The Judicial Integration of the Deep South* (1978); J. W. Peltason, *Fifty-Eight Lonely Men, Southern Federal Judges and School Desegregation* (1961).

Charles D. Lowery

THE WOMAN'S ERA. This periodical, the first to be owned and published by African-American women, was edited by Josephine St. Pierre Ruffin* of Boston; the first issue was dated 24 March 1894. Referred to as both a newspaper and a magazine, *The Woman's Era* focused on the activities of black women's clubs and organizations with particular emphasis on racial advancement, civil rights, and the vote for women. With the creation of a national network of black women's clubs, *The Woman's Era* expanded beyond the Northeast and included states of the far West and the Deep South, but by the end of the century it had ceased publication.

SELECTED BIBLIOGRAPHY
Robert L. Allen, *Reluctant Reformers: Racism and Social Reform Movements in the United States* (1975); Penelope L. Bullock, *The Afro-American Periodical Press: 1838–1900* (1981); Paula Giddings, *When and Where I Enter: The Impact of Black Women on Race and Sex in America* (1984); Gerda Lerner, ed., *Black Women in White America: A Documentary History* (1972); Wilson Jeremiah Moses, *The Golden Age of Black Nationalism* (1978).

Willi Coleman

WOODSON, CARTER GODWIN (19 December 1875, New Canton, Va.–3 April 1950, Washington, D.C.). An African-American educator and historian, Woodson received his secondary education at Fayette, Virginia. He earned his B.A. and M.A. degrees at the University of Chicago and his Ph.D. at Harvard in 1912. Woodson travelled to North Africa, Europe, and Asia before completing his doctorate. His travel, study, and research experience taught him that American historians ignored black contributions to America's development. He and others decided to form the Association for the Study of Afro-American Life and History* in 1915. The association published its first issue of *The Journal of Negro History** in 1916. While Woodson served as chief editor of the journal, he was also the dean of the College of Arts and Sciences at Howard University.* In 1920 he left Howard to become dean of West Virginia Collegiate Institute. While in West Virginia, Woodson founded the Associated Publishers to help young black scholars publish their works. In 1922 Woodson decided to resign his deanship at West Virginia to concentrate on black-related research. His important works on blacks include *Education of the Negro prior to 1861* (1915), *A Century of Negro Migration* (1918), *The Negro in Our History* (1922), and *The Mind of the Negro as Reflected in Letters Written during the Crisis* (1926). No wonder that Woodson is called the Father of Black History.

SELECTED BIBLIOGRAPHY
Lorenzo J. Greene, *Working with Carter G. Woodson, the Father of Black History: A Diary, 1928–1930* (1989); Mary Anthony Scally, *Carter G. Woodson: A Bio-Bibliography* (1985); Mary Anthony Scally, *Walking Proud, the Story of Dr. Carter G. Woodson* (1989); Earl E. Thorpe, *Black Historians* (1971).

Amos J. Beyan

WORK, MONROE NATHAN (15 August 1866, Iredell County, N.C.–2 May 1945, Tuskegee, Ala.). An African-American sociologist who collected and disseminated information on the history of black peoples in order to empower them, Work received baccalaureate and master's degrees from the University of Chicago. As director of the Department of Records and Research at Tuskegee Institute,* Work kept annual tabulations on lynchings of African Americans and edited *The Negro Year Book*. In 1928 he published the *Bibliography of the Negro*, a seminal reference book. In 1945 Work began research on his most ambitious project, unpublished due to his death, entitled "A Bibliography of European Colonization, and the Resulting Contacts of Peoples, Races, Nations and Culture."

SELECTED BIBLIOGRAPHY
Robert J. Norrell, *Reaping the Whirlwind: The Civil Rights Movement in Tuskegee* (1985); Anne Kendrick Walker, *Tuskegee and the Black Belt: A Portrait of a Race* (1944); *Who Was Who in America, 1943–1950* (1950); Linda O. McMurry, *Recorder of the Black Experience: A Biography of Monroe Nathan Work* (1985).

Nancy E. Fitch

WRIGHT, J. SKELLY (14 January 1911, New Orleans, La.–6 August 1988, Westmorland Hills, Md.). A self-acknowledged judicial activist, educated at Loyola University in New Orleans, J. Skelly Wright was appointed to the federal bench in 1949. As a district judge he ordered the admission of black students to the Louisiana State University (LSU) School of Law on the grounds that the law facilities the state provided for blacks at Southern University were not equal. Soon afterward he ordered LSU to admit a black undergraduate for the same reason. These rulings, both of which preceded *Brown v. Board of Education,** made Wright unpopular with white Louisianians. In 1956 he was part of a three-judge panel which, in *Bush v. Orleans Parish School Board,** struck down Louisiana's public school segregation laws. Then, in what was the first such action undertaken by a federal judge in the Fifth Judicial Circuit, he instructed the New Orleans school board to desegregate all of its public schools "with all deliberate speed." Delays followed and finally, in May 1960, Wright set a date in September to begin desegregation of the public schools. A major confrontation followed between Wright and state officials, who were determined to maintain segregated schools. With the support of the United States Court of Appeals for the Fifth Judicial Circuit* and the U.S. Justice Department, Wright faced down the state officials and successfully integrated New Orleans public schools. In addition to abolishing the dual school system, he desegregated the parks and city buses of New Orleans and championed voting rights for blacks. Because of his unwavering enforcement of *Brown v. Board of Education** in Louisiana, including the issuance of numerous injunctions against the state legislature's obstructive efforts, Senator Russell Long prevented his elevation from federal district judge to the Court of Appeals for the Fifth Circuit. He was then appointed to the Court of Appeals for the District of Columbia Circuit where he held de facto segregation in Washington, D.C., schools to be unconstitutional. In Louisiana and Washington, he rendered decisions protecting voting rights.

SELECTED BIBLIOGRAPHY
Jack Bass, *Unlikely Heroes* (1981); Michael S. Bernick, "The Unusual Odyssey of
J. Skelly Wright," *Hastings Constitutional Law Quarterly* 7 (1980), 971–99; Arthur
Selwyn Miller, *A "Capacity for Outrage": The Judicial Odyssey of J. Skelly Wright*
(1984); J. W. Peltason, *Fifty-Eight Lonely Men: Southern Federal Judges and School
Desegregation* (1961); Geoffrey R. Stone, "A Passion for Justice," *Yale Law Journal*
98 (1988), 207–19; J. Skelly Wright, "The Judicial Right and the Rhetoric of
Restraint: A Defense of Judicial Activism in an Age of Conservative Judges,"
Hastings Constitutional Law Quarterly 14 (1987), 487–523.

Patricia A. Behlar

WRIGHT, RICHARD (4 September 1908, Roxie, Miss.–28 November
1960, Paris, France). From his birth on a Mississippi plantation to his
death in Paris, Richard Wright was a man plagued by hunger for the
acceptance and recognition of one's humanity that a racist society seeks
desperately to deny. After a deprived childhood, which included minimal formal education, Wright migrated to Chicago in 1927. In the
Depression years he worked at various odd jobs until he found employment with the Federal Theater Project and the Federal Writers' Project. He also became a member of the John Reed Club, which promoted
the publication of his proletarian poetry in such magazines as *Left Front,
The Anvil,* and *New Masses.* His association with left-wing literary circles
led him to become a member of the Communist party,* but Wright was
too independent to adhere to the party's regimentation, and he broke
with the party in 1942. Wright's experiment with Marxism, however,
did sharpen his perspective on how to write about racial discrimination
and class problems. In 1937 he moved to New York to work as a journalist
with the Harlem bureau of the *Daily Worker.* In 1938, he won the *Story
Magazine* prize for "Fire and Cloud" and published *Uncle Tom's Children,**
a collection of stories about racial tensions and black resistance in the
rural South. The success of his first book enabled Wright to write *Native
Son** (1940), a portrait of life for a black youth in the Chicago ghettoes,
for which he was awarded the Spingarn Medal* in 1941. He followed
this overwhelmingly successful novel with *Twelve Million Black Voices*
(1941), a folk history, and *Black Boy,** the autobiography that made him
the spokesman for an entire generation of black Americans. With a
passion matched only in the classic slave narratives, Wright sought to
alert the world to the deepest feelings of people shaped and mangled
by racist oppression. Ironically, American racism was more than Wright
could endure, and he chose to exile himself to France in 1947. In the
1950s, Wright was often criticized for having lost any perspective on the
development of civil rights in the United States, especially in *The Long
Dream* (1958), the last book published before his death. Nevertheless,
one could argue that Wright developed a broader view of the struggle
for human rights in the work produced during his European exile. In

The Outsider (1953), *Black Power* (1954), *The Color Curtain* (1956), *Pagan Spain* (1957), and in the essays in *White Man, Listen!* (1957), Wright projects a prophetic vision of the global issues that eventually changed the nature of civil rights activities in the United States.

SELECTED BIBLIOGRAPHY

Russell C. Brignano, *Richard Wright: An Introduction to the Man and His Works* (1970); Michel Fabre, *The Unfinished Quest of Richard Wright* (1973); Addison Gayle, *Richard Wright: Ordeal of a Native Son* (1980); Yoshinobu Hakutani, ed., *Critical Essays on Richard Wright* (1982); Keneth Kinnamom, *The Emergence of Richard Wright* (1972); Margaret Walker, *Richard Wright, Daemonic Genius, A Portrait of the Man, A Critical Look at His Works* (1988); Constance Webb, *Richard Wright: A Biography* (1968).

Jerry Ward

WRIGHT, RICHARD ROBERT, JR. (16 April 1878, Cuthbert, Ga.–12 December 1967, Philadelphia, Pa.). Wright conducted some of the most significant studies of black northern workers done before World War I. After studying theology and sociology at the University of Chicago (B.D., 1901; A.M., 1904), he earned a doctorate in sociology from the University of Pennsylvania in 1911. His social studies were influenced and encouraged by W.E.B. Du Bois.* A political moderate, Wright used his editorship of the African Methodist Episcopal (A.M.E.) Church's *Christian Recorder* (1909–1928) to urge the church to take a more active role in social reform and to promote an increased awareness of black history. He was president of Wilberforce College (1932–1936), in Wilberforce, Ohio, and was elected fifty-seventh A.M.E. bishop in 1936.

SELECTED BIBLIOGRAPHY

Francille R. Wilson, "The Segregated Scholars: Black Labor Historians, 1895–1950" (Ph.D. diss., University of Pennsylvania, 1988); R. R. Wright, Jr., *Eighty-Seven Years behind the Black Curtain* (1965); R. R. Wright, Jr., "The Negro in Times of Industrial Unrest," *Charities* 15 (7 October 1905), 69–73.

Francille Rusan Wilson

WRIGHT, RICHARD ROBERT, SR. (16 May 1855?, Dalton, Ga.–2 July 1947, Philadelphia, Pa.). Slave-born educator, Wright was the principal of Georgia's first black public high school (1880–1890) and the president of Georgia State Industrial College for Negroes (1890–1921). A Republican party activist in the 1880s and 1890s, Wright became a major and an army paymaster during the Spanish American War, but he was simultaneously forced out of state politics by segregationists. Wright thereafter publicly aligned himself and his college with Booker T. Washington,* but, as an alumni trustee of Atlanta University,* he cofounded its research conference in 1896 and urged the hiring of W.E.B. Du Bois.* In 1921 Wright and his family established the Citizens and Southern Bank and Trust in Philadelphia. He lobbied for a postage stamp honoring Booker T. Washington and the establishment of a National Freedom Day to commemorate emancipation.

SELECTED BIBLIOGRAPHY

James D. Anderson, *The Education of Blacks in the South, 1860–1935* (1988); Elizabeth Ross Haynes, *Black Boy of Atlanta* (1952); June O. Patton, "Major Richard R. Wright" (Ph.D. diss., University of Chicago, 1980); Rayford W. Logan and Michael R. Winston, eds., *Dictionary of American Negro Biography* (1982).

Francille Rusan Wilson

Y

YOUNG, ANDREW (12 March 1932, New Orleans, La.–   ). A dynamic clergyman and civil rights leader, with an outstanding record as a public official, Andrew Young attended Dillard University, in New Orleans, Louisiana, before he earned a B.S. degree at Howard University* in 1951 and a B.D. degree from Hartford Theological Seminary in 1955. Active in interracial and civil rights projects since his seminary days, Young joined the staff of the Southern Christian Leadership Conference* (SCLC) in 1961. A skillful strategist and negotiator, Young soon gained prominence as one of Martin Luther King, Jr.'s,* lieutenants. From 1964 to 1970 Young served as the executive director of SCLC and between 1967 and 1970 as the organization's executive vice president as well. He now sits on its board of directors and on the board of the Martin Luther King, Jr., Center for Social Change. In 1972 Andrew Young became the first African American to be elected to the United States House of Representatives since Reconstruction. In 1977 President Jimmy Carter appointed him the first black United States ambassador to the United Nations. Between 1982 and 1990 he served as mayor of Atlanta, but, in 1990, Young lost his bid to become Georgia's first African-American governor.

SELECTED BIBLIOGRAPHY

Hamilton Bims, "A Southern Activist Goes to the House: King Lieutenant Andrew Young Is Declared Winner in Georgia," *Ebony* 28 (February 1973), 83; David J. Garrow, *Bearing the Cross: Martin Luther King, Jr., and the Southern Christian Leadership Conference* (1986); W. Augustus Low and Virgil A. Clift, eds., *Encyclopedia of Black America* (1981); Stephen B. Oates, *Let the Trumpet Sound: The Life of Martin Luther King, Jr.* (1982); Eleanora W. Schoenebaum, ed., *Political Profiles*, vol. 5 (1979).

                                                          Barbara L. Green

YOUNG, CHARLES (12 March 1864, Mayslick, Ky.–8 January 1922, Lagos, Nigeria). An army officer and cartographer, Charles Young was the third African American to graduate (1884–1889) from the United States Military Academy, at West Point. His military career included tours of duty in Haiti, Mexico, the Philippines, and Liberia. In 1916 Young received the NAACP's* annual Spingarn Medal* for his exceptional work in Liberia. In 1917 the army medical board found him unfit for service because of high blood pressure and retired him with the rank of colonel. On 6 November 1918, the army returned him to active duty and shortly thereafter sent him to Liberia. On 8 January 1922, Young died of nephritis in Lagos, Nigeria. He is buried in Arlington National Cemetery. His retirement and various other aspects of his military career remain a source of controversy.

Colonel Charles Young. (Negro Almanac Collection, Amistad Research Center, Tulane University, New Orleans.)

SELECTED BIBLIOGRAPHY
Robert E. Greene, *Black Defenders of America, 1775–1973* (1974); in Rayford W. Logan and Michael R. Winston, eds., *Dictionary of American Negro Biography* (1982).

Barbara L. Green

YOUNG, P.(LUMMER) B.(ERNARD). (27 July 1884, Littleton, N.C.–9 October 1962, Norfolk, Va.). Editor and publisher of the largest black newspaper in the South during the first half of the twentieth century, a member of the Fair Employment Practice Committee,* and a black higher education leader, P. B. Young attended St. Augustine College, in Raleigh, North Carolina, from 1900 to 1906. In 1907 he moved to Norfolk, Virginia, to become a foreman for the *Norfolk Journal and Guide,** the newspaper of the Knights of Gideon. He soon became a part of the city's black elite, and he established a relationship with Booker T. Washington.* In 1910 he bought the *Journal and Guide* from the Gideons. Despite a disastrous fire in 1913, the newspaper grew in circulation and influence. It reflected Booker T. Washington's accommodationist philosophy, which was expressed in Young's slogan, "Build Up, Don't Tear Down." He maintained his conservative approach to race relations all his life. Before and after the *Brown v. Board of Education** decision in 1954 he supported the "equal" in separate but equal* when he spoke to whites and talked of integration to blacks. Politically, he changed from being a fervent Republican to a New Deal Democrat. He was the epitome of the black bourgeoisie, a pillar of the African-American press, and a key spokesman to white society for Norfolk blacks.

SELECTED BIBLIOGRAPHY
Rayford W. Logan and Michael R. Winston, eds., *Dictionary of American Negro Biography* (1982); Henry Lewis Suggs, "Black Strategy and Ideology in the Segregation Era: P. B. Young and the *Norfolk Journal and Guide*, 1910–1954," *Virginia Magazine of History and Biography* 91 (April 1983), 161–90; Henry Lewis Suggs, *P. B. Young Newspaperman: Race, Politics, and Journalism in the New South* (1988); Henry Lewis Suggs, "P B. Young of the *Norfolk Journal and Guide*: A Booker T. Washington Militant, 1904–1928," *Journal of Negro History* 64 (Fall 1979), 365–76.

John F. Marszalek

YOUNG, WHITNEY MOORE, JR. (31 July 1921, Lincoln Ridge, Ky.–11 March 1971, Lagos, Nigeria). Often called the nation's most creative civil rights leader, Whitney Young led the National Urban League* during the height of the civil rights movement. After completing high school at Lincoln Institute, Young attended Kentucky State College and taught briefly before joining the U.S. Army during World War II. He spent 1942–1943 studying engineering at Massachusetts Institute of Technology. His experiences of working with people in the military caused him to decide on a career in the field of race relations. He earned a master's

Whitney Young. (Negro Almanac Collection, Amistad Research Center, Tulane University, New Orleans.)

degree from the University of Minnesota in 1947 and spent the next seven years with the Urban League branch offices in Saint Paul, Minnesota, and Omaha, Nebraska. Then, in 1954, he accepted the deanship of the Atlanta University* School of Social Work. Under his leadership, Atlanta became one of the leading schools of social work in the South. He interrupted his work there in 1960 to accept a Rockefeller grant to study at Harvard. The following year he succeeded Lester B. Granger* as executive director of the National Urban League. During the militant protests of the 1960s, when faced with a choice, business executives preferred to talk to Young rather than to those black leaders they considered more militant. Young took advantage of these opportunities to open jobs for black workers and to build financial support for his organization. By the mid–1960s, the National Urban League's budget had increased from $270,000 to $3 million, and the number of branches had risen from sixty-two to eighty-two. Young realized that this was not enough. In 1963 he proposed that the nation undertake a domestic Marshall plan to help black Americans catch up. He presented a full discussion of his plan in *To Be Equal*. President Lyndon B. Johnson's War on Poverty* owed much to Young's proposal. Young was aware that he and his organization must not lose credibility among black Americans. He insisted that the Urban League participate in the March on Washington* in 1963 and in the other major civil rights events. Although he was reluctant to bring his organization into the Meredith March* in 1966, he did participate in its final phase. He, along with Roy Wilkins* of the NAACP* and Martin Luther King, Jr.,* was slow to embrace the new Black Power* philosophy. When he determined that there were elements of this philosophy that reflected the mood of black Americans, he came to see its positive possibilities. In his book *Beyond Racism: Building an Open Society*, he explained how black power could move the nation toward a more democratic society. Young's brilliant career as a civil right's leader was cut short when he died on 11 March 1971 while attending a conference of American and African leaders in Lagos, Nigeria.

SELECTED BIBLIOGRAPHY

L. E. Lomax, *Negro Revolt* (1963); George R. Metcalf, *Black Profiles* (1968); Guichard Parris and Lester Brooks, *Blacks in the City: A History of the National Urban League* (1971); Edgar A. Toppin, *A Biographical History of Blacks in America since 1528* (1971); *Who Was Who in America* (1973); Nancy J. Weiss, *Whitney M. Young, Jr., and the Struggle for Civil Rights* (1990).

Arvarh E. Strickland

YOUNGE, SAMUEL, JR. (17 November 1944, Tuskegee, Ala.–3 January 1966, Tuskegee, Ala.). This twenty-one-year-old Tuskegee Institute* student and civil rights activist spent 3 January 1966 (the day of his death) working as a voter registration volunteer at the Macon County, Alabama, courthouse. That night he stopped at a service station in town to buy some cigarettes and use the restroom. When attendant Marvin Segrest directed him to a rear bathroom—which Younge believed was a Jim Crow* facility—an argument started. Younge armed himself with a golf club and Segrest picked up his pistol. Segrest fatally shot Younge as the latter ran away from him. The death of the fifth civil rights worker in Alabama since the beginning of the voter registration campaign just a year earlier sparked immediate protest. Tuskegee blacks marched through the rain to the site of Younge's murder. Segrest was arrested, and Mayor Charles Kever promised justice would be done "regardless of race." These words seemed empty when an all-white jury in nearby Lee County determined that Segrest had acted in self-defense and acquitted him of murdering Sammy Younge.

SELECTED BIBLIOGRAPHY

James Forman, *Sammy Younge, Jr.: The First Black College Student to Die in the Black Liberation Movement* (1968); *Montgomery Advertiser*, 5–6 January 1966; Robert J. Norell, *Reaping the Whirlwind: The Civil Rights Movement in Tuskegee* (1985); *Tuskegee News*, 6 January 1966.

William Warren Rogers, Jr.

CHRONOLOGY

1861   First American Missionary Association school for blacks established at Fortress Monroe, Virginia.

First Confiscation Act empowers federal government to confiscate slaves of rebelling Southerners.

1862   Second Confiscation Act passed.

National Freedmen's Relief Association established.

1863   Emancipation Proclamation issued.

New York City draft riots occur.

1864   National Equal Rights League formed.

President Lincoln pocket vetoes Wade-Davis bill.

1865   Thirteenth Amendment outlawing slavery ratified.

Black Codes passed to restrict freedmen.

Freedman's Bank chartered by Congress.

Congress creates the Freedmen's Bureau.

Black conventions meet.

President Andrew Johnson announces restoration of the Union.

Congressional Joint Committee of Fifteen created to examine restoration issue.

1866   Civil Rights Act of 1866 passed by Congress.

Congress passes Fourteenth Amendment granting citizenship to freedmen.

Fisk University founded.

Memphis race riot occurs.

New Orleans race riot occurs.

Southern Homestead Act passed by Congress.

First Reconstruction Act passed over Andrew Johnson's veto.

1867 Peonage Abolition Act passed by Congress.

Atlanta University established by American Missionary Association.

Howard University established.

Morehouse College established.

Peabody Education Fund established.

1868 Fourteenth Amendment ratified.

W.E.B. Du Bois born.

Hampton Institute admits first students.

1869 Congress passes Fifteenth Amendment granting freedmen the right to vote.

Tougaloo College founded in Mississippi by American Missionary Association.

1870 Fifteenth Amendment ratified.

Enforcement Acts passed to protect freedmen in exercising Fourteenth and Fifteenth Amendment rights.

Great Migration of blacks from rural South to urban North begins.

Hiram R. Revels elected to U.S. Senate from Mississippi.

1871 Enforcement Acts passed.

Fisk University's Jubilee Singers conduct fund-raising tour.

1873 Supreme Court's *Slaughterhouse Cases* ruling limits scope of Fourteenth Amendment.

1874 New Orleans race riot occurs.

1875 Congress passes Civil Rights Act of 1875.

1876 Hamburg, South Carolina, race riot occurs.

1877 Compromise of 1877 leads to end of Reconstruction.

1878 Chicago's first black newspaper, the *Chicago Conservator*, is established.

1879 Exodus of southern blacks to Kansas and Southwest begins.

1882 Slater Fund established to aid education for blacks.

1883 Supreme Court's *Civil Rights Cases* strike down Civil Rights Act of 1875.

1886 Colored Farmers' National Alliance and Cooperative Union established.

T. Thomas Fortune founds *New York Age*.

1887 The all-black town of Mound Bayou is founded in Mississippi.

1888 *Indianapolis Freeman* begins publication.

Booker T. Washington opens doors of Tuskegee Institute.

1890 T. Thomas Fortune founds Afro-American League.

Force Bill passed to protect black suffrage.

Lake Mohonk Conference held.

Second Morrill Act passed creating black land-grant colleges.

New Mississippi state constitution becomes model for other southern states.

1891 Second Lake Mohonk Conference meets.

1894 Hampton Conference enhances reputation of Booker T. Washington.

1895 Booker T. Washington delivers Atlanta Compromise Speech.

Frederick Douglass dies.

1896 Supreme Court's *Plessy v. Ferguson* decision enunciates separate but equal doctrine.

W.E.B. Du Bois establishes the Atlanta University Conference for the Study of Negro Problems.

Kowaliga Industrial Community founded.

National Association of Colored Women founded.

1897 T. Thomas Fortune founds the Afro-American Council.

Alexander Crummel founds American Negro Academy.

1898 Grandfather clause written into new Louisiana constitution restricts black suffrage.

Blacks fight in Spanish-American War.

1899 Capon Springs Conference promotes industrial education for southern blacks.

Sam Hose lynching in Georgia.

1900 National Negro Business League formed by Booker T. Washington.

New Orleans race riot occurs.

Norfolk Journal and Guide begins publication.

1901 The African-American protest newspaper *Boston Guardian* established.

Southern Education Board founded to promote education.

Booker T. Washington's *Up from Slavery* published.

Booker T. Washington dines with President Theodore Roosevelt at the White House.

1902 John D. Rockefeller establishes General Education Board to aid education for blacks.

1903   All-black town of Boley, Oklahoma, founded.

1904   At Carnegie Hall Meeting, W.E.B. Du Bois and Booker T. Washington part ways.

1905   Anna T. Jeanes Fund established to improve educational opportunities for southern blacks.

         Chicago Defender is launched.

         Niagara Movement launched by W.E.B. Du Bois and others.

1906   Atlanta race riot occurs.

         Brownsville, Texas, affray occurs.

1907   *Horizon*, journal of the Niagara Movement, begins publication.

1908   Springfield, Illinois, race riot stimulates formation of the National Association for the Advancement of Colored People (NAACP).

1909   New York weekly newspaper *Amsterdam News* founded.

1910   NAACP formally established by W.E.B. Du Bois and others.

         Pittsburgh Courier founded.

         NAACP journal, the *Crisis*, launched.

1911   National Urban League founded.

         Phelps-Stokes Fund established to aid black education.

1915   Carter G. Woodson establishes the Association for the Study of Afro-American Life and History.

1916   *The Journal of Negro History* founded by Carter G. Woodson.

1917   In landmark *Buchanan v. Warley* decision, Supreme Court strikes down residential segregation ordinances.

         East St. Louis race riot and Houston race riot occur.

         Marcus Garvey establishes Universal Negro Improvement Association branch in United States and launches "Back to Africa" movement.

         The radical black newspaper *The Messenger* begins publication.

         Julius Rosenwald Fund established to aid black education.

         Blacks fight in World War I.

1918   The monthly magazine, *The Crusader*, is launched.

1919   Associated Negro Press established.

         During Red Summer, major race riots occur in Charleston, South Carolina; Chicago, Illinois; Knoxville, Tennessee; Omaha, Nebraska; Washington, D.C.; and elsewhere.

         Houston Informer begins publication.

1920   Harlem Renaissance flourishes.

James Weldon Johnson becomes executive secretary of the NAACP.

1921   Marcus Garvey establishes the Black Star Steamship Line.

Antilynching bill introduced in Congress.

1922   Dyer antilynching bill fails in Congress.

Harmon Foundation founded to honor black artistic achievements.

1923   National Urban League begins publication of *Opportunity*.

1925   A. Philip Randolph founds Brotherhood of Sleeping Car Porters and Maids.

Alain Locke's New Negro movement is precursor of black pride.

1926   Negro History Week launched.

1929   Martin Luther King, Jr., born January 15.

Oscar DePriest is elected to Congress, the first black to be elected in the twentieth century.

"Don't Buy Where You Can't Work" movement launched.

"Jobs for Negroes" movement gets under way.

1931   Scottsboro Trials get under way.

1932   *Journal of Negro Education* established at Howard University.

Black voters begin moving into Democratic party.

1933   Black Cabinet advises President Franklin D. Roosevelt on African-American issues.

Joint Committee on National Recovery established to help blacks.

1934   Eleanor Roosevelt entertains Mary McLeod Bethune at White House.

Costigan-Wagner Antilynching Bill fails in Congress.

Claude Neal lynching in Florida.

Elijah Muhammad (Elijah Poole) assumes command of the Nation of Islam.

Arthur W. Mitchell, a black Democrat, is elected to Congress.

1935   Harlem race riot occurs.

National Negro Congress established.

1936   Jesse Owens wins four gold medals at Olympic games in Berlin.

1937   *Negro History Bulletin* founded by Carter G. Woodson.

1938   Supreme Court's *Missouri ex rel. Gaines v. Canada* decision erodes *Plessy* doctrine.

NAACP Legal Defense and Educational Fund established to challenge segregated education.

Southern Conference for Human Welfare founded to promote civil rights.

1939   Civil Liberties Unit (subsequently retitled the Civil Rights Section) is created in the U.S. Department of Justice.

Thurgood Marshall becomes director of NAACP Legal Defense Fund.

1940   Wagner-Gavagan Antilynching Bill fails in Congress.

Phylon founded by W.E.B. Du Bois.

1941   Blacks fight in World War II.

Supreme Court decision *Taylor v. Georgia* strikes blow to black peonage.

A. Philip Randolph launches March on Washington movement.

National Committee to Abolish the Poll Tax formed.

1942   Congress of Racial Equality (CORE) founded.

President Franklin D. Roosevelt's Executive Order 8802 creates Fair Employment Practice Committee.

1943   Detroit race riot occurs.

Harlem race riot occurs.

1944   Supreme Court's *Pollock v. Williams* decision deals death blow to black peonage.

Southern Regional Council founded to improve educational and economic opportunities in the South.

United Negro College Fund established.

Supreme Court in *Smith v. Allwright* strikes down white primary.

1945   Adam Clayton Powell, Jr., begins long congressional career.

1946   President Harry S. Truman's Executive Order 9808 creates the President's Committee on Civil Rights.

1947   CORE sponsors Journey of Reconciliation.

Jackie Robinson breaks the color barrier in major league baseball.

Special report *To Secure These Rights* is released.

1948   President Truman unsuccessfully seeks strong civil rights legislation abolishing poll tax, punishing lynching, and establishing a Fair Employment Practice Commission.

President Truman's Executive Order 9981 integrates armed forces.

President Truman appoints Fahy Committee.

1950 Supreme Court in *Sweatt v. Painter* declares unequal educational facilities for blacks unconstitutional.

1954 *Brown v. Board of Education* abolishes separate but equal doctrine.

1955 *Brown v. Board of Education* II calls for desegregation of public schools with "all deliberate speed."

Montgomery bus boycott catapults Martin Luther King, Jr., into national prominence.

Montgomery Improvement Association founded.

Emmett Louis Till murdered in Mississippi.

Roy Wilkins becomes executive secretary of the NAACP.

1956 Autherine Juanita Lucy enrolls as first black student at the University of Alabama.

Tallahassee, Florida, bus boycott launched.

1957 Civil Rights Act of 1957 passed by Congress.

Civil Rights Commission created.

Civil Rights Division in Department of Justice established.

Martin Luther King, Jr., forms Southern Christian Leadership Conference(SCLC).

President Dwight D. Eisenhower calls on the National Guard to handle Little Rock desegregation crisis.

Durham, North Carolina, sit-ins begin.

1958 Martin Luther King, Jr.'s, *Stride toward Freedom* published.

Taconic Foundation established to help improve the status of blacks.

1960 Civil Rights Act of 1960 passed by Congress.

Greensboro, North Carolina, sit-in begins.

New Orleans, Louisiana, elementary schools integrated by court order.

Student Nonviolent Coordinating Committee (SNCC) founded.

Supreme Court's *Boynton v. Virginia* decision declares segregation in railway and bus terminals unconstitutional.

Nashville sit-ins begin.

Tallahassee, Florida, sit-ins begin.

1961 University of Georgia admits first black students.

Freedom Riders attacked in Alabama and Mississippi.

Martin Luther King, Jr., launches Albany, Georgia, sit-in.

President John F. Kennedy calls for affirmative action to ensure nondiscrimination in awarding government contracts.

Northern Student Movement launched at Yale University.

Leontyne Price debuts at New York Metropolitan Opera.

1962   Council of Federated Organizations (COFO) established.

Voter Education Project launched.

James Meredith integrates the University of Mississippi.

1963   Birmingham Confrontation: black boycotts and demonstrations highlight racial injustices.

March on Washington for Jobs and Freedom.

Martin Luther King, Jr., delivers "I Have a Dream" speech at the Lincoln Memorial in Washington, D.C.

Medgar W. Evers assassinated in Mississippi.

Governor George Wallace "stands in school house door" to block admission of black students to the University of Alabama.

Martin Luther King, Jr., writes "Letter from Birmingham Jail."

Chattanooga Freedom Walk takes place.

1964   President Lyndon B. Johnson declares War on Poverty.

Economic Opportunity Act passed.

Civil Rights Act of 1964 passed by Congress.

Ratification of Twenty-Fourth Amendment abolishes poll tax.

Martin Luther King, Jr., receives Nobel Peace Prize.

Three young civil rights workers—James Earl Chaney, Andrew Goodman, and Michael Henry Schwerner—are murdered near Philadelphia, Mississippi.

Equal Employment Opportunity Commission established.

Harlem race riot and race riots in other northern cities occur.

Freedom Summer of 1964 launched in Mississippi.

1965   Selma to Montgomery March accompanied by violence and murder of Viola Liuzzo and Reverend James J. Reeb.

Voting Rights Act of 1965 passed by Congress.

The Watts race riot, in California, is the worst racial riot in the nation's history.

Chicago race riot occurs.

Malcolm X is assassinated.

President Johnson creates Federal Office of Grant Compliance to supervise affirmative action in awarding government contracts.

Mississippi Freedom Democratic party founded.

1966   James Meredith shot during the Meredith March, the "March against Fear."

Black Panther party organized by Bobby Seale and others.

Stokely Carmichael coins "Black Power" phrase.

White House Conference "To Fulfill These Rights" meets.

Widespread racial rioting occurs during the summer in the northern cities of Chicago, Illinois; Cleveland, Ohio; New York; and elsewhere.

Edward William Brooke elected by Massachusetts as first black to serve in U.S. Senate since Reconstruction.

Chicago Freedom Movement led by Martin Luther King, Jr., gets under way.

Robert C. Weaver becomes first black to hold a cabinet post in the federal government.

1967   Black college students riot on campuses of Fisk, Jackson State, Southern University, and elsewhere.

Detroit race riot and Newark, New Jersey, race riot occur in the summer.

President Lyndon B. Johnson establishes the Commission on Civil Disorders (Kerner Commission) to study civil disorder.

Thurgood Marshall becomes first black Supreme Court justice.

1968   Civil Rights Act of 1968 passed with provisions for open housing.

Shirley Chisholm elected to Congress.

Kerner Commission report released.

Sanitation workers strike in Memphis, Tennessee.

Martin Luther King, Jr., assassinated in Memphis on April 4.

Poor People's March on Washington is led by Ralph Abernathy.

Eldridge Cleaver publishes bestselling *Soul on Ice*.

Knoxville riot occurs.

Resurrection City erected in Washington, D.C.

1969   Office of Minority Business Enterprise established.

1971   Congressional Black Caucus founded.

Jesse Jackson runs for mayor of Chicago.

Jesse Jackson founds People United to Save Humanity.

Public school busing to achieve integration begins.

1972   Equal Employment Opportunity Act of 1972 passed.

Barbara C. Jordan elected to Congress from Texas.

Andrew Young elected to Congress from Georgia.

1973   Maynard Jackson elected first black mayor of Atlanta.

1976   Alex Haley's *Roots: The Saga of an American Family* becomes best-seller.

1977   Benjamin Hooks becomes executive director of NAACP.

Ernest N. Morial elected first black mayor of New Orleans.

Andrew Young appointed as first black U.S. Ambassador to the United Nations.

1978   U.S. Supreme Court in *University of California Regents v. Bakke* rejects racial quotas.

1982   Voting Rights Act of 1965 renewed for another twenty-five years.

1983   Harold Washington elected first black mayor of Chicago.

1984   Jesse Jackson seeks Democratic party nomination for president.

1985   Anti-apartheid rallies are held throughout the world.

1986   Martin Luther King, Jr.'s., birthday declared a national holiday.

1988   Jesse Jackson seeks Democratic party nomination for president.

1989   Lawrence Douglas Wilder becomes governor of Virginia—first black to be elected by popular vote to the governorship of any state.

1990   Civil Rights Bill of 1990 vetoed by President George Bush.

SELECTED
BIBLIOGRAPHY

Abraham, Henry J. *Freedom and the Court, Civil Rights and Liberties in the United States* (1988).

Anderson, James D. *The Education of Blacks in the South: 1860–1935* (1988).

Bardolph, Richard, ed. *The Civil Rights Record: Black Americans and the Law, 1849–1970* (1970).

Barnes, Catherine A. *Journey from Jim Crow: The Desegregation of Southern Transit* (1983).

Bartley, Numan V. *The Rise of Massive Resistance: Race and Politics in the South during the 1950s* (1969).

Belknap, Michael R. *Federal Law and Southern Order: Racial Violence and Constitutional Conflict in the Post-Brown South* (1987).

Bell, Derrick A., Jr. *Race, Racism and American Law*, 2nd ed. (1980).

Belz, Herman. *Emancipation and Equal Rights: Politics and Constitutionalism in the Civil War Era* (1978).

Berman, William C. *The Politics of Civil Rights in the Truman Administration* (1970).

Blumberg, Rhoda Lois. *Civil Rights: The 1960s Freedom Struggle* (1991).

Branch, Taylor. *Parting the Waters: America in the King Years, 1954–1963* (1989).

Brauer, Carl M. *John F. Kennedy and the Second Reconstruction* (1977).

Brisbane, Robert H. *Black Activism: Radical Revolution in the United States, 1954–1970* (1974).

———. *The Black Vanguard: Origins of the Negro Social Revolution, 1900–1960* (1970).

Brooks, Thomas R. *Walls Came Tumbling Down: A History of the Civil Rights Movement, 1940–1970* (1974).

Bullock, Henry Allen. *The History of Negro Education in the South from 1619 to the Present* (1967).

Bullock, Penelope L. *The Afro-American Periodical Press: 1838–1900* (1981).

Bunche, Ralph J. *The Political Status of the Negro in the Age of FDR* (1973).

Burk, Robert Frederick. *The Eisenhower Administration and Black Civil Rights* (1984).

Burstein, Paul. *Discrimination, Jobs, and Politics: The Struggle for Equal Employment Opportunity in the United States since the New Deal* (1985).

Carson, Clayborne. *In Struggle: SNCC and the Black Awakening of the 1960s* (1981).

Combs, Michael W., and John Gruhl, eds. *Affirmative Action Theories, Analysis and Prospects* (1986).

Cortner, Richard C. *The Supreme Court and the Second Bill of Rights: The Fourteenth Amendment and the Nationalization of Civil Liberties* (1981).

Couch, Harvey C. *A History of the Fifth Circuit, 1891–1981* (1984).

Cruden, Robert. *The Negro in Reconstruction* (1969).

Dalfiume, Richard M. *Desegregation of the U.S. Armed Forces: Fighting on Two Fronts, 1939–1953* (1969).

Daniel, Pete. *The Shadow of Slavery: Peonage in the South, 1901–1969* (1972).

Daniel, Walter C. *Black Journals of the United States* (1982).

Davis, Arthur P. *From the Black Tower: Afro-American Writers, 1900 to 1960* (1974).

Davis, George, and Gregg Watson. *Black Life in Corporate America* (1982).

Davis, Marianna W., ed. *Contributions of Black Women to America*, vol. 1, *The Arts, Media, Business, Law, Sports* (1982).

Du Bois, W.E.B. *Black Reconstruction in America* (1935).

Fairclough, Adam. *To Redeem the Soul of America: The Southern Christian Leadership Conference and Martin Luther King, Jr.* (1987).

Fairman, Charles. *History of the Supreme Court of the United States, Vol. VII: Reconstruction and Reunion, 1864–1888, Part II* (1986).

Fletcher, Marvin E. *The Black Soldier and Officer in the United States Army* (1974).

Foner, Eric. *Reconstruction: America's Unfinished Revolution, 1863–1877* (1988).

Foner, Philip S. *American Socialism and Black Americans: From the Age of Jackson to World War II* (1977).

———. *Organized Labor and the Black Worker, 1619–1981* (1982).

Foner, Philip S., and Ronald L. Lewis, eds. *The Black Worker: A Documentary History from Colonial Times to the Present*, vol. V., *The Black Worker from 1900 to 1919* (1980).

Foner, Philip S., and George E. Walker, eds. *Proceedings of the Black National and State Conventions, 1865–1900* (1986).

Franklin, John Hope. *The Emancipation Proclamation* (1963).

Franklin, John Hope, and August Meier, eds. *Black Leaders of the Twentieth Century* (1982).

Franklin, John Hope, and Alfred A. Moss, Jr. *From Slavery to Freedom: A History of Negro Americans*, 6th ed. (1988).

Friedman, Leon, and Fred L. Israel, eds. *The Justices of the United States Supreme Court, 1789–1969: Their Lives and Major Opinions*, 5 vols. (1969–1978).

Fullinwider, S. P. *The Mind and Mood of Black America* (1969).

Garrow, David J. *Bearing the Cross: Martin Luther King, Jr., and the Southern Christian Leadership Conference* (1986).

———. *Protest at Selma: Martin Luther King, Jr., and the Voting Rights Act of 1965* (1978).

Gillette, William. *Retreat from Reconstruction, 1869–1879* (1979).

Gillon, Steven M. *Politics and Vision: The ADA and American Liberalism, 1947–1985* (1987).

Goings, Kenneth W. *The NAACP Comes of Age: The Defeat of Judge John J. Parker* (1990).

Goldfied, David R., Jr. *Black, White, and Southern: Race Relations and Southern Culture, 1940 to the Present* (1990).

Graham, Hugh Davis. *The Civil Rights Era* (1990).

Grant, Donald B. *The Anti-Lynching Movement, 1883–1932* (1975).

Greenberg, Jack. *Race Relations and American Law* (1959).

Greene, Kathanne W. *Affirmative Action and Principles of Justice* (1989).

Grossman, James R. *Land of Hope: Chicago, Black Southerners and the Great Migration* (1989).

Gutman, Herbert G. *The Family in Slavery and Freedom, 1750–1925* (1976).

Habenstreit, Barbara. *Eternal Vigilance: The American Civil Liberties Union in Action* (1971).

Hampton, Henry, and Steve Fayer. *Voices of Freedom: An Oral History of the Civil Rights Movement from the 1950s through the 1980s* (1990).

Harlan, Louis R. *Booker T. Washington: The Making of a Black Leader, 1856–1901* (1972).

———. *Booker T. Washington: The Wizard of Tuskegee, 1901–1915* (1983).

Harris, Fred, and Roger W. Wilkins, eds. *Quiet Riots: Race and Poverty in the United States, The Kerner Report Twenty Years Later* (1988).

Hogan, Lawrence D. *A Black National News Service, the Associated Press and Claude Barnett, 1919–1945* (1984).

Huggins, Nathan Irvin. *Harlem Renaissance* (1977).

Kaczorowski, Robert. *The Politics of Judicial Interpretation: The Federal Courts, Department of Justice and Civil Rights, 1866–1876* (1985).

Kellner, Bruce, ed. *The Harlem Renaissance: A Historical Dictionary for the Era* (1984).

Kellogg, Charles Flint. *NAACP: A History of the National Association for the Advancement of Colored People* (1967).

Kirby, John B. *Black Americans in the Roosevelt Era* (1980).

Kluger, Richard. *Simple Justice: The History of Brown v. Board of Education and Black America's Struggle for Equality* (1976).

Lawson, Steven F. *Black Ballots: Voting Rights in the South, 1944–1969* (1976).

———. *In Pursuit of Power: Southern Blacks and Electoral Politics, 1965–1982* (1985).

———. *Running for Freedom: Civil Rights and Black Politics in America since 1941* (1991).

Lewis, David Levering. *King: A Critical Biography* (1970).

Lincoln, C. Eric. *The Black Muslims in America* (1973).

———. *Race, Religion and the Continuing American Dilemma* (1984).

Litwack, Leon, and August Meier, eds. *Black Leaders of the Nineteenth Century* (1988).

Lofgren, Charles A. *The Plessy Case: A Legal-Historical Interpretation* (1987).

Logan, Rayford W., and Michael R. Winston, eds. *Dictionary of American Negro Biography* (1982).

MacGregor, Morris J. *Integration of the Armed Forces, 1940–1965* (1981).

McPherson, James M. *The Abolitionist Legacy: From Reconstruction to the NAACP* (1975).

———. *The Struggle for Equality, Abolitionists and the Negro in the Civil War and Reconstruction* (1964).

Meier, August. *Negro Thought in America, 1880–1915: Racial Ideologies in the Age of Booker T. Washington* (1963).

Meier, August, and Elliott Rudwick. *Black History and the Historical Profession, 1915–1980* (1986).

———. *CORE: A Study in the Civil Rights Movement, 1942–1968* (1973).

Mendelsohn, Jack. *The Martyrs: Sixteen Who Gave Their Lives for Racial Justice* (1966).

Miller, Loren. *The Petitioners: The Story of the Supreme Court of the United States and the Negro* (1966).

Moore, Jesse Thomas, Jr. *A Search for Equality: The National Urban League, 1910–1961* (1981).

Morris, Aldon D. *The Origins of the Civil Rights Movement: Black Communities Organizing for Change* (1984).

Moses, Wilson J. *The Golden Age of Black Nationalism, 1850–1925* (1978).

Muse, Benjamin. *The American Negro Revolution: From Nonviolence to Black Power, 1963–1967* (1968).

Myrdal, Gunnar. *An American Dilemma: The Negro Problem and Modern Democracy* (1944).

Nalty, Bernard C. *Strength for the Fight: A History of Black Americans in the Military* (1986).

National Advisory Commission on Civil Disorders, *Report* (1968).

Nelson, William E. *The Fourteenth Amendment: From Political Principle to Judicial Doctrine* (1988).

Nieman, Donald G. *Promises to Keep: African-Americans and the Constitutional Order, 1776 to the Present* (1991).

Norrell, Robert J. *Reaping the Whirlwind: The Civil Rights Movement in Tuskegee* (1985).

Oates, Stephen B. *Let the Trumpet Sound: The Life of Martin Luther King, Jr.* (1982).

Oppenheimer, Martin. *The Sit-In Movement of 1960* (1989).

Peltason, J. W. *Fifty-Eight Lonely Men: Southern Federal Judges and School Desegregation* (1961).

Ploski, Harry A., and James Williams, eds. *The Negro Almanac: A Reference Work on the African American*, 5th ed. (1989).

Rabinowitz, Howard N. *Race Relations in the Urban South, 1865–1890* (1978).

Read, Frank T., and Lucy S. McGough. *Let Them Be Judged: The Judicial Integration of the Deep South* (1978).

Shapiro, Herbert. *White Violence and Black Response from Reconstruction to Montgomery* (1988).

Sitkoff, Harvard. *A New Deal for Blacks: The Emergence of Civil Rights as a National Issue, The Depression Decade* (1978).

———. *The Struggle for Black Equality, 1954–1980* (1981).

Southern, David W. *Gunnar Myrdal and Black-White Relations: The Use and Abuse of An American Dilemma, 1944–1969* (1987).

Southern, Eileen. *Biographical Dictionary of Afro-American and African Musicians* (1982).

Stoper, Emily. *The Student Nonviolent Coordinating Committee* (1989).

Suggs, Henry Lewis, ed. *The Black Press in the South, 1865–1979* (1983).

Toppin, Edgar A. *A Biographical History of Blacks in America since 1528* (1971).

Trefousse, Hans L. *Lincoln's Decision for Emancipation* (1975).

———. *The Radical Republicans: Lincoln's Vanguard for Racial Justice* (1969).

Tushnet, Mark V. *The NAACP's Legal Strategy against Segregated Education, 1925–1950* (1987).

U.S. Equal Employment Opportunity Commission. *A History of the Equal Employment Opportunity Commission, 1965–1984* (1984).

Waskow, Arthur I. *From Race Riot to Sit-In, 1919 and the 1960s: A Study in the Connections between Conflict and Violence* (1966).

Weisbrot, Robert. *Freedom Bound: A History of America's Civil Rights Movement* (1990).

Weiss, Nancy J. *Farewell to the Party of Lincoln* (1983).

———. *The National Urban League, 1910–1940* (1974).

Wilkinson, J. Harvie III. *From Brown to Bakke: The Supreme Court and School Integration, 1954–1978* (1979).

Williams, Juan. *Eyes on the Prize: America's Civil Rights Years, 1954–1965* (1987).

Williamson, Joel. *The Crucible of Race: Black-White Relations in the American South since Emancipation* (1984).

Wilmore, Gayraud S. *Black Religion and Black Radicalism: An Interpretation of the Religious History of Afro-American People* (1983).

Wolters, Raymond. *The Burden of Brown: Thirty Years of School Desegregation* (1984).

———. *Negroes and the Great Depression* (1970).

Woodward, C. Vann. *The Strange Career of Jim Crow*, 2nd ed. (1974).

Zangrando, Robert L. *The NAACP Crusade against Lynching, 1909–1950* (1980).

Zinn, Howard. *SNCC: The New Abolitionists* (1964).

INDEX

Page numbers in bold refer to main entries.